AN INTELLECTUAL HISTORY

OF MODERN EUROPE

AN INTELLECTUAL HISTORY

OF MODERN EUROPE

Marvin Perry

Baruch College, City University of New York

George W. Bock, Editorial Associate

HOUGHTON MIFFLIN COMPANY   BOSTON   TORONTO

Geneva, Illinois   Palo Alto   Princeton, New Jersey

Sponsoring editor: *Sean W. Wakely*
Senior development editor: *Frances Gay*
Senior project editor: *Carol Newman*
Production/design coordinator: *Caroline Ryan*
Senior manufacturing coordinator: *Holly Schuster*

Cover credit: *Theodore Duret,* Chester Dale Collection © 1992
National Gallery of Art, Washington, 1912.

Printed in the U.S.A.

Library of Congress Catalog Card Number: 92-72647

ISBN: 0-395-65348-7

6789-QF-02 01 00 99

Contents

Part II
THE ENLIGHTENMENT TRADITION PRESERVED,
EXPANDED, AND CHALLENGED   171

Preface

Over the course of centuries Western thinkers have discussed the crucial questions of human existence. In the process, they have forged the instruments of reason that made possible a rational and systematic investigation of physical nature and human culture, conceived the idea of political liberty, and recognized the intrinsic worth of the individual. *An Intellectual History of Modern Europe* is written with the conviction that the Western intellectual tradition has something valuable to tell students. Without an adequate understanding of the historical evolution of the West's core ideals—how they were forged, interpreted, implemented, opposed, violated, and defended—commitment to them will diminish.

Characteristics of the Book

An Intellectual History of Modern Europe contains an overarching theme that provides unity and a sense of direction to modern European intellectual history and permits students to see key relationships. The theme is contained in the heading of Part II—The Enlightenment Tradition Preserved, Expanded, and Challenged. The Enlightenment is treated as the culmination of the movement toward modernity that began with the Renaissance. The nineteenth and first half of the twentieth centuries are treated in relation to the promise (and limitations) of the Enlightenment. The text strives to interpret, structure, and synthesize in order to provide readers with a frame of reference with which to comprehend the evolution of modern European thought.

The text contains two introductory chapters that survey the foundations and development of Western thought in the ancient world, the Middle Ages, and early modern times. This overview discusses the evolution and essential meaning of the Judeo-Christian and Greco-Roman traditions; the medieval view of the universe, the individual, and reason; and the rise of the modern outlook during the era of the

Renaissance and the Reformation. Instructors will find this compre-hensive overview a useful introduction to the course.

Not all key ideas in the modern West derive from the application of reason to the great questions of human existence. Because many non-rational ideas have profoundly affected modern European conscious-ness and politics, the text devotes considerable attention to the theme of irrationalism. It discusses both those thinkers who celebrated the irrational and those who struggled to comprehend it; it treats creative expressions of the irrational in the arts; and it explores the irrational in political thinking, particularly in the form of extreme nationalism, racism, and fascism.

An Intellectual History of Modern Europe is written with the stu-dent in mind: chapter introductions provide a clear focus; difficult ideas are clearly explained; and an historical context is provided for ideas and thinkers. Several chapters contain concluding essays that strive to present the larger meaning of the material discussed. Numer-ous extracts from primary sources are integrated into the narrative.

Acknowledgments

There is a symbiotic relationship between this work and my chapters in *Western Civilization: Ideas, Politics, and Society,* Fourth Edition, by Marvin Perry, Myrna Chase, James R. Jacob, Margaret C. Jacob, Theodore H. Von Laue. Since I worked on both projects simultane-ously, some of the material from the intellectual history was incorpo-rated into various editions of the Western civilization text. Conversely, suitable material from the Western civilization text has been inte-grated into this work. I have also drawn extensively from my *Sources of the Western Tradition,* Second Edition.

I would like to thank the following instructors for their critical read-ing of sections of the manuscript:

William J. Greenwald, Arkansas State University
Isabel F. Knight, The Pennsylvania State University
W. Warren Wagar, State University of New York at Binghamton
Steven Werner, University of Wisconsin Center–Waukesha County
Ken Wolf, Murray State University

Several of their suggestions were incorporated into the final version. I am also grateful to the staff of Houghton Mifflin Company who lent their considerable talents to the project. In particular, I would like to thank Frances Gay, developmental editor, and Carol Newman, project editor, for their careful attention to detail, and Irmina Plaszkiewicz-

Pulc, whose copyediting skills are reflected in the manuscript. I am especially grateful to my friend George Bock who read the manuscript with an eye for organization, major concepts, and essential relationships. Our often heated but always fruitful discussions demonstrate to me the intrinsic value of the Socratic dialogue. And once more, I thank my wife Phyllis G. Perry for her encouragement.

M.P.

AN INTELLECTUAL HISTORY

OF MODERN EUROPE

Europe

Reykjavik ⊛ ICELAND

ATLANTIC
OCEAN

Norwegian
Sea

FINLAND

NORWAY
Oslo ⊛   SWEDEN   Helsinki ⊛

North
Sea

⊛ Stockholm   Tallinn ⊛
ESTONIA   RUSSIA

DENMARK   Riga ⊛   Moscow ⊛
Baltic Sea   LATVIA
Copenhagen ⊛   LITHUANIA

IRELAND
Dublin ⊛

GREAT
BRITAIN   THE   Vilnius ⊛   ⊛ Mensk
NETHERLANDS   BELARUS
London ⊛   ⊛ Amsterdam

The Hague ⊛ Berlin ⊛   POLAND
Brussels ⊛   Kiev ⊛
BELGIUM   GERMANY   Warsaw ⊛
Paris ⊛   UKRAINE
⊛ Luxembourg
LUXEMBOURG   Prague ⊛
CZECHOSLOVAKIA   MOLDOVA
LIECHTENSTEIN   Vienna ⊛   Kishinev ⊛
FRANCE   Budapest
Bern ⊛ ⊛ Vaduz   AUSTRIA   ⊛
SWITZERLAND   SLOVENIA HUNGARY   ROMANIA
Ljubljana ⊛ Zagreb ⊛
PORTUGAL   CROATIA Vojvodina   Bucharest ⊛
ANDORRA   BOSNIA-   ⊛ Belgrade   Black Sea
Lisbon ⊛   ⊛ Madrid   HERCEGOVINA Serbia
Sarajevo ⊛ YUGOSLAVIA
SPAIN   ITALY   MONTE-   BULGARIA
NEGRO   Kosovo ⊛ Sofia
Titograd ⊛   ⊛ Skopje
⊛ Rome   Tirane ⊛ MACEDONIA
ALBANIA
GREECE   TURKEY

Mediterranean Sea   Athens ⊛

MOROCCO   ALGERIA   TUNISIA

0   200   400   600 km

0   200   400 mi

INTRODUCTION

FOUNDATIONS OF THE WESTERN

INTELLECTUAL TRADITION

1

The Judeo-Christian and

Greco-Roman Traditions

Over the course of some 2,500 years, Western thinkers, at times with great perception, have explored the crucial questions of life, death, and the nature of the universe. Despite its great diversity and complexity, the Western intellectual tradition does reveal several integrating principles. Surpassing mythical thinking, Western intellects forged the instruments of reason that made possible a rational and systematic investigation of physical nature and human culture, conceived the idea of political liberty, and recognized the intrinsic worth of the individual. These ideals of reason, freedom, and human dignity—what constitute the Western *idea*—are not inherent components of human nature; nor are they self-evident principles. Rather, they are human creations, among humanity's finest achievements.

The history of modern Western civilization is a grand but tragic drama. Despite the value that westerners have given to reason, freedom, and human dignity, they have shown a frightening capacity for irrational behavior and a fascination for irrational ideologies and violence. They have also willingly sacrificed liberty and negated human dignity for security and national grandeur. The world wars and totalitarian movements of the twentieth century have demonstrated that Western civilization, despite its extraordinary achievements, is fragile and perishable.

The Western intellectual tradition, like Western civilization itself, is a confluence of two traditions that arose in the ancient world: the Judeo-Christian and the Greco-Roman. Both the ancient Hebrews and the Greeks inherited and assimilated the many achievements of the Egyptians and the Mesopotamians, the creators of the world's first civilizations. But even more important for an understanding of the essential meaning of Western civilization are the ways in which Hebrews and Greeks rejected or transformed elements of the older Near Eastern tradition to create new departures for the human mind. The great achievement of the Greeks lay in the development of rational thought; with the Greeks, the mind discovered its own capacities for thinking. The Hebrews' genius lay in the sphere of religious-ethical thought.

To understand and appreciate the monumental achievements of the Hebrews and the Greeks, it is necessary to examine the myth-making world-view of the older civilizations of ancient Mesopotamia and Egypt from which both the Hebrews and the Greeks, each in their own way, departed.

THE MYTH-MAKING OUTLOOK OF THE ANCIENT NEAR EAST

All features of Near Eastern society—law, kingship, art, and science— were generally intertwined with and dominated by religion. Religion was the source of the vitality and creativity of Mesopotamian and Egyptian civilizations. Near Eastern art drew its inspiration from religion; literature and history dealt with the ways of the gods; science was permeated by religion. And priest-kings or god-kings, their power sanctioned by divine forces, furnished the necessary authority to organize large numbers of people in cooperative ventures.

A religious or mythopoeic (myth-making) view of the world gives Near Eastern civilization its distinctive form and allows us to see it as an organic whole. Myth-making was humanity's first way of thinking. Appealing primarily to the imagination and emotions, not to reason, myth-making was the earliest attempt to make nature and life comprehensible.

Originating in sacred rites, ritual dances, feasts, and ceremonies, myths depicted the deeds of gods, who, in some remote past, had brought forth the world and human beings. Holding that human destiny was determined by the gods, Near Eastern people interpreted their experiences through myths. Myths also enabled Mesopotamians and Egyptians to make sense out of nature, to explain the world of phenomena. Through myths, the Near Eastern mind sought to give coherence to the universe, to make it intelligible. These myths offered Near Eastern peoples a framework with which to pattern their experiences into a meaningful order, justify their rules of conduct, and try to overcome the uncertainty of existence. Mythical explanations of nature, human origins, and human experience made life seem less overwhelming, less filled with fears.

The civilizations of the ancient Near East were based on a way of thinking that is fundamentally different from the modern scientific outlook. The difference between scientific and mythical thinking is profound. The scientific mind views physical nature as an *it*—inanimate, impersonal, and governed by universal law. The myth-making mind of the Near East saw every object in nature as a *thou*—personified, alive, with an individual will, a god or demon that manipulates things according to its desires. The sun and stars, the rivers and mountains, the wind and lightning were either gods or the dwelling places of gods. An Egyptian or a Mesopotamian experienced natural phenomena—a falling rock, a thunderclap, a rampaging river—as life facing life. If a river flooded the region, destroying crops, it was because it wanted to; the river or the gods decided to punish the people.

> In other words, the ancients told myths instead of presenting an analysis or conclusions. We would explain, for instance, that certain atmospheric changes broke a drought and brought about rain. The Babylonians observed the same facts but experienced them as the intervention of the gigantic bird Imdugud which came to their rescue. It covered the sky with the black storm clouds of its wings and devoured the Bull of Heaven, whose hot breath had scorched the crops.[1]

The Egyptians believed that the sun rose in the morning, traveled across the sky, and set into the netherworld beyond the western horizon. After warding off the forces of chaos and disruption, the sun reappeared the next morning. For the Egyptians, the rising and setting of the sun were not natural occurrences—a celestial body obeying impersonal law—but a religious drama.

The scientific mind holds that natural objects obey universal rules; hence the location of planets, the speed of objects, and the onset of a hurricane can be predicted. The myth-making mind of the ancient Near East was not troubled by contradictions; it did not seek logical consistency. It had no awareness of repetitive laws inherent in nature. Rather, it attributed physical occurrences to divine powers whose behavior was often erratic and unpredictable. The scientific mind appeals to reason—it analyzes nature logically and systematically and searches for general principles that govern phenomena. The myth-making mind appeals to the imagination and feelings and proclaims a truth that is emotionally satisfying, not one that has been arrived at through intellectual analysis and synthesis. Mythical explanations of nature and human experience enriched perception and feeling; they also eased life's burdens and made death less frightening.

Mesopotamians and Egyptians did not distinguish between the *subjective*—how nature appears to us through feelings, illusions, and dreams—and the *objective*—what nature really is, a system governed by laws that can be apprehended through intellectual analysis and synthesis. Of course, Near Eastern people did engage in rational forms of thought and behavior. They certainly employed reason in building irrigation works, in preparing a calendar, and in performing mathematical operations. But because rational or logical thought remained subordinate to a mythic-religious world-view, Near Eastern people did not arrive at a *consistently* and *self-consciously* rational method of inquiring into physical nature and human culture. They did not fashion a body of philosophic and scientific ideas that were logically structured, discussed, and debated.

Near Eastern civilization reached the first level in the development of science: observing nature, recording data, and improving technology in mining and metallurgy, and architecture. But it did not advance to the level of self-conscious philosophic and scientific thought, that is, logically deduced abstractions, hypotheses, and generalizations. These later developments were the singular achievement of Greek philosophy; it gave a "rational interpretation to natural occurrences which had previously been explained by ancient mythologies. . . . With the study of nature set free from the control of mythological fancy, the way was opened for the development of science as an intellectual system."[2]

THE HEBREWS: ETHICAL MONOTHEISM

Ancient Mesopotamia and Egypt, the birthplace of the first civilizations, are not the spiritual ancestors of the West. For the origins of the Western tradition, we must turn to the Hebrews and the Greeks. As Egyptologist John A. Wilson says,

> The Children of Israel built a nation and a religion on the rejection of things Egyptian. Not only did they see God as one, but they ascribed to Him consistency of concern for man and consistency of justice to man. . . . Like the Greeks, the Hebrews took forms from their great neighbors; like the Greeks, they used these forms for very different purposes.[3]

The Hebrews' conception of God and their affirmation of moral autonomy and human dignity are crucial to the shaping of the Western intellectual tradition.

God: One, Sovereign, Transcendent, Good

Monotheism, the belief in one God, became the central force in the life of the Hebrews, and marked a profound break with Near Eastern religious thought. The gods of other Near Eastern peoples were not truly free; their power was not without limits. Unlike Yahweh, the Hebrew divinity, Near Eastern gods were not eternal, but were born or created; they issued from some prior realm. They were also subject to biological conditions, requiring food, drink, sleep, and sexual gratification. Sometimes they became ill, or grew old, or died. When they behaved wickedly, they had to answer to fate, which demanded punishment as retribution; even the gods were subject to fate's power.

The Hebrews, or Jews, regarded God as *fully* sovereign. He ruled all and was subject to nothing. Yahweh's existence and power did not derive from a pre-existing realm, as was the case with the gods of other peoples. The Hebrews believed that no realm of being preceded God in time or surpassed Him in power. They saw God as eternal, the source of all in the universe, and having a supreme will. He created and governed the natural world and shaped the moral laws that govern human beings. He was not subservient to fate but determined what happened.

Whereas Near Eastern divinities dwelt within nature, the Hebrew God was *transcendent*, above nature and not part of it. Yahweh was not identified with any natural force and did not dwell in a particular place in heaven or on earth. Since God was the creator and ruler of nature, there was no place for a sun-god, a moon-god, a god in the river, or a demon in the storm. Nature was God's creation but was not itself divine. Therefore, when the Hebrews confronted natural phenomena, they experienced God's magnificent handiwork, not objects with wills of their own. All natural phenomena—rivers, mountains, storms, and stars—were divested of any supernatural quality. The stars and planets were creations of Yahweh, not divinities or the abodes of divinities. The Hebrews neither regarded them with awe nor worshiped them.

This removal of the gods from nature is a necessary prerequisite for scientific thought. The Hebrews demythicized nature, but concerned with religion and morality, they did not create theoretical science. As testimony to God's greatness, nature inspired people to sing the praises of the Lord; it invoked worship of God, not scientific curiosity. When Hebrews gazed at the heavens, they did not seek to discover mathematical relationships but admired God's handiwork. The Jews did not view nature as a system governed by self-operating principles or natural law. Rather, they saw the rising sun, spring rain, summer heat, and winter cold as God intervening in an orderly manner in his creation. Unlike the Greeks, the Hebrews were not philosophical or scientific thinkers. They were concerned with God's will, not the human intellect; with the feelings of the heart, not the power of the mind; with righteous behavior, not abstract thought. Human wickedness stemmed not from ignorance but from disobedience and stubbornness.

Unlike the Greeks, the Jews did not speculate about the origins of all things and the operations of nature; they knew that God had created everything. For the Hebrews, God's existence was based on religious conviction, not on rational inquiry; on revelation, not reason. It was the Greeks, not the Hebrews, who originated rational thought. But Christianity, born of Judaism, retained the Hebrew view of a transcendent God and the orderliness of his creation—concepts that could accommodate Greek science.

The Jews also did not speculate about God's nature. They knew only that he was *good* and that he made ethical demands on his people. Unlike Near Eastern gods, Yahweh was not driven by lust or motivated by evil but was "gracious, and full of compassion; slow to anger, and of great mercy." (Psalm 145:8).* In contrast to pagan gods, who were indifferent to human beings, Yahweh was attentive to human needs.

By asserting that God was one, sovereign, transcendent, and good, the Hebrews effected a religious revolution that separated them from the world-view held by the other peoples of the ancient Near East.

The Individual and Moral Autonomy

This new conception of God made possible a new awareness of the individual. In confronting God, the Hebrews developed an awareness of *self*, or *I*; the individual became conscious of his or her own person, moral autonomy, and personal worth. The Hebrews believed that God, who possessed total freedom himself, has bestowed on his people moral freedom: the capacity to choose between good and evil.

Fundamental to Hebrew belief was the insistence that God did not create people to be his slaves. The Hebrews regarded God with awe and humility, with respect and fear, but they did not believe that God wanted people to grovel before him; rather, he wanted them to fulfill their moral potential by freely making the choice to follow or not to follow God's Law. Thus, in creating men and women in his own image, God granted them autonomy and sovereignty. In God's plan for the universe, human beings were the highest creation, subordinate only to

---

*The biblical passages in this chapter are quoted from *The Holy Scriptures* published by the Jewish Publication Society of America.

God. Of all his creations, only they had been given the freedom to choose between righteousness and wickedness, between "life and good, and death and evil" (Deuteronomy 30:15).

God demanded that the Hebrews have no other gods and that they should neither make, bow down to, nor serve idols. The Jews believed that the worship of idols deprived people of their freedom and dignity; people cannot be fully human if they surrender themselves to a lifeless idol. Hence, the Hebrews rejected images and all other forms of idolatry. A crucial element of Near Eastern religion was the use of images— art forms that depicted divinities—but the Hebrews believed that God, the Supreme Being, could not be represented by pictures or sculpture fashioned by human hands. The Jews rejected entirely the belief that an image possessed divine powers, which could be manipulated for human advantage. Ethical considerations, not myth or magic, were central to Hebrew religious thought.

By making God the center of life, Hebrews could become free moral agents; no person, no human institution, and no human tradition could claim their souls. Because God alone was the supreme value in the universe, only he was worthy of worship. Thus, to give ultimate loyalty to a king or a general violated God's stern warning against the worship of false gods. The first concern of the Hebrews was supposed to be righteousness, not power, fame, or riches, which were only idols and would impoverish a person spiritually and morally.

There was, however, a condition to freedom. For the Hebrews, people were not free to create their own moral precepts, their own standards of right or wrong. Freedom meant voluntary obedience to commands that originated with God. Evil and suffering were not caused by blind fate, malevolent demons or arbitrary gods; they resulted from people's disregard of God's commands. The dilemma is that, in possessing freedom of choice, human beings are also free to disobey God, to commit sin, which leads to suffering and death. Thus, in the Genesis story, Adam and Eve were punished for disobeying God.

For the Jews, to know God did not mean to comprehend him intellectually, define him, or prove his existence; to know God was to be righteous and loving, merciful and just. When men and women loved God, the Hebrews believed, they were uplifted and improved. Gradually, they learned to overcome the worst elements of human nature and to treat people with respect and compassion. The Jews came to interpret the belief that man was created in God's image to mean that each human being has a divine spark in him or her, giving every person a unique dignity that cannot be taken away.

By their devotion to God, the Hebrews also asserted the dignity and autonomy of human beings. Thus, the Hebrews conceived the idea of moral freedom: that each individual is responsible for his or her own actions. These ideas of human dignity and moral autonomy, which Christianity inherited, are central to the Western tradition.

The Prophets

Jewish history was marked by the emergence of prophets—spiritually inspired persons who felt compelled to act as God's messengers. The prophets cared nothing for money or possessions, feared no one, and preached without invitation. Often emerging in times of social distress and moral confusion, the prophets pleaded for a return to the covenant and the Law. They taught that when people forgot God and made themselves and their own creations the center of all things they would bring disaster on themselves and their community.

Social Justice   The flowering of the prophetic movement—the age of classical, or literary, prophecy—began in the eighth century B.C. In attacking oppression, cruelty, greed, and exploitation of the poor and the weak, the prophets added a new dimension to Israel's religious development. To the prophets, social evils were religious sins. In the name of God, the mid-eighth-century prophet Amos denounced the hypocrisy, pomp, and heartlessness of the rich and demanded that "justice well up as waters. And righteousness as a mighty stream" (Amos 5:24). God is compassionate, insisted the prophets; he cares for all, especially the poor, the unfortunate, the suffering, and the defenseless. God's injunctions, declared Isaiah, were to "Seek justice, relieve the oppressed, Judge the fatherless, plead for the widow" (Isaiah 1:17).

Prophets stressed the direct spiritual-ethical encounter between the individual and God. The inner person concerned them more than the outer forms of religious activity. They criticized priests whose commitment to rites and rituals was not supported by a deeper spiritual insight or matched by a zeal for morality in daily life. To the prophets, an ethical sin was far worse than an omission in ritual. Above all, said the prophets, God demands righteousness, living justly before God. To live unjustly, mistreat one's neighbors, and act without compassion was to violate God's law and endanger the entire social order.

The prophets thus helped shape a social conscience that has become part of the Western tradition. This revolutionary social doctrine states that everyone has a God-given right to social justice and fair treatment; that each person has a religious obligation to denounce evil and oppose mistreatment of others; and that the community has a moral responsibility to assist the unfortunate. The prophets held out the hope that life on earth could be improved, that poverty and injustice need not be accepted as part of an unalterable natural order, and that the individual was capable of elevating himself or herself morally and could respect the dignity of others.

Universalism and Individualism   Two tendencies were present in Hebrew thought: parochialism and universalism. Parochial-mindedness stressed the special nature, destiny, and needs of the chosen people, a nation set apart from others. This narrow outlook was offset by universalism, a concern for all humanity, which found expression in those prophets who saw all people as equally precious to God and envisioned the unity of all people under God.

> In that day there shall be a highway out of Egypt to Assyria, and the Assyrian shall come into Egypt, and the Egyptian into Assyria; and the Egyptians shall worship with the Assyrians.
>   In that day shall Israel be the third with Egypt and with Assyria . . . for that the Lord of hosts hath blessed him saying: "Blessed be Egypt My people and Assyria the work of My hands and Israel Mine inheritance." [Isaiah 19:23–24]

The prophets were not pacifists, particularly if a war was being waged against the enemies of Yahweh. But some prophets denounced war as obscene and looked forward to its elimination. In a world where virtually everyone glorified the warrior, the prophets of universalism envisioned the day when peace would reign over the earth—when nations "shall beat their swords into plowshares, And their spears into pruning-hooks; Nation shall not lift up sword against nation, Neither shall they learn war any more" (Isaiah 2:4). These prophets maintained that when people glorify force they dehumanize their opponents, brutalize themselves, and dishonor God. When violence rules, there can be no love of God and no regard for the individual.

The prophets' universalism was accompanied by an equally profound awareness of the individual and his or her worth to God. Before Moses and the later prophets, virtually all religious tradition in the Near East had been produced communally and anonymously. The prophets, however, spoke as fearless individuals, who, by affixing their signatures to their thoughts, took full responsibility for their religious inspiration and conviction.

Prophets emphasized the individual's responsibility for his or her own actions. In coming to regard God's law as a *command to conscience, an appeal to the inner person,* the prophets heightened the awareness of the human personality. They indicated that the individual could not know God only by following edicts and by performing rituals; the individual must experience God. Precisely this I-Thou relationship could make the individual fully conscious of self and could deeply enrich his or her own personality. During the Exodus, the Hebrews were a tribal people who obeyed the Law largely out of awe and group compulsion. By the prophets' time, the Jews appeared to be autonomous individuals who heeded the Law because of a deliberate, conscious, and inner commitment.

For the Jews, monotheism had initiated a process of self-discovery and self-realization unmatched by other peoples of the Near East. The prophets' ideals helped sustain the Jews throughout their long and often painful historical odyssey and remain a vital force for Jews today. Incorporated into the teachings of Jesus, these ideals, as part of Christianity, are embedded in the Western tradition.

THE GREEKS: FROM MYTH TO REASON

The Hebrew conception of ethical monotheism, with its stress on human dignity, is one source of the Western tradition. The other source is ancient Greece. The Greeks broke with the mythopoeic outlook of the Near East and conceived a new way of viewing nature and human society that is the basis of the Western scientific and philosophic tradition. After an initial period of mythical thinking, the Greek mind by the fifth century B.C., had gradually applied reason to the physical world and to all human activities. As Greek society evolved, says British historian James Shiel, there

> was a growing reliance on independent reason, a devotion to logical precision, progressing from myth to logos [reason]. Rationalism permeated the whole social and cultural development. . . . Architecture . . . developed from primitive cultic considerations to sophisticated mathematical norms; sculpture escaped from temple image to a new love of naturalism and proportion; political life proceeded from tyranny to rational experiments in democracy. From practical rules of thumb, geometry moved forward in the direction of the impressive Euclidian synthesis. So too philosophy made its way from "sayings of the wise" to the Aristotelian logic, and made men rely on their own observation and reflection in facing the unexplained vastness of the cosmos.[4]

The Greeks conceived of nature and society as following general rules, not acting according to the whims of gods or demons. They saw human beings as having a capacity for rational thought, a need for freedom, and a worth as individuals. Although the Greeks never dispensed with the gods, they increasingly stressed the importance of human reason and human decisions; they came to assert that reason is the avenue to knowledge and that people—not the gods—are responsible for their own behavior. In this shift of attention from the gods to human beings, the Greeks created the rational, humanist outlook that is a distinctive feature of Western civilization.

Philosophy in the Hellenic Age

The development of rational thought in Greece was a process, a trend, not a finished achievement. The process began when some original thinkers became skeptical of Homer's gods and went beyond mythical explanations for natural phenomena. The nonphilosophic majority did not, however, entirely eliminate the language, attitudes, and beliefs of myth from their life and thought. Even in the mature philosophy of Plato and Aristotle, mythical modes of thought persisted. What is of immense historical importance is not the degree to which the Greeks successfully integrated the norm of reason, but that they originated this norm, defined it, and applied it in their intellectual and political life.

Cosmologists: A Rational Inquiry into Nature The first theoretical philosophers in human history emerged in the sixth century B.C. in the Greek cities of Ionia in Asia Minor. Curious about the essential composition of nature and dissatisfied with earlier creation legends, the Ionians—Thales, Anaximander, and Anaximenes—sought physical, rather than mythic-religious, explanations for natural occurrences. In the process, they arrived at a new concept of nature and a new method of inquiry. They maintained that nature was not manipulated by arbitrary and willful gods and that it was not governed by blind chance. The Ionians said that underlying the seeming chaos of nature were principles of order—general laws ascertainable by the human mind. The Ionians revolutionized thought because they omitted the gods from their accounts of the origins of nature and searched for natural explanations for physical happenings. This approach marks the beginning of scientific and philosophical thought. The early Greek thinkers are called cosmologists, because they were concerned with the nature of the universe, or Pre-Socratics, because they came before Socrates, a pivotal thinker in the evolution of Greek thought.

Concepts essential to scientific thought emerged in embryonic form with the cosmologists: natural explanations for physical occurrences (Ionians), the mathematical order of nature (Pythagoras), logical proof (Parmenides), and the mechanical structure of the universe (Democritus). By giving to nature a rational, rather than a mythical, foundation and by holding that theories should be grounded in evidence and that one should be able to defend them logically, these early Greek philosophers pushed thought in a new direction. Their achievement made possible theoretical thinking and the systematization of knowledge—as distinct from the mere observation and collection of data.

This systematization of knowledge extended into several areas. Greek mathematicians, for example, organized the Egyptians' practical experience with land measurements into the logical and coherent science of geometry. Both Babylonians and Egyptians had performed fairly complex mathematical operations, but unlike the Greeks, they made no attempt to prove underlying mathematical principles. In another area, Babylonian priests had observed the heavens for religious reasons, believing that the stars revealed the wishes of the gods. The Greeks used the data collected by the Babylonians, but not for a religious purpose; they sought to discover the geometrical laws underlying the motions of heavenly bodies. A parallel development occurred in medicine. No Near Eastern medical text explicitly attacked magical beliefs and practices. In contrast, Greek doctors associated with the medical school of Hippocrates asserted that diseases have a natural, not a supernatural, cause.

The Sophists: A Rational Investigation of Human Culture   In their effort to understand the external world, the cosmologists had created the tools of reason. Greek thinkers then turned away from the world of nature and attempted a rational investigation of the human world. Exemplifying this shift in focus were the Sophists, professional teachers who wandered from city to city teaching rhetoric, grammar, poetry, gymnastics, mathematics, and music. The Sophists insisted that it was futile to speculate about the first principles of the universe, for such knowledge was beyond the grasp of the human mind; they urged instead that individuals improve themselves and their cities by applying reason to the tasks of citizenship and statesmanship. The Sophists answered a practical need in Athens, which had been transformed into a wealthy and dynamic imperial state after the defeat of Persia in 479 BC Because the Sophists claimed that they could teach *political areté*— the skill to formulate the right laws and policies for cities and the art of eloquence and persuasion—they were sought as tutors by politically ambitious young men, especially in Athens. The Western humanist tradition owes much to the Sophists, who examined political and ethical problems, cultivated the minds of their students, and invented formal secular education.

In applying reason to human affairs, the Sophists undermined the traditional religious and moral values of Athenian society. Some Sophists taught that speculation about the divine was useless; others went further and asserted that religion was just a human invention to ensure obedience to traditions and laws. The Sophists also applied reason to law, with the same effect—the undermining of traditional authority. The laws of a given city, they asserted, did not derive from the gods; nor were they based on any objective and universal standards of justice and good, for such standards did not exist. Some Sophists argued that law was merely something made by the most powerful citizens for their own benefit. This view had dangerous implications: since law rested on no higher principle than might, it need not be obeyed.

Some Sophists combined the assault on law with an attack on the ancient Athenian idea of *sophrosyne*—moderation and self-discipline—because it denied human instincts. Instead of moderation, they urged that people should maximize pleasure and trample underfoot those traditions that restricted them from fully expressing their desires.

In subjecting traditions to the critique of reason, the radical Sophists triggered an intellectual and spiritual crisis. Their doctrines encouraged disobedience to law, neglect of civic duty, and selfish individualism. These attitudes became widespread during and after the Peloponnesian War, dangerously weakening community bonds. Conservatives sought to restore the authority of law and a respect for moral values by renewing allegiance to the sacred traditions undermined by the Sophists.

Socrates: The Rational Individual   Socrates (c. 470–399 B.C.), one of the most extraordinary figures in the history of Western civilization, took a different position and attacked the Sophists' relativism. His central concern was the perfection of individual human character, the achievement of moral excellence. Moral values, for Socrates, did not derive from a transcendent God as they did for the Hebrews. They were attained when the individual regulated his life according to universal standards arrived at through rational reflection, that is, when reason became the formative, guiding, and ruling agency of the soul. For Socrates, true education meant the shaping of character according to values discovered through the active and critical use of reason.

By examining critically all human beliefs and behavior, Socrates wanted to remove ethics from the realm of authority, tradition, dogma, superstition, and myth. He believed that reason was the only proper guide to the most crucial problem of human existence—the question of good and evil.

In urging Athenians to think rationally about the problems of human existence, Socrates offered no systematic ethical theory, no list of ethical precepts. What he did supply was a method of inquiry called *dialectics*, or logical discussion. As Socrates used it, a dialectical exchange between individuals, a *dialogue*, was the essential source of knowledge. It forced people out of their apathy and smugness and

compelled them to examine their thoughts critically, to confront illogical, inconsistent, dogmatic, and imprecise assertions, and to express
their ideas in clearly defined terms.

The dialogue compelled the individual to play an active role in acquiring the ideals and values by which to live. In a dialogue, individuals became thinking participants in a search for knowledge. Through
relentless cross-examination, Socrates induced his partner to explain
and justify his opinions through reason, for only thus did knowledge
become a part of one's being.

Dialogue implied that reason was meant to be used in relations between human beings and that they could learn from each other, help
each other, teach each other, and improve each other. It implied further
that the human mind could and should make rational choices. To deal
rationally with oneself and others is the distinctive mark of being
human.

Socrates devoted much of his life to his mission of persuading his
fellow Athenians to think critically about how they lived their lives.
Through probing questions, he tried to stir people out of their compla-
cency, to make them realize how directionless and purposeless their
lives were. For many years, Socrates challenged Athenians without
suffering harm, for Athens was generally distinguished by its freedom
of speech and thought. However, in the uncertain times during and
immediately after the Peloponnesian War (431–404 BC), Socrates made
enemies. When he was seventy, he was accused of corrupting the youth
of the city and of not believing in the city's gods but in other, new
divinities. Underlying these accusations was the fear that Socrates was
a troublemaker, a subversive who threatened the state by subjecting
its ancient and sacred values to the critique of thought.

Socrates denied the charges and conducted himself with great dignity at his trial, refusing to grovel and beg forgiveness. Convicted by
an Athenian court, he was ordered to drink poison. Had he attempted
to appease the jurors, he probably would have been given a light punishment, but he would not alter his principles even under threat of
death.

Socrates did not write down his philosophy and beliefs. We are able
to construct a coherent account of his life and ideals largely through
the works of his most important disciple, Plato.

Plato: The Rational Society   Plato (c. 429–347 B.C.) used his master's
teachings to create a comprehensive system of philosophy that embraced both the world of nature and the social world. Virtually all the
problems discussed by Western philosophers for the past two millennia
were raised by Plato. We focus on two of his principal concerns: the
theory of Ideas and that of the just state. Plato expanded Socrates' con-

ception of reason in his theory of Ideas and Socrates' notion of the rational individual and moral character in his conception of the just state.

Socrates had taught that universal standards of right and justice exist and that they are arrived at through thought. Building on the insights of his teacher, Plato insisted on the existence of a higher world of reality, independent of the world of things that we experience every day. This higher reality, he said, is the realm of Ideas, or Forms—unchanging, eternal, absolute, and universal standards of beauty, goodness, justice, and truth.

Truth resides in this world of Forms and not in the world made known through the senses. For example, a person can never draw a perfect square, but the properties of a perfect square exist in the world of Forms. Similarly, the ordinary person only forms an opinion of what beauty is from observing beautiful things; the philosopher, aspiring to true knowledge, goes beyond what he sees and tries to grasp with his mind the Idea of beauty. The ordinary individual lacks a true conception of justice or goodness; such knowledge is available only to the philosopher, whose mind can leap from worldly particulars to an ideal world beyond space and time. Thus, true wisdom is obtained through knowledge of the Ideas, not the imperfect reflections of the Ideas that are perceived with the senses. Plato was a champion of reason who aspired to study and to arrange human life according to universally valid standards. Rejecting sophistic relativism, he maintained that objective and eternal standards do exist.

In adapting the rational legacy of Greek philosophy to politics, Plato constructed a comprehensive political theory. What the Greeks had achieved in practice—the movement away from mythic and theocratic politics—Plato accomplished on the level of thought: the fashioning of a rational model of the state.

Plato had experienced the ruinous Peloponnesian War and Socrates' trial and execution. Disillusioned by the corruption of Athenian morality and democratic politics, he came to believe that under the existing Athenian constitution neither the morality of the individual Athenian nor the good of the state could be enhanced and that Athens required moral and political reform founded on Socrates' philosophy.

Fundamental to Plato's political theory as formulated in his great dialogue, *The Republic*, was his criticism of Athenian democracy. An aristocrat by birth and temperament, Plato believed that it was foolish to expect the common man to think intelligently about foreign policy, economics, or other vital matters of state. Plato rejected the fundamental principle of Athenian democracy: that the average person is capable of participating sensibly in public affairs. People would not entrust the care of a sick person to just anyone, said Plato, nor would they allow a novice to guide a ship during a storm. Yet in a democracy, amateurs were permitted to run the government and to supervise the education of the young; no wonder Athenian society was disintegrating. Plato felt that these duties should be performed only by the best people in the city, the philosophers who would approach human problems with reason and wisdom derived from knowledge of the world of unchanging and perfect Ideas. Only these possessors of truth would be competent to rule, said Plato.

Aristotle: Synthesis of Knowledge   Aristotle (384–322 B.C.) stands at the apex of Greek thought because he achieved a creative synthesis of the knowledge and theories of earlier thinkers. The range of Aristotle's interests and intellect is extraordinary. He was the leading expert of his time in every field of knowledge, with the possible exception of mathematics.

Aristotle undertook the monumental task of organizing and systematizing the thought of the Pre-Socratics (cosmologists), Socrates, and Plato. He shared with the natural philosophers a desire to understand the physical universe; he shared with Socrates and Plato the belief that reason was a person's highest faculty and that the polis was the primary formative institution of Greek life.

To the practical and empirically minded Aristotle, the Platonic notion of an independent and separate world of Forms beyond space and time seemed contrary to common sense. To comprehend reality, said Aristotle, one should not escape into another world. For him, Plato's two-world philosophy suffered from too much mystery, mysticism, and poetic fancy; moreover, Plato undervalued the world of facts and objects revealed through sight, hearing, and touch—a world that Aristotle valued. Like Plato, Aristotle desired to comprehend the essence of things and held that understanding universal principles is the ultimate aim of knowledge. But unlike Plato, he did not turn away from the world of things to obtain such knowledge. Possessing a scientist's curiosity to understand nature, Aristotle respected knowledge obtained through the senses.

For Aristotle, the Forms were not located in a higher world outside and beyond phenomena, but existed in things themselves. He said that through human experience with such things as men, horses, and white objects the essence of man, horse, and whiteness can be discovered through reason; the Form of Man, the Form of Horse, and the Form of Whiteness can be determined. These universals, which apply to all men, all horses, and all white things, were for both Aristotle and Plato the true objects of knowledge. For Plato, these Forms existed independently of particular objects; the Forms for men or horses or whiteness or triangles or temples existed, whether or not representations of these

Aristotle *(Alinari/Art Resource, NY)*

Ideas in the form of material objects were made known to the senses. For Aristotle, however, universal Ideas could not be determined without examination of particular things. Whereas Plato's use of reason tended to stress otherworldliness, Aristotle tried to bring philosophy back to earth.

By holding that certainty in knowledge comes from reason alone and not from the senses, Plato was predisposed toward mathematics and metaphysics—pure thought that transcends the world of change and material objects. By stressing the importance of knowledge acquired through the rational examination of sense experience, Aristotle favored the development of empirical sciences—physics, biology, zoology, botany, and other disciplines based on the observation and investigation of nature and the recording of data.

Ethical Thought   Like Socrates and Plato, Aristotle believed that a knowledge of ethics was possible and that it must be based on reason. For Aristotle, the good life was the examined life; it meant making intelligent decisions when confronted with specific problems. People could achieve happiness when they exercised the distinctively human trait of reasoning, when they applied their knowledge relevantly to life, and when their behavior was governed by intelligence and not by whim, tradition, or authority.

Aristotle recognized, however, that people are not entirely rational, that there is a passionate element in the human personality that can never be eradicated or ignored. Aristotle held that surrendering completely to desire meant descending to the level of beasts, but that denying the passions and living as an ascetic was a foolish and unreasonable rejection of human nature. Aristotle maintained that by proper training people could learn to regulate their desires. They could achieve moral well-being, or virtue, when they avoided extremes of behavior and rationally chose the way of moderation. "Nothing in excess" is the key to Aristotle's ethics.

Political Thought   Aristotle's *Politics* complements his *Ethics*. To live the good life, he said a person must do it as a member of a political community. Only the polis, the self-governing city-state, would provide people with an opportunity to lead a rational and moral existence. With this assertion, Aristotle demonstrated a typically Greek attitude. Like Plato, Aristotle presumed that political life could be rationally understood and intelligently directed. He emphasized the importance of the rule of law. He placed his trust in law rather than in individuals, for they are subject to passions. Although Aristotle recognized that at times laws should be altered, he recommended great caution; otherwise, people would lose respect for law and legal procedure.

Tyranny and revolution, Aristotle said, can threaten the rule of law and the well-being of the citizen. To prevent revolution, the state must maintain "the spirit of obedience to law. . . . [M]en should not think it slavery to live according to the rule of the constitution, for it is their salvation."[5] Aristotle held "that the best political community is formed by citizens of the middle class, and that those states are likely to be well-administered, in which the middle class is large and stronger if possible than the other classes [the wealthy and the poor]."[6] Both the rich, who excel in "beauty, strength, birth, [and] wealth," and the poor, who are "very weak or very much disgraced [find it] difficult to follow rational principle. Of these two the one sort grow into violent and great criminals, the others into rogues and petty rascals." The rich are unwilling "to submit to authority. . . . for when they are boys, by reason of the luxury in which they are brought up, they never learn even at school, the habit of obedience." Consequently, the wealthy "can only rule despotically." On the other hand, the poor "are too degraded. . . . to command and must be ruled like slaves."[7] Middle-class citizens are less afflicted by envy than the poor and are more likely than the rich to view their fellow citizens as equals.

The Hellenistic Age: Stoicism

Greek civilization, or Hellenism, passed through three distinct stages: the Hellenic Age, the Hellenistic Age, and the Greco-Roman Age. The Hellenic Age began around 800 BC with the early city-states, reached its height in the fifth century BC, and lasted until the death of Alexander the Great in 323 BC At that time, the ancient world entered the Hellenistic Age, which ended in 30 BC, when Egypt, the last major Hellenistic state, fell to Rome. The Greco-Roman Age spanned five hundred years: the period of the Roman Empire up to the collapse of the Empire's western half in the last part of the fifth century AD

As a result of Alexander the Great's conquests of the lands between Greece and India, tens of thousands of Greek soldiers, merchants, and administrators settled in eastern lands. This mixing of Greek and Near Eastern peoples and cultures defines the Hellenistic Age.

Hellenistic thinkers preserved and enlarged the rational tradition of Greek philosophy. In the Hellenic Age, Greek philosophers had a limited conception of humanity, dividing the world into Greeks and non-Greeks, who were called barbarians. In the Hellenistic Age, the intermingling of Greeks and peoples of the Near East caused a shift in focus from the city to the *oikoumene* (the inhabited world). Parochialism gave way to universalism and cosmopolitanism as people began to think of themselves as members of a world community. Philosophers came to regard the civilized world as one city, the city of humanity.

By teaching that the world constituted a single society, Stoicism, the leading philosophy in the Hellenistic world, gave theoretical expression to the world-mindedness of the age. By arriving at the concept of a world-state, the city of humanity, Stoicism offered an answer to the problem of community and alienation posed by the decline of the city-state. By stressing inner strength in dealing with life's misfortunes, Stoicism offered an avenue to individual happiness in a world fraught with uncertainty.

At the core of Stoicism was the belief that the universe contained a principle of order, variously called the Divine Fire, God, and Divine Reason (logos). This ruling principle underlay reality and permeated all things; it accounted for the orderliness of nature. The Stoics reasoned that because people are part of the universe, they too shared in the logos that operated throughout the cosmos. The logos was implanted in every human soul; it enabled people to act intelligently, and to comprehend the principles of order that governed nature. Since reason was common to all, human beings were essentially brothers and fundamentally equal. Reason gave individuals dignity and enabled them to recognize and respect the dignity of others. To the Stoics, all people, Greek and barbarian, free and slave, rich and poor, were fellow human beings, and one law, the law of nature, applied to all of them. Thus, the Stoics, like the Hebrews, arrived at the idea of the oneness of humanity.

Like Socrates, the Stoics believed that a person's distinctive quality was the ability to reason and that happiness came from the disciplining of emotions by the rational part of the soul. Like Socrates, too, the Stoics maintained that individuals should progress morally, should perfect themselves. In the Stoic view, wise persons ordered their lives according to the natural law—the law of reason—that underlay the cosmos. This harmony with the logos would give them the inner strength to resist the torments inflicted by others, by fate, and by their own passionate natures. Self-mastery and inner peace, or happiness, would follow. Such individuals remain undisturbed by life's misfortunes, for their souls are their own. Even slaves were not denied this inner freedom; although their bodies were subjected to the power of their masters, their minds still remained independent and free.

Stoicism had an enduring influence on the Western mind. To some Roman political theorists, the Roman Empire fulfilled the Stoic ideal of a world community in which people of different nationalities held citizenship and were governed by a worldwide law that accorded with the law of reason, or natural law, operating throughout the universe. Stoic beliefs—that by nature we are all members of one family, that each person is significant, that distinctions of rank and race are of no account, and that human law should not conflict with natural law— were incorporated into Roman jurisprudence, Christian thought, and modern liberalism. There is continuity between Stoic thought and the principle of inalienable rights stated in the American Declaration of Independence.

The Greek Achievement: Reason, Freedom, Humanism

Like other ancient peoples, the Greeks warred, massacred, and enslaved; they could be cruel, arrogant, contentious, and superstitious; and they often violated their ideals. But their achievement unquestionably had a profound historical significance. Western thought begins with the Greeks, who first defined the individual by his capacity to reason. It was the great achievement of the Greek spirit to rise above magic, miracles, mystery, authority, and custom and to discover the means of giving rational order to nature and society. Every aspect of Greek civilization—science, philosophy, art, literature, politics, historical writing—showed a growing reliance on human reason and a diminishing dependence on the gods.

In Mesopotamia and Egypt, people had no clear conception of their individual worth and no understanding of political liberty. They were not citizens, but subjects who marched to the command of a ruler whose absolute power originated with the gods. Such royal power was not imposed on an unwilling population but was religiously accepted and obeyed.

In contrast, the Greeks created political freedom. They saw the state as a community of free citizens who made laws in their own interest. The Greeks held that men are capable of governing themselves and they valued active citizenship. For the Greeks, the state was a civilizing agent that permitted people to live the good life. Greek political thinkers arrived at a conception of the rational or legal state in which law was an expression of reason, not of whim or divine commands; of justice, not of might; of the general good of the community, not of self-interest.

The Greeks also gave to Western civilization a conception of inner, or ethical, freedom. People were free to choose between shame and honor, cowardice and duty, moderation and excess. The heroes of Greek tragedy suffered, not because they were puppets being manipulated by higher powers, but because they possessed the freedom of decision. The idea of ethical freedom reached its highest point with Socrates. To shape oneself according to ideals known to the mind—to develop into an autonomous and self-directed person—was for the Greeks the highest form of freedom.

During the Hellenistic Age, the Greeks, like the Hebrews before them, arrived at the idea of universalism, the oneness of humanity. Stoic philosophers taught that all people, because of their ability to reason, are fundamentally alike and can be governed by the same laws. This idea is at the root of the modern principle of natural, or human, rights which are the birthright of each individual.

Underlying everything accomplished by the Greeks was a humanist attitude toward life. The Greeks expressed a belief in the worth, significance, and dignity of the individual; they called for the maximum cultivation of human talent, the full development of human personality, and the deliberate pursuit of excellence. Greek art, for example, made the human form the focal point of attention and exalted he nobility, dignity, self-assurance, and beauty of the human being. In valuing the human personality, the Greek humanists did not approve of living without restraints; they aimed at creating a higher type of man. Such a man would mold himself according to worthy standards; he would make his life as harmonious and flawless as a work of art. This aspiration required effort, discipline, and intelligence. Fundamental to the Greek humanist outlook was the belief that man could master himself. Although people could not alter the course of nature, for there was an order to the universe over which neither human beings nor gods had control, the humanist believed that people could control their own lives.

By discovering theoretical reason, by defining political freedom, and by affirming the worth and potential of human personality, the Greeks broke with the past and founded the rational and humanist tradition of the West. "Had Greek civilization never existed," says poet W. H. Auden, "we would never have become fully conscious, which is to say that we would never have become, for better or worse, fully human."[8]

THE ROMANS

By constructing a world community that broke down barriers between nations, by preserving and spreading Greek civilization, and by developing a rational system of law that applied to all humanity, Rome completed the trend toward universalism and cosmopolitanism that had emerged in the Hellenistic Age. Rome's great achievement was to transcend the narrow political orientation of the city-state and to create a world-state that unified the different nations of the Mediterranean world. Regarding the polis as the only means to the good life, the Greeks had not desired a larger political unit and had almost totally excluded foreigners from citizenship. Although Hellenistic philosophers had conceived the possibility of a world community, Hellenistic politics could not shape one. But Rome overcame the limitations of the city-state mentality and developed an empirewide system of law and citizenship. The Hebrews were distinguished by their prophets, and the Greeks by their philosophers; Rome's genius found expression in law and government.

Historians divide Roman history into two broad periods: the period of the Republic began in 509 B.C. with the overthrow of the Etruscan monarchy, and that of the Empire started in 27 B.C., when Octavian (Augustus) became in effect the first Roman emperor, ending almost five hundred years of republican self-government. By conquering the Mediterranean world and extending its law and, in some instances, citizenship to different nationalities, the Roman Republic transcended the parochialism typical of the city-state. The Republic initiated the trend toward political and legal universalism, which reached fruition in the second phase of Roman history, the Empire.

Philosophy and Law

A chief consequence of expansion was increased contact with Greek culture. Romans acquired from Greece knowledge of scientific thought, philosophy, medicine, and geography. Roman writers and orators used Greek history, literature, and oratory as models. Adopting the humanist outlook of the Greeks, the Romans came to value human intelligence and eloquent and graceful prose and poetry. Wealthy Romans retained Greek tutors, poets, and philosophers in their households and sent their sons to Athens to study. Thus, Rome creatively assimilated the Greek achievement and transmitted it to others, extending the orbit of Hellenism.

Stoicism was the principal philosophy of the Roman world, and its leading exponents were Cicero, Seneca, Epictetus, and Marcus Aurelius. Perpetuating the rational tradition of Greek philosophy, Roman Stoics saw the universe as governed by reason and esteemed the human intellect. Like Socrates, they sought the highest good in this world, not in an afterlife, and envisioned no power above human reason. Moral values were obtained from reason alone. The individual was self-sufficient, and depended entirely on rational faculties for knowing and doing good. Stoics valued the self-sufficient person who attains virtue and wisdom by exercising rational control over his life. The Stoic doctrine that all people, because of their capacity to reason, belong to a common humanity coincided with the requirements of the multinational Roman Empire.

Expressing the Roman yearning for order and justice, law was Rome's great legacy to Western civilization. During the period of the Republic's expansion outside Italy, contact with the Greeks and other peoples led to the development of a branch of Roman law called the law of nations *(jus gentium)*, which combined Roman civil law with principles selectively drawn from the legal tradition of Greeks and other peoples. Roman jurists identified the jus gentium with the natural law *(jus naturale)* of the Stoics. The jurists said that a law should accord with rational principles inherent in nature—uniform norms that can be discerned by rational people. Serving to bind different peoples together, the law of nations harmonized with the requirements of a world empire and with Stoic ideals, as Cicero pointed out: "True law is right reason in agreement with nature; it is of universal application, unchanging and everlasting. And there will not be different laws at Rome and at Athens or different laws now and in the future, but one eternal and unchangeable law will be valid for all nations and all times."[9] The law of nations came to be applied throughout the Empire, although it never entirely supplanted local law. In the eyes of the law, a citizen was not a Syrian or a Briton or a Spaniard, but a Roman.

The Roman Achievement

Rome left the West a rich heritage that endured for centuries. The idea of a world empire united by a common law and effective government never died. In the centuries following the collapse of Rome, people continued to be attracted to the idea of a unified and peaceful world-state. By preserving and adding to the philosophy, literature, science, and arts of ancient Greece, Rome strengthened the foundations of the Western cultural tradition. Latin, the language of Rome, lived on long after Rome perished. The Western church fathers wrote in Latin, and during the Middle Ages, Latin was the language of learning, literature, and law. From Latin came Italian, French, Spanish, Portuguese, and Romanian. When the Roman Empire collapsed, Roman law, the quintessential expression of Roman genius, fell into disuse in western Europe. Gradually reintroduced in the twelfth century, it came to form the basis of the common law in all Western lands except Britain and its dependencies. Finally, Christianity, the core religion of the West, was born within the Roman Empire and was greatly influenced by Roman law and organization.

EARLY CHRISTIANITY: A WORLD RELIGION

As confidence in human reason and hope for happiness in this world waned in the last centuries of the Roman Empire, a new outlook began to take hold. Evident in philosophy (particularly in Neo-Platonism, which sought to reach the Absolute not through reason but through spiritual intoxication—a mystical experience) and in the popularity of oriental religions, this viewpoint stressed escape from an oppressive world and communion with a higher reality. Christianity evolved and expanded within this setting of declining classicism and heightening otherworldliness. As one response to a declining Hellenism, Christianity offered a reason for living to a spiritually disillusioned Greco-Roman world: the hope of personal immortality. The triumph of Christianity marked a break with classical antiquity and a new stage in the evolution of the West, for there was a fundamental difference between the classical and the Christian concepts of God, the individual, and the purpose of life.

The triumph of Christianity was related to a corresponding decline in the vitality of Hellenism and a shift in cultural emphasis—a movement from reason to emotion and revelation. Offering comforting solutions to the existential problems of life and death, religion demonstrated a greater capacity to stir human hearts than reason did. Hellenism had invented the tools of rational thought, but the power of mythical thought was never entirely subdued. By the Late Roman Empire, science and philosophy were unable to compete with mysticism and myth. Mystery cults, which promised personal salvation, were spreading and gaining followers. Neo-Platonists yearned for a mystical union with the One. Astrology and magic, which offered supernatural explanations for the operations of nature, were also popular. This drift from rational and worldly values helped prepare the way for Christianity. In a culturally stagnating and spiritually troubled Greco-Roman world, Christianity gave life a new meaning and offered disillusioned men and women a new hope.

The Christian message of a divine Savior, a concerned Father, and brotherly love inspired people who were dissatisfied with the world of the here-and-now, who felt no attachment to city or empire, who derived no inspiration from philosophy, and who suffered from a profound sense of loneliness. Christianity offered the individual what the city-state and the Roman world-state could not: a profoundly personal relationship with God, an intimate connection with a higher world, and membership in a community of the faithful who cared for one another.

Stressing the intellect and self-reliance, Greco-Roman thought did not provide for the emotional needs of the ordinary person. Christianity addressed itself to this defect in the Greco-Roman outlook. The poor, the oppressed, and the slaves were attracted to the personality, life, death, and resurrection of Jesus, his love for all, and his concern for suffering humanity. They found spiritual sustenance in a religion that offered a hand of love, and taught that a person of worth need not be well-born, rich, educated, or talented. To people burdened with misfortune and terrified by death, Christianity held out the promise of eternal life, a kingdom of heaven where they would be comforted by God the Father. Thus, Christianity gave to the common person what the aristocratic values of Greco-Roman civilization generally did not—hope and a sense of dignity.

Christianity and Greek Philosophy

Christianity synthesized both the Hebrew and the Greco-Roman traditions. Having emerged from Judaism, it assimilated Hebrew monotheism and prophetic morality and retained the Old Testament as the Word of God. As the new religion evolved, it also assimilated elements of Greek philosophy. But there was a struggle between conservatives, who wanted no dealings with pagan philosophy, and those believers who recognized the value of Greek thought to Christianity.

To conservative church fathers, classical philosophy was all in error because it did not derive from divine revelation. As the final statement of God's truth, Christianity superseded both pagan philosophy and pagan religions. These conservatives feared that studying classical authors would contaminate Christian morality (did not Plato propose a community of wives, and did not the dramatists treat violent passions?) and promote heresy (was not classical literature replete with references to pagan gods?). For these church fathers there could be no compromise between Greek philosophy and Christian revelation.

Some early church fathers, however, defended the value of studying classical literature. They maintained that Greek philosophy contained a dim glimmer of God's truth, a pre-Christian insight into divine wisdom. Christ had corrected and fulfilled an insight reached by the philosophical mind. Knowledge of Greek philosophy, they argued, helped a Christian to explain his beliefs logically and to argue intelligently with pagan critics of Christian teachings.

Utilizing the language and categories of Greek philosophy, Christian intellectuals transformed Christianity from a simple ethical creed into a theoretical system, a theology. This effort to express Christian beliefs in terms of Greek rationalism is referred to as the Hellenization of Christianity. Greek philosophy enabled Christians to explain in rational terms God's existence and revelation. Christ was depicted as the divine logos (reason) in human form. The Stoic teaching that all people are fundamentally equal because they share in universal reason could be formulated in Christian terms—that all are united in Christ. Stoic ethics, which stressed moderation, self-control, and brotherhood, could be assimilated by Christian revelation. Particularly in Platonism, which drew a distinction between a world perceived by the senses and a higher order open to the intellect, Christian thinkers found a congenial vehicle for expressing Christian beliefs. The perfect and universal Forms, or Ideas, which Plato maintained were the true goal of knowledge and the source of ethical standards, were held by Christians to exist in God's mind.

That Greek philosophy exercised a hold over church doctrine is of immense importance; it meant that rational thought, the priceless achievement of the Greek mind, was not lost. But this Hellenization of Christianity was not a triumph of classicism over Christianity. The reverse is the essential truth: Christianity triumphed over Hellenism. Greek philosophy had to sacrifice its essential autonomy to the requirements of Christian revelation—that is, reason had to fit into a Christian framework. Moreover, although Christianity made use of Greek philosophy, Christian truth ultimately rested on faith, not reason.

Saint Augustine: The Christian World-View

During the early history of Christianity, many learned men, "fathers of the church," explained and defended church teachings. The most important Christian theoretician in the Late Roman Empire was Saint Augustine (A.D. 354–430), bishop of Hippo in North Africa and author of *The City of God*. Augustine became the principal architect of the Christian outlook that succeeded a dying classicism.

In 410, when Augustine was in his fifties, Visigoths sacked Rome— a disaster for which the classical consciousness was unprepared. Throughout the Empire people panicked. Pagans blamed the tragedy on Christianity. Even Christians expressed anxiety. Why were the righteous also suffering? Where was the kingdom of God on earth that had been prophesied? In *The City of God*, Augustine maintained that the worldly city could never be the central concern of Christians. The misfortunes of Rome, therefore, should not distress Christians unduly, for the true Christian was a citizen of a heavenly city that could not possibly be pillaged by ungodly barbarians but would endure forever. Compared with God's heavenly city, the decline of Rome was unimportant. What really mattered in history, said Augustine, was not the coming to be or the passing away of cities and empires, but the individual's entrance into heaven or hell.

However, Augustine did not hold that by his death Christ had opened the door to heaven for all. Most people were wicked sinners condemned to eternal punishment, said Augustine. Everywhere in human society we see

> love for all those things that prove so vain . . . and breed so many heartaches, troubles, griefs, and fears; such insane joys in discord, strife, and war . . . such fraud and theft and robbery; such . . . homicide and murder, cruelty and savagery, lawlessness and lust; all the shameless passions of the impure . . . the sins against religion . . . the iniquities against our neighbors . . . cheating, lies, false witness, violence to persons and property.[10]

Augustine held that only a handful had the gift of faith and the promise of heaven. People could not by their own efforts overcome a sinful nature; a moral and spiritual regeneration stemmed not from human will power but from God's grace. The small number endowed with God's grace constituted the City of God. These people lived on earth as visitors only, for they awaited deliverance to the Kingdom of Christ. Most inhabitants of the earthly city were destined for eternal punishment in hell. A perpetual conflict existed between the two cities and between their inhabitants; one city stood for sin and corruption, the other for God's truth and perfection. For Augustine, the highest good was not of this world but consisted of eternal life with God. His distinction between this higher world of perfection and a lower world of corruption remained influential throughout the Middle Ages.

Augustine repudiated the distinguishing feature of classical humanism—the autonomy of reason. For him, ultimate wisdom could not be achieved through rational thought alone; reason had to be guided by faith. Without faith there could be no true knowledge, no understanding. Philosophy had no validity if it did not first accept as absolutely true the existence of God and the authority of his revelation. Thus, Augustine upheld the primacy of faith, but he did not necessarily regard reason as an enemy of faith, and he did not call for an end to rational speculation. What he denied of the classical view was that reason alone could attain wisdom. The wisdom that Augustine sought was Christian wisdom, God's revelation to humanity. The starting point for this wisdom, he said, was belief in God and the Scriptures. For Augustine, secular knowledge for its own sake was of little value; the true significance of knowledge lay in its role as a tool for comprehending God's will. Augustine adapted the classical intellectual tradition to the requirements of Christian revelation.

With Augustine, the human-centered outlook of classical humanism—which for centuries had been undergoing transformation—gave way to a God-centered world-view. The fulfillment of God's will, not the full development of human talent, became the central concern of life.

Christianity and Classical Humanism:
Alternative World-Views

Christianity and classical humanism are the two principal components of the Western tradition. The value that modern Western civilization places on the individual derives ultimately from classical humanism and the Judeo-Christian tradition. Classical humanists believed that individual worth came from the individual's capacity to reason, to shape his character and his life according to rational standards. Christianity also places great stress on the individual. In the Christian view, God cares for each person; he wants people to behave righteously and to enter heaven; Christ died for all because he loves humanity. Christianity espouses active love and genuine concern for fellow human beings.

But Christianity and classical humanism also represent two essentially different world-views. The triumph of the Christian outlook signified a break with the essential meaning of classical humanism; it pointed to the end of the world of antiquity and the beginning of an age of faith, the Middle Ages. With the victory of Christianity, the ultimate goal of life shifted. Life's purpose was no longer to achieve excellence in this world through the full and creative development of human talent, but to attain salvation in a heavenly city. A person's worldly accomplishments amounted to very little if he or she did not accept God and his revelation.

In the classical view, history had no ultimate end, no ultimate meaning; periods of happiness and misery repeated themselves endlessly. In the Christian view, history is filled with spiritual meaning. It is the profound drama of individuals struggling to overcome their original sin in order to gain eternal happiness in heaven. History began with Adam and Eve's defiance of God and would end when Christ returns to earth, when evil is eradicated, and when God's will prevails.

Classicism held that there was no authority above reason; early Christianity taught that, without God as the starting point, knowledge was formless, purposeless, and prone to error. Classicism held that ethical standards were laws of nature that reason could discover. Through reason, individuals could arrive at those values by which they should regulate their lives. Reason would enable them to govern desires and will; it would show them where their behavior was wrong and teach them how to correct it. Early Christianity, on the other hand, maintained that ethical standards emanated from the personal will of God. Without obedience to God's commands, people would remain wicked forever; the human will, essentially sinful, could not be transformed by the promptings of reason. Only when individuals turned to God for forgiveness and guidance—only then would they find the inner strength to overcome their sinful nature. People could not perfect themselves through scientific knowledge; spiritual insight and belief in God must serve as the first principle of their lives.

In classicism, the ultimate good was to be sought through independent thought and action; in Christianity, ultimate good comes through knowing, obeying, and loving God. In early Christianity, the good life was identified not with worldly achievement but with eternal life. Each person must make entrance into God's kingdom the central aim of life. For the next thousand years, this distinction between heaven and earth, this otherworldly, theocentric outlook, would define the Western mentality.

NOTES

1. Henri Frankfort et al., *Before Philosophy* (Baltimore: Penguin Books, 1949), p. 15.

2. Samuel Sambursky, *The Physical World of the Greeks* (New York: Collier Books, 1962), pp. 18–19.

3. John A. Wilson, "Egypt—the Kingdom of the 'Two Lands,'" in *At the Dawn of Civilization*, ed. E. A. Speiser, (New Brunswick, N. J.: Rutgers University Press, 1964), pp. 267–268. Vol. I in *The World History of the Jewish People.*

4. James Shiel, ed., *Greek Thought and the Rise of Christianity* (New York: Barnes and Noble, 1968), pp. 5–6.

5. *Politics*, in *Basic Works of Aristotle*, ed. Richard McKeon (New York: Random House, 1941), pp. 1246, 1251.

6. Ibid., p. 1221.

7. Ibid., pp. 1220–1221.

8. W. H. Auden, ed., *The Portable Greek Reader* (New York: Viking, 1952), p. 38.

9. Cicero, *De Re Publica*, trans. C. W. Keyes (Cambridge, Mass.: Harvard University Press, Loeb Classical Library, 1928), 3.22, p. 211.

10. Saint Augustine, *The City of God.* An abridged version from the translation by Gerald G. Walsh et al. (Garden City, N. Y.: Doubleday Image Books, 1958), p. 519.

SUGGESTED READING

The Ancient Near East

Frankfort, Henri, *Ancient Egyptian Religion* (1948).

Frankfort, Henri et al. *The Intellectual Adventure of Ancient Man* (1946); paperback edition is entitled *Before Philosophy.*

Moscati, Sabatino, *The Face of the Ancient Orient* (1962).

Saggs, H. W. F., *Civilization Before Greece and Rome* (1989).

Wilson, John A., *The Culture of Ancient Egypt* (1951).

Ancient Hebrews

Anderson, Bernhard, *Understanding the Old Testament*, 2nd ed. (1966).

Boadt, Lawrence, *Reading the Old Testament* (1984).

Bright, John, *A History of Israel* (1972).

Heschel, Abraham, *The Prophets*, 2 vols. (1962).

Kaufmann, Yehezkel, *The Religion of Israel* (1960).

Scott, R. B. Y., *The Relevance of the Prophets* (1968).

Snaith, N. H., *The Distinctive Ideas of the Old Testament* (1964).

Greece

Boardman, John et al., eds., *The Oxford History of the Classical World* (1986).

Copleston, Frederick, *A History of Philosophy*, I (1962).

Cornford, F. M., *Before and After Socrates* (1968).

Dodds, E. R., *The Greeks and the Irrational* (1957).

Ferguson, John, *The Heritage of Hellenism* (1973).

Guthrie, W. K. C., *The Greek Philosophers from Thales to Aristotle* (1960).

Hadas, Moses, *Hellenistic Culture* (1972).

Jaeger, Werner, *Paideia: The Ideals of Greek Culture*, 3 vols. (1939–1944).

Jones, W. T., *A History of Western Philosophy*, I (1962).

Lloyd, G. E. R., *Early Greek Science* (1970).

Peters, F. E., *The Harvest of Hellenism* (1970).

Robinson, J. M., *An Introduction to Early Greek Philosophy* (1968).

Snell, Bruno, *The Discovery of the Mind* (1953).

Taylor, A. E., *Socrates* (1951).

Vernant, Jean-Pierre, *The Origins of Greek Thought* (1982).

Rome and Early Christianity

Armstrong, A. H., and Markus, R. A., *Christian Faith and Greek Philosophy* (1960).

Benko, Stephen, *Pagan Rome and the Early Christians* (1984).

Boardman, John et al., eds., *The Oxford History of the Classical World* (1986).

Clarke, M. L., *The Roman Mind* (1968).

Cochrane, C. N., *Christianity and Classical Culture* (1957).

Dodds, E. R., *Pagan and Christian in an Age of Anxiety* (1965).

Jaeger, Werner, *Early Christianity and Greek Paideia* (1961).

Meeks, Wayne A., *The Moral World of the First Christians* (1986).

Nock, A. D., *St. Paul* (1963).

———, *Early Christianity and Its Hellenistic Background* (1964).

Pelikan, Jaroslav, *The Christian Tradition* (1971).

Perkins, Pheme, *Reading the New Testament* (1978).

Segal, Allan F., *Rebecca's Children* (1986).

Wardman, Alan, *Rome's Debt to Greece* (1976).

White, Lynn, ed., *The Transformation of the Roman World* (1973).

2

The Middle Ages and the Rise

of Modernity

The triumph of Christianity and the establishment of Germanic kingdoms on once-Roman lands constituted a new phase in Western history: the end of the ancient world and the beginning of the Middle
Ages, a period that spanned a thousand years. During the Middle Ages,
a common European civilization evolved that integrated Christian,
Greco-Roman, and Germanic traditions. Christianity was at the center
of medieval civilization; Rome was the spiritual capital, and Latin the
language of intellectual life; Germanic customs pervaded social and
legal relationships. The church more than anything else gave form and
direction to the emerging civilization; it served as a unifying and civilizing agent and provided people with an intelligible and purposeful
conception of life and death. Men and women saw themselves as participants in a great drama of salvation. There was only one truth—
God's revelation to humanity. There was only one avenue to heaven,
and it passed through the church. Membership in a universal church
replaced citizenship in a universal empire. Across Europe from Italy to
Ireland, a new society centered on Christianity was forming. In the
Early Middle Ages (500–1050), the new civilization was struggling to
take form; in the High Middle Ages (1050–1300), medieval civilization
reached its height.

THE EARLY MIDDLE AGES AND THE WANING OF CLASSICAL CULTURE

The Roman world was probably too far gone to be rescued, but even if this were not so, the Germans were culturally unprepared to play the role of rescuer. By the end of the seventh century, the old Roman lands in the West showed a marked decline in central government, town life, commerce, and learning. Greco-Roman humanism, which had been in retreat since the Late Roman Empire, continued its decline in the centuries immediately following Rome's demise. The old Roman upper classes abandoned their heritage and absorbed the ways of their Germanic conquerors; the Roman schools closed, and Roman law faded into disuse. Few people besides clerics could read and write Latin, and even learned clerics were rare. Knowledge of the Greek language in western Europe was almost totally lost, and the Latin rhetorical style deteriorated. Many literary works of classical antiquity were either lost or neglected. European culture was much poorer than the high civilizations of Byzantium, Islam, and ancient Rome.

During this period of cultural poverty, the few persons who were learned generally did not engage in original thought but salvaged and transmitted remnants of classical civilization. These scholars—Boethius (480–c. 525), Cassiodorus (c. 490–575), and Isidore of Seville (c. 576–636)—retained respect for the inheritance of Greece and Rome at the same time that they remained devoted to Christianity. In a rudimentary way, they were struggling to create a Christian culture that combined the intellectual tradition of Greece and Rome with the religious teachings of the Christian church. The translations and compilations made by Boethius, Cassiodorus, and Isidore, the books collected and copied by monks and nuns, and the schools established in monasteries (particularly those in Ireland, England, and Italy) kept intellectual life from dying out completely in the Early Middle Ages.

Charlemagne (r. 768–814), the great Frankish ruler who was crowned emperor of the Romans by the pope in the year 800, fostered education in his realm. He gathered some of the finest scholars in Europe. Alcuin of Northumbria, England (735–804), was given charge of the palace school, attended by Charlemagne and his family, high lords, and youths training to serve the emperor.

The focus of the Carolingian Renaissance was predominantly Christian—an effort to train clergymen and improve their understanding of the Bible and the writings of the church fathers. This process raised the level of literacy and improved the Latin style. Most important, monastic copyists continued to preserve ancient texts, which otherwise might not have survived: the oldest surviving manuscripts of many ancient works are Carolingian copies.

Compared with the Greco-Roman past, with the cultural explosion of the twelfth and thirteenth centuries, or with the great Italian Renaissance of the fifteenth century, the Carolingian Renaissance seems slight indeed. But we must bear in mind the cultural poverty that prevailed before the era of Charlemagne. The Carolingian Renaissance reversed the process of cultural decay that characterized much of the Early Middle Ages. Learning would never again fall to the low level it had reached in the centuries following the decline of Rome. Carolingian scholars thus helped to fertilize the cultural flowering known as the Twelfth-Century Awakening—the high point of medieval civilization.

THE HIGH MIDDLE AGES: AN INTELLECTUAL FLOWERING

In the late eleventh century, Latin Christendom began to experience a cultural revival; all areas of life showed vitality and creativeness. In the twelfth and thirteenth centuries, a rich civilization with a distinctive style united an educated elite in the lands from Britain to Sicily. Gothic cathedrals, an enduring testament to the creativity of the religious impulse, were erected throughout Europe. Universities sprang up in scores of cities. Roman authors were again read and their style imitated; the quality of written Latin—the language of the church, learning, and education—improved, and secular and religious poetry, both in Latin and in the vernacular, abounded. Roman law emerged anew in Italy, spread to northern Europe, and regained its importance (lost since Roman times) as worthy of study and scholarship. Some key works of ancient Greece were translated into Latin and studied in universities. Employing the rational tradition of Greece, men of genius harmonized Christian doctrines and Greek philosophy.

The Medieval World-View

A distinctive world-view, based essentially on Christianity, evolved during the Middle Ages. This outlook differed from both the Greco-Roman and the modern scientific and secular views of the world. In the Christian view, not the individual but the Creator determined what constituted the good life. Thus, reason that was not illuminated by revelation was either wrong or inadequate, for God had revealed the proper rules for the regulation of individual and social life. Ultimately, the good life was not of this world but came from a union with God in a higher world. This Christian belief, as formulated by the church, made life and death purposeful and intelligible. It was the outlook that dominated the thought of the Middle Ages.

The Universe: Higher and Lower Worlds   Medieval thinkers sharply differentiated between spirit and matter, between a realm of grace and an earthly realm composed of base matter that stood just above hell, between a higher world of perfection and a lower world of imperfection. Moral values were derived from the higher world, which was also the final destination for the faithful. Two sets of laws operated in the medieval universe, one for the heavens and one for the earth. The cosmos was a giant ladder of ascending quality—stones, plants, animals, humans, angels, and ultimately God at the summit.

The medieval individual's understanding of himself or herself related to a comprehension of the universe as a hierarchy culminating in God. On earth, the basest objects were lifeless stones devoid of souls; higher than stones were plants, which possessed a primitive type of soul that allowed for reproduction and growth. Still higher were animals, which had the capacity for motion and sensation. The highest of the animals were human beings, who, unlike other animals, could grasp some part of universal truth. Far superior to them were the angels, who apprehended God's truth without difficulty. At the summit of this graduated universe (the Great Chain of Being) was God, who was pure Being, without limitation, and the source of all existence. God's revelation reached down to humanity through the hierarchical order. From God, revelation passed to the angels, who were also arranged hierarchically. From the angels, the truth reached men and women, grasped first by prophets and apostles and then by the multitudes. Thus, all things in the universe, from angels to men and women to the lowest earthly objects, occupied a place peculiar to their nature and were linked by God in a great, unbroken chain.

From Aristotle and Ptolemy, medieval thinkers inherited the theory of an earth-centered universe—the geocentric theory—which they imbued with Christian symbolism. The geocentric theory held that revolving around the motionless earth at uniform speeds were seven transparent spheres in which were embedded each of the seven "planets"—the moon, Mercury, Venus, the sun, Mars, Jupiter, and Saturn. A sphere of fixed stars enclosed this planetary system. Above the firmament of the stars were the three heavenly spheres: the outermost, the Empyrean Heaven, was the abode of God and the Elect. An earth-centered universe accorded with the Christian idea that God created the universe for men and women and that salvation was the primary aim of life. Because God had created people in his image, they deserved this central position in the universe. Although they might be living at the bottom rung of the cosmic ladder, only they, of all living things, had the capacity to ascend to heaven, the realm of perfection.

Also acceptable to the Christian mentality was the sharp distinction drawn by Aristotle between the world above the moon and the one below it. Aristotle held that terrestrial bodies were made of four elements: earth, water, air, fire. Celestial bodies that occupied the region above the moon were composed of a fifth element, the ether, too clear, too pure, too perfect to be found on earth. The planets and stars existed in a world apart; they were made of the divine ether and followed celestial laws that did not apply to earthly objects. Whereas earthly bodies underwent change—ice converting to water, a burning log converting to ashes—heavenly objects were incorruptible, immune to all change. Unlike earthly objects, they were indestructible.

Heavenly bodies also followed different laws of motion from earthly objects. Aristotle said that it was natural for celestial bodies to move eternally in uniform circles, such motion being considered a sign of perfection. According to Aristotle, it was also natural for heavy bodies (stone) to fall downward and for light objects (fire, smoke) to move upward toward the celestial world; the falling stone and the rising smoke were finding their natural place in the universe. This view of the universe would be shattered by the Scientific Revolution of the sixteenth and seventeenth centuries.

The Individual: Sinful but Redeemable   At the center of medieval belief was the idea of a perfect God and a wretched and sinful human being. God had given Adam and Eve freedom to choose; rebellious and presumptuous, they had used their freedom to disobey God. In doing so, they made evil an intrinsic part of the human personality. In *On the Misery of the Human Condition,* the future Pope Innocent III described the human being's sinful nature in Augustinian terms:

> For sure man was formed out of earth, conceived in guilt, born to punishment. What he does is depraved and illicit, is shameful and improper. . . . He will become fuel for eternal fires, food for worms, a mass of rottenness. . . . Man was formed . . . of the filthiest seed. He was conceived from . . . the stench of lust. . . . He commits depraved acts by which he offends God, his neighbor, and himself; shameful acts by which he defiles his name, his person, and his conscience.[1]

But God, who has not stopped loving human beings, had shown them the way out of sin. God became man and died so that human beings might be saved. Men and women were weak, egocentric, and sinful.

With God's grace they could overcome their sinful nature and gain salvation; without grace, they were utterly helpless.

Medieval individuals derived a sense of security from the hierarchical universe, in which the human position was clearly defined. True, they were sinners who dwelt on a corruptible earth at the bottom of the cosmic hierarchy. But they could ascend to the higher world of perfection above the stars. As children of God, they enjoyed the unique distinction that each human soul was precious and commanded respect.

Arranging knowledge in a hierarchical order, medieval thinkers held that knowledge of spiritual things, of God's revelation, surpassed all worldly knowledge, all human sciences. To know what God wanted of the individual was the summit of self-knowledge and permitted entrance into heaven. Thus, God was both the source and the end of knowledge. The human capacity to think and to act freely constituted the image of God within each individual; it ennobled men and women and offered them the promise of associating with God in heaven. Human nobility might derive from intelligence and free will, but if individuals used these attributes to disobey God, they brought misery on themselves.

The Social Hierarchy   To the medieval mind, God had also arranged society in a hierarchical order. The entire social structure constituted a hierarchy in which each person's duties and rights were defined by his or her divinely appointed place: the clergy guided society according to Christian standards; lords and kings, who derived their right to rule from God, defended Christian society against its enemies; and serfs, at the bottom of the social order, toiled for the good of all. Society functioned smoothly when each person accepted his or her status and performed his or her proper role, when inferiors obeyed their superiors, and when superiors led society in accordance with divine teachings. One's rights, duties, and relationship to law depended on one's ranking in the social order, and to change one's position was to upset the organic unity of society. However, no one, serfs included, should be deprived of the traditional rights associated with his or her rank. Every person, no matter how humble, occupied a vital link in God's divine chain. This hierarchical ordering was justified by the clergy:

> God himself has willed that, among men, some must be lords and some serfs, in such a fashion that the lords venerate and love God, and that the serfs love and venerate their lord following the word of the Apostle: serfs obey your temporal lords with fear and trembling; lords treat your serfs according to justice and equity.[2]

Philosophy

Medieval philosophy, or *scholasticism,* attempted to apply reason to revelation. It tried to explain and clarify Christian teachings by means of concepts and principles of logic derived from Greek philosophy. Scholastics tried to show that the teachings of faith, although not derived from reason, were not contrary to reason. They tried to prove through reason what they already held to be true through faith. For example, the existence of God and the immortality of the soul, which every Christian accepted as articles of faith, could also, they thought, be demonstrated by reason. In struggling to harmonize faith with reason, medieval thinkers constructed an extraordinary synthesis of Christian revelation and Greek rationalism.

The scholastic masters used reason not to challenge faith but to serve faith—to elucidate, clarify, and buttress it. They did not break with the central concern of Christianity, that of earning God's grace and achieving salvation. Although this goal could be realized solely by faith, scholastic thinkers insisted that a science of nature did not obstruct the pursuit of grace and that philosophy could assist the devout in the contemplation of God. They did not reject Christian beliefs that were beyond the grasp of human reason and therefore could not be deduced by rational argument. Instead, they held that such truths rested entirely on revelation and were to be accepted on faith. To medieval thinkers, reason did not have an independent existence but ultimately had to acknowledge a suprarational, superhuman standard of truth. They wanted rational thought to be directed by faith for Christian ends and guided by scriptural and ecclesiastical authority. Ultimately, faith had the final word.

Not all Christian thinkers welcomed the use of reason. Regarding Greek philosophy as an enemy of faith, a fabricator of heresies, and an obstacle to achieving communion of the soul with God, conservative theologians opposed the application of reason to Christian revelation. In a sense, the conservatives were right. By giving renewed vitality to Greek thought, medieval philosophy nurtured a powerful force that would eventually shatter the medieval concepts of nature and society and weaken Christianity. Modern Western thought was created by thinkers who refused to subordinate reason to Christian authority. Reason proved a double-edged sword: it both ennobled and undermined the medieval world-view.

Thomas Aquinas: The Synthesis of Reason and Christianity   The introduction into Latin Christendom of the major works of Aristotle created a dilemma for religious authorities. Aristotle's comprehensive philosophy of nature and man, a product of human reason alone, con-

Thomas Aquinas *(The Bettmann Archive)*

flicted in many instances with essential Christian doctrine. Whereas Christianity taught that God created the universe at a specific point in time, Aristotle held that the universe was eternal. Nor did Aristotle believe in the personal immortality of the soul, another cardinal principle of Christianity. Church officials feared that the dissemination of Aristotle's ideas and the use of Aristotelian logic would endanger faith. At various times in the first half of the thirteenth century, they forbade teaching the scientific works of Aristotle at the University of Paris. But because the ban did not apply throughout Christendom and was not consistently enforced in Paris, Aristotle's philosophy continued to be studied.

Rejecting the position of the conservatives who insisted that philosophy would contaminate faith, Saint Thomas Aquinas (c. 1225–1274) upheld the value of human reason and natural knowledge. He set about reconciling Aristotelianism with Christianity. Aquinas taught at Paris and organized the Dominican school of theology in Naples. His greatest work, *Summa Theologica,* is a systematic exposition of Christian thought.

Can the teachings of faith conflict with the evidence of reason? For Aquinas, the answer was emphatically no. Since both faith and reason came from God, they were not in competition with each other but, properly understood, supported each other and formed an organic unity. Consequently, reason should not be feared, for it was another avenue to God. Because there was an inherent agreement between true faith and correct reason—they both ultimately stemmed from God—contradictions between the two were only a misleading appearance. Although philosophy had not yet been able to resolve the dilemma, for God no such contradictions existed. In heaven, human beings would attain complete knowledge, as well as complete happiness. While on earth, however, they must allow faith to guide reason; they must not permit reason to oppose or undermine faith.

Because reason was no enemy of faith, its application to revelation should not be feared. Thus, in exalting God, Aquinas also paid homage to human intelligence, proclaimed the value of rational activity, including the investigation of the natural world, and asserted the importance of physical reality discovered through human senses. Therefore, he valued the natural philosophy of Aristotle. Correctly used, Aristotelian thought would provide faith with valuable assistance. Aquinas's great effort was to synthesize Aristotelianism with the divine revelation of Christianity, for he had no doubt that the two could be harmonized. He made use of Aristotelian categories in his five proofs of God's existence. For example, in his first proof, Aquinas argued that a thing cannot move itself. Whatever is moved must be moved by something else, and that by something else again. "Therefore, it is necessary to arrive at a first mover, moved by no other; and this everyone understands to be God."[3]

Aquinas upheld the value of reason. To love the intellect was to honor God and not to diminish the truth of faith. He had confidence in the power of the rational mind to comprehend most of the truths of revelation, and he insisted that in nontheological questions about specific things in nature—those questions not affecting salvation—people should trust only to reason and experience. Thus, Aquinas gave new importance to the empirical world and to scientific speculation and human knowledge. The traditional medieval view, based largely on Saint Augustine, drew a sharp distinction between the higher world of grace and the lower world of nature, between the world of spirit and the world of sense experience. Knowledge derived from the natural world was often seen as an obstacle to true knowledge. Aquinas altered this tradition by affirming the importance of knowledge of the social order and the physical world. He gave human reason and worldly knowledge a new dignity. Thus, the City of Man was not merely a sinful place from which people tried to escape in order to enter God's city; it was worthy of investigation and understanding. But Aquinas remained a medieval and not a modern thinker, for he always subordinated reason to the needs of faith, and he never questioned the truth of the medieval Christian view of the world and the individual.

Science

During the Early Middle Ages, few scientific works from the ancient world were available to western Europeans. Scientific thought was at its lowest ebb since it had originated more than a thousand years earlier in Greece. In contrast, both Islamic and Byzantine civilizations preserved and in some instances added to the legacy of Greek science. However, in the High Middle Ages, many ancient texts were translated from Greek and Arabic into Latin and entered Latin Christendom for the first time. The principal centers of translation were Spain, where Christian and Muslim civilizations met, and Sicily, which had been controlled by Byzantium up to the last part of the ninth century and then by Islam until Christian Normans completed conquest of the island by 1091. The translated works stimulated interest in a rational inquiry into nature.

In the thirteenth and fourteenth centuries, a genuine scientific movement did occur. Impressed with the naturalistic and empirical approach of Aristotle, some medieval schoolmen spent time examining physical nature. Among them was the Dominican Albert the Great (Albertus Magnus). Albert (c. 1206–1280) was born in Germany, studied at Padua, and taught at the University of Paris, where Thomas Aquinas was his student. To Albert, philosophy meant more than employing Greek reason to contemplate divine wisdom: it also meant making sense of nature. Albert devoted himself to editing and commenting on the vast body of Aristotle's works.

While retaining the Christian stress on God, revelation, the supernatural, and the afterlife, Albert (unlike many earlier Christian thinkers) considered nature a valid field for investigation. In his writings on geology, chemistry, botany, and zoology, Albert, like Aristotle, displayed a respect for the concrete details of nature, utilizing them as empirical evidence.

Other scholars of the scientific movement included Robert Grosseteste (c. 1175–1253), the chancellor of Oxford University. He declared that the roundness of the earth could be demonstrated by reason. In addition, he insisted that mathematics was necessary in order to understand the physical world, and he carried out experiments on the refraction of light. Another Englishman, the monk and philosopher Roger Bacon (c. 1214–1294), foreshadowed the modern attitude of using science to gain mastery over nature. Bacon valued the study of mathematics and read Arabic works on the reflection and refraction of light. Among his achievements were experiments in optics and the observation that light travels much faster than sound. His description of the anatomy of the vertebrate eye and optic nerves was the finest of that era, and he recommended dissecting the eyes of pigs and cows to obtain greater knowledge of the subject.

Medieval scholars did not make the breakthrough to modern science. They kept the belief that the earth was at the center of the universe and that different sets of laws operated on earth and in the heavens. They did not invent analytic geometry or calculus or arrive at the modern concept of inertia. Moreover, medieval science was never wholly removed from a theological setting. Modern science deliberately seeks the advancement of specifically scientific knowledge, but in the Middle Ages, many questions involving nature were raised merely to clarify a religious problem.

Medieval scholars and philosophers did, however, advance knowledge about optics, the tides, and mechanics. They saw the importance of mathematics for interpreting nature, and they performed experiments. By translating and commenting on ancient Greek and Arabic works, medieval scholars provided future ages with ideas to reflect on and to surpass, a necessary precondition for the emergence of modern science. Medieval thinkers also developed an anti-Aristotelian physics that some historians of science believe influenced Galileo, the creator of modern mechanics, more than two centuries later.

THE MIDDLE AGES AND THE MODERN WORLD: CONTINUITY AND DISCONTINUITY

Medieval civilization began to decline in the fourteenth century, but no dark age comparable to the three centuries following Rome's fall descended on Europe; its economic and political institutions and technological skills had grown too strong. Instead, the waning of the Middle Ages opened up possibilities for another stage in Western civilization—the modern age.

The modern world is linked to the Middle Ages in innumerable ways. European cities, the middle class, the state system, English common law, universities—all had their origins in the Middle Ages. During medieval times, important advances were made in business practices, including partnerships, systematic bookkeeping, and the bill of exchange. By translating and commenting on the writings of Greek and Arabic thinkers, medieval scholars preserved a priceless intellectual heritage, without which the modern mind could never have evolved. And between the thought of the scholastics and that of early modern philosophers there are numerous connecting strands.

During the Middle Ages, Europeans began to take the lead over the Muslims, the Byzantines, the Chinese, and all other peoples in the use of technology. Medieval technology and inventiveness stemmed in part from Christianity, which taught that God had created the world specifically for human beings to subdue and exploit. Consequently, medieval people tried to employ animal power and laborsaving machinery to relieve human drudgery. Moreover, Christianity taught that God was above nature, not within it; so the Christian had no spiritual obstacle to exploiting nature, unlike, for instance, the Hindu. In contrast to classical humanism, the Christian outlook did not consider manual work degrading—even monks combined it with study.

The Christian stress on the sacred worth of the individual and on the higher law of God has never ceased to influence Western civilization. Although in modern times the various Christian churches have not often taken the lead in political and social reform, the ideals identified with the Judeo-Christian tradition have become part of the Western heritage. As such, they have inspired social reformers who may no longer identify with their ancestral religion.

Believing that God's law was superior to state or national decrees, medieval philosophers provided a theoretical basis for opposing tyrannical kings who violated Christian principles. The idea that both the ruler and the ruled are bound by a higher law would, in a secularized form, become a principal element of modern liberal thought.

Feudalism also contributed to the history of liberty. According to feudal theory, the king, as a member of the feudal community, was duty-bound to honor agreements made by his vassals. Lords possessed personal rights that the king was obliged to respect. Resentful of a king who ran roughshod over customary feudal rights, lords also negotiated contracts with the crown, such as the famous Magna Carta (1215), to define and guard their customary liberties. To protect themselves from the arbitrary behavior of a king, feudal lords initiated what came to be called *government by consent* and the *rule of law*.

Thus, in the Middle Ages there gradually emerged the idea that law was not imposed on inferiors by an absolute monarch but required the collaboration of the king and his subjects; that the king, too, was bound by the law; and that lords had the right to resist a monarch who violated agreements. A related phenomenon was the rise of representative institutions with which the king was expected to consult on the realm's affairs. The most notable such institution was the British Parliament, which, although subordinate to the king, became a permanent part of the state. Later, in the seventeenth century, Parliament would successfully challenge royal authority. Thus, continuity exists between the feudal tradition of a king bound by law and the modern practice of limiting the authority of the head of state.

Although the elements of continuity are clear, the characteristic outlook of the Middle Ages is as different from that of the modern age as it was from that of the ancient world. Religion was the integrating feature of the Middle Ages, whereas science and secularism—a preoccupation with worldly life—determine the modern outlook. The period from the Italian Renaissance of the fifteenth century through the eighteenth-century Age of Enlightenment constituted a breaking away from the medieval world-view—a rejection of the medieval conception of nature, the individual, and the purpose of life. The transition from medieval to modern was neither sudden nor complete, for there are no sharp demarcation lines separating historical periods. While many distinctly medieval ways endured in the sixteenth, seventeenth, and even eighteenth centuries, these centuries saw as well the rise of new intellectual, political, and economic forms that marked the emergence of modernity.

Medieval thought began with the existence of God and the truth of his revelation as interpreted by the church, which set the standards and defined the purposes for human endeavor. The medieval mind rejected the fundamental principle of Greek philosophy—the autonomy of reason. Without the guidance of revealed truth, reason was seen as feeble.

Scholastics reasoned closely and carefully, drew fine distinctions, and at times demonstrated a critical attitude. They engaged in genuine philosophical speculation, but they did not allow philosophy to challenge the basic premises of their faith. Unlike either ancient or modern thinkers, medieval schoolmen believed ultimately that reason alone could not provide a unified view of nature or society. A rational soul had to be guided by a divine light. For all medieval philosophers, the natural order depended on a supernatural order for its origin and purpose. To understand the natural world properly, it was necessary to know its relationship to the higher world. The discoveries of reason had to conform with Scripture as interpreted by the church. In medieval thought, says historian-philosopher Ernst Cassirer,

> neither science nor morality, neither law nor state, can be erected on its own foundations. Supernatural assistance is always needed to bring them to true perfection. . . . Reason is and remains the servant of revelation; within the sphere of natural intellectual and psychological forces, reason leads toward, and prepares the ground for revelation.[4]

In the modern view, both nature and the human intellect are self-sufficient. Nature is seen as a mathematical system that operates without miracles or any other form of divine intervention. To comprehend nature and society, the mind needs no divine assistance; it accepts no authority above reason. The modern mentality finds it unacceptable to reject the conclusions of science on the basis of clerical authority and revelation or to base politics, law, or economics on religious dogma; it refuses to settle public issues by appeals to religious belief.

Rejecting the medieval division of the universe into higher and lower realms and superior and inferior substances, modern thinkers came to regard the universe as one and nature as uniform. The Scientific Revolution of the sixteenth and seventeenth centuries removed earth from its central position in the universe and made it just another planet that revolves about the sun. It dispensed with the medieval division of the universe into higher and lower worlds and postulated the uniformity of nature and of nature's laws. The cosmos knows no privilege of rank; heavenly bodies follow the same laws of nature as earthly objects do; and space is geometric and homogeneous, not hierarchical, heterogeneous, and qualitative. The universe was no longer seen as finite and closed but as infinite, and the operations of nature were explained mathematically. The modern thinker studies mathematical law and chemical composition, not grades of perfection. Spiritual meaning is not sought in an examination of the material world. Roger Bacon, for example, described seven coverings of the eye and then concluded that God had fashioned the eye in this manner in order to express the seven gifts of the Spirit. This way of thinking is alien to the modern outlook.

The modern outlook also broke with the rigid division of medieval society into three orders: clergy, nobles, and commoners. Opposing the feudal principle that an individual's obligations and rights are a function of his or her rank in society, the modern intellect stressed equality of opportunity and equal treatment under the law. It rejected the idea that society should be guided by clergy who possessed a special wisdom, by nobles who were entitled to special privileges, and by a monarch who received his or her power from God.

The modern mind also rejected the personal and customary character of feudal law. As the modern state developed, law assumed an impersonal and objective character. For example, if the lord demanded more than the customary forty days of military service, the vassal might refuse to comply, seeing the lord's request as an unpardonable violation of custom and agreement and an infringement on his liberties. In the modern state, with a constitution and a representative assembly, if a new law increasing the length of military service is passed, it merely replaces the old law. People do not refuse to obey it because the government has broken faith or violated custom.

In the modern world, the individual's relationship to the universe has been radically transformed. Medieval people lived in a geocentric universe that was finite in space and time. The universe was small, enclosed by a sphere of fixed stars, beyond which were the heavens. The universe, it was believed, was some four thousand years old, and in the not too distant future, Christ would return and human history would come to an end. People in the Middle Ages knew why they were on earth and what was expected of them; they never doubted that heaven would be their reward for living a Christian life. Preparation for heaven was the ultimate aim of life. J. H. Randall, Jr., a historian of ideas, eloquently sums up the medieval view of a purposeful universe in which the human being's role was clearly defined:

> The world was governed throughout by the omnipotent will and omnis-cient mind of God, whose sole interests were centered in man, his trial, his fall, his suffering and his glory. Worm of the dust as he was, man was yet the central object in the whole universe. . . . And when his destiny was completed, the heavens would be rolled up as a scroll and he would dwell with the Lord forever. Only those who rejected God's freely offered grace and with hardened hearts refused repentance would be cut off from this eternal life.[5]

This comforting medieval vision is alien to the modern outlook. To-day, in a universe 15 billion years old, in which the earth is a tiny speck floating in an endless cosmic ocean, where life evolved over tens of millions of years, many westerners are no longer certain that human beings are special children of God; that heaven is their ultimate goal; that under their feet is hell; and that God is an active agent in human history. To many intellectuals, the universe seems unresponsive to the religious supplications of people and life's purpose is sought within the limits of earthly existence. Science and secularism have driven Christianity and faith from their central position to the periphery of human concerns.

From the Italian Renaissance of the fifteenth century through the eighteenth-century Age of Enlightenment, the outlook and institutions of the Middle Ages were progressively dismantled and distinctly modern forms developed. The radical change in European civilization could be seen on every level of society. On the economic level, commerce and industry expanded greatly and capitalism replaced medieval forms of economic organization. On the political level, central government grew stronger at the expense of feudal and religious authorities. On the religious level, the rise of Protestantism fragmented the unity of Christendom. On the social level, middle-class townspeople, increasing in number and wealth, were playing a more important role in economic and cultural life. On the cultural level, the clergy lost its monopoly over learning, and the otherworldly orientation of the Middle Ages gave way to a secular outlook in literature and art.

During these centuries, the modern outlook gradually emerged. Mathematics rendered the universe comprehensible. Economic and political thought broke free of the religious frame of reference. Science became the great hope of the future. The thinkers of the Enlightenment wanted to liberate humanity from superstition, ignorance, and traditions that could not pass the test of reason. They saw themselves as emancipating culture from theological dogma and clerical authority. Rejecting the Christian idea of a person's inherent sinfulness, they held that the individual was basically good and that evil resulted from faulty institutions, poor education, and bad leadership. Thus, the concept of a rational and free society in which individuals could realize their potential slowly emerged.

THE RENAISSANCE

For many historians, the Renaissance, which was characterized by a rebirth of interest in the human-centered culture and secular outlook of ancient Greece and Rome, marks the starting point of the modern era. The Renaissance began in the fourteenth century in the northern Italian city-states, which had grown prosperous from the revival of trade in the Middle Ages. Italian merchants and bankers had the wealth to acquire libraries and fine works of art and to support art, literature, and scholarship. Surrounded by reminders of ancient Rome—amphitheaters, monuments, and sculpture—the well-to-do took an interest in classical culture and thought. In the late fifteenth and sixteenth centuries, Renaissance ideas spread to Germany, France, Spain, and England through books available in great numbers due to the invention of the printing press.

Although Renaissance individuals were by no means anti-Christian, they valued worldly activities and interests to a much greater degree than did people of the Middle Ages, whose outlook was dominated by Christian otherworldliness. Renaissance individuals were fascinated by *this* world and by life's joys and possibilities; they aspired to live a rich and creative life on earth and to fulfill themselves through artistic and literary activity. In his folk epic, *Gargantua and Pantagruel*, the French humanist François Rabelais (c. 1495–c. 1553) criticized medieval philosophy for its overriding concern with obscure and irrelevant questions, which provided no insights into the human condition; he also censured the narrow-minded clergy, who deprived people of life's joys.

Expressing his aversion to medieval asceticism, Rabelais attacked monasticism as life-denying and regarded worldly pleasure as a legitimate need and aim of human nature. He imagined a monastery where people's lives were not regulated by "laws, statutes, or rules, but according to their own free will and pleasure." They slept and ate when they desired and learned "to read, write, sing, play musical instruments, speak five or six languages, and compose in them."[6] Only one rule did they observe: "DO WHAT YOU WILL."

Thus, the Renaissance gave rise to the secular outlook that characterizes the modern mentality. The new secularism bestowed intrinsic worth on worldly pleasure and activity. Reviving the Greco-Roman view that the complete man is a political animal who participates actively in civic affairs, Renaissance figures were critical of monastic withdrawal and asceticism and of the scholastics' purely contemplative life. The humanist Coluccio Salutati (1331–1406) admonished a friend who intended to withdraw into a monastery: "Do not imagine, Pellegrino, that one can seek perfection by fleeing from the crowd, shunning the sight of everything beautiful and locking oneself up in a monastery or a hermitage."[7] In the centuries to come, a growing secular outlook would hold that the individual should be emancipated from domination by otherworldly concerns, theological dogma, and ecclesiastical authority and should focus on the full development of human talents and on improving the quality of earthly existence.

Individualism was another hallmark of the Renaissance. The urban elite sought to demonstrate their unique talents, to assert their own personalities, and to gain recognition for their accomplishments. Traditional feudal values of birth and place in a fixed hierarchy were superseded by a desire for individual achievement. And individual worth was interpreted far more broadly than it had been by feudal lords, who had equated worth with military prowess. Renaissance Italy produced a distinctive human type, the "universal man": a many-sided person, who demonstrated mastery of the ancient classics, an appreciation of and even talent for the visual arts, and a concern for the day-to-day affairs of his city, someone who aspired to mold his life into a work of art. Disdaining Christian humility, Renaissance individuals took pride in their talents and worldly accomplishments—"I can work miracles," said the great Leonardo da Vinci. Renaissance artists portrayed the individual character of human beings, captured the rich diversity of human personality, produced the first portraits since Roman times, and affixed their signatures to their works. Renaissance writers probed their own feelings, demonstrating a self-awareness that characterizes the modern outlook.

In the opening section of his *Oration on the Dignity of Man*, Giovanni Pico della Mirandola (1463–1494) declared that, unlike other creatures, man has not been allotted a fixed place in the universe; human beings are not part of a world scheme that assigns every living thing a fixed nature and purpose. Our destiny is not determined by anything outside us, said Pico. Rather, God has bestowed on human beings a unique distinction, a unique dignity—the liberty to determine the form and value that their lives shall acquire. Man, said Pico, can be whatever he wills; he can choose his own destiny.

> I have come to understand why man is the most fortunate of creatures and consequently worthy of all admiration. . . . [God] took man as a creature of indeterminate nature and, assigning him a place in the middle of the world, addressed him thus: The nature of all other things is limited and constrained within the bounds of laws prescribed by Us. Thou, constrained by no limits, in accordance with thine own free will . . . shalt ordain for thyself the limits of thy nature. We have set thee at the world's center that thou mayest from thence more easily observe whatever is in the world. We have made thee neither of heaven nor of earth, neither mortal nor immortal, so that with freedom of choice and with honor, as though the maker and moulder of thyself, thou mayest fashion thyself in whatever shape thou shalt prefer.[8]

The notion that people are self-sufficient beings, with the power to shape their own lives according to the ideals that they embrace through reason, not authority, is a key characteristic of the modern outlook.

Medieval thinkers often expressed contempt for the worldly life. For them, people had dignity essentially because they were created in God's image and could attain salvation, not because they possessed worldly talents. They agreed with Saint Augustine that it was presumptuous for human beings to think that they could achieve excellence through their own powers. Human nature, which is corrupt, said Augustine, always depends on God's grace. Innocent III's *On the Misery of the Human Condition*, which emphasized humanity's sinful state, echoed Saint Augustine's low estimation of the individual.

Renaissance figures, both in thought and deed, repudiated Augustine's view of the individual's fallen and dependent nature. In *Hamlet*, Shakespeare eloquently expressed the new conception of man: "What a piece of work is a man! How noble in reason, how infinite in faculties, in form and moving how express and admirable, in action how like an angel, in apprehension, how like a god; the beauty of the world, the paragon of animals."[9] In the tradition of the ancient Greeks, Renaissance figures expressed confidence in human nature and urged talented people to realize their capacities. They ascribed to human beings a special dignity: they had the intelligence and talent to accomplish wonders on earth and a special duty to realize this potential. The realization of excellence, of greatness, depended on human intelligence and will, not on God's providence. British student of political thought Quentin Skinner concludes: "This emphasis on man's creative powers. . . . helped to foster a new interest in the individual personality. It came to seem possible for man to use his freedom to become the architect and the explorer of his own character."[10]

To be sure, the Renaissance was not a complete or abrupt break with the Middle Ages. Many medieval elements and attitudes, particularly scholastic learning, persisted into the Renaissance and beyond, and several components of Renaissance culture have medieval antecedents. For example, the revival of classical learning, which is the distinguishing feature of the Renaissance, dates back to the cultural awakening of the twelfth and thirteenth centuries.

Yet there are three important differences between the Twelfth-Century Awakening, which was the high point of medieval civilization, and the Renaissance. First, many more ancient works were restored to circulation during the Renaissance than during the cultural revival of the Middle Ages. While Roman authors were widely known in the Middle Ages, some Latin writers, such as Lucretius and Tacitus, were rediscovered only during the Renaissance. Renaissance scholars had much better knowledge of classical Latin and of Latin authors than did their medieval forebears. For the most part, medieval thinkers did not know the Greek language and were unfamiliar with many important works of Greek literature, which remained untranslated into Latin. Renaissance scholars mastered Greek and translated into Latin the whole corpus of ancient Greek literature, making many texts available to western Europeans for the first time; and they produced new and better translations of Roman works. Second, medieval scholastics had tried to fit the ideas of the ancients into a Christian framework; they used Greek philosophy to explain Christian teachings. Renaissance scholars, on the other hand, valued ancient literature for its own sake. They admired its graceful style and believed that Greek and Roman authors could teach much about the art of living and the performance of civic duties. Third, Renaissance humanists approached ancient civilization with a critical attitude; they studied texts in a historical context and examined them for authenticity and accuracy. In contrast, Medieval thinkers generally did not relate a text to its times but accepted it uncritically as an authoritative work of wisdom.

Lorenzo Valla (c. 1407–1457) expressed the new critical spirit in *Declamation Concerning the False Decretals of Constantine*. The so-called Donation of Constantine, which was used by popes to support their claim to temporal authority, stated that the fourth-century Roman Emperor Constantine had given the papacy dominion over the western Empire. By showing that some of the words in the document were unknown in Constantine's time and therefore could not have been used by the emperor, Valla proved that the document was forged by church officials several hundred years after Constantine's death. And in his *Notes to the New Testament,* Valla said that "none of the words of Christ have come down to us, for Christ spoke in Hebrew and never wrote down anything."[11] By viewing ancient works as historical phenomena—products of a particular people at a particular time—Renaissance humanists helped create a more critical historical awareness.

Renaissance figures were aware that they were living in a new and special time. They regarded the centuries immediately preceding them (unfairly, as we now know) as a dark age, in which antiquity's cultural brilliance had been snuffed out; and they described their own age as a rebirth of the arts and learning after an interval of medieval darkness and sterility. It was Renaissance humanists who arranged history into three periods: ancient, medieval, and modern. The humanists also conceived the embryo of the modern idea of progress. In their exuberance and self-confidence, they dared to believe that they, "the moderns," could surpass the cultural brilliance of the ancient Greeks and Romans.

As noted earlier, the distinguishing feature of the Renaissance period was the revival of classical learning. It was fostered by the humanist movement, an educational and cultural program based on the study of ancient Greek and Latin literature. By studying the humanities—literature, history, rhetoric, and moral and political philosophy—humanists aimed to revive the worldly spirit and civic virtue of the ancient Greeks and Romans, which they believed had been lost during the Middle Ages. Humanists were fascinated by the writings of the ancients. From the works of Thucydides, Plato, Cicero, Seneca, and other ancient authors, humanists sought guidelines for living well in this world and looked for stylistic models for their own literary efforts. Their appreciation of Greek literature led them to introduce the study of Greek into the university curriculum.

Humanists believed that the study of Greek and Roman literature was the only fitting education for a gentleman or someone engaged in public service. To the humanists, the ancients had written brilliantly, in an incomparable literary style, on friendship, citizenship, statesmanship, love, bravery, beauty, excellence, and every other topic devoted to the enrichment of human life. Humanists admired ancient authors for their insights into the human condition and viewed them as guides for moral self-development. Humanists strove to imitate the style of the ancients, to speak as eloquently and to write as gracefully as the Greeks and Romans. Toward these ends, they sought to read, print and restore to circulation every scrap of ancient literature that could still be found. They searched monastery libraries for these lost treasures. Humanists were not anti-Christian or irreligious, but in contrast to medieval thinkers, they did not subordinate secular studies to the requirements of Christian teachings, and they placed the human being at the center of their world outlook.

Like the humanist movement, Renaissance art also marked a break with medieval culture. The art of the Middle Ages had served a religious function: its purpose was to lift the mind to God. It depicted a spiritual universe in which the supernatural was the supreme reality. The Gothic cathedral, with its flying buttresses, soared toward heaven, rising in ascending tiers; it reflected the medieval conception of a hierarchical universe, with God at its apex.

Medieval painting visually depicted spirituality. Traditionally, the left side of a painting portrayed the damned, the right side the saved; dark colors expressed evil, light colors good. Spatial proportion was relative to spirituality—the less spiritually valuable a thing was, the less form it had (or the more deformed it was). Medieval art perfectly expressed the Christian view of the universe and the individual.

Renaissance artists, of course, utilized religious themes. But at the same time, they shifted attention from heaven to the natural world and to the human being, shattering the dominance of religion over art. With unmatched brilliance, Raphael, Michelangelo, da Vinci, and other Renaissance artists depicted the human qualities of men and women and celebrated the human form. Renaissance art also developed a new conception of visual space, which was defined from the standpoint of the individual observer. It was quantitative space, in which the artist, employing reason and mathematics, portrayed the essential form of the object as it appeared in three dimensions to the human eye. This attempt to represent reality in a mathematical way is a distinctive feature of the modern outlook.

THE REFORMATION

The Renaissance broke with medieval art and literary forms and ushered in a vibrant secularism and individualism. At first glance, it might seem that the Reformation, which began in the early sixteenth century with Martin Luther's (1483–1546) attack on the church, marked a break with the secular humanism initiated by the Renaissance and was a regression to medieval religiosity. Whereas the humanists fostered free discussion and criticism, the Reformation, at times, degenerated into fanaticism, narrow-mindedness, and intolerance. Attracted to the ancient Stoic doctrine of the autonomous will, Renaissance humanists had broken with Augustine's stern view of original sin—a corrupt human nature and the person's inability to achieve salvation through his or her own efforts. However, both Luther and John Calvin (1509–1564) saw human beings as essentially depraved and corrupt and rejected completely the notion that individuals can do something for their own salvation. Such an assertion of human will, they held, revealed a dangerous self-confidence in human beings. Men and women must always humble themselves before God, depend entirely on his will, and despair completely of securing salvation through their own deeds.

Yet in several important ways, the Reformation contributed to the shaping of modernity. By dividing Christendom into Catholic and Protestant, the Reformation destroyed the religious unity of Europe, the distinguishing feature of the Middle Ages, and weakened the church, the chief institution of medieval society. By strengthening monarchs at the expense of church bodies, the Reformation furthered the growth of the modern secular and centralized state. Protestant rulers repudiated all papal claims to temporal authority and extended their power over the newly established Protestant churches in their lands. In Catholic lands, the weakened church was reluctant to challenge monarchs, whose support it now needed more than ever. This subordination of clerical authority to the throne permitted kings to build strong centralized states, which characterize the political life of the modern West.

While absolute monarchy was the immediate beneficiary of the Reformation, indirectly Protestantism contributed to the growth of political liberty—another feature of the modern West. To be sure, neither Luther nor Calvin championed political freedom. Luther believed that a good Christian was an obedient subject, and he explicitly stated that subjects should obey their rulers' commands: "It is no wise proper for anyone who would be a Christian to set himself up against his government, whether it act justly or unjustly."[12] He also declared: "Those who sit in the office of magistrate sit in the place of God, and their judgment is as if God judged from heaven. . . . If the emperor calls me, God calls me."[13] When the long-suffering German peasants rose up against the lords, Luther, regarding the uprising as a threat to the social order, approved its suppression by the lords. Calvinists created a theocracy in Geneva that closely regulated the citizens' private lives, and Calvin strongly condemned resistance to political authority as wicked. He held that rulers are selected by God and punishment of bad rulers belongs only to God and not to the rulers' subjects.

Nevertheless, the Reformation also provided a basis for challenging monarchical authority. Some Protestant theorists, mainly Calvinists, finding themselves an oppressed minority, supported resistance to political authorities whose edicts, they believed, contravened God's law as expressed in the Bible. This religious justification for revolution against tyrannical authority helped to fuel the resistance of English Calvinists, or Puritans, to the English monarchy in the seventeenth century. Like their English counterparts, American Puritans believed that the Bible was infallible and its teachings a higher law than the law of the state. They, too, challenged political and religious authorities who, in their view, contravened God's law. Thus, American Puritans acquired two habits that were crucial to the development of political liberty: dissent and resistance. When transferred to the realm of politics, these Puritan tendencies led Americans to resist authority that they considered unjust. Both the English Revolution and the American Revolution were instrumental in creating the modern constitutional state, which limits the powers of government.

The Reformation advanced the idea of equality. Equality is rooted in the Judeo-Christian belief that all people are the creatures of a single God. In two important ways, however, medieval society contravened the principle of equality. First, feudalism stressed hereditary distinctions between nobles and commoners. Medieval society was a hierarchy of legal orders, or estates—ascending from commoners to nobles and then to clergy. Second, the medieval church taught that only the clergy could administer the sacraments, which provided people with the means of attaining salvation; for this reason, the clergy were above the laity. Luther, in contrast, held that there was no spiritual distinction between laypeople and clergy. There was a spiritual equality of all believers: all were equally Christian; all were equally priests.

The Reformation fostered a religious individualism that was the counterpart of the intellectual individualism of the Renaissance. In their rebellion against clerical authority and accepted orthodoxy, Protestant reformers asserted the primacy of private judgment and individual conscience. When Luther was ordered by the authorities to recant, he answered in the spirit of a rebellious and self-determining religious individualism: "Unless I am convinced by Scripture and plain reason— I do not accept the authority of popes and councils, for they have contradicted each other—my conscience is captive to the Word of God. I cannot and I will not recant anything, for to go against conscience is neither right nor safe. God help me."[14]

Since for Protestants there was no official interpreter of Scripture as there was for Catholics, each person had the responsibility of interpreting the Bible according to the commands of his or her own conscience. Everyone had to decide individually which path to take toward God. Thus, Protestants confronted the prospect of salvation or damnation entirely on their own. No church provided them with security or certainty, and no priesthood interceded between them and God. The Protestant church was a community of equal believers guided by their own consciences, not a hierarchy of offices with special powers and prerogatives. Piety was not determined by the church but by the autonomous individual, whose conscience, illuminated by God, was the source of judgment and authority.

For the Protestant, faith was personal and inward. This new arrangement called for a personal relationship between each person and God and called attention to the individual's inner religious capacities. Certain that God had chosen them for salvation, many Protestants developed the inner self-assurance and assertiveness that characterized the modern westerner. Thus, the Protestant emphasis on private judgment in religious matters—on an inner personal conviction—helped to mold a new and distinctly modern European, who had confidence in his own judgment and was unafraid to resist authority.

The Reformation's stress on individual conscience may have contributed to the development of the capitalist spirit, which underlies modern economic life. So argued German sociologist Max Weber in *The Protestant Ethic and the Spirit of Capitalism* (1904). Weber acknowledged that capitalism existed in Europe before the Reformation; for example, merchant bankers in medieval Italian and German towns engaged in capitalistic activities. But, he argued, Protestantism (particularly Calvinism) gave to capitalism a special dynamism. Protestant businessmen believed that they had a religious obligation to make money, and their faith gave them the self-discipline to do so. Convinced that prosperity was God's blessing and poverty his curse, Calvinists had a spiritual inducement to labor industriously and to avoid sloth. According to Calvin's doctrine of predestination, God had already determined in advance who would be saved; salvation could not be attained through any worldly actions. Although there was no definite way of determining who had received God's grace, Calvin's followers came to believe that certain activities were signs that God had chosen them: hard work, diligence, dutifulness, efficiency, frugality, and a disdain for hedonism (all virtues that contribute to rational and orderly business procedures and to business success) were signs of election. Thus, argued Weber, Protestantism, unlike Catholicism, gave religious approval to moneymaking and the businessman's way of life. Moreover, Calvinists seemed to believe that they had attained a special insight into their relationship with God; this attitude fostered a sense of self-assurance and righteousness. Protestantism, therefore, produced a highly individualistic religiosity that valued inner strength, self-discipline, and methodical and sober behavior—necessary traits for a middle class seeking business success in a highly competitive world.

Did the Protestant emphasis on individual conscience and individual interpretation of Scripture promote liberty of conscience, that is, toleration of differing religious views, which is another fundamental characteristic of the modern world? There is no easy answer to this question. Luther himself opposed propagation of beliefs that in his view misinterpreted Scripture. Calvin ordered that Michael Servetus, who held unorthodox views on the trinity be burned to death as a heretic, and the Lutheran princes slaughtered Anabaptists. However, the killings and the disruption of the body politic caused by sectarian conflicts prompted some thinkers, including some clergy, to proclaim the principle of toleration. Toleration became one of the chief concerns of the secular-minded eighteenth-century Enlightenment thinkers, who were disgusted by Christianity's brutal history of persecution.

The Reformation released a torrent of religious fanaticism, culminating in persecution and the "wars of religion" between Protestants and Catholics, which devastated Europe until 1648, the end of the Thirty Years' War. Nor did Europe rid itself of this fanaticism. In a broad view of Western history, it could be argued that the fanaticism of the wars of religion was channeled in the nineteenth and twentieth centuries into the even more destructive wars of nationality.

NOTES

1. Lothario dei Segni (Pope Innocent III), *On the Misery of the Human Condition*, ed. Donald R. Howard, trans. Margaret Mary Dietz (Indianapolis: The Library of Liberal Arts, 1969), p. 6.

2. Quoted in V. H. H. Green, *Medieval Civilization in Western Europe* (New York: St. Martin's, 1971), p. 35.

3. Thomas Aquinas, *Summa Theologica*, excerpted in *Introduction to Saint Thomas Aquinas*, ed. Anton C. Pegis (New York: Modern Library, 1948), pt. 1, quest. 2, art. 3, p. 25.

4. Ernst Cassirer, *The Philosophy of the Enlightenment*, (Boston: Beacon, 1955), p. 40.

5. J. H. Randall, Jr., *The Making of the Modern Mind* (Boston: Houghton Mifflin, 1940), p. 34.

6. François Rabelais, *The Histories of Gargantua and Pantagruel*, trans. J. M. Cohen (Baltimore: Penguin, 1967), p. 159.

7. Quoted in Eugenio Garin, *Italian Humanism*, trans. Peter Munz (New York: Harper and Row, 1965), p. 28.

8. Giovanni Pico della Mirandola, *Oration on the Dignity of Man*, trans. Elizabeth Livermore Forbes, excerpted in *The Renaissance Philosophy of Man*, ed. Ernst Cassirer, P. O. Kristeller, and John Herman Randall, Jr. (Chicago: University of Chicago Press, 1948), pp. 223–225.

9. William Shakespeare, *Hamlet*, in *The Riverside Shakespeare*, ed. G. Blakemore Evans (Boston: Houghton Mifflin Company), act 2, sc. 2, lines 303–307, p. 1156. Used with permission.

10. Quentin Skinner, *The Founda-*

tions of Modern Political Thought (Cambridge: Cambridge University Press, 1978), I, 98.

11. Quoted in Garin, *Italian Humanism*, p. 16.

12. Quoted in George H. Sabine, *A History of Political Thought* (New York: Holt, Rinehart and Winston, 1961), p. 361.

13. Quoted in Roland H. Bainton, *Here I Stand* (New York: Abingdon, l950), p. 238.

14. Quoted in Roland H. Bainton, *The Reformation of the Sixteenth Century* (Boston: Beacon, 1952), p. 61.

SUGGESTED READING

Middle Ages

Baldwin, John W., *The Scholastic Culture of the Middle Ages* (1971).

Benson, Robert L. and Constance Giles, eds., *Renaissance and Renewal in the Twelfth Century* (1982).

Brooke, Christopher, *The Twelfth-Century Renaissance* (1969).

Copleston, F. C., *Aquinas* (1955).

Crombie, A. C., *Medieval and Early Modern Science*, 2 vols. (1959).

Gilson, Etienne, *Reason and Revelation in the Middle Ages* (1966).

Knowles, David, *The Evolution of Medieval Thought* (1964).

Laistner, M.L.W., *Thought and Letters in Western Europe* A.D. *500 to 900* (1957).

Mâle, Emile, *The Gothic Image* (1958).

Pieper, Josef, *Scholasticism* (1964).

Piltz, Anders, *The World of Medieval Learning* (1981).

Wieruszowski, Helene, *The Medieval University* (1966).

Renaissance and Reformation

Bainton, Roland H., *The Reformation of the Sixteenth Century* (1952).

Garin, Eugenio, *Italian Humanism* (1965).

Hannock, Ralph C., *Calvin and the Foundations of Modern Politics* (1989).

Kelley, Donald R., *Renaissance Humanism* (1991).

Kristeller, Paul O., *Renaissance Concepts of Man* (1972).

———, *Renaissance Thought* (1955).

———, *Renaissance Thought and Its Sources* (1979).

———, *Eight Philsophers of the Italian Renaissance* (1964).

Panofsky, Erwin, *Renaissance and Renascences in Western Art* (1960).

Ralph, Philip L., *The Renaissance in Perspective* (1973).

Reardon, Bernard M. G., *Religious Thought in the Reformation* (1981).

Stephens, John, *The Italian Renaissance* (1990).

I

SHAPING OF

THE MODERN

MENTALITY

3

The Scientific Revolution: A New

Cosmology and Methodology

The movement toward modernity initiated by the Renaissance was greatly advanced by the Scientific Revolution of the seventeenth century. The Scientific Revolution destroyed the medieval world picture and established the scientific method—rigorous and systematic observation and experimentation—as the essential means of unlocking nature's secrets. Increasingly, Western thinkers emphasized the importance of mathematics, which had grown more sophisticated with the discovery of the calculus; they maintained that nature was a mechanical system governed by laws that could be expressed mathematically. The new discoveries electrified the imagination. Science displaced theology as the queen of knowledge, and reason, which had been subordinate to religion in the Middle Ages, asserted its autonomy. The great confidence in reason inspired by the Scientific Revolution helped give rise to the Enlightenment, which explicitly rejected the ideas and institutions of the medieval past and articulated the essential norms of modernity. As British historian Herbert Butterfield notes, because the Scientific Revolution transformed our way of thinking about the world, it

> outshines everything since the rise of Christianity and reduces the Renaissance and Reformation to the rank of mere episodes, mere internal displacements, within the system of medieval Christendom. Since it changed the character of men's habitual mental operations even in the conduct of the non-material sciences, while transforming the whole

diagram of the physical universe and the very texture of human life itself, it looms so large as the real origin both of the modern world and of the modern mentality.[1]

THE MEDIEVAL VIEW OF THE UNIVERSE

Medieval thinkers constructed a coherent picture of the universe that blended the theories of two ancient Greeks, Aristotle and Ptolemy of Alexandria, with Christian teachings (see pages 37–38). To the medieval mind, the cosmos was a giant ladder, a qualitative order, ascending toward heaven. God was at the summit of this hierarchical universe and the earth, base and vile, just above hell. Still adhering to medieval cosmology, Michel de Montaigne, the sixteenth-century French humanist, called the earth "the filth and mire of the world, the worst, lowest, most lifeless part of the universe, the bottom story of the house."[2] In the medieval world-picture, a motionless earth stood in the center of the universe; Aristotle and other ancient thinkers had held that all heavy matter, including the earth, by nature moved to the center of the world, its final destination, and remained there. In the medieval view, the earth's central location meant that the universe centered on human beings, that by God's design human beings—the only creatures on whom God had bestowed reason and the promise of salvation—were lords of the earth. Around the earth revolved seven transparent spheres, each of which carried a "planet"—the moon, Mercury, Venus, the sun, Mars, Jupiter, and Saturn. (Since the earth did not move, it was not considered a planet.) The eighth sphere, in which the stars were embedded, also revolved about the earth. Beyond the stars was a heavenly sphere, the *primum mobile*, which imparted motion to the planets and the stars, so that in one day the entire celestial system turned around the stationary earth. Enclosing the entire system was another heavenly sphere, the Empyrean, where God sat on his throne, attended by angels.

Medieval thinkers inherited Aristotle's view of a qualitative universe. Earthly objects were composed of earth, water, air, and fire, whereas celestial objects, belonging to a higher world, were composed of the ether—an element too pure and perfect to be found on earth, which consisted of base matter. In contrast to earthly objects, heavenly bodies were incorruptible, that is they experienced no change. This two-world orientation blended nicely with the Christian outlook.

Like Aristotle, Ptolemy held that planets moved in perfect circular orbits and at uniform speeds around the earth. Since, in reality, the path of planets is not a circle but an ellipse and since planets do not move at uniform speed but accelerate as they approach the sun, problems arose that required Ptolemy to incorporate into his system certain ingenious devices that had been employed by earlier Greek astronomers. To save the appearance of uniform motion, Ptolemy placed the earth at a point on the circle's diameter somewhat off center of the planet's orbit and established another point (later called an equant) along the same diameter. When measured from the equant, a planet's motion seemed uniform. To save the appearance of circular orbits, Ptolemy made use of epicycles. A planet revolved uniformly around a small circle, an epicycle, which in turn revolved about the earth in a larger circle. If one ascribed a sufficient number of epicycles to a planet, the planet could seem to move in perfectly circular orbits.

The Aristotelian-Ptolemaic model of the cosmos did appear to accord with common sense and raw perception—the earth does indeed seem and feel to be at rest. And it appeared to be confirmed by evidence, for it enabled thinkers to predict with considerable accuracy the movement and location of celestial bodies and the passage of time. The geocentric model and the division of the universe into higher and lower worlds also accorded with passages in Scripture. Scholastic philosophers harmonized Aristotelian and Ptolemaic science with Christian theology, producing an intellectually and emotionally satisfying picture of the universe, in which everything was arranged according to a divine plan.

In the sixteenth and seventeenth centuries, the schools and universities were dominated by Aristotelian scholastics committed to an all-embracing conceptual scheme encompassing nature, society, and the individual's relationship to God. For them, Scripture, the church fathers, and, in matters of natural knowledge, Aristotle were the ultimate authorities. They believed that knowledge derived from experience should confirm what we already know to be true on the basis of these authorities. Innovation and the questioning of authority were undesirable. Clearly, many thinkers would resist attempts to dismantle this world-picture, which rested on the authority of Aristotle and Ptolemy and on the even higher authority of Scripture and which made life and death both intelligible and purposeful.

RENAISSANCE BACKGROUND OF
THE SCIENTIFIC REVOLUTION

In several ways, the Renaissance contributed to the Scientific Revolution. The revival of interest in antiquity during the Renaissance led to the rediscovery of some ancient scientific texts, including the works of Archimedes (287–212 B.C.) that fostered new ideas in mechanics, and to the improved translations of Galen's treatises that stimulated the study of anatomy.

Renaissance art, which linked an exact representation of the human body to mathematical proportions and called for the accurate observation of natural phenomena, was another factor in the rise of modern science. In his work, *On Painting*, Leon Battista Alberti (1404–1472), the first modern art theoretician, formulated the mathematical theory of perspective. His purpose was to enable artists to depict three-dimensional objects on a two-dimensional surface, thus creating the illusion of depth. To do this, Alberti had to establish a precise mathematical relationship between the object and the observer. "No investigation can claim to be a true science," said Leonardo da Vinci, "if it doesn't proceed by mathematical demonstrations."[3] Renaissance painters also strove for a detailed and accurate knowledge of the structure of objects, an attitude that coincided with the emergence of the modern sciences of observation. By defining visual space and the relationship between the object and the observer in mathematical terms and by delineating the natural world with unprecedented scientific precision, Renaissance art helped to foster a new view of nature, which later found expression in the astronomy of Copernicus and Kepler and the physics of Galileo.

The Renaissance revival of ancient Pythagorean and Platonic ideas, which stressed mathematics as the key to comprehending reality, also contributed to the Scientific Revolution. Extending the mathematical harmony found in music to the universe at large, Pythagoras (c. 580–507 B.C.) and his followers believed that all things have form, which can be expressed numerically; reality consists fundamentally of number relations that the mind can grasp. The Pythagoreans blended this brilliant scientific insight—that the cosmos is an ordered system—with religious mysticism. Holding that knowledge of this cosmic harmony purified the soul, Pythagoreans pursued wisdom in order to liberate the soul from earthly dependence and to attain spiritual redemption. Plato maintained that beyond the world of everyday objects made known to us through the senses lies a higher reality, the world of Forms, which contains an inherent mathematical order apprehended only by thought. The great thinkers of the Scientific Revolution were influenced by these ancient ideas of nature as a harmonious mathematical system knowable to the mind.

We are so used to drawing a sharp distinction between scientific thought and mysticism and magic—between a rational attempt to investigate nature and the belief that occult forces control the operations of nature—that it is easy to overlook links between a nonrational occult tradition and the rise of modern science. In recent years scholars, have suggested just such a connection between a mystical-magical Hermeticism, which enjoyed popularity during the Renaissance, and the Scientific Revolution.

Hermes Trismegistus (the thrice great) was thought to be an Egyptian priest and a contemporary of Moses. His treatises, containing the wisdom of ancient Egypt, it was believed, inspired Greek philosophers. In reality, no such person had ever lived; the treatises attributed to Hermes were actually written much later, between A.D. 100 and 300, by people in Egypt who had received some instruction in Greek philosophy. The Hermetic writings mixed astrology, alchemy, Jewish creation accounts, and mystical yearnings with elements of Greek philosophy, particularly Platonism and Pythagoreanism. Around 1460, a monk brought to Florence a Greek manuscript containing these Hermetic writings. The document, subsequently known as the *Corpus Hermeticum*, was given to the Florentine merchant-prince Cosimo dé Medici, who ordered the humanist scholar Marsilio Ficino (1433–1499) to translate it into Latin.

The importance of the Hermetic tradition to science is that it assimilated Pythagorean and Neo-Platonic ideas. The *Corpus Hermeticum* contains the beliefs that an unseen mathematical harmony pervades the cosmos; that mathematics is an activity akin to religious contemplation, for it yields a divine truth, the key to ultimate reality; and that human beings ennoble their souls when they acquire knowledge of the cosmic order, which God transmits to the world.

The influence of Pythagorean number mysticism and of Neo-Platonism on the Scientific Revolution is most apparent in the thought of Johannes Kepler, one of the luminaries of seventeenth-century science. Drawing his inspiration from a quasi-mystical tradition, Kepler sought to discover the musical harmonies governing the motion of planets. He described this quest as follows: "I feel carried away and possessed by an unalterable rapture over the divine spectacle of the heavenly harmony."[4]

NICHOLAS COPERNICUS:
THE DETHRONEMENT OF THE EARTH

Modern astronomy begins with Nicholas Copernicus (1473–1543) astronomer, mathematician, and church canon, who proclaimed that earth is a planet that orbits a centrally located sun together with the other planets. This heliocentric theory served as the kernel of a new world picture that supplanted the medieval view of the universe. Copernicus did not base his heliocentric theory on new observations and new data. What led him to remove the earth from the center of the universe was the complexity and cumbersomeness of the Ptolemaic system, which offended his sense of mathematical order. To Copernicus, the numerous epicycles (the number had been increased since Ptolemy, making the model even more cumbersome) and the equant violated the Platonic vision of the mathematical symmetry of the universe.

Fearful that his theories would spark a controversy, Copernicus refused to publish his work, but persuaded by his friends, he finally relented, and his masterpiece, *On the Revolutions of the Heavenly Spheres*, appeared in 1543. According to tradition, a copy reached Copernicus on his deathbed, just a few hours before he expired. The book contained an unsigned preface, which stated that the new cosmology was intended merely as an hypothesis, not as the truth. Because the preface was unsigned, it appeared that Copernicus had written it; the real author, however, was Andreas Osiander, a Lutheran theologian, who knew of Luther's opposition to the heliocentric theory on biblical grounds. Copernicus himself had no doubt of the correctness of heliocentrism.

Copernican astronomy disposed of the equant, resolved some problems that had perplexed astronomers, particularly the retrograde motion of the planets,* and eliminated some epicycles—he could not do away with epicycles entirely, for he believed with the ancients that circular motion was a sign of perfection. So the Copernican system of the universe was only slightly less complex than the Ptolemaic model.

Attack on Copernicanism

As Copernicus had feared, his views stirred up controversy, but the new astronomy did not become a passionate issue until the early seventeenth century, more than fifty years after the publication of *On the Revolutions*. The Copernican theory frightened clerical authorities, who controlled the universities as well as the pulpits, for it seemed to conflict with Scripture. For example, Psalm 93 says: "Yea, the world is established, that it cannot be moved." And Psalm 103 says that God "fixed the earth upon its foundation not to be moved forever." Learned

---

*To an observer on earth a planet moves eastward through the heavens; this is called direct motion. But at times the planet stops moving in eastward motion and for a short distance moves westward; this westward motion is called retrograde. A planet's apparent reversal of direction could not be adequately accounted for in the Ptolemaic system. But a heliocentric model makes it readily apparent that retrograde motion is due to the relative speeds of planets. Copernicus explained that Mars seems to reverse its direction because it is orbiting the sun more slowly than the earth is.

men knew of Copernicus's work even before it was published. Thus, in 1539, Luther had said of Copernicus:

> People gave ear to an upstart astrologer who strove to show that the earth revolves, not the heavens or the firmament, the sun and the moon. Whoever wishes to appear clever must devise some new system which of all systems is of course the very best. This fool wishes to reverse the entire science of astronomy; but sacred Scripture tells us that Joshua commanded the sun to stand still, and not the earth.[5]

Shortly after the publication of *On the Revolutions*, Giovanni Maria Tolosani (c. 1471–1549), a Dominican friar, attacked Copernicus for contradicting Aristotle, Ptolemy, and the Bible:

> Nicholas Copernicus neither read nor understood the arguments of Aristotle the philosopher and Ptolemy the astronomer. . . . Read Book 1 of Nicholas Copernicus' *Revolutions* and from what I have written here you will clearly recognize into how many and how great errors he has tumbled, even contrary to Holy Writ. Where he wished to show off the keenness of his mind, . . . by his own words and writings he rather revealed his own ignorance.[6]

For seventy years, the Catholic church (but not individual clergymen) refrained from attacking Copernican astronomy; then in the early seventeenth century, it joined the struggle against Copernicanism. Alarmed by the Protestant Reformation, Catholic authorities were seeking to avoid any lapses in church discipline and belief. These officials feared that if they "bent" the Scriptures to accommodate the new cosmology, Protestant publicists would have another issue with which to attack the church. In 1616, the church placed *On the Revolutions* and all other works that ascribed motion to the earth on the Index of forbidden books.

In their rejection of a moving earth, the critics of Copernicus did not rely just on Scripture. Using Aristotelian arguments, they insisted that a body as heavy as earth cannot move through space at the speed required by the Copernican system; that if the earth is spinning on its axis, a stone dropped from a height would land at a point behind where it was dropped rather than directly below; that if the earth is in motion, objects would fly off it; and that it is impossible for the moon to orbit both the earth and the sun simultaneously. It is important to realize that before the invention of the telescope there was little compelling evidence to support the Copernican theory.

In theologians' resistance to an earth that moves, far more was at stake than the commitment of scholastic thinkers to Aristotle and Ptolemy and the meaning of a few lines of Scripture. The real problem was that Copernicanism undermined the entire system of a hierarchically ordered universe—a cosmology deemed central to the Christian view of life, death, and the individual's relationship to God. Historian of science Thomas Kuhn reflects on this larger meaning of the new cosmology for the traditional medieval world-view:

> Copernicanism was potentially destructive of an entire fabric of thought. . . . if the earth is a planet and therefore a celestial body located away from the center of the universe, what becomes of man's intermediate but focal position between the devils and the angels? If the earth, as a planet, participates in the nature of celestial bodies, it cannot be a sink of iniquity from which man will long to escape to the divine purity of the heavens. Nor can the heavens be a suitable abode for God if they participate in the evils and imperfections so clearly visible on a planetary earth. Worst of all, if the universe is infinite, as many of the later Copernicans thought, where can God's Throne be located? In an infinite universe how is man to find God or God man? Copernicanism required a transformation in man's view of his relation to God and of the bases of his morality. Such a transformation could not be worked out overnight.[7]

Illustrating the church's fear of Copernicanism was its treatment of the Late Renaissance philosopher Giordono Bruno (1548–1600). An Italian and a former Dominican who had fled the order, Bruno was an eager student of Hermeticism. Accused of heresy, he spent more than eight years in the prisons of the Inquisition until he was burned alive. The Inquisition then scoured Europe for his writings, which it also consigned to the flames. Bruno's Hermeticism led him to embrace and to embellish Copernican heliocentricity. In Hermetic philosophy, movement is the energy of life, and the living earth orbits the divine sun. For Bruno, Copernicanism confirmed this fundamental Hermetic doctrine, and he became a staunch defender of the new astronomy. Bruno brought to his Copernicanism an ecstatic mysticism, which led him to produce a new vision of the universe: the earth was a living being, space was infinite, and there were innumerable inhabited worlds. In Bruno, Copernicanism evoked not despair, as it did for Pascal (see below), but awe; nature itself is God and it is worthy of both worship and investigation. Bruno did not find his sustenance in organized religion or in the supernatural as would Pascal in the next century; rather, in the spirit of a mystic, he called for the rapturous worship, glorification, and contemplation of nature. He wanted such a religion to replace the teachings of the organized churches.

Copernicanism and the Modern Mind

In later centuries, further implications of the new cosmology caused great anguish. The conviction that the earth was fixed beneath their feet, that God had created the universe for them, and that He had given the earth the central position in his creation had provided medieval people with a profound sense of security. They knew why they were here and never doubted that heaven was the final resting place for the faithful. Copernican astronomy dethroned the earth, expelled human beings from their central position in the universe, and implied an in-finite universe. In the sixteenth and seventeenth centuries, few think-ers comprehended the full significance of this displacement. However, in succeeding centuries, this radical cosmological transformation proved as traumatic for the modern mind as did Adam and Eve's ex-pulsion from the Garden of Eden for the medieval mind. Today we know that earth is one of billions and billions of celestial bodies, a tiny speck in an endless cosmic ocean, and that the universe is some 15 billion years old. Could such a universe have been created just for hu-man beings? Could it contain a heaven that assures eternal life for the faithful and a hell with its eternal fires and torments for sinners?

Few people at the time were aware of the full implications of the new cosmology. One who did understand was Blaise Pascal (1623–1662), a French scientist and mathematician. A devout Catholic, Pas-cal was frightened by what he called "the eternal silence of these infi-nite spaces," and realized that the new science could foster doubt, uncertainty, and anxiety, which threatened belief.

> I see those frightful spaces of the universe which surround me, and I find myself tied to one corner of this vast expanse, without knowing why I am put in this place rather than in another, nor why the short time which is given me to live is assigned to me at this point rather than at another of the whole eternity which was before me or which shall come after me. I see nothing but infinities on all sides, which surround me as an atom, and as a shadow which endures only for an instant and returns no more. All I know is that I must soon die. . . .
>
> When I consider the short duration of my life, swallowed up in the eternity . . . the little space which I fill, and even can see, engulfed in the infinite immensity of spaces of which I am ignorant, and which know me not, I am frightened, and am astonished at being here rather than there; for there is no reason why here rather than there, why now rather than then. Who has put me here? By whose order and direction have this little place and time been allotted to me?[8]

To ward off atheism and religious skepticism, Pascal urged a strength-ened commitment to Christianity; this is achieved, he said, by seeking God intuitively with the heart, through love and faith, rather than through thought.

GALILEO: SHAPING THE MODERN
SCIENTIFIC OUTLOOK

Galileo Galilei (1564-1642) is a principal reason that the seventeenth century has been called "the century of genius." A talented musician and artist and a cultivated humanist, Galileo knew and loved the Latin classics and Italian poetry. He was also an astronomer and physicist who helped shatter the medieval conception of the cosmos and shape the modern scientific outlook. Galileo was indebted to the Platonic tradition, which tried to grasp the mathematical harmony of the universe, and to Archimedes, the Hellenistic mathematician-engineer who had sought a geometric understanding of space and motion. Galileo's opposition to Aristotelian physics and his attempt to mathematize physical concepts also had antecedents in the work of late medieval scholars, but the extent to which he was influenced by this earlier work is not certain.

Uniformity of Nature and Experimental Physics

Galileo rejected the medieval division of the universe into higher and lower realms and proclaimed the modern idea of nature's uniformity. Learning that a telescope had been invented in Holland, Galileo built one for himself and used it to investigate the heavens—the first person to do so. From his observations of the moon, Galileo concluded:

> I have been led to the opinion and conviction that the surface of the moon is not smooth, uniform, and precisely spherical as a great number of philosophers believe it (and the other heavenly bodies) to be, but is uneven, rough, and full of cavities and prominences, being not unlike the face of the earth, relieved by chains of mountains and deep valleys.[9]

This discovery of the moon's craters and mountains led Galileo to break with the Aristotelian notion that celestial bodies were pure, perfect, and unchangeable. It implied that the moon, a celestial body, was made of the same material as the earth. Galileo's discovery of sunspots a few years later was further evidence that celestial matter was not intrinsically immutable. For Galileo, there was no difference in quality between celestial and terrestrial bodies. Nature was not a hierarchical order, in which physical entities were ranked according to their possession or lack of quality; rather it was a homogeneous system, the same throughout. Those committed to the conventional Aristotelian view dismissed Galileo's discovery, denying that the the moon, a crystalline sphere, could be marred by craters, or the sun, the symbol of celestial perfection, could be blemished by spots. Galileo's telescope was deceiving observers, they contended.

With his telescope, Galileo discovered the four moons that orbit Jupiter, an observation that overcame a principal objection to the Copernican system. Galileo showed that a celestial body could indeed move around a center other than the earth; that the earth was not the common center for all celestial bodies; and that a celestial body (the earth's moon or Jupiter's moons) could orbit a planet at the same time that the planet revolved around another body (namely the sun). One Florentine astronomer, steeped in medieval thinking, attacked Galileo as follows:

> There are seven windows given to animals through which the air is admitted to the tabernacle of the body. . . . Two nostrils, two eyes, two ears, and a mouth. So in the heavens, as in the macrocosmos, there are two favorable stars, two unpropitious, two luminaries and mercury undecided and indifferent. From this and many other similarities in nature, such as the seven metals . . . we gather that the number of planets is necessarily seven. Moreover, these planets of Jupiter are invisible to the naked eye and therefore would be useless and therefore do not exist. Besides the Jews and other ancient nations, as well as modern Europeans, have adopted the division of the week into seven days and have named them after the seven planets. Now if we increase the number of planets, this whole and beautiful system falls to the ground.[10]

Galileo pioneered in experimental physics and advanced the modern idea that knowledge of motion should be derived from direct observation and from mathematics. In dealing with problems of motion, Aristotle did not proceed by observation and mathematical calculation but relied largely on a priori principles and common-sense logic; by contrast, Galileo insisted on applying mathematics to the study of moving bodies and did in fact study acceleration by performing experiments, which required careful mathematical measurement. By rolling a ball down an inclined plane and designating its positions after a series of equal times, Galileo confirmed his hypothesis that the distance traversed by a falling body is in proportion to the square of the time that has elapsed from the instant the body began to fall. For Aristotelian scholastics, a rock fell because it was striving to reach its proper place in the universe, thereby fulfilling its nature; it was acting in accordance with the purpose God had assigned it. Galileo completely rejected the view that motion is due to a quality inherent in an object. Rather, he said, motion is the relationship of bodies to time and distance. By holding that bodies fall according to uniform and quantifiable laws, Galileo posited an entirely different conceptual system. This system requires that we study angles and distances and search for mathematical ratios but avoid inquiring into an object's quality and purpose—the role God assigned it in a hierarchical universe.

For Galileo, the universe was a "grand book which . . . is written in the language of mathematics and its characters are triangles, circles, and other geometric figures without which it is humanly impossible to understand a single word of it."[11] In the tradition of Plato, Galileo sought to grasp the mathematical principles governing nature and ascribed to mathematics absolute authority. Like Copernicus and Kepler, he believed that mathematics expresses the harmony and beauty of God's creation.

Attack on Authority

Insisting that physical truth is arrived at through observation, experimentation, and reason, Galileo strongly denounced reliance on authority. Scholastic thinkers regarded Aristotle as the supreme authority on questions concerning nature, and university education was based on his works. These doctrinaire Aristotelians angered Galileo, who protested that they sought truth not by opening their eyes to nature and new knowledge but by slavishly relying on ancient texts. In 1590, he wrote: "Few there are who seek to discover whether what Aristotle says is true; it is enough for them that the more texts of Aristotle they have to quote, the more learned they will be thought."[12] In *Dialogue Concerning the Two Chief World Systems—Ptolemaic and Copernican* (1632), Galileo upheld the Copernican view and attacked the unquestioning acceptance of Aristotle's teachings.

> Is it possible for you to doubt that if Aristotle should see the new discoveries in the sky he would change his opinions and correct his books and embrace the most sensible doctrines, casting away from himself those people so weak-minded as to be induced to go on abjectly maintaining everything he had ever said? . . . It is the followers of Aristotle who have crowned him with authority, not [Aristotle] who has . . . appropriated it for himself. . . . I do not mean that a person should not listen to Aristotle; indeed, I applaud the reading and careful study of his works, and I reproach only those who give themselves up as slaves to him in such a way as to subscribe blindly to everything he says and take it as an inviolable decree without looking for any other reasons.[13]

Aristotle himself, said Galileo, never claimed the authority ascribed to him by his scholastic followers; therefore, when these misguided men insist on holding manifestly false propositions as true, they detract from the reputation of the great Athenian.

Galileo also criticized Roman Catholic authorities for attempting to suppress the Copernican theory. In 1615, in a letter addressed to Grand Duchess Christina of Tuscany but intended to catch the eye of theologians, Galileo argued that passages from the Bible had no authority in questions involving nature; he denounced his opponents for making "a shield for their fallacies out of the mantle of pretended religion and the authority of the Bible. These they apply, with little judgment, to the refutation of arguments that they do not understand and have not even listened to." These people, he continued, "would extend such authorities in purely physical matters—where faith is not involved—they would have us altogether abandon reason and the evidence of our senses in favor of some biblical passage though under the surface meaning of its words this passage may contain a different sense."[14] Galileo also pointed out that,

> Copernicus never discusses matters of religion or faith. . . . He stands always upon physical conclusions . . . founded primarily upon sense experiences and very exact observations. . . . in discussions of physical problems we ought to begin not from the authority of Scriptural passages, but from sense-experience and necessary demonstrations.[15]

A sincere Christian, Galileo never intended to use the new science to undermine faith; what he desired was to separate science from faith so that reason and experience alone would be the deciding factors on questions involving nature. He could not believe that "God who has endowed us with senses, reason and intellect,"[16] did not wish us to use these faculties in order to acquire knowledge. For Galileo, the aim of Scripture was to teach people the truths necessary for salvation, not to instruct them in the operations of nature, which is the task of science. The epigram that he cited in the letter to the Grand Duchess—probably acquired in conversation with a cardinal—aptly sums up his position: "That the intention of the Holy Ghost is to teach us how one goes to heaven, not how heaven goes."[17] Since the weight of evidence indicated that the earth does indeed move, Galileo considered it a terrible mistake for the church to use biblical passages to convey astronomical truths. He feared that if the church persisted in challenging the new astronomy with the authority of Scripture, which was never intended as a guide to knowledge of the physical world, faith as well as science would suffer. In his old age, Galileo wrote:

> Take note, theologians that in your desire to make matters of faith out of propositions relating to the fixity of sun and earth, you run the risk of eventually having to condemn as heretics those who would declare the earth to stand still and the sun to change position—eventually, I say, at such a time as it might be physically or logically proved that the earth moves and the sun stands still.[18]

Galileo's support of Copernicus aroused the ire of both scholastic philosophers and the clergy, who feared that the brash scientist threatened a world picture that had the support of venerable ancient authorities, Holy Writ, and scholastic tradition. Galileo was proclaiming a truth about the fundamental structure of nature that was not based on the testimony of Scripture—indeed that seemed to contradict it—and contravened accredited theological interpretation. In effect, Galileo was removing the new science from any theological control. Already traumatized by the Protestant threat, Catholic officials were fearful of ideas that might undermine traditional belief and authority.*

In 1616, the Congregation of the Index, the church's censorship organ, condemned the teaching of Copernicanism. Cardinal Bellarmine, who headed the Inquisition, ordered Galileo to cease his defense of the new astronomy. When Galileo published his *Dialogue Concerning the Two Chief World Systems*, his enemies succeeded in halting further printing. In 1633, the aging and infirm scientist was summoned to Rome. Tried and condemned by the Inquisition, he was ordered to abjure the Copernican theory. Not wishing to bring harm to himself and certain that the truth would eventually prevail, Galileo bowed to the Inquisition. On his knees he recited these words as the Inquisition required:

> ... with sincere heart and unfeigned faith I abjure, curse, and detest the aforesaid errors and heresies [that the sun is the center of the world and immovable and that the earth is not the center of the world] and generally every other error ... contrary to the Holy Church and I swear that in the future I will never again say or assert, verbally or in writing, anything that might furnish occasion for a similar suspicion regarding me.[19]

Galileo was sentenced to life imprisonment—largely house arrest at his own villa near Florence—the *Dialogue* was banned, and he was forbidden to write on Copernicanism. Not until 1820 did the church lift the ban on Copernicanism.

The meaning of Galileo's trial and sentencing by the Inquisition is still a matter of debate. Galileo's contemporaries viewed the trial as a

---

*A careful investigation of Vatican files has pointed perhaps to another reason why the church condemned Galileo. Galileo subscribed to an atomic theory of matter, which seemed to contradict the Council of Trent's decision on the dogma of the Eucharist. The council had ruled that when the bread and wine miraculously convert into the body and blood of Christ, nothing remains of the substance of the bread and wine. But Galileo's physics, as presented in *The Assayer*, taught the permanence of substantial particles. If applied to the Eucharist, this could be interpreted to mean that the bread and wine remain even after the consecration, thereby casting doubt on the miracle. See Pietro Redondi, *Galileo Heretic* (Princeton: Princeton University Press, 1987).

victory for clerical authority. John Milton, who visited Galileo five years after his imprisonment, wrote: "There it was that I found and visited the famous Galileo, grown old, a prisoner to the Inquisition for thinking in Astronomy otherwise than the Franciscan and Dominican licensers thought."[20] Traditionally, Galileo has been viewed as a martyr to truth, the victim of an authoritarian religious institution that sought to bend science to the overriding concern of theology—the classic example of the conflict between science and organized religion.

In recent years, the trial has been studied with greater care, and more consideration has been given to the predicament of church authorities. These men knew that if Copernicus was correct, Scripture would have to be reinterpreted to fit the new theory. Before initiating such a hazardous venture, they had to have more convincing proof than Galileo could provide. Had Galileo been willing to treat Copernicanism as a hypothesis rather than as an established fact, the authorities most likely would have left him alone. But this Galileo could not do, for he believed completely in the physical truth of Copernicanism.

Regardless of the bind that that church authorities found themselves in, their condemnation of Galileo did enormous harm to the church. In succeeding generations, many educated people would see an inevitable conflict between religious dogma and scientific knowledge, between clerical authority and the scientific spirit. As Margaret C. Jacob notes, the immediate effect of the Inquisition's condemnation of Galileo was to stifle scientific activity in Catholic lands:

> After the condemnation of Galileo, books at the vanguard of the new science—that is, those that advocated the mechanical philosophy and heliocentricity—had to be published where the Inquisition had no authority. In practice that meant in Protestant Europe.[21]

JOHANNES KEPLER: LAWS OF PLANETARY MOTION

Johannes Kepler (1571–1630), a German mathematician and astronomer, exemplified the influence exerted by the Renaissance revival of Pythagoreanism and Platonism. Kepler combined the Pythagorean-Platonic quest to comprehend the mathematical harmony within nature with a deep commitment to Lutheran Christianity. He contended that Plato's Ideas were eternal archetypes in God's mind, that God had prescribed a geometric harmony to his creation, and that God gave human beings the ability to understand these laws of harmony and proportion. It was the divine regularity of nature—a manifestation of God's wisdom—that Kepler wanted to understand and explain mathematically. Like other people of his day, both simple and learned, Kepler believed in astrology—"the last major astronomer, in fact, to be in any degree a convinced astrologer,"[22] notes historian of science I. B. Cohen. Kepler considered celestial signs to be divine portents and furnished patrons and friends with horoscopes.

After having discovered numerical harmonies in the musical intervals, the ancient Pythagoreans, in a remarkable leap of the imagination, had asserted that the universe, too, depends on numerical principles. As a true Pythagorean, Kepler yearned to discover the geometric harmony of the planets, what he called the "music of the spheres." Such knowledge, he believed, would provide supreme insight into God's mind. No doubt, this mystical quality triggered the creative potential of the imagination, but to be harnessed for science, it had to be disciplined by the rational faculties. Fortunately, Kepler's skill in mathematics and respect for empirical facts enabled him to do just that. Thus, he attacked Robert Fludd, the English follower of Paracelsus* and a Hermeticist, for holding that the essence of nature could be grasped through a mystical experience or pseudoscience:

> It is obvious that he derives his main pleasure from unintelligible charades about the real world, whereas my purpose is, on the contrary, to draw the obscure facts of nature into the bright light of knowledge. His method is the business of alchemists, hermeticists, and Paracelsians, mine is the task of the mathematician.[23]

Although Kepler speculated in a mystical vein and was a convinced astrologer, Ernst Cassirer states that Kepler "could never have become the founder of the new astronomy if he had not been able to remove magic from his path, a slow and steady effort which we can follow in his writings." In his condemnation of Fludd, continues Cassirer, Kepler restricted his mystical

> speculations within very definite limits. Once this was done, his mysticism no longer endangered his empirical cosmology. . . . The Pythagorean mysticism never lost its aesthetic attraction for him. But he became the creator of mathematical astronomy by ultimately refusing to use pseudo-science as a *basis* for his work even though he still continued to derive *inspiration* from it. It did not mislead him or lessen his achievement as an empirical researcher, because more and more he learned to discipline himself in a logical manner.[24]

Kepler discovered three basic laws of planetary motion that shattered Ptolemaic cosmology. In doing so, he utilized the data collected

---

*The thought of Paracelsus (1493–1547), a Swiss-born German physician, was replete with Neo-Platonic mysticism, magic, alchemy, and the occult.

by Tycho Brahe, a Danish astronomer, who for twenty years systematically observed the planets and stars and recorded their positions with far greater accuracy than had ever been done. Kepler sought to fit Brahe's observations into Copernicus's heliocentric model.

Kepler's first law states that planets move in elliptical orbits—not circular ones, as Aristotle and Ptolemy (and Copernicus) had believed—and that the sun is one focus of the ellipse. Kepler was reluctant to abandon circular orbits, for in the Pythagorean tradition, the circle was seen as a perfect geometric form. However, this discovery that a planet's path was one simple oval eliminated all the epicycles that had been used to save the appearance of circular motion. Kepler's second law showed that planets do not move at uniform speed, as had been believed, but accelerate as they near the sun, and he provided the rule for deciphering a planet's speed at each point in its orbit: a planet's velocity in its orbit varies in such a way that a line drawn from the planet to the sun sweeps out equal areas of space in equal intervals of time. The third law drew a mathematical relationship between the time it takes a planet to complete its orbit and its average distance from the sun: the square of the time required by a planet to revolve around the sun is proportional to the cube of its mean distance from the sun. On the basis of these laws, one could calculate accurately a planet's position and velocity at a particular time—another indication that the planets were linked together in a unified mathematical system.

Kepler's laws of planetary motion, derived from carefully observed facts, provided additional support for Copernicanism, for they made sense only in a heliocentric universe, one in which the sun provides the force that accounts for the planets' motion. But why did the planets move in elliptical orbits? Why didn't they fly off into space or crash into the sun? For these questions Kepler had no satisfactory explanation, although he did suggest that the sun possessed a continuously acting physical force that kept the planets moving. It was Isaac Newton (1642–1727), the great British mathematician-scientist, who arrived at a celestial mechanics that linked the astronomy of Copernicus and Kepler with the physics of Galileo and accounted for the behavior of planets.

THE NEWTONIAN SYNTHESIS

The publication in 1687 of Isaac Newton's *The Mathematical Principles of Natural Philosophy* marks the climax of the Scientific Revolution. Newton postulated three laws of motion that joined all

Isaac Newton *(The Bettmann Archive)*

celestial and terrestrial objects into a vast mechanical system, all of
whose parts worked in perfect harmony and whose connections could
be expressed in mathematical terms. Since Copernican astronomy was
essential to his all-encompassing theory of the universe, Newton had
provided mathematical proof for the heliocentric system and opposition to it dissipated.

Newton's first law is the principle of inertia: that a body at rest remains at rest unless acted on by a force and a body in rectilinear motion continues to move in a straight line at the same velocity unless a
force acts on it. A moving body does not require a force to keep it in
motion, as ancient and medieval thinkers had believed. Once started,
bodies continue to move; motion is as natural a condition as rest.
Newton's second law states that a given force produces a measurable
change in a body's velocity; a body's change of velocity is proportional
to the force acting on it. Newton's third law holds that for every action
or force there is an equal and opposite reaction or force. The sun pulls
the earth with the same force that the earth exercises on the sun. An
apple falling to the ground is being pulled by the earth, but the apple

is also pulling the earth toward it. (However, since the mass of the apple is so small in comparison with the earth, the force that the apple exercises on the earth causes no visible change in the earth's motion.)

Newton held that the same laws of motion and gravitation that operate in the celestial world also govern the movement of earthly bodies. Ordinary mechanical laws explain why apples fall to the ground and why planets orbit the sun. Newtonian physics ended the medieval division of the cosmos into higher and lower worlds with different laws operating in each realm. The universe is an integrated, harmonious mechanical system held together by the force of gravity. By demonstrating that the universe contains an inherent mathematical order, Newton realized the Pythagorean and Platonic visions.

To his contemporaries, it seemed that Newton had unraveled all of nature's mysteries: the universe was fully explicable. It was as if Newton had penetrated God's mind. Alexander Pope expressed this admiration for Newton's achievement in these famous lines:

> Nature and Nature's laws lay hid in night;
> God said, Let Newton be! and all was light.

Newton, who was deeply committed to Anglican Christianity, retained a central place for God in his world system. He wrote:

> This most beautiful system of the sun, planets, and comets could only proceed from the counsel and dominion of an intelligent and powerful Being. And if the fixed stars are the centers of other like systems, these being formed by the like wise counsel, must be all subject to the dominion of the One. . . . This Being governs all things . . . as Lord over all. . . . The Supreme God is a Being eternal, infinite, absolutely perfect. . . . He endures forever and is everywhere present.[25]

For Newton, God was the grand architect whose wisdom and skill accounted for nature's magnificent design. Newton also believed that God could intervene in his creation and that there was no conflict between divine miracles and a clockwork universe. However, in future generations, thinkers called deists (see Chapter 5) came to regard miracles as incompatible with a universe governed by impersonal mechanical principles.

Newton, whose discovery of the composition of light, laid the foundation of the science of optics, was a cautious experimentalist who valued experimental procedures, including drawing appropriate conclusions from accumulated data. He helped formulate the scientific method, as the following passages illustrate:

> For the best and safest methods of philosophizing seems to be, first, to inquire diligently into the properties of things and to establish those properties by experiments, and to proceed later to hypotheses for the explanation of things themselves.[26]

And again:

> ... the proper method for inquiring after the properties of things is to deduce them from experiments. ... the theory which I propounded was evinced to me, not by inferring *'tis thus because not otherwise*, that is, not by deducing it only from a confutation of contrary suppositions, but by deriving it from experiments concluding positively and directly. ... The way therefore to examine it is by considering whether the experiments which I propound do prove those parts of the theory to which they are applied, or by prosecuting other experiments which the theory may suggest for its examination.[27]

Both Newton's mechanical universe and his championing of the experimental method were foundation blocks of the Age of Enlightenment.

PROPHETS OF MODERN SCIENCE

The accomplishments of the Scientific Revolution extend beyond the creation of a new model of the universe. They also include the formulation of a new method of inquiry into nature and the recognition that science could serve humanity. Two thinkers instrumental in articulating the implications of the Scientific Revolution were Francis Bacon and René Descartes. Both repudiated the authority of Aristotle and other ancients in scientific matters and urged the adoption of new methods for seeking and evaluating truth. The growing importance of mathematical thinking and of the new conception of nature as an orderly system also found expression in the thought of Benedict Spinoza, who designed a philosophical system on the model of Euclidian geometry and regarded traditional religious views as incompatible with reason.

Francis Bacon: The Inductive Method

Sir Francis Bacon (1561–1626), an English statesman and philosopher, vigorously supported the advancement of science and the scientific method. Although he himself had no laboratory and made no discoveries, for his advocacy of the scientific method he is deservedly regarded as a prophet of modern science. Bacon recognized that Aristotelian scholasticism, which dominated the schools and was considered the true and final philosophy, was not suited for an emerging age of science. He attributed the limited progress of science over the ages to the interference of scholastic philosophers, who sought to bend theories of nature to the requirements of Scripture. "[F]rom this unwholesome mixture of things human and divine," wrote Bacon in the *New Organon* (1620), "there arises not only a fantastic philosophy but also an heretical religion. Very meet it is therefore that we be soberminded, and give to faith that only which is faith's."[28] Bacon also denounced scholastic thinkers for their slavish attachment to Aristotelian doctrines, which prevented independent thinking and the acquisition of new information about nature.

> But even though Aristotle were the man he is thought to be I should still warn you against receiving as oracles the thoughts and opinions of one man. What justification can there be for this self-imposed servitude?... But if you will be guided by me you will deny, not only to this man but to any mortal now living or who shall live hereafter, the right to dictate your opinions.... You will never be sorry for trusting your own strength, if you but once make the trial of it. You may be inferior to Aristotle on the whole, but not in everything. Finally, and this is the head and front of the whole matter, there is at least one thing in which you are far ahead of him—in precedents, in experience, in the lessons of time.... Are you of a mind to cast aside not only your own endowments but the gifts of time? Assert yourselves before it is too late. Apply yourselves to the study of things themselves. Be not forever the property of one man.[29]

Bacon also attacked scholastic thinkers for engaging in an arid verbalism and constructing elaborate systems that had little to do with the empirical world. Aristotelian scholastics, he said, were more concerned with winning arguments than with diligent inquiry; the intricate webs they spun were ingenious but barren, for they did not increase our understanding of nature or give us power over the environment. To acquire new knowledge and improve the quality of human life, said Bacon, we should not depend on ancient texts; old authorities must be discarded. Knowledge must be pursued and organized in a new way. In *The New Organon*, Bacon wrote:

> The sciences we now possess are merely systems for the nice ordering and setting forth of things already invented; not methods of invention or direction of new works. . . .
>
> The logic now in use serves rather to fix and give stability to the errors which have their foundation in commonly received notions, than to help the search after truth. So it does more harm than good. . . .
>
> In order to penetrate into the inner and further recesses of nature, it is necessary that . . . a method of intellectual operation be introduced altogether better and more certain.[30]

Bacon also described those "idols," or false notions, that hamper human understanding. The Idols of the Tribe derive from human nature that is common to the human race: "the human understanding is like a false mirror, which, receiving rays irregularly, distorts and discolours the nature of things by mingling its own nature with it."[31] Thus our senses might deceive us, or our emotions might interfere with our judgment. The Idols of the Cave derive from the peculiar nature of individual experience. One's understanding, said Bacon, has been influenced by one's upbringing, education, and by the people that one admires. This personal cave hampers understanding. So do the Idols of the Marketplace. In their discourse with each other, people employ ambiguous words and concepts that "overrule the understanding and throw all into confusion and lead men away into numberless empty controversies and idle fancies."[32] The Idols of the Theater also obstruct understanding; these idols are the individual's commitment to various philosophical dogmas and scientific theories, "which by tradition, credulity, and negligence have come to be believed."[33]

The method that Bacon advocated as the way to truth and useful knowledge was the inductive approach: careful observation of nature and the systematic accumulation of data; drawing general laws from the knowledge of particulars; and testing these laws through constant experimentation. In his discovery of the circulation of the blood, Bacon's contemporary, British physician William Harvey (1578–1657), successfully employed the inductive method championed by Bacon.

Because he gave supreme value to the direct observation of nature, Bacon is one of the founders of the empirical tradition in modern philosophy. Grasping the essential approach of modern natural science, Bacon attacked practitioners of astrology, magic, and alchemy for their errors, secretiveness, and enigmatic writings, advocating instead cooperative and methodical scientific research that could be publicly criticized.

Bacon was among the first to appreciate the new science's value for human life. The function of thought, he argued, is not to contemplate the purpose that God gave each object in nature and to explain how everything fits into God's design. Rather, said Bacon, knowledge should help us utilize nature for human advantage; it should improve the quality of human life by advancing commerce, industry, and agriculture. Holding that knowledge is power, Bacon urged the state to found scientific institutions and praised progress in technology and the mechanical arts.

René Descartes *(The Bettmann Archive)*

René Descartes: The Deductive Method

The scientific method encompasses two approaches to knowledge that usually complement each other—the empirical (inductive) and the rational (deductive). In the inductive approach, which is employed in such descriptive sciences as biology, anatomy, and geology, general principles are derived from analyzing data collected through observation and experiment. The essential features of the inductive method, as we have seen, were championed by Bacon, who regarded sense data as the foundation of knowledge. In the deductive approach, which is employed in mathematics and theoretical physics, truths are derived in successive steps from first principles, indubitable axioms. In the seventeenth century, the deductive method was formulated by René Descartes (1596–1650), a French mathematician and philosopher, who is also regarded as the founder of modern philosophy.

In the *Discourse on Method* (1637), Descartes expressed his disenchantment with the learning of his day. Since much of what he had believed on the basis of authority had come to be shown as untrue, Descartes resolved to seek no other knowledge than that which he might find within himself or within nature. Rejecting as absolutely false anything about which he could have the least doubt, Descartes searched for an incontrovertible truth that could serve as the first principle of knowledge, the basis of an all-encompassing philosophical system.

Descartes' quest for certainty was, in part, a response to the revival of ancient Greek skeptical philosophy, which maintained that we are incapable of achieving certainty. In contrast to "the sceptics who doubt only for doubting's sake, and affect to be always undecided," Descartes sought "assurance and the rejection of shifting ground and sand in order to find rock or clay."[34]

Descartes began his search for certainty by agreeing with the skeptics that the knowledge we attain through the senses is often deceiving. (For example, to the eye, the sun looks much smaller and much closer than it really is.) He also agreed with the skeptics that the conclusions we arrive at might be based on faulty logic. Nor can we be certain that what we are now experiencing is really happening. We might be dreaming. But Descartes found that there was one truth that was certain and unshakable: that it was he who was doing the doubting and thinking. In his dictum "I think therefore I am," Descartes had his starting point of knowledge. Descartes is viewed as the founder of modern philosophy because he called for the individual to question and if necessary to overthrow all traditional beliefs, and he proclaimed the mind's inviolable autonomy and importance, its ability and right to comprehend truth. With his assertions on the power of thought, human beings became fully aware of their capacity to comprehend the world through their own mental powers.

Descartes believed that through reason the individual could establish permanent and universal truths and find certainty, even if previous attempts had failed. But everything depended on the appropriate method. Descartes held that the method used in mathematics is the most reliable avenue to certain knowledge. By applying mathematical reasoning to philosophic problems, we can achieve the same certainty and clarity evidenced in geometry. Mathematics is the key to understanding both the truths of nature and the moral order underlying human existence.

The mathematical, or deductive, approach favored by Descartes consists of finding a self-evident principle, such as a geometric axiom, and then deducing other truths from it through logical reasoning. In essence, Descartes' method consists of breaking a problem down into its elementary components and then, by logically reassembling the units, progressing toward more complex knowledge. Descartes was convinced that this method, which had enabled geometricians to solve the most complex problems, allowed the apprehension of all reality.

Proceeding step by step from the indubitable fact of his own existence as a thinking human being, Descartes then deduced the existence of the physical world and of God. (Like Copernicus, Kepler, Galileo, Bacon, and Newton, Descartes considered himself a Christian.) Everywhere we experience imperfect beings, said Descartes; nevertheless, the mind still possesses the idea of a Perfect Being. Employing a train of thought reminiscent of medieval scholastics, Descartes then concluded that the very idea of a Perfect Being necessitates God's objective existence. We would not have the capacity to conceive this Perfect Being if such a being did not exist, did not create us, and did not implant the idea of God in us. Moreover, since perfection is an attribute of existence—that is, without existence God would be less than perfect—God must exist.

Pursuing this train of thought, Descartes maintained that God ordered the universe in such a way that it functioned in harmony with the human mind: that is, God gave human beings the intellectual capacity to understand the natural world. The structure of nature, he said, corresponds to the clear and distinct ideas inherent in the mind. Descartes believed that both celestial and terrestrial bodies obeyed fixed mechanical laws established by God. He was convinced that the physical universe possessed an essential mathematical character and was knowable to the mind, which God has predisposed to comprehend nature's truths. Yet although Descartes believed in God, his philosophy of methodical doubt would ultimately undermine Christianity. Moreover, once God set the universe in motion, he served no significant function in Descartes' philosophical system; God is virtually dispensed with as the devout Pascal protested: "I cannot forgive Descartes. In all his philosophy he would have been quite willing to dispense with God. But he had to make him give a fillip to set the world in motion; beyond this, he has no further need of God."[35]

Descartes' deductive approach presumed that inherent in the mind are mathematical principles, logical relationships, the principle of cause and effect, concepts of size and motion, and so on—ideas that exist independently of human experience with the external world. For example, Descartes would say that the principles of a right angle triangle are implicit in human consciousness prior to any experience one might have with a triangle. These innate ideas, said Descartes, permit the mind to give order and coherence to the physical world. Descartes held that the mind arrives at truth when it "intuits," or comprehends the logical necessity of its own ideas, and expresses these ideas with clarity and accuracy. Descartes' deductive method, with its mathe-matical emphasis, perfectly complements Bacon's inductive approach, which stresses observation and experimentation. The scientific achievements in modern times have arisen from the skillful synchro-nization of both induction and deduction.

A fundamental feature of Descartes' philosophy was dualism, the division of reality into two fundamentally different substances: mind, whose principal attribute is consciousness and thinking; and matter, which is characterized by spatial extension. But how can these com-pletely distinct substances interact? What, for example, is the relation-ship between the human mind, which is immaterial, and the material body, in which it resides? This question has intrigued and troubled philosophers to this day.

Descartes sought to free scientific inquiry from clerical interference and theological constraints. His confidence in human reason, his de-sire to liberate the mind from authority and beliefs not authorized by reason, his support of the new scientific spirit, and his faith in the ability of human beings to think for themselves undermined dogma and helped form the inquiring and skeptical outlook of the Enlighten-ment.

Benedict Spinoza: Nature as an Intelligible System

Benedict or Baruch Spinoza (1632–1677), descendant of Spanish Jews who fled to the Netherlands to escape the Inquisition, studied tradi-tonal Jewish religious and philosophic works, medieval scholasticism, and the new science and philosophy of his day, particularly the works of Descartes and Hobbes (see Chapter 4). Influenced by the new critical spirit, Spinoza disputed rabbinical interpretations of Scripture. Ac-cused of heresy, he was excommunicated by Jewish religious authori-ties. Living simply—he was a lens grinder—and with great dignity, Spi-noza devoted his life to the pursuit of truth. As his reputation spread, leading figures, including Christian Huygens, the great mathematician and physicist, Henry Oldenburg, a diplomat and man of learning, and Gottfried Wilhelm von Leibnitz, the great philosopher and mathema-tician, corresponded or visited with him.

Spinoza's conception of nature as mathematical and law-abiding and his naturalistic approach to ethics derived largely from the new science with which he was very familiar—he himself engaged in experi-ments in optics. Like Descartes, Spinoza contended that reality is an intelligible whole that can be comprehended by pure reasoning. A tho-roughgoing rationalist, he agreed with Descartes that the deductive method is the truest avenue to certainty. Using Euclid's geometry as a model, Spinoza began with what seemed to be universally valid premises, from which through rigorous logic he deduced other truths.

Like medieval scholastics, Spinoza held that the highest form of knowledge was knowledge of God. Spinoza stated specifically that the "intellectual love of God" is the ultimate human goal. However, his conception of God marked a radical break with both traditional Jewish and Christian thought. For Spinoza, God was not a transcendent crea-tor or miracle maker; he was not a superhuman being who possessed an intellect and free will; he was not a personal being, a loving father who cared for each individual and heeded prayers. Inspired by the new science, Spinoza identified God with the order of nature: nature, a sin-gle all-inclusive system of unchangeable, universal laws in which all things have a determinate place, is also God. God and nature are indis-tinguishable. Since nature is a unified, intelligible, causal system, God is knowable to the human mind. Spinoza insisted that human reason alone can decipher the properties of everything in nature. There are no mysteries that reason cannot unravel; there are no questions for which reason must turn to revelation for answers.

Consistent with his commitment to reason, Spinoza rejected many religious beliefs as superstition and called for a critical reading of the Bible. In his view the Bible was not the literal word of God but an ancient text written by humans with a specific intent. To understand the Hebrew Bible, said Spinoza, requires a thorough knowledge of He-brew and an investigation into the life and times of its authors. Spi-noza's linguistic, scientific, and historical approach—his call for the critical examination of sources—foreshadowed the "higher criticism" of Scripture that emerged in the nineteenth century.

Traditionalists denounced Spinoza as an atheist, who denied the God of the Judeo-Christian tradition and rejected the authority of Scripture. Some early nineteenth-century romantics praised him as a pantheist, a mystic who saw God's presence everywhere in nature. More recent-ly, Spinoza has been viewed as a herald of modernity. Supporters of this interpretation refer to Spinoza's refusal to subordinate thinking to revelation or priestly authority; his rejection of miracles and the efficacy of prayers; his critical approach to the study of Scripture; his attack on superstition and commitment to scientific objectivity; his plea for freedom of thought and religious toleration; and his advocacy of constitutional government which sets limits on state authority.

THE MEANING OF
THE SCIENTIFIC REVOLUTION

The radical transformation of our conception of the physical universe produced by the Scientific Revolution ultimately transformed our understanding of the individual, society, and the purpose of life. The Scientific Revolution, therefore, was a decisive factor in the shaping of the modern world. It destroyed the medieval world-picture, in which the earth occupied the central position, heaven lay just beyond the fixed stars, and every object had its place in a hierarchical and qualitative order. It replaced this view with the modern conception of a homogeneous universe of unbounded space and an infinite number of celestial bodies. Gone were the barriers that separated the heavens and the earth. Gone also was the medieval notion that God had assigned an ultimate purpose to all natural objects and to all plant and animal life, that in God's plan everything had an assigned role: we have eyes because God wants us to see and rain because God wants crops to grow. Eschewing ultimate purposes, modern science examines physical nature for mathematical relationships and chemical composition.

Medieval thinkers deemed the eternal and the unchangeable as most worthy of contemplation. Thus, theology, which studied God, who is immutable, and his truths, which are eternal, was regarded as the queen of the sciences. Because it investigated the immutable heavens, astronomy ranked high in the hierarchy of knowledge, but not as high as theology. Little value was given to the study of physical nature or of animal and plant life. Increasingly, the new outlook initiated by the Scientific Revolution aspired to understand all aspects of the natural environment.

The conception of reason advanced by Galileo and other thinkers of the period differed fundamentally from that of medieval scholastics. Scholastic thinkers viewed reason as a useful aid for contemplating divine truth; as such, reason always had to serve theology. Influenced by the new scientific spirit, thinkers now saw the investigation of nature as reason's principal concern. And this was viewed as an autonomous activity not subject to theological authority.

The Scientific Revolution fostered a rational and critical spirit among the intellectual elite, who were guided by Descartes' first rule of method: "never to accept anything as true that I did not know to be evidently so: that is to say, carefully to avoid precipitancy and prejudice, and to include in my judgements nothing more than what presented itself so clearly and distinctly to my mind that I might have no occasion to place it in doubt."[36] Descartes' methodical doubt, rejection of authority, and insistence on the clarity, precision, and accuracy of

an idea and Francis Bacon's insistence on verification pervaded the outlook of the eighteenth-century Enlightenment thinkers, who denounced magic, spells, demons, witchcraft, alchemy, and astrology as
vulgar superstitions. Phenomena attributed to occult forces, they argued, could be explained by reference to natural forces. A wide breach
opened up between the intellectual elite and the masses, who remained steeped in popular superstitions and committed to traditional
Christian dogma.

The creators of modern science had seen no essential conflict between traditional Christianity and the new view of the physical universe and made no war on the churches. Indeed, they believed that they
were unveiling the laws of nature instituted by God at the Creation—
that at last the human mind could comprehend God's magnificent
handiwork. And Newton specifically allowed for God's occasional intervention in nature's operations in order to assure mechanical precision. But the new cosmology and new scientific outlook ultimately
weakened traditional Christianity.

The new critical spirit led the thinkers of the Enlightenment to
doubt the literal truth of the Bible and to dismiss miracles as incompatible with what science teaches about the regularity of nature. So
brilliantly had God crafted the universe, they said, so exquisite a mechanism was nature, that its operations did not require God's intervention. In the generations after the Scientific Revolution, theology, long
considered the highest form of contemplation, was denounced as a barrier to understanding or even dismissed as irrelevant, and the clergy
rapidly lost their position as the arbiters of knowledge. To many intellectuals, theology seemed sterile and profitless in comparison with the
new science. Whereas science promised the certitude of mathematics,
theologians seemed to quibble endlessly over unfathomable and, even
worse, inconsequential issues. That much blood had been spilled over
these questions discredited theology even more. In scientific acade-
mies, in salons, and in coffee houses, educated men and some women
met to discuss the new ideas, and journals published the new knowledge for eager readers. European culture was undergoing a great transformation, marked by the triumph of a scientific and secular spirit
among the intellectual elite.

The Scientific Revolution repudiated reliance on Aristotle, Ptolemy,
and other ancient authorities for questions concerning nature and substituted in their place knowledge derived from observation, experimentation, and mathematical thinking. Citing an ancient authority
was no longer sufficient to prove a point or to win an argument. The
new standard of knowledge derived from experience with the world,
not from ancient texts or inherited views. This new outlook had far-
reaching implications for the Age of Enlightenment. If the authority of

ancient thinkers regarding the universe could be challenged, could not inherited political beliefs be challenged as well—for example, the divine right of kings to rule? Impressed with the achievements of science, many intellectuals started to urge the application of the scientific method to all fields of knowledge.

The new outlook generated by the Scientific Revolution served as the foundation of the Enlightenment. The Scientific Revolution gave thinkers great confidence in the power of the mind, which had discovered nature's laws, reinforcing the confidence in human abilities expressed by Renaissance humanists. It was believed that in time the scientific method would unlock all nature's secrets, and humanity, gaining ever greater knowledge and control of nature, would progress rapidly. The remarkable achievements in science provided a hope for advances and improvements in all areas of human endeavor. In the words of Sir Isaiah Berlin,

> . . . the entire programme of the Enlightenment, especially in France, was consciously founded on Newton's principles and methods, and derived its confidence and its vast influence from his spectacular achievement. And this, in due course, transformed—indeed largely created—some of the central concepts and directions of modern culture in the west, moral, political, technological, historical, social—no sphere of thought or life escaped the consequence of this cultural mutation.[37]

NOTES

1. Herbert Butterfield, *The Origins of Modern Science* (New York: Free Press, 1965), pp. 7–8.
2. Quoted in Arthur Koestler, *The Sleepwalkers* (New York: Macmillan, 1968), p. 97.
3. Quoted in John Herman Randall, Jr., *The Career of Philosophy* (New York: Columbia University Press, 1962), I, 305.
4. Quoted in Hugh Kearney, *Society and Change 1500–1700* (New York: McGraw Hill, 1971), p. 138.
5. Quoted in Thomas S. Kuhn, *The Copernican Revolution* (Cambridge: Harvard University Press, 1957), p. 191.
6. Excerpted in Edward Rosen, *Copernicus and the Scientific Revolution* (Malabar, Fla.: Krieger, 1984), p. 191.
7. Kuhn, *The Copernican Revolution*, pp. 192–193.
8. Blaise Pascal, *Pensées* (New York: Dutton, 1958), nos. 206, 194, 205, pp. 61, 55.
9. Galileo Galilei, *The Starry Messenger*, in *Discoveries and Opinions of Galileo*, trans. and ed. Stillman Drake (Garden City, N.Y.: Doubleday Anchor Books, 1957), p. 31.
10. Quoted in E. N. da C. Andrade, *Sir Isaac Newton* (New York: Macmillan, 1954; paperback reprint, Garden City, N.Y.: Doubleday, n. d.), pp. 12–13.
11. Galileo Galilei, *The Assayer*, in

Discoveries and Opinions of Galileo, pp. 237–238.

12. Quoted in James J. Langford, *Galileo, Science and the Church* (Ann Arbor: University of Michigan Press, 1977), p. 21.

13. Galileo Galilei, *Dialogue Concerning the Two Chief World Systems—Ptolemaic and Copernican*, trans. Stillman Drake (Berkeley: University of California Press, 1962), pp. 110–112.

14. Galileo Galilei, "Letter to the Grand Duchess Christina," in *Discoveries and Opinions of Galileo*, pp. 177, 179.

15. Ibid., pp. 179, 182.

16. Ibid., p. 183.

17. Ibid., p. 186.

18. Quoted in Stillman Drake, *Galileo* (New York: Hill and Wang, 1980), p. 19.

19. Excerpted in Giorgio de Santillana, *The Crime of Galileo* (Chicago: University of Chicago Press, 1955), p. 312.

20. Quoted in J. J. Fahie, *Galileo His Life and Work* (London: John Murray, 1903), p. 389.

21. M. C. Jacob, *The Cultural Meaning of the Scientific Revolution* (New York: Knopf, 1987), p. 25.

22. I. B. Cohen, *Revolution in Science* (Cambridge: Harvard University Press, 1985), p. 197.

23. Quoted in Koestler, *The Sleepwalkers*, p. 397.

24. Ernst Cassirer, "Mathematical Mysticism and Mathematical Science," in *Galileo Man of Science*, ed. Ernan McMullen (New York: Basic Books, 1967), p. 349.

25. Isaac Newton, *The Mathematical Principles of Natural Philosophy*, trans. Andrew Motte (London: Symonds, 1803), bk. 3, p. 310.

26. Excerpted in H. J. Thayer, ed., *Newton's Philosophy of Nature* (New York: Hafner Press, 1953), p. 5.

27. Ibid., pp. 7–8.

28. Francis Bacon, *The New Organon* in *The Works of Francis Bacon*, eds. James Spedding, R. L. Ellis, and D. D. Heath (Boston: Taggard and Thompson, 1863), VIII, sec. 65.

29. Francis Bacon, *Redargutio Philosophiarum (The Refutation of Philosophy)*, trans. and ed. Benjamin Farrington (Liverpool: Liverpool University Press, 1970), pp. 114–15.

30. Francis Bacon, *The New Organon*, secs. 8, 12, 18.

31. Ibid., sec. 41.

32. Ibid., sec. 43.

33. Ibid., sec. 44.

34. René Descartes, *Discourse on Method*, trans. F. E. Sutcliffe (Baltimore: Penguin Books, 1968), p. 50.

35. Pascal, *Pensées*, sec 2, no. 77, p. 23.

36. Descartes, *Discourse on Method*, p. 41.

37. Quoted in I. B. Cohen, *Revolution in Science*, p. 127.

SUGGESTED READING

Andrade, da C. E. N., *Sir Isaac Newton* (1954).

Armitage, Angus, *John Kepler* (1966).

———, The World of Copernicus (1951).

Butterfield, Herbert, *The Origins of Modern Science* (1965).

Cohen, I. B., *Revolution in Science* (1985).

———, *The Birth of a New Physics* (1960).

Drake, Stillman, *Galileo* (1980).

Grant, Edward, *Physical Science in the Middle Ages* (1951).

Hampshire, Stuart, *Spinoza* (1951).

Kearney, Hugh, *Society and Change 1500–1700* (1971).

Koestler, Arthur, *The Sleepwalkers* (1968).

Kuhn, Thomas, S., *The Copernican Revolution* (1957).

Langford, James, J., *Galileo, Science and the Church* (1977).

McMullen, Ernan, ed., *Galileo Man of Science* (1967).

Randall, John Herman, Jr., *The Career of Philosophy*, vol 1, *from the Middle Ages to the Enlightenment* (1962).

Redondi, Pietro, *Galileo Heretic* (1981).

Rosen, Edward, *Copernicus and the Scientific Revolution* (1984).

Rossi, Paolo, *Francis Bacon from Magic to Science* (1968).

Santillana, Giorgio de, *The Crime of Galileo* (1955).

Shapere, Dudley, *Galileo* (1974).

4

Revolution in Political Thought:

Machiavelli, Hobbes, Locke

The skeptical and critical attitude, the breaking with traditional modes of thinking, and the secularization of intellectual life initiated by the Renaissance and furthered by the Scientific Revolution also marked early modern political thought. Some sixteenth- and seventeenth-century political theorists argued that the state was a purely human creation: its authority did not derive from God, and its actions should not be measured by norms originating in a higher world. They contended that revelation did not extend to politics, that churches should exercise no political authority; and that assisting a church in the saving of souls was not the state's function. This deliberate rejection of otherworldly interpretations and valuations of political life signaled a fundamental break with medieval political thought and is a distinguishing feature of the modern outlook.

By the end of the seventeenth century, a revolution in political thinking had occurred that paralleled and complemented the revolution in Western thinkers' perception of the physical universe. The study of both nature and politics had largely become autonomous fields of inquiry. Both the new cosmology and the new political philosophies rested on their own intellectual foundations; they did not depend on principles that originated in a higher world and required clerical clarification. In both instances, theorists, some quite self-consciously, were departing from the medieval division of the universe into a lower earthly realm and a higher realm beyond the stars, which determined the standards for all earthly endeavors. This growing secularization and rationalization of thought marked a radical departure from the essential outlook of the Middle Ages.

The revolution in political thinking also reflected the changing realities of political life in the sixteenth and seventeenth centuries—a period that saw the dissolution of the old medieval political order and the emergence of the modern centralized, territorial state, which subordinated religious institutions to national control.

TOWARD THE MODERN STATE

During the Middle Ages, kings had to share political power with feudal lords, the clergy, free cities, and representative assemblies. Central authority was tempered by overlapping jurisdictions and numerous and competing allegiances. People saw themselves as members of an estate—clergy, aristocracy, or commoners—rather than as subjects or citizens of a state. Church theorists envisioned Christian Europe as a unitary commonwealth in which spiritual concerns prevailed over secular authority. According to this view, kings, who received their power from God, must never forget their religious obligation to rule in accordance with God's commands as interpreted by the clergy.

Emphasizing the superiority of the spiritual power of the church over the temporal power of the state, church theorists insisted that it was the duty of earthly authority to aid the church in the performance of its spiritual duties. Thus, Pope Gregory VII (1073–1085) who sought to assert the pre-eminence of the papacy over secular rulers, declared that princes should not attempt to subject the church to temporal authority. He asked: "Does anyone doubt that the priests of Christ are to be considered as fathers and masters of kings and princes and of all believers? Would it not be regarded as pitiable madness if a son should try to rule his father or a pupil his master?"[1] Gregory's exaltation of the spiritual authority of the church encouraged future popes to challenge the state whenever it threatened the supremacy of Christian moral teachings or the church's ability to carry out its mission of leading men and women to salvation.

In the Late Middle Ages, Marsilius of Padua (c. 1275–1342) made a radical break with traditional medieval political theory. He argued in *Defender of the Peace* that Christ never intended that his Apostles or their successors, the bishops, should exercise political power; nor did he intend that the clergy should be exempt from civil laws. Religion dealt with a supernatural world and with principles of faith that could not be proved by reason, said Marsilius. Politics, on the other hand, dealt with a natural world and with the affairs of the human community. Political life operated according to its own principles and required no guidance from a higher authority; the state, therefore, should not be made to conform to articles of faith. Thus, Marsilius denied the essential premises of medieval papal theory: that the state, as part of a divinely ordered world, must conform to and fulfill supernatural ends; that the pope, as God's vicar, was empowered to guide kings; and that the clergy were above the laws of the state. Marsilius felt that the church should be a spiritual institution with no temporal power. Pope John XXII branded him a heretic for publishing this work, and Marsilius was forced to seek the protection of the German prince Louis of Bavaria.

In the sixteenth and seventeenth centuries, kings successfully asserted their authority over competing powers, continuing a trend that had begun in the Late Middle Ages. Everywhere strong monarchs dominated or crushed the parliaments, which, during the Middle Ages, had acted as a brake on royal power; increasingly, lords and ecclesiastical authorities were made subject to royal control. The old medieval political order—characterized by feudal particularism and the strength of local authorities on the one hand, and the supranational claims and goals of a universal church on the other—dissolved, and the national, territorial state, the hallmark of the modern world, gradually became the essential political unit.

During this period of declining feudal and clerical power, several essential features of the modern state emerged. A definition of the modern state in its maturity would include the following points: the modern state is supreme in its own territory and has a strong central government, which issues laws that apply throughout the land; it maintains and pays a permanent army of professional soldiers, as well as trained bureaucrats, who are responsible to the central government and collect taxes, enforce laws, and administer justice; it is also a secular state, for promotion of religion is not its concern and churches do not determine state policy. These features of the modern state had been largely absent in the Middle Ages, when the privileges of nobles, church, and towns impeded central authority and when kings were expected to rule in accordance with Christian teachings. In the sixteenth and seventeenth centuries, monarchs were exercising central authority with ever greater effectiveness at the expense of clerical and feudal authority. The secularized character of the state, although still incomplete, became firmly established after the Thirty Years' War (1618-1648). With their countries worn out by Catholic-Protestant conflicts, kings came to act less for religious motives than for reasons of national security and power.

Absolutism, which was justified by divine right, was the form of government favored by early modern kings. During the Middle Ages,

royal absolutism had been blocked by the feudal lords' power and customary rights, the townspeople's vigorous sense of personal freedom
and urban autonomy, the church's countervailing power, and the evolution of representative assemblies. With varying degrees of success,
early modern European monarchs subjected these competing political
authorities to their will. In this new balance of political forces, monarchs claimed that they were chosen by God to rule and were responsible only to him. According to the theory of divine right, the king's
office and person were sacred and rebellion was sacrilege, a crime
against God. Thus, in a speech before the English Parliament in 1610,
James I claimed that the "state of monarchy is the supremest thing
upon earth: for kings are not only God's lieutenants upon earth and sit
upon God's throne, but even by God himself they are called gods. . . .
as to dispute what God may do is blasphemy, . . . so is it sedition in
subjects to dispute what a king may do."[2]

The emergence of the modern state coincided with the gradual
breakdown of a medieval socioeconomic system based on tradition,
hierarchy, and estates. In the medieval system, every group—clergy,
lords, serfs, guildsmen—occupied a particular place and had a unique
function. Society functioned best when each person fulfilled the role
allotted to him or her by God and tradition. Early modern times saw
the growth of a capitalist market economy whose central focus was
the self-sufficient individual, striving, assertive, and motivated by self-
interest. This nascent market economy, greatly boosted by the voyages
of discovery and the conquest and colonization of other parts of the
world, subverted the hierarchically arranged and tradition-bound medieval community.

In responding to these changing political realities, thinkers precipi-
tated a revolution in political ideas, which accelerated the development of the modern outlook. The three most important political theorists of early modern Europe were Niccolò Machiavelli, Thomas
Hobbes, and John Locke.

NICCOLO MACHIAVELLI

The Renaissance revival of classical literature and art marks the beginning of the modern era. The break with the Middle Ages also occurred
on the level of political thought, which, like Renaissance art and literature, moved in a secular direction The emergence of the modern
political spirit during the Renaissance is exemplified in the writings of
Niccolò Machiavelli (1469–1527), the Florentine statesman and political theorist. In his two principal works, *The Prince*, written in 1513,

and *Discourses on the First Decade of Titus Livius*, written between 1512 and 1516, Machiavelli gave expression to the new direction in which politics was moving in European lands.

In the last part of the fifteenth century, Italy was divided into several small, independent city-states, each controlling the surrounding territory and eyeing its neighbors suspiciously; the church, based in Rome, ruled central Italy. The various political units in Italy engaged in frequent conflicts, which sometimes led to the intervention of the German emperor and French and Spanish monarchs. In 1512, a Spanish army allied to Pope Julius II overthrew the Florentine republic, and the Medici family was restored to power. The new leaders dismissed Machiavelli from his government position and forced him into exile. The following year, a conspiracy against the Medici failed and the conspirators were executed. Suspected of involvement in the conspiracy (probably mistakenly), Machiavelli was arrested and tortured but confessed to nothing. On his release, he retired to his farm in the country and devoted himself to study and writing. But never resigned to forced retirement, Machiavelli tried to win the favor of the Medicis in order to regain a position in the Florentine government. Thus, he dedicated *The Prince* to Lorenzo, the duke of Urbino and a Medici (grandson of Lorenzo the Magnificent). But Lorenzo showed no interest in the manuscript, which was circulated privately and not published until 1532, five years after Machiavelli's death.

Machiavelli's political thought reflected the condition of politics in Renaissance Italy. Although less national in scope than the monarchies of England, Spain, and France, the Italian cities were still territorial states, most of them headed by despots, whose chief priority was power (for a time, Venice and Florence survived as republics). Emerging in the Middle Ages, the city-states of northern and central Italy had, by the fifteenth century, become the first truly secular states in Christian Europe. In Italian political life as in the arts, the Christian worldview was being undermined by a growing secularism, as Garrett Mattingly explains:

> Everywhere else, temporal powers were masked and sanctified by religious forms and immemorial customs. Elsewhere, kings, anointed with holy oils and crowned by high priests with special, sacred ceremonies, ruled in accordance with laws considered to be eternal. . . . But in Italy, the city republics were temporal powers in the purest sense of the word. . . . their welfare and their survival depended on their cunning and their strength. . . . In each city the party, the social class, the tyrant temporarily in power had climbed there by force or craft and had to stay there by the same means.[3]

A keen observer of Italian politics, Machiavelli regarded the Italian city-states, ruled by men whose authority rested solely on their cunning and effective use of force, as a new phenomenon, which traditional political theory, concerned with ideal ends, could not adequately explain. Italian princes looked to their own interests, employed force ruthlessly, and made no effort to justify their policies on religious or idealistic grounds. In the endemic warfare, powerful cities devoured weaker ones, and diplomacy was riddled with intrigue, betrayal, and bribery. Moreover, Italy was continually being overrun by foreign invaders, who caused much suffering, In such a tooth-and-claw political world, survival depended on alertness, cleverness, and strength.

The Politics of Reality

Machiavelli believed that, under these circumstances, medieval theorists, who called for an earthly realm that accorded with standards revealed by God, or classical theorists, who sought to base the state on moral norms apprehended by reason, were irrelevant. A supreme realist, Machiavelli wanted rulers to understand how to preserve and expand the state's power and to provide security in a dangerous world. What people require, he maintained, is not a just or virtuous state, but a secure and safe one, and it is the object of politics to attain it. Machiavelli also hoped that a ruler properly guided could end Italy's suffering by restoring its unity and reviving its ancient greatness. He expounded a new political morality, which coincided with the emergence of the modern secular state and the hard world of power politics.

"We are much beholden to Machiavelli and others that write what men do and not what they ought to do,"[4] said Francis Bacon, who was born thirty-four years after Machiavelli's death. Both ancient and medieval theorists sought to define the best form of constitution, the just regime, the ideal state. Classical political thought maintained that ethics and politics are interrelated, that it is the state's purpose to promote the virtuous life. Greek philosophers wanted the human community to accord with natural law—rules of conduct whose principles were ascertainable by reason. Christian thinkers wanted to fashion the earthly city according to the divine commandments revealed in Scripture and interpreted by the church.

Machiavelli had no patience with an approach—for instance, Platonism—that sought to shape political life in accordance with ideal standards. Such visionary expectations, he held, bring the state to ruin, for we do not live in the world of the "ought," the fanciful utopia, but in the world of the "is," the real world of real human beings. Machiavelli aimed to discover how states functioned in the real world, and how rulers must behave if they are to protect their states against the threats posed by domestic and foreign enemies and the unruly passions of their subjects.

Machiavelli's rigorous investigation of politics led him to examine human nature from the standpoint of its limitations and imperfections; a bleak and pessimistic view of human nature pervades his works. The astute prince looks at men as they are and not as he would like them to be. He recognizes that human beings are by nature selfish, corrupt, cowardly, faithless, base, dishonest, and prone to violence and that deception and coercion are necessary to hold in check a flawed human nature that threatens civil order. In his *Discourses*, Machiavelli stressed that

> it must needs be taken for granted that all men are wicked and that they will always give vent to the malignity that is in their minds when opportunity offers. . . . men never do good unless necessity drives them to it.[5]

Machiavelli believed that his study of ancient history and his observations of contemporary politics produced insights into human behavior and statesmanship that were invaluable for rulers seeking to make informed policy decisions. It was Machiavelli's empiricism—his drawing of principles of political behavior from accumulated data—that Bacon, himself an ardent advocate of the empirical method in the study of nature, so admired. Machiavelli was aware that this approach of studying politics in the cold light of reason, free of illusions about human nature, and devoid of idle speculation about higher worlds and imaginary and unattainable commonwealths, represented a new departure.

> . . . it appears to me more proper to go to the real truth of the matter than to its imagination; and many have imagined republics and principalities which have never been seen or known to exist in reality; for how we live is so far removed from how we ought to live, that he who abandons what is done for what ought to be done, will rather learn to bring about his own ruin than his preservation.[6]

Both ancient and medieval theorists had taught that political behavior must be guided by the highest ideals and that rulers should demonstrate a genuine concern for their subjects and be faithful to obligations, magnanimous, and compassionate. Schooled in the rough-and-tumble world of Italian power politics, Machiavelli warned that rulers who aspire to do what is usually considered good and recoil from what is considered bad will be destroyed by their rivals. For Machiavelli, no moral imperative governs state policy. Politics is not the pursuit of moral virtue but the pursuit of the state's security and well-being. When conditions require it, the wise prince sets aside conventional morality and does what is necessary, even if these actions are generally considered morally wrong.

Machiavelli did not advocate wickedness. However, he did say that actions condemned in personal behavior are permissible in politics. The successful prince separates political morality from private morality; no private conscience delimits his public acts. History, said Machiavelli, affords numerous examples of persons who lived exemplary private lives but failed as leaders and statesmen because they confused politics with virtue. Conversely, men who demonstrated despicable character traits in their personal lives proved to be wise and successful rulers. As Machiavelli sums it up in *The Prince*,

> A man who wishes to make a profession of goodness in everything must necessarily come to grief among so many who are not good. Therefore it is necessary for a prince, who wishes to maintain himself, to learn how not to be good, and to use this knowledge and not use it, according to the necessity of the case.[7]

Machiavelli's *The History of Florence* contains a passage that illustrates this point. He describes party disputes and lower class unrest that exploded into violence in 1378. The lower class engaged in arson and looting, but now it feared punishment, for the whole city was united against it. At this point, a fiery worker urged increasing the level of violence, for "where many err, no body is punished; little faults are punished, great and serious ones are rewarded." To those acting out of conscience and wishing to refrain from further violence, Machiavelli has the plebs' spokesman respond in these revealing words:

> Neither conscience nor ill fame ought to frighten you, for those who conquer . . . never because of it come to disgrace. Of conscience we need take no account, for when people fear hunger and prison, as we do, they cannot and should not have any fear of Hell.
>
>   If you will observe the way in which men act, you will see that all those who attain great riches and great power have attained them by means of either fraud or force. . . . But those who, through either lack of prudence or great folly, avoid these ways, always are smothered in servitude and poverty, for faithful servants are always servants, and good men are always poor. . . . From this it comes that men devour one another; and they who are weakest always come off worst. We ought, then, to use force when we get a chance.[8]

Machiavelli maintained that the state was purely a human creation and that the actions of princes should be governed solely by necessity. The successful prince, concerned only with preserving and strengthening the state's power, dismisses issues of morality and immorality as irrelevant. The course of action that he chooses is determined by the needs of a particular situation and not by any moral purpose or by any system of justice given to man by God or rooted in the natural order of things. All means are permitted the prince if the state's survival is at stake.

> For when the safety of one's country wholly depends on the decision to be taken, no attention should be paid either to justice or injustice, to kindness or cruelty, or to its being praiseworthy or ignominious. On the contrary, every other consideration being set aside, that alternative should be wholeheartedly adopted which will save the life and preserve the freedom of one's country.[9]

Successful princes, Machiavelli contended, have always been indifferent to moral and religious considerations—a lesson of history that rulers ignore at their own peril.

> How laudable it is for a prince to keep good faith and live with integrity, and not with astuteness, every one knows. Still the experience of our times shows those princes to have done great things who have had little regard for good faith, and have been able by astuteness to confuse men's brains. . . . You must know, then, that there are two methods of fighting, the one by law, the other by force: the first method is that of men, the second of beasts; but as the first method is often insufficient, one must have recourse to the second. It is therefore necessary for a prince to know well how to use both the beast and the man. . . .
> . . . Therefore, a prudent ruler ought not to keep faith when by so doing it would be against his interest, and when the reasons which made him bind himself no longer exist. If men were all good, this precept would not be a good one; but as they are bad, and would not observe their faith with you, so you are not bound to keep faith with them.[10]

A wise prince gives the appearance of being virtuous, for such a pretense will assist him in governing his subjects. But when the security of the state requires it, the prince is prepared to abandon all virtue. In the world of politics, blunders—not crimes—are unpardonable.

> Thus it is well to seem merciful, faithful, humane, sincere, religious, and also to be so; but you must have the mind so disposed that when it is needful to be otherwise you may be able to change to the opposite qualities. And it must be understood that a prince, and especially a new prince, cannot observe all those things which are considered good in men, being often obliged in order to maintain the state, to act against faith, against charity, against humanity, and against religion.[11]

If the prince's policy proves successful, his ruthlessness will be forgiven and forgotten: ". . . in the actions of men, and especially of princes . . . the end justifies the means. Let a prince therefore aim at conquering and maintaining the state and the means will always be judged honourable and praised by everyone, for the vulgar is always taken by appearances."[12]

In justifying unscrupulous behavior, Machiavelli did not intend to provide guidelines for a tyrant who merely sought to gain personal power for private ends. He had no love for cruel and megalomaniacal despots. Rather, he wanted the prince to identify with the body politic, to aspire to do what is best for the state in its quest for survival and stability. If the prince succeeds in this goal, he earns ultimate glory— a reputation that will survive long after his death. Nor did Machiavelli condone needless acts of cruelty and violence: the prince resorts to repression and terror for reasons of state, never for private passion, pride, whim, or petty revenge, and he employs violence judiciously and deftly.

> A prince, therefore, must not mind incurring the charge of cruelty for the purpose of keeping his subjects united and faithful; for, with a very few examples, he will be more merciful than those who, from excess of tenderness, allow disorders to arise, from whence spring bloodshed and rapine; for these as a rule injure the whole community, while the executions carried out by the prince injure only individuals.[13]

Breaking with the Medieval Outlook

Machiavelli's interpretation of history and politics is devoid of any overarching Christian meaning. Themes that occupied a central place for Christian moralists—the coming of Christ to earth, human sin, the salvation of souls, the unity of Christian civilization guided by the papacy—were of no concern to Machiavelli. Nor did he give any indication that he viewed Christianity as a religion of revelation. Machiavelli did not claim that Christianity derived from a transcendental realm, that Christian morality should guide political life, or that there existed universal moral values prescribed by God. But will not the prince be punished on the day of judgment for violating Christian teachings? In startling contrast to medieval theorists, Machiavelli simply ignored the question. Only the world of the here and now concerned him.

In a world where states compete for power, Christian otherworldly concerns and values were unworkable guides, said Machiavelli; indeed, by glorifying the unmanly virtues of humility and meekness, Christianity undermined the state. He compared Christian virtues unfavorably with those of classical civilization. The religion of the ancient Greeks and Roman, he said,

> did not beatify men unless they were replete with worldly glory: army commanders, for instance, and rulers of republics. Our religion has glorified humble and contemplative men, rather than men of action. It has assigned as man's highest good humility, abnegation, and contempt for

mundane things, whereas the other identified it with magnanimity, bodily strength, and everything else that conduces to make men very bold. And, if our religion demands that in you there be strength, what it asks for is strength to suffer rather than strength to do bold things.[14]

Machiavelli regarded Christian ideals of compassion, meekness, humility, turning the other cheek, yearning for salvation, and contempt for the worldly life as detrimental to the state's well-being. The ruler who tries to govern on the basis of Christian teachings condemns himself to political impotence. On the other hand, the morality of Pericles' Athens and Scipio's Rome, which valued personal achievement, courage, strength, pride, glory, civic responsibility, and patriotism, fosters the development of a strong and vigorous republic.

For Machiavelli, religion had value not because it was revelation or truth but because it was socially useful; a wise ruler should utilize religion to unite his subjects and to promote civic obedience, public-spiritedness, and patriotism. It was a weapon employed by the state in its struggle for survival. Religion serves the same purpose for the prince that the noble lies do for Plato's philosophers. In each case, rulers employ pious fictions for a worthwhile civic end.

> It will also be seen by those who pay attention to Roman history, how much religion helped in control of the armies, in encouraging the plebs, in producing good men, and in shaming the bad. . . . Nor in fact was there ever a legislator who, in introducing extraordinary laws to a people, did not have recourse to God, for otherwise they would not have been accepted, since many benefits of which a prudent man is aware, are not so evident to reason that he can convince others of them. . . . The rulers of a republic or of a kingdom, therefore, should . . . keep their commonwealths religious, and, in consequence, good and united.[15]

Such an outlook requires that churches always remain subordinate to the interests of the state—a complete reversal of the essential character of medieval political thought. For Machiavelli, says Giuseppe Prezzolini, "veneration of the supernatural. . . . is a weapon of illusion, for the use of politics in the state's fight for survival."[16] Machiavelli, who substituted the primacy of the state for the primacy of faith, would have approved of Napoleon's observation:

> Society cannot exist without inequality of fortunes and inequality of fortunes cannot exist without religion. When a man is dying of hunger alongside another who stuffs himself, it is impossible to make him accede to the difference unless there is an authority which says to him God wished it thus; there must be some poor and some rich in the world, but hereafter and for all eternity the division will be made differently.[17]

Machiavelli broke with the distinguishing feature of medieval thought—the division of the universe into higher and lower worlds. To this extent, he did for political thought what Galileo did a century later for scientific thought. Medieval thinkers held that the ruler derived his power from God and had a religious obligation to govern in accordance with God's precepts and that God expressed his will in mysterious ways. In their view, the best state was one that assisted in the saving of souls. Rejecting completely this otherworldly, theocentric orientation, Machiavelli ascribed no divine origin or purpose to the state but saw it entirely as a natural entity. He considered it utterly absurd to believe that the power of principalities and states had anything to do with God's intent and explicitly rejected the principle that kings should adhere to Christian moral teachings.

Over the centuries, the term *machiavellianism* has come to mean the justification of any form of opportunism, duplicity, and wickedness in politics; the adjective *machiavellian* is used to refer to politicians and statesmen who stop at nothing to achieve their political ends. But Machiavelli's true significance is not as a proponent of immoral or amoral behavior. He is a great political thinker because, for good or for ill, he removed political thought from a religious frame of reference and viewed the state and political behavior in the detached and dispassionate manner of a scientist.

In secularizing and rationalizing political philosophy, Machiavelli initiated trends in political thought that we recognize as distinctly modern. He was doing on a theoretical level what Italian rulers were doing in fact, asserting the state's temporal character and autonomy— its independence from a transcendental realm, from theological principles, and from clerical authority. Like the Italian princes, Machiavelli viewed the state as an autonomous entity that recognized no higher religious-ethical power and considered self-interest, that is, survival and power, the only legitimate standards in political life. In succeeding centuries, all Europe would be broken up into sovereign secular states that mirrored the political behavior and outlook of the Italian Renaissance states. Increasingly, thinkers would proclaim that both nature and the human intellect are also autonomous—that, like the state, they require no direction from a higher world. The two-world orientation of the Middle Ages was in disarray.

THOMAS HOBBES

"It was Machiavelli, that greater Columbus, who had discovered the continent on which Hobbes could erect his structure,"[18] Leo Strauss reminds us. Like Machiavelli, the English philosopher and political theorist Thomas Hobbes (1588–1679) had a gloomy view of human nature, rejected religious interpretations of political life, and sought to fashion a theory of the state that accorded with the reality of the human condition. Both Hobbes and Machiavelli paid no mind to the view of medieval theologians that the political community should conform to God's revelation, and both regarded the attempts of ancient philosophers to design commonwealths modeled on an ideal of human perfection as useless utopian dreams. In contrast to Plato particularly, both Machiavelli and Hobbes sought political arrangements that were realistic and realizable—that accorded with the way people actually behave. Focusing on the dark, unsocial side of human nature, both thinkers saw society threatened by insatiable human desires and ambitions, which they wanted the state to hold in check. Thus, in contrast to the idealistic Plato, who designed a state based on standards of justice and virtue, the realistic Hobbes fashioned a state intended to provide security in an unsafe and violent world.

Like Machiavelli's, Hobbes's political thought reflected the new economic, political, and cultural forces that were transforming western Europe. The agonies of the English civil war, including the execution of Charles I, fortified Hobbes's conviction that absolute monarchy was the most logical and desirable form of government, a position that he developed fully in *Leviathan* (1651), his principal work of political theory. (The title *Leviathan* comes from the Book of Job and refers to the great monster that rules "over all the children of pride.") Hobbes attributed the civil war to Parliament, which undermined royal sovereignty, and to militant religious leaders, who set their personal vision of Christianity against the established church and settled law. He believed that a proper understanding of the state, particularly its need for power in order to restrain willful human passions, would avert future rebellions against established authority and their threat to domestic order. Without the coercive power of the state, society would degenerate into anarchy.

Also influenced by the Scientific Revolution, particularly by Galileo's mathematical physics, Hobbes aimed to build a political philosophy on a scientific foundation. He maintained that just as moving bodies obey mechanical principles so too does the behavior of human beings proceed according to laws. Hence, thinkers who study politics in a scientific way can predict with some certainty what will be the outcome of a specific constellation of conditions. Similarly, Hobbes believed that the construction of a proper government depends on adherence to set rules, which are as regular and timeless as the rules of geometry. He had no doubt that he was the first theorist to deduce these rules and to unite them into a logical system, a true political philosophy. He believed that he had created a scientific model of the political world that was as precise and accurate as Euclid's system. Yet, as Dante Germino points out,

> we would wholly fail to understand his greatness as a political philosopher if we thought of him as a servant of any rigid and simplistic method or system claiming to be 'scientific.' Throughout his . . . political writings, a basic openness of mind and spirit triumphs over the rigidities of the abstract and rationalistic models he often purports to emulate. . . . As any reader of the *Leviathan* must know, Hobbes' subject is man, not the machine. For all his borrowings from the methods and material of the natural sciences, Hobbes does not treat man in nonhuman terms.[19]

Human Nature as Flawed

Hobbes maintained that to build the right political order we must first understand human behavior. Using geometry as a model, he began with what he believed were self-evident axioms regarding human nature from which he deduced other truths regarding the nature of political life. Convinced that people are innately selfish, grasping, envious, distrustful, and treacherous, he asserted that competition and dissension, rather than cooperation, characterize human relations.

> For as to the strength of body, the weakest has strength enough to kill the strongest, either by secret machination or by confederacy with others. . . . And as to the faculties of the mind . . . men are . . . [more] equall than unequall. . . . From this equality of ability, ariseth equality of hope in the attaining of our Ends. And therefore if any two men desire the same thing, which neverthelesse they cannot both enjoy, they become enemies; and in the way to their End, . . . endeavour to destroy, or subdue one another. . . . If one plant, sow, build, or possesse a convenient Seat, others may probably be expected to come prepared with forces united to dispossesse and deprive him, not only of the fruit of his labour, but also of his life, or liberty.[20]

Because human beings are by nature competitive, they "use Violence, to make themselves Masters of other men's persons, wives, children, and cattell;"[21] because they inherently fear and mistrust each other, they resort to force to defend themselves; and because they naturally aspire to glory, they will use violence "for trifles, as a word, a smile, a different opinion, and any other signe of undervalue, either direct in their Persons, or by reflexion in their Kindred, their Friends, their Nation, their Profession, or their Name."[22] Consequently, "without a common Power to keep them all in awe, they are in that condition which is called Warre; and such a warre, as is of every man, against every man."[23]

In a passage that is remarkably Freudian, Hobbes succinctly defines human beings as creatures governed by unruly passions: "The secret thoughts of man run over all things, holy, profane, clean, obscene, grave and light, without shame or blame."[24] When reason teaches that cooperation is more advantageous than competition people are reluctant to alter their ways, because their behavior is governed more by passion than by reason. "All men agree," says Hobbes, that "Peace is Good," and therefore also the ". . . means of Peace, which . . . are *Justice, Gratitude, Modesty, Equity, Mercy*, and the [other moral virtues] are good."[25] But driven by rapaciousness, they will sacrifice peace and virtue to the altar of power. More than avarice, however, leads people to seek ever more power. They are also driven by insecurity and fear. Living in a hostile and dangerous world, individuals (and states) aspire to greater power in order to safeguard their lives, property, and status.

> . . . in the first place, I put for a generall inclination of all mankind a perpetuall and restless desire of Power after power, that ceaseth only in Death. And the cause of this, is not always that a man hopes for a more intensive delight, than he has already attained to; or that he cannot be content with a moderate power: but because he cannot assure the power and means to live well, which he hath present, without the acquisition of more. And from hence it is, that Kings, whose power is greatest, turn their endeavours to the assuring it at home by Lawes, or abroad by Wars; and when that is done, there succeedeth a new desire; in some of Fame from new Conquest; in others, . . . of admiration, or being flattered.[26]

Hobbes's theory of government was intended to contain the strife provoked by a flawed human nature. Hobbes postulated a state of nature, a hypothetical condition of humanity prior to the formation of the state. He did not ascribe an actual historical existence to the state of nature. Rather, he intended it as a logical abstraction, a device employed to demonstrate that powerful antisocial forces are present in human beings and to afford a rational foundation for a strong ruling entity—the state—in order to hold in check an aggressive and socially harmful human nature. For Hobbes, the state of nature is what society would be like if there were no common power to restrain man's natural inclinations; without an authority to make and to enforce law, life would be miserable, a war of every man against every man.

> Whatsoever therefore is consequent to a time of Warre, where every man is Enemy to every man; the same is consequent to the time, wherein men live without other security, than what their own strength and their own invention shall furnish them withall. In such condition, there is no place for Industry; because the fruit thereof is uncertain: and consequently no Culture of the Earth; no Navigation, nor use of commodities that may be imported by Sea; no commodious Building; no Instruments of moving and removing such things as require much force;

no Knowledge of the face of the Earth; no account of Time; no Arts; no Letters; no Society; and which is worst of all, continuall feare and danger of violent death. And the life of man, solitary, poore, nasty, brutish, and short.[27]

Aristotle had stated that by nature man is a social being. For Hobbes, the natural condition of man is one of strife and chaos. Driven by competitiveness, distrust, and a yearning for power, which is the means to satisfy desires, individuals in the state of nature quarrel and war with each other; each person is at the mercy of every other person. Consequently, people live always in fear of violent death, and without a ruling authority to impose order, every man has to rely on his own strength and cleverness, for protection against others.

The perpetual strife and lack of protection against both outside invaders and the acts of others cause people to live in fear of their lives and prevent them from securing the benefits of their labor and the fruits of the earth.

Human behavior in the state of nature represents, for Hobbes, the way we naturally are. Thus, contemporary society is never far removed from the ferocity, fear, and insecurity that marked the state of nature.

The intolerable conditions in the state of nature make people desperate, says Hobbes. Finally they recognize that the only way to break this cycle of violence and anxiety

is to conferre all their power and strength upon one Man, or upon one Assembly of men, that may reduce all their Wills, by plurality of voices, unto one Will. . . . and therein to submit their Wills, every one to his Will, and their Judgements to his Judgement. This is more than Consent, or Concord: it is a reall Unitie of them all, in one and the same Person, made by Covenant of every man with every man, in such manner, as if every man should say to every man, I authorise and give up my Right of Governing my selfe, to this Man, or to this Assembly of men, on the condition, that thou give up thy Right to him, and Authorise all his Actions in like manner. This done, the Multitude so united in one Person, is called a COMMON-WEALTH.[28]

Hobbes derives the need for the state from human nature itself, whose failings are made manifest in the prepolitical state of nature. Desiring peace and security—that is, seeking to escape from the specter of violent death—each person contracts to renounce the freedom of his natural condition. Men surrender their right to take whatever action is necessary to preserve their lives and property to one ruler, or to an assembly, and agree to submit to the will of authority. In effect, they contract to establish a state headed by a sovereign whose duty is to protect his subjects and safeguard their natural right of self-preservation. The ruler does this by instilling a fear of punishment in his subjects, for people are dissuaded from harming each other when they realize that the punishment outweighs the gain from a criminal act.

The same deficiencies in human nature that necessitate the creation of a commonwealth require that the sovereign exercise absolute power, for if the sovereign's power is shackled, he cannot protect the lives of the subjects, which is the reason why a commonwealth was established in the first place. Hobbes denies that the sovereign can be called to account by his subjects and deprives them of any legitimate justification for rebellion. Subjects are bound by the social contract to obey the sovereign's commands, for in the creation of civil society each person has transferred the powers that he had exercised in the state of nature to the sovereign. Thus, subjects cannot disobey the sovereign's commands by accusing him of violating his contract with them, for the people have only covenanted with each other, not with the sovereign. The sovereign, says Hobbes, must have supreme and unlimited power, or society will collapse and the anarchy of the state of nature will return. Nor can the covenant that had granted full authority to the sovereign be revoked.

> And therefore, they that are subjects to a Monarch, cannot without his leave cast off Monarchy, and return to the confusion of a disunited Multitude; nor transferre their Person from him that beareth it, to another Man, or other Assembly of men. . . . if they depose him, they take from him that which is his own, and so again it is injustice. . . . and consequently none of his Subjects, by any pretense of forfeiture, can be freed from his Subjection.[29]

While the sovereign could be an assembly or a monarch, for Hobbes the best form of government is hereditary monarchy, for it is best able to control a human being's rapacious nature and to provide a secure environment. Hobbes recognized that the abuse of absolute power was a distinct possibility, but the alternative was far worse—civil war and anarchy. Thus Hobbes disagreed totally with the view held by some ancient and medieval theorists that killing a tyrant was both lawful and praiseworthy.

Shaping the Modern Outlook

Leviathan is a rational and secular political statement. In this modern approach, rather than in Hobbes's justification of absolutism, lies the work's true significance. Like Machiavelli, Hobbes was a distinctly modern thinker, who rejected the authority of tradition and church as inconsistent with a science of politics and made no attempt to fashion the earthly city in accordance with Christian teachings. In contrast to medieval theorists, Hobbes dispensed with revealed religion as the source of political authority. Thus, although he supported absolute monarchy, he dismissed the idea advanced by other theorists of absolutism that the monarch's power derived from God. For him, the state was a human invention organized by human beings to deal with a human problem, and its legitimacy and power rested purely on human authority. Also in contrast with medieval theorists, Hobbes rejected the idea that the sovereign's commands need not be obeyed if they conflicted with God's law. The ruinous religious conflicts in England demonstrated religion's ability to provoke civil discord; they convinced Hobbes that the authority of the state must prevail over that of the church. For Hobbes, the state was not God's creation; it was merely a useful arrangement that permitted individuals to exchange goods and services in a secure environment.

Hobbes claimed that he had done something unique: he was the first political philosopher to deduce with scientific precision the natural laws governing human nature and the social order, the first to elevate politics to the rank of a science. His success, he said, derived from the fact that he understood what was most powerful in people—their passions. And no passion was more powerful than the fear of violent death at the hands of others. The individual's natural desire for self-preservation is the fundamental fact of existence; if people are to live in peace, they must accept external restraints on their behavior.

Medieval thinkers had assigned each group of people—clergy, lords, serfs, guildsmen—a place in a fixed social order; an individual's social duties were set by ancient traditions believed to have been ordained by God. During early modern times, the great expansion of commerce and capitalism spurred the new individualism already pronounced in Renaissance culture; group ties were shattered by competition and accelerating social mobility. Hobbes gave expression to an emerging society where people confront each other as competing individuals pursuing their own ends and where they are bound neither by a transcendental system of morality nor by the rules and customs that support a fixed ordering of society. Hobbes feared that these changed conditions jeopardized peaceful behavior among men, which for him was the highest virtue. For this reason he championed hereditary absolute monarchy, holding that only the unlimited authority of a sovereign could contain human passions that threatened the social order with disintegration and provide an environment in which people were free to pursue their individual interests in a peaceful way.

Hobbes's construction, in rational and secular terms, of a theory of the state based on the premise that self-interest dominates human behavior makes him the first major theorist of modern individualism.

While Hobbes's absolute state is antithetical to the spirit of modern liberalism, his focus on providing an orderly environment in which individuals were able to pursue their own aims is central to the modern liberal outlook. Also crucial to the liberal outlook is Hobbes's idea of the social contract, according to which the people, rather than God, are the source of the ruler's authority. As already noted Hobbes held that the power granted by the people to the sovereign was irrevocable. Later political theorists, however, would advance the liberal view that the people are both the original and the continuing source of governmental authority, that the people have the power both to institute and to revoke political authority, and that sovereignty resides permanently with the people. Although we reject Hobbes's justification of absolutism, his insight that civilization is forever in danger of collapsing into anarchy and savagery is still a poignant message for our times.

JOHN LOCKE

John Locke (1632–1704), an English physician, statesman, philosopher, and political theorist, shared Hobbes's rational and secular approach to political thought but diverged from Hobbes's conceptions of human nature and of the state. Locke regarded the individual as essentially good and rational and rejected Hobbes's absolute state. Seeking to preserve individual freedom, Locke advocated constitutional government, in which the power to govern derives from the consent of the governed and the state's authority is limited by agreement. Locke's psychological and educational thought, as well as his political thought, was instrumental in the shaping of the liberal tradition. In this chapter, we discuss Locke's political thought as expressed in his *Second Treatise of Government*; in the next chapter, we treat other aspects of Locke's thought.

The *Two Treatises of Government* were published anonymously in 1690, and only some years later did Locke acknowledge authorship. In the preface, Locke stated that he intended the treatises to vindicate the Glorious Revolution of 1688, in which James II was overthrown and William and Mary acceded to the throne. It was Locke's purpose "to justify to the World the People of England, whose love of their Just and Natural Rights, with their Resolution to preserve them, saved the Nation when it was on the very Brink of Slavery and Ruine."[30] We now know that Locke had composed the treatises several years before the revolution—the first was written in 1683 and the second probably between 1679 and 1681.

John Locke *(The Bettmann Archive)*

Recognizing the need for a reasoned defense of the events of 1688, Locke quickly adapted the manuscript and wrote an appropriate preface. The *First Treatise* is a refutation of Robert Filmer's *Patriarcha*, which tried to trace back to Adam the supposed divine right of Charles II to rule. In trying to justify absolutism, Filmer argued that kings have the same authority over their subjects that Adam had over his children; and in both cases this authority derived originally from God. The *Second Treatise,* enunciated the principle of natural rights, attacked arbitrary government, and affirmed government by consent of the people in the interests of the people; it established Locke as a seminal thinker in the shaping of the liberal-democratic tradition. Locke gave theoretical expression to what many progressive Britons had come to regard as inextricable components of English tradition—a rejection of monarchical absolutism, parliamentary government under the rule of law, and protection of private property.

Human Nature and Natural Rights

Locke had a greater confidence than Hobbes in the human being's rational capacities and moral potential. Whereas Hobbes saw human beings as utterly selfish animals, promoting perpetual strife with their relentless pursuit of creature comforts, fame, and power, Locke held that individuals participate in a moral order whose existence can be grasped through reason and that rational people can recognize that their behavior ought to correspond to the requirements of the moral order. Because human beings are rational by nature and are moved by a sense of moral obligation, they are capable of transcending a narrow selfishness and of respecting the inherent dignity of others.

This is not to imply that Locke was a naive optimist; he knew very well that people do not inevitably and consistently behave rationally and virtuously. Locke maintained that human beings often display rationality, sociability, and virtue but that there are occasions when they are ignorant, irrational, contentious, covetous, and wicked, when they ignore the voice of duty and pay no heed to the dictates of conscience. Hobbes's advocacy of absolutism flowed logically from his low estimation of human nature: strong government is required to hold in check unruly passions. On the other hand, Locke's support of limited government and the safeguarding of individual rights derived from a more positive image of the human being's rational and moral potential.

Like Hobbes, Locke made use of "the state of nature," the presumed condition of humanity before the creation of the state, as a means of developing his views of human nature and his political philosophy. In the state of nature, said Locke, individuals are born free, rational, and equal. God has not set some people above others, as Filmer had claimed. Locke considered it self-evident that all men, because they belong to the same species and have the same nature, are created equal. Consequently, one person should not be placed in subjection to another. Nor for Locke was the state of nature a Hobbesian war of all against all; instead, he saw it as governed by a law of nature, "which willeth the Peace and *Preservation of all Mankind*." Locke viewed the law of nature as a law of reason, which the rational mind can apprehend:

> [It] obliges everyone: And Reason, which is that law, teaches all Mankind who will but consult it, that being all equal and independent, no one ought to harm another in his Life, Health, Liberty, or Possessions. For Men being all the Workmanship of one Omnipotent and infinitely wise Maker . . . and being furnished with like Faculties, sharing all in one Community of Nature, there cannot be supposed any such *Subordination* among us, that may Authorize us to destroy one another, as if we

were made for one anothers Uses, as the inferior ranks of Creatures are for ours.[31]

In the state of nature, all individuals are required not to harm others. But since men are capable of acting contrary to reason, they do violate the law of nature by invading the rights of others. And since there is no authority to restrain people from such behavior, wronged parties have the right to punish the evildoer, who "declares himself to live by another Rule than that of *reason* and common Equity, which is the measure God has set to the Actions of Men for their mutual security."[32] The degree of punishment and the amount of reparation should be dictated by reason and conscience and should be in proportion to the transgression.

Although the state of nature is not as frightening and chaotic as Hobbes described it, it still suffers from basic weaknesses: the lack of an authority to deal with transgressors of the law of nature and the lack of fixed penalties. When each person behaves as judge and executioner, conditions are ripe for further tensions and conflicts. Because of the uncertainties inherent in the state of nature, men consent to organize a civil government and to submit to the will of the majority. These last points are crucial. By asserting that human beings enter into a social contract in order to create their own government, Locke rejects the theory that rulers derive their power from God, which had served as a prop for Stuart absolutism. In its place, he affirms the principle that all legitimate authority derives from the consent of the majority, which coincided with Parliament's goal of limiting the monarch's power.

Locke begins with the assumption that as rational beings people are endowed by nature (and God) with fundamental rights, among which are the right to their life, liberty, and property. In developing the theory of natural rights, Locke drew on the ancient Stoic conception of natural law, which applies to all human beings, and the medieval Christian view that God's eternal law was a law of reason apprehensible by the mind. In establishing a government, the people do not surrender these natural rights to any authority but intend the new political society to recognize and secure these rights. In contrast to that of Hobbes, the Lockean state cannot be an absolute and arbitrary power, for such a political organization would not aspire to protect the natural rights of the individual, which is the very reason for the existence of political society. Indeed, rule by a tyrant is a far worse condition than the uncertainties of the state of nature.

A ruling authority that attempts to govern absolutely and arbitrarily fails to fulfill the purpose for which it was established; it has placed itself in a state of war with the people. Under these circumstances, the people have the moral right to dissolve the government, something which Hobbes had denied them. When the

> *Legislators endeavour to take away, and destroy the Property of the People*, or to reduce them to Slavery under Arbitrary Power, they put themselves into a state of War with the People, who are thereupon absolved from any further Obedience. . . . Whensoever therefore the *Legislative* shall transgress this fundamental Rule of Society; and either by Ambition, Fear, Folly or Corruption, *endeavour to grasp* themselves, *or put into the hands of any other, an Absolute Power* over the Lives, Liberties, and Estates of the People; By this breach of Trust they *forfeit the Power*, the People had put into their hands, for quite contrary ends.[33]

To the charge that his ideas will foster frequent rebellion, Locke replies that the true rebels are the magistrates who, in pursuit of "absolute dominion," break their trust and cease to be legitimate governors. Moreover, Locke justifies rebellion only in the most extreme circumstances—only after a long train of abuses has demonstrated the ruler's tyrannical intentions.

Cornerstone of Liberalism

Locke's political thought is crucial in the shaping of the liberal-democratic tradition. In the Lockean state, laws are intended for the general welfare of the people and not for the private advantage of the ruler. Whereas Hobbes feared the destructive passions of subjects, Locke's chief concern was to protect people from absolutism, from the arbitrary, predatory, and capricious acts of ruling authorities. For Hobbes, the gravest evil was the breakdown of security; for Locke, nothing was worse than the loss of individual liberty. In opposition to advocates of the theory of divine right, who insisted that rulers were answerable only to God, for God had chosen them to rule, Locke advanced the idea that sovereignty resides with the people and that government rests on the consent of the governed. The ruler governs in the people's name and is bound by the same natural law that binds his subjects. This law, which God had embedded within nature and which is discoverable by reason, is superior to the king's law. Government is obliged through its laws to respect and to implement the law of nature. This recognition that there is a higher law above human law, which people and governing authorities are obligated to obey, is the cornerstone of modern liberalism. Raymond Polin captures the essence of Locke and of liberalism when he states: "For Locke, freedom exists and is meaningful only if it is bound to the obligation to achieve a reasonable order and a moral one. This principle lies at the bottom of any true and efficient liberalism."[34]

The Lockean state is also a constitutional state, another essential feature of modern liberalism. It follows established rules and sets barriers to arbitrary dictates. Rulers hold their authority under law; when they act outside the law, they forfeit their right to govern. Locke wanted the legislature—the British Parliament—to have greater power than the monarch. He believed that members of Parliament, sensible and industrious property owners—the emerging middle class—with a stake in society, were more likely than monarchs not to act impetuously, not to interfere with personal liberty and property, not to violate established law and procedures, and not to raise taxes without the nation's consent.

Both Hobbes and Locke agreed that the state exists in order to ensure the tranquility, security, and well-being of its citizens. But they proposed radically different ways for attaining this end. Unlike Hobbes, Locke believed that social well-being encompassed personal freedom. Rejecting Hobbes's view that absolute power can remedy the defects of the state of nature, Locke stated the case for limited government, the rule of law, the protection of fundamental human rights, and the right of resistance to arbitrary power. Underlying Locke's conception of the state is the conviction that people have the capacity for reason and freedom: "we are born Free as we are born Rational."[35]

The value that Locke gave to reason and freedom and his theories of natural rights and the right of rebellion against unjust authority had a profound effect on the Enlightenment and the liberal revolutions of the late eighteenth and early nineteenth centuries. Thus, in the Declaration of Independence, Thomas Jefferson restated Locke's principles to justify the American Revolution. Locke's tenets that property is a natural right and that state interference with personal property leads to the destruction of liberty also became core principles of modern liberalism.

NOTES

1. Ephraim Emerton, ed. and trans., *The Correspondence of Pope Gregory VII* (New York: Columbia University Press, 1932; New York: Octagon Press, 1966), p. 169.

2. Excerpted in G. W. Prothero, ed., *Select Statutes and Other Constitutional Documents Illustrative of the Reigns of Elizabeth and James I* (Oxford: Clarendon Press, 1906), pp. 293–294.

3. Garrett Mattingly, "Changing Attitudes Towards the State During the Renaissance," in *Facets of the Renaissance*, ed. William H.

Werkmeister (New York: Harper Torchbooks, 1963) pp. 28–29.

4. Quoted in Ernst Cassirer, *Myth of the State* (New Haven: Yale University Press, 1946), p. 119.

5. Niccolò Machiavelli, *The Discourses*, trans. Leslie J. Walker, rev. Brian Richardson (Baltimore: Penguin Books, 1986), bk. 1, chap. 3, p. 111–112.

6. Niccolò Machiavelli, *The Prince*, trans. Luigi Ricci, rev. E.R.P. Vincent (New York: New American Library, Mentor Books, 1955; in arrangement with Oxford University Press), chap. 15. By permission of Oxford University Press.

7. Ibid., chap. 15.

8. Niccolò Machiavelli, *The History of Florence*, bk. 3, chap. 12, in *Machiavelli: The Chief Works and Others* ed. and trans. Albert Gilbert (Durham, N.C.: Duke University Press, 1965), III, 1160.

9. Machiavelli, *The Discourses*, bk. 3, chap. 41, p. 515.

10. Machiavelli, *The Prince*, chap. 18.

11. Ibid., chap. 18.

12. Ibid.

13. Ibid., chap. 17.

14. Machiavelli, *The Discourses*, bk 2, chap. 2, p. 278.

15. Ibid., chap. 11–12, pp. 140–141, 143.

16. Giuseppi Prezzolini, *Machiavelli* (New York: Noonday, 1967), p. 30.

17. Quoted in Robert B. Holtman, *The Napoleonic Revolution* (Philadelphia: Lippincott, 1967), pp. 123–124.

18. Leo Strauss, *Natural Right and History* (Chicago: University of Chicago Press, 1953), p. 177.

19. Dante Germino, *Machiavelli to Marx: Modern Western Political Thought* (Chicago: University of Chicago Press, 1972), p. 94.

20. Thomas Hobbes, *Leviathan*, ed. C. B. Macpherson (Baltimore: Penguin Books, 1968), pt. 1, chap. 13, p. 183. Introduction and notes copyright © C. B. Macpherson, 1968. Reproduced by permission of Penguin Books Ltd.

21. Ibid., p. 185.

22. Ibid.

23. Ibid.

24. Ibid., chap. 8, p. 137.

25. Ibid., chap. 15, p. 216.

26. Ibid., chap. 11, p. 161.

27. Ibid., chap. 13, p. 186.

28. Ibid., pt. 2, chap. 17, p. 227.

29. Ibid., chap. 18, pp. 229–230.

30. John Locke, *Two Treatises of Government*, ed. Peter Laslett (New York: New American Library, Mentor Book, 1963), preface, p. 171.

31. Ibid., *The Second Treatise*, chap. 2, sec. 7, p. 312.

32. Ibid., sec. 8, p. 312.

33. Ibid., chap. 19, sec. 222, p. 460.

34. Raymond Polin, "John Locke's Conception of Freedom," in *John Locke: Problems & Perspectives*, ed. John W. Yolton, (Cambridge: Cambridge University Press, 1969), p. 18.

35. Locke, *The Second Treatise*, chap. 6, sec. 61, p. 350.

SUGGESTED READING

Chabod, Federico, *Machiavelli and the Renaissance* (1958).

Cranston, Maurice, *John Locke: A Biography* (1957).

Cranston, Maurice and Richard Peters, eds., *Hobbes and Rousseau: A Collection of Critical Essays* (1972).

Dunn, John, *Locke* (1984).

Germino, Dante, *Machiavelli to Marx: Modern Western Political Thought* (1972).

Goldsmith, M. M., *Hobbes's Science of Politics* (1966).

Gouch, J. W., *John Locke's Political Philosophy* (1973).

McDonald, Lee Cameron, *Western Political Theory* (1968).

Prezzolini, Giuseppe, *Machiavelli* (1967).

Raphael, D. D., *Hobbes* (1977).

Sabine, George, H., *A History of Political Theory* (1961).

Strauss, Leo and Joseph Cropsey, eds., *History of Political Philosophy* (1963).

Skinner, Quentin, *Machiavelli* (1981).

Warrender, Howard, *The Political Philosophy of Thomas Hobbes* (1957).

Yolton, John W., ed., *John Locke: Problems and Perspectives* (1969).

5

The Age of Enlightenment:

Affirmation of Reason and Freedom

The Enlightenment of the eighteenth century culminated the movement toward modernity initiated by the Renaissance. The thinkers of the Enlightenment, called philosophes, aspired to create a more rational and humane society. Toward these ends, they attacked medieval otherworldliness, rejected theology as an avenue to truth, denounced the Christian idea of people's inherent depravity, and sought to understand nature and society through reason alone, unaided by revelation or priestly authority. Adopting Descartes' method of systematic doubt, they questioned all inherited opinions and traditions. "We think that the greatest service to be done to men," said Denis Diderot, "is to teach them to use their reason, only to hold for truth what they have verified and proved."[1] An aged Thomas Jefferson reflected on the integrating principle of his times: "We believed that man was a rational animal, endowed by nature with rights. . . . We believed that men, habituated to thinking for themselves, and to follow their reason as guide, would be more easily and safely governed than with minds nourished in error and vitiated and debased . . . by ignorance."[2] Jean Le Rond d'Alembert summed up the critical spirit of his fellow philosophes:

> Our century has called itself the philosophic century par excellence. . . . from the principles of the profane sciences to the foundations of revelation, from metaphysics to questions of taste, from music to morals, from the scholastic disputes of theologians to commercial affairs, from the rights of princes to those of people, from the natural law to the

arbitrary law of nations . . . everything has been discussed, analyzed and disputed.[3]

The philosophes believed that they were inaugurating an enlightened age. Through the power of reason, humanity was at last liberating itself from the fetters of ignorance, superstition, and despotism with which tyrants and priests had bound it in past ages.

The Enlightenment was a cosmopolitan movement linking together intellectuals from various Western lands. Paris was the center of the Enlightenment, but there were philosophes and adherents of their views in virtually every leading city in western Europe and North America. The philosophes saw themselves as citizens of the world who had the best interests of humanity at heart.

In a spacious view of Western history, several traditions flowed into the Enlightenment: the rational outlook born in ancient Greece; the Stoics' conception of natural law as applying to all people; and the Christian belief that all are equal in God's eyes. A more immediate source of the Enlightenment was the secular and individualistic spirit of the Renaissance, its admiration for classical antiquity, and the humanists' critique of medieval learning for its preoccupation with questions that seemed unrelated to the human condition. The philosophes viewed their own age as the completion of a movement initiated by the Renaissance—a movement whose ultimate aim was the liberation of the human mind from all things medieval. But the philosophes' secularism was much more thoroughgoing than that of the Renaissance humanists and artists, who had combined a worldly outlook with Christian convictions.

In many ways, the Enlightenment grew directly out of the Scientific Revolution. The philosophes admired the discoveries of the Scientific Revolution and valued the method that made them possible. They celebrated Newton as a rare genius who had deciphered nature's mysteries and put humanity on a new course—Voltaire called Newton "the Columbus of the eighteenth century."[4] And they shared with Bacon and Descartes the conviction that science was a great boon to humanity. The Scientific Revolution made people aware of the immense power of the rational faculties. The philosophes sought to expand knowledge of nature and to apply the scientific method to the human world in order to uncover society's defects and to achieve appropriate reforms.

The philosophes embraced Newtonian science, but they carefully ignored Newton's strong religious beliefs. They drew a sharp distinction between theology, a fanciful construction that impeded clear thinking—"a mere castle in the air" is the way Baron d'Holbach described religion—and science, which provided knowledge that was both certain and useful. Whereas theological dogmas had produced endless disputations and many bloody conflicts, reasonable people could assent to the conclusions of science; "there are no sects in geometry," quipped Voltaire. The philosophes saw themselves engaged in a monumental struggle against superstition, ignorance, and arbitrary power, all of which, they said, drew sustenance from religion.

THE ENLIGHTENMENT OUTLOOK: REASON AND SCIENCE

Newton had uncovered universal laws that explained the physical phenomena. Are there not general rules that also apply to human behavior and social institutions, asked the philosophes? Could a "science of man" be created that would correspond to and complement Newton's science of nature—that would provide clear and certain answers to the problems of the social world in the same way that Newtonian science had solved the mysteries of the physical world? The philosohes believed that the true laws of society are laws of nature. "How exact and regular is everything in the *natural* world," noted Benjamin Franklin, the acknowledged leader of the American Enlightenment. "How wisely in every part contriv'd. . . . All the heavenly Bodies, the Stars and Planets, are regulated with the utmost wisdom! And can we suppose less care to be taken in the order of the Moral than in the Natural System?"[5] "Oh! Nature," declared Diderot, "all that is good is enclosed within your breast. You are the fertile source of all truths."[6]

The social order was defective, railed the philosophes, for it lacked the rationality evidenced in nature. By relying on the same methodology that Newton had employed to establish certain knowledge of the physical universe, the philosophes hoped to arrive at the irrefutable laws that operated in the realm of human society. They aspired to shape religion, government, law, morality, and economics in accordance with these natural laws. To be valid, they said, human institutions, morals, systems, and beliefs must rest on nature's self-evident truths that were common to and beneficial to the human race and that could be grasped by the rational mind. All things should be re-evaluated to see if they accorded with nature, that is, if they promoted human well-being.

The philosophes preferred Bacon's and Newton's method of analysis and synthesis—drawing inferences and eventually universal principles from a careful evaluation of observed phenomena—to the methodology of the seventeenth-century system builders, Descartes, Spinoza, and Leibnitz, who deduced vast intellectual systems from what they perceived to be self-evident axioms. To the philosophes, such systems were fanciful constructs that often did not accord with observed fact.

The proper method of reasoning, they said, was to arrive at general laws through an analysis of observed phenomena and then to explain and predict other phenomena on the basis of these laws. When facts are analyzed and structured into a system that fits the data—enabling one to discern the true from the false—the empirical world becomes accessible to the mind. Seeking to transfer to the social world the method that scientists had used so successfully to explain the physical universe, the philosophes examined society as if it were a physical entity. From its component parts, carefully observed and analyzed, they constructed general laws that applied to the individual and society. Knowledge of these laws, they believed, would make possible the resolution of social problems that had persistently burdened humanity.

In championing the methodology of science, the philosophes affirmed respect for the mind's capacities and for human autonomy. Individuals are self-governing, they insisted. The mind is self-sufficient; rejecting appeals to clerical or princely authority, it relies on its own ability to think, and it trusts the evidence of its own experience. In an essay entitled "What is Enlightenment?" (1784), the German philosopher Immanuel Kant (1724–1804) expressed this central principle of the Enlightenment.

> Enlightenment is man's leaving his self-caused immaturity. Immaturity is the incapacity to use one's intelligence without the guidance of another. Such immaturity is self-caused if it is not caused by lack of intelligence, but by lack of determination and courage to use one's intelligence without being guided by another. *Sapere aude!* [Dare to know!] Have the courage to use your own intelligence! is therefore the motto of the enlightenment.[7]

Rejecting the authority of tradition, the philosophes wanted people to have the courage to break with beliefs and institutions that did not meet the test of reason and common sense and to seek new guideposts derived from reason. To this extent they were disciples of Descartes, who maintained that doubting inherited knowledge is the first step toward the discovery of truth. In the spirit of Descartes, Diderot, the principal editor of the *Encyclopedia* (see page 151), wrote:

> All things must be examined, debated, investigated without exception and without regard for anyone's feelings. . . . We must ride roughshod over all those ancient puerilities, overturn the barriers that reason never erected, give back to the arts and sciences the liberty that is so precious to them. . . . We have for quite some time needed a reasoning age when men would no longer seek the rules in classical authors but in nature.[8]

Never before had westerners placed such confidence in the power of the mind. Reason was more than an abstract exercise; it was an effective tool for reforming society. The numerous examples of injustice, inhumanity, and superstition in society outraged the philosophes. Behind their devotion to reason and worldly knowledge lay an impassioned moral indignation against institutions and beliefs that degraded human beings. For these thinkers, philosophy, science, history, and literature had an ethical component; they provided knowledge that improved the individual and society and promoted human happiness. Thus, Diderot said of Voltaire: "Other historians tell us facts in order to teach us facts. You do it in order to excite in the depth of our souls a strong indignation against mendacity, ignorance, hypocrisy, superstition, fanaticism, tyranny; and that indignation remains when the memory of facts has gone."[9] Baron d'Holbach summed up this link between knowledge and the improvement of the human condition, philosophy and public spiritedness, and thought and social action.

> Ignorance and servitude are calculated to make men wicked and unhappy. Knowledge, Reason, and Liberty, can alone reform them, and make them happier. . . . Men are unhappy, only because they are ignorant; they are ignorant, only because everything conspires to prevent their being enlightened; they are wicked only because their reason is not sufficiently developed.[10]

The Age of Faith, which had been in retreat for centuries, had given way to an Age of Reason.

CHRISTIANITY ASSAILED

The philosophes waged an unremitting assault on traditional Christianity, denouncing it for harboring superstition, promulgating unreason, and fostering fanaticism and persecution.

Opposition to Dogma, Fanaticism, and Persecution

Relying on the facts of experience as Bacon had taught, the philosophes dismissed miracles, angels, and devils as violations of nature's laws and figments of the imagination, which could not be substantiated by the norms of evidence. Applying the Cartesian spirit of careful reasoning to the Bible, they pointed out flagrant discrepancies between various biblical passages and rejected as preposterous the theologians' attempts to resolve these contradictions. "Theology amuses me," wrote Voltaire, "that's where we find the madness of the human spirit in all its plenitude."[11] And David Hume, the Scottish skeptic, wrote in *Natural History of Religion* (1757):

> Examine the religious principles, which have, in fact, prevailed in the world. You will scarcely be persuaded, that they are anything but sick men's dreams: Or perhaps will regard them more as the playsome, whimsies of monkies in human shape, than the serious, positive, dogmatical asseverations of a being, who dignifies himself with the name rational. . . . No theological absurdities so glaring that they have not, sometimes, been embraced by men of the greatest and most cultivated understanding.[12]

With science as an ally, the philosophes challenged Christianity's claim that it possessed infallible truths, and they ridiculed theologians for wrangling over pointless issues and for compelling obedience to doctrines that defied reason.

The philosophes also assailed Christianity for viewing human nature as evil and human beings as helpless without God's assistance; for focusing on heaven at the expense of human happiness on earth; for fostering fanaticism and persecution; and for impeding the acquisition of useful knowledge by proclaiming the higher authority of dogma, and revelation. Frightened and confused by religion, people have been held in subjection by clergy and tyrants, the philosophes argued. To establish an enlightened society, clerical power must be broken, Christian dogmas repudiated, and the religious fanaticism that produced the horrors of the Crusades, the Inquisition, and the Wars of Religion, purged from the European soul. The philosophes shared Voltaire's disdain for Christian dogma, fanaticism, and institutions exemplified in his famous battle cry against the Roman Catholic church: "écrasez l'infâme" (crush the infamous thing). They broke with the Christian past, even if they retained the essential elements of Christian morality.

François-Marie Arouet (1694–1778), known to the world as Voltaire, was the recognized leader of the French Enlightenment. Few of the philosophes had a better mind and none had a sharper wit. Spending more than two years in Great Britain, Voltaire acquired a great admiration for English liberty, commerce, science, and religious toleration. Voltaire's angriest words were directed against established Christianity, to which he attributed many of the ills of French society. He regarded Christianity as "the Christ-worshiping superstition" that someday would be destroyed "by the weapons of reason."[13] Voltaire's respect for reason and disdain for revelation, as well as his sly wit, are demonstrated in the following passage:

> I wholeheartedly long to eat of the fruit that hung from the tree of knowledge, and it seems to me that the prohibition against eating it is strange; having given man reason, God should have encouraged him to

Voltaire *(The Bettmann Archive)*

learn. Did he want to be served by a dunce? I should also like to speak to the serpent since he made so much sense; but I should like to know what language he spoke.[14]

Many Christian dogmas are incomprehensible, said Voltaire, yet Christians have slaughtered one another to enforce obedience to these doctrines.

Is Jesus the Word? If He be the Word, did He emanate from God in time or before time? If He emanated from God, is he co-eternal and con-substantial with Him, or is He of similar substance? Is He distinct from Him, or is he not? Is He made or begotten?. . . Is the Holy Ghost made? or begotten? or produced? or proceeding from the Father? or proceeding from the Son? or proceeding from both?. . . is His hypostasis consubstan-tial with the hypostasis of the Father and the Son? . . . Assuredly, I un-derstand nothing of this; no one has ever understood any of it, and that is why we have slaughtered one another. The Christians tricked, ca-villed, hated, and excommunicated one another, for some of these dog-mas inaccessible to human intellect.[15]

Voltaire was appalled by all the crimes committed in the name of God. He condemned religious fanaticism, such as "that exhibited on the night of St. Bartholomew, when the people of Paris rushed from house to house to stab, slaughter, throw out of the window, and tear to pieces their fellow citizens who did not go to mass."[16] He also condemned religious superstition that had led to the torture and burning of thousands of people accused of witchcraft. "If to these murders are added the infinitely superior number of massacred heretics, [Christian lands] will seem to be nothing but a vast scaffold covered with torturers and victims surrounded by judges, guards, and spectators."[17]

Voltaire saw the church as a resolute opponent of reason and a more humane society. That is why he devoted so much energy to discredit its doctrines and to publicize its institutional failures and excesses. Like other philosophes, he was a deist (see the next section) who wanted to reduce religion to its barest essentials: belief in one righteous God and the performance of his moral commandments.

Paul-Henri Thiry, Baron d'Holbach (1723–1789), the Enlightenment's foremost exponent of atheism, regarded the idea of God as a product of ignorance, fear, and superstition. Terrified by storms, fire, and floods—natural phenomena that they could not explain—humanity's primitive ancestors attributed these occurrences to unseen spirits, whom they tried to appease through rituals. Belief in invisible powers and subservience to priestly authority, said Holbach, thwarted the progress of the human mind and stifled the growth of liberty.

> How could the human mind make any considerable progress, while tormented with frightful phantoms, and guided by men, interested in perpetuating its ignorance and fears? Man has been forced to vegetate in his primitive stupidity: he has been taught nothing but stories about invisible powers upon whom his happiness was supposed to depend. Occupied solely by his fears, and by unintelligible reveries, he has always been at the mercy of his priests, who have reserved to themselves the right of thinking for him, and directing his actions. . . . The human mind, confused by its theological opinions, ceased to know its own powers, mistrusted experience, feared truth and disdained reason, in order to follow authority. Man has been a mere machine in the hands of tyrants and priests, who alone have had the right of directing his actions. Always treated as a slave, man has contracted the vices of a slave.
>
> Such are the true causes of the corruption of morals. . . . Priests cheat [men], tyrants corrupt, the better to enslave them. Tyranny ever was, and ever will be, the true cause of man's depravity. . . . To discover the true principles of Morality, men have no need of theology, of revelation, or of gods, they have need only of common sense. . . . Men are . . . . wicked only because their reason is not sufficiently developed.[18]

Denis Diderot *(UPI/Bettmann)*

Like the other philosophes, Denis Diderot (1713–1784) attacked Christianity for promoting superstition, fanaticism, and persecution. But in his *Supplement to the Voyage of Bouganville* (1772), Diderot added what was generally a novel criticism of Christianity: that its sexual mores were contrary and hurtful to human nature. By regarding lust as a mortal sin, said Diderot, Christianity impeded the natural and healthy expression of the passions. To prohibit people their passions is to forbid them to be fully human and to deny them happiness.

Diderot reviewed Louis Antoine de Bouganville's *Voyage Around the World* (1771) and later wrote *Supplement*, in which he denounced European imperialism and the exploitation of non-Europeans and questioned Christian sexual standards. In one passage, Diderot has a Tahitian elder rebuke Bouganville and his companions for bringing the evils of European civilization, including sexual shame and guilt, to his land. Before the Christian Europeans arrived, says the elder,

> . . . the young Tahitian girl blissfully abandoned herself to the embraces of a Tahitian youth. . . . She was proud of her ability to excite men's de-

sires. . . . The notion of crime and the fear of [venereal] disease have come
among us only with your coming. Now our enjoyments, formerly so
sweet, are attended with guilt and terror. That man in black [a priest] . . .
has spoken to our young men, and I know not what he has said to our
young girls, but our youth are hesitant and our girls blush.[19]

The philosophes arrived at a simple equation: science and its advocates are on the side of good, whereas theology and its priestly exponents promote wickedness. Thus, in his "Discourse of a Philosopher
to a King," Diderot states: "If you want priests you do not need philosophers and if you want philosophers you do not need priests; for the
one being by their calling the friends of reason and the promoters of
science, the other the enemies of reason and favourers of ignorance, if
the first do good, the others do evil."[20]

Deism and Skepticism

While some philosophes were atheists, most were deists, who rejected
miracles, mysteries, prophecies, and other fundamentals of revealed
Christianity and sought to fashion a natural religion that accorded
with reason and science. They attempted to adapt the Christian tradition to the requirements of the new science. Eighteenth-century deists
were influenced by late seventeenth-century critics of traditional
Christianity: the French skeptic Pierre Bayle and English freethinkers.

Son of a French pastor, Pierre Bayle (1647–1706) experienced the religious intolerance of Louis XIV's realm, which culminated in the re-
vocation of the Edict of Nantes in 1685. In 1681, Bayle went into exile
to Holland, where he devoted himself to scholarship. In an early work,
*Philosophical Commentary on the Words of Jesus "Constrain them to
Come in"* (1686), Bayle pleaded for religious toleration, even for Jews
and atheists. In his *Historical and Critical Dictionary* (1695, 1697), he
took the astonishing position that atheists, from Socrates to Spinoza,
had frequently evidenced good moral character, while biblical heroes
and Christian clergy often behaved immorally. "Nothing is more common," he declared, "than to see orthodox Christians living evil lives,
and free thinkers living good ones."[21]

Holding that reason and revelation stood in sharp opposition to each
other, Bayle dismissed the efforts of thinkers to prove by reason the
claims of revealed Christianity. Bayle insisted that he merely intended
to point out the weaknesses of reason, its inability to arrive at certainty, and to reaffirm reliance on faith as the one true guide. In maintaining that the mysteries of Christianity were beyond human comprehension, Bayle intended to stress that religious people cannot rely

solely on philosophy and that religion should be a matter of quiet faith. But his insistence on the essential incompatibility between reason and faith and his critique of Christian theologians who attempted to bridge the gap were so convincing that his opponents attacked him as an unbeliever who undermined Christian faith and morality. The philosophes praised Bayle for having the courage to teach the validity of doubting accepted convictions, the intellectual acuteness to reveal the inadequacy and failings of religious orthodoxy, and the humanity to urge religious toleration.

English freethinkers John Toland (1670–1722) and Matthew Tindal (c. 1657–1733) attacked clerical authority and rejected religious dogmas that seemed to contradict common sense. Their advocacy of a natural religion, one that accorded with reason, was the foundation of the philosophes' deism. In his most famous work, *Christianity Not Mysterious* (1696), which was denounced by members of Parliament and the clergy, Toland argued that if the truth of an idea cannot be demonstrated by reason, we should reserve judgment. Toland applied this standard to Christian teachings: we should not be required to believe in anything that seemed contradictory or inconceivable to the rational mind. There is no purpose in threatening intelligent people with damnation if they refuse to believe what they cannot comprehend or what seems patently absurd. Although Toland maintained that Christian mysteries were not above reason, the damage had been done, for Christianity and mystery are inseparably linked. Sir Leslie Stephen, the nineteenth-century student of English thought, astutely observed: "in truth, there is one way, and only one way, in which mystery may be expelled from religion, and that is by expelling theology. A religion without mystery is a religion without God."[22]

The arguments put forward in Matthew Tindal's *Christianity as Old as the Creation* (1730) were widely accepted by eighteenth-century deists. Tindal held that God, who is wise and just, prescribed a perfect moral law for human beings which he implanted in human hearts. True religion consists in doing all the good we can. In essence religion consists of a few elemental moral truths that are ascertainable to the mind. Rituals, miracles, and asceticism are merely priestly accretions; they have nothing to do with God's original moral law. Indeed, said Tindal, by promoting superstition, persecution, and bloody religious warfare, priestly authority impeded the imposition of God's law. To the philosophes, it seemed that Tindal was advocating a natural religion, one that valued reason, made people cognizant of their moral duties, condemned persecution, and had little to do with priests, miracles, and revelation.

To eighteenth-century deists, of whom Voltaire and Thomas Paine (1737–1809), the English-American radical, are typical, it seemed

reasonable that this magnificently designed universe, operating with
clockwork precision, was created at a point in time by an all-wise Creator. But once God had set the universe in motion he refrained from
interfering with its operations. Thus, the deists did not follow Newton,
who allowed for divine intervention in the world. In addition to the
argument from design, deists argued from the necessity of a final cause
in the manner of Voltaire:

> I exist, hence something exists. If something exists, then something
> must have existed from all eternity. . . . Whence then have the particles
> of matter which think and feel received sensation and thought? . . . they
> must have received these gifts from the hands of a Supreme Being, intel-
> ligent, infinite, and the original cause of all beings.[23]

To the arguments of design and final cause, Voltaire added a practical
reason for belief in God.

> I want my lawyer, my tailor, my servants, even my wife to believe in
> God, because it means that I shall be cheated and robbed and cuckolded
> less often . . . God is needed to provide a divine sanction for morality. It
> is absolutely necessary not only for ordinary people, but also for princes
> and rulers to have an idea of the Supreme Being, Creator, governor, re-
> warder, and avenger profoundly engraven on their minds . . . . If God did
> not exist, it would be necessary to invent him.[24]

Holding that God had endowed human beings with the ability to
reason, which enables them to discover and comprehend God's physical and moral laws, deists rejected entirely revelation, miracles, and
original sin. To deists, the essence of religion was morality, a commitment to justice and humanity, and not adherence to rituals, doctrines,
or clerical authority. In *The Age of Reason* (1794–95), Paine declared:
"I believe in the equality of man; and I believe that religious duties
consist in doing justice, loving mercy, and endeavoring to make our
fellow-creatures happy."[25] After death, said deists, those who fulfilled
God's moral law would be rewarded, while those who did not would
be punished. This seemed entirely reasonable.

Deists denied that the Bible was God's revelation, rejected clerical
authority, and dismissed Christian mysteries, prophecies, and miracles—the virgin birth, Jesus walking on water, and the resurrection,
and others—as violations of a lawful natural order. Thus, to the question of the virgin birth, Paine applied the critical spirit of the Enlightenment. Neither Joseph nor Mary wrote that she gave birth without
any cohabitation with a man, said Paine, "it is only reported by others
that *they said so*—it is hearsay upon hearsay, and I do not choose to
rest my belief upon such evidence."[26] With his unsurpassable wit, Voltaire expressed the deists' belief in God but without revelation or a
resurrection. Voltaire and a companion had climbed a hill in order to

see the sunrise. Moved by the magnificent scene, the aged philosopher stretched out on the ground and exclaimed: "I believe! I believe in you! Powerful God, I believe!" Then he stood up and added: "As for Monsieur the Son and madame His Mother, that's a different story."[27] To the philosophes, Jesus was not divine but an inspiring teacher of morality. Many deists still considered themselves Christians; the clergy, however, regarded their views with horror, agreeing with Jonathan Edwards, an American minister and theologian:

> The Deists wholly cast off the Christian religion and are professed infidels. . . [T]hey deny the whole Christian religion. . . . [T]hey deny that Christ was the Son of God . . . and they deny the whole Scripture. They deny any of it is the word of God. . . . They deny any revealed religion, or any word of God at all; and say that God has given mankind no other light to walk on but their own reason.[28]

The deists' natural religion also came under attack from skeptics, such as the Scottish philosopher David Hume. Like other Enlightenment thinkers, Hume believed that religion was replete with superstitions and doctrines that affronted reason, but he did not think that deism had resolved the problem of God's existence. Hume dismissed as unreasonable the deist argument that this orderly universe could not be a product of chance but required a conscious, designing mind to create it. He argued that the universe might very well be eternal and that the seemingly orderly universe is simply a natural condition that requires no explanation. There is no necessary connection between a universal order and a lawful Creator. Hume also rejected the watch analogy: we have seen a watchmaker fashion a watch, but no one has seen a world constructed. Nor, on the basis of human experience where the good often suffer and the wicked do not, can we conclude that there is an afterlife in which rewards and punishments are distributed fairly. Hume demolished the deists attempt to construct a natural religion that placed Christianity on a Newtonian foundation; deist beliefs were not logically superior to Christian beliefs. Ultimately, said Hume, all religious ideas, including belief in God, derive from human feelings, from a fear of death, and from a longing for eternal life. The distance between skepticism and atheism was not great and was easily traversed.

POLITICAL THOUGHT

For the philosophes, established religion was one source of the evil that afflicted humanity; another source was despotism. If human beings were to achieve happiness, they had to extirpate revealed religion and check the power of their rulers. "Every age has its dominant idea," wrote Diderot; "that of our age seems to be Liberty."[29] Eighteenth-century political thought is characterized by a thoroughgoing secularism; an indictment of despotism, the divine right of kings, and the special privileges of the aristocracy and the clergy; a respect for English constitutionalism because it enshrined the rule of law; and an affirmation of John Locke's theory that government had an obligation to protect the natural rights of its citizens. Central to the political outlook of the philosophes was the conviction that political solutions could be found for the ills that afflicted society.

Several entries in the *Encyclopedia* expressed essential elements of the philosophes' political thought. Thus, Louis, Chevalier de Jaucourt, in his article "Government," declared that

> . . . the good of the people must be the great purpose of the *government*. The governors are appointed to fulfill it; and the civil constitution that invests them with this power bound therein by the laws of nature and by the law of reason. . . . The greatest good of the people is its liberty. . . . If it happens that those who hold the reins of *government* find some resistance when they use their power for the destruction and not the conservation of things that rightfully belong to the people, they must blame themselves, because the public good and the advantage of society are the purpose of establishing a *government*. Hence it necessarily follows that power cannot be arbitrary and that it must be exercised according to the established laws so that people may know its duty and be secure within the shelter of laws, and so that governors at the same time should be held within just limits and not be tempted to employ the power they have in hand to do harmful things to the body politic.[30]

In his article "Political Authority," Diderot held that the monarch's authority "is limited by the laws of nature and the state." Although the king may inherit the throne, the government "is not private property, but public property that consequently can never be taken from the people, to whom it belongs exclusively, fundamentally, and as a freehold."[31]

In general, the philosophes favored constitutional government that protected citizens from the abuse of power. With the notable exception of Rousseau, the philosophes' concern for liberty did not lead them to embrace democracy, for they placed little trust in the masses. Several philosophes, notably, Voltaire placed their confidence in reforming despots, like Frederick II of Prussia, who were sympathetic to enlightened ideas. However, the philosophes were less concerned with the form of government—monarchy or republic—than they were with preventing the authorities from abusing their power.

Montesquieu

The contribution of Charles Louis de Secondat, Baron de Montesquieu (1689–1755) to political theory rests essentially on his *The Spirit of the Laws* (1748), a work of immense erudition covering many topics. Montesquieu held that the study of political and social behavior is not an exercise in abstract thought, but must be undertaken in relationship to geographic, economic, and historic conditions. Toward this end, Montesquieu accumulated and classified a wide diversity of facts, from which he tried to draw general rules governing society. Montesquieu's effort to explain social and political behavior empirically—to found a science of society based on the model of natural science—makes him a forerunner of modern sociology.

Montesquieu concluded that different climactic and geographic conditions and different national customs, habits, religions and institutions give each nation a particular character; each society requires constitutional forms and laws that pay heed to the character of its people.

> . . . the political and civil laws of each nation . . . . should be adapted . . . to the people for whom they are framed. . . . They should be in relation to the climate of each country, to the quality of its soil, to its [location] and extent, to the principal occupation of the natives, whether husbandmen, huntsmen, or shepherds: they should have relation . . . to the religion of the inhabitants, to their inclinations, riches, numbers, commerce, manners, and customs.[32]

Like other philosophes, Montesquieu believed in the existence of natural law—universal norms that apply to all humanity—and he used this standard to attack laws and institutions that contradicted it. At the same time, he was a cultural relativist who recognized that positive law could take different forms because of differing environmental conditions and historical development. Montesquieu was trying to do for human society what natural scientists had done for the physical universe: to discover the fundamental principles governing the phenomena. Such knowledge would permit a rational, sensible reformation of society. But he also recognized that universal laws had to be adapted to particular social and physical conditions. It was this relationship between law and culture, what he called the "Spirit of Law," that Montesquieu set out to investigate.

Montesquieu juggled two potentially contradictory viewpoints: belief in absolute standards, that is, in natural law, and the recognition that differing environmental conditions and cultural evolution produce differing institutions, customs, and laws in different nations. Inevitably, this led to a certain amount of ambiguity and inconsistency in his thought. Thus, Montesquieu held that a law ought to conform to a universal standard of justice, but at the same time, he argued that laws ought to reflect the general spirit of a nation, which is a product of its peculiar physiography and history.

An ardent reformer, Montesquieu used learning, logic, and wit to denounce the abuses of his day—despotism, intellectual repression, religious intolerance, torture, militarism, slavery. In an earlier work, *The Persian Letters*, published anonymously in Holland in 1721, Montesquieu satirized French (and European) institutions and traditions, demonstrating in the process, a concern for liberty and a tolerant and humanitarian spirit. In the guise of letters written by two imaginary Persian travelers in Europe, Montesquieu makes a statement. He denounces French absolutism, praises English parliamentary government, and attacks religious persecution, as in this comment on the Spanish Inquisition:

> I have heard that in Spain and Portugal there are dervishes who do not understand a joke, and who have a man burned as if he were straw. . . . Even though he swears like a pagan that he is orthodox, they may not agree, and burn him for a heretic. It is useless for him to submit distinctions, for he will be in ashes before they even consider giving him a hearing.[33]

He also expresses admiration for religious toleration:

> The Christians are beginning to lose that spirit of intolerance which animated them. It is now seen that it was a mistake to chase the Jews from Spain, and to persecute French Christians whose belief differed a bit from that of the king. They now perceive that zeal for the expansion of religion is different from dutiful devotion to it, and that love and observance of a religion need not require hatred and persecution of those who do not believe.[34]

In *The Spirit of the Laws*, Montesquieu, in the tradition of Aristotle, distinguishes three basic forms of government—republic, monarchy, and despotism—and defines the special nature of each. In a republican government, the people possess supreme power. If power is possessed by the entire people, the republic is a democracy; if a part of the people is sovereign, then it is an aristocracy. In a monarchy, one person governs by established laws. In a despotism, the worst form of government for Montesquieu, a single ruler dispenses with established laws and governs arbitrarily and capriciously. Despots depend on the fear of their subjects to retain their power. A republic, Montesquieu says, is fit for small states, like ancient Athens and Sparta. For a democratic republic to endure, there must be no great extremes in wealth; devotion to the community must outweigh self-interest, and the behavior of the citizens must not degenerate into license. If these conditions are not met, social cohesion breaks down. Montesquieu's analysis of the reasons for the breakdown of a democratic republic was carefully read by the founding fathers of the United States.

A monarchy is best suited for large areas that require centralized authority to hold it together; its success depends on a military aristocracy imbued with a sense of honor and on respect for fixed laws. Montesquieu offers England as the best example of a monarchy and is unrestrained in his admiration of England, a nation "that has for the direct end of its constitution political liberty."[35] As an aristocrat fearful of royal despotism, Montesquieu championed the English form of constitutional monarchy for France.

Montesquieu regarded despotism as a pernicious form of government, corrupt by its very nature. Ruling as he wishes and unchecked by law, the despot knows nothing of moderation and institutionalizes cruelty and violence. The slavelike subjects, wrote Montesquieu, know only servitude, fear, and misery. Driven by predatory instincts, the despotic ruler involves his state in wars of conquest, caring not at all about the suffering this causes his people. In a despotic society, economic activity stagnates, for merchants, fearful that their goods will be confiscated by the state, lose their initiative. "Under this sort of government nothing is repaired or improved . . . everything is drawn from, but nothing restored to the earth; the ground lies untilled, and the whole country becomes a desert."[36] Like Aristotle, Montesquieu saw Asiatic governments as the archetype of despotism.

To safeguard liberty from despotism, Montesquieu advocated the principle of separation of powers. In every government, said Montesquieu, there are three sorts of powers: legislative, executive, and judiciary. When one person or one body exercises all three powers—if the same body both prosecutes and judges, for example—liberty cannot be preserved. Where sovereignty is monopolized by one person or body, power is abused and political liberty is denied. In a good government, one power balances and checks another power, an argument that impressed the framers of the U. S. Constitution.

Several of Montesquieu's ideals were absorbed into the liberal tradition—constitutional government and the rule of law, separation of powers, freedom of thought, religious toleration, and protection of individual liberty. The conservative tradition drew on Montesquieu's respect for traditional ways of life and his opposition to sudden reforms that ignored a people's history and culture. Nineteenth-century positivists and sociologists valued the systematic way in which Montesquieu studied human institutions.

Voltaire

Unlike Hobbes and Locke, Voltaire was not a systematic political theorist but a propagandist and polemicist who hurled pointed barbs at all the abuses of the Old Regime. Nevertheless, Voltaire's writings do contain ideas that form a coherent political theory, which in many ways expresses the outlook of the Enlightenment.

Voltaire disdained arbitrary power, for it is based on human whim rather than on established law. He described a prince who imprisons or executes his subjects unjustly and without due process as "nothing but a highway robber who is called 'Your Majesty.'" For Voltaire, freedom consisted in being governed by an established and standard code of law that applies equally to all. Without the rule of law, wrote Voltaire, there is no liberty of person, no freedom of thought or of religion, no protection of personal property, no impartial judiciary, and no protection from arbitrary arrest. Underlying Voltaire's commitment to the rule of law was his conviction that power should be used rationally and beneficially.

Voltaire's respect for the rule of law was strengthened by his stay in England between 1726 and 1729, which led to the publication of *The English Letters* in 1733. In this work, Voltaire presents an idealized and, at times, inaccurate picture of English politics and society. More important, however, is the fact that his experience with English liberty gave him hope that a just and tolerant society was not a utopian dream, thereby strengthening his resolve to attack the abuses of French society; *The English Letters* was an indictment of the Old Regime.

Voltaire was impressed with the large measure of religious toleration and freedom of thought prevailing in England—a situation that contrasted markedly with the strict censorship imposed by the clergy and the court on French writers. Like Montesquieu, Voltaire liked the English system of constitutional monarchy.

> The English are the only people on earth who have been able to prescribe limits to the power of kings by resisting them, and who, by a series of struggles, have at length established that wise and happy form of government where the prince is all-powerful to do good, and at the same time is restrained from committing evil; where the nobles are great without insolence or lordly power, and the people share in the government without confusion.[37]

England served as a foil for the deficiencies of French society. In Voltaire's view, the enlightened English system fostered commercial prosperity and the flowering of the arts, whereas France was held back by irrational customs, particularly the privileges bestowed on an undeserving nobility.

> A peer or nobleman in ... [England] pays his share of the taxes as others do, all of which are regulated by the House of Commons. . . . [When a tax law is passed], then every person is to pay his quota without distinction; and that not according to his rank or quality, which would be absurd, but in proportion to his revenue. . . .
>
> In France everybody is a marquis; and a man just come from the obscurity of some remote province, with money in his pocket and a name that ends with an '*ac*' or an '*ille*,' may give himself airs, and usurp such phrases as, "A man of my quality and rank"; and hold merchants in the most sovereign contempt. The merchant again, by dint of hearing his profession despised on all occasions at last is fool enough to blush at his condition. I will not, however, take upon me to say which is the most useful to his country, and which of the two ought to have preference; whether the powdered lord, who knows to a minute when the king rises or goes to bed, perhaps to stool, and who gives himself airs of importance in playing the part of a slave in the antechamber of some minister; or the merchant who enriches his country, and from his counting-house sends his orders into Surat or Cairo, thereby contributing to the happiness and convenience of human nature.[38]

Several of Voltaire's heroes were English. He admired Newton for unlocking nature's secrets; Locke for his practical and empirical philosophy, for enshrining liberty of person and property in the theory of natural rights, and for castigating religious persecution; and Bacon for identifying progress with the advancement of science and technology and for denouncing metaphysical and theological speculation as hindrances to knowledge.

Voltaire was no democrat. He had little confidence in the capacities of the common people whom he saw as prone to superstition and fanaticism. Nor did he advocate revolution. What he did favor was reforming society through the advancement of reason and the promotion of science and technology. Voltaire himself fought to introduce several reforms into France, including freedom of the press, religious toleration, a fair system of criminal justice, proportional taxation, and striking at the privileges of the clergy and nobility.

Voltaire believed that enlightened rulers, who used their power to end abuses and to promote the common good, were the best hope for reform. The aristocratic Montesquieu feared royal power and sought to check it by strengthening the aristocracy; the bourgeois Voltaire, on the other hand, saw the nobility, along with the aristocracy-dominated church, as the principal barriers to enlightened reform. Although Voltaire saw enlightened kings as the best vehicle for reform, his thought ultimately undermined royal power, as Maurice Cranston astutely points out:

> . . . he swept away, one by one, all the things that made a king feel safe on his throne: religion, habit, customs, and the established order of

society. . . . he took away . . . old motives for obedience. And thus, paradoxically, Voltaire proved to be even more subversive of absolute government in defending it than Montesquieu in attacking it.[39]

Rousseau

To the philosophes, advances in the arts and sciences were hallmarks of progress. Jean-Jacques Rousseau (1712–1778), the Geneva-born French thinker, however, argued that the accumulation of knowledge improved human understanding but corrupted the human species morally. In *A Discourse on the Origin of Inequality* (1755) and *A Discourse on the Arts and Sciences* (1751), Rousseau questioned advances in knowledge and spurned the glorification of reason that was central to the outlook of the philosophes. The philosophes, he was saying, have given people better reasoning but have destroyed them morally. The price paid for cultural and intellectual progress has been the moral deterioration of the individual, a condition that can no longer be endured.

Rousseau drew a sharp distinction between "civilized or societal man" and "natural or savage man." Natural man—the individual prior to the creation of civil society—was superior to civilized man in several ways. He was stronger and healthier and had greater compassion for a suffering human being. Separated from nature and living an artificial existence, civilized man has become effeminate, feeble and anxious. Not content with satisfying natural needs, he has become envious and greedy, obsessively pursuing luxury and sinking into debauchery. Most important, modern man has lost much of his natural compassion for a fellow being. When a glimmer of compassion surfaces, he reasons it away: this is not my concern, he says.

> A murder may with impunity be committed under his window; he has only to put his hands to his ears and argue a little with himself, to prevent nature, which is shocked within him, from identifying itself with the unfortunate sufferer. Uncivilized man has not this admirable talent; and for want of reason and wisdom is always foolishly ready to obey the first promptings of humanity.[40]

Rousseau rejected Hobbes's view that the individual is innately brutish and violent and that each person is by nature the enemy of every other. Instead, he saw human beings as inherently good. Every human being possesses an inner voice, a conscience, in which resides a sense of justice and compassion. This inner voice does not depend on intelligence; illiterate peasants as well as Parisian intellectuals possessed it. But society distorts and perverts our nature.

In the state of nature, says Rousseau, there was little difference between individuals. When private property emerged, however, this natural equality ended, with disastrous results: insatiable ambition, jealousy, and rivalry. Force and guile swept aside primitive people's natural goodness and pity.

> The first man who, having enclosed a piece of ground, bethought himself of saying "This is mine," and found people simple enough to believe him, was the real founder of civil society. From how many crimes, wars, and murders, from how many horrors and misfortunes might not any one have saved mankind, by pulling up the stakes, or filling up the ditch, and crying to his fellows: "Beware of listening to this impostor; you are undone if you once forget that the fruits of the earth belong to us all, and the earth itself to nobody."[41]

To protect his property, "the rich man . . . conceived at length the profoundest plan that ever entered the mind of man"—the creation of civil society. But the state was really a form of slavery, "which bound new fetters on the poor, and gave new powers to the rich; which irretrievably destroyed natural liberty, eternally fixed the law of property and inequality . . . and, for the advantage of a few ambitious individuals, subjected all mankind to perpetual labour, slavery, and wretchedness."[42] The creation of civil society enabled the rich and the clever to dominate others; it also led to national wars, which were far more destructive than the occasional acts of violence between individuals that had marred the serenity of the state of nature before the institution of property.

Rousseau seemed to hold the startling thesis that civilization has ruined humanity, that natural, instinctual, feeling man was morally superior to thinking man of modern society, that the accumulation of knowledge was a burden that must be cast off if man is to be rescued from unhappiness and depravity. Because of his recognition and glorification of the emotions' primitive power, Rousseau is an important forerunner of the Romantic Movement.

Rousseau's attack on civilization, however, had a deeper, more complex meaning; he was too sophisticated to urge forsaking civilization in favor of a return to an imagined idyllic state of nature, such as that depicted in eighteenth-century travel literature. Rousseau was not railing against civilization in general but against the civilization of his day, which had corrupted people morally, and against its political agent, the unjust and despotic state, which had deprived them of their freedom. Rousseau maintained that compassion is required for mutual preservation; concern for each other is our ultimate security. But a materialistic modern society has desensitized us, stifling our compassionate nature. Society's institutions must be reshaped in order to restore to the individual his original freedom and goodness. Rousseau believed that once the abuses of contemporary society, particularly inequality, despotism, and selfish individualism, were understood, appropriate reforms could be instituted. In the new society, reason would be used to enhance man's innate goodness and to make him free. This is precisely what Rousseau attempted to express in his writings on government and education.

"Man is born free and everywhere he is in chains."[43] With these stirring words, Rousseau began *The Social Contract* (1762), his celebrated work of political thought. Rousseau says that the state as it is presently constituted is unjust and corrupt. It is dominated by the rich and the powerful, who use it to further their interests, while the weak know only oppression and misery. The modern state deprives human beings of their natural freedom and fosters a selfish individualism that undermines feelings of mutuality and a concern for the common good.

Rousseau wanted the state to be a genuine democracy, a moral association that binds together the people in freedom, equality, and civic devotion. For Rousseau, individuals fulfill their moral potential not in isolation, but as committed members of the community; human character is ennobled when people cooperate with each other and care for each other. Rousseau admired the ancient Greek city-state, the polis, for it was an organic community in which citizens set aside private interests in order to attain the common good. Welded together in a spirit of fraternity, the citizens viewed their polis as a second family that instructed them in proper morality and promoted cultural and intellectual life. Consequently, they never regarded the state as a despotism from which they needed protection. Thus, Rousseau's ideal polity is a small state, like the polis, in which people have the opportunity to know each other and to participate actively in public affairs. Such a political environment produces free and committed citizens; in contrast, the large territorial states ruled by absolute monarchs produce servile subjects.

In *The Social Contract*, Rousseau sought to recreate the community spirit and the political freedom that characterized the Greek city-state. Like Hobbes and Locke, he refers to an original social contract that terminates the state of nature and establishes the civil state. The clash of particular interests in the state of nature compels people to enter into a social contract and create civil society. The fundamental problem of the social contract, says Rousseau, "is to find a form of association which will defend and protect with the whole common force the person and goods of each associate, and in which each, while uniting himself with all may still obey himself alone, and remain as free as before [in the state of nature]."[44]

Rousseau's solution is for each person to surrender unconditionally all his rights to the community as a whole and to submit to its authority. To prevent the assertion of private interests over the common good, Rousseau wants the state to be governed in accordance with the general will—an underlying principle that expresses what is best for the community. The general will is not a majority or even a unanimous vote, both of which may be wrong. Rather, it is a plainly visible truth that is easily discerned by common sense, by reason, and by listening to our hearts. The general will expresses the best in human beings. Transcending any particular or selfish interest, it is the voice of humanity within us, our concern with doing what is right. It resembles the Stoic conception of "right reason," of thinking purged of self-interest and unworthy motives so that it accords with the natural law underlying the universe.

Rousseau holds that "the general will is always right and tends always to the public advantage"[45] and that "It is solely on the basis of this common interest that every society should be governed."[46] The well-being of each person is served when the welfare of the community becomes the prime concern of the citizen. Just and enlightened citizens imbued with a public spirit would have the good sense and moral awareness to legislate in accordance with the general will. For Rousseau, true freedom consists of obedience to laws that coincide with the general will—that serve the community's common interests. Obedience to the general will transforms an individual, motivated by self-interest, appetites, and passions, into a higher type of person: a citizen committed to the community as a whole, one who realizes that personal happiness is inextricably tied to the happiness of others, to the general good.

Like ancient Athens, Rousseau's state is a direct democracy, in which the citizens themselves, not their representatives, constitute the lawmaking body; in this way, the governed and the government are one and the same. For Hobbes, the most satisfactory sovereign is the hereditary monarch; for Rousseau, the citizens as a collective body constitute the sovereign. Rousseau believes that people will obey the laws that they have a voice in making and that they will rise above self-interest and rationally seek the common good when they see themselves as participating citizens rather than as subjects of a tyrant. The state imagined by Rousseau enshrines equality: its citizens are equally subject to the law that they participate equally in making.

By definition, the general will is what is best for the community. Only when the general will is given primacy can justice and social well-being prevail. For this reason, says Rousseau, it ought to be the will of each citizen of the community. What happens, however, if a person's private will—that is, expressions of particular, selfish interests—clashes with the general will? When people enter the social contract, says Rousseau, they exchange natural liberty for "civil liberty, which is limited by the general will."[47] The social contract gives the body politic absolute power over all its members. Since private interests could ruin the polity, "whoever refuses to obey the general will shall be compelled to do so by the whole body. This means nothing less than that he will be forced to be free."[48] Rousseau believes that the realization of the general will constitutes a moral end: it bestows freedom and equality on the citizenry. Therefore, it is morally justifiable to compel obedience to its requirements. Rousseau would force people to be free.

Rousseau is a leading theorist of democratic thought. He condemned arbitrary and despotic monarchy, the divine-right theory of kings, and the traditional view that people should be governed by their betters, lords and clergy, who were entitled to special privileges. He granted sovereignty to the people as a whole, affirmed the principle of equality, and sought to replace a corrupt and arbitrary political order with one that allowed individuals to fulfill their moral potential, to regain the natural goodness that had been corrupted by civil society. He intended to devise a political system in which the individual would be

> substituting justice for instinct in his conduct, and giving his actions the morality they had formerly lacked. Then only when the voice of duty takes the place of physical impulses and right of appetite, does man, who so far had considered only himself, find that he is forced to act on different principles, and to consult his reason before listening to his inclinations.[49]

As Ernst Cassirer notes, "Rousseau wants to transform the present improvised form of the state into a rational state; he wants to change society from a product of blind necessity to one of freedom."[50] Moreover, Rousseau maintained that by fostering a sense of mutual cooperation, a genuine community spirit, democratic politics provides citizens with a sense of security; they do not feel threatened by each other. Both Machiavelli and Hobbes sought security through punitive measures imposed by the ruler. Rousseau, in contrast, held that cooperation with fellow citizens—a heightened sense of community—was the avenue to security.

Rousseau's critics assert that his political thought, whose goal is a body of citizens who think alike, buttresses a dangerous collectivism and even totalitarianism. These critics argue that Rousseau grants the sovereign—the people constituted as a corporate body—virtually unlimited authority over the citizenry; the rights of the individual are sacrificed to the omnipotence of the state. In practical terms, concludes George H. Sabine, Rousseau's notion of "forcing a man to be free is a euphemism for making him blindly obedient to the mass or the strongest party."[51]

Rousseau started from diametrically opposing premises with regard to the state than did exponents of liberalism (see Chapter 7). To liberals, the state was a potential threat to individual freedom and self-development. To Rousseau, the state, by overcoming selfishness and strife among competing interests, enhanced freedom and self-development. Unlike Locke, Montesquieu, and nineteenth-century liberals, Rousseau did not treat governmental authority with caution. He did not place constitutional limitations on sovereignty or erect safeguards to protect individual and minority rights from a potentially tyrannical majority; he also rejected entirely the Lockean principle that citizens possess rights independently of and against the state. This last point was an absurdity to Rousseau. Since the individual constitutes the state, how can he have rights against himself? Thus, in several ways, Rousseau's state contradicts liberal ideals: it possesses unlimited power, demands submission in the name of the the general will, requires the individual to identify his personal life with the totality, deplores diversity, and is intolerant of dissenting minorities.

Rousseau's critics maintain that the concept of the general will—of a sole truth whose realization is the aim of politics—has opened the gates to dictatorships and mass murder, all in the name of the people. Social theorist Robert Nisbet declares:

> To strike off the chains was the objective Rousseau sent to all future revolutionaries and reformers, but with this message went another, more subtle but more powerful. True freedom lies in the individual's total surrender of self and all possessions, including rights, to the absolute community. From Rousseau to Lenin, that has been the essentially collectivist—or communal—interpretation of true freedom.[52]

Particularly distressing to these critics is Rousseau's notion of the legislator: a charismatic leader who knows what the general will is and feels duty-bound to guide the people, leading them to make the right choice. Thus, during the radical stage of the French Revolution, Robespierre (see page 158), a disciple of Rousseau, justified the Terror, claiming that he and his fellow Jacobins represented the will of the French people and that opponents were sinners who had to be liquidated for the good of the nation. Hitler also claimed that his will represented the will of the German people, that he was a man of destiny who intuitively knew what was best for the nation. To oppose *Der Fuehrer* was to oppose the best interests of the German community; such persons were enemies of the people and deserved scorn and the severest punishment. Israeli historian J. L. Talmon sees only danger in Rousseau's theory of the general will:

> The general will assumes thus the character of a purpose and as such lends itself to definition in terms of . . . a pre-ordained goal, towards

which we are irresistibly driven; a solely true aim, which we will, or are bound to will, although we may not will it yet, because of our backwardness, prejudices, selfishness or ignorance.

In this case the idea of a people becomes naturally restricted to those who identify themselves with the general will and the general interest. Those outside are not really of the nation. They are aliens. This conception of the nation (or people) was soon to become a powerful political argument. . . .

The very idea of an assumed pre-ordained will, which has not yet become the actual will of the nation . . . gives those who claim to know and to represent the real and ultimate will of the nation . . . a blank cheque to act on behalf of the people.[53]

SOCIAL THOUGHT

The philosophes rejected the Christian belief that human beings are endowed with a sinful nature, a consequence of Adam and Eve's disobedience of God. They knew from experience, of course, that human beings behave wickedly and seem hopelessly attached to nonrational modes of thinking. While they retained a certain pessimism about human nature, the philosophes generally believed in individuals' essential goodness and in their capacity for moral improvement. "Nature has not made us evil." wrote Diderot, "it is bad education, bad models, bad legislation that corrupt us."[54] And Voltaire declared that a person is "born neither good nor wicked; education, example, the government into which he is thrown—in short, occasion of every kind—determines him to virtue or vice."[55] The philosophes' conception of human nature rested heavily on John Locke's epistemology, or theory of knowledge. To the philosophes, it seemed that Locke had discovered the fundamental principles governing the human mind, an achievement comparable to Newton's discovery of the laws governing physical bodies.

Epistemology, Psychology, and Education

In his *Essay Concerning Human Understanding* (1690), a work of immense significance in the history of philosophy, Locke argued that human beings are not born with innate ideas (the idea of God, principles of good and evil, and rules of logic, for example), divinely implanted in their minds as Descartes had maintained. Rather, said Locke, the human mind is a blank slate upon which are imprinted sensations derived from contact with the phenomenal world. Knowledge is derived from experience.

Let us then suppose the mind to be, as we say, white paper, void of all characters, without any ideas:—how comes it to be furnished? . . . To this I answer, in one word, from experience: in that all our knowledge is founded; and from that it ultimately derives itself. Our observation employed either about external sensible objects, or about the internal operations of our minds perceived and reflected on by ourselves, is that which supplies our understanding with all the materials of thinking. These two are the fountains of knowledge, from whence all the ideas we have, or can naturally have, do spring.[56]

The implications of Locke's theory of knowledge are profound. First, Locke's epistemology is a principal foundation of the school of philosophy known as empiricism, which is closely associated with British thinkers. Following Locke, British empiricists rejected Descartes' theory that self-evident ideas are imprinted on the mind. When the mind transcends the realm of concrete experience, they said, it engages in flights of fancy, vain dreams, and idle speculation—barriers to the accumulation of knowledge. Building on Locke's empiricism, Enlightenment thinkers held that people should not dwell on unanswerable questions, particularly sterile theological ones, but should seek practical knowledge that enlightens human beings and gives them control over their environment. They argued that all theories must be analyzed, judged, and confirmed on the basis of actual human experience. Locke's empiricism insisted on clarity and verification and aspired to useful knowledge. This approach coincided with Francis Bacon's call for an inductive science and with advances in the empirical sciences. It also stimulated an interest in political and ethical questions that focused on concrete human concerns. Thus, it helped to mold the utilitarian and reformist spirit of the Enlightenment.

Second, if there are no innate ideas, said the philosophes, then human beings, contrary to Christian doctrine, are not born with original sin, are not depraved by nature. All that individuals are derives from their particular experiences. If people are provided with a proper environment and education, they will behave morally; they will become intelligent and productive citizens. By the proper use of their reason, people could bring their beliefs, their conduct, and their institutions into harmony with the natural law. This was how the reform-minded philosophes interpreted Locke. They preferred to believe that evil stemmed from faulty institutions and poor education, both of which could be remedied, rather than from a defective human nature. In *Some Thoughts Concerning Education* (1693), Locke gave support to the new importance ascribed to the environment: "Men's happiness or misery is [mainly] of their own making. . . . of all the men we meet with, nine . . . of ten are what they are, good or evil, useful or not, by their education."[57]

Claude-Adrien Helvétius (1715–1771) carried Locke's sensationalist psychology to its logical extreme, interpreting the *tabula rasa* to mean that human beings are born with equal abilities and that differences in intellect result solely from the individual's cumulative experiences from birth. Helvétius held that at birth there is no essential difference between individuals; the inequality of minds is the effect of a known cause, and this cause is the difference in education.

> If I could demonstrate that man is indeed but the product of his education, I should undoubtedly have revealed a great truth to the nations. They would then know that they hold within their own hands the instrument of their greatness and their happiness, and that to be happy and powerful is only a matter of perfecting the science of education.
>
> The general conclusion of this discourse is that genius is common. . . . The man of genius is only the product of the circumstances in which he has found himself.[58]

While Helvétius's theory belies all that experience teaches us about human beings, it nevertheless served a positive function for later ages. It contributed to the democratic idea of equality, provided a theoretical justification for public education for the masses, and reinforced the reformers' belief that human nature was not a barrier to progress.

The most important work of Enlightenment educational thought was Rousseau's *Émile* (1762). In his *A Discourse on the Origin of Inequality*, Rousseau had diagnosed the illnesses of contemporary society, particularly despotism, inequality, and a mean-spirited and selfish individualism. In the *Social Contract*, he provided a theoretical foundation for political liberty and a healthy community life. In *Émile*, he suggested educational reforms that would instill in children self-confidence, self-reliance, and emotional security, necessary qualities if they were to become productive adults and responsible citizens. If the young are taught to think for themselves, said Rousseau, they will learn to cherish personal freedom. Underlying Rousseau's educational philosophy is a belief in the essential goodness of human nature. Like Helvétius, Rousseau assumed that youngsters have an equal capacity to learn; differences in intelligence are due largely to environmental factors.

Rousseau understood that children should not be treated like little adults, for children have their own ways of thinking and feeling. He railed against those who robbed children of the joys and innocence of childhood by chaining them to desks, ordering them about, and filling their heads with rote learning. Instead, he urged that children experience direct contact with the world to develop their body and senses and their curiosity, ingenuity, resourcefulness, and imagination. It is the whole child that concerns Rousseau:

Give his body constant exercise, make it strong and healthy, in order to make him good and wise; let him work, let him do things, let him run and shout, let him be always on the go; make a man of him in strength, and he will soon be a man in reason. Of course by this method you will make him stupid if you are always giving him directions, always saying come here, go there, stop, do this, don't do that. If your head always guides his hands, his own mind will become useless.[59]

Rousseau's emphases on self-reliance and on learning by doing rather than by rote—the first book that Émile will read is *Robinson Crusoe*—make him a forerunner of the progressive education advocated by John Dewey (see pages 434–436), the American philosopher and educational reformer.

Toleration

The philosophes regarded religious persecution—whose long and bloodstained history included the burning of heretics in the Middle Ages, the slaughter of Jews and Muslims during the First Crusade, and the massacres of the Wars of the Reformation—as humanity's most depraved offense against reason. While the worst excesses of religious fanaticism had dissipated by the eighteenth century, examples of religious persecution still abounded, particularly in Catholic lands.

One incident of religious persecution that infuriated Voltaire was the famous Calas affair. In 1761, Marc-Antoine Calas, the son of Jean Calas, a Huguenot cloth merchant, committed suicide. According to French law, the corpse of a suicide was to be dragged through the streets and then hung. To avoid this, the Calas family at first claimed that Marc-Antoine had been murdered. A rumor quickly spread that the family had strangled the youth in order to prevent him from converting to Catholicism. Although his body was stretched on the rack and his bones broken on the wheel, Jean Calas continued to proclaim his innocence; finally, he was cruelly executed. An enraged Voltaire wrote to d'Alembert: "Shout everywhere, I beg you, for the Calas and against fanaticism, for it is *l'infâme* [the infamous church] that has caused their misery."[60]

Four years later, Chevalier de la Barre, an eighteen-year-old Catholic, was convicted of mutilating a crucifix and of using blasphemous language. The court ordered that the young man's tongue be cut out and his right hand amputated prior to execution. After enduring prolonged torture, La Barre was decapitated and his body burned. Thrown into the flames was a copy of Voltaire's *Philosophical Dictionary*.

Atrocities like these stirred the humanitarian instincts of the philosophes, who waged a relentless campaign for toleration, continuing a struggle initiated by enlightened sixteenth- and seventeenth-century thinkers and statesmen on both sides of the Atlantic. Thus, Spinoza (see pages 88–89) had insisted that religious belief was a matter of private conscience and urged the state not to favor one religion over another. Baron Samuel von Pufendorf (1632–1694), a German jurist, had argued against the prince imposing his own religious belief on his subjects and urged the toleration of dissenting sects. William Penn (1644–1718), the Quaker leader, maintained that religious persecution contradicted the teachings of Jesus and violated the individual's right to the free use of his reason. Roger Williams (1603–1683), who fled persecution in Massachusetts, wrote *The Bloody Tenet of Persecution for Causes of Conscience* (1644); he, too, saw a contradiction between intolerance and the true spirit of Christianity. Richard Overton, who, during the revolutionary decade of the 1640s, wrote pamphlets calling for the transformation of England into a democratic republic in which the masses would have a voice, also called for religious freedom, even for Jews. He declared: "To force men and women against their consciences is worse than to ravish the bodies of women and Maides against their wills."[61] As already noted, Pierre Bayle argued that even atheists should be tolerated.

Because of his reputation as the leading philosopher of his day, John Locke's passionate plea for toleration commanded great respect. Like other seventeenth-century supporters of toleration, Locke was reacting to the sectarian bitterness and persecution that marred English political life. In *A Letter Concerning Toleration* (1689), he argued that since the doctrines of faith cannot be proven, no one has the right to compel others to believe. "I esteem toleration to be the chief characteristic mark of the true church."[62] Those zealots who torture and execute in order to impose conformity of belief violate Jesus' teachings of love and charity. Christ's apostles went to the nations

> not armed with the sword or other instruments of force, but prepared with the Gospel of peace and with the exemplary holiness of their conversation. . . . The toleration of those that differ from others in matters of religion is so agreeable to the Gospel of Jesus Christ, and to the genuine reason of mankind, that it seems monstrous for men to be so blind as not to perceive the necessity and advantage of it in so clear a light.[63]

For Locke, persuasion, not coercion, was the appropriate means of winning souls. Since even sincere and honest people may hold different religious opinions, the only alternative to mutual tolerance is endless persecution, which threatens civil society.

Locke did limit religious liberty in two important ways. He denied tolerance to atheists because their oaths could not be trusted and to all those (he meant Catholics) who gave their loyalty to a foreign prince. Locke was expressing a common fear that the papacy controlled the conscience of English Catholics to the detriment of the state. Moreover, a strong advocate of constitutional government, Locke associated Catholicism with political absolutism. The Glorious Revolution, which had deposed the Catholic ruler James II for his leanings to absolutism, was still fresh in Locke's mind.

The philosophes were unanimous in their condemnation of religious persecution. In his pleas for tolerance, Voltaire spoke for all the philosophes:

> It is clear that every private individual who persecutes a man, his brother, because he is not of the same opinion, is a monster. . . . Of all the religions, the Christian ought doubtless to inspire the most tolerance, although hitherto the Christians have been the most intolerant of all men.[64]

And he vowed:

> I shall never cease . . . to preach tolerance from the housetops . . . until persecution is no more. The progress of reason is slow, the roots of prejudice lie deep. Doubtless, I shall never see the fruits of my efforts, but they are seeds which may one day germinate.[65]

Freedom of the Press

Censorship was a serious and ever present problem for the philosophes. After the publication of *The English Letters*, Voltaire's printer was arrested and the book confiscated and publicly burned as irreligious. On another occasion, when Voltaire was harassed by the authorities, he was prompted to write: "It is easier for me to write books than to get them published."[66] Denounced by ecclesiastical and ministerial authorities as a threat to religion and constituted authority, Helvétius' *On the Mind* (1758) was burned by the public executioner. Diderot, who served as principal editor of the thirty-eight-volume *Encyclopedia*, whose 150 or more contributors included the leading Enlightenment thinkers, had to contend with French authorities, who, at times, suspended publication. After the first two volumes were published, the authorities denounced the work for containing "maxims that would tend to destroy royal authority, foment a spirit of independence and revolt . . . and lay the foundations for the corruption of morals and religion."[67] In 1759, Pope Clement XIII condemned the *Encyclopedia* for having "scandalous doctrines [and] inducing scorn for religion."[68] It required careful diplomacy and clever ruses to finish the project and still incorporate ideas considered dangerous by religious and governmental authorities. With the project's completion in 1772, Diderot and Enlightenment opinion triumphed over clerical, royal, and aristocratic censors.

One of de Jaucourt's articles in the *Encyclopedia*, "The Press," expressed the philosophes' yearning for freedom of thought and expression. For them, the term *press* designated more than newspapers and journals; it encompassed everything in print, particularly books.

> People ask if freedom of the *press* is advantageous or prejudicial to a state. The answer is not difficult. It is of the greatest importance to conserve this practice in all states founded on liberty. I would even say that the disadvantages of this liberty are so inconsiderable compared to the advantages that this ought to be the common right of the universe, and it is certainly advisable to authorize its practices in all governments.[69]

Humanitarianism

A humanitarian spirit, which no doubt owed something to Christian compassion, pervaded the outlook of the philosophes. It found expression in attacks on torture, which was commonly used to obtain confessions in many European lands, on cruel punishments for criminals, on slavery, and on war. The philosophes' humanitarianism rested on the conviction that human beings were endowed with benevolent feelings toward each other and that human nature was essentially virtuous.

In *On Crimes and Punishments* (1764), Cesare Beccaria (1738–1794), an Italian economist and criminologist inspired in part by Montesquieu, condemned torture as inhuman, "a criterion fit for a cannibal,"[70] and as an irrational way of determining guilt or innocence, for an innocent person, unable to withstand the agonies of torture, will confess to anything and a criminal with a high threshold for pain will be exonerated. Influenced by Beccaria's work, reform-minded jurists, legislators, and ministers called for the elimination of torture from codes of criminal justice, and several European lands abolished torture in the eighteenth century.

While not pacifists, the philosophes denounced war as barbaric and an affront to reason, a scourge promoted by power-hungry monarchs and supported by fanatical clergy, wicked army leaders, and ignorant commoners. In his literary masterpiece, *Candide* (1759), Voltaire ridiculed the rituals of war. The article "Peace" in the *Encyclopedia* described war as

> the fruit of man's depravity; it is a convulsive and violent sickness of the body politic. . . . [It] depopulates the nation, causes the reign of disorder.

... makes the freedom and property of citizens uncertain ... disturbs and causes the neglect of commerce; land becomes uncultivated and abandoned .... If reason governed men and had the influence over the heads of nations that it deserves, we would never see them inconsiderately surrender themselves to the fury of war; they would not show that ferocity that characterizes wild beasts.[71]

Montesquieu, Voltaire, Hume, Benjamin Franklin, Thomas Paine, and other philosophes condemned slavery and the slave trade. In Book 15 of *The Spirit of the Laws*, Montesquieu scornfully refuted all justifications for slavery. Ultimately, he said, slavery, which violates the fundamental principle of justice underlying the universe, derived from base human desires to dominate and exploit other human beings. Adam Smith (see pages 221–222), the Enlightenment's leading economic theorist, demonstrated that slave labor was inefficient and wasteful. In *The Social Contract*, Rousseau said of slavery: "So, from whatever aspect we regard the question, the right of slavery is null and void, not only as being illegitimate, but also because it is absurd and meaningless. The words *slave* and *right* contradict each other and are mutually exclusive."[72] An examination of ancient slavery, said Hume, demonstrates its loathsome character:

> The little humanity, commonly observed in persons, accustomed from their infancy, to exercise so great authority over their fellow-creatures, and to trample upon human nature, were sufficient alone to disgust us with that unbounded dominion. ... every man of rank was rendered a petty tyrant, and educated amidst the flattery, submission, and low debasement of his slaves.[73]

In 1780, Paine helped draft the act abolishing slavery in Pennsylvania. Five years earlier, he wrote:

> Our Traders in Men ... must know the wickedness of that SLAVE-TRADE, if they attend to reasoning, or the dictates of their own hearts; and [those who] shun and stifle all these wilfully sacrifice Conscience, and the character of integrity to that Golden Idol. ... Most shocking of all is alleging the sacred Scriptures to favour this wicked practice.[74]

In 1787, Benjamin Franklin became president of the Pennsylvania Society for Promoting the Abolition of Slavery.

In another of his articles in the *Encyclopedia*, "The Slave Trade," de Jaucourt denounced slavery as a violation of the individual's natural rights.

> Negroes .... are bought from their own princes who claim to have the right to dispose of their liberty. ... If commerce of this kind can be justified by a moral principle, there is no crime, however atrocious it may be, that cannot be made legitimate. Kings, princes, and magistrates are not the proprietors of their subjects: they do not, therefore, have the right

to dispose of their liberty and to sell them as slaves. On the other hand, no one has the right to buy them or to make himself their master. Men and their liberty are not objects of commerce; they can be neither sold nor bought. . . . There is not, therefore, a single one of these unfortunate people regarded only as slaves who does not have the right to be declared free.[75]

Progress

The philosophes were generally optimistic about humanity's future progress. Two principal assumptions contributed to this optimism. First, accepting Locke's theory of knowledge, the philosophes attributed evil to a flawed but remediable environment, not to an inherently wicked human nature. Hopeful that a reformed environment would bring out the best in people, they looked forward to a day when reason would prevail over superstition, prejudice, intolerance, and tyranny. Second, the philosophes' veneration of science led them to believe that the progressive advancement of knowledge would promote material and moral progress. The belief in a golden age of earthly happiness held by some philosophes is in many ways a secularized version of the millenarian Christian belief in humanity's cumulative spiritual growth, a process that would culminate with Christ's return.

A work written near the end of the century epitomized the philosophes' vision of the future: *Sketch for a Historical Picture of the Progress of the Human Mind* (1794) by Marie-Jean-Antoine-Nicholas Caritat, Marquis de Condorcet (1743–1794). A mathematician and historian of science who contributed to the *Encyclopedia,* Condorcet campaigned for religious toleration and the abolition of slavery. During the French Revolution, Condorcet attracted the enmity of the dominant Jacobin party and in 1793 was forced to go into hiding. Secluded in Paris, he wrote *Sketch.* Arrested in 1794, Condorcet died during his first night in prison from either exhaustion or self-inflicted poison. In *Sketch,* Condorcet lauded recent advances in knowledge that enabled reason to "lift her chains [and] shake herself free"[76] from superstition and tyranny. He praised the French Revolution for attacking the royal despotism, aristocratic privileges, and clerical power and intolerance. Passionately affirming the Enlightenment's confidence in reason and science, Condorcet expounded a theory of continuous and indefinite human improvement:

> . . . nature has set no terms to the perfection of human faculties . . . the progress of this perfectibility, from now onwards independent of any power that might wish to halt it, has no other limit than the duration of the globe upon which nature has cast us. This progress . . . will never be

reversed as long as the earth occupies its present place in the vast system of the whole universe, and as long as the general laws of this system produce, neither a general cataclysm nor such changes as will deprive the human race of its present faculties and its present resources.[77]

He pointed toward a future golden age characterized by the triumph of reason and freedom.

> Our hopes for the future condition of the human race can be subsumed under three important heads: the abolition of inequality between nations, the progress of equality within each nation, and the true perfection of mankind. . . .
>
> The time will therefore come when the sun will shine only on free men who know no other master but their reason; when tyrants and slaves, priests and their stupid or hypocritical instruments will exist only in works of history and on the stage; and we shall think of them only to pity their victims and their dupes; to maintain ourselves in a state of vigilance by thinking on their excesses; and to learn how to recognize and so to destroy, by force of reason, the first seeds of tyranny and superstition, should they ever dare to reappear amongst us.[78]

But the philosophes were not starry-eyed dreamers. They knew that progress was painful, slow, and reversible. Voltaire's *Candide* was a protest against a naive optimism that ignored the granite might of human meanness, ignorance, and irrationality. "Let us weep and wail over the lot of philosophy," said Diderot. "We preach wisdom to the deaf and we are still far indeed from the age of reason."[79] "Barbarism," said d'Alembert, "lasts for centuries and seems to be our natural element; reason and good taste are merely transient."[80] Hume, ever the skeptic, cautioned: "All plans of government which suppose great reformation in the manners of mankind, are plainly imaginary."[81] And Rousseau, that great voice of dissent, challenged the very notion that advances in the sciences and the arts constituted progress.

THE ENLIGHTENMENT AND THE FRENCH REVOLUTION

The philosophes were not themselves revolutionaries, and by 1789 almost all of the principal philosophes were dead, but their ideas helped to trigger the French Revolution. Ideological considerations alone, of course, cannot account for the French Revolution. It originated in the tensions between the aristocracy and the throne, the bourgeoisie, and the peasantry; in the failures of absolutism; and in a mounting financial crisis. Nevertheless, ideas are weapons. By drawing attention to the abuses of the Old Regime and by holding that rational reforms were possible, the philosophes helped create a revolutionary mentality. They made people believe, wrote Alexis de Tocqueville (see pages 217–219) in *The Old Regime and the French Revolution* (1856), that many eighteenth-century institutions "had ceased to have any present value" and that society should be reorganized "on entirely new lines." These views acquired "the driving force of a new political passion."[82] Revolutions are born in the realm of the spirit; they require, notes George Rudé, "some unifying body of ideas, a common vocabulary of hope and protest, something, in short, like a common revolutionary psychology."[83] The ideas of the philosophes engendered such a revolutionary psychology. As Henri Peyre observes,

> Eighteenth-century philosophy taught the Frenchman to find his condition wretched, or in any case, unjust and illogical and made him disinclined to the patient resignation to his troubles that had long characterized his ancestors. The propaganda of the "Philosophes" perhaps more than any other factor accounted for the fulfillment of the preliminary condition of the French Revolution, namely discontent with the existing order of things.[84]

The outbreak of the French Revolution in 1789 stirred the imagination of westerners. Both participants and observers sensed that they were living in a pivotal age. On the ruins of the Old Order, founded on privilege and despotism, a new era was forming that promised to realize the ideals of liberty and equality championed by the philosophes. It seemed that the natural rights of the individual—a distant ideal until then—would now reign on earth, ending centuries of oppression and misery. Never before had people shown such confidence in the power of human intelligence to shape the conditions of existence. Never before had the future seemed so full of hope. This lofty vision kindled emotions akin to religious enthusiasm and attracted converts throughout the Western world. In August 1789, Count Mirabeau, echoing the cosmopolitanism of the philosophes, told his fellow deputies in the National Assembly: "You will usher in the fortunate era when . . . common liberty will banish from the whole earth the absurd oppressions that weigh men down, the prejudices of ignorance and cupidity that divide them. . . and will bring about the rebirth of a worldwide brotherhood."[85] "If we succeed," wrote the French poet André Chénier, "the destiny of Europe will be changed. Men will regain their rights and the people their sovereignty."[86] The editor of the Viennese publication *Wiener Zeitung* wrote to a friend: "In France a light is beginning to shine which will benefit the whole of humanity."[87] British reformer John Cartwright expressed the hopes of reformers everywhere: "Degenerate must be that heart which expands not with sentiments of delight at what is now transacting in . . . France. The French . . . are not only asserting their own rights, but they are asserting and advancing the general liberties of mankind."[88] Because of the revolutionaries' desire to regenerate society, Tocqueville compared the Revolution to a religious movement:

> Not only did it have repercussions beyond French territory, but like all great religious movements it resorted to propaganda and broadcast a gospel. This was something quite unprecedented: a political revolution that sought proselytes all the world over and applied itself as ardently to converting foreigners as compatriots. . . . [T]he ideal the French Revolution set before it was not merely a change in the French social system but nothing short of a regeneration of the whole human race. It created an atmosphere of missionary fervor and indeed, assumed all the aspects of a religious revival. . . . [T]his strange religion has, like Islam, overrun the whole world with its apostles, militants, and martyrs.[89]

The French Revolution attempted to reconstruct society on the basis of Enlightenment thought, which had passionately embraced and propagated Locke's theory of natural rights. The Declaration of the Rights of Man and of the Citizen (1789), whose spirit permeated the reforms of the Revolution, expressed the liberal and universal goals of the philosophes. It proclaimed the inalienable right to liberty of person, conscience, and thought and to equal treatment under the law; it asserted that government belonged to the people as a whole and insisted that the state has no higher duty than to promote the freedom and autonomy of the individual; and it held that all citizens had a right to participate in lawmaking and the voting of taxes. Maximilien Robespierre (1758–1794), the principal figure in the Jacobin Reign of Terror, summed up the link between eighteenth-century philosophy and the Revolution: "It is not enough to have overturned the throne; our concern is to erect upon its remains holy Equality and the Sacred Rights of Man."[90]

Inspired by the ideals of the philosophes, the French reformers eliminated the feudal rights and privileges of the nobility, opened careers to talent rather than birth, and provided for equality under the law and the protection of human rights—habeas corpus, trial by jury, and freedom of religion, speech, and the press. Absolutism and the divine right of monarchy, repudiated in theory by the philosophes, were invalidated by constitutions that set limits to the power of government and by elected parliaments that represented the governed. By abolishing both slavery in the French colonies (at least, in theory) and imprisonment for debt and by making plans for free public education, the Jacobins revealed their links to the philosophes' humanitarianism. By depriving the church of its special position, the Revolution accelerated the secularization of Europe, another goal of the philosophes. Sweeping aside the administrative chaos of the old Regime, the Revolution attempted to impose rational norms on the state. The sale of public offices that produced inefficient and corrupt administrators was eliminated and the highest positions in the land were opened to qualified men, regardless of birth. The Revolution abolished the peasant's manorial obligations, which hampered agriculture, and swept away barriers to economic expansion. It based taxes on income and streamlined their collection. In the nineteenth century, liberal reformers in other lands would follow the lead set by France.

Inspired by the ideals of equality voiced in the Enlightenment and the French Revolution, women began to demand equal rights. How could the political condition of women be reconciled with the progressive view that governments derive their just power from the consent of the governed? Thus, shortly after the National Assembly passed the Declaration of the Rights of Man, Olympe de Gouges published the *Declaration of the Rights of Women* (1791), and in 1792, Mary Wollstonecraft, an English writer closely associated with the radicals of her day, wrote the *Vindication of the Rights of Women* (see page 283).

The Revolution also unleashed forces—terror as government policy, political extremism, total war, and nationalism—that threatened to negate the liberties desired by the philosophes: When the newly established republic was threatened by foreign invasion and internal enemies, the Jacobin leadership, with Robespierre playing a leading role, initiated the Reign of Terror. A disciple of Rousseau, Robespierre conceived the national general will as ultimate and infallible. Its realization meant the establishment of a Republic of Virtue, founded on reason, virtue, and good citizenship; its denial meant the death of an ideal and a return to despotism. Robespierre felt certain that he and his colleagues in the Committee of Public Safety had correctly ascertained the needs of the French people and that they were the genuine interpreters of the general will. To establish the Republic of Virtue and to preserve republican liberty, the Jacobins urged harsh treatment for enemies of the republic. Robespierre said:

> Does not liberty, that inestimable blessing have the . . . right to sacrifice lives, fortunes, and even, for a time, individual liberties? Is not the French Revolution . . . a war to the death between those who want to be free and those content to be slaves? . . . There is no middle ground; France must be entirely free or perish in the attempt, and any means are justifiable in fighting for so fine a cause.[91]

Deeply devoted to republican democracy, Robespierre and his fellow Jacobins viewed themselves as bearers of a higher faith. Like all vision-aries, Robespierre was convinced that he knew the right way, that the new society he envisaged would benefit all humanity, and that those who impeded its implementation were not just opponents but sinners who had to be liquidated for the good of humanity. With the Robespierrists, we see the crystallization of a revolutionary mentality that aspired to regenerate the world in accordance with a new and secular world-view that carried the force of an absolute faith. They were true believers who resorted to terror in order to create a "new man" and a new social and political order; they sought to carry out Rousseau's conviction that it is proper to force people to be free.

The Reign of Terror, which took the lives of twenty thousand people (some estimates are higher), many of them innocent of any crime against the republic, poses fundamental questions about the meaning of the French Revolution and the validity of the Enlightenment conception of man. To what extent was the Terror a reversal of the ideals of the Revolution as formulated in the Declaration of the Rights of Man? To what extent did the feverish passions and fascination for violence demonstrated in the mass executions in the provinces and in the public spectacles in Paris indicate a darker side of human nature beyond control of reason? Did Robespierre's religion of humanity revive the fanaticism and cruelty of the wars of religion that had so disgusted the philosophes? Did the Robespierrists, who considered themselves the staunchest defenders of the Revolution's ideals, soil and subvert these ideals by their zeal? Did the Robespierrists unleash a new force—total commitment to a political ideology—that would fuel twentieth-century totalitarian movements?

To fight the war against foreign invaders, the Jacobins mobilized the nation's human and material resources. The levy in mass decreed by the Convention in 1793 heralded the emergence of modern total war.

> [Article] I. Henceforth, until the enemies have been driven from the territory of the Republic, the French people are in permanent requisition for army service.
>
> The young men shall go to battle; the married men shall forge arms and transport provisions; women shall make tents and clothes, and shall serve in the hospitals; the children shall turn old linen into lint; the old men shall repair to the public places, to stimulate the courage of the warriors and preach the unity of the Republic and hatred of kings.[92]

In a remarkable demonstration of administrative skill, the republic equipped an army of more than 800,000 men and infused the soldiers with a love for *la patrie* (the nation). The aroused citizen-soldiers of the republic overcame the armies of the European monarchs.

Acting in the name of the general will, the state could mobilize the entire citizen body. And all citizens had a moral and legal obligation to defend the state, which served as the protector of the individual's natural rights. The world wars of the twentieth century are the terrible fulfillment of this new development in warfare. Whereas eighteenth-century wars were fought by professional soldiers for limited aims, the French Revolution, says British historian Herbert Butterfield,

> brings conscription, the nation in arms, the mobilization of all the resources of the state for unrelenting conflict. It heralds the age when peoples, woefully ignorant of one another, bitterly uncomprehending, lie in uneasy juxtaposition watching one another's sins with hysteria and indignation. It heralds Armageddon, the giant conflict for justice and right between angered populations each of which thinks it is the righteous one. So a new kind of warfare is born—the modern counterpart to the old conflicts of religions.[93]

The philosophes would have regarded the nation in arms as a violent sickness that threatened the European body politic.

In calling for complete devotion to the nation, the French Revolution also heralded the rise of modern nationalism. "The image of the *Patrie* as the sole divinity which it is permissible to worship,"[94] read a petition to the Legislative Assembly in June 1792. With its potential to trample upon the rights of the individual and other nations, nationalism clashed with the outlook of the philosophes, who were cosmopolites with a warm concern for humanity. "I write as a citizen of the world." said Friedrich von Schiller (1759–1805), the great German humanist, "I lost my fatherland in order to trade it for the whole world."[95] The philosophes would have deemed nationalism, which demanded dedication of body and soul to the nation and, in the process, submerged thought in a torrent of emotion to be a repudiation of their cosmopolitanism. It was a new dogma capable of evoking wild and dangerous passions and a setback for the progress of reason.

The reforms of the French Revolution upheld the dignity of the individual, demanded respect for the individual, attributed to each person natural rights, and barred the state from denying these rights. The tragedy of the Western experience is that this humanist vision, brilliantly expressed by the Enlightenment and given recognition in the reforms of the Revolution, would be undermined in later generations. And, ironically, by spawning total war, nationalism, terror as government policy, and a revolutionary mentality that sought to change the world through violence, the French Revolution itself contributed to the shattering of this vision.

THE ENLIGHTENMENT AND
THE MODERN MENTALITY

The philosophes articulated core principles of the modern outlook. Human beings, they asserted, are capable of thinking independently of authority. Pascal (see page 70), the great French mathematician-scientist and proponent of faith, had warned of just such a glorification of the autonomous intellect:

> What will become of you . . . O man, who try by your natural reason to discover what is your true condition? . . . Know then, proud creature, what a paradox you are to yourself. Be humble, impotent reason; be quiet, imbecile nature . . . and learn from your Master of our true condition, of which you are ignorant. Hearken unto God.[96]

In dismissing these warnings and asserting the mind's self-sufficiency, the philosophes defined the modern outlook and accelerated its development.

The philosophes insisted on a thoroughgoing rational and secular interpretation of nature and society. They critically scrutinized authority and tradition and valued science and technology as a means for promoting human betterment. They sought to emancipate the mind from the bonds of ignorance and superstition and to rescue people from intolerance, cruelty, and oppression. Because of their efforts, torture (which states and Christian churches had endorsed and practiced) was eventually abolished in Western lands, and religious toleration and freedom of speech and of the press became the accepted norms. The arguments that the philosophes marshaled against slavery were utilized by those who fought against the slave trade and called for emancipation. Enlightenment economic thought, particularly Adam Smith's *Wealth of Nations* gave theoretical support to a market economy based on supply and demand, an outlook that fostered commercial and industrial expansion. The philosophes' denunciation of despotism and championing of natural rights, equality under the law, and constitutional government are the chief foundations of modern liberal government.

The ideals of the Enlightenment traversed the Atlantic and helped shape the political thought of the Founding Fathers. The Declaration of Independence clearly articulated Locke's basic principles: that government derives its authority from the governed, that human beings are born with natural rights, which government has a responsibility to protect, and that citizens have the right to resist a government that deprives them of their rights. The Constitution asserted that the people are sovereign: "We the People of the United States . . . do ordain and establish this Constitution for the United States of America." And it contained several safeguards against despotic power, including Montesquieu's principle of separation of powers which was also written into several state constitutions. Both the bills of rights drawn up by the various states and the federal Bill of Rights gave recognition to the individual's inherent rights and explicitly barred government from tampering with them—a principal concern of the philosophes. The *Federalist Papers*, the major American contribution to eighteenth-century political thought, in many ways epitomized Enlightenment thinking. It incorporated specific ideas of Locke, Montesquieu, Hume, and the *Encyclopedia*, analyzed political forms in a rational, secular, and critical spirit, regarded the protection of personal freedom as a principal goal of the state, and expressed a willingness to break with past traditions when they conflicted with good sense. The new American republic, says Peter Gay, was "convincing evidence, to the philosophes . . . . that men had some capacity for self-improvement and self-government, that progress might be a reality instead of a fantasy, and that reason and humanity might become governing rather than merely critical principles."[97]

The philosophes broke with the traditional Christian view of human nature and the purpose of life. In that view, men and women were born in sin; suffering and misery were their lot, and relief could come only from God; and for many, eternal damnation was a deserved final destination. In contrast, the philosophes expressed confidence in people's ability to attain happiness by improving the conditions of their earthly existence and articulated a theory of human progress that did not require divine assistance. Rejecting the idea of a static and immutable order of society instituted by God, the philosophes had confidence that human beings could improve the conditions of their existence and they pointed to advances in science and technology as evidence of progress.

Thus, the idea of secular progress, another key element of modernity, also grew out of the Enlightenment. After two world wars and countless other conflicts, after Auschwitz and other examples of state-sponsored mass murder, and with the development of weapons of mass destruction, it is difficult to realize that at the beginning of the twentieth century most westerners were committed to a doctrine of perpetual progress that embodied the hopes of the philosophes.

To be sure, the promise of the Enlightenment has not been achieved. More education for more people and the spread of constitutional government have not eliminated fanaticism and superstition, violence and war, or evil and injustice. In the light of twentieth-century events, it is difficult to subscribe to Condorcet's belief in linear progress. As Peter Gay observes:

The world has not turned out the way the philosophes wished and half expected that it would. Old fanaticisms have been more intractable, irrational forces more inventive than the philosophes were ready to conjecture in their darkest moments. Problems of race, of class, of nationalism, of boredom and despair in the midst of plenty have emerged almost in defiance of the philosophes' philosophy. We have known horrors, and may know horrors, that the men of the Enlightenment did not see in their nightmares.[98]

The world-view of the philosophes also suffered from inherent weaknesses, some of which were pointed out by their romantic and conservative critics (see Chapters 6 and 7). According to some critics, since the philosophes emphasized the abuses of religious authorities and the fetters religion had placed on reason and since they felt no need themselves for the spiritual sustenance of religion, they had trouble understanding or empathizing with Christianity's capacity to uplift men and women morally and emotionally. Blinded by their hostility to Christianity, the philosophes viewed the Middle Ages solely as an era of barbarism. They could neither comprehend nor appreciate the richness of the civilization that had produced the Gothic cathedral, Aquinas, and Dante. Instead, they shared the attitude of English writer Henry Fielding, who dismissed the medieval past as "centuries of monkish dullness when the whole world seems to have been asleep."[99]

The philosophes' contempt for the Christian Middle Ages, critics have argued, reveals a larger failing of the philosophes: they did not seek to understand a past age on its own terms but judged it according to preconceived norms, disdaining and rejecting anything that contradicted their idea of truth and their view of the good society. Such an outlook, say the critics, led the philosophes to underestimate the extent to which the past governs the present. Holding with Hume that human nature remains the same in all nations and ages, the philosophes, regarded differences between peoples and civilizations as superficial and inconsequential. Since reason was common to humanity, government, law, morality, education, and all other institutions and systems of thought could be based on universal principles and could apply to all peoples throughout the globe regardless of their cultures and history. Historian of ideas Arthur O. Lovejoy comments on this feature of Enlightenment thought:

> Thus for two centuries the efforts made for improvement and correction in beliefs, in institutions, and in art had been, in the main, controlled by the assumption that, in each phase of his activity, man should conform as nearly as possible to a standard conceived as universal, uncomplicated, immutable, uniform for every rational human being. The Enlightenment was, in short, an age devoted, at least in its dominant

tendency, to the ... simplification and standardization of thought and life — to their standardization by means of their simplification.

Spinoza summed it up. . . : 'The purpose of Nature is to make men uniform, as children of a common mother.' The struggle to realize this supposed purpose of nature, the general attack upon the differences of men and their opinions and valuations and institutions . . . was the central and dominating fact in the intellectual history of Europe from the late sixteenth to the late eighteenth century.[100]

In reality, this meant that the outlook of a small party of thinkers would become normative for all peoples and cultures. Such an undervaluing of the complex relationship between past and present, of human diversity, and of the immense appeal of familiar beliefs, traditions, and institutions—even if they seem so blatantly in opposition to reason—promotes the presumptuous and dangerous belief that society and government can be easily and rapidly molded to fit abstract principles and that reformers need pay only scant attention to historically conditioned cultural forms.

The philosophes' belief in universality, in timeless truths that apply to all peoples at all times, also contains an inherent danger. In politics, it could create true believers totally committed to an abstraction, such as the exploited class or the infallible party. To realize their ideal, these devotees will employ terror and mass murder with a clear conscience. As Isaiah Berlin notes, "Of course, nobody believed in universality more than the Marxists: Lenin, Trotsky, and the others who triumphed saw themselves as disciples of the Enlightenment thinkers, corrected and brought up to date by Marx."[101] Robespierre and the Reign of Terror might be viewed as an early manifestation of this attempt to make society adhere to a conceptual grid.

Perhaps this criticism is too harsh. True, the philosophes were committed to natural law, but as Steven Seidman points out, they also

> distinguished between universal moral laws and their concrete realization in positive law and social institutions. The philosophes maintained that these universal laws had to be fitted to the unique natural and social conditions of specific societies. . . . [T]he philosophes could be critical, in the sense of preserving a transcendent standard and yet remain sensitive to historical particularity.[102]

Thus, Étienne Condillac insisted that the legislator "should not seek the most perfect government in his imagination. . . . He must study the character of the people, investigate their usages and customs. . . . Then he will preserve what is found to be good, and replace what is found to be bad, but only by means which conform most to the *moeurs* [customs] of the citizens."[103]

Building on the attack of early nineteenth-century romantics, critics have accused the philosophes of overvaluing the intellect at the expense of human feelings. According to this view, the philosophes did not recognize the value of the feelings as a source of creativity and did not call for their full development. Rather, they viewed the emotions as impediments to clear thinking that had to be overcome. Although there is much truth to this argument, like the previous indictment of the philosophes, it is also overstated. There are numerous instances where the philosophes recognized the intrinsic value of the passions. Thus, Diderot wrote in his *Philosophic Thoughts* (1746):

> People are continually inveighing against the passions; we impute all man's troubles to them and forget that they are also the source of all his pleasures. They are an element in his constitution of which it is impossible to speak either too well or too ill. But what makes me angry is that no one ever considers anything but their bad side, as though it would be an insult to reason to say a single word in defense of its rivals. And yet it is the passions alone, great passions, that can raise the soul to great deeds. Without them, there would be an end of sublimity both in human actions and in art; the fine arts would return to their infancy, and virtue would become quibble.[104]

Another criticism is that the philosophes' exuberant view of science and reason prevented them from realizing that reason is a double-edged sword: it could demean as well as ennoble human personality. The philosophes believed that removing thought from the realm of myth and religion and eliminating irrational forms of social organization would foster human emancipation. They could not foresee that modern bureaucracy and technology, both creations of the rational mind, could fashion a social order that devalues and depersonalizes the individual. In its determination to make the social world accord with a theoretical model, rationalism strives for uniformity and efficiency; in the process, it threatens to regulate, organize, and manipulate the individual as it would any material object. Future periods would not only reveal the limitations of reason—its inability to cope with powerful irrational drives and instincts that incite acts of inhumanity—but also the dangers of reason—its capacity to subordinate and sacrifice the individual to theoretical systems, particularly political ideologies.

The limitations of the philosophes, however, should not lead us to undervalue their achievement. Their ideals became an intrinsic part of the liberal-democratic tradition and inspired nineteenth- and twentieth-century reformers. The spirit of the Enlightenment will always remain indispensable to all those who cherish the traditions of reason and freedom.

NOTES

1. Quoted in Frank E. Manuel, *Age of Reason* (Ithaca, N.Y.: Cornell University Press, 1951), p. 28.
2. Quoted in Henry Steele Commager, *The Empire of Reason* (Garden City, N.Y.: Doubleday, 1977), p. 41.
3. Ibid., p. 42.
4. Quoted in Thomas J. Schlereth, *The Cosmopolitan Ideal in Enlightenment Thought* (Notre Dame, Ind.: University of Notre Dame Press, 1977), p. 26.
5. Ibid., p. 2.
6. Quoted in Alain Besançon, *Rise of the Gulag: Intellectual Origins of Leninism*, trans. Sarah Matthews (New York: Continuum, 1981), p. 30.
7. Immanuel Kant, "What is Enlightenment," in *The Philosophy of Kant*, ed. Carl J. Friedrich (New York: Modern Library, 1949), p. 132.
8. Excerpted in Stephen J. Gendzier, ed. and trans., *Denis Diderot's The Encyclopedia Selections* (New York: Harper Torchbooks, 1967), p. 93. Reprinted by permission of Stephen J. Gendzier.
9. Quoted in Peter Gay, *The Enlightenment: An Interpretation*, vol. 1, *The Rise of Modern Paganism* (New York: Vintage Books, 1966), p. 188.
10. Paul-Henri Thiry, Baron d'Holbach, *Good Sense or Natural Ideas Opposed to Ideas that are Supernatural*, excerpted in *Sources of the Western Tradition*, ed. Marvin Perry et al. 2nd ed. (Boston: Houghton Mifflin, 1991), II, 69–70.
11. Quoted in Peter Gay, *The Party of Humanity* (New York: Norton, 1971), p. 37.
12. David Hume, *The Natural History of Religion*, ed. H. E. Root (London: Adam and Charles Black, 1956), p. 75.
13. Quoted in Ben Ray Redman, ed., *The Portable Voltaire* (New York: Viking Press, 1949), p. 26.
14. Voltaire, *Zapata's Questions*, excerpted in *Voltaire on Religion*, ed. Kenneth W. Applegate (New York: Ungar, 1974), p. 22.
15. Voltaire, *Philosophical Dictionary*, in *Candide and Other Writings*, ed. Haskell M. Block, (New York: Modern Library, 1956), p. 385.
16. Ibid., p. 406.
17. Voltaire, *A Commentary on the Book of Crimes and Punishments*, ibid., p. 375.
18. Holbach, *Good Sense*, in *Sources of the Western Tradition*, II, 69–70.
19. Denis Diderot, *Supplement to Bouganville's 'Voyage,'* trans. Jacques Barzun and Ralph H. Bowen, in *Rameau's Nephew and Other Works* (Indianapolis: Library of Liberal Arts, 1956), p. 191.
20. Denis Diderot, "Discourse of a Philosopher to a King," in *Diderot, Interpreter of Nature: Selected Writings*, ed. Jonathan Kemp, trans. Jean Stewart and Jonathan Kemp (New York: International Publishers, 1943), p. 214.
21. Quoted in Friedrich B. Artz, *The Enlightenment in France* (Kent, Ohio: Kent State University Press, 1968), p. 26.
22. Sir Leslie Stephen, *History of*

English Thought in the Eighteenth Century (New York: Harcourt, Brace, and World, 1962), I, 92.

23. Quoted in John Herman Randall, Jr., *The Making of the Modern Mind* (Boston: Houghton Mifflin, 1940), p. 296.

24. Quoted in Maurice Cranston, *Philosophers and Pamphleteers* (New York: Oxford University Press, 1986), p. 44.

25. Thomas Paine, *The Age of Reason* (New York: Eckler, 1892), p. 5.

26. Ibid., p. 6.

27. Quoted in Gay, *The Enlightenment*, I, p. 122.

28. Quoted in Peter Gay, ed., *Deism An Anthology* (Princeton: Van Nostrand, 1968), p. 11.

29. Quoted in Paul Hazard, *European Thought in the Eighteenth Century* (New Haven: Yale University Press. 1954), p. 174.

30. Excerpted in Gendzier, *Denis Diderot's The Encyclopedia Selections*, p. 124.

31. Ibid., pp. 186–187.

32. Baron de la Brède et de Montesquieu, *The Spirit of the Laws*, trans. Thomas Nugent (New York: Hafner, 1949), bk. 1, chap. 3, pp. 6–7.

33. Montesquieu, *The Persian Letters*, trans. George R. Healy (Indianapolis: Library of Liberal Arts, 1964), chap. 29, p. 53.

34. Ibid., chap. 60, pp. 101–102.

35. *Spirit of the Laws*, bk 11, chap. 5, p. 151.

36. Ibid., bk 5, chap. 14, p. 59.

37. Voltaire, *The English Letters*, excerpted in Redman, *The Portable Voltaire*, p. 513.

38. Ibid., pp. 520–521, 523.

39. Cranston, *Philosophers and Pamphleteers*, pp. 60–61.

40. Jean Jacques Rousseau, *A Discourse on the Origin of Inequality*, in *The Social Contract and Discourses*, ed. and trans. G. D. H. Cole, (New York: Dutton, 1950), p. 226.

41. Ibid., pp. 234–235.

42. Ibid., pp. 250–252

43. Rousseau, *The Social Contract*, bk. 1, chap. 1, p. 3.

44. Ibid., bk. 1, chap. 6, pp. 13–14.

45. Ibid., bk. 2, chap. 3, p. 26.

46. Ibid., bk. 2 chap. 1, p. 23.

47. Ibid., bk. 1, chap. 8, p. 19.

48. Ibid., bk. 1, chap. 7, p. 18.

49. Ibid.

50. Ernst Cassirer, *The Philosophy of the Enlightenment*, trans. Fritz C. A. Koelln and James Pettegrove (Boston: Beacon, 1951), p. 272.

51. George Sabine, *A History of Political Theory* (New York: Holt, Rinehart and Winston, 1961), p. 591.

52. Robert Nisbet, *Conservatism: Dream or Reality* (Minneapolis: University of Minnesota Press, 1986), p. 48.

53. J. L. Talmon, *Origins of Totalitarian Democracy* (New York: Praeger, 1960), p. 48.

54. Quoted in Gay, *The Enlightenment*, vol. 2, *The Science of Freedom*, p. 170.

55. Quoted in Steven Seidman, *Liberalism and the Origins of European Social Theory* (Berkeley: University of California Press, 1983), p. 30.

56. John Locke, *Essay Concerning Human Understanding*, in *Locke: Selections*, ed. Sterling P. Lamprecht (New York: Scribner's, 1928), pp. 110–111.

57. John Locke, *Some Thoughts Concerning Education*, in *Locke: Selections*, p. 3.

58. Quoted in John Herman Ran-

dall, Jr., *The Career of Philosophy*, vol. 1, *From the Middle Ages to the Enlightenment* (New York: Columbia University Press, 1962), pp. 933–934.

59. Jean Jacques Rousseau, *Émile*, trans. Barbara Foxley (New York: Dutton, 1974), p. 82.

60. Quoted in Peter Gay, *Voltaire's Politics* (New York: Random House, Vintage Books, 1965), p. 277.

61. Quoted in Henry Kamen, *The Rise of Toleration* (New York: McGraw Hill, 1967), p. 176.

62. John Locke, *A Letter Concerning Toleration* (Indianapolis: The Library of Liberal Arts, 1955), p. 13.

63. Ibid., p. 16.

64. Voltaire, *Philosophical Dictionary*, p. 443.

65. Voltaire, "Letter to M. Bertrand," in *Candide and Other Writings*, p. 525.

66. Quoted in Gay, *Voltaire's Politics*, p. 71.

67. Quoted in Gendzier, *Denis Diderot's The Encyclopedia Selections*, p. xxv.

68. Ibid., p. xxvi.

69. Excerpted in ibid., p. 199.

70. Cesare Beccaria, *On Crimes and Punishments*, trans. Henry Paolucci (Indianapolis: Library of Liberal Arts, 1963), p. 32.

71. Excerpted in Gendzier, *Denis Diderot's The Encyclopedia Selections*, pp. 183–184.

72. Rousseau, *The Social Contract*, bk. 1, chap. 4, p. 12.

73. David Hume, "Of the Populousness of Ancient Nations," in *David Hume: Writings on Economics*, ed. Eugene Rotwein (Madison: University of Wisconsin Press, 1970), p. 113.

74. Excerpted in Moncure Daniel Conway, ed., *The Writings of Thomas Paine* (New York: Burt Franklin, 1969), pp. 4–5.

75. Excerpted in Gendzier, *Denis Diderot's The Encyclopedia Selections*, pp. 229–230.

76. Antoine Nicolas de Condorcet, *Sketch for a Historical Picture of the Progress of the Human Mind*, trans. June Barraclough (London: Weidenfeld & Nicholas, 1955), p. 124.

77. Ibid., pp. 4–5.

78. Ibid., pp. 173–179.

79. Quoted in Gay, *The Enlightenment*, I, 20.

80. Quoted in J. H. Brumfitt, *The French Enlightenment* (Cambridge, Mass: Schenkmann, 1972), p. 154.

81. David Hume, "Idea of a Perfect Commonwealth," in *David Hume's Political Essays*, ed. Charles W. Hendel (Indianapolis: The Library of Liberal Arts, 1953), p. 154.

82. Alexis de Tocqueville, *The Old Regime and the French Revolution*, trans. Stuart Gilbert (Garden City, N.Y.: Doubleday Anchor Books, 1955), pp. 140, 139.

83. George Rudé, *Revolutionary Europe 1783–1815* (New York: Harper Torchbooks, 1966), p. 74.

84. Henri Peyre, "The Influence of Eighteenth Century Ideas on the French Revolution," *Journal of the History of Ideas*, 101 (1949), 73.

85. Quoted in Hans Kohn, *Prelude to Nation-States: The French and German Experiences, 1789–1815* (Princeton: Van Nostrand, 1967), p. 14.

86. Quoted in G. P. Gooch, *Germany and the French Revolu-*

tion (New York: Russell & Russell, 1966), p. 39.

87. Quoted In Ernst Wangermann, *From Joseph II to the Jacobin Trials* (New York: Oxford University Press, 1959), p. 24.

88. Excerpted in Alfred Cobban, ed., *The Debate on the French Revolution* (London: Adam & Charles Black, 1960), p. 41.

89. Tocqueville, *The Old Regime and the French Revolution*, pp. 11–13.

90. Quoted in Christopher Dawson, *The Gods of Revolution* (New York: New York University Press, 1972), p. 83.

91. Excerpted in E. L. Higgins, ed., *The French Revolution* (Boston: Houghton Mifflin, 1938), pp. 306–307.

92. Excerpted in John Hall Stewart, ed., *A Documentary Survey of the French Revolution* (New York: Macmillan, 1969), pp. 472–473.

93. Herbert Butterfield, *Napoleon* (New York: Collier Books, 1962), p. 18.

94. Quoted in Connor Cruise O'Brien, "Nationalism and the French Revolution," in *The Permanent Revolution*, ed. Geoffrey Best (London: Fontana, 1988), p. 177.

95. Quoted in Koppel S. Pinson, *Modern Germany* (New York: Macmillan, 1954), p. 16.

96. Quoted in Cassirer, *Philosophy of the Enlightenment*, p. 144.

97. Gay, *The Enlightenment*, II, 555.

98. Ibid., p. 567.

99. Quoted in Norman Hampson, *The Enlightenment* (Baltimore: Penguin Books, 1968), p. 149.

100. Arthur O. Lovejoy, *The Great Chain of Being* (Cambridge, Mass.: Harvard University Press, 1964), pp. 292–293.

101. Nathan Gardels, "Two Concepts of Nationalism: An Interview with Isaiah Berlin," *The New York Review of Books*, November 21, 1991, p. 20.

102. Seidman, *Liberalism and the Origins of European Social Theory*, pp. 24–25.

103. Ibid., p. 24.

104. Denis Diderot, *Philosophic Thoughts*, in *Diderot's Selected Writings*, ed. Lester G. Crocker, trans. Derek Coltman (New York: Macmillan, 1966), pp. 1–2.

SUGGESTED READING

Anchor, Robert, *The Enlightenment Tradition* (1967).

Artz, Frederick B., *The Enlightenment in France* (1968).

Brumfitt, J. H., *The French Enlightenment* (1972).

Cranston, Maurice, *Philosophers and Pamphleteers* (1986).

Cobban, Alfred, *In Search of Humanity* (1960).

Commager, Henry Steele, *The Empire of Reason* (1977).

Einaudi, Mario, *The Early Rousseau* (1967).

France, Peter, *Diderot* (1983).

Gay, Peter, *The Enlightenment an Interpretation*, 2 vols. (1966).

———, *Voltaire's Politics* (1959).

———, *The Party of Humanity* (1971).

———, ed., *The Enlightenment A Comprehensive Anthology* (1973).

Gendzier, Stephen J., ed., *Denis Diderot The Encyclopedia Selections* (1967).

Grimsley, Ronald, *The Philosophy of Rousseau* (1973).

Hampson, Norman, *The Enlightenment* (1968).

Hazard, Paul, *European Thought in the Eighteenth Century* (1954).

Hulliung, Mark, *Montesquieu and the Old Regime* (1976).

Martin, Kingsley, *French Liberal Thought in the Eighteenth Century* (1962).

Randall, J. H. Jr., *The Career of Philosophy: from the Middle Ages to the Enlightenment* (1962).

Redman, Ray Ben, ed., *The Portable Voltaire* (1949).

Roche, Kennedy, *Rousseau: Stoic and Romantic* (1974).

Schlereth, Thomas J., *The Cosmopolitan Ideal in Enlightenment Thought* (1977).

Wilson, Arthur M., *Diderot* (1972).

Yolton, John W. ed., *The Blackwell Companion to the Englightenment* (1991).

II

THE ENLIGHTENMENT TRADITION

PRESERVED, EXPANDED,

AND CHALLENGED

6

Romanticism and German Idealism

The early nineteenth century saw the flowering of a new cultural orientation. Romanticism, with its plea for the liberation of human emotions and the free expression of personality and imagination, challenged the Enlightenment's stress on rationalism. Although primarily a literary and artistic movement, romanticism also permeated philosophy and political thought, particularly conservatism, and nationalism.

Historians recognize the prominence of romanticism in nineteenth-century cultural life, but the movement was so complex and the differences among the various romantic writers, artists, and musicians so numerous that historians cannot agree on a definition of romanticism. Romantics were both liberals and conservatives, revolutionaries and reactionaries; some were preoccupied with religion and God, while others paid little attention to faith.

Most of Europe's leading cultural figures in the early nineteenth century came under the influence of the Romantic Movement. Among the exponents of romanticism were the poets Shelley, Wordsworth, Keats, Coleridge, and Byron in England; the novelist Victor Hugo and the Catholic novelist and essayist Chateaubriand in France; the writers A. W. and Friedrich Schlegel, the dramatist and poet Schiller, and the philosopher Schelling in Germany. Caspar David Friedrich in Germany and John Constable in Britain expressed the romantic mood in art, and the later Beethoven, Schubert, Chopin, and Wagner expressed it in music.

EXALTING IMAGINATION AND FEELINGS

Perhaps the central message of the romantics was that the imagination of the individual should determine the form and content of an artistic creation. This outlook ran counter to the rationalism of the Enlightenment, which itself had been a reaction against the otherworldly Christian orientation of the Middle Ages. The philosophes had attacked faith because it thwarted and distorted reason; romantic poets, philosophers, and artists denounced the scientific rationalism of the philosophes because it stifled the emotions and impeded creativity.

Like the philosophes, romantics believed in the individual's personal significance; indeed, it was just this high value that they gave to the individual that led romantics to criticize the philosophes. They denounced the philosophes for turning flesh-and-blood human beings into soulless thinking machines. The Enlightenment's geometric spirit, which sought to fit all life into a mechanical framework, said romantics, had diminished and demeaned the individual. Such shallow thinking had separated people from their feelings; it had crushed spontaneity and individuality, stifling the creative imagination and preventing people from realizing their human potential.

In *Faust,* Johann Wolfgang von Goethe (1749–1832), Germany's greatest poet, described the emptiness of a man whose pursuit of science and philosophy had separated him from a deeper wisdom that is the source and sustainer of life. The learned Dr. Faustus, restless and striving, now yearns to plumb the depths of the senses. His revolt against quietude and his yearning for the joy and excitement of life's experiences exemplify the romantics' passionate intensity. In the opening scene, Faust laments that a life of calm and contemplation devoid of experience is empty:

> Ah me! I've now studied thoroughly and with ardent effort philosophy, law, medicine, and even, alas! theology. And here I stand, poor fool, and am no wiser than before. I've the title of Master, even Doctor, and for ten years now I've been leading my pupils by the nose, up and down and back and forth—and realize that we can't know anything! And that is eating my heart out. . . . I'm deprived of all joy. . . .
>
> O light of the full moon, would that you were gazing for the last time upon my pain, you whom I have seen, as I sat awake at this desk, rise through so many a midnight hour. Then, as now, it was over books and papers, mournful friend, that you appeared to me. Ah! could I but walk on mountain heights in your beloved radiance, hover with spirits about mountain caverns, rove over meadows in your dimness, and unburdened of all this fog of learning, find health by bathing in your dew.
>
> Woe! still stuck in this dungeon here? Accursed, musty hole-in-the-

wall, where even the blessed light of heaven breaks but dimly through the painted panes! Hemmed in by this pile of books, which is gnawed by worms and covered with dust.[1]

To restore human beings to their true nature, to make them whole again, said romantics, they must be emancipated from the tyranny of excessive intellectualizing. The feelings must again be nurtured and expressed. The romantics agreed with Rousseau, a romantic in an age of reason, that feeling not thinking is the essential part of our being and that a good heart—the moral self—is superior to a powerful intellect. Taking up one of Rousseau's ideas, romantics yearned to rediscover a pristine freedom and creativity in the human soul that had been squashed by habits, values, rules, and standards imposed by civilization. Romantics cherished the creative experience, which they linked with the transcendent. During such a moment of exhilaration, it seems that one "hath . . . drunk the milk of Paradise," as Samuel Taylor Coleridge (1772–1834) wrote in "Kubla Khan."

The philosophes had concentrated on people in general—those elements of human nature shared by all people. Romantics, on the other hand, emphasized human diversity and uniqueness—those distinctive traits that set one human being apart from others. The conscious pursuit of diversity and uniqueness was romanticism's first commandment. Discover and express your true self: cultivate your own imagination; play your own music; write your own poetry; paint your own personal vision of nature; experience love and suffering in your own way. The philosophes had asserted the *autonomy of the mind*—its capacity to think for itself independently of authority; romantics, on the other hand, gave primary importance to the *autonomy of the personality*—the individual's need and right to find and fulfill the inner self. This intense introspection—the individual's preoccupation with his or her own feelings—is the distinguishing feature of romanticism. In the opening lines of his autobiography, *Confessions*, Rousseau expressed the subjectivism, the yearning for the liberation of the self, that characterized the Romantic Movement:

> I am commencing an undertaking, hitherto without precedent and which will never find an imitator. I desire to set before my fellows the likeness of a man in all the truth of nature, and that man myself. Myself alone! I know the feelings of my heart, and I know men. I am not made like any of those I have seen. I venture to believe that I am not made like any of those who are in existence. If I am not better, at least I am different.[2]

Through rational argument, the philosophes had sought to expose the inadequacies of existing conventions and institutions; through intelligent planning, they hoped to reform society. Regarding the feelings as an obstacle to clear thinking, the philosophes held that the rational faculties should exercise tight control over imagination, intuition, inspiration, and sentiments. To the romantics, however, feelings were the human essence. People could not live by reason alone, they said. Romantics agreed with Rousseau, who wrote: "For us, to exist is to feel and our sensibility is incontestably prior to our reason."[3] For the romantics, reason was cold and dreary, its understanding of people and life meager and inadequate. Reason could not comprehend or express the complexities of human nature nor the richness of human experience. By always dissecting and analyzing, by imposing deadening structure and form, and by demanding adherence to strict rules, reason crushed inspiration and creativity, barring true understanding. In his poem "Milton," William Blake (1757–1827), British poet, artist, and mystic, expressed the romantics' distaste for the rationalist-scientific outlook of the Enlightenment and their affirmation of the creative potential of the imagination.

> . . . the Reasoning Power in Man;
> This is a false Body; an Incrustation over
>   my Immortal
> Spirit; a Selfhood, which must be put off & annihilated
>   alway [for all time]
> To cleanse the Face of my Spirit by Self-
>   Examination
> . . . .
> To cast off Rational Demonstration by
>   Faith in the Saviour,
> To cast off the rotten rags of Memory by
>   Inspiration,
> To cast off Bacon, Locke & Newton
>   from Albion's [England's] covering
> To take off his filthy garments & clothe
>   him with Imagination,
> To cast aside from Poetry all that is not
>   Inspiration . . .[4]

For the romantics, the avenue to truth was not the intellect; the rationalist's conceptual schemes and scientific abstractions provided only a superficial understanding of the individual and nature. "God forbid that Truth should be Confined to Mathematical Demonstration!"[5] protested Blake. The scientific spirit is cold, its vision narrow, its effect fragmentation and dehumanization of consciousness. William Wordsworth (1770–1850) said that by viewing nature as "dead and spiritless," science wages "an impious warfare with the very life of our own souls!"[6]

William Wordsworth *(The Bettmann Archive)*

John Keats (1795–1821) also protested against the dissecting scientific spirit: ". . . Do not charms fly / At the mere touch of cold philosophy? . . . / Philosophy will clip an Angel's wings, / Conquer all mysteries by rule and line. . . . / Unweave a rainbow."[7]

And Coleridge argued that "deep thinking is attainable only by a man of deep feeling, and that all truth is a species of revelation."[8] Reality is too intricate, too immense to be grasped by reason's formulas. A deeper insight into the world and life comes from spontaneous human emotions, from intuition, from the soul spreading its wings. Thus, the musician Franz Schubert (1797–1828) exclaimed:

> Oh imagination, thou supreme jewel of mankind, thou inexhaustible source from which artists and scholars drink! Oh, rest with us—despite the fact that thou art recognized only by a few—so as to preserve it from so-called Enlightenment, that ugly skeleton without flesh or blood.[9]

By cultivating the passions and the imagination, individuals could then experience true reality and discover their authentic selves. The romantics wanted people to feel and to experience—to "bathe in the Waters of Life,"[10] said Blake. Or as Goethe wrote in *Faust:* "All theory, dear friend is gray, and the golden tree of life is green."[11]

Holding with Goethe that "feeling is all" and with Keats that "but to think is to be full of sorrow," romantics insisted that imaginative poets had a greater insight into life and truth than analytical philosophers. Coleridge defined the poet as one "with a soul unsubdued by habit, unshackled by custom, [who] contemplates all things with the freshness and wonders of a child."[12] Poetry is a true philosophy, the romantics said: it can do what rational analysis and geometric calculations cannot—speak directly to the heart, clarify life's deepest mysteries, and penetrate to the depths of human personality. Madame de Staël (1776–1817), novelist and critic, said that "the poet knows how to restore the union between the natural and the moral world: his imagination forms a connecting tie between the one and the other."[13] German literary theorist Friedrich Schlegel (1772–1829) declared that the Romantic Movement's supreme goal was to carry the poetic spirit to all spheres of human endeavor—religion, history, even science.

The poet's imagination, said the romantics, is an avenue to a higher reality beyond the visible world; it enables the individual to participate in the eternal and to discover the transcendent. For Blake, to exercise the poetic imagination was to partake in God's creative activity; God manifests himself in the human imagination.

> The world of the Imagination is the world of Eternity; it is the divine bosom into which we shall all go after the death of the Vegetated body. This World of Imagination is Infinite and Eternal, whereas the world of Generation, or Vegetation, is Finite and Temporal. There Exist in that Eternal World the Permanent Realities of Every Thing which we see reflected in this Vegetable Glass of Nature. All Things are comprehended in their Eternal Forms of the divine body of the Saviour, the True Vine of Eternity, The Human Imagination.[14]

To think profoundly, one has to feel deeply, the romantics said. For reason to function best, it must be nourished by the poetic imagination, which alone extricates and ennobles feelings hidden in the soul. "I am certain of nothing but of the holiness of the heart's affections and the truth of the Imagination," wrote Keats. "O for a Life of Sensations rather than of Thoughts."[15] In his Preface to *The Lyrical Ballads* (1798), often called the manifesto of romanticism, Wordsworth held that poetry—that is, imagination, intuition, and feeling—not mathematics and logic, yielded the highest truth. From the poet's heart, said Goethe in *Wilhelm Meister*, "the beautiful flower of wisdom grows."

The Enlightenment mind had been clear, critical, and controlled. It had adhered to standards of esthetics thought to be universal that had dominated European cultural life since the Renaissance. It stressed technique, form, order, and changeless patterns and tended to reduce the imagination to mechanical relationships. "Analysis and calculation make the poet, as they make the mathematician," wrote Etienne Condillac, a prominent French philosophe. "Once the material of a play is given, the invention of the plot, the characters, the verse, is only a series of algebraic problems to be worked out."[16] Following in this tradition, Népomucène Lemercier determined that there were twenty-six rules for tragedy, twenty-three for comedy, and twenty-four for the epic; he proceeded to manufacture plays and epics according to this formula.

Romantic poets, artists, and musicians broke with the traditional styles and austere rules and created new cultural forms and techniques. "We do not want either Greek or Roman models," said Blake, but should be "just & true to our own imaginations."[17] Victor Hugo (1802–1885), the dominant figure among French romantics, sought art forms free of restraints imposed by inherited standards.

> But still we hear the same refrain and doubtless we shall hear it for years to come, "Follow the rules! Copy the models!" . . . Let us speak out boldly. The time has come to do it. . . . Let us take the hammer to their theories and systems and treatises. Let us tear down the old stucco-work which conceals the façade of art! There are no rules or models or rather there are no other rules than the general laws of nature, which extend over the whole domain of art. . . . Let the poet above all things beware of copying anyone, Shakespeare no more than Molière, Schiller no more than Corneille.[18]

Dismissing a belief in eternal models, the romantics valued esthetic freedom and diversity. The romantics, says historian of ideas A. D. Lovejoy, maintained "that diversity itself is the essence of excellence; and that of art, in particular, the objective is . . . [not] the attainment of some single ideal perfection of form . . . which is shared by all mankind in all ages, but rather the fullest possible expression of the abundance of differences that there is, actually or potentially, in nature and human nature."[19]

For the romantics, yearning as they did for unhindered self-expression, one did not learn how to write poetry or paint by following textbook rules; nor could one understand the poet's or artist's intent by judging works according to fixed standards and immutable ideals. Only by looking within themselves, by trusting to their own feelings could individuals attain their creative potential and achieve self-realization. "I do not make poetry," stated Polish poet Adam Mickiewicz (1798–1855), "I strike my heart and eloquence flows from it."[20] "It is precisely individuality that is the original and eternal thing in men." declared Friedrich Schlegel. "The cultivation and development of this individuality . . . [is] one's highest vocation."[21]

As the romantics saw it, the most creative works of art were not photographic imitations of nature but authentic and spontaneous expressions of the artist's feelings, fantasies, and dreams. American painter Washington Allston urged: "Listen to the voice within you, and sooner or later she will make herself understood not only to you, but she will enable you to translate her language to the world, and this it is which forms the only real merit of any work of art."[22] Similarly, the romantics were less impressed by the constructions of Ludwig van Beethoven (1770–1827) than by the intensity and passion of his music. Thus, E.T.A. Hoffmann (1776–1822), a composer and critic who was Beethoven's contemporary, declared: "Beethoven's music moves the levers that open the floodgates of fear, terror, of horror, of pain and arouses that longing for the eternal which is the essence of Romanticism."[23]

In their zeal to convey the immediacy of the inner experience, the romantics explored the inner life of the mind, which Freud would later call the unconscious. "It is the beginning of poetry," wrote Friedrich Schlegel, "to abolish the law and the method of the rationally proceeding reason and to plunge us once more into the ravishing confusion of fantasy, the original chaos of human nature."[24] It was this layer of the mind, the wellspring of creativity—mysterious, primitive, more elemental and more powerful than reason—that the romantics yearned to revitalize and release.

NATURE, GOD, HISTORY

The philosophes had viewed nature as a lifeless machine—a giant clock, all of whose parts worked together in perfect precision and harmony. Nature's laws, operating with mathematical certainty, were uncovered by the methodology of science. Reflecting this viewpoint, neoclassical art theory called for artists to portray nature's inherent order. Rejecting this impersonal mechanical model, romantics reacted to nature in an emotional way, inspired and awed by its beauty, majesty, and hidden powers. In *Childe Harold's Pilgrimage*, Lord Byron (1788–1824) wrote:

> Are not the mountains, waves, and skies a part
> Of me and of my soul, as I of them?

Is not the love of these deep in my heart
With a pure passion?[25]

Wordsworth immortalized these same feelings:

My heart leaps up when I behold
    A rainbow in the sky;
So was it when my life began;
So is it now I am a man. . . .[26]

To the romantics, nature was alive and suffused with God's presence;
one sought to enter into communion with God's creation. Thus, German artist Otto Runge declared in unmistakably romantic tones:

When the sky above me teems with innumerable stars, the wind blows
through the vastness of space, the wave breaks in the immense night;
when above the forest the reddish morning light appears and the sun
begins to illuminate the world, the mist rises in the valley and I throw
myself in grass sparkling with dew, every blade and stalk of grass teems
with life, the earth awakes and stirs beneath me, and everything harmonizes in one great chord; then my soul rejoices and soars in the immeasurable space around me, there is no high or low, no time, no beginning and no end. I hear and feel the living breath of God who holds and
supports the world, in whom everything lives and acts: this is our highest feeling—God![27]

Nature stimulated the creative energies of the imagination, and it
taught human beings a higher form of knowledge. As Wordsworth expressed it,

Books! 'tis a dull and endless strife:
Come, hear the woodland linnet,
How sweet his music! on my life,
There's more wisdom in it.
. . . .
One impulse from a vernal wood
May teach you more of man
Of moral evil and of good
Than all the sages can.
. . . .
Enough of Science and of Art;
Close up those barren leaves;
Come forth, and bring with you a heart
That watches and receives.[28]

Interaction with nature also fostered self-discovery. Wordsworth saw
in nature

The anchor of my purest thoughts, the nurse,
The guide, the guardian of my heart, and soul
Of all my moral being.[29]

For the romantics, nature did not consist of mechanical parts but of trees, lakes, mountains, clouds, and stars, which filled "The mind . . . With lofty thoughts."[30] One experienced nature in a personal and emotional way. Not the mathematician's logic but the poet's imagination unlocked nature's most important secrets. In perhaps the most impassioned application of this principle, English romantics decried their country's drab factories—the "dark satanic mills" that polluted streams, blackened towns with grime and soot, separated people from natural beauty, and deprived life of its joy.

The philosophes had seen God as a great watchmaker—a detached observer of a self-operating mechanical universe—and they tried to reduce religion to a series of scientific propositions. Many romantics, on the other hand, deplored the decline of Christianity. Christian moral commands, compassionate and just, elevated human behavior to a higher level; the cathedrals and ceremonies, poetic and mysterious, satisfied the esthetic impulse. "The Man who never in his Mind & Thoughts travel'd to Heaven Is No Artist,"[31] wrote Blake. In *Genius of Christianity* (1802), François René de Chateaubriand (1768–1848), a French Catholic writer, stressed the interconnection between Christianity and artistic creativity: both aspired to contemplate the infinite.

The romantics condemned the philosophes for undermining Christianity by subjecting its dogmas to reason's critical scrutiny. Regarding God as a spiritual force that enriched life, they recoiled with anger at the philosophes' relegation of God to the role of a watchmaker, a remote being, who, after setting the universe in motion, remains aloof from his creation. Thus, Coleridge condemned "a doctrine which degrades the Deity into a bland hypothesis, and that the hypothesis of a clockwork-maker . . . : a godless nature, and a natureless, abstract God . . . the Sunday name of gravitation."[32] For the romantics, religion was not science and syllogism but a passionate and authentic expression of human nature. Faith, they said, did not derive from the mind's acceptance of dogma but from an awareness of God's presence in nature and the human heart. The deeper we retreat into ourselves, the closer we get to the fount of faith. The romantics' call to acknowledge and cultivate the spiritual side of human nature accorded with their goal of restoring to wholeness a personality fragmented by an excessive stress on the intellect.

The philosophes had viewed the Middle Ages as an era of darkness, superstition, and fanaticism and regarded surviving medieval institutions and traditions as barriers to progress. The romantics, on the other hand, revered the Middle ages. The years of the French Revolution and Napoleon and the breakdown of political equilibrium had produced a sense of foreboding about the future. Some sought spiritual security by looking back to the Middle Ages, when Europe was united by a single faith. Then, said the romantics, no rationalist's blade dissected and slashed Christian mysteries; no wild-eyed revolutionaries tore apart the fabric of society. To the romantic imagination, the Middle Ages abounded with heroic and chivalrous deeds, noble sentiments, and social harmony.

The leading Protestant thinker of the Age of Romanticism was Friedrich Schleiermacher (1768–1834), who is called the "father of modern theology." Schleiermacher did not deem it a weighty matter that some details of the Gospel story are historically inaccurate. It is much more important, he said, to penetrate beneath the dogma and attain a spiritual feeling. True religion is not dogma but an intuitive piety; originating in our innermost being, it makes us aware that we have a relationship with God. Our own religious consciousness and experience of the divine are crucial to our humanity; without it the human spirit is diminished. This spiritual component of our human nature must be acknowledged and cultivated, along with our esthetic and moral capacities. Thus, it is the task of theologians to rediscover the faith in Christ as redeemer and mediator between the individual and God that had inspired the first Christians and was the source of Christian dogma.

The romantics and the philosophes held differing conceptions of history. For the philosophes, history served a didactic purpose by providing examples of human folly. Such knowledge assisted people in preparing for a better future, and for that reason alone, history should be studied. To the romantics, a historical period, like an individual, was a unique entity with its own soul; it could not be described in terms of universal principles. They wanted the historian to portray and to analyze the variety of nations, traditions, and institutions that constituted the historical experience. The romantics' feeling for the uniqueness of phenomena—their appreciation of cultural differences—and their command to study the specific details of history and culture and to consider them within the context of their times are also the foundation of modern historical scholarship.

Searching for universal principles, the philosophes had dismissed folk traditions as peasant superstitions and impediments to knowledge and progress. By contrast the romantics, rebelling against the standardization of culture, saw native languages, myths, songs, and legends as the unique creation of a people and the deepest expression of national feeling—the wellspring of poetry and art, the spiritual source of a people's cultural vitality and creativity; these ancient traditions also enabled individuals to find their identity within the context of a historical community. For these reasons, romantics examined a people's earliest cultural expressions with awe and reverence, an activity that was instrumental in shaping modern nationalism.

THE IMPACT OF
THE ROMANTIC MOVEMENT

The romantic revolt against the Enlightenment had an important and enduring impact on European history. By focusing on the creative capacities inherent in the emotions—intuition, instinct, passion, spontaneity, empathy, and compassion—the romantics shed light on a side of human nature that the philosophes had often overlooked or undervalued. By encouraging freedom of expression and diversity in art, music, and literature, they greatly enriched European cultural life. Future artists, writers, and musicians would proceed along the path opened by the romantics. Modern art, for example, owes much to the Romantic Movement's emphasis on the legitimacy of human feeling and its exploration of the hidden world of dreams and fantasies. By recognizing the distinctive qualities of historical periods, peoples, and cultures, the romantics helped create the modern historical outlook. By valuing the nation's past, romanticism contributed to modern nationalism and conservatism.

The romantics' emphasis on feelings sometimes found expression in humanitarian movements that fought slavery, child labor, and poverty. In "Song to the Men of England," Percy Bysshe Shelley (1792–1822) protested against the exploitation of the poor.

> Men of England, wherefore plough
> For the Lords who lay ye low?
> Wherefore weave with toil and care
> The rich robes your tyrants wear?
>
> Wherefore feed, and clothe, and save,
> From the cradle to the grave,
> Those ungrateful drones who would
> Drain your sweat—nay, drink your blood?[33]

Romantics were among the first to attack the emerging industrial capitalism for subordinating individuals to the requirements of the industrial process and treating them as mere things.

But there was a potentially dangerous side to the Romantic Movement, and it serves as background to the extreme nationalism of the twentieth century. As Ernst Cassirer points out, the romantics "never meant to politicize but to 'poeticize' the world,"[34] and their deep respect for human individuality and national diversity was not compatible with Hitler's racial nationalism. However, by waging their attack on reason with excessive zeal, the romantics undermined respect for the rational tradition of the Enlightenment and thus set up a precondition for the rise and triumph of fascist movements. Although their intention was cultural and not political, by idealizing the past and glorifying ancient folkways, legends, native soil, and native language, the romantics introduced a highly charged nonrational component into political life. In the generations to come, romanticism, particularly in Germany, fused with political nationalism to produce, says Horst von Maltitz, "a general climate of inexact thinking, an intellectual . . . dreamworld and an emotional approach to problems of political action to which sober reasoning should have been applied."[35]

The philosophes would have regarded the romantics' veneration of a people's history and traditions and their search for a nation's soul in an archaic culture as barbarous—a regression to superstition and the triumph of myth over philosophy. Indeed, when transferred to the realm of politics, the romantics' idealization of the past and fascination for inherited national myths as the source of a higher wisdom led to a way of thinking about history and the national community that rested more on feeling than on reason. In the process, people became committed to nationalist and political ideas that were fraught with danger. Thus, in 1937, Alfred Baeumler, a German professor and Nazi enthusiast, unfavorably compared Enlightenment individualism with the romantics' quest for the folk community. The Enlightenment, he said, viewed man "as a wholly individual entity . . . a fictionalized person responsible only to himself. In contrast, romanticism saw man again in the light of his natural and historical ties. Romanticism opened our eyes to the night, the past, our ancestors, . . . to the mythos and the Volk." [36]

This glorification of myth and the folk community constitutes a link, however unintended, between romanticism and the extreme nationalism that culminated in the world wars of the twentieth century.

BACKGROUND TO GERMAN IDEALISM: THE CHALLENGE POSED BY HUME'S SKEPTICISM

Romantics held that feelings are the path to truth. This stress on the inner person also found expression in the school of German philosophy called idealism. Romantics valued philosophical idealism, for it seemed to support their view that the creative imagination, as expressed in poetry and art, is the formative force in comprehending truth. Idealists gave primacy to spirit over matter and explained the world in spiritual terms. It is the activity of human consciousness that determines the form of the physical world. A higher reality, a world of ultimate Truth, does exist; it is something spiritual and is reached through our own inner nature, our spiritual self. German idealism arose in part as a response to the challenge posed by David Hume, the great British empiricist and skeptic.

Enlightenment thinkers believed that the physics and astronomy epitomized by Newton provided the kind of certainty that other forms of inquiry, notably theology, could not. However, in his *Treatise of Human Nature* (1739–40) and *Enquiry Concerning Human Understanding* (1748), Hume cast doubt on the view that scientific certainty was possible. As discussed in Chapter 5, Hume demolished the religious argument for miracles and the deist argument for a Creator; he also called into question the very notion of scientific law.

Science rests on the conviction that regularities observed in the past and the present will be repeated in the future—that there exists an objective reality, which rational creatures can comprehend. Hume, however, argued that science cannot demonstrate a *necessary connection* between cause and effect. Because we repeatedly experience a burning sensation when our fingers have contact with a flame, we assume a cause and effect relationship. This is unwarranted, says Hume. All we can acknowledge is that there is a constant conjunction between the flame and the burning sensation. It is merely habit and the mind's capacity to make associations that lead us to link events in a cause and effect relationship. According to Hume, a thoroughgoing empiricist, sense perception is the only legitimate source of knowledge, and our sense experiences can never prove a necessary connection between what we customarily perceive as cause and effect. We can only have impressions of happenings, not of causation or of links between happenings. We can see things happening, but we cannot see why they happen. Experience tells us only what happens at a particular moment; it cannot tell us with certainty that the same combination of events will be repeated in the future. Based on past experience, the mind expects the flame to burn, but we cannot prove that there is a law at work in nature guaranteeing that a specific cause will produce a specific effect. What we mean by cause and effect is simply something that the mind, through habit, imposes on our sense perceptions. For practical purposes we can say that two events are in association with each other, but we cannot conclude with certainty that the second was caused by the first, that natural law is operating within the physical universe.

It is one thing to argue, as Hume did, that we cannot prove God's existence or the immortality of the soul. True believers could always turn to faith as a sufficient basis for belief; moreover, in an age of growing secularism, many thinkers were giving less thought to God and an afterlife. But it is another matter to suggest that scientific knowledge is not unqualifiedly certain, that it is habit and not necessity that leads us to conclude that the sun will rise tomorrow. Such a radical empiricism undermines the very foundations of science so revered by progressive thinkers.

IMMANUEL KANT

In the *Critique of Pure Reason* (1781), Immanuel Kant (1724–1804), the great German philosopher and proponent of Newtonianism and the scientific method, undertook the challenge of rescuing reason and science from Hume's skepticism. In doing so he advanced a new theory of epistemology, which marks a major turning point in the history of philosophy.

Rescuing Scientific Validity

Kant rejected Hume's (and Locke's) underlying premise that all knowledge derives from sense experience, which imprints impressions on the mind. The mind, said Kant, is not a *tabula rasa*, a blank slate that passively receives sense impressions, but an active instrument that structures, organizes, and interprets the multiplicity of sensations that it receives. The mind can coordinate a chaotic stream of sensations because it contains its own inherent logic; it is equipped with several categories of understanding, including, space, time, and cause and effect. These categories are a priori and universal—that is they are necessary constituents of all human minds and they exist independently of and prior to experience.

Kant agreed with Hume that from experience alone we cannot conclude that a necessary link—which we customarily call cause and effect—exists between two experiences. However, he rejected Hume's contention that mere habit leads us to conclude that a necessary connection exists between event A and event B. For Kant, cause and effect has an objective existence as an a priori component of human consciousness. Because of the way our mind is constituted, we presuppose a relationship of cause and effect in all our experiences with the objects of this world. The mind does not treat the physical world in an arbitrary or random way but imposes structure and order on our sense experiences. Cause and effect and the other categories of the mind permit us to attribute certainty to scientific knowledge. This cognitive form that we impose on nature permits us to ascribe to it an objective order: we have not had an experience in which the law of causality was violated, and we cannot conceive of a future experience where this will occur.

The physical world must possess certain definite characteristics because these characteristics conform to the categories of the mind. The object, said Kant, must "accommodate itself to the subject." We see nature in a certain way because of the mental apparatus that we bring to it. The mind is a lawgiver; its operative concepts of cause and effect, space, time, unity, totality, necessity, limitation, and so forth give coherence and law to the raw materials of sense experience. The mind does not derive the laws of nature from the physical world. Indeed, it is just the reverse: the mind imposes its own laws on nature—on the raw impressions received by the senses—giving the physical world form, structure, and order. Kant rescued science from Hume's assault— the laws of science are universally valid. But in the process, Kant made scientific law dependent on the mind and its a priori categories.

By holding that objects must conform to the rules of the human mind, that it is the knowing subject that creates order within nature, Kant gave primacy to the knower rather than to the objects of knowledge. He saw the mind as an active agent, not a passive receptacle for sensations. This new relationship between subject and object, which Kant considered as revolutionary for philosophy as the Copernican theory had been for astronomy, gave unprecedented importance to the mind's power—to the active and creative knower—as T. Z. Lavine explains:

> Here we have the most startling and influential significance of the new turn which Kant gave to philosophy. It is the turn from the external world of independent nature to the inner world of the activity and powers of the mind as the key to what we experience and what we know. . . . After Kant, and under his influence, whatever is experienced or known will be shown in part to be due to the mind itself, to the concepts by which the mind understands things. . . . [T]he Kantian turn in philosophy, in which the object is always in some degree the creation of the subject . . . opened wholly new horizons for philosophy, for the sciences, and the humanities.[37]

Rescuing Christianity and Morality

Refuting Hume's skepticism in order to justify scientific law was one concern of Kant; another was to preserve the validity of Christianity and the certainty of morality. This he attempted in *The Critique of Practical Reason* (1788). In applying reason to religion, several eighteenth-century thinkers had concluded that crucial Christian teachings—the resurrection, miracles, immortality of the soul, even God's existence—could not be rationally demonstrated. To preserve religious faith and universal morality, Kant had to place limitations on the scientific method. He had to show that certain moral and religious truths lay beyond the realm of experience and science. These truths precede our experiences and do not depend on them for certainty.

According to Kant, we cannot know ultimate reality. Our knowledge is limited to the phenomenal world, the realm of natural occurrences. We can only know things that we experience, that is, things as they appear to us through the active intervention of the mind's categories. We can have no knowledge of a thing-in-itself, that is of an object's ultimate or real nature, its nature as it is independently of the way we experience it, apart from the way our senses receive it. The human mind can only acquire knowledge of that part of reality that is revealed through sense experience. We can say nothing about the sun's true nature; we can only describe the way the sun appears to us—that is, our impression of the sun formed by the mind's ordering of our sense experiences with it. Thus, at the same time that Kant reaffirmed the validity of scientific law, he also limited the range of science and reason.

Science deals with the world of appearances, of sense experience, and not with ultimate reality—this is a fundamental principle of Kant's philosophy. Since the categories of the mind can never reach beyond the objects of experience—and by their very nature some phases of reality cannot be apprehended by the senses—a science that grasps total reality is impossible. Thus, on the basis of our experiences with the phenomenal world, says Kant, we cannot prove that the individual has an immortal soul and free will, that there are invariable moral laws, that there was a creation, or that God exists. Nor, argued Kant, can we derive these essential Christian beliefs from speculative thought; for example, all the arguments offered by rational theology to prove God's existence are easily refuted.

Nevertheless, says Kant, there does exist an unquestionable basis for religious faith and moral norms: the moral law in our hearts. Human beings are not only rational but also moral beings. Like Rousseau, Kant held that our inner voice, the conscience, is the source of morality; it tells us what is right and commands us to do our duty. It leads us to act as if God were observing and judging us. For Kant, in effect, God reveals himself in the human conscience. The presence of such a moral regulator justifies for Kant the belief in God, universal moral standards, free will, and an afterlife—the belief in the existence of a higher reality beyond experienced phenomena, which he called the noumenal world. Thus, the furthest reaches of reality, more ultimate than what we attain through experience, may be revealed not through the senses, but nonsensuously, through moral experience. God must exist and the soul must be immortal because morality demands it. Theoretical reason cannot give us proof of God's existence, but we do have a moral proof for God. It is the moral conscience and not speculative theology that enables us with certainty to know that God exists.

Kant set forth the categorical imperative that remains a crucial principle in moral philosophy. He asserted that when confronted with a moral choice people should ask themselves: "Can you will that your maxim should also be a general law?"[38] By this he meant that people should ponder whether they would want the moral principle underlying their action to be elevated to a universal law that would govern others in similar circumstances. If their conclusion were no, it should not, then the maxim should be rejected and the action avoided. A corollary of this categorical imperative is that people should be treated as ends, not as means: we should at all times respect a person's humanity and one's right to make moral decisions based on one's own conscience.

Kant's moral philosophy is founded on the assumption that there are universal and rational norms of morality and that each individual has the capacity to discover them through his or her conscience. Conscience is the portal to the noumenal world: it reveals to us the universal law and commands that we do our duty and obey it. A person cannot be free if he or she is coerced from without or is governed by spontaneous and unruly passions. Individuals are free when their will is autonomous, when with full awareness and through a sense of duty, they adhere to the moral law.

G.W.F. HEGEL

Kant had insisted that knowledge of what lies beyond the phenomena—knowledge of ultimate or absolute reality itself—is beyond the mind's reach and is forever denied us. Georg Wilhelm Friedrich Hegel (1770–1831) another German philosopher, could not accept this. He constructed an all-embracing metaphysical system that attempted to explain reality, to uncover the fundamental nature and meaning of the

G.W.F. Hegel *(The Bettmann Archive)*

universe and of human history. In the process, he synthesized the leading currents of thought of his day: the rationalism of the Enlightenment, romanticism, and Kantian philosophy.

Hegel inherited from the philosophes a respect for reason and the conviction that the universe is intelligible—that the human intellect can make sense out of nature and the human experience. The romantics taught him to appreciate the wide diversity of human experience and to search for truth in the varieties of cultural life and history rather than in an unchanging natural order. From the romantics, he learned to appreciate the importance of desire and passion in motivating human behavior. Like the romantics, Hegel held that the scientific method provided only a partial and limited view of reality. From the romantics, Hegel also acquired the idea that we should aspire to see things wholly, as an organic unity of interdependent parts, rather than as separate atoms in isolation. He shared their conviction that the infinite—the full meaning of human existence—finds expression in the finite world.

Adopting Kant's notion that the mind imposes its categories on the world, Hegel emphasized the importance of the thinking subject in the quest for truth. However, Kant held that we can have knowledge only of how a thing appears to us, not of the thing-in-itself. Hegel, in contrast, maintained that ultimate reality is knowable to the human mind: the mind can comprehend the conceptual truths underlying all existence; it can grasp the essential meaning of human experience.

The same thought may be expressed in another way. Kant had asserted the essential idealist position that it is the knowing subject that organizes our experiences of the phenomenal world. Hegel took a giant step beyond that by contending that there exists a universal Mind—Absolute Spirit—which differentiates itself in the minds of thinking individuals. Mind, the thing-in-itself, is a universal agent—the soul of the human species—whose nature can be apprehended through thought.

Reason and History

Absolute Spirit is truth in its totality and wholeness. Plato believed that true reality, the Idea, was static, timeless, and unchanging and existed in a higher superterrestrial world, apart from the transitory world of phenomena that we observe every day. Hegel, however, held that ultimate reality was characterized by change and development and was to be found in the concrete world of human experience; in cultural life, institutions, and political conflicts, the Idea or Spirit becomes actualized. To discover ultimate truth, the human mind does not flee from the objects of this world to a higher reality; rather it aspires to a deeper understanding of existing things. Every element of human existence contains a fundamental and intelligible structure, a conceptual truth that is knowable to the human mind. It is the task of philosophy, says Hegel, to synthesize these manifestations of Absolute Spirit, these partial insights into ultimate reality, and to grasp truth in its unity and totality.

Because Hegel viewed Absolute Spirit not as fixed and static but as evolving and developing, history plays a central role in his philosophical system. In the arena of world history, truth unfolds and makes itself known to the human mind. History, for Hegel, is the development of Spirit in time. Stated another way, history may be seen as the development and actualization of an immanent God. Like the romantics, Hegel said that each historical period has a distinctive spirit or character that separates it from every preceding age and enables us to see it as an organic whole. The art, science, philosophy, religion, politics, and leading events are so interconnected that the period may be said to possess an organic unity, a historical coherence. Thus, we may speak of the spirit of the Renaissance, for a secular and humanist outlook pervaded the cultural life of the times; or of the Age of Enlightenment, for all phases of eighteenth-century culture and thought gave expression to the mechanical model of the universe developed by Newton. But since for Hegel history is a dynamic process, a particular historical period must also be viewed temporally, that is, in relationship to what preceded and followed it. Every age inherits elements from the past and contains in its womb the seeds of the future. Historians must rise above merely recording the events of an age; they must distinguish between those happenings, as well as the cultural expressions that are merely the sterile, decaying remnants of a dying period, and the dynamic forces that are giving rise to the future.

Does history contain an overarching meaning? Are past, present, and future linked together by something more profound, more unifying than random chance? The belief that history proceeds according to a purposeful plan derives ultimately from the Judeo-Christian tradition. The ancient Hebrews saw history as a spiritual encounter between people and God. God made his will known through historical events, and in the future God will establish on earth a great age of peace, prosperity, and happiness. For Christians, the historical process would culminate with the second coming of Christ.

Hegel believed that world history reveals a rational process; an internal principle of order underlies historical change. "Reason is the Sovereign of the World . . . the history of the world, therefore, presents us with a rational process,"[39] he declared. There is a purpose and an end to history: the unfolding of Absolute Spirit. In the course of history, an immanent Spirit manifests itself; gradually, progressively, and nonrepetitively, it actualizes itself, becoming itself fully, realizing its ultimate goal, which is self-knowledge. Nations and exceptional human beings, "World-Historical" individuals—such as Alexander, Caesar, or Napoleon—are the mediums through which Spirit realizes its potentiality, achieves self-consciousness.

Hegel's philosophy of history is a modern form of theodicy that gives meaning, purpose and direction to historical events. Where is history taking us? What is its ultimate meaning? For Hegel, history is humanity's progress from lesser to greater freedom:

> . . . the final cause of the World at large, we allege to be the consciousness of its own freedom on the part of Spirit, and ipso facto, the reality of that freedom. . . . This result it is, at which the process of the World's History has been continually aiming; and to which the sacrifices . . . through the long . . . ages have been offered. . . . [T]he idea of freedom . . . [is] the nature of Spirit, and the absolute goal of History.[40]

Hegel said that Spirit manifests itself in history through a dialectical tension between two opposing ideas or forces; the struggle between one force (thesis) and its adversary (antithesis) is evident in all spheres of human activity. This clash of opposites gains in intensity and ends in a resolution that unifies both opposing ideas. Thought and history then enter a new and higher stage, that of synthesis, which, by absorbing the truths within both the thesis and the antithesis, achieves a higher level of truth and a higher stage of history. Soon this synthesis itself becomes another thesis, resulting in another conflict between another set of opposing forces; this conflict, too, is resolved by a still higher synthesis. Thus, the dynamic struggle between thesis and antithesis—sometimes expressed in revolutions and war, sometimes in art, religion, and philosophy—and its resolution into a synthesis accounts for movement in history. Or, in Hegelian language, Spirit is closer to realization—its rational structure is progressing from potentiality to actuality. The dialectic is the march of Spirit through human affairs. Since Hegel held that freedom is the essence of Spirit, it is through history that human beings progress toward consciousness of their own freedom. They become aware of their own self-determination, their ability to regulate their lives rationally according to their own consciousness. This applies not only to individuals but to humanity at large. With experience and maturity, a person acquires wisdom and an awareness of his or her innate potential. So too does collective humanity, as it moves progressively from epoch to epoch, gain insight into the meaning and purpose of its nature and development.

Hegel traced the evolution of freedom, which he considered the goal of world history. In the ancient oriental world, only one person was free, the despotic ruler. The orientals did not attain the knowledge that "Man *as such* is free."[41] The awareness of freedom first arose among the Greeks. However, because "their splendid liberty was implicated with the institution of slavery,"[42] the Greeks and likewise the Romans "knew only that *some* are free—not man as such." The Germanic peoples "under the influence of Christianity were the first to attain the consciousness that man, as man, is free,"[43] that the human personality has infinite value. It would take centuries for this principle of subjective freedom, originating first in early Christianity and culminating in the Lutheran Reformation, to be applied to political relations.

Political Thought

But for individual freedom to be realized, says Hegel, social and political institutions must be rationally determined and organized—that is, the will of the individual must be harmonized with the needs of the community. Freedom is not a matter of securing abstract natural rights for the individual, as was the goal of the French Revolution. Rather, true freedom is attained only within the social group. Thus, in Hegel's view, human beings discover their essential character, their moral and spiritual potential, only as citizens of a cohesive political community—a view that goes back to the city-states of ancient Greece, which Hegel admired.

Liberals saw the state as a necessary arrangement that provided a secure environment for individuals to pursue their own interests. For Hegel, the state fulfilled a loftier function: it was an ethical idea that made possible the individual's full development as a human being. Like Rousseau, Hegel sought to bring the individual's freedom to choose into harmony with the needs of society as a whole. Hegel linked freedom to obedience to the state's commands. In the state's laws and institutions, which are manifestations of reason, the objectivization of Spirit, the individual finds a basis for rationally determining his own life. In this way, the private interests of citizens become one with the common interests of the community. For Hegel, reason realizes itself in the state, the highest form of human association. The state joins isolated individuals together into a community and substitutes a rule of justice for the rule of instincts. It permits individuals to live ethical lives and to develop their human potential. An individual cannot achieve these goals in isolation.

The rationally organized community favored by Hegel was a constitutional monarchy. But he also reached the perplexing conclusion that the pinnacle of the consciousness of freedom was to be found in the Germany of his day. Germans recognized the value of monarchical leadership, he said, but also assimilated the Christian principle of the individual's infinite worth.

In deeming the Prussian state—which had an autocratic king, no constitution, no popularly elected parliament, and government-imposed censorship—to be the summit of freedom, the goal for which history had been striving, Hegel has been accused of exalting the state and subordinating the individual to it. For Hegel, the national state was the supreme achievement of Absolute Spirit.

> It must . . . be understood that all the worth which the human being possesses—all spiritual reality, he possesses only through the State. . . . Thus only is he fully conscious; thus only is he a partaker of morality— of a just and moral social and political life. For Truth is the unity of the universal . . . and the Universal is to be found in the State, in its laws, its universal and rational arrangements. The state is the Divine Idea as it exists on Earth.[44]

Hegel's apotheosis of the state, his liberal critics have said, threatens individual liberty.

Several other ideas advanced by Hegel distressed nineteenth-century liberals and their twentieth-century heirs. Hegel held that the state does not acknowledge abstract rules of good or bad but is bound only by the duty of self-preservation. He justified war as something fundamentally moral and necessary, the means by which Spirit unfolds in history. He also extolled power. Hegel claimed that in every historical epoch the World-Spirit hands over to a particular people a mission of world-historical importance. Against this nation chosen to be the agent of the World-Spirit, the spirits of other nations are without rights. This romantic and mystical conception, much abused by German nationalists to justify conquest, has led some commentators to regard Hegel as a spiritual precursor of fascist totalitarianism.

Defenders of Hegel point out that Nazi theorists made very little use of his works, that Hegel was a very complex thinker and abstruse writer who is easily misread and misinterpreted, and that a careful reading of his works within the context of his entire philosophical system shows trends in his thought that are inimical to fascism. For example, Hegel endorsed no biological racism and rejected anti-Semitism. His criticism of absolute monarchy for draining the souls of its subjects cannot be reconciled with the Fuehrer principle, which justified Hitler's dictatorial power. His recognition of the need and value of social and cultural diversity and his opposition to subordinating religion, art, and philosophy to the state flies in the face of the totalitarian state's goal of creating an organic unity by forcibly effacing differences.

Hegel attempted to reconcile tradition and modernity—to resolve the tensions in European political life in the wake of the upheavals of the French Revolution. There is a strong conservative bent to his political thought. At first he supported the French Revolution for attempting to make political life accord with rational principles. But then he denounced the reformers for their recklessness, their overzealous commitment to abstractions about the individual. In their frenzy to restructure French society on the basis of abstract thought, said Hegel, the reformers destroyed the ancient French institutions of monarchy and aristocracy and through terror achieved the "freedom of the void." Like other conservatives (see Chapter 7), Hegel held that a constitution is not something made by the human intellect but grows out of a people's historical experience. German conservatives employed Hegel's idea that existing institutions have a rational legitimacy to support their opposition to rapid change. Existing reality, even if it appears cruel and hateful, is the actualization of Universal Divine Reason. Therefore, it is inherently necessary and rational; it should not be radically altered but should be permitted to fulfill itself.

YOUNG HEGELIANS

Hegel's central idea that history is a necessary progression, that it contains an inherent meaning and purpose, had a profound impact on nineteenth-century thought. Hegel's political and religious thought also had a wide influence.

Political Radicalism

Some of Hegel's followers, known as Young Hegelians or Left Hegelians, interpreted Hegel in a radical sense. (Right Hegelians saw Hegel as a defender of the conservative Prussian state.) They rejected his view that the Prussian state, or any German state, was the goal of world history, the realization of freedom. The Germany of their day, held the Young Hegelians, had not attained a harmony between the individual and society: it was not rationally organized and did not foster freedom. These Young Hegelians saw Hegel's philosophy as a justification for radically altering the world to make existing society truly rational.

The most important of the radical Young Hegelians was Karl Marx. Marx retained Hegel's overarching principles that history contains an inner logic, that it is an intelligible process, and that a dialectical struggle propels history from a lower stage to a higher stage. Marx also adopted Hegel's conviction that human beings operate within an arena of historical necessity. Marx's insistence that historical circumstances must be ripe before socialists should attempt to overthrow capitalism was an adaptation of Hegel's insight that history was a rational process moving through identifiable stages. But whereas Hegel believed that philosophy cannot change but only interpret the world, Marx, a radical revolutionary, insisted that philosophy must be transformed into action, that it could and should change the world. For Hegel, the state was a spiritual entity that overcame the self-interest running rampant in modern economic life. For Marx, the state was a product of class antagonisms, an agent of the class that wielded economic power. Applying Hegel's dialectical method, Marx concluded that a classless society, not the Prussian state, was the end of history, the condition of true freedom.

Religious Radicalism

Hegel's notion that history is the self-development of God in time was open to various criticisms and interpretations. Orthodox theologians, who saw God as perfect by nature, scorned the idea that God progressed toward self-awareness, self-realization, and self-perfection in the course of historical time. However, other theologians—Right Hegelians—regarded Hegel's philosophy as a useful instrument for reinterpreting historical Christianity in a way that would justify it to the modern world. Left Hegelians, notably David Friedrich Strauss, Ludwig Feuerbach, and Marx criticized Hegel for not going far enough in overcoming Christian faith and launched their own radical critique of Christianity.

David Friedrich Strauss   David Friedrich Strauss (1808–1874) came under the influence of Hegel's philosophy at the University of Berlin. In his *Life of Jesus* (1835–36), Strauss examined the Gospels in a critical spirit, attempting to discern what was historically valid. He maintained that the New Testament was replete with myths, unconscious inventions that expressed the hopes and longings of Jesus' early followers. For centuries, said Strauss, Christians regarded the Gospels' accounts of Jesus' birth, life, and death as objective facts, failing to recognize their mythical content. The Gospels do not provide historical support for Christian assertions about Jesus' uniqueness and divinity.

Jesus' Jewish contemporaries, the first Christians, had no critical-historical consciousness, said Strauss. Consequently, the Gospel writers embellished Jesus' life and words with their own messianic longings and with inherited legends. For example, said Strauss, the miracles purported to be performed by Jesus spring from the rich folklore of the ancient Mediterranean world. The Gospels contain much mythical-religious content, he said, but little history. Prior to the publication of Strauss's work, most students of religion had viewed the Gospels as a reliable historical source. But Strauss argued that the Jesus of faith is not the same as the Jesus of history. The belief that history, as presented in the Gospels, provided a firm basis for belief in Christian teachings had been permanently undermined.

In ensuing generations, scholars would undertake the challenge raised by Strauss and engage in a quest for the historical Jesus, employing the critical historical approach that he had suggested. They sought to place Jesus and early Christianity within the cultural matrix of the ancient world: they related Jesus' teachings to developments within the Judaism of his day; investigated the relationship between early Christian thought and practices and the mystery religions of the ancient Mediterranean world; and explored the influence of Greek thought on Christian dogma.

Ludwig Feuerbach   Ludwig Feuerbach (1804–1872), a philosopher and theologian, criticized Hegel, and indeed all traditional philosophy, for

harboring a religious world-view. Hegel's philosopy of Spirit, he declared "is the last grandiose attempt to restore lost, ruined, Christianity with the aid of philosophy. . . . he who does not renounce the philosophy of Hegel does not renounce theology."[45] In *Essence of
Christianity* (1841), Feuerbach argued that the starting point of philosophy should be the human being and the material world, not God. For
Feuerbach, nothing existed outside nature and human beings. "Religion is the dream of the human mind,"[46] he said, and God was a human
creation, a product of human feelings and wishes. Human beings believe in the divine because they seek assistance from it in life and fear
death. He called theology a "web of contradictions and illusions."[47]
The first principle of his philosophy, he said, was that man is a sensible
creature, "a real being."

Feuerbach treated religion as an expression of mythical thinking and
God as an unconscious projection of human hopes, fears, and self-
doubts. Christianity diminishes human beings in order to affirm God,
said Feuerbach; Christians deny their own worth and goodness that
they might ascribe all value to God. The human being, weak and self-
hating,

> sets God before him as the antithesis of himself. . . . God is the infinite,
> man the finite being; God is perfect, man imperfect; God eternal, man
> temporal; God almighty, man weak; God holy, man sinful. God and
> man are extremes: God is the absolutely positive, the sum of all realities;
> man the absolutely negative. . . .
>
> But in religion man contemplates his own latent nature. Hence it
> must be shown that this antithesis, this differencing of God and man,
> with which religion begins, is a differencing of man with his own na-
> ture.[48]

Religion, said Feuerbach, is a form of self-alienation, for human
beings diminish their humanity when they invest their finest qualities
in a nonexistent God and reserve their worst qualities for themselves.
God represents the externalization of an idealized human being. When
individuals measure themselves against this God-ideal, they see only
miserable, contemptible, and worthless creatures. "To enrich God,
man must become poor; that God may be all, man must become nothing. . . . [M]an is wicked, corrupt, incapable of good; but, on the other
hand, God is only good—the Good Being."[49]

Feuerbach naturalized Hegel's idea of alienation. For Hegel, Spirit
seeks to overcome its estrangement from itself by actualizing its potential over the course of historical time. Feuerbach saw alienation as
a human, not a metaphysical, problem. Man's estrangement from himself, a product of his religious illusions, is the existential condition of
human life. Alienation results when human beings project a portion of

their being onto God, an illusory being. Hegel confused and mystified the issue, said Feuerbach, when he made imaginary Spirit, and not man, the focal point of alienation. Humanity liberates itself when it rejects God's existence and religion's claims to truth. Feuerbach said that it was his aim to change the friends of God into friends of human beings and the seekers of heaven into active, productive, and life-affirming individuals.

Karl Marx Feuerbach's approach to religion strengthened a naturalist-humanist strand of German philosophy, which had emerged in reaction to Hegelian idealism. Marx's thoroughgoing materialism was also representative of this new orientation. Marx praised Feuerbach for distinguishing between the real world of human beings and Hegel's imaginary world of Spirit and for seeing human alienation as a crucial feature of human existence. Like Feuerbach, Marx stressed the illusory character of religion and attacked it for contributing to human alienation. Religion, said Marx, was an expression of an unrewarding and unfulfilled existence. For Marx, religion was also a profoundly reactionary force. Ideologists of the ruling class used it to legitimatize economic and social privilege and to protect the bourgeois state from revolution. The promise of immortality lured workers away from their historic responsibility of changing the social order.

But in two important ways Marx went beyond Feuerbach. First, Feuerbach sought to liberate human beings from alienation caused by religion. For Marx, the problem of alienation was much broader; it covered economic, political, and social, as well as religious, factors and its causes were rooted in the relations of production and class conflicts. Second, Feuerbach believed that by seeing religion in its true light, people could liberate themselves from alienation. For Marx, humanity's liberation required more than knowledge; it entailed a radical reconstruction of society and this necessitated a working-class revolution as a preliminary condition.

NOTES

1. Johann Wolfgang von Goethe, *Faust*, trans. Bayard Quincy Morgan (Indianapolis: Library of Liberal Arts, 1954), pp. 13–14.

2. Jean Jacques Rousseau, *Confessions* (New York: Modern Library, 1950), p. 2.

3. Quoted in H. G. Schenk, *The Mind of the European Romantics* (Garden City, N.Y.: Doubleday, 1969), p. 4.

4. William Blake, "Milton," bk. 2, stanzas 46 and 48, in *Poetry and Prose of William Blake*, ed. Geof-

frey Keynes (New York: Random House, 1927), p. 546.

5. William Blake, "Annotations to Sir Joshua Reynolds's Discourses," ibid., p. 1009.

6. William Wordsworth, "The Excursion," bk. 4, lines 962, 967, 968, in *The Poetical Works of William Wordsworth*, eds. E. D. Selincourt and Helen Darbishire (Oxford: Clarendon Press, 1966), I, p. 141.

7. John Keats, "Lamia," pt. 2, lines 229–237, in *The Complete Poetry and Selected Prose of John Keats*, ed. Harold Edgar Briggs (New York: Modern Library, 1951), p. 367.

8. Coleridge to Thomas Poole, March 23, 1801, in *Samuel Taylor Coleridge: Selected Letters*, ed. H. J. Jackson (Oxford: Oxford University Press, 1987), p. 89.

9. Quoted in Schenk, *The Mind of the European Romantics*, p. 5.

10. Blake, "Milton," bk. 2, stanza 48, in *Poetry and Prose of William Blake*, p. 546.

11. Goethe, *Faust*, p. 47.

12. Quoted in C. M. Bowra, *The Romantic Imagination* (Oxford: Oxford University Press, 1961), p. 286.

13. Anne L.G.N. de Staël Holstein, *Germany*, excerpted in Le Van Baumer, ed., *Main Currents of Western Thought* (New Haven: Yale University Press, 1978), p. 474.

14. William Blake, "A Vision of the Last Judgment," in *Poetry and Prose of William Blake*, p. 830.

15. Letter of Keats, November 22, 1817, in Hyder E. Rollins, ed., *The Letters of John Keats* (Cambridge, Mass.: Harvard University Press, 1958), I, 184–185.

16. Quoted in John Herman Randall, Jr., *The Career of Philosophy* (New York: Columbia University Press, 1965), II, 80.

17. Blake, "Milton," preface, in *Poetry and Prose of William Blake*, p. 464.

18. Victor Hugo, *Preface to Cromwell*, in *Hugo's Works, Dramas*, trans. and ed. I. G. Burnham (Philadelphia: George Barrie and Son, 1896), IX, 67–69.

19. A. D. Lovejoy, *The Great Chain of Being* (Cambridge: Harvard University Press, 1964), p. 293.

20. Excerpted in A. K. Thorlby, ed., *The Romantic Movement* (New York: Barnes and Noble, 1966), p. 153.

21. Quoted in Lovejoy, *The Great Chain of Being*, pp. 9–10.

22. Quoted in Hugh Honour, *Romanticism* (New York: Harper and Row, 1979), p. 16.

23. Quoted in Frederic Ewen, *Heroic Imagination* (Secaucus, N.J.: Citadel, 1984), p. 276.

24. Quoted in Ernst Cassirer, *An Essay on Man* (New York: Bantam Books, 1970), p. 178.

25. Lord Byron, *Childe Harold's Pilgrimage*, ed. Samuel C. Chew (New York: Odyssey, 1936), canto 3, stanza 75, p. 112.

26. William Wordsworth, "My Heart Leaps Up," in *The Poetical Works of William Wordsworth*, I, p. 226.

27. Quoted in Honour, *Romanticism*, p. 73.

28. William Wordsworth, "The Tables Turned," lines 9–12, 21–24, 29–32, *The Poetical Works of William Wordsworth*, IV, p. 57.

29. William Wordsworth, "Lines Composed a Few Miles Above Tintern Abbey," lines 109–111, ibid, II, p. 262.

30. Ibid., lines 126, 128.

31. William Blake, "Annotations to Sir Joshua Reynolds' Discourses," in *Poetry and Prose of William Blake*, p. 987.

32. Quoted in R. W. Harris, *Romanticism and the Social Order 1780–1830* (New York: Barnes and Noble, 1969), pp. 223–224.

33. Percy Bysshe Shelly, "Song to the Men of England," lines 1–8, in *Shelley's Complete Poetical Works*, ed. George Edward Woodberry (Boston: Houghton Mifflin, 1901), pp. 363–365.

34. Ernst Cassirer, *The Myth of the State* (New Haven: Yale University Press, 1946), p. 184.

35. Horst von Maltitz, *The Evolution of Hitler's Germany* (New York: McGraw Hill, 1973), p. 217.

36. Excerpted in George L. Mosse, ed., *Nazi Culture* (New York: Grosset and Dunlap, 1966), p. 97.

37. T. Z. Lavine, *From Socrates to Sartre: The Philosophic Quest* (New York: Boston, 1984), pp. 197–198.

38. Immanuel Kant, *Metaphysical Foundations of Morals*, in *The Philosophy of Kant*, ed. Carl J. Friedrich (New York: The Modern Library, 1949), p. 151.

39. G.W.F. Hegel, *The Philosophy of History*, trans. J. Sibree (New York: Dover, 1956), p. 9.

40. Ibid., pp. 19, 23.

41. Ibid., p. 18.

42. Ibid.

43. Ibid.

44. Ibid., p. 31

45. Quoted in Robert Tucker, *Philosophy and Myth in Karl Marx* (Cambridge: Cambridge University Press, 1972), p. 83.

46. Ludwig Feuerbach, *The Essence of Christianity*, trans. George Eliot (New York: Harper Torchbooks, 1957), p. xxxix.

47. Ibid., p. xxxvi.

48. Ibid., p. 33.

49. Ibid., pp. 26–28.

SUGGESTED READING

Avineri, Shlomo, *Hegel's Theory of the Modern State* (1972).

Bowra, C. M., *The Romantic Imagination* (1969).

Cassirer, Ernst, *The Myth of the State* (1946).

Harris, R. W., *Romanticism and the Social Order 1780–1830* (1969).

Honour, Hugh, *Romanticism* (1979).

Jones, W. T., *A History of Western Philosophy*, IV, *Kant to Witgenstein and Sartre* (1969).

Kaufmann, Walter, *Hegel: A Reinterpretation* (1965).

Kemp, John, *The Philosophy of Kant* (1968).

Korner, S., *Kant* (1955).

Lavine, T. Z., *From Socrates to Sartre: The Philosophic Quest* (1984).

Mure, G.R.G., *The Philosophy of Hegel* (1965).

Peyre, Henri, *What Is Romanticism?* (1977).

Schenk, H. G., *The Mind of the European Romantics* (1969).

Singer, Peter, *Hegel* (1983).

Solomon, Robert C., *History and Human Nature* (1979).

———, *From Hegel to Existentialism* (1987).

Wilkins, Burleigh T., *Hegel's Philosophy of History* (1974).

7

Rise of Ideologies

In 1815, the armies of France no longer marched across the Continent, and Napoleon was imprisoned on an island a thousand miles off the coast of Africa. Much of the Old Regime outside France had survived the stormy decades of the French Revolution and Napoleon. Monarchs still held the reins of political power. Aristocrats, particularly in central and eastern Europe, retained their traditional hold over the army and administration, controlled the peasantry and local government, and enjoyed tax exemptions. The traditional rulers of Europe, some of them just restored to power, were determined to protect themselves and society from future Robespierres who organized reigns of terror and Napoleons who obliterated traditional states. As defenders of the Old Order of Europe and its social arrangements, they attacked the reformist spirit of the philosophes, which had produced the Revolution. In conservatism, which championed tradition over reason, hierarchy over equality, order and authority over liberty, and the community over the individual, they found a philosophy to justify their assault on the Enlightenment and the French Revolution.

The reactionary rulers tried to to turn the clock back to the Old Regime, but the forces unleashed by the Revolution were too powerful to contain. Between 1820 and 1848, a series of revolutions rocked Europe. The principal causes were liberalism, which demanded constitutional government and the protection of the freedom and rights of the individual, and nationalism which called for the reawakening and unification of the nation and its liberation from foreign domination.

Still another force emerging in the post-Napoleonic period was socialism. Reacting to the problems produced by the Industrial Revolution, socialists called for creating a new society based on cooperation rather than on capitalist competition. A minor movement in the first half of the century, socialism in its Marxist version became a major force in the last part of the century.

Conservatism, liberalism, nationalism, and socialism were generated by the dual revolutions of the late eighteenth century—the French and the Industrial revolutions. They are termed ideologies because they are relatively coherent systems of beliefs—"social formulas" or "secular religions"—that have the capacity to unite and stir large numbers of people to political action. In some ways, ideologies came to fill the spiritual void left by a retreating Christianity and a disintegrating Old Order. Ideological commitment would gain in intensity in the late nineteenth century. In the twentieth century, a radicalized nationalism on the one hand and a radicalized socialism on the other threatened to destroy the liberal-rational tradition.

EUROPE 1815–1848: LIBERAL AND NATIONALIST REVOLUTIONS

In 1815, the Great Powers of Europe, meeting at Vienna, drew up a peace settlement awarding territory to the states that had fought Napoleon and restored to power some rulers dethroned by the French emperor. The Congress of Vienna also organized the Concert of Europe to preserve the Vienna settlement and to guard against the resurgence of the revolutionary spirit that had kept Europe in turmoil for some twenty-five years. Determined to enforce obedience to traditional authority and to smother liberal and nationalist ideals, the conservative ruling elites, particularly in central and eastern Europe, resorted to censorship, secret police, and armed force. They took their cue from Prince Klemens Metternich (1773-1859) of Austria, the pivotal figure in the period 1815 to 1848. Belonging to the old order of courts and kings, Metternich believed that domestic order and international stability depended on rule by monarchy and respect for aristocracy. He hated the new forces of nationalism and liberalism, which threatened the traditional order. He regarded liberalism as a dangerous disease carried by middle-class malcontents, who were guilty of "denying . . . the value of the past, and declaring themselves the masters of the future."[1] The misguided liberal belief that society could be reshaped according to the ideals of liberty and equality, said Metternich, had led to years of revolution, terror, and war. To restore stability and peace, the Old Order must suppress liberal ideas and quash the first signs of revolution. If the European powers did not destroy the revolutionary spirit, said Metternich, they would be devoured by it.

Metternich also feared the new spirit of nationalism. As a multinational empire, Austria was particularly vulnerable to nationalist unrest. If its ethnic minorities—Poles, Czechs, Magyars, Italians, South Slavs, and Romanians—became infected with the nationalist virus, they would shatter the Hapsburg Empire. A highly cultured, multilingual, and cosmopolitan aristocrat, Metternich considered himself the defender of European civilization. He felt that by arousing the masses and setting people against people nationalism could undermine the foundations of the European civilization, which he cherished.

Fearful of what Metternich called "the disorganized excitement which has taken possession of men's minds,"[2] conservatives in their respective countries took measures to prevent liberal and nationalist uprisings. Thus, in 1819, Metternich and representatives from leading German states met at Carlsbad and drew up several decrees calling for the dissolution of the *Burschenschaft*, a student fraternity that favored German national unity, for the imposition of strict censorship over the press, and for the dismissal of professors who disseminated liberal ideals. But repression could not hold in check the liberal and nationalist ideas aroused by the French Revolution. In the period 1820 to 1848, three separate waves of revolution swept across Europe.

In the 1820s, the Concert of Europe crushed a quasi-liberal revolution in Spain and liberal uprisings in Italy. In addition, Tsar Nicholas I subdued an uprising by liberal aristocrats who challenged tsarist autocracy. The Greeks, however, imbued with the new liberal and nationalist ideals, successfully fought for independence from the Ottoman Turks.

Between 1830 and 1832, another wave of revolutions swept over Europe. In France, a revolution led to the overthrow of the reactionary Charles X in 1830 and his replacement with a more moderate ruler, Louis Philippe; a little later, Belgium gained its independence from Holland. But Italian liberals and patriots failed to free Italy from foreign rule or to wrest reforms from autocratic princes, and the tsar's troops crushed a Polish uprising against Russian rule.

The year 1848 was decisive in the struggle for liberty and nationhood. In France, democrats overthrew Louis Philippe and established a republic. In Italy and Germany, revolutions attempting to unify each land failed, as did a bid in Hungary for independence from the Hapsburg empire. After enjoying initial successes, the revolutions in Italy and central Europe were crushed by superior might. The liberal and nationalist objectives of the revolutionaries remained largely unfulfilled, but liberal gains were not insignificant. All French men obtained the right to vote; the labor services of peasants were abolished in Austria and the German states; parliaments, albeit dominated by princes and aristocrats, were established in Prussia and other German states. In later decades, liberal reforms would become more widespread. These reforms were introduced peacefully, for the failure of the Revolutions of 1848 convinced many people, including liberals, that popular uprisings were ineffective ways of changing society. The Age of Revolution initiated by the French Revolution of 1789 had ended.

CONSERVATISM: THE VALUE OF TRADITION

To the traditional rulers of Europe—kings, aristocrats, and clergy—the French Revolution was a great evil that had inflicted a near-fatal wound on civilization. They condemned the revolutionaries for confiscating church lands, destroying the privileges of the aristocracy, executing Louis XVI, and instituting the Reign of Terror. Compounding this wickedness, said conservatives, was the fact that the Revolution gave rise to Napoleon, who deposed kings, continued the assault on the aristocracy, and sought to dominate Europe. Disgusted and frightened by revolutionary violence, terror, and warfare, the traditional rulers of Europe sought to refute the philosophes' world-view, which had spawned the Revolution. To them, natural rights, equality, the goodness of man, and perpetual progress were perverse doctrines that had produced the Jacobin "assassins." In conservatism, they found a political philosophy to counter the Enlightenment ideology and to reassert the importance of authority.

Hostility to the Enlightenment and the French Revolution

Edmund Burke's *Reflections on the French Revolution* (1790) was instrumental in shaping conservative thought. "Rarely in the history of thought has a body of ideas been as closely dependent upon a single man and a single event as modern conservatism is upon Edmund Burke and his fiery reaction to the French Revolution,"[3] observes Robert Nisbet. Burke (1729-1797), an Anglo-Irish political theorist and statesman, wanted to warn his compatriots of the dangers inherent in the ideology of the revolutionaries. Although writing in 1790, he astutely predicted

Edmund Burke *(The Bettmann Archive)*

that the Revolution would lead to terror and military dictatorship. To Burke, fanatics armed with pernicious principles—abstract ideas divorced from historical experience—had dragged France through the mire of revolution. Burke developed a coherent political philosophy that served as a counterweight to the ideology of the Enlightenment and the Revolution.

The leading conservative theorists on the Continent were Joseph de Maistre (1753-1821) and Vicomte Louis de Bonald (1754–1840). Maistre, who fled his native Piedmont in 1792 and again in 1793, after the invasion by the armies of the new French republic, was vociferous in his denunciation of the philosophes for undermining belief and authority; he called their activity an "insurrection against God." In *Reflections on the State of France* (1796) and other works, he attacked the philosophes and the French Revolution, which he blamed them for inciting. Committed to authority and order, Maistre fought any kind of political or religious liberalism. To him, the Revolution was a satanic evil, a horrible example of human depravity; all its pronouncements must be totally condemned and its roots expunged from the soil of Christian Europe.

Like Maistre, Bonald, a French émigré, detested the French Revolution, staunchly defended monarchy, and attacked the rational spirit of the Enlightenment as an enemy of faith. His Catholicism and monarchism are summarized in his famous remark: "When God wished to punish France, he took away the Bourbon from her governance."

The philosophes and the French reformers, entranced by the great discoveries in science, had believed that the human mind could also transform social institutions and ancient traditions according to rational models. Progress through reason became their faith. Dedicated to creating a new future, the revolutionaries had little respect for traditional society; they abruptly dispensed with old habits, with established authority, and with familiar ways of thought. To conservatives, who like the romantics venerated the past, this was supreme arrogance and wickedness—a "philosophic frenzy," Maistre called it. Conservatives regarded the revolutionaries as presumptuous men who recklessly severed society's links with ancient institutions and traditions and condemned venerable religious and moral beliefs as ignorance. Maistre called Voltaire the man "into whose hands hell has given all its power."[4] The philosophes and the revolutionaries envisioned the good society in some future age when reason and freedom would prevail over tyranny and superstition. Conservatives, on the other hand, saw the good society in an idealized medieval past, when the chivalric code of a Christian gentleman prevailed, religious values pervaded social and political life, and the various orders of society—clergy, nobility, commoners—bonded together into a healthy social organism in which liberty and authority were successfully balanced.

Conservatives castigated the revolutionaries for forgetting or for never knowing that the traditions and institutions they wanted to destroy did not belong solely to them. Past generations and indeed future generations had a claim to these creations of French genius. By attacking time-honored ways, the revolutionaries had deprived French society of moral leadership and opened the door to anarchy and terror. The revolutionaries, insisted the conservatives, did not comprehend that we defile the future when we reject our past. "You began ill," said Burke of the revolutionaries, "because you began by despising everything that belonged to you. . . . When ancient opinions and rules of life are taken away, the loss cannot possibly be estimated. From that moment we have no compass to govern us; nor can we know distinctly to what port we steer."[5] To Burke, the French Revolution was quite different from the Glorious Revolution of 1688, which he valued, and the American Revolution, which he had supported. These earlier revolutions, he said, were attempts to restore traditional liberties that had been violated by tyrannical governments; unlike the French Revolution, they did not try to remake society from top to bottom. Burke, who was committed to the perpetuation of traditional English ways and liberties, praised the English people for rejecting the radicalism of the French philosophes and the revolutionaries:

> ... we still bear the stamp of our forefathers. ... We are not the converts of Rousseau; we are not the disciples of Voltaire; Helvétius has made no progress amongst us. Atheists are not our preachers; madmen are not our lawgivers. We know that *we* have made no discoveries, and we think that no discoveries are to be made, in morality nor many in the great principles of government. ... We fear God; we look up with awe to kings, with ... duty to magistrates, with reverence to priests, and with respect to nobility.[6]

Conservatives did not regard human beings as good by nature. Human wickedness was not due to a faulty environment, as the philosophes had proclaimed, but was at the core of human nature, as Christianity taught. Not reason but tried and tested institutions, traditions, and beliefs held evil in check. Without these habits inherited from ancestors, said conservatives, the social order was threatened by sinful human nature. Human beings are too evil and aggressive to be free; they require the authority of a church and a state to restrain their dark and destructive instincts.

Because monarchy, aristocracy, and the church had endured for centuries, argued the conservatives, they had worth. The clergy taught proper rules of conduct; monarchs preserved order and property; aristocrats guarded against despotic kings and the tyranny of the common people. All protected and spread civilized ways. By despising and uprooting these ancient institutions, the revolutionaries had hardened the people's hearts, perverted their morals, and caused them to commit terrible outrages on each other and on society.

The philosophes and French reformers had expressed unlimited confidence in the power of the human intellect to understand and to change society. While appreciating human rational capacities, conservatives also recognized the limitations of reason. "We are afraid to put men to live and trade each on his own private stock of reason," said Burke, "because we suspect that this stock in each man is small, and that the individuals would do better to avail themselves of the general bank and capital of nations and of ages."[7] Reason cannot control a corrupt human nature, insisted conservatives. Moreover, an overly critical spirit promotes discontent, fosters atheism, and undermines established authority.

Conservatives saw the Revolution and the Terror that it spawned as a natural outgrowth of an arrogant Enlightenment philosophy that overvalued reason and sought to reshape society in accordance with abstract principles and contrived formulas. Moderate conservatives would accept reforms provided that reformers were not contemptuous of history and tradition, did not seek to level society according to some artificial or mechanical scheme—timeless abstractions that ignored historical realities—and did not move at a pace that disrupted the social order. For conservatives, society was not a machine with replaceable parts, but a complex and delicate organism. Tamper with its vital organs, as the revolutionaries had done, and it would die.

The Quest for Social Stability

Conservatives detested attempts to transform society according to a theoretical model. They considered human nature too intricate and social relations too complex for such social engineering. In the conservatives' view, the revolutionaries had reduced people and society to abstractions divorced from their historical settings; consequently, they had destroyed ancient patterns that seemed inconvenient and had drawn up constitutions based on the unacceptable principle that government derives its power from the consent of the governed. The art of politics, argued Burke, entails practical reason. The wise statesman, said traditionalists, abhors abstract principles and spurns ideal models. Rather, he values the historical experiences of his nation, and is concerned with real people in specific historical situations; he recognizes that institutions and beliefs do not require theoretical excellence and do not have to meet the test of reason or of nature in order to be useful and beneficial to society. Statesmen who ignore these truisms and attempt to reform a commonwealth in accordance with a priori models, political formulas that do not accord with the realities of history and the social order, plunge the nation into anarchy. To Burke, the revolutionaries were zealots who, like the religious radicals during the Reformation, resorted to force and terror in order to create a new individual and a new society. In politics, experience is the best teacher and prudence the best method of proceding: "it is with infinite caution that any man ought to venture upon pulling down an edifice which has answered in any tolerable degree for ages the common purposes of society, or on building it up again, without having models and patterns of approved utility before his eyes."[8]

For conservatives, God and history were the only legitimate sources of political authority; states were not made but were an expression of the nation's moral, religious, and historical experience. No legitimate or sound constitution could be drawn up by a group assembled for that purpose. Scraps of paper with legal terminology and philosophical visions could not produce an effective government. Thus, Maistre castigated the philosophes:

> One of the greatest errors of a century which professed them all was to believe that a political constitution could be created and written *a priori*, whereas reason and experience unite in proving that a constitution is a divine work and that precisely the most fundamental and essentially constitutional of a nation's laws could not possibly be written. . . . Was it not a common belief everywhere [in the eighteenth century] that a constitution was the work of the intellect, like an ode or a tragedy? Had not Thomas Paine declared with a profundity that charmed the universities, that a constitution does not exist as long as one cannot put it in his pocket? The unsuspecting, overweening self-confidence of the eighteenth century balked at nothing, and I do not believe that it produced a single stripling of any talent who did not make three things when he left school: an educational system, a constitution, and a world.[9]

A sound political system, said conservatives, evolved gradually and inexplicably in response to circumstances and gave expression to the unwritten and fundamental laws that bind people into a nation. For this reason, conservatives admired the English constitution. It was not a product of abstract thought; no assembly had convened to fashion it. Because it grew imperceptibly out of the historical experiences and needs of the English people, it was durable and effective.

The liberal philosophy of the Enlightenment and the French Revolution started with the individual. The philosophes and the revolutionaries envisioned a society in which the individual was free and autonomous. For conservatives, however, society was a living organism held together by centuries-old bonds, not a mechanical arrangement of disconnected units. Alone, a person would be selfish, unreliable, frail; it was only as a member of a social group—family, guild, church, or state—that one acquired the ways of cooperation and the manners of civilization. By exalting the individual, the revolutionaries had steered Europe along the path of political and spiritual anarchy. Individualism overturned the very bases of human society: it shattered traditional ties that made people care for each other and the community; it destroyed obedience to law and authority and fragmented society into disconnected parts, isolated, self-seeking atoms devoid of any spiritual or civic purpose. Bonald summed up the view of conservative thinkers. "The schools of modern philosophy," he said, "have produced the philosophy of individual man, the philosophy of *I* . . . I want to produce the philosophy of social man, the philosophy of *we*."[10] Bonald, Maistre, and other Catholic conservatives blamed Luther and the Reformation for inaugurating a rebellious individualism that weakened traditional authority.

Conservatives denounced the social contract theory—that people voluntarily enter into an agreement to establish a political community and that government rests on the consent of the governed—as a threat to established monarchical power. Holding that the community was more important than the individual, conservatives also rejected the philosophy of natural rights. Rights were not abstractions that preceded an individual's entrance into society and pertained to all people everywhere. Rather, the state, always remembering the needs of the entire community and its links to past generations, determined what rights and privileges its citizens might possess. There were no "rights of man," only rights of the French, the English, and so forth, as determined and allocated by the particular state.

Conservatives viewed equality as another pernicious abstraction that contradicted all historical experience. For conservatives, society was naturally hierarchical; they believed that some men by virtue of their intelligence, education, wealth, and birth were best qualified to rule and instruct the less able. They maintained that the revolutionaries, by uprooting a long-established ruling elite that had learned its art through experience, had deprived society of effective leaders, brought internal disorder, and prepared the way for the Terror and Napoleon.

The philosophes had attacked Christianity for promoting superstition and fanaticism. Holding with Maistre that the philosophes' irreligion was "an insurrection against God," conservatives saw Christianity as the basis of civil society; the social bond, civilization itself, depends on religious commitments, for "no other known force can influence the savage." Maistre discerned "a *satanic* element in the French Revolution," which manifested itself in attacks on religion.

> [This] scorn for God brings an irrevocable curse on the human works stained by it. Every conceivable institution either rests on a religious idea or is ephemeral. Institutions are strong and durable to the degree that they partake of divinity. Not only is human reason, or what is ignorantly called philosophy, unable to replace those foundations ignorantly called superstitions, but philosophy is, on the contrary, an essentially destructive force. . . . It would be interesting to go thoroughly through our European institutions and to show how they are all *christianized*, how religion, touching on everything, animates and sustains everything.[11]

Catholic conservatives, in particular, held that God had constituted the church and monarchy to check sinful human behavior. "Christian monarchs are the final creation of the development of political society and of religious society," said Bonald. "The proof of this lies in the fact that when monarchy and Christianity are both abolished society returns to savagery."[12] Excessive liberty, the weakening of religion, and an exclusively scientific and secular education, argued Maistre, had brutalized people and shattered the foundations of society. "If the guidance of education is not returned to the priests," he said, "and if science is not uniformly relegated to a subordinate rank, incalculable evils await us. We shall become brutalized by science, and that is the worst sort of brutality."[13]

Conservatism pointed to a limitation of the Enlightenment. It showed that human beings and social relationships are far more complex than the philosophes had imagined. People do not always respond to the rigorous logic of the philosopher and are not eager to break with ancient ways, however illogical they appear to the intellect. They often find familiar customs and ancestral religions more satisfying guides to life than the blueprints of philosophers. The power of tradition remains an obstacle to all the visions of reformers.

LIBERALISM: THE VALUE OF
THE INDIVIDUAL

The decades after 1815 saw a spectacular rise of the bourgeoisie. Talented and ambitious bankers, merchants, manufacturers, professionals, and officeholders wanted to break the stranglehold of the landed nobility—the traditional elite—on political power and social prestige and to ensure individual freedom. The political philosophy of the bourgeoisie was most commonly liberalism. While conservatives sought to strengthen the foundations of traditional society, which had been severely shaken in the period of the French Revolution and Napoleon, liberals wanted to alter the status quo and to carry out the promise of the Enlightenment and the Revolution. Conservatives concentrated on the community, whereas liberals stressed individual freedom. Conservatives tried to preserve a social hierarchy based on hereditary aristocracy, whereas liberals insisted that a person's worth was measured not by birth but by achievement. Conservatives held that the state rests on tradition, whereas liberals sought the rational state, in which political institutions and procedures were based on intelligible principles. Conservatives wanted individuals, inherently wicked, to obey their betters. Liberals, on the other hand, had confidence in the goodness of human nature and the capacity of individuals to control their own lives.

The Sources of Liberalism

In the long view of Western civilization, liberalism is an extension and development of the democratic practices and rational outlook that originated in Greece. Also flowing into the liberal tradition is the Judeo-Christian principle of the worth and dignity of each individual and the belief that God has endowed all human beings with the freedom to make moral choices. But the immediate historical roots of nineteenth-century liberalism extended back to seventeenth-century England. At that time, the struggle for religious toleration by English Protestant dissenters established the principle of freedom of conscience, which is easily transformed into freedom of opinion and expression in all matters. The Glorious Revolution of 1688 set limits on the power of the English monarchy and firmly established parliamentary government under the rule of law. At the same time, John Locke's natural rights philosophy declared that the individual was by nature entitled to freedom, and it justified revolutions against rulers who deprived citizens of their lives, liberty, or property.

The French philosophes helped shape liberalism. From Montesquieu, liberals derived the theory of the separation of powers and of checks and balances—principles intended to guard against autocratic government. The philosophes had supported religious toleration, freedom of thought, and the critical use of the intellect. They had also expressed confidence in the capacity of the human mind to reform society, maintained that human beings are essentially good, and believed in the future progress of humanity—all fundamental tenets of liberalism.

The American and French Revolutions were crucial phases in the history of liberalism. The Declaration of Independence gave expression to Locke's theory of natural rights; the Constitution of the United States incorporated Montesquieu's principles and demonstrated that people could create an effective government; the Bill of Rights protected the person and rights of the individual. In destroying the special privileges of the aristocracy and opening careers to talent, the French National Assembly of 1789 had implemented the liberal ideal of equality under the law. It also drew up the Declaration of the Rights of Man and of the Citizen, which affirmed the dignity and rights of the individual, and a constitution that limited the king's power. Both the American and French revolutions explicitly called for the protection of property rights, another basic premise of liberalism.

Individual Liberty

The liberals' central concern was the enhancement of individual liberty. They agreed with Immanuel Kant that all persons exist as ends in themselves and·not as an object to be used arbitrarily by others. Uncoerced by government and churches and properly educated, a person could develop into a good, productive and self-directed human being. Individuals could make their own decisions, base actions on universal moral laws, and respect each others' rights.

Liberals rejected a legacy of the Middle Ages: the classification of the individual as a commoner or aristocrat on the basis of birth and the assignment of the individual to a fixed social position with a definite role. They held that a man was not born into a certain station in life but made his way through his own efforts. Taking their cue from the French Revolution, liberals called for an end to all hereditary privileges of the aristocracy.

In the tradition of the philosophes, liberals stressed the pre-eminence of reason as the basis of political and social life. Unfettered by ignorance and tyranny, the mind could eradicate traditions and prejudices that had burdened people for centuries and begin an age of free institutions and responsible citizens. For this reason, liberals supported the advancement of education. They believed that educated people apply reason to their political and social life; such people act in ways beneficial to themselves and to society and are less likely to submit to tyrants or to endure injustice. Liberals also endorsed the open-mindedness of science, open debate between opposing viewpoints, and the toleration of dissent. British philosopher John Stuart Mill's *On Liberty* (see pages 275–276) is the classic statement of freedom of thought. Their confidence in human reasoning, the efficacy of education, and the essential goodness of human nature led liberals to be generally optimistic about the future.

Liberals agreed with John Locke that "Man [is] *Proprietor of his own Person*,"[14] that he is the guardian of his own affairs, and that his life is his own to do with as he wishes; it does not belong to a church or a state. (Except for a few radicals, most liberals would have placed limitations on this and other liberal principles if people tried to extend them to women.) Holding that the individual could handle his own affairs better than any church or government could, liberals attacked the state and other authorities that prevented people from exercising the right of free choice, deprived them of their privacy, interfered with the right of free expression, and hindered their self-determination and self-development. "There is . . . a part of human life," said Benjamin Constant (1767-1830), a leading French liberal theorist, "which of necessity remains individual and independent and which as of right remains outside the jurisdiction of society."[15] Liberals concurred with Mill's dictum "That the only purpose for which power can be rightfully exercised over any member of a civilized community against his will, is to prevent harm to others. . . . Over himself, over his own body and mind, the individual is sovereign."[16]

The great question that confronted nineteenth-century liberals was the relationship between state authority and individual liberty. Regarding individual freedom as the supreme value, liberals were always suspicious of collective power, particularly when exercised by the state. To guard against the absolute and arbitrary authority of rulers, liberals demanded written constitutions that granted freedom of speech, of the press, and of religion, freedom from arbitrary arrest, and the protection of property rights. To prevent the abuse of political authority, liberals called for a freely elected parliament and the distribution of power among the various branches of government. Liberals held that a government that derived its authority from the consent of the governed, as given in free elections, was least likely to violate the individual's freedom and privacy. A corollary of this principle was that the best government is the one that governs least—that is, one that interferes as little as possible with the economic activities of its citizens and does not involve itself in their private lives or their beliefs.

How did liberals interpret the individual's relationship to the community? In ancient Athens, the citizen did not see himself as an isolated entity but as a member of a community, the city-state (polis). He viewed the polis as a second family and community spirit as a prerequisite for political life, indeed for life itself. Only as a citizen of a polis, said Aristotle, could a man develop himself politically, morally, and intellectually. The Greek view that nature intended that people live in communities was inherited by medieval thinkers, who expressed it in Christian terms: the community should adhere to norms that originated with God. Liberals broke with this tradition. For them, each individual was an independent unit whose needs took precedence over communal concerns. Their conservative opponents argued that the liberals' focus on self-interest weakened the bonds that held society together; they accused liberals of fragmenting a community into isolated, anti-social units, all pursuing their own selfish interests at the expense of the common good. Liberals disagreed. They held that self-interest worked to the advantage of both the individual and the community. When individuals are free to pursue their own ends and to fulfill their human potential, they promote the general good of society. Moreover, liberals assumed that self-interest would be tempered by reason and a natural benevolence that would deter people from engaging in anti-social behavior.

Liberalism and Democracy

The French Revolution presented a dilemma for liberals. They supported the reforms of the moderate stage: the destruction of the special privileges of the aristocracy, the drawing up of a declaration of rights and a constitution, the establishment of a parliament, and the opening of careers to talent. But they repudiated Jacobin radicalism. Liberals were frightened by the excesses of the Jacobin regime: its tampering with the economy, which liberals regarded as a threat to private property; its appeal to the "little people," which liberals viewed as undermining orderly and responsible government; its use of the guillotine, which awakened the basest human feelings.

Although many liberals adhered to the doctrine of natural rights—the theory underlying the reforms of the Revolution—some who were disturbed by the Jacobin experience discarded it. These liberals, fearing social disorder as much as conservatives did, did not want to ignite revolutions by the masses, whom they referred to as the "wild ones," or the "vile mob." In the hands of the lower classes, the natural-rights philosophy was too easily translated into the democratic creed that all people should share in political power—a prospect that the bourgeois regarded with horror. To them, the participation of commoners in politics meant a vulgar form of despotism and the end to individual liberty. The masses—uneducated, unpropertied, inexperienced, and impatient—had neither the ability nor the temperament to maintain liberty, protect property, and preserve culture. Roger Henry Soltau, a student of French political thought, explains the attitude of early nineteenth-century liberals:

> Liberalism believed as fully as Conservatism in the maintenance of social order and in the essential limitation of power to certain well-defined classes, but it believed that social order would be not disturbed but strengthened by the accession to power of the hitherto excluded middle class. It was rigidly opposed to any wide extension of the suffrage, and as anti-democratic as any Conservative.[17]

Few thinkers in the first half of the nineteenth century grasped the growing significance of the masses in politics as did Alexis de Tocqueville (1805–1859), the French political theorist and statesman. In the wake of the French Revolution, Tocqueville, an aristocrat by birth but a liberal by temperament, recognized that the destruction of aristocracy, a system based on rank, and the march toward democracy could not be curbed. In *Democracy in America* (1835–1840), based on his travels in the United States, Tocqueville with cool detachment and brilliance, analyzed the nature, merits, and weaknesses of American democratic society. In contrast to France of the Old Regime, said Tocqueville, American society had no hereditary aristocracy with special privileges, and the avenues to social advancement and political participation were open to all.

Tocqueville held that democracy was more just than aristocratic government, and he predicted that it would be the political system of the future, but he also recognized its inherent dangers. In a democratic society, he said, people's passion to be equal outweighs their desire for liberty. Spurred by the ideal of equality, citizens in a democracy desire the honors and possessions that they think are their due. They demand that the avenues to social, economic, and political advancement be opened to all, and they no longer accept the disparity in wealth and position as part of the natural order. However, since people are not naturally equal in ability, many are frustrated and turn to the state to secure for them those possessions and advantages that they cannot obtain by themselves. They are willing to sacrifice political liberty to improve their material well-being. Consequently, democracies face an ever-present danger in that people, craving to achieve equality, will surrender their liberty to a central government that promises to provide them with property and other advantages. Granted ever more power by the people, the state would regulate its citizens' lives and crush local institutions that impede centralized control, and impose the beliefs of the majority on the minority. Liberty would be lost not to the despotism of kings, but to the tyranny of the majority. To prevent democracy from degenerating into state despotism, Tocqueville urged strengthening institutions of local government, forming numerous private associations over which the state had no control, protecting the independence of the judiciary, and preserving a free press—all of which would promote active and responsible citizenship.

In a democratic society, said Tocqueville, there is a danger that the majority will impose its viewpoint on the minority. The majority demands conformity of belief. Its power is so great and irresistible, held Tocqueville, that the minority is fearful to stray from the track which the majority prescribes. Tocqueville declared: "I think that liberty is endangered when this power [of the majority] is checked by no obstacles which may retard its course and force it to moderate its own vehemence."[18]

According to Tocqueville, democracy also spawned a selfish individualism that could degenerate into vulgar hedonism. Driven by an overriding concern for possessions and profits, people would lose their taste for political participation and their concern for the public good. If preoccupation with private concerns prevails over a sense of public duty, liberty cannot long endure.

Although recognizing the limitations of democracy, Tocqueville did not seek to reverse its growth. In this new age that is dawning, he said,

> . . . all who shall attempt . . . to base freedom upon aristocratic privilege will fail . . . all who shall attempt to draw and to retain authority within a single class, will fail. . . . All . . . who would establish or secure the independence and the dignity of their fellow-men, must show themselves the friends of equality. . . . Thus the question is not how to reconstruct aristocratic society, but how to make liberty proceed out of that democratic state of society in which God had placed us.[19]

The problems of democracy, declared Tocqueville, must be resolved without jeopardizing political freedom. The task of a democratic society is to temper extreme individualism and unrestrained acquisitiveness by fostering public-spiritedness. Without direct participation by cooperating citizens—that is, without a concern for the common good—democracy faces a bleak future. Freedom depends less on laws than on cultivating the sentiments and habits of civic virtue.

Because bourgeois liberals feared that democracy could quash personal freedom as ruthlessly as any absolute monarch, they called for property requirements for voting and officeholding. They wanted political power to be concentrated in the hands of a safe and reliable— that is, a propertied and educated—middle class. Such a government would prevent revolution from below, a prospect that caused anxiety among bourgeois liberals.

Early nineteenth-century liberals engaged in revolutions, to be sure, but their aims were always limited. Once they had destroyed absolute monarchy and gained a constitution and a parliament or a change of government, they quickly tried to terminate the revolution. When the fever of revolution spread to the masses, bourgeois liberals either withdrew or turned counterrevolutionary, for they feared the stirrings of the multitude.

Although liberalism was the political philosophy of a middle class generally hostile to democracy, the essential ideals of democracy flowed logically from liberalism. Eventually, democracy became a later stage in the evolution of liberalism because the masses, their political power enhanced by the Industrial Revolution, would press for greater social, political, and economic equality. Moreover, the ideals of liberty and equality are by nature universal and inclusive; denying them to people on the basis of class (and race or gender) cannot be convincingly defended. Thus, by the early twentieth century, many European states had introduced universal manhood suffrage, abandoned property requirements for officeholding, and enacted laws to improve conditions for workers.

But the fears of nineteenth-century liberals were not without foundation. In the twentieth century, the participation of common people in politics has indeed threatened freedom. Impatient with parliamentary procedures and seduced by appeals to passions and prejudices, the masses, particularly when troubled by economic problems, have in some instances turned their support to demagogues who promised swift and decisive action. The granting of political participation to the masses has not always made people freer. The confidence of democrats has been shaken in the twentieth century by the seeming willingness of common people to trade freedom for authority, order, economic security, and national power. Liberalism is based on the assumption that human beings can and do respond to rational argument, and that reason will prevail over base feelings. The history of our century shows that this may be an overly optimistic assessment of human nature.

Classical Liberal Economic Thought

In the last part of the eighteenth century, as a revolution for liberty and equality swept across France and sent shock waves through Europe, a different kind of revolution, a revolution in industry, was transforming life in Great Britain. In the nineteenth century, the Industrial Revolution spread to the United States and to the European continent.

Rapid industrialization caused hardships for the new class of industrial workers, many of them recent arrivals from the countryside. Arduous and monotonous factory labor was geared to the strict discipline of the clock, the machine, and the production schedule. Employment was never secure. Sick workers received no pay and were often fired; aged workers suffered pay cuts or lost their jobs. During business slumps, employers lowered wages with impunity and laid-off workers had nowhere to turn for assistance. Because factory owners often did not consider safety to be important, accidents were frequent. Municipal authorities were unable to cope with the rapid pace of urbanization, and without adequate housing, sanitation, or recreational facilities, the exploding urban centers were another source of working-class misery. In preindustrial Britain, most people had lived in small villages. They knew where their roots were; relatives, friends, and the village church gave them a sense of belonging. The industrial centers, however, separated people from nature and from their origins, shattering traditional ways of life that had given men and women a sense of security.

The plight of the working class created a demand for reform, but the British government, committed to laissez-faire economic principles that militated against state involvement, was slow to act. The ascendancy of laissez faire, which called for the free movement of goods and capital, showed how far western Europe had moved from traditional medieval society, with its fixed status and limits on accumulation of wealth.

Adam Smith   *The Wealth of Nations* (1776), written by Adam Smith, professor of moral philosophy in Scotland, became the foundation of liberal economic theory. Smith attacked the theory of mercantilism, which held that a state's wealth was determined by the amount of gold and silver it possessed. According to this theory, to build up its reserves of precious metals, the state should promote domestic industries, encourage exports, and discourage imports. Mercantilist theory called for government regulation of the economy so that the state could compete successfully with other nations for a share of the world's scarce resources. Smith argued that the real basis of a country's wealth was measured by the quantity and quality of its goods and services and not by its storehouse of precious metals. Government intervention, he said, retards economic progress; it reduces the real value of the annual produce of the nation's land and labor. On the other hand, when people pursue their own interests—when they seek to better their condition—they foster economic expansion, which benefits the whole society.

> Every individual is continually exerting himself to find out the most advantageous employment for whatever capital he can command. It is his own advantage, indeed, and not that of the society, which he has in view. But the study of his own advantage, naturally or necessarily, leads him to prefer that employment which is most advantageous to the society. . . . By pursuing his own interest he frequently promotes that of society more effectually than when he intends to promote it. I have never known much good done by those who affected to trade for the publick good.[20]

Smith limited the state's authority to maintaining law and order, administering justice, and defending the nation. He believed that competition was self-regulating, as if an "invisible hand" held greed in check and promoted the general good. For example, if a merchant charged too high a price, he would be driven out of business by a competitor willing to accept a lesser profit. Left to its own devices, Smith maintained, the market mechanism works ultimately for the benefit of all members of society, a view that supported the Enlightenment's belief in progress.

Smith, who sought to expand the wealth of the entire nation, did not intend his work to serve as an apologia for bourgeois interests. He was critical of the manufacturers who, driven by greed, deceived and oppressed the public. The free market functioned best, he said, when business people in pursuit of their own interests did not take unfair advantage of others and did not neglect the common good. Nor, unlike political economists Malthus, Ricardo, and a host of bourgeois factory owners, did he view poverty as an ineradicable law of nature. He neither dismissed nor demeaned the poor:

> Servants, labourers and workmen of different kinds make up the far greater part of every great political society. . . . No society can surely be flourishing and happy, of which the far greater part of the members are poor and miserable. It is but equity, besides, that they who feed, cloath and lodge the whole body of the people, should have such a share of the produce of their own labour as to be themselves tolerably well fed, cloathed and lodged.[21]

To those who argued that low wages were necessary to reduce costs and to discourage the poor from working fewer hours, Smith replied:

> The liberal reward of labour . . . increases the industry of the common people. The wages of labour are the encouragement of industry, which like every other human quality, improves in proportion to the encouragement it receives. A plentiful subsistence increases the bodily strength of the labourer, and the comfortable hope of bettering his condition, and of ending his days perhaps in ease and plenty, animates him to exert that strength to the utmost. Where wages are high, accordingly, we shall always find the workmen more active, diligent, and expeditious than where they are low.[22]

Nevertheless, the principle of laissez faire—that government should not interfere with the market—was used by the bourgeoisie to justify its opposition to humanitarian legislation intended to alleviate the misery of the factory workers. Liberals regarded such social reforms as unwarranted and dangerous meddling with the natural law of supply and demand.

Thomas Malthus and David Ricardo   Another theorist favored by bourgeois liberals was Thomas R. Malthus (1766–1834), an Anglican cleric and professor of history and political economy. In his *Essay on the Principle of Population* (published in 1798 and then in a second, much enlarged, edition in 1803), Malthus asserted that the population grows at a much faster rate than the food supply. This results in food shortages, irregular employment, lowered wages, and high mortality. The poor's distress, said Malthus, was not due to faulty political institutions or existing social and property relations. Its true cause was the number of children they had.

> When the wages of labour are hardly sufficient to maintain two children, a man marries and has five or six. He of course finds himself miserably distressed. . . . He accuses his parish. . . . He accuses the avarice of the rich. He accuses the partial and unjust institutions of society. . . . In searching for objects of accusation, he never adverts to the quarter

from which all his misfortunes originate. The last person that he would think of accusing is himself.[23]

The state cannot ameliorate the poor's misery, said Malthus: "the means of redress are in their own hands, and in the hands of no other persons whatever."[24] This "means of redress" would be lowering the birthrate through late marriages and chastity, but Malthus believed that the poor lacked the self-discipline to refrain from sexual activity. When they receive higher wages, they have more children, thereby upsetting the population-resource balance and bringing misery to themselves and others. This view of poverty as an iron law of nature, which could not be undone by the good intentions of the state or through philanthropy, buttressed supporters of strict laissez faire and eased the consciences of the propertied classes. Compassion for the poor was simply a misplaced emotion; government reforms were doomed to fail, and higher wages provided no relief. Malthus's theory also flew in the face of adherents of human perfectibility and inevitable progress. Poverty, like disease, was simply a natural phenomenon, one of nature's laws, that could not be eliminated. No wonder his contemporaries called economics "the dismal science."

In *Principles of Political Economy* (1817),. David Ricardo (1772–1823) gave support to Malthus's gloomy outlook. Higher wages, said Ricardo, lead workers to have more children, causing an increase in the labor supply. Competition for jobs by an expanding labor force brings wages down. This "iron law of wages" offered bleak prospects for the working poor.

> When, however, by the encouragement which high wages give to the increase of population, the number of labourers is increased, wages again fall to their natural price [to a subsistence level] and indeed from a reaction sometimes fall below it. . . . It is a truth which admits not a doubt, that the comforts and well-being of the poor cannot be permanently secured without some regard on their part, or some effort on the part of the legislature, to regulate the increase of their numbers, and to render less frequent among them early and improvident marriages.[25]

Early nineteenth-century liberals saw poverty and suffering as part of the natural order and beyond government's scope. They feared that state intervention in the economy to redress social ills disrupted the free market, threatening personal liberty and hindering social well-being. Thus, an editorial in the *Economist* of May 13, 1848, protesting against a bill before Parliament that sought to improve housing and sanitation in cities, declared: "Suffering and evil are nature's admonitions; they cannot be got rid of; and the impatient attempts of benevolence to banish them from the world by legislation . . . have always been productive of more evil than good." Government interference, liberals also argued, discouraged the poor from finding work, thereby promoting idleness. According to liberal political economy, unemployment and poverty stemmed from individual failings. The New Poor Law (1834) put into practice these liberal assumptions. The workhouses were deliberately designed to deter and punish the idle; the diet was kept virtually on a starvation level, and, in accordance with the Malthusian goal of checking the population growth of the poor, wives and husbands were separated.

A particularly glaring example of the coldness and harshness of liberals toward suffering was their response to the Irish famine of 1845–1849. While the Irish were dying of starvation, the liberal leadership in Britain, fearing that government intervention would promote dependence, did little to alleviate the suffering. "The more I see of government interference," wrote Sir Charles Wood, chancellor of the Exchequer, "the less I am disposed to trust to it, and I have no faith in anything but private capital employed under the individual charge."[26] To hard-hearted liberals, the famine, which killed about 1.5 million people, was simply nature's way of dealing with Ireland's excess population. A dogmatic commitment to laissez faire discouraged British officials from dealing humanely with this disaster.

Malthus, Ricardo, and their supporters departed from the general view of the philosophes, which saw natural law as beneficent and a model for human law. But for adherents of the "dismal science" of economics, natural law entailed human suffering and provided no relief. How could this be squared with Condorcet's optimism? In the last part of the century, liberals modified their adherence to strict laissez faire, accepting the principle that the state had a responsibility to protect the poor against the worst abuses of rapid industrialization (see Chapter 8).

RADICALISM AND DEMOCRACY: THE EXPANSION OF LIBERALISM

In the early nineteenth century, democratic ideals were advanced by thinkers and activists called radicals. Inspired by the Jacobin stage of the French Revolution and by the democratic principles expressed in Rousseau's *Social Contract*, early nineteenth-century French radicals championed popular sovereignty—rule by the people. In contrast to liberals, who were generally fearful and disdainful of the masses, French radicals trusted the common person. Advocating universal manhood suffrage and a republic, radicalism gained the support of many French workers and the lower bourgeois in the 1830s and 1840s.

British radicals, like their liberal cousins, inherited the Enlightenment's confidence in reason and its belief in the essential goodness of the individual. In the 1790s, British radicals expressed sympathy for the French Revolution, approving its concern for natural rights and its attack on feudal privileges. In the first half of the nineteenth century, radicals sought parliamentary reforms, because some heavily populated districts were barely represented in Parliament, while lightly populated districts were overrepresented. They demanded payment for members of Parliament to permit the nonwealthy to hold office; they sought universal manhood suffrage to give the masses representation in Parliament; and they insisted on the secret ballot to prevent intimidation of voters. Radicals attacked the hereditary aristocracy and fought corruption; some, like William Cobbett, a crusading journalist, supported the struggle of the working class to improve its condition. He declared:

> A labouring man in England with a wife and only three children, though he never lose a day's work, though he and his family be economical, frugal and industrious in the most extensive sense of these words, is not now able to procure himself by his labour a single meal of meat from one end of the year into the other. Is this a state in which the labouring man ought to be?[27]

English radicalism embodied the desires of parliamentary reformers for broader political representation and the hopes of the laboring poor for a better life. Two important theorists of the movement were Thomas Paine and Jeremy Bentham.

Thomas Paine

Thomas Paine (see Chapter 5), responding to Burke's *Reflections on the French Revolution* with the *Rights of Man* (published in two parts, in 1791 and 1792), denounced reverence for tradition, defended the principle of natural rights, and praised as progress the destruction of the Old Regime. Paine shared the conviction of other Enlightenment thinkers that superstition, intolerance, and despotism had interfered with human progress in the past, and he staunchly supported both the American and French revolutions. To initiate a true age of enlightenment, he said, it is necessary to recognize that "all the great laws of society are laws of nature,"[28] and to reconstitute the social and political order in line with these principles inherent in nature. Paine denounced all hereditary monarchy and aristocracy as wretched systems of slavery that deprived people of their inherent right to govern themselves and exploited them financially in order to raise money for war. "Kings succeed each other, not as rationals," he wrote, "but as animals. It signifies not what their mental or moral characters are."[29] The only legitimate government, he claimed, was representative democracy, in which the right of all men to participate was assured. Paine believed that republican governments would be less inclined than hereditary ones to wage war and more concerned with the welfare of the common person.

Paine supported revolution as the means of creating a truly just society, one that took reason and nature as its guide. The overthrow of traditional governments, he contended, would promote justice, prosperity, and peace. In *Rights of Man*, Paine answered Burke's argument that a country should be guided by its inherited traditions.

> The circumstances of the world are continually changing, and the opinions of men change also; and as government is for the living and not for the dead, it is the living only that has any right to it. That which may be thought right and found convenient in one age may be thought wrong and found inconvenient in another. In such cases, who is to decide, the living or the dead?[30]

As the French Revolution turned more violent, Paine revealed his basic humanitarianism, decrying the massacres and urging clemency, not execution, for Louis XVI. Arrested during the Terror, he barely escaped execution himself. Nevertheless, his attitude toward revolution was somewhat naive, as British historian John W. Derry notes:

> Paine talked much of revolution, posing as its prophet; but he persistently underestimated the social consequences of violent change. He thought of revolution as giving effect to several elementary truths, such as the folly of hereditary right and the benefits of representative democracy, but he did not understand the anatomy of revolutions, their tendency to devour their children, their propensity to distort the certainties of liberal belief in order to gratify their appetite for power. He was horrified by the Reign of Terror, but he could not explain it. . . . [W]hy had the revolutionaries allowed [their] high ideals to be compromised and perverted? Paine had no answer to this.
>
> He was happy to talk of the blissful consequences of revolution but he persistently failed to grasp the social and economic tensions which made his principles so difficult to apply in the complex world of power politics.[31]

From Paine, the English radical tradition acquired a faith in reason and human goodness, a skeptical attitude toward established institutions, an admiration for the open and democratic society being shaped in the United States, and a dislike of organized religion. It also gained the conviction that the exclusion of common people from political participation was an injustice, indeed, that the essential purpose of government was to foster the well-being of ordinary people. Paine's ideas stimulated organized political activity among working people who were excluded from political participation. Influenced in part by Paine, they formed societies that endorsed the reforms of the French Revolution and demanded similar reform in Britain. But most English radicals rejected Paine's praise of revolution as something inherently desirable.

Jeremy Bentham

In contrast to Paine, Jeremy Bentham (1748–1832) rejected the doctrine of natural rights as an abstraction that had no basis in reality. He regarded the French Revolution as an absurd attempt to reconstruct society according to principles as misguided as those that had supported the Old Regime. Bentham's importance to the English radical tradition derives from his principle of utility, which he offered as a guide to reformers. The central fact of human existence, said Bentham, is that human beings seek to gratify their desires, that they prefer pleasure to pain, and that pleasure is intrinsically good and pain bad. In Bentham's view, human beings are motivated solely by self-interest, which they define in terms of pleasure and pain: "Nature has placed mankind under the governance of two sovereign masters, *pain* and *pleasure*. It is for them alone to point out what we ought to do, as well as to determine what we shall do."[32] Consequently, any political, economic, judicial, or social institution and any legislation should be judged according to a simple standard: does it bring about the "greatest happiness for the greatest number"? If not, it should be swept away.

Bentham believed that he had found an objective and scientific approach to the study and reform of society. By focusing on the need for change and improvement on every level of society and by urging a careful and objective analysis of social issues, Bentham and his followers, called philosophical radicals, contributed substantially to the shaping of the English reform tradition.

Bentham pointed out that those in power had always used what they had considered the highest principles—God's teachings, universal standards, honored traditions—to justify their political and social systems, their moral codes, and their laws. On the basis of these principles, they persecuted and abused people, instituted practices rooted in ignorance and superstition, and imposed values that made people miserable because they conflicted with human nature and the essential needs of men and women. He contended that the principle of utility—to act always so as to derive the greatest happiness for the greatest number of people—permits the reforming of society in accordance with people's true nature and needs. It does not impose unrealistic standards on men and women but accepts people as they are. Utilitarianism, he declared, bases institutions and laws on an objective study of human behavior—on enlightened self-interest, rather than on unsubstantiated religious beliefs, unreliable traditions, and mistaken philosophical abstractions. Its goal is to propose measures that augment rather than diminish the community's happiness. In his desire to make people happier, Bentham was representative of the humanitarianism of the Enlightenment.

Bentham's utilitarianism led him to press for social and political reforms. The aristocratic ruling elite, he said, were not interested in producing the greatest happiness of the greatest number but in furthering their own narrow interests. Only if the rulers came from the broad masses of people would government be amenable to reforms based on the greatest happiness principle. Thus, he supported extension of the suffrage and a secret ballot and attacked political corruption and clerical control over education. Bentham wanted to do away with the monarchy and the House of Lords, and to disestablish the Anglican church. In contrast to laissez-faire liberals, Benthamites argued for legislation to protect women and children in the factories; they also sought to improve sanitation in the cities and to reform the archaic British prison system.

EARLY SOCIALISM: NEW POSSIBILITIES FOR SOCIETY

A new group of social theorists called socialists went further than either the liberals or the radicals in dealing with the problems created by industrialization. Socialists argued that the liberals' concern for individual freedom and the radicals' demand for extension of the suffrage had little impact on the poverty, oppression, and gross inequality of wealth that plagued modern society. Asserting that the liberals' doctrine of individualism degenerated into selfish egoism, which harmed community life, socialists called for the creation of a new society based on cooperation rather than competition. Reflecting the spirit of the Enlightenment and the French Revolution, socialists, like liberals, denounced the status quo for perpetuating injustice and held that people could create a better world. Like liberals, too, they placed the highest value on a rational analysis of society and on transforming society in accordance with scientifically valid premises, whose truth rational people could comprehend. Socialists believed that they had discerned a pattern in human society, which, if properly understood and acted upon, would lead men and women to an earthly salvation. Thus, socialists were also romantics, for they dreamed of a new social order, a future utopia, where each individual could find happiness and self-fulfillment.

An early expression of socialist thinking emerged during the French Revolution, when Gracchus Babeuf (1760–1797), an ardent supporter of the *sans-culottes*, the laboring poor, attacked the Directory, the governing body established at the end of 1795, in his journal, *Tribune of the People*, and played a leading role in a conspiracy to overthrow the Directory. Seeking to end the division of society into exploiter and exploited, Babeuf called for the abolition of private property—a goal that separated him from earlier French revolutionaries. At his trial, Babeuf quoted from his writings in *Tribune of the People*, which revealed his revolutionary socialist ideals:

> The masses can no longer find a way to go on living; they see that they possess nothing and that they suffer under the harsh and flinty oppression of a greedy ruling class. The hour strikes for great and memorable revolutionary events . . . when a general overthrow of the system of private property is inevitable, when the revolt of the poor against the rich becomes a necessity that can no longer be postponed. . . .
>
> Happiness is a new idea in Europe. . . . Do not tolerate a single instance of poverty and misery in the State. Let Europe know that you will permit no more downtrodden people and no more oppressors on French soil. . . . It is the destiny of the wretched of the earth to rule it; theirs is the right to talk as masters to the governments that neglect them. . . . In a truly just social order there are neither rich nor poor. The rich, who refuse to give up their superfluous wealth for the benefit of the poor, are enemies of the people.[33]

Early nineteenth-century socialists regarded the organization of society as inept and unjust. They denounced as hollow and hypocritical the liberals' preoccupation with liberty and equality, arguing that to the lower classes devastated by poverty these ideals were merely formal principles: they protected the person and property of the wealthy while the majority were mired in poverty and helplessness. Denying that human beings fared best as competing individuals, socialists contended that people achieved more happiness for themselves and for others as members of a cooperative community, which lived, worked, and planned together for the common good. Some socialists proposed communes or model factory towns as places to realize socialist ideals. The most important early nineteenth-century socialist thinkers—Saint-Simon, Fourier, and Owen—espoused a new social and economic system in which production and distribution of goods would be

planned for the general good of society. Their thought influenced Karl
Marx and Friedrich Engels, who in the second half of the nineteenth
century, became the most influential formulators and propagators of
socialism. There were also Christian communitarians who protested
the unsettling conditions caused by industrialization and the treatment of the poor; these Christian socialists urged believers to share
their property and labor and live together cooperatively in new communities.

Saint-Simon: Technocratic Socialism

Descended from a distinguished French aristocratic family, Henri
Comte de Saint-Simon (1760–1825) renounced his title during the
French Revolution and enthusiastically preached the opportunity for a
new society. He regarded his own society as defective and in need of
reorganization: the critical philosophy of the Enlightenment had shattered the Old Order, but it had not provided a guide for reconstructing
society. Saint-Simon believed that he had a mission to set society right
by providing an understanding of the new age being shaped by science
and industry. Many of the brightest young people believed in his mission.

Saint-Simon argued that just as Christianity had provided social
unity and stability during the Middle Ages, scientific knowledge
would bind the society of his time. The scientists, engineers, industrialists, bankers, artists, and writers would replace the unproductive
classes—clergy, aristocracy, and the idle rich—as the social elite; Saint-
Simon had a romantic love of genius and talent. In the new industrial
age, he thought, the control of society must pass to the "industriels"—
productive people who would harness technology for the betterment
of humanity and eliminate the causes of social conflicts. Saint-Simon's
disciples championed efforts to build great railway and canal systems,
including the Suez and Panama canals. His vision of a rationally
planned and efficiently run society led by trained experts was a powerful force among intellectuals in the nineteenth century.

Like the philosophes, Saint-Simon valued science, had confidence in
the power of reason to improve society, and believed in the certainty
of progress according to laws of social development. Also like the philosophes, he attacked the clergy for clinging to superstition and dogma
at the expense of morality. The essence of Christianity, he said, was
the Golden Rule—the sublime command that people should treat each
other like brothers and sisters. According to Saint-Simon, the traditional clergy, having placed dogma above moral law, had forfeited its
right to lead Europe, just as the aristocracy had before the French Rev-

olution. He called for a "new Christianity" (the title of one of his books) to serve as an antidote to selfish interests.

Saint-Simon's thought reveals several socialist elements: industrial society constituted a new stage in history; unchecked individualism was detrimental to society; and creative and collective planning was necessary to cope with social ills. But a conception crucial to Marxist socialism was absent from his thought: he did not view society as divided into classes with competing interests.

Fourier: Psychological Socialism

Another early French socialist was Charles Fourier (1772–1837), who believed that society conflicted with the natural needs of human beings and that this tension was responsible for human misery. Only the reorganization of society so that it would fulfill people's desires for pleasure and satisfaction would end that misery. Whereas Saint-Simon and his followers had elaborate plans to reorganize society on the grand scale of large industries and giant railway and canal systems, Fourier sought to create small communities to allow men and women to enjoy life's simple pleasures. These communities of about 1,600 people, called phalansteries, would be organized according to the unchanging needs of human nature. In phalansteries, no force would coerce or thwart innocent human drives. Holding that human beings have been degraded by dehumanizing manual labor, Fourier sought to make work emotionally satisfying. All people would work at tasks that interested them and would produce things that brought them and others pleasure; consequently, work would seem like play. Along with Adam Smith, Fourier understood that specialization bred boredom and alienation from work and life. Unlike Smith, he did not believe that vastly increased productivity compensated for the evils of specialization.

In the phalansteries, money and goods would not be equally distributed; those with special skills and responsibilities would be compensated accordingly. This system of rewards accorded with nature, said Fourier, because people have a natural desire to be rewarded.

Both Fourier and Saint-Simon supported female equality; they were among the first social thinkers to do so. Fourier did not define female equality merely in political terms. He thought that marriage distorted the natures of both men and women because monogamy restricted their sexual needs; in the bedroom, as well as in the work place, human nature, ever prone to boredom, required variety. Because married women had to devote all their strength and time to household and children, they had no time or energy left to enjoy life's pleasure. Fourier did not call for the abolition of the family, but he did hope that it would disappear of its own accord as society adjusted to his theories. Men and women would find new ways of fulfilling themselves sexually and the community would be organized so that it would care for the children.

Fourier's ideas found some acceptance in the United States where in the 1840s at least twenty-nine communities were founded on Fourierist principles. But none lasted more than five or six years.

Owen: Industrial Socialism

In 1799, Robert Owen (1771–1858) became part owner and manager of the New Lanark cotton mills in Scotland. Distressed by widespread mistreatment of workers, Owen resolved to improve the lives of his employees and to demonstrate that it was possible to do so without destroying profits. He raised wages, upgraded working conditions, refused to hire children under ten, and provided workers with neat homes, food, and clothing, all at reasonable prices. He set up schools for children and for adults. In every way, he demonstrated his belief that healthier, happier workers produced more than less-fortunate ones. Like Saint-Simon, Owen believed industry and technology could, and would, enrich humankind if organized according to the proper principles. Visitors came from all over Europe to see Owen's factories.

Just like many philosophes, Owen also held that the environment was the principal shaper of character—that the ignorance, alcoholism and crime of the poor derived from bad living conditions. Public education and factory reform, said Owen, would make better citizens of the poor. When Parliament balked at reforms, Owen even urged the creation of a grand national trade union of all the workers in England. In the earliest days of industrialization, with very few workers organized in unions, this dream seemed an impossible one. Owen came to believe that the entire social and economic order must be replaced by a new system based on harmonious group living, rather than on competition. He established a model community at New Harmony, Indiana, but it was short-lived. Even in his factory in Scotland, Owen had some difficulty holding on to the workers, many of whom were devout Christians and resented his secular ideas and the dancing taught to their children in his schools.

NATIONALISM

Nationalism is a conscious bond shared by a group of people who feel strongly attached to a particular land and who possess a common language, culture, and history marked by shared glories and sufferings. Nationalists contend that one's highest loyalty and devotion should be given to the nation. They exhibit great pride in their people's history and traditions and often feel that their nation has been specially chosen by God or history. They assert that the nation—its culture and history—gives meaning to an individual's life and actions. Like a religion, nationalism provides the individual with a sense of community and with a cause worthy of self-sacrifice.

In an age when Christianity was in retreat, nationalism became the dominant spiritual force in nineteenth-century European life. Nationalism provided new beliefs, martyrs, and "holy" days that stimulated reverence; it offered membership in a community, which satisfied an overwhelming psychological need of human beings for fellowship and identity. And nationalism supplied a mission—the advancement of the nation—to which people could dedicate themselves.

Rise of Modern Nationalism

The essential components of modern nationalism emerged during the French Revolution. The Revolution asserted the principle that sovereignty derived from the nation, from the people as a whole—the state was not the private possession of the ruler but the embodiment of the people's will. The nation-state was above king, church, estate, guild, or province; it superseded all other loyalties. The French people must view themselves not as subjects of the king, not as Bretons or Normans, not as nobles or bourgeois, but as citizens of a united fatherland, la patrie. These two ideas—that the people possess unlimited sovereignty and that they are united in a nation—were crucial in the fashioning of modern nationalism.

As the Revolution moved from the moderate to the radical stage, French nationalism intensified. In August 1793, when the Republic was threatened by foreign invasion, the Jacobins decreed the levy in mass, which called for the mobilization of all the nation's human and material resources. War was no longer a conflict between kings fought by small armies of professional soldiers; it had become the struggle of the whole people. Young men were required to serve as soldiers, married men to forge arms, women to make clothing, and old men to deliver patriotic speeches. The Jacobins demanded ever greater allegiance to and sacrifice for the nation, and called for the expansion of France's borders to the Alps and the Rhine. In the schools, in newspapers, speeches, and poems, on the stage, and at rallies and meetings of patriotic societies, the French people were told of the glory won by the republican soldiers on the battlefield and were reminded of their duties to *la patrie.* "The citizen is born, lives, and dies, for the fatherland."[34] These words were written in public places for all citizens to read and ponder. The soldiers of the Revolution fought not for money or for a king but for the nation. "When *la Patrie* calls us for her defense," wrote a young soldier to his mother, "we should rush to her. . . . Our life, our goods, and our talents do not belong to us. It is to the nation, to la patrie, to which everything belongs."[35] Under the Jacobins, the French became converts to a secular faith preaching total reverence for the nation: "In 1794 we believed in no supernatural religion; our serious interior sentiments were all summed up in the one idea, how to be useful to the fatherland. Everything else . . . was, in our eyes, only trivial. . . . It was our only religion."[36]

Was not the heightened sense of nationality that concentrated on the special interests of the French people a rejection of the philosophes' cosmopolitanism, exemplified by Paine's dictum: "My country is the World, my countrymen are Mankind"?[37] Could it be reconciled with the Declaration of the Rights of Man, whose principles were addressed to all humanity? In Rousseauistic language, Louis Antoine de Saint-Just, an ardent Robespierrist, urged sacrificing individual liberty to the requirements of the nation. "You have to punish not only the traitors, but even those who are indifferent; you have to punish whoever is passive in the Republic and does nothing for her. For, since the French people has manifested its will, everything opposed to it is outside the sovereign; whatever is outside the sovereign is an enemy."[38]

The revolutionaries themselves did not understand the implications of the new force that they had unleashed. Few suspected that the new religion of nationalism generated passions that threatened the ideals of reason, freedom, and equality championed by the philosophes and the reformers of 1789. Saint-Just was gazing into our own century when he declared: "There is something terrible in the sacred love of the fatherland. This love is so exclusive that it sacrifices everything to the public interest, without pity, without fear, with no respect for the human individual."[39]

The Romantic Movement also awakened nationalist feelings. Just as all individuals had their own singular personalities, said the romantics, so too did national communities. Johann Gottfried Herder (1744–1803) conceived the idea of the *Volksgeist*—the soul of the people. For Herder, each people was unique and creative; each expressed its genius in language, literature, monuments, and folk traditions. Herder did not make the theoretical leap from a spiritual and cultural nationalism to political nationalism; he did not call for the formation of states based on nationality. Nor did he believe that one people was biologically or culturally superior to another. But his emphasis on the unique culture of a people stimulated a national consciousness among Germans and the various Slavic peoples who lived under foreign rule. The *Volksgeist* led intellectuals to investigate the past of their own people, to rediscover their ancient traditions, and to extol their historic language and culture. By examining the languages, literature, and folkways of their people, romantic thinkers instilled a sense of national pride in their compatriots. From this cultural nationalism it was only a short step to a political nationalism that called for national liberation, unification, and statehood.

The romantics were the earliest apostles of German nationalism. They restored to consciousness memories of the German past, and they emphasized the peculiar qualities of the German folk and the special destiny of the German nation. The romantics expressed an ardent appreciation of the native countryside and ancient folksongs and legends, glorified medieval Germany, and valued hereditary monarchy and aristocracy as vital links to the nation's past. They saw the existence of each individual as inextricably bound up with ancestors, folk, and fatherland, and they found the self-realization for which they yearned by merging their own egos with the national soul. To these romantics, the national community was a vital force that gave the individual both an identity and a purpose in life. The original intent of romanticism, the liberation of individual genius and originality, particularly in poetry and art, was transformed in Germany into a theory of nationalism that saw identification with the national spirit as the avenue to self-fulfillment. And the nation, which bound isolated souls into a community of brethren, stood above the individual. Thus, Ernst Moritz Arndt (1769–1860), the German nationalist poet who glorified the War of Liberation against Napoleon in 1813, said that "the most beautiful thing about all this holy zeal" demonstrated by Germans during the struggle "was that all differences of position, class, and age were forgotten . . . that the one great feeling for the Fatherland, its freedom and honor, swallowed all other feelings, caused all other considerations to be forgotten."[40]

The Napoleonic wars kindled nationalist sentiments in the German states. Hatred of the French occupier evoked a feeling of outrage and a desire for national unity among some Germans, who, before the French occupation, had thought not of a German fatherland but of their own states and princes. These Germans called for a war of liberation against Napoleon. Attracting mostly intellectuals, the idea of political unification had limited impact on the rest of the people, who remained loyal to local princes and local territories. Nevertheless, the embryo of nationalism was conceived in the German uprising against Napoleon in 1813. Arndt's writings vividly express the emerging nationalism. In unmistakably romantic tones, Arndt urged Germans to unite against Napoleon:

> German man, feel again God, hear and fear the eternal, and you hear and fear also your Volk [people], you feel again in God the honor and dignity of your fathers, their glorious history rejuvenates itself in you, their firm and gallant virtue reblossoms in you, the whole German Fatherland stands again before you in the august halo of past centuries. . . . No longer Catholics and Protestants, Prussians and Austrians, Saxons and Bavarians, Silesians and Hanovarians, no longer of different faith, different mentality, and different will—be Germans, be one, will to be one by love and loyalty and no devil [Napoleon] will vanquish you.[41]

Most German romantics expressed hostility to the liberal ideals of the French Revolution. They condemned the reforms of the Revolution for trying to reconstruct society by separating individuals from their national past, for treating them as isolated abstractions. They held that the German folk spirit should not be polluted by foreign French ideas. To the philosophes, the state was a human institution, a rational arrangement between individuals that safeguarded human rights. To German romantics, such a state was an artificial and lifeless construction. The true German state was something holy, the expression of the divine spirit of the German people; it could not be manufactured to order by the intellect. The state's purpose was neither the protection of natural rights nor the promotion of economic well-being; rather, the state was a living organism that linked each person to a sacred past and reconciled and united heterogeneous wills, imbuing them with a profound sense of community. "This 'Romantic' image of a state, founded not on any rational idea of the functions and purposes of a state but on love and perfect communion, is of course a formula for totalitarianism," observes R. J. Hollingdale, "and it was towards a state modeled on this formula that German nationalism continually moved."[42]

Nationalism and Liberalism

In the early nineteenth century, liberals were the principal leaders and supporters of nationalist movements. They viewed the struggle for national rights—the freedom of a people from foreign rule—as an extension of the struggle for the rights of the individual. There could be no liberty, said liberal nationalists, if people were not free to rule themselves in their own land. Liberal nationalists called for the unification of Germany and Italy, the rebirth of Poland, the liberation of Greece from Turkish rule, and the granting of autonomy to the Hungarians of the Austrian Empire. They envisioned a Europe of independent states based on nationality and popular sovereignty. Free of foreign domination and tyrant princes, these newly risen states would protect the rights of the individual and strive to create a brotherhood of nationalities in Europe.

Exemplifying the outlook of liberal nationalism was Giuseppe Mazzini (1805–1872), who dedicated his life to the creation of a united and republican Italy—a goal he pursued with extraordinary moral intensity and determination. Mazzini was both a romantic and a liberal. As a liberal, he fought for republican and constitutional government and held that national unity would enhance individual liberty. As a romantic, he sought truth through heightened feeling and intuition and believed that an awakened Italy would lead to the regeneration of humanity. Mazzini believed that, just as Rome had provided law and unity in the ancient world and the Roman pope had led Latin Christendom during the Middle Ages, a third Rome, a newly united Italy, would usher in a new age of free nations, personal liberty, and equality. This era would represent great progress for humanity; peace, prosperity, and universal happiness would replace conflict, materialism, and self-interest. Given to religious mysticism, Mazzini saw a world of independent states founded on nationality, republicanism, and democracy as the fulfillment of God's plan. Young Italy, a society founded by Mazzini, consisted of dedicated Italian revolutionaries, many of them students. Young Italy was intended to serve as the instrument for the awakening of Italy and the transformation of Europe into a brotherhood of free peoples.

In the first half of the nineteenth century, few intellectuals recognized the dangers inherent in nationalism or understood the fundamental conflict between liberalism and nationalism. For the liberal, the idea of universal natural rights transcended all national boundaries. Inheriting the cosmopolitanism of the Enlightenment, liberalism emphasized what all people had in common, called for all individuals to be treated equally under the law, and preached toleration. Many nationalists, manifesting the particularist attitude of the in-group and the tribe, regarded the nation as the essential fact of existence; it stood before all and above all. Consequently, they often willingly subverted individual liberty for the sake of national grandeur, held that their own nation constituted the highest good, and designated other nationalities as evil. Whereas the liberal sought to protect the rights of all within the state, the nationalist often ignored or trampled on the rights of individuals and national minorities. Whereas liberalism grew out of the rational tradition of the West, nationalism derived from an emotional attachment to ancient customs and bonds, often evoking a mythic and romantic past that distorted history. Because it fulfilled an elemental yearning for community and kinship, nationalism exerted a powerful hold over human hearts, often driving people to political extremism.

During the Revolutions of 1848 in central Europe, the dangers of nationalism became apparent. In March 1848, German liberals clamored for a constitution, parliamentary government, freedom of thought, and an end to police intimidation. Some also called for the creation of a unified Germany governed by a national parliament. Liberals took advantage of their initial success in Prussia and other German states to form a national assembly charged with the task of creating a unified and liberal Germany. It was soon clear that liberal ideals would be sacrificed to nationalist hopes. Democratic deputies urged the assembly to support the rebirth of Poland, which had been partitioned in the late eighteenth century. German nationalists, however, opposed the surrender of Polish lands, an early sign of the triumph of nationalism over liberalism. In an emotional speech, Wilhelm Jordan declared:

> Our right is none other than the right of the stronger, the right of the conqueror. . . . The German conquests in Poland were a natural necessity. The law of history is not like that of the legal code. It knows only the laws of nature, and one of these laws tells us that a people does not have the right to political independence merely by virtue of its mere existence. This comes only as a result of the force to assert itself as a state among other states.[43]

The delegates voted 342 to 31 to keep the Polish lands German.

In 1848, the Magyars sought first local autonomy and then independence from the Hapsburg Empire. The Hungarian leadership introduced liberal reforms—suffrage for all males who could speak Magyar and owned some property, freedom of religion, freedom of the press, the termination of serfdom, and the end of the privileges of nobility and church. Within a few weeks, the Hungarian parliament changed Hungary from a feudal to a modern liberal state. But the Hungarian leaders' nationalist dreams towered above their liberal ideals. The Magyars intended to incorporate lands inhabited by Serbs, Slovaks, and Romanians into their kingdom and transform these people, whom they regarded as cultural inferiors, into Hungarians. As Hugh Seton-Watson has written,

> Kossuth and his friends genuinely believed that they were doing the non-Hungarians a kindness by giving them a chance of becoming absorbed in the superior Hungarian culture. To refuse this kindness was nationalist fanaticism; to impose it by force was to promote progress. The suggestion that Rumanians, Slovaks, or Serbs were nations, with a national culture of their own, was simply ridiculous nonsense.[44]

Before 1848, democratic idealists like Mazzini had envisioned the birth of a new Europe of free peoples and liberated nations. The revolutions of 1848 showed that for many Europeans, including liberals, nationalism was a more important sentiment than liberalism, that nationalism and liberalism were not natural allies, that to many people national power was more important than individual liberty. In 1848, Nicholas Balescu, a Romanian patriot, voiced these sentiments:

> For my part, the question of nationality is more important than liberty. Until a people can exist as a nation, it cannot make use of liberty. Liberty can easily be recovered when it is lost, but not nationality. Therefore I believe that in the present position of our country we must aim rather at the preservation of our . . . nationality and seek only as much liberty as is necessary for the development of nationality.[45]

That nationalism seemed to prevail over liberalism was a dangerous portent for the future. Disheartened by these nationalist antagonisms, John Stuart Mill lamented that "the sentiment of nationality so far outweighs the love of liberty that the people are willing to abet their rulers in crushing the liberty and independence of any people not of their race or language."[46] In the Revolutions of 1848, concludes British historian Lewis Namier, "nationality, the passionate creed of the intellectuals, invades the politics of central and east-central Europe, and with 1848 starts the Great European War of every nation against its neighbors."[47]

In the last part of the nineteenth century, the irrational and mythical quality of nationalism would intensify. By stressing the unique qualities and history of a particular people, nationalism would promote hatred between nationalities. By kindling deep love for the past, including a longing for ancient borders, glories, and power, nationalism would lead to wars of expansion. By arousing the emotions to fever pitch, nationalism would shatter rational thinking, drag the mind into a world of fantasy and myth, and introduce extremism into politics. Love of nation would become an overriding passion threatening to extinguish the liberal ideals of reason, freedom, and equality.

NOTES

1. Excerpted in Marvin Perry et al., eds., *Sources of the Western Tradition*, 2nd ed. (Boston: Houghton Mifflin, 1991), II, 119.
2. Ibid.
3. Robert Nisbet, *Conservatism: Dream and Reality* (Minneapolis: University of Minnesota Press, 1986), p. 1.
4. Quoted in George Brandes, *Rev-*

olution and Reaction in Nineteenth Century French Literature (New York: Russell & Russell, reprint, n. d), pp. 106–107.

5. Edmund Burke, *Reflections on the Revolution in France* (New York: Liberal Arts Press, 1955), pp. 40, 89.

6. Ibid., p. 97.

7. Ibid., p. 99.

8. Ibid., p. 70.

9. Joseph de Maistre, *Essay on the Generative Principle of Political Constitutions*, in *On God and Society*, ed. Elisha Greifer and trans. Elisha Greifer with the assistance of Lawrence Porter (Chicago: Regnery, Gateway, 1959), pp. 3, 12.

10. Quoted in Jerzy Szacki, *History of Sociological Thought* (Westport, Conn.: Greenwood, 1979), pp. 95–96.

11. Joseph de Maistre, *Consideration on France*, excerpted in *The Works of Joseph de Maistre* ed. and trans. Jack Lively (New York: Schocken Books, 1971), pp. 71–72.

12. Quoted in Friedrich B. Artz, *Reaction and Revolution, 1814–1832* (New York: Harper Torchbooks, 1963), p. 73.

13. Maistre, *Essay on the Generative Principle of Political Constitutions*, p. 54.

14. John Locke, the *Second Treatise* in *Two Treatises of Government*, ed. Peter Laslett (New York: New American Library, Mentor Books, 1963), chap. 5, sec. 44, pp. 340–341.

15. Excerpted in W. M. Simon, ed., *French Liberalism, 1789–1848* (New York: Wiley, 1972), p. 65.

16. John Stuart Mill, *On Liberty*, ed. Currin V. Shields (Indianapolis: Library of Liberal Arts, 1956), chap. 1, p. 13.

17. Roger Henry Soltau, *French Political Thought in the Nineteenth Century* (New York: Russell & Russell, 1931), p. 33.

18. Alexis de Tocqueville. *Democracy in America*, trans. Henry Reeve (New York: Oxford University Press, 1924), p. 162.

19. Ibid., pp. 493–494.

20. Adam Smith, *An Inquiry into the Nature and Causes of the Wealth of Nations*, eds. R. H. Campbell et al. (Oxford: Clarendon Press, 1976), I, 454, 456.

21. Ibid., p. 96.

22. Ibid., p. 99.

23. Thomas Robert Malthus, *First Essay on Population*, reprinted for the Royal Economic Society (London: Macmillan, 1926), p. 16.

24. Ibid., p. 17.

25. David Ricardo, *The Principles of Political Economy and Taxation*, ed. Ernest Rhys (London: Dent, Everyman's Library, 1911), pp. 53, 61.

26. Quoted in Anthony Arblaster, *The Rise and Decline of Western Liberalism* (Oxford: Blackwell, 1984), p. 258.

27. Quoted in Raymond William, *Culture and Society, 1780–1945* (New York: Columbia University Press, 1983), p. 14.

28. Thomas Paine, *Rights of Man*, in *Common Sense and Other Political Writings*, ed., Nelson F. Adkins (Indianapolis: Library of Liberal Arts, 1953), p. 118.

29. Ibid., p. 122.

30. Ibid., p. 80.

31. John W. Derry, *The Radical Tradition* (New York: St. Martin's, 1967), p. 42.

32. Jeremy Bentham, *An Introduc-*

tion to the *Principles of Morals and Legislation* and a *Fragment on Government* (London: Blackwell, 1948), chap. 1, sec. 1, p. 125.

33. *The Defense of Gracchus Babeuf,* ed. and trans. John Anthony Scott (New York: Schocken Books, 1972), pp. 45–47.

34. Quoted in Hans Kohn, *Nationalism: Its Meaning and History* (Princeton: Van Nostrand, 1965), p. 25.

35. Quoted in Carlton C. J. H. Hayes, *The Historical Evolution of Modern Nationalism* (New York: Richard R. Smith, 1931), p. 55.

36. Ibid.

37. Quoted in Thomas J. Schlereth, *The Cosmopolitan Ideal in Enlightenment Thought* (Notre Dame, Indiana: University of Notre Dame Press, 1977), p. 203.

38. Quoted in Hans Kohn, *Prelude to Nation-States* (Princeton: Van Nostrand, 1962), p. 62.

39. Quoted in Hans Kohn, *Making of the Modern French Mind* (New York: Van Nostrand, 1955), p. 17.

40. Excerpted in Louis L. Snyder, ed., *The Dynamics of Nationalism* (Princeton: Van Nostrand, 1964), p. 146.

41. Ibid., pp. 146–147.

42. R. J. Hollingdale, *Nietzsche* (London: Routledge & Kegan Paul, 1973), p. 25.

43. Quoted in Koppel S. Pinson, *Modern Germany* (New York: Macmillan, 1954), p. 99.

44. Hugh Seton-Watson, *Nations and States* (Boulder, Colo.: Westview, 1977), p. 162.

45. Quoted in Hans Kohn, *The Twentieth Century* (New York: Macmillan, 1949), p. 15.

46. Quoted in Kohn, *Nationalism,* pp. 51–52.

47. Lewis Namier, *1848: The Revolution of the Intellectuals* (Garden City, N.Y.: Doubleday Anchor Books, 1964), p. 38.

SUGGESTED READING

Arblaster, Anthony, *The Rise and Decline of Western Liberalism* (1984).

Bullock, Alan, and Shock, Maurice, eds., *The Liberal Tradition* (1956).

Derry, John W., *The Radical Tradition* (1967).

Drescher, Seymour, *Dilemmas of Democracy: Tocqueville and Modernization* (1968).

Epstein, Klaus, *The Genesis of German Conservatism* (1966).

Fried, Albert, and Sanders, Ronald, eds., *Socialist Thought* (1964).

Gray, John, *Liberalism* (1986).

Hayes, Carlton, J. H., *Historical Evolution of Modern Nationalism* (1931).

Kohn, Hans, *The Idea of Nationalism* (1961).

Lively, Jack, ed., *The Works of Joseph de Maistre* (1971).

MacCoby, S., ed., *The English Radical Tradition, 1763–1914* (reprint 1952).

Manuel, Frank, *The Prophets of Paris* (1962).

Markham, F.M.H., ed., *Henri Comte de Saint-Simon* (1952).

Nisbet, Robert, *Conservatism* (1986).

Poster, Mark, ed., *Harmonian Man* (1971).

Schapiro, J. S., *Liberalism, Its Meaning and History* (1958).

Shafer, B. C., *Faces of Nationalism* (1972).

Simon, W. M., *French Liberalism 1789–1848* (1972).

Smith, A. D., *Theories of Nationalism* (1972).

Soltau, Roger H., *French Political Thought in the Nineteenth Century* (1931).

Strauss, Leo and Cropsey, Joseph, eds., *History of Political Philosophy* (1963).

Weiss, John, *Conservatism in Europe, 1770–1945* (1977).

8

Thought and Culture in an Age of Science and Industrialism

The second half of the nineteenth century was characterized by great progress in science, a surge in industrialization, and a continuing secularization of life and thought. The principal intellectual currents of the century's middle decades reflected these trends. Realism, positivism, Darwinism, Marxism, and liberalism all reacted against romantic, religious, and metaphysical interpretations of nature and society and focused on the empirical world. In one way or another, each movement derived from and expanded the Enlightenment tradition. Adherents of these movements relied on careful observation and strove for scientific accuracy. This emphasis on objective reality helped to stimulate a growing criticism of social ills, for despite unprecedented material progress, reality was often sordid, somber, and dehumanizing. In the last part of the century, reformers, motivated by an expansive liberalism, revolutionary or evolutionary socialism, or a socially committed Christianity, pressed for the alleviation of social injustice.

REALISM

Realism, the dominant movement in art and literature in the mid-nineteenth century, opposed the romantic veneration of the inner life and romantic sentimentality. The romantics exalted passion and intuition, let their imaginations transport them to a presumed idyllic medieval past, and sought subjective solitude amid nature's wonders. Realists, on the other hand, concentrated on the actual world, on social conditions and contemporary mores, and on the familiar details of everyday life. With clinical detachment and meticulous care, they analyzed how people looked, worked, and behaved.

Like scientists, realist writers and artists investigated the empirical world. For example, Gustave Courbet (1819–1877), who exemplified realism in painting, sought to practice what he called a "living art," painting common people and commonplace scenes—laborers breaking stones, peasants tilling the soil or returning from a fair, a country burial, wrestlers, bathers, family groups. In a matter-of-fact style, without any attempt at glorification, and refraining from interjecting their own personalities and their own subjective feelings, realist artists also depicted floor scrapers, rag pickers, prostitutes, and beggars. Gustave Flaubert (1821–1880), said of *Madame Bovary*, his masterpiece of realist literature: "Art ought . . . to rise above personal feelings and nervous susceptibilities! It is time to give it the precision of the physical sciences by means of a pitiless method."[1] E. M. de Vogüé, a nineteenth-century French writer, described realism as follows:

> They [realists] have brought about an art of observation rather than of imagination, one which boasts that it observes life as it is in its wholeness and complexity with the least possible prejudice on the part of the artist. It takes men under ordinary conditions, shows characters in the course of their everyday existence, average and changing. Jealous of the rigour of scientific procedure, the writer proposes to instruct us by a perpetual analysis of feelings and of acts rather than to divert us or move us by intrigue and exhibition of the passions. . . . The new art seeks to imitate nature.[2]

Romantic writers had written lyrics, for lyric poetry is the language of feeling; the novel, because it lends itself admirably to depicting human behavior and social conditions, was the literary genre used by realist writers. Numerous realist novels were serialized in the inexpensive newspapers and magazines that the many newly literate common people could read. Thus, the commoners' interests helped shape the content of the novels. Seeking to portray reality as it is, realist writers frequently dealt with social abuses and the sordid aspects of human behavior and social life. In his novels, Honoré de Balzac (1799–1850) described how social and economic forces affected people's behavior. In *Dead Souls*, (1842) an early work of Russian realism, Nikolai Gogol depicted the injustices of serfdom. Ivan Turgenev's *Sketches* (1852) described rural conditions in Russia and expressed compassion for the brutally difficult life of serfs. The angered authorities arrested Turgenev and exiled him to his country estate. In *War and Peace* (1863–

1869), Leo Tolstoy vividly described the manners and outlook of the Russian nobility and the tragedies that attended Napoleon's invasion of Russia. In *Anna Karenina* (1873–1877), he treated the reality of class divisions and the complexities of marital relationships. Fyodor Dostoevski's *Crime and Punishment* (1866) is a psychological novel that provides penetrating insights into human behavior. Eugène Sue's serialized novel, *Les Mystères de Paris* (1842–1843) offered harrowing accounts of slum life and crime in Paris. George Sand's* *Indiana* (1832), which saw the married woman as a victim, was praised by a reviewer for presenting "a true, living world, which is our world . . . characters and manners just as we can observe them around us, natural conversations, scenes in familiar settings, violent, uncommon passions, but sincerely felt or observed . . ."[3]

Many regard Gustave Flaubert's *Madame Bovary* (1857) as the prototype of the realistic novel; it tells the story of a self-centered bourgeois wife who shows her disdain for her devoted, hardworking, but dull husband by committing adultery. One observer, commenting on the realistic character of the novel, said that it "represents an obsession with description. Details are counted one by one, all are given equal value, every street, every house, every room, every book, every blade of grass is described in full. . . . There is neither emotion nor feeling for life in this novel."[4]

The novels of Charles Dickens—*Bleak House* (1853), *Hard Times* (1854), and several others—depicted in detail the squalor of life, the hypocrisy of society, and the drudgery of labor in British industrial cities. Elizabeth Gaskell, the wife of a Unitarian minister in Manchester, dealt compassionately with the plight of industrial workers in her *Mary Barton* (1848) and *North and South* (1855).

Literary realism evolved into naturalism when writers tried to demonstrate that there was a causal relationship between human character and the social environment—that certain conditions of life produced predictable character traits in human beings. This belief that human behavior was governed by a law of cause and effect reflected the immense prestige attached to science in the closing decades of the nineteenth century. Émile Zola (1840–1902), the leading naturalist novelist, had an unreserved confidence in the scientific method. He described the task of the writer in an age of science as follows:

> Man is not alone; he lives in society, in a social condition; and consequently, for us novelists, this social condition unceasingly modifies the phenomena. Indeed our great study is just there, in the reciprocal effect of society on the individual and the individual on society. . . . And this

*George Sand was the pseudonym for the female French novelist Amandine Aurore Lucie Dupin (1804–1876).

is what constitutes the experimental novel. . . . [which] is a consequence of the scientific evolution of the century; it continues and completes physiology, which itself leans for support on chemistry and medicine; it substitutes for the study of the abstract and the metaphysical man the study of the natural man, governed by physical and chemical laws, and modified by the influences of his surroundings; it is in one word the literature of our scientific age, as the classical and romantic corresponded to a scholastic and theological age.[5]

In his novels, Zola searched for laws of human development, aspiring to do for social relations what Darwin did for humanity's physical development. He probed the slums, brothels, mining villages, and cabarets of France, examining how people were conditioned by the squalor of their environment. In *Germinal* (1885), his greatest novel, Zola graphically depicted the terrible toil and drudgery that coal miners had to endure.

The Norwegian Henrik Ibsen, the leading naturalist playwright, examined with clinical precision the commercial and professional classes—their personal ambitions and family relationships. In the *Pillars of Society* (1877), Ibsen treated bourgeois social pretensions and hypocrisy; in *A Doll's House* (1879), a woman leaves her husband and the "doll house" environment he had created for her in search of a more fulfilling life, a theme that shocked a late-nineteenth-century bourgeois audience.

In aiming for a true-to-life portrayal of human behavior and the social environment, realism and naturalism coincided with an attitude of mind shaped by science, industrialism, and secularism. Their empirical approach to the world and their social criticism link realist and naturalist writers to the Enlightenment. Both movements reasserted the importance of the external world. The same outlook also gave rise to positivism in philosophy.

POSITIVISM

In the nineteenth century, science and technology continued to make astonishing strides, which, combined with striking economic advancement, led many westerners to believe that they were living in an era of such progress that a golden age was on the horizon. In *The Future of Science* (1849), Ernest Renan (1823–1892), a French historian and man of letters, viewed science as a force for human liberation from superstition, ignorance, and prejudice. It "free[d] us spiritually," he claimed. "It broke the tyranny of the old holy lies. It extinguished the funeral piles of witches and heretics," and it fostered a rational and humanitarian outlook that led to the emancipation of Jews and the abolition of the slave trade. "The triumph of scientific methods," continued Renan "will appear to posterity as just such a landmark in the development of humanity as the triumph of monotheism 1800 years earlier. . . . if there is one criterion which for us indicates the progress of humanity, it is . . . the level attained of power over nature."[6]

Regarding science as the highest achievement of the mind, many intellectuals sought to apply the scientific method to other areas of thought. They believed that this method was a reliable way to approach all problems. They insisted that history could be studied scientifically and society reorganized according to scientific laws of social development. Marxism was one attempt to fashion a science of society; another attempt was positivism.

Positivists held that although people's knowledge of nature was vastly expanding they did not understand society. This deficiency could be remedied by using a strict empirical approach in the study of society. The philosopher must proceed like a scientist, carefully assembling and classifying data and formulating general rules that demonstrate regularities in the social experience. Such knowledge, based on concrete facts, would provide the social planner with useful insights. Positivists rejected metaphysics, which in the tradition of Plato tried to discover ultimate principles through reason alone, rather than through observation of the empirical world. For the positivist, any effort to go beyond the realm of experience to a deeper reality would be a mistaken and fruitless endeavor. The positivist restricted human knowledge to what could be experienced and saw the method of science as the only valid approach to knowledge.

The leading figure in the emergence of positivism was Auguste Comte (1798–1857), an engineer with thorough scientific training. Comte served as secretary to Saint-Simon (see page 230) until their association, punctuated by frequent quarrels, ended in 1824. But much of Saint-Simon's thought found its way into Comte's philosophy. Like Saint-Simon (and Marx), Comte called for a purely scientific approach to history and society: only by a proper understanding of the laws governing human affairs could society, which was in a state of intellectual anarchy, be rationally organized. Again like Saint-Simon, Comte held that the Enlightenment and the French Revolution had shattered the Old Regime but had not replaced it with new institutions and a new ideology; this was the pressing need of the age.

Comte called his system positivism because he believed that it rested on sure knowledge derived from observed facts and was therefore empirically verifiable. Like others of his generation, Comte believed that scientific laws operated in human affairs and that they were discoverable through the methods of the empirical scientist, that is, through recording and systematizing observable data. "I shall bring factual proof," he said, "that there are just as definite laws for the development of the human race as there are for the fall of a stone."[7]

One of the laws that Comte believed he had discovered was the "law of the three stages." Comte held that the human mind had progressed through three broad historical stages: the theological, the metaphysical, and the scientific. In the theological stage—the most primitive—the mind found a supernatural explanation for the origins and purpose of things, and society was ruled by priests. In the metaphysical stage, which included the Enlightenment, the mind tried to explain things through abstractions—nature, equality, natural rights, popular sovereignty—that rested on hope and belief rather than on empirical investigation. The metaphysical stage was a transitional period between the infantile theological stage and the highest stage of society, the scientific, or positive, stage. In this culminating stage, the mind breaks with all illusions inherited from the past, formulates laws based on careful observation of the empirical world, and reconstructs society in accordance with these laws. People remove all mystery from nature and base their social legislation on laws of society similar to the laws of nature discovered by Newton.

Regarding religion as a necessary outlet for human emotional needs, Comte proposed a Religion of Humanity, in which the human race, its past and future, would become an object of veneration, replacing the God of Christianity. A scientific-industrial elite would replace the Christian priesthood. The new nontheistic religion, complete with dogmas, rituals, and heroes, would help men and women cope with the grim realities of life; it would bind society together and promote morality.

Because Comte advocated the scientific study of society, he is regarded as a principal founder of sociology—it was he who coined the term. Comte's effort inspired many thinkers to collect and analyze critically all data pertaining to social phenomena. Émile Durkheim (see pages 322–324), a pioneer in the science of sociology, declared his indebtedness to Comte and, despite criticisms of Comte's work, recommended it as a superb introduction to the study of sociology. In trying to make the study of civilization an exact science, English historian, Henry T. Buckle (1821–1862), proceeded in the positivist manner. Buckle saw human culture as a product of climate, soil, and food; consequently, he thought that the achievements of western Europe were due to a favorable environment and the backwardness of Russia and Africa to an unfavorable one. Buckle believed that rigorous laws operated in the social world and that they could be uncovered best through statistical studies. Positivism also appealed to freethinkers and secularists, who supported Comte's effort to devise a system of ethics independent of traditional theistic religion.

Although Comte attacked the philosophes for delving into abstractions instead of fashioning laws based on empirical knowledge, he was also influenced by the spirit of eighteenth-century philosophy. Like the philosophes, he valued science, criticized supernatural religion, and believed in progress. In this way, he accepted the Enlightenment's legacy, including the empirical and antitheological spirit of Diderot's *Encyclopedia* and Montesquieu's quest for historical laws governing society. Comte also acknowledged his debt to Condorcet, who saw intellectual and social progress as an inevitable condition of humanity.

DARWINISM

Many contributed to the steady advance of science in the nineteenth century. In 1808, John Dalton, an English chemist, formulated the atomic theory. In 1831, another English chemist, Michael Faraday, discovered the principle of electromagnetic induction, on which the electric generator and electric motor are based. In 1847, Hermann von Helmholtz, a German physicist, formulated the law of conservation of energy, which states that the total amount of energy in the universe is always the same; energy that is used up is not lost but is converted into heat. In 1887, another German physicist, Heinrich Hertz, discovered electromagnetic waves, which later made possible the invention of radio, television, and radar. In 1869, Dmitri Mendeleev, a Russian chemist, constructed a periodic table for the elements, helping make chemistry more systematic and mathematical. In 1861, Louis Pasteur, a French scientist, proved that diseases were caused by microbes and devised vaccines to prevent them.

Perhaps the most important scientific advance was the theory of evolution formulated by Charles Darwin (1809–1882), an English naturalist. Darwin did for his discipline what Newton had done for physics: he made biology an objective science based on general principles. The Scientific Revolution of the seventeenth century had produced a new conception of space; Darwin radically altered our conception of time.

Natural Selection

During the eighteenth century, almost all people had adhered to the biblical account of creation contained in Genesis: God had instantaneously created the universe and the various species of animal and plant life; and he had given every river and mountain and each species of animal and plant life a finished and permanent form distinct from every other species. God had designed the bird's wings so that it could fly, the fish's eyes so that it could see under water, and the human legs so that people could walk. All this, it was believed, had occurred some five thousand years ago.

Gradually, this view was questioned. Already in 1794, Erasmus Darwin, the grandfather of Charles Darwin, had published *Zoonomia, or the Laws of Organic Life*, which offered evidence that the earth had existed for millions of years before the appearance of people and that animals experienced modifications that they passed on to their offspring. Between 1830 and 1833, Sir Charles Lyell published his three-volume *Principles of Geology*, which showed that the planet had evolved slowly over many ages.

In December 1831, Charles Darwin sailed as a naturalist on the H.M.S. *Beagle*, which surveyed the shores of South America and some Pacific islands. During the five-year expedition, Darwin collected and examined specimens of plant and animal life. He concluded that many animal species had perished, that new species had emerged, and that there were links between extinct and living species.

Influenced by Lyell's achievement, Darwin sought to interpret distant natural occurrences by means of observable processes that were still going on. He could not accept that a fixed number of distinct and separate species had been instantaneously created a mere five thousand years ago. In the *Origin of Species* (1859) and the *Descent of Man* (1871), Darwin used empirical evidence to show that the wide variety of animal species was due to a process of development over many millennia, and he supplied a convincing theory that explained how evolution operates.

Darwin adopted the Malthusian idea that the population reproduces faster than the food supply, causing a struggle for existence. Not all infant organisms grow to adulthood; not all adult organisms live to old age. The principle of natural selection determines which members of the species have a better chance of survival. The offspring of a lion, giraffe, or insect are not exact duplications of their parents. A baby lion might have the potential for being slightly faster or stronger than its parents; a baby giraffe might grow up to have a longer neck than its parents; an insect might have a slightly different color. These small variations give the organism a crucial advantage in the struggle for food and against natural enemies. The organism favored by nature is more likely to reach maturity, to mate, and to pass on its superior qualities to its offspring, some of which will acquire the advantageous trait to an even greater degree than the parent. Over many generations, the favorable characteristic becomes more pronounced and more wide-spread within the species. Over many millennia, natural selection causes the death of old species and the creation of new ones. Very few of the species that dwelt on earth 10 million years ago still survive, and many new ones, including human beings, have emerged. People themselves are products of natural selection, evolving from earlier, lower, nonhuman forms of life.

In *The Descent of Man*, Darwin stated unequivocally:

> The main conclusion here arrived at . . . is that man is descended from some less highly organised form. The grounds upon which this conclusion rests will never be shaken, for the close similarity between man and the lower animals in embryonic development, as well as in innumerable points of structure and constitution . . . are facts which cannot be disputed. . . . The great principle of evolution stands up clear and firm. . . . He who is not content to look, like a savage, at the phenomena of nature as disconnected, cannot any longer believe that man is the work of a separate act of creation. . . .
>
> We must . . . acknowledge . . . that man with all his noble qualities, with sympathy which feels for the most debased, with benevolence which extends not only to other men but to the humblest living creatures, with his god-like intellect which has penetrated into the movements and constitution of the solar system—with all these exalted powers—Man still bears in his bodily frame the indelible stamp of his lowly origin.[8]

Darwinism and Christianity

Like Newton's law of universal gravitation, Darwin's theory of evolution had revolutionary consequences in areas other than science. Evolution challenged traditional Christian belief. To some, it undermined the infallibility of Scripture and called into question crucial Christian doctrines—the Fall, Original Sin, Atonement, Redemption, and human uniqueness—that rested on the history of humanity as presented in the Bible. Natural selection could explain the development of the organic world without reference to any divine design. Indeed, references to God's design and purpose now seemed superfluous and an obstacle to a scientific understanding of nature.

Darwin's theory touched off a great religious controversy between outraged fundamentalists, who defended a literal interpretation of Genesis, and advocates of the new biology. One theologian asserted that the Darwinian theory "does open violence to everything which the Creator himself has told us in the *Scriptures* of the methods and results of his work."[9] Another declared: "If the Darwinian theory is true, Genesis is a lie, the whole framework of the book of life falls to pieces, and the revelation of God to man, as we Christians know it, is a delusion and a snare."[10] A Methodist publication contended: "We regard this theory, which seeks to eliminate from the universe the immediate, ever-present, all pervasive action of a living and personal God, which excludes the possibility of the supernatural and the miraculous . . . as practically destructive of the authority of divine revelation, and subversive of the foundation of religion and morality."[11] Taking a rigidly uncompromising stance, fundamentalists, who were likely to be evangelical Protestants, outright rejected evolution and every other scientific discovery that seemed to conflict with a literal reading of Scripture.

In time, most religious thinkers tried to reconcile evolution with the Christian view that there was a Creation and that it had a purpose. These Christian thinkers held that God was the creator and director of the evolutionary process. The Bible, they contended, was a work of spiritual truth; it was never intended to serve as a textbook in science or as a work of historical scholarship. Many sections had an allegorical meaning and should not be taken literally.

Darwinism ultimately helped to end the practice of relying on the Bible as an authority in questions of science, completing a trend initiated by Galileo. Scientists concerned with empirical data, with the corroboration of conclusions, and with how nature operates had little in common with theologians, whose belief in a teleological purpose to life could not be scientifically tested and whose spiritual concerns were seen as beyond the province of science. Increasingly, theology came under attack as obscurantist and an obstacle to the advancement of knowledge—a theme richly developed by Andrew D. White in his *A History of the Warfare of Science with Theology in Christendom* (1896).

Darwinism contributed to the waning of religious belief and to a growing secular attitude that dismissed or paid scant attention to the Christian view of a universe designed by God and a soul that rises to heaven. For many, the conclusion was inescapable: nature contained no divine design or purpose, and the human species itself was a chance product of impersonal forces. The core idea of Christianity—that people were children of God participating in a drama of salvation—rested more than ever on faith rather than reason. Some declared God an "unnecessary hypothesis," rejected completely that the Bible was the Word of God, and even talked openly of the "death of God."

The notion that people are sheer accidents of nature, that they dwell in a purposeless and uncaring universe in which death and not God reigns, was shocking. Copernicus had deprived people of the comforting belief that the earth had been placed in the center of the universe just for them; Darwin deprived people of the privilege of being God's special creation, thereby contributing to the feeling of anxiety that characterizes the twentieth century. Historian Carl Becker eloquently described the new outlook produced by modern science in general and Darwinism in particular:

> Edit and interpret the conclusions of modern science as tenderly as we like, it is still quite impossible for us to regard man as the child of God for whom the earth was created as a temporary habitation. Rather must we regard him as little more than a chance deposit on the surface of the world, carelessly thrown up between two ice ages by the same forces that rust iron and ripen corn. . . . What is man that the electron should be mindful of him! Man is but a foundling in the cosmos abandoned by the forces that created him. Unparented, unassisted, and undirected by omniscient or benevolent authority, he must fend for himself, and with the aid of his own limited intelligence find his way about in an indifferent universe.[12]

Social Darwinism

Darwin's theories were extended by others beyond the realm in which he had worked. Social thinkers, who recklessly applied Darwin's conclusions to the social order, produced theories that had dangerous consequences for society. Social Darwinists—those who transferred Darwin's scientific theories to social and economic issues—used the terms "struggle for existence" and "survival of the fittest" to buttress economic individualism and political conservatism. They contended that social reforms instituted by the government upset the competitive order decreed by nature; by favoring the least fit, these ill-conceived reforms weakened the nation. Successful businessmen, they said, had demonstrated their fitness to succeed in the competitive world of business. Their success accorded with nature's laws and therefore was beneficial to society; those who lost out in the socioeconomic struggle had demonstrated their unfitness. Thus, American industrialist Andrew Carnegie (1835–1919) wrote in *The Gospel of Wealth* (1900),

> We accept and welcome . . . the concentration of business, industrial and commercial, in the hands of a few and the law of competition . . . as being, not only beneficial, but essential to the future progress of the race. . . . We start, then, with a condition of affairs under which the best interests of the race are promoted, but which inevitably gives wealth to the few.[13]

John D. Rockefeller (1839–1937) held that "The growth of a large business is merely the survival of the fittest. . . . This is not an evil tendency in business. It is merely the working out of a law of nature and a law of God."[14]

Using Darwin's model of organisms evolving and changing slowly over tens of thousands of years, conservatives insisted that society too should experience change at an unhurried pace. Instant reforms conflicted with nature's laws and wisdom and resulted in the deterioration of the social body. The application of Darwin's biological concepts to the social world, where they did not apply, also buttressed imperialism, racism, nationalism, and militarism—doctrines that preached progress through relentless conflict among nations and races (see Chapter 10).

MARXISM

The failure of the revolutions of 1848 and a growing fear of working-class violence led liberals to abandon revolution and to press for reforms through the political process. In the last part of the nineteenth century, Marxists and anarchists became the chief proponents of revolution. Both liberals and Marxists shared common principles derived from the Enlightenment. Both believed in the essential goodness and perfectibility of human nature and claimed that their doctrines rested on rational foundations. Both aspired to liberate individuals from accumulated superstition, ignorance, and prejudices of the past and to fashion a more harmonious and rational society. And both believed in social progress and valued the full realization of human talents.

Despite these similarities, the differences between liberalism and Marxism are profound. The goal of Marxism—the seizure of power by the working class and the destruction of capitalism—was inimical to bourgeois liberals; so too was the Marxist belief that class struggle and violence were the essence of history, the instruments of progress, and the vehicle to a higher stage of humanity. Liberals, who placed the highest value on the individual, held that through education and self-discipline people could overcome inequality and poverty. Marxists, on the other hand, insisted that, without a transformation of the economic system, individual effort by the downtrodden would amount to very little.

Karl Marx (1818–1883) was born of German-Jewish parents (both descendants of prominent rabbis). To save his career as a lawyer, Marx's father converted to Lutheranism. Enrolled in a university to study law, Marx switched to philosophy, embracing elements of Hegel's thought. In 1842, Marx was editing a newspaper that was soon suppressed by the Prussian authorities for its outspoken ideas. Leaving his native

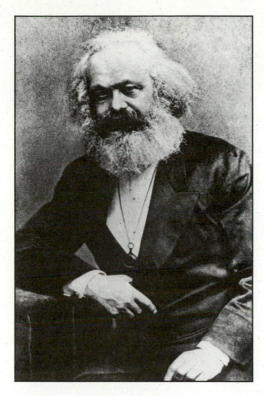

Karl Marx *(The Bettmann Archive)*

Rhineland, Marx went to Paris, where he met another German, Friedrich Engels (1820–1895), who was the son of a prosperous textile manufacturer. Marx and Engels entered into a lifelong collaboration and became members of socialist groups. In February 1848, they published the *Communist Manifesto*, which called for a working-class revolution to overthrow the capitalist system. Forced to leave France in 1849 because of his political views, Marx moved to London, where he spent the rest of his life. Although supported by Engels, Marx was continually short of funds, and at times he and his wife and daughters lived in dreadful poverty. In London, Marx spent years writing *Capital* (1867)*—a study and critique of the modern capitalist economic system, which, he predicted, would be destroyed by a socialist revolution.

*Edited by Engels, volumes 2 and 3 of *Capital* were published in 1885 and 1894.

A Science of History

As did other thinkers influenced by the Enlightenment, Marx believed that human history, like the operations of nature, was governed by scientific law. He insisted that he had discovered the laws of nature operating in history and society. Marx was a strict materialist, rejecting all religious and metaphysical interpretations of both nature and society. He viewed religion as a human creation—a product of people's imagination and feelings, a consolation for the oppressed—and considered the happiness it brought an illusion. Real happiness would come, said Marx, not by transcending the natural world but by improving it. Rather than deluding oneself by seeking refuge from life's misfortunes in an imaginary world conjured up by religion or Hegelian metaphysics, one must confront the ills of society directly and remedy them. This last point is crucial: "The philosophers have only *interpreted* the world in different ways; the point is to *change* it."[15] Philosophy should seek to understand the past in order to alter the present, Marx insisted. It should not be disinterested speculation but a force for social liberation. There must be a unity of thought and practice.

The world could be rationally understood and changed, said Marx. People were free to make their own history, but to do so effectively, they must comprehend the inner meaning of history—the laws governing human affairs in the past and operating in the present. Marx adopted Hegel's view that history was not an assortment of unrelated and disconnected events but rather a progressive development, which, like the growth of a plant, proceeded according to its own inner laws. For both Hegel and Marx, the historical process was governed by objective and rational principles; it was intelligible. Marx also adopted Hegel's view that history advanced dialectically, that the clash of opposing forces propelled history into higher stages and toward a final destination: a harmonious society.

However, Marx also broke with Hegel in crucial ways. For Hegel, history was the unfolding of the metaphysical Spirit or Idea. According to Marx, Hegel's system suffered from mystification. It transcended the realities of the known world; it downgraded the real world, which becomes a mere attribute of Spirit. Marx saw Hegel's abstract philosophy as diverting attention from the real world and its problems, which cry out for understanding and solution; it was a negation of life. For Marx, history was explainable solely in terms of natural processes, empirically verifiable developments; reality could not be reduced to something metaphysical or spiritual.

Building on Feuerbach's naturalistic approach to religion (see pages 198–200), Marx, as it is often said, turned Hegel upside down. Hegel began with a metaphysical consciousness, the Idea, Spirit, or God, which unfolded itself in human existence. Human beings and the human situation were attributes or emanations of the universal Idea, whose self-actualization gave essential meaning to the historical process. For Marx, the real relation of thought to human life was the exact reverse. The starting point and ultimate significance of history is found in the human social and economic environment, the natural conditions of life; thought is a product of these conditions. Marx valued Hegel's insight that history is a progressive and purposeful process, but he criticized Hegel for embedding this insight in metaphysical-theological fantasy. Hegel, said Marx, had made a mystical principle the real subject of history and thought. But in truth, it is the "real man," the person who lives in and is conditioned by the objective world, who is the only true reality and the center of history. History is not Spirit aspiring to self-actualization but human beings becoming fully human, fulfilling their human potential. The moving forces in history, said Marx, were economic and technological factors: the ways in which goods are produced and wealth distributed. They accounted for historical change and were the basis of all culture—politics, law, religion, morals, and philosophy. "The history of humanity," he concluded, "must therefore always be studied and treated in relation to the history of industry and exchange."[16]

For Hegel, it was the dialectical clash of opposing ideas that propelled history into a higher stage; for Marx, it was the clash of opposing classes, what is called dialectical materialism, that accounted for historical change and progress. Marx divided past history into three broad stages: slavery, feudalism, and capitalism. Each stage constitutes a thesis that in turn gives rise to an antithesis in the form of a class that feels deprived by the existing socioeconomic relations. For example, during the Middle Ages, feudalism constituted the thesis, and an emerging middle class, the bourgeoisie, hostile to the established order, represented the antithesis. The victory of the bourgeoisie over the feudal aristocracy produced a synthesis, capitalism, which marked a higher stage of history. Constituting the new thesis, capitalism gave rise to its own antithesis, the working class, or proletariat. Like the bourgeoisie in relationship to the feudal aristocracy, the proletariat is a productive class that is denied the fruits of its labor. The clash between the working class, awakened to its revolutionary role, and the bourgeoisie will produce a still higher synthesis and another stage of history—socialism.

Marx said that material technology—the methods of cultivating land and the tools for manufacturing goods—determined society's social and political arrangements and its intellectual outlooks. For example, the hand mill, the loose yoke, and the wooden plow had given rise to feudal lords, whereas power-driven machines had spawned the industrial capitalists. As material technology expanded, it came into conflict with established economic, social, and political forms, and the resulting tension produced change. Thus, feudal patterns could not endure when power machinery became the dominant mode of production. Consequently, medieval guilds, communal agriculture, and even the domestic production of goods gave way to free labor, private property, and the factory system of manufacturing. As Marx put it, the expansion of technology triggered a change from feudal social and economic relationships to capitalist ones. Ultimately, the change in economic-technological conditions becomes the cause for great social, political, and cultural changes.

This process was most clearly demonstrated by the French Revolution. Radical changes in the economic foundations of society had taken place since the Middle Ages without corresponding political changes, said Marx. However, the forces of economic change could not be contained in outdated political forms, which protected the power and privileges of the aristocracy. In France, this tension exploded into revolution. Whatever their conscious intentions, said Marx, the bourgeois leaders of the French Revolution had scattered feudal remnants to the wind; they had promoted free competition and commercial expansion, destroyed the special privileges of the aristocracy and the clergy, and transferred power from the landed aristocracy to the leaders of finance and industry. Whenever major economic changes take place, said Marx, political, social, and cultural changes must follow. Thus, the French Revolution and the other political upheavals of the late eighteenth and early nineteenth centuries were attempts of the bourgeoisie to gain political power commensurate with the economic power that it had derived from changing modes of production.

Class Conflict

Throughout history, said Marx, there has been a class struggle between those who own the means of production and those whose labor is exploited to provide wealth for this upper class. This dialectical, or opposing, tension between classes in pursuit of their interests has pushed history forward into higher stages. In the ancient world, when wealth was based on land, the struggle was between master and slave, patrician and plebeian; during the Middle Ages, when land was still the predominant mode of production, the struggle was between lord and serf. In the modern industrial world, two sharply opposed classes were confronting each other: the capitalists, who owned the factories, mines, banks, and transportation systems, and the exploited wage earners, the proletariat.

Marx and Engels held that political and economic power are interlocked; the class with economic power also controlled the state, said Marx. That class used political power to protect and increase its property and to hold down the laboring class. "Thus the ancient State was above all the slaveowners' state for holding down the slaves," said Engels, "as a feudal State was the organ of the nobles for holding down the . . . serfs, and the modern representative State is the instrument of the exploitation of wage-labor by capital."[17]

According to Marx and Engels, the class that controlled material production also controlled mental production: that is, the philosophies, moral codes, and religious views held by the ruling class became the dominant ideas of society. These ideas and ideals, presented as laws of nature, or moral and religious standards, may be regarded as the truth by oppressor and oppressed alike. In reality, however, these bodies of belief, or ideologies, merely masked the special economic interests of the ruling class. This class used the false images or ideologies to support and legitimize the social order from which it derived its property, power, and privileges.

> The ideas of the ruling class are, in every epoch, the ruling ideas: i.e., the class, which is the ruling material force of society, is at the same time its ruling intellectual force. The class which has the means of material production at its disposal, has control at the same time over the means of mental production. . . . For each new class which puts itself in the place of one ruling before it, is compelled, merely in order to carry through its aims, to represent its interest as the common interest of all the members of society, put in an ideal form of universality, and represent them as the only rational, universally valid ones.[18]

Thus, said Marx, bourgeois theorists were merely apologists for the capitalist system. For example, these theorists argued that natural rights and laissez faire were laws of nature having universal validity. But, said Marx, these "laws" were born of the needs of the bourgeoisie in its struggle to wrest power from an obsolete feudal regime and to protect its property from the state. Similarly, nineteenth-century slave holders convinced themselves that slavery was morally right—that it had God's approval and was good for the slave. Slave owners and capitalist employers alike may have defended their labor systems by citing universal principles that they thought were true and in the interests of all, but in reality their systems rested on simple and selfish economic considerations. Slave labor was good for the pocketbook of the slave owner, and wage labor was good in the same way for the capitalist.

The Destruction of Capitalism

Since for Marx history is a progressive process, the triumph of capitalism over feudalism was both necessary and beneficial: necessary, because history now entered a higher stage, bringing it closer to fulfillment in a classless society; beneficial, because industrial capitalism, by breaking free from the restraints of outdated feudal modes of production, enormously increased productivity, making possible an improved standard of living, even the end of scarcity, which had burdened all previous societies. But the capitalists' unlimited greed for profits prevented a rational and socially beneficial deployment of the new technology. Under capitalism, said Marx, workers, the true producers, knew only poverty. They worked long hours for low wages, suffered from periodic unemployment, and lived in squalid, overcrowded dwellings. Most monstrous of all, they were forced to send their young children into the factories. In *Capital*, Marx quotes a British official who declared in 1860:

> Children of nine or ten years are dragged from their squalid beds at two, three, or four o'clock in the morning and compelled to work for a bare subsistence until ten, eleven, or twelve at night, their limbs wearing away, their frames dwindling, their faces whitening, and their humanity absolutely sinking into a stone-like torpor, utterly horrible to contemplate.[19]

Dehumanization and Alienation   Capitalism also produced another kind of poverty, according to Marx—poverty of the human spirit. Under capitalism, the worker was reduced to a laboring beast, performing tedious and repetitive tasks in the factory—a dark, dreary, dirty cave, an altogether inhuman environment. Unlike the artisans in their own shops, factory workers found no pleasure and took no pride in their work, which they performed under compulsion; they did not have the satisfaction of creating a finished product that expressed their skills. Whereas artisans made use of tools, factory workers were tools of the machine. Work, said Marx, is a basic human need and should be a source of fulfillment. It is a way that people affirm their personalities and develop their potential. Capitalism, however, distorted this natural need for work, turning it into a torment. Now people flee from it, said Marx.

Exploiting human beings in order to satisfy their greed, declared Marx, capitalists treated people not as human beings but as cogs in the production process. They "distort the workers into a fragment of a man, they degrade him to the level of a machine,"[20] depriving him of control over his own life. By depersonalizing men and women and stripping them of their dignity and personal identity, capitalism alienated them from their work, from their own humanity, and from one another. The conditions of labor in capitalist industry, said Marx, produced stunted and stultified individuals. As Marx stated in his early writings,

> [T]he worker . . . does not fulfill himself in his work but denies himself, has a feeling of misery rather than well-being, does not develop freely his mental and physical energies but is physically exhausted and mentally debased. . . . His work is not voluntary but imposed, forced labour. It is not the satisfaction of a need, but only a means for satisfying other needs. Its alien character is clearly shown by the fact that as soon as there is no physical or other compulsion it is avoided like the plague. . . .
> . . . [T]he more the worker expends himself in work, . . . the poorer he becomes in his inner life, and the less he belongs to himself. . . . The worker puts his life into the object, and his life then belongs to the object.[21]

Marx noted, however, that capitalism dehumanized not only the workers, but the capitalists as well. Consumed by greed and a ruthless competitiveness, they abused workers and each other and lost sight of life's true meaning—the fulfillment of the individual's creative potential. Marx's view of the individual owed much to the Western humanist tradition, which aspired to shape self-sufficient, productive, active, striving human beings who develop their intellectual, esthetic, and moral capacities and relate to others as subjects, not as objects. By reducing people to commodities and human relations to a cash nexus, said Marx, capitalism thwarted the realization of this humanist vision.

Revolution　Marx believed that capitalist control of the economy and the government would not endure forever. The capitalist system would perish just as the feudal society of the Middle Ages and the slave society of the ancient world had perished. The destruction of capitalism was inevitable, said Marx; it was necessitated by the law of historical materialism. From the ruins of a dead capitalist society, a new socio-economic system, socialism, would emerge.

Marx predicted how capitalism would be destroyed. Periodic unemployment would increase the misery of the workers and intensify their hatred of capitalism. Small-business owners and shopkeepers, unable to compete with the great capitalists, would sink into the ranks of the proletariat, greatly expanding its numbers. Society would become polarized into a small group of immensely wealthy capitalists and a vast proletariat, poor, embittered, and desperate. This monopoly of capital by the few inhibits the productive process—that is the capitalist system of organizing production becomes unable to make effective use of natural resources, machinery, and human labor. Aroused, educated, and organized by communist intellectuals, the industrial workers grow increasingly conscious of their misery and the communality of their interests. They realize their historical role by forcibly overthrowing capitalism and creating a socialist society. "Revolution is necessary," said Marx, "not only because the *ruling* class cannot be overthrown in any other way, but also because only in a revolution can *the class which overthrows it* rid itself of the accumulated rubbish of the past and become capable of reconstructing society."[22] The working-class revolutionaries smash the government that helped the capitalists maintain their dominance. Then they confiscate the capitalists' property, abolish private property, place the means of production in the workers' hands, and organize a new society. The *Communist Manifesto* ends with a ringing call for revolution:

> The Communists . . . openly declare that their ends can be attained only by the forcible overthrow of all existing social conditions. Let the ruling classes tremble at a Communist revolution. The proletarians have nothing to lose but their chains. They have a world to win.
> Workingmen of all countries, unite![23]

Although revolution was an intrinsic part of Marx's political philosophy, he also held out the possibility of a peaceful progression to socialism in England, the United States, and Holland—countries with deeply ingrained democratic traditions. In these lands, said Marx, workers might succeed in voting themselves into power.

A Classless Society   Marx did not say a great deal about the new society that would be ushered in by the socialist revolution. With the destruction of capitalism, the distinction between capitalist and worker would cease and so would the class conflict and the exploitation of one human being by another. No longer would society be divided into haves and have-nots, oppressors and oppressed. Since this classless society would contain no exploiters, there would be no need for a state, which was merely an instrument for maintaining and protecting the power of the exploiting class. Thus, the state would eventually wither away. The production and distribution of goods would be carried out through community planning and communal sharing, replacing the capitalist system of competition. People would work at varied tasks rather than being confined to one form of employment, just as Fourier (see page 231) had advocated.

A revolutionary change in the conditions of life, Marx predicted, will produce a radical transformation of the self. The abolition of classes will liberate individuals from an alienation that has marred their relationship to their work, to others, and to their own humanity. No longer debased by the self-destructive pursuit of profit and property and no longer victims of capitalist exploitation, people would become finer human beings—altruistic, sensitive, cooperative, and creative. United with others in a classless society free of exploitation and no longer divided by divergent interests, individuals would become truly communal beings (realizing Rousseau's and Hegel's quest for a genuine social spirit). They would also become truly free beings, surpassing the merely political freedom achieved in the bourgeois state: that is, they would become truly human.

The Appeal and Influence of Marx

Marxism had immense appeal for both the downtrodden and intellectuals. It promised to end the injustices of industrial society and assured adherents that history guaranteed the triumph of their cause. It also offered explanations for all the crucial events of history—explanations that claimed the certainty of science. As Lenin wrote, "the materialist conception of history is no longer a hypothesis, but a scientifically demonstrated proposition."[24] This identification with science, and therefore truth, greatly increased Marxism's appeal.

Marx's influence grew during the second wave of industrialization in the closing decades of the nineteenth century, when class bitterness between the proletariat and the bourgeoisie seemed to worsen. Many workers thought that liberals and conservatives had no sympathy for their plight and that the only way to improve their lot was through socialist parties. It seemed to Marx's advocates that his predictions would be realized: capitalist monopolies in the advanced nations would swallow small competitors and, for the sake of profit, draw all the world into capitalism. Besides, severe economic depressions seemed to force more and more people out of farming or small business and into the ranks of the destitute working class. Others disagreed with this scenario, pointing out that the workers were not getting poorer; on the contrary, because of their unions, increased productivity, and protection by the state, they had improved their lives considerably. Marx's picture, these socialists argued, may have been accurate for the midcentury but not for the end of the century. Rejecting Marx's call for revolution, they appealed for the peaceful creation of a socialist society through gradual reforms within the democratic process (see pages 268–270). Thus, in our own century, both the socialist parties of Western Europe, which pressed for reform through parliamentary methods, and the communist regimes in Russia and China, which came to power through revolution, claimed to be heirs of Marx.

Marx's emphasis on economic forces has immeasurably broadened the perception of historians, who now explore the economic factors in historical developments and in the transformation of culture. This approach has greatly expanded our understanding of Rome's decline, the outbreak of the French Revolution and the American Civil War, and other crucial developments. Marx's theory of class conflict has provided social scientists with a useful tool for analyzing social process. His theory of alienated labor has been adapted by sociologists and psychologists. Partly because of Marx, we are aware that work in modern industrial society can be a very shallow and distasteful activity. Of particular value to social scientists is Marx's insight that the ideas people hold to be true and the values they consider valid are not autonomous products of human rationality but veil economic interests and are instruments in power struggles. Finally, Marx has forced us to confront an issue that does not go away: of what value is our vaunted political freedom to the desperately poor? To many poor, it means no more than saying that both the poor and the rich are equally free to be homeless. Despite the great strengths of the capitalist economy, there remains in Western countries, notably in the United States, an immense disparity between the rich and the poor—a small percentage of society controls vast amounts of wealth, whereas some people live in appalling poverty.

Critics of Marx

Critics point out serious weaknesses in Marxism. The rigid Marxist who tries to squeeze all historical events into an economic framework is at a disadvantage. Economic forces alone will not explain the triumph of Christianity in the Roman Empire, the fall of Rome, the Crusades, the French Revolution, World War I, or the rise of Hitler. Economic explanations fall particularly flat when we try to fathom modern nationalism, whose appeal, stemming from deeply ingrained emotional needs, crosses class lines. Before World War I, the international Marxist movement committed itself to engage in a general strike if war did break out. Had not Marx said that nationalism was moribund, that workers had no country but were members of a universal class fighting for all humanity? However, in August 1914, French workers did not make common cause with German workers against the ruling capitalists in their respective countries. Rather, the workers of both countries entered into a sacred union with their capitalist kindred. In defiance of Marxist ideology, their prime allegiance went to their nation and not to their class. The great struggles of the twentieth century have not generally been between classes but between nations. The Marxist dogma that nationalism is a by-product of capitalism and will not outlive capitalism's demise has proven to be a fallacy.

Marx could be accused of having a naive view of human nature. He believed that the destruction of the capitalist economic system, which is based on competition, would lead to the elimination of conflicts between individuals, who would now work together for the common good. It seems more logical to propose that if people did not compete with each other for material possessions they would engage in struggles for status and power. Will a change in the economic structure eliminate ethnic, racial, and religious animosities, which are often rooted in the irrational?

Many of Marx's predictions or expectations have not materialized. Workers in Western lands did not become the oppressed and impoverished working class that Marx had described in the mid-nineteenth century. Because of increased productivity, as well as the efforts of labor unions and reform-minded governments—Marx greatly underestimated the capacity of capitalist governments to rectify the abuses of industrialization—Western workers improved their lives considerably, so that they now enjoy the highest standard of living in history. The tremendous growth of a middle class of professionals, civil service employees, and small-business persons belies Marx's prediction that capitalist society would be polarized into a small group of very rich capitalists and a great mass of destitute workers.

Marx believed that socialist revolutions would break out in the advanced industrialized lands. But the socialist revolutions of the twentieth century occurred in underdeveloped, predominantly agricultural countries. The state in communist lands, far from withering away, grew more centralized, powerful, and oppressive. In no country where communist revolutionaries seized power did the individual achieve the personal autonomy, liberty, and opportunity for self-fulfillment that Marx had desired. Rather, Marxist ideology provided new rulers with new means and new justifications for oppression. Marx's dictatorship of the proletariat turned out to be a dictatorship of a new class over the proletariat, just as Bakunin had predicted (see pages 267–269).

Marxism produced true believers with a totalitarian frame of mind. The destruction of the bourgeoisie, which is ordained by history, said Marxists, is the price that humanity is compelled to pay for progress. Carried to its logical conclusion, the annihilation of class enemies—which ultimately entails the killing of men and women in revolutionary violence—is neither avoidable nor regrettable. Those engaged in liquidation need feel no remorse. Acting as agents of history, they are advancing the progress of reason and the good of humanity. The liquidated—members of a historically obsolete class or other "enemies of the people"—are expendable.

All these failed predictions and expectations and the phenomenal collapse of communist regimes in Russia and Eastern Europe in recent years profoundly contradict Marx's claim that his theories rested on an unassailable scientific foundation. They call into question Marx's fundamental conviction that there are laws of history operating with iron necessity. Indeed, far from being a scientific system, Marxism had the features of a religious myth. In many ways, Marxism was a secular religion that provided people with an emotionally satisfying world outlook: the proletariat is a chosen class endowed with a mission to achieve worldly salvation for humanity, the end of servitude and exploitation. It adapted and secularized several Judeo-Christian themes: an apocalyptic struggle between good and evil brings history to an end; humanity's messianic hopes are realized in an end-of-days when human beings, emancipated from the slavery of exploitation, undergo spiritual regeneration and fulfill the promise of their human nature; and militant proletarians serve as the agents of worldly salvation. In his railing against injustice, Marx himself seemed very much like an Old Testament prophet. Ultimately, faith, not science, assures the triumph of the proletariat and the redemption of humanity. The writings of Marx (and later those of Lenin and Mao) became official dogma for the faithful. Those who deviated were branded as heretics and were condemned for their sins. During its heyday, Marxism's capacity to win converts and to influence behavior was comparable with that of the major world religions.

As Robert Tucker notes, it was this religious quality in Marxism that attracted many people to its cause. Like medieval Christianity, Marx's system undertakes to

> provide an integrated all-inclusive view of reality, an organization of all significant knowledge in an interconnected whole, a frame of reference within which all possible questions of importance are answered. . . . This, of course, indicates a source of his system's appeal to some modern men in whom the hold of traditional religion has loosened but the craving for an all-inclusive world-view remains alive and strong.[25]

ANARCHISM

Anarchism was another radical movement that attacked capitalism. Like Marxists, anarchists protested the exploitation of workers and denounced the coercive authority of government. Radical individualists, anarchists were suspicious of bureaucracies and centralized authority and envisioned a stateless society. Only by abolishing the state, they said, could the individual live a free and full life. Some anarchists advocated revolutionary terrorism—bomb throwing and assassinations— against the state. Others, like the great Russian novelist Leo Tolstoy, rejected all violence. These anarchists sought to destroy the state by refusing to cooperate with it.

Anarchists engaged in several acts of political terrorism, including the attempted assassination of heads of state and key ministers, but they never waged a successful revolution. They failed to reverse the trend toward the concentration of power in industry and government that would characterize the twentieth century.

Pierre Joseph Proudhon

Anarchists drew inspiration from Pierre Joseph Proudhon (1809–1865), a self-educated French printer and typesetter. Proudhon criticized social theorists who devised elaborate systems that regimented daily life, conflicted with human nature, and deprived people of their personal liberty. He desired a new society that maximized individual freedom. He looked back longingly to preindustrial society, which he saw as free of exploitation and corruption and of great manufacturers and financiers. He had great respect for the dignity of labor and wanted to liberate workers from the exploitation and false values of industrial capitalism. An awakened working class would construct a new moral and social order. Proudhon believed that people would deal justly with one another, respect one another, and develop their full potential in a society of small peasants, shopkeepers, and artisans. Such a society would not require a government. Government only fosters privilege and suppresses freedom:

> To be governed is to be watched over, inspected, spied on, directed, legislated at, regulated, docketed, indoctrinated, preached at, controlled . . . censored, ordered about, by men who have neither the right nor the knowledge nor the virtue. To be governed means to be, at each operation, at each transaction, at each movement . . . registered, controlled, taxed . . . hampered, reformed, rebuked, arrested. It is to be, on the pretext of the general interest, taxed, drilled . . . exploited . . . repressed, fined, abused. . . . That's government, that's its injustice, that's its morality.[26]

Proudhon was less a theorist than a man who could express passionately the disillusionment and disgust with the new industrial society that was developing in Europe.

Mikhail Bakunin

Anarchism had a particular appeal in Russia, where there was no representative government and no way, other than petitions to the tsar, to redress injustice legally. A repressive regime, economic backwardness, a youth movement passionately committed to improving the lives of the masses, and a magnetic leader, Mikhail Bakunin (1814–1876), all contributed to shaping the Russian anarchist tradition. Bakunin was a man of action who organized and fought for revolution and set an example of revolutionary fervor. The son of a Russian noble, he left the tsar's army to study philosophy in the West, where he was attracted to the ideas of Proudhon and Marx. He was arrested for participating in the German revolution of 1848 and turned over to tsarist officials. He served six years in prison and was then banished to Siberia, from which he escaped in 1861.

Maintaining that "the history of ancient and modern States is nothing more than a series of revolting crimes,"[27] Bakunin devoted himself to organizing secret societies that would lead the oppressed in revolt against political authority. Whereas Marx held that revolution would occur in the industrial lands through the efforts of a class-conscious proletariat, Bakunin wanted all oppressed people to revolt, including the peasants (the vast majority of the population in central and eastern Europe). Toward this end, he favored secret societies and terrorism, such as the assassination of a hated official, which could spark the revolution.

Marx and Bakunin disagreed on one crucial issue of strategy. Marx wanted to organize the workers into mass political parties; Bakunin, on the other hand, held that revolutions should be fought by secret societies of fanatical insurrectionists. Bakunin feared that after the Marxists overthrew the capitalist regime and seized power, they would become the new masters and exploiters, using the state to enhance their own power. They would, said Bakunin, become a "privileged minority . . . of *ex-workers*, who once they become rulers or representatives of the people, cease to be workers and begin to look down upon the toiling people. From that time on they represent not the people but themselves and their claims to govern the people."[28] Therefore, said Bakunin, once the workers capture the state, they should destroy it forever. Bakunin's astute prediction that a socialist revolution would lead state power to intensify rather than disappear has been borne out in the twentieth century.

MARXISM AFTER MARX: REVISIONISM AND LENINISM

In the closing years of the nineteenth century, several socialist theorists questioned central Marxist premises regarding the course of capitalism and the inevitability of the proletarian revolution. While still remaining within the Marxist camp, these *revisionists* called for a modification of Marx's theories in the light of failed predictions.

Revisionism

The leading revisionist was Eduard Bernstein (1850–1932), who was born in Berlin of nonpracticing Jewish parents. Dwelling for a dozen years in England, where he observed the strength of the English economy, Bernstein became convinced that the Marxist doctrine of the imminent demise of capitalism was an illusion. No doubt Bernstein was influenced by the Fabian Society's (discussed later) program of gradual reform (see pages 280–281) and by the empirical spirit of British political theory.

Bernstein approached philosophy with an empiricist attitude—if a theory did not accord with observed facts, it had to be abandoned. In *Evolutionary Socialism* (1899), Bernstein argued that contrary to Marxist theory the collapse of the capitalist system was not imminent: the middle class of small capitalists was not sinking into the ranks of the proletariat but was increasing, and through the efforts of working class organizations and political democracy, living standards were improving for workers. Given these unrealized Marxist expectations, said Bernstein, workers should concentrate their efforts not on a catastrophic revolution but on increasing step by step their political power and improving the material conditions of their lives. Most socialist goals, he said, could be achieved peacefully and lawfully. "No one has questioned the necessity for the working classes to gain the control of government," he wrote, but "in my judgment a greater security for lasting success lies in a steady advance than in the possibilities offered by a catastrophic crash."[29]

Although Bernstein concurred with Marx regarding the importance of economic forces in the shaping of history, he also argued that noneconomic factors cannot be underestimated. Socialist theorists, he said,

> must make full allowance for the ideas of law and morals, the historical and religious traditions of every epoch, the influences of geographical and other circumstances of nature—to which also the nature of man and his spiritual disposition belong. . . .
>
> Modern society is much richer than earlier societies in ideologies which are not determined by economics. . . . Sciences, arts, a whole series of social relations are today much less dependent on economics than was formerly the case.[30]

For Bernstein socialism meant social democracy—gradual reform, not a catastrophic revolution that expropriates the capitalists—and parliamentary democracy that is representative of all groups, not a dictatorship of the proletariat. He hoped that the spread of liberal values and institutions would make possible the peaceful transition to a socialist society. Thus, revisionism may be viewed as "a compromise between liberalism and Marxian socialism, or a socialist variant of liberalism."[31]

From the late 1890s until World War I, revisionists and defenders of Marxist orthodoxy waged a war of words. Orthodox Marxists viewed revisionists as heretics and attacked them with the same fervor that medieval guardians of the faith attacked religious reformers. Karl Kautsky (1854–1938), the principal defender of orthodoxy, argued that, despite errors, Marx and Engels had correctly interpreted the past and astutely assessed the current and future direction of Western economic development. Marxism, he insisted, was the only valid system for explaining history and society; it required no revision. Kautsky denounced as naive Bernstein's hope for cooperation between the bourgeoisie and the proletariat for the purpose of implementing sociodemocratic reforms in authoritarian Germany. The German middle class, said Kautsky, feared popular government and was unsympathetic to the workers' plight. Moreover, the German ruling elite would never willingly and peacefully surrender their control over the government.

During World War I, socialists chose to cooperate with the bourgeois parties and support the war effort. In effect, the party lost its revolutionary character and came to favor reform through constitutional methods. Revisionism had triumphed. There is great continuity between Bernstein's thought and the policies of contemporary democratic socialist movements in Western lands. With the ascendancy of revisionism in Germany, the center of gravity of revolutionary Marxism moved eastward to Russia.

Leninism

As Russia underwent industrialization in the 1880s and 1890s, it experienced many of the same wretched conditions that beset Britain in the early days of the Industrial Revolution. Workers, largely ex-peasants unused to the discipline and pace of the factory, toiled twelve to sixteen hours a day in unsafe plants and mines and were prohibited from striking. Many Russian intelligentsia saw in Marxism a means of dealing with the monumental distress of the laboring masses and of overthrowing the reactionary and autocratic tsarist government. An early Russian exponent of Marxism was Georgi Plekhanov (1857–1918), a nobleman who, prior to embracing Marxism, had participated in the going-to-the-people movement—a movement of radical urban intellectuals who flocked to the countryside in order to stir up revolutionary sentiments among the peasants. The movement was a complete failure; the peasants did not understand or have patience with the abstract ideas of the intellectuals, and they had no liking for a revolt against the tsar, whom they viewed as their father and protector against the aristocratic landlords. Disillusioned by this total failure to organize the peasants and by the ineffectiveness of terrorism, Plekhanov went into exile in Switzerland and moved toward Marxism.

Becoming the leader of an emerging Russian socialist movement, Plekhanov adopted the Marxist tenet that the proletariat, not the peasantry, were the agents of revolution. He also accepted the Marxist formula that history moves in a progressive fashion—from a feudal stage to a capitalist stage to a socialist stage. Since Russia was a largely feudal society, argued Plekhanov, a socialist revolution was premature. The laws of history required that a liberal-bourgeois-capitalist society must first be established on the ruins of tsarist autocracy; then, when the objective conditions for revolution are present, the working class would overthrow the bourgeois government and impose a socialist system.

Thus, Plekhanov was essentially an orthodox Marxist who followed the formula expounded by the founder. Under the leadership of Vladimir Ulyanov, who took the revolutionary name of Lenin, Russian socialism deviated from Marx's formula.

Vladimir Lenin (1870–1924), the son of a school inspector, became attracted to Marxism as a young student. No doubt his revolutionary consciousness was heightened by the execution of his brother for his role in a plot to assassinate Alexander III. Lenin himself was sentenced to Siberia for antigovernment activity and in 1900 was expelled from the country.

An uncompromising revolutionary, Lenin dismissed reforms generated by labor unions and progressive political parties as harmful to the movement, for they detracted from the proletariat's concentration on the destruction of capitalism through class mobilization and revolutionary action. In 1902, Lenin wrote *What Is to Be Done?*—a seminal document in the history of Russian Marxist thought. He argued in this work that the workers by themselves could never achieve a successful revolution. Ignorant and given to undisciplined and spontaneous actions, they could not rise above a petty trade union consciousness—"the conviction that it is necessary to combine in unions, fight the employers, and strive to compel the government to pass necessary labor legislation."[32] Enticed by higher wages and better working conditions, the proletariat would compromise with capitalism and seek to join the middle class rather than triumph over it; it would accept bourgeois ideology and make its peace with rather than destroy the bourgeois state. Possessing insufficient scientific-socialist consciousness, the workers require the leadership of a close-knit vanguard of dedicated and disciplined professional revolutionaries who, understanding the laws of history discovered by Marx, would seek not piecemeal reform but the abolition of the social system that exploited and degraded the propertyless.

Kautsky and other orthodox Marxists held that as the internal contradictions of capitalism worsened, the proletariat's class consciousness would intensify, leading to a spontaneous but inevitable revolution. Lenin, however, argued that the masses of workers, ignorant of history's laws and blind to their true class needs, cannot be trusted to their own devices; they require leaders who know what is right, who understand the laws of history and social development—who know when conditions are ripe for the revolution and know how to organize the liberated masses into a rationally planned society. Possessing true knowledge and aware of its historical role, the revolutionary elite will guide the masses, whose behavior is driven more by spontaneous and irrational instincts than by a rational comprehension of history. (Once the revolutionary vanguard gains power, it will, through proper education, instill a true consciousness in the proletariat.) By holding that the proletariat's having a fully developed class consciousness was not a prerequisite for revolution—that it was sufficient for the revolutionary elite to possess such consciousness—Lenin deviated from classical Marxism.

Lenin's view of a general staff of revolutionaries leading independently of a popular mandate aroused the ire of many Marxists. In 1904, Leon Trotsky (born Lev Bronstein), who was to play an important role in the Bolshevik Revolution, astutely predicted: "Lenin's methods lead to this: the party organization at first substitutes itself for the party as a whole, then the Central Committee substitutes itself for the organization, and finally a single 'dictator' substitutes himself for the Central Committee."[33]

Many nineteenth-century socialists viewed Marxism as a force for liberating human beings from economic exploitation and political oppression and, no less than liberals, were dedicated to the realization of individual liberty, albeit in a new socialist society. For Lenin, however, democratic ideals had no intrinsic value; without qualms, he would sacrifice the rights of the individual if the revolution demanded it.

Lenin's theory of a self-designated and self-perpetuating leadership using every means possible to attain its objective stamped a totalitarian character on Marxism. The self-appointed revolutionary vanguard alone possesses truth and has a historical mandate to make this truth prevail. It alone has the determination and the skill to overthrow the Old Order and to lead and organize effectively the ignorant and unruly masses. Force, terror, and the suppression of all competing views both within and without the party are legitimate instruments for seizing and maintaining power; the liberal notion of the inviolability of the person could be sacrificed to the needs of the class revolution. And yet, in one of history's great ironies, the leaders of this party believed that they were charged with the historical responsibility of rescuing humanity from a socioeconomic system that exploits, oppresses, degrades, and alienates and of ushering in a socialist-communist age of humanism and freedom.

Lenin's call for a tightly controlled, exclusive party that demanded unswerving loyalty, his will-to-power, and, once he gained power, his ruthless suppression of dissent and purging of "enemies of the people" prepared the soil for Stalin's totalitarian state. When Lenin died in January 1924, after six years of rule, the machinery of terror was in place, and the *Gulag*, the forced-labor camps in which millions of Stalin's victims perished, were already functioning.

BRITISH LIBERALISM AND SOCIALISM: TOWARD THE WELFARE STATE

In the early part of the nineteenth century, British liberals were preoccupied with protecting the rights of the individual against the demands of the state. Their commitment to the free market and the autonomous individual led them to support Jefferson's dictum that the best state is the one that governs the least. They championed laissez faire because they feared that state interference in the economy to redress social evils would threaten individual rights and the free market that they thought were essential to personal liberty; they favored property requirements for voting and officeholding, because they were certain that the unpropertied and uneducated masses lacked the wisdom and experience to exercise political responsibility.

In opposing state involvement, liberals often gave expression to what is called "the capitalist or bourgeois ethic"—that diligent and responsible hard work directed by an internal discipline produced success regardless of one's social background. When the state over-guides and overgoverns, it saps the individual's initiative. Best exemplifying the bourgeois ethic were the works of Samuel Smiles (1812–1904), a Scottish physician turned journalist. (His father, a paper maker and merchant, had died early, leaving his eleven children to fend for themselves.) In *Self-Help* (1859), which became an instant success, Smiles articulated the outlook of many bourgeois liberals.

> The spirit of self-help is the root of all genuine growth in the individual; and, exhibited in the lives of many, it constitutes the true source of national vigour and strength. Help from without is often enfeebling in its effect, but help from within invariably invigorates.
>
> . . . But in all times men have been prone to believe that their happiness and well-being were to be secured by means of institutions rather than by their own conduct. Hence the value of legislation as an agent to human advancement has usually been much over-estimated. . . . [N]o laws, however stringent, can make the idle industrious, the thriftless provident, or the drunken sober. Such reforms can only be effected by means of individual action, economy, and self-denial; by better habits, rather than by greater rights.
>
> National progress is the sum total of individual industry, energy, and uprightness, as national decay is of individual idleness, selfishness, and vice. What we are accustomed to decry as great social evils, will, for the most part, be found to be but the outgrowth of man's own perverted life; and though we may endeavour to cut them down and extirpate them by means of Law, they will only spring up again with fresh luxuriance in some other form, unless the conditions of personal life and character are radically altered. If this view be correct, then it follows that the highest patriotism and philanthropy consist, not so much in altering laws and modifying institutions, as in helping and stimulating men to elevate and improve themselves by their own and independent individual action.[34]

But the persistent problems created by rapid industrialization and urbanization, the painful awareness that the vaunted principle of individual freedom also provided the economically strong with a license to exploit the weak, and the growing solidarity of workers who pressed for reforms compelled late nineteenth-century liberals to abandon pure laissez-faire doctrines and favor a more activist state. In the last part of the century, liberals began to support—though not without reservation and qualification—extended suffrage and government intervention to remedy the abuses of unregulated industrialization. This growing concern for the welfare of the poor—"the left out millions," Winston Churchill was to call them—coincided with and was influenced by an unprecedented proliferation of humanitarian movements on both sides of the Atlantic. Nurtured by both the Enlightenment and Christian traditions, reform movements called for the prohibition of child labor, schooling for the masses, humane treatment for prisoners and the mentally ill, equality for women, the abolition of slavery, and an end to war. By the beginning of the twentieth century, liberalism had evolved into liberal democracy, and laissez faire had been superseded by the acceptance, however reluctant, of social legislation and government regulation. The foundations for the British welfare state were being laid.

On the Continent, too, social welfare laws were enacted. To be sure, the motives behind such legislation were quite diverse and at times had little to do with liberal sentiments. Nevertheless, in several countries, liberalism was expanding into political and social democracy, a trend that would continue in the twentieth century.

John Stuart Mill

The transition from laissez-faire liberalism to a more socially conscious and democratic liberalism is seen in the thought of John Stuart Mill (1806–1873), a British philosopher and statesman. Mill's *On Liberty* (1859) is the classic defense of individual freedom—that the government and the majority have no right to interfere with the liberty of another human being whose actions do no injury to others. The only legitimate ground for the state to use its power of coercion in order to restrict an individual's liberty, said Mill, is to prevent that person from causing genuine harm to others. Mill contended that

> human liberty . . . . comprises first the inward domain of consciousness, demanding liberty of conscience in the most comprehensive sense, liberty of thought and feeling, absolute freedom of opinion and sentiment on all subjects, practical or speculative, scientific, moral, or theological. No society in which these liberties are not, on the whole, respected is free, whatever may be its form of government. . . . If all mankind minus one were of one opinion, mankind would be no more justified in silencing that one person than he, if he had the power, would be justified in silencing mankind.[35]

Like Tocqueville, Mill feared that the majority, operating through public opinion, would seek to impose its outlook on the entire population, stifling dissent in the process. Mill insisted that the individual should be protected "against the tyranny of the prevailing opinion and feeling; against the tendency of society to impose . . . its own ideas and practices as rules of conduct on those who dissent from them . . . and compel all characters to fashion themselves upon the model of its own."[36]

Mill regarded freedom of thought and expression, the toleration of opposing and unpopular viewpoints, as a necessary precondition for the shaping of a rational, moral, and civilized citizen. When we silence an opinion, said Mill, we hurt present and future generations. If the opinion is correct, "we are deprived of the opportunity of exchanging error for truth." If the opinion is wrong—and of this we can never be entirely certain—we "lose the clearer perception and livelier impression of truth produced by its collision with error."[37] Therefore, government has no right to force an individual to hold a view

> because it will be better for him to do so, because it will make him happier, because in the opinions of others, to do so would be wise, or even right. These are good reasons for remonstrating with him, or reasoning with him, or persuading him, or entreating him, but not for compelling him or visiting him with any evil in case he do otherwise.[38]

Mill would place limits on the power of government, for in an authoritarian state citizens cannot develop their moral and intellectual potential. Although he feared the state as a threat to individual liberty, Mill also recognized the necessity for state intervention to promote opportunities for individual self-development—the expansion of individual moral, intellectual, and esthetic capacities For example, he maintained that it was permissible for the state to require children to attend school against the wishes of their parents, to limit the hours of labor, to promote public health, and to provide workers' compensation and old age insurance. Mill moved in the direction of socialism:

> . . . [In time] our ideal of ultimate improvement went far beyond Democracy, and would class us decidedly under the general designation of Socialists. While we repudiated with the greatest energy that tyranny of society over the individual which most Socialistic systems are supposed to involve, we yet looked forward to a time when society will no longer be divided into the idle and the industrious. . . . The social problem of the future we considered to be, how to unite the greatest individual liberty of action with a common ownership in the raw material of the globe, and an equal participation of all in the benefits of combined labor.[39]

Among Mill's socialistic proposals were restrictions on inheritance in order to reduce inequality of wealth and the replacement of the wage system with a cooperative "association of the laborers themselves on the basis of equality, collectively owning the capital with which they carry on their operations, and working under managers elected and removed by themselves."[40]

In *Considerations on Representative Government* (1861), Mill endorsed the active participation of all citizens, including the lower classes, in the political life of the state. However, he also proposed a system of plural voting in which education and character would determine the number of votes each person was entitled to cast. In this way, Mill, a cautious democrat, sought to protect the individual from the tyranny of a politically unprepared majority—"the uncultivated herd" is the way he referred to the masses in his autobiography.

Thomas Hill Green

The leading late-nineteenth-century figures in the shaping of a new liberal position were Thomas Hill Green (1836–1882), an Oxford University professor, D. G. Ritchie (1853–1903), who taught philosophy at Oxford and St. Andrews, J. A. Hobson (1858–1940), a social theorist, and L. T. Hobhouse (1864–1929), an academic who also wrote for the *Manchester Guardian*. In general, these thinkers argued that laissez faire protected the interests of the economically powerful class and ignored the welfare of the nation. For example, Green valued private property but could not see how this principle helped the poor. "A man who possesses nothing but his powers of labor and who has to sell these to a capitalist for bare daily maintenance, might as well . . . be denied rights of property altogether."[41] Green argued that the do-nothing state advocated by traditional laissez-faire liberalism condemned many citizens to destitution, ignorance, and despair. The state must preserve individual liberty while at the same time secure the common good by promoting conditions favorable for the self-development of the great majority of the population.

Green agreed with earlier liberals that freedom "is the greatest of blessings." But he broadened the meaning of freedom:

> When we measure the progress of a society by its growth in freedom, we measure it . . . by the greater power on the part of the citizens as a body to make the most and best of themselves. . . . If the ideal of true freedom is the maximum of power for all members of human society alike to make the best of themselves, we are right in refusing to ascribe the glory of freedom to a state in which the apparent elevation of the few is founded on the degradation of the many.[42]

For Green, liberalism encompassed more than the protection of individual rights from an oppressive government; a truly liberal society, he said, gives individuals the opportunity to fulfill their moral potential and human capacities. And social reforms initiated by the state assisted in the realization of this broader conception of liberty.

Green and other advocates of state intervention contended that the government has a moral obligation to create social conditions that permit the individual's self-realization. Toward that end, the state should promote public health, ensure decent housing, and provide for education. An ignorant person, Green held, cannot be morally self-sufficient or a good citizen. Since many parents will not voluntarily make provisions for the education of their children, it behooves the state to install a system of compulsory education.

Green sought to base political philosophy on moral principles that promoted the common good and led people to recognize that they had a duty to be concerned with their neighbor's well-being. In developing his political thought, Green was influenced by both Rousseau and Hegel. He agreed with Rousseau that good government requires citizens motivated by public-spiritedness and that the political community has a responsibility to promote the individual's moral development. He accepted Hegel's conviction that a spiritual principle that realizes itself in human society underlies reality. If the infinite is manifested in the finite, then human beings are not disconnected abstractions but are tied together by a moral-spiritual bond. Human beings are essentially social, and they fulfill their human potential through relations with each other in a community. From this it follows that the state is a moral association, an ethical idea, committed to the self's realization through positive community relations.

L. T. Hobhouse concurred: "Democracy is not founded merely on the right of the private interest of the individual. . . . It is founded equally on the function of the individual as a member of the community."[43] Consequently, the state had a duty "to secure the conditions upon which the mind and character may develop themselves"—conditions that will enable people to behave as good and productive citizens.

> It is not fit for the State to feed, house, or clothe them. It is for the State to take care that the economic conditions are such that the normal man who is not defective in mind or body or will can by useful labor feed, house, and clothe himself and his family. The "right to work" and right to a "living wage" are just as valid as the rights of person or property. That is to say, they are integral conditions of a good social order. A society in which a single honest man of normal capacity is definitely unable to find the means of maintaining himself by useful work is to that extent suffering from malorganization. There is somewhere a defect in the social system, a hitch in the economic machine.[44]

The individual worker, continued Hobhouse, cannot be faulted if he loses his job due to "overproduction in his industry, or if a new and cheaper process has been introduced which makes his particular skill, perhaps the product of years of application, [obsolete]."[45] The worker has no control over the vicissitudes of the market. Therefore, it is the duty of the state to secure justice for him.

Green and other progressives remained advocates of capitalism but rejected strict laissez faire, which, they said, benefited only a particular class at the expense of the common good. Overcoming a traditional liberal mistrust of state power, they assigned the state a positive role in improving social conditions and insisted that state actions need not threaten individual freedom. Thus, D. G. Ritchie wrote:

> The main reason for desiring more State action is in order to give the individual a greater chance of developing all his activities in a healthy way. The State and the individual are not sides of an antithesis between which we must choose; and it is possible, though, like all great things, difficult for a democracy to construct a strong and vigorous individuality, not selfish nor isolated, but finding its truest welfare in the welfare of the community.[46]

Such a turn in the thinking of British liberals served as the theoretical foundation for the British welfare state that emerged in the twentieth century.

Herbert Spencer: Resistance to State Intervention

To be sure, many traditional liberals regarded state intervention—"creeping socialism," they called it—as a betrayal of the liberal principle of individual freedom and held to the traditional liberal view that the plight of the downtrodden was not a legitimate concern of the state. They argued, much as did Samuel Smiles, that the new liberalism would make people dependent on the state, thereby stifling industriousness, self-reliance, and thrift. Paternalistic government, they insisted, would cripple the working class morally by turning it into "grown up babies."

In *The Man versus the State* (1884), British philosopher Herbert Spencer (1820–1903) rejected the idea "that evils of all kinds should be dealt with by the State." Given the "defects of human nature, many evils can only be thrust out of one place or form into another place or form—often being increased by the change." The outcome of state intervention, he said, is that "each member of the community as an individual would be a slave to the community as a whole . . . and the slavery will not be mild."[47] Committed to a philosophy of extreme individualism, Spencer never abandoned the view that the state was an evil and oppressive institution. He favored a society in which government would play the smallest role possible and individual freedom would be maximized. When the power of the state is extended, however well-intentioned the motive, the freedom of the individual is restricted. Spencer's extreme laissez faire and "rugged individualism" led him to oppose various forms of government intervention, including factory inspection, sanitary laws, pure food and drug requirements, a state postal system, compulsory public education, and public relief for the poor. "The function of Liberalism in the past was that of putting a limit to the powers of kings," he declared. "The function of true Liberalism in the future will be that of putting a limit to the powers of Parliament."[48]

A thoroughgoing Social Darwinist, Spencer saw the poor as incapable, weak, imprudent, and lazy—unfit to compete in the struggle for existence. Their poverty was nature's stern discipline. For Spencer, state action was always misguided, for it tampered with nature's laws. "Instead of diminishing suffering, it eventually increases it. It favours the multiplication of those worst fitted for existence, and, by consequence, hinders the multiplication of those best fitted for existence— leaving, as it does, less room for them."[49] Governmental assistance creates an attitude of dependency among the poor; because they expect things to be done for them, they do not do things for themselves. States that cater to the nation's weak, said Spencer, will lose out in the struggle for existence with other states:

> ... when the struggle for existence between societies by war having ceased, there remains only the industrial struggle for existence, the final survival and spread must be on the part of those societies which produce the largest number of the best individuals—individuals best adapted for life in the industrial state. Suppose two societies, otherwise equal, in one of which the superior are allowed to retain for their own benefit and the benefit of their offspring, the entire proceeds of their labour; but in the other of which the superior have taken from them part of these proceeds for the benefit of the inferior and their offspring. Evidently the superior will thrive and multiply more in the first than in the second. A greater number of the best children will be reared in the first; and eventually it will outgrow the second.[50]

Fabian Socialism

While discontent with laissez-faire capitalism was widespread in Britain, neither intellectuals nor workers were attracted to Marxism. Marxism's revolutionary rhetoric, its rigid doctrines, and the bitter controversies engaged in by the master's heirs did not appeal to the pragmatic and cautious English temperament.

In 1884, several socialistically inclined British intellectuals organized the Fabian Society, which in time attracted figures destined for prominence, including dramatist George Bernard Shaw, political scientists Graham Wallas (see page 329) and Harold Laski, historian G. D. H. Cole, and political-social commentators Sidney and Beatrice Webb. Fabians held that social ills cannot be remedied within the context of capitalist society, which was fundamentally unjust. But influenced by the British liberal-radical reformist tradition, particularly as expressed by John Stuart Mill, Fabians rejected the Marxist call for revolution, urging instead an evolutionary path to socialism. Fabians viewed socialism as an inevitable outgrowth of liberalism.

Fabians advocated state involvement to aid the underprivileged, to provide what the Webbs called "The National Minimum"—standards of living below which people should not be permitted to fall. Toward this end, Fabians pressed for the eight-hour day, workers' compensation, old-age pensions, and better housing and education for the poor. Fabians favored a system of state socialism in which key industries and services would be publicly owned and operated by local authorities or by the central state.

Fabians did not aspire to become a working-class party. Rather, they intended to act as an educational body in order to heighten awareness of the defects of capitalist society and to make socialism palatable to the English people. In the future society envisioned by the Fabians, each person would be a civil servant performing functions assigned to him or her by an administrative elite. Freed from the anxiety of earning enough to feed their families and from the tyranny of capitalist selfishness and ruthlessness, people would be able to fulfill themselves as human beings. One Fabian described the society's utopian vision:

> Then will come to the front all those multifarious motives which are at work in the complex human organism. . . . The desire to excel, the joy in creative work, . . . the eagerness to win social approval, the instinct of benevolence: all these will start into full life, and will serve at once as the stimulus to labour and the reward of excellence. . . . Humanity will rise to heights undreamed of now; and the most exquisite Utopias, as sung by the poet and the idealist, shall, to our children, seem but dim and broken lights compared with their perfect day.[51]

What never occurred to the Fabians is that the state is potentially a greater exploiter than the private entrepreneur and that, as the state exercises greater control over the individual, the realization of the humanist goals sought by the Fabians becomes increasingly less attainable.

FEMINISM: EXTENDING THE PRINCIPLE OF EQUALITY

Another example of the expansion of liberalism was the emergence of feminist movements in western Europe and the United States. Feminists insisted that the principles of liberty and equality expressed by the philosophes and embodied in the French Declaration of the Rights of Man and of the Citizen and the American Declaration of Independence be applied to women. Thus, Olympe de Gouges' *Declaration of the Rights of Women* (1791), modeled after the Declaration of the Rights of Man and of the Citizen (1789), the French Revolution's tribute to Enlightenment ideals, stated: "Woman is born free and remains equal to man in rights. . . . The aim of every political association is the preservation of the natural . . . rights of man and woman."[52] And in 1837, English novelist and economist Harriet Martineau observed: "One of the fundamental principles announced in the Declaration of Independence is that governments derive their just power from the consent of the governed. How can the political condition of women be reconciled with this?"[53]

In their struggle for equality, feminists had to overcome attitudes deeply ingrained in Western culture that subordinated women to men. In ancient Greece, women were denied legal and political rights. Most Greeks no doubt agreed with Aristotle, who said: "The male is by nature superior, and the female inferior, and . . . the one rules and the other is ruled." Sharing in the patriarchal tradition of Jewish society, early Christianity subjected the wife to her husband's authority. "Wives, be subject to your husbands, as to the Lord," declared Saint Paul. "For the husband is the head of the wife as Christ is the head of the church" (Ephesians 5:22–23). Although the medieval church taught that both men and women were precious to God and spiritual equals, the tradition evolved that women were evil temptresses, who, like the biblical Eve, lured men into sin.

Traditional premises about female inferiority and deficiencies persisted into the modern world. Even the philosophes, who often enjoyed the company of intelligent and sophisticated women in the famous salons, continued to view women as intellectually and morally inferior to men. Some philosophes, notably Condorcet, who wrote *Plea for the Citizenship of Women* (1791), argued for female emancipation, but they were the exception. Most philosophes concurred with Hume, who held that "nature has subjected" women to men and that their "inferiority and infirmities are absolutely incurable."[54] Rousseau, who believed that nature had granted men power over women, regarded traditional domesticity as a woman's proper role:

> I would a thousand times rather have a homely girl, simply brought up, than a learned lady and a wit who would make a literary circle of my house and install herself as its president. A female wit is a scourge to her husband, her children, her friends, her servants, to everybody. From the lofty height of her genius, she scorns every womanly duty, and she is always trying to make a man of herself.[55]

Nevertheless, by clearly articulating the ideals of liberty and equality, the philosophes made a women's movement possible. The growing popularity of these ideals could not escape women who measured their own position by them. Moreover, by their very nature these ideals are expansive. Denying them to women would ultimately be seen as an indefensible contradiction.

An early figure in the development of feminism was Mary Wollstonecraft (1759–1797), whose *Vindication of the Rights of Women* (1792), written under the influence of the French Revolution, protested against the prevailing subordination and submissiveness of women and the limited opportunities afforded them to cultivate their minds. She pleaded that family life and society in general were best served by well-educated, self-reliant, and strong women capable of holding their own in the world. She considered it an act of tyranny for women "to be excluded from a participation of the natural rights of mankind . . . and tyranny, in whatever part of society it rears its brazen front, will ever undermine morality."[56]Female emancipation would benefit both men and women:

> Would men but generously snap our chains, and be content with rational fellowship instead of slavish obedience, they would find us more observant daughters, more affectionate sisters, more faithful wives, more reasonable mothers—in a word, better citizens. We would then love them with true affection, because we should learn to respect ourselves.[57]

In the United States, in the 1830s, Angelina and Sarah Grimké spoke in public—something women rarely did—against slavery and for women's rights. In 1838, Sarah Grimké published *Letters on the Equality of the Sexes and the Condition of Women*, where she stated emphatically: "Men and women were Created Equal: they are both moral and accountable beings, and whatever is *right* for man to do is *right* for women. . . . How monstrous, how anti-Christian, is the doctrine that woman is to be dependent on man!"[58] The Woman's Suffrage Movement, holding its first convention in 1848 in Seneca Falls, New York, drew up a Declaration of Statements and Principles that broadened the Declaration of Independence: "We hold these truths to be self-evident: that all men and women are created equal." The document protested "that woman has too long rested satisfied in the circumscribed limits which corrupt customs and a perverted application of the Scriptures have marked out for her" and called for the untiring effort of both men and women to secure for women "an equal participation with men in the various trades, professions, and commerce."[59]

Opponents argued that feminist demands would threaten society by undermining marriage and the family. An article in the *Saturday*

Mary Wollstonecraft *(Culver Pictures)*

Review, an English periodical declared that "It is not the interest of States . . . to encourage the existence of women who are other than entirely dependent on man as well for subsistence as for protection and love. . . . Married life is a woman's profession."[60] And in 1870, a member of the House of Commons wondered "what would become, not merely of woman's influence, but of her duties at home, her care of the household, her supervision of all those duties and surroundings which make a happy home . . . if we are to see women coming forward and taking part in the government of the country."[61] This concern for the family combined with a traditional biased view of woman's nature, as one writer for the *Saturday Review* revealed:

> The power of reasoning is so small in women that they need adventi-
> tious help; and if they have not the guidance and check of a religious
> conscience, it is useless to expect from them self-control on abstract
> principles. They do not calculate consequences, and they are reckless
> when they once give way; hence they are to be kept straight only through

their affections, the religious sentiment and a well-educated moral sense.[62]

In contrast to most of their contemporaries, some prominent men did support equal rights for women. "Can man be free if woman be slave?"[63] asked Shelley, who favored female suffrage. So too did Bentham and political economist William Thompson, who wrote *Appeal of One Half of the Human Race* (1825). John Stuart Mill thought that differences between the sexes (and between the classes) were due far more to education than to inherited inequalities. Believing that all people—women as well as men—should be able to develop their talents and intellects as fully as possible, Mill was an early champion of female equality, including women's suffrage. In 1867, Mill, as a member of Parliament, proposed that the suffrage be extended to women (the proposal was rejected by a vote of 194 to 74). In 1851, Mill married Harriet Taylor, a long-time friend and a recent widow. An ardent feminist, Harriet Mill influenced her husband's thought. In the *Subjection of Women* (1869), Mill argued that male dominance of women constituted a flagrant abuse of power. He described female inequality as a single relic of an old outlook that has been exploded in everything else. It violated the principle of individual rights and hindered the progress of humanity.

> . . . the principle which regulates the existing social relations between the two sexes—the legal subordination of one sex to the other—is wrong in itself, and now one of the chief hindrances to human improvement: and . . . it ought to be replaced by a principle of perfect equality, admitting no power or privilege on the one side, nor disability on the other.[64]

Mill considered it only just that women be admitted to all the functions and occupations until then reserved for men.

Agitation in Great Britain for women's suffrage reached a peak during the turbulent years of parliamentary reform, 1909–1911. Under the leadership of Emmeline Pankhurst (1858–1928) and her daughter Christabel, women engaged in demonstrations, disrupted political meetings, and when dragged off to jail, resorted to passive resistance and hunger strikes. Emmeline Pankhurst, who maintained that this new militancy was justifiable because all other means had failed to secure justice, showed the link between the feminist movement and the other great movements for liberty that shaped the liberal tradition. Addressing an audience in the United States in 1913, she declared:

> Our hearts burn within us when we read the great mottoes which celebrate the liberty of your country; when we go to France and we read the words, liberty, fraternity and equality, don't you think that we appreciate the meaning of these words? And then when we wake to the knowledge

that these things are not for us, they are only for our brothers, then there comes a sense of bitterness into the hearts of some women, and they say to themselves, "Will men never understand?"[65]

During World War I, women worked in offices, factories, and service industries, at jobs formerly held by men. Their wartime service made it clear that women played an essential role in the economic life of nations, and many political leaders argued for the extension of the vote to them. In 1918, British women over the age of thirty gained the vote, and in 1928, Parliament lowered the voting age for British women to twenty-one, the same as for men. In the United States, Congress approved an amendment granting the vote to women in 1918. Gaining the suffrage resolved one major injustice, but other grievances of women persisted; the Women's Liberation Movement that emerged in the 1960s sought to address them.

NOTES

1. Quoted in George J. Becker, *Master European Realists of the Nineteenth Century* (New York: Ungar, 1982), pp. 30–31.
2. Quoted in Damian Grant, *Realism* (London: Methuen, 1970), pp. 31–32.
3. Quoted in F.W.J. Hemming, ed., *The Age of Realism* (Atlantic Highlands, N.J.: Humanities Press, 1978), p. 152.
4. Quoted in Leonard J. Davis, "Gustave Flaubert," in *European Writers*, ed. Jacques Barzun and George Stade, vol. 7, *The Romantic Century* (New York: Scribner's, 1985), p. 1382.
5. Émile Zola, *The Experimental Novel*, trans. Belle M. Sherman (New York: Haskell House, 1964), pp. 20–21, 23.
6. Excerpted in Roland N. Stromberg, ed., *Realism, Naturalism, and Symbolism: Modes of Thought and Expression in Europe, 1848–1914* (New York: Harper Torchbooks, 1968), pp. 27–28, 30.
7. Quoted in Ernst Cassirer, *The Problem of Knowledge*, trans. William H. Woglom and Charles W. Hendel (New Haven: Yale University Press, 1950), p. 244.
8. Charles Darwin, *The Descent of Man* (New York: Appleton, 1876), pp. 606–607, 619.
9. Quoted in Andrew D. White, *A History of the Warfare of Science with Theology in Christendom* (New York: Appleton, 1896), I, 71.
10. Ibid., p. 71.
11. Excerpted in Richard Olson, ed., *Science as Metaphor* (Belmont, Calif.: Wadsworth, 1971), p. 124.
12. Carl Becker, *The Heavenly City of the Eighteenth-Century Philosophers* (New Haven: Yale University Press, 1932), pp. 14–15.
13. Andrew Carnegie, *The Gospel of Wealth* (New York: Century, 1900), pp. 4, 11.

14. Excerpted in Olson, *Science as Metaphor*, p. 111.

15. Karl Marx, *Theses on Feuerbach*, excerpted in *Karl Marx: Selected Writings in Sociology and Social Philosophy*, ed. T. B. Bottomore and Maximilien Rubel (London: Watts, 1956), p. 69.

16. Karl Marx, *The German Ideology* (New York: International Publishers, 1939), p. 18.

17. Friedrich Engels, *The Origins of the Family, Private Property & the State*, in *A Handbook of Marxism*, ed. Emile Burns (New York: Random House, 1935), p. 330.

18. Marx, *The German Ideology*, pp. 39–41.

19. Karl Marx, *Capital*, vol. 1, trans. Ben Fowkes (New York: Vintage Books, 1976), p. 353.

20. Ibid., p. 799.

21. Karl Marx, *Economic and Philosophical Manuscripts*, in *Karl Marx: Early Writings*, ed. T. B. Bottomore (New York: McGraw-Hill, 1963), pp. 122, 124–125.

22. Marx, *The German Ideology*, p. 69.

23. Karl Marx, *Communist Manifesto*, trans. Samuel Moore (Chicago: Henry Regnery, 1954), pp. 81–82.

24. Quoted in Alain Besançon, *The Rise of the Gulag: Intellectual Origins of Leninism*, trans. Sarah Matthews (New York: Continuum, 1981), p. 5.

25. Robert Tucker, *Philosophy and Myth in Karl Marx* (Cambridge: Cambridge University Press, 1972), p. 22.

26. Quoted in James Joll, *The Anarchists* (New York: Grosset and Dunlap, 1964), pp. 78–79.

27. Excerpted in G. P. Maximoff, ed., *The Political Philosophy of Bakunin* (Glencoe, Ill.: Free Press, 1953), p. 141.

28. Ibid., p. 287.

29. Eduard Bernstein, *Evolutionary Socialism*, trans. Edith C. Harvey (New York: Schocken, 1961), p. xviii.

30. Ibid., pp. 12–15.

31. Leszek Kolakowski, *Main Currents of Marxism*, vol. 2, *The Golden Age* (New York: Oxford University Press, 1978), p. 114.

32. V. I. Lenin, "What Is to Be Done," in *Collected Works of V. I. Lenin* (Moscow: Progress Publishers, 1964), V, 375.

33. Quoted in Isaac Deutscher, *The Prophet Armed* (New York: Oxford University Press, 1954), p. 90.

34. Samuel Smiles, *Self-Help* (London: John Murray, 1897), pp. 1–3.

35. John Stuart Mill, *On Liberty*, ed. Currin V. Shields (Indianapolis: Library of Liberal Arts, 1956), pp. 16, 21.

36. Ibid., p. 7.

37. Ibid., p. 21.

38. Ibid., p. 13.

39. *Autobiography of John Stuart Mill* (New York: Columbia University Press, 1924), p. 162.

40. John Stuart Mill, *Principles of Political Economy*, ed. W. J. Ashley (London: Longmans, Green, 1904), bk. 4, chap. 7, par. 6.

41. Thomas Hill Green, *Lectures on the Principles of Political Obligation* (Ann Arbor, Mich.: University of Michigan Press, 1967), p. 219.

42. Thomas Hill Green, *Liberal Legislation and Freedom of Contract, A Lecture* (Oxford: Slattery & Rose, 1861), p. 9.

43. L. T. Hobhouse, *Liberalism* (West-

port, Conn.: Greenwood, 1964), p. 116.

44. Ibid., pp. 83–84.

45. Ibid., p. 84.

46. D. G. Ritchie, *The Principles of State Interference*, excerpted in *The Liberal Tradition*, ed. Alan Bullock and Maurice Shock (London: Adam and Charles Black, 1956), p. 189.

47. Herbert Spencer, *The Man versus the State* (London: Watts, 1940), pp. 34, 49–50.

48. Ibid., p. 152.

49. Ibid., p. 83.

50. Herbert Spencer, *Principles of Sociology* (New York: Appleton, 1909), II, 610.

51. Quoted in Lane W. Lancaster, *Hegel to Dewey* (Boston: Houghton Mifflin, n.d.), p. 323; vol. 3 in *Masters of Political Thought*.

52. Excerpted in Eleanor S. Riemer and John C. Fout, eds., *European Women: A Documentary History, 1789–1945* (New York: Schocken, 1980), pp. 63–64.

53. Excerpted in Gayle Graham Yates, ed., *Harriet Martineau on Women* (New Brunswick, N.J.: Rutgers University Press, 1985), p. 134.

54. Quoted in Bonnie S. Anderson and Judith P. Zinsser, *A History of Their Own* (New York: Harper and Row, 1988), II, 113.

55. Jean Jacques Rousseau, *Émile*, trans. Barbara Foxley (London: Dent, Everyman's Library, 1974), p. 370.

56. Mary Wollstonecraft, *Vindication of the Rights of Women* (London: Dent, 1929), pp. 11–12.

57. Ibid., p. 164.

58. Excerpted in Miriam Schneir, ed., *Feminism: the Essential Historical Writings* (New York: Vintage Books, 1972), pp. 40–41.

59. Ibid., pp. 76, 82.

60. Quoted in J. A. and Olive Banks, *Feminism and Family Planning in Victorian England* (Liverpool: Liverpool University Press, 1965), p. 43.

61. Ibid., p. 46.

62. Ibid., p. 47.

63. "The Revolt of Islam," canto 2, stanza 43, in *The Complete Poetical Works of Percy Bysshe Shelley* ed. Thomas Hutchinson (London: Oxford University Press, 1929), p. 63.

64. John Stuart Mill, *The Subjection of Women*, in *On Liberty, Etc.*, (London: Oxford University Press, 1924), p. 427.

65. Excerpted in Marvin Perry et al., *Sources of the Western Tradition*, vol. 2, *From the Renaissance to the Present*, 2nd ed. (Boston: Houghton Mifflin, 1991), pp. 189–190.

SUGGESTED READING

Anderson, Bonnie S., and Judith P. Zinsser, *A History of Their Own* (1988).

Andreski, Stanislav, ed., *The Essential Comte* (1974).

Arblaster, Anthony, *The Rise and Decline of Liberalism* (1984).

Becker, George J., *Master European Realists of the 19th Century* (1982).

Bullock, Alan, and Maurice Shock, eds., *The Liberal Tradition* (1956).

de Ruggiero, G., *The History of European Liberalism* (1927).

Farrington, Benjamin, *What Darwin Really Said* (1966).

Grant, Damian, *Realism* (1970).

Greene, J. C., *The Death of Adam* (1961).

Hemmings, F.W.J., ed., *The Age of Realism* (1978).

Hofstadter, Richard, *Social Darwinism in American Thought* (1955).

Joll, James, *The Anarchists* (1964).

Maximoff, G. P., ed., *The Political Philosophy of Bakunin* (1953).

McLellan, David, *Karl Marx: His Life and Thought* (1977).

Manuel, Frank E., *The Prophets of Paris* (1965).

Matthews, Betty, ed., *Marx: A Hundred Years On* (1983).

Nochlin, Linda, *Realism* (1971).

Schnier, Miriam, ed., *Feminism: The Essential Historical Writings* (1972).

Stromberg, Roland N., ed., *Realism, Naturalism, and Symbolism* (1968).

Richter, Melvin, *The Politics of Conscience* (1964).

Tucker, Robert, *The Marxian Revolutionary Idea* (1969).

———, ed., *The Marx-Engels Reader* (1972).

———, *Philosophy and Myth in Karl Marx* (1972).

III

THE CRISIS OF

THE EUROPEAN MIND

9

Modern Consciousness: New Views of Nature, Human Nature, and the Arts

The modern mentality may be said to have passed through two broad phases—an early modernity and a late modernity. Formulated during the era of the Scientific Revolution and the Enlightenment, the outlook of early modernity stressed confidence in reason, science, human goodness, and humanity's capacity to improve society. In the late nineteenth and early twentieth centuries a new outlook took shape.

Late modern thinkers and scientists achieved revolutionary insights into human nature, the social world, and the physical universe; and writers and artists opened up hitherto unimagined possibilities for artistic expression. These developments produced a shift in European consciousness. The mechanical model of the universe that had dominated the Western outlook since Newton was altered; the Enlightenment view of human rationality and goodness was questioned; the belief in natural rights and objective standards governing morality was attacked; rules of esthetics that had governed the arts since the Renaissance were discarded. Shattering old beliefs, late modernity left Europeans without landmarks—without generally accepted cultural standards or agreed upon conceptions of human nature and life's meaning.

The end of the nineteenth and beginning of the twentieth centuries were marked by extraordinary creativity in thought and the arts. However imaginative and fruitful these changes were for Western intellectual and cultural life, they also helped to create the disoriented, fragmented, and troubled era that is the twentieth century.

IRRATIONALISM

While many intellectuals continued to adhere to the outlook identified with the Enlightenment, some thinkers in the late nineteenth century challenged the basic premises of the philosophes and their nineteenth-century heirs. In particular, they repudiated the Enlightenment conception of human rationality, stressing instead the irrational side of human nature. Regarding reason as sovereign, the philosophes had defined human beings by their capacity to think critically; now thinkers saw blind strivings and animal instincts as the primary fact of human existence. It seemed that reason exercised a very limited influence over human conduct, that impulses, drives, instincts—all forces below the surface—determined behavior much more than did logical consciousness.

The problem of irrationalism is manifold. Some thinkers, recognizing the weakness of reason, continued to value it and sought to preserve it as an essential ingredient of civilized life. Others, concentrating on the creative potential of the irrational, urged nourishing the feelings, which they considered vital to artistic creativity and a richer existence. Still others, rebelling against the insistence of scientists and positivists that a calculating and analytical reason was the supreme arbiter of knowledge and the only path to certainty, took a more extreme position. The truths discovered by the intellect, they said, were less profound than those grasped by our interior sentiments. Like the romantics, proponents of the nonrational placed more reliance on feeling, spontaneity, instinct, intuition, and other nonrational sources of knowledge than on reason. They belittled the intellect's attempts to comprehend reality, scorned the liberal-rational tradition, praised outbursts of the irrational, and in some instances lauded violence.

The new insights into the irrational side of human nature and the growing assault on reason had immense implications for political life. In succeeding decades, these currents of irrationalism would become ideologized and politicized by unscrupulous demagogues, who sought to mobilize and manipulate the masses. The popularity of fascist movements, which openly denigrated reason and exalted race, blood, action, and will, demonstrated the naiveté of nineteenth-century liberals, who believed that reason had triumphed in human affairs.

Friedrich Nietzsche

The principal figure in the "dethronement of reason" and the glorification of the irrational was German philosopher Friedrich Nietzsche

Friedrich Nietzsche *(The Bettmann Archive)*

(1844–1900). Most of Nietzsche's writings are not systematic treatises but collections of aphorisms, often vague and sometimes containing internal contradictions. For this reason, his philosophy lends itself to misinterpretation and misapplication, as manifested by Nazi theorists who distorted and exploited Nietzsche to justify their theory of the German master race.

Critic of European Values   Nietzsche attacked the accepted views and convictions of his day as a hindrance to a fuller and richer existence for man. He denounced social reform, parliamentary government, and universal suffrage, ridiculed the vision of progress through science, condemned Christian morality, and mocked the liberal belief in man's essential goodness and rationality. He said that man must understand that life, which abounds in cruelty, injustice, uncertainty, and absurdity, is not governed by rational principles. There exist no absolute standards of good and evil, no timeless principles, whose truth can be demonstrated by reflective reason. The higher world of metaphysics is a myth; so too is the Christian heaven. Nothing is true. There is only naked man living in a godless, chaotic, meaningless, and absurd world. The strong must face this reality. The weak cannot, so they invent fables about a higher reality and a future life.

Modern bourgeois society, said Nietzsche, was decadent and enfeebled—a victim of the excessive development of the rational faculties at the expense of will and instinct. Against the liberal-rationalist stress on the intellect, Nietzsche urged recognition of the dark mysterious world of instinctual desires, the true forces of life. Smother the will with excessive intellectualizing and you destroy the spontaneity that sparks cultural creativity and ignites a zest for living. The critical and theoretical outlook has for too long stifled the creative instincts. For man's manifold potential to be realized, he must forgo relying on the intellect and nurture again the instinctual roots of human existence, Nietzsche said.

In *The Birth of Tragedy* (1872), his first major work, Nietzsche offered an unconventional interpretation of ancient Greek culture. Traditionally, scholars and philosophers had lauded the Greeks for their rationality—for originating scientific and philosophical thought and for aspiring to achieve balance, harmony, and moderation both in the arts and in ethics. Nietzsche chose to emphasize the emotional roots of Greek culture—the Dionysian spirit that springs from the soil of myth and ritual, passion and frenzy, instinct and intuition, heroism and suffering. He maintained that this Dionysian spirit, rooted in the nonrational, was the source of Greek creativity in art and drama. Greek tragedy declined, said Nietzsche, when serenity, clarity, order, structure, form, and cold calculation—the Apollonian spirit—predominated over noble ecstasy and creative intuition. Greek tragedy was killed by a life-undermining rationalism.

Nietzsche attributed to Socrates the rise of a theoretical outlook, of scientific thought, which seeks to separate truth from myth, illusion, and error. He said that this scientific outlook, which began essentially with Socrates and attained its height in the Hellenistic Age in Alexandria, had become the basis of modern culture. Modern westerners value the theoretical man and not the man of instinct and action; consequently, they do not appreciate the creative potential of the nonrational side of human nature. But, said Nietzsche, we are beginning to recognize the limitations of science and of the cognitive faculty itself. Kantian philosophy, in particular, has produced doubts about science's claim to the attainment of certainty.

> Whereas the current optimism had treated the universe as knowable, in the presumption of eternal truths, and space, time, and causality as absolute and universally valid laws, Kant showed how these supposed

laws serve only to raise appearance ... to the status of true reality,
thereby rendering impossible a genuine understanding of that reality. . . .
Socratic culture has been shaken and has begun to doubt its own infallibility.[1]

Christianity, with all its prohibitions and demands to conform, also
crushes the human impulse for life, said Nietzsche. Christian morality
must be obliterated, for it is fit only for the weak, the slave. The
triumph of Christianity in the ancient world, he said, was a revolution
of the lowest elements of society, the meek, the weak, and the ignoble
to inherit the earth from their aristocratic superiors. It was nothing
less than an attempt of the resentful slaves and the slavelike plebeians
to prevent superior people from expressing their heroic natures and to
strike back at those noble spirits, whom they envied. The worthless
rabble did this by holding that the needy, the weak, the poor, and the
lowly are good and blessed, by condemning as evil the very traits that
they lacked—strength, assertiveness, ability, and a zest for life—and by
making their own base, wretched, and life-negating values—pity, kind-
ness, self-denial, the pursuit of heaven—the standard for all things.
Then they saddled people with guilt if they deviated from these contemptible values. What a clever act of revenge against their superiors! This transvaluation of values engineered by Christianity, said
Nietzsche, led to a deterioration of life and culture. In The *Anti-Christ*
(1888), Nietzsche wrote:

> Christianity . . . has waged a *war to the death* against this *higher* type of
> man. . . . Christianity has taken the side of everything weak, base, ill-
> constituted, it has made an ideal out of *opposition* to the preservative
> instincts of strong life. . . . Christianity is called the religion of *pity*. Pity
> stands in antithesis to the basic emotions which enhance the energy of
> the feeling of life; it has a depressive effect. One loses force when one
> pities. . . . Christianity is a revolt of everything that crawls along the
> ground directed against that which is elevated.[2]

But, adds Nietzsche, these virtues of love, compassion, and pity are
really only a facade; they hide the Christians' true feelings of envy,
resentment, hatred, and revenge against their superiors, betters, and
tormentors. One reason why the lowly aspire to heaven is that there
they will take their revenge; they will be able to peer into hell, as Aquinas noted, and take pleasure in the torments of the damned, including
their old enemies.

Although the philosophes had rejected Christian doctrines, they had
largely retained Christian ethics. Nietzsche, however, did not attack
Christianity because it was contrary to reason, as the philosophes had,
but because it was a "declaration of hostility towards life, nature, the
will to life."[3] By blocking the free and spontaneous exercise of human

instincts and making humility and self-abnegation virtues and pride a vice, said Nietzsche, Christianity gave man a sick soul. These depraved ideals of blessedness, piety, righteousness, suffering, and salvation have made us miserable. In short, Christianity put out the spark of life in man. This spark of life, this inner yearning which is man's true essence, must again burn.

"God is dead," proclaimed Nietzsche. God is man's own creation. There are no higher worlds, no transcendental or metaphysical truths, no higher morality that derives from God or nature. Dead too are the secular ideals of natural rights, scientific socialism, and faith in inevitable progress. All the old values and truths, both secular and religious, have lost their intelligibility; they are merely bankrupt sentiments devoid of certainty. But we need not despair, said Nietzsche. The death of God and of all transcendental truth can mean the liberation of man. Man can surmount nihilism by creating new values that further his instincts for life and foster self-mastery. In the process, he can overcome the deadening uniformity and mediocrity of modern civilization; he can undo democracy and socialism, which have made masters out of the cattlelike masses, and quash the shopkeeper's spirit, which has made man soft and degenerate.

European society lacks heroic figures, said Nietzsche. Everyone belongs to a vast herd but there are no shepherds: "in the dwarfing and levelling of the European man lurks *our* greatest peril, for it is this outlook which fatigues—we see today nothing which wishes to be greater, . . . the process is . . . towards something more . . . comfortable, more mediocre."[4] European culture has been debased by a crude materialism. The vulgar masses have imposed their tastes and values on all phases of life.

The Superman   Europe can be saved only by the emergence of a higher type of man, the *superman*, or *overman*, who would not be held back by the egalitarian rubbish preached by democrats and socialists. "A declaration of war on the masses by *higher men* is needed," said Nietzsche, to end "the dominion of *inferior* men." Europe requires "the annihilation of *suffrage universel*; i. e., the system through which the lowest natures prescribe themselves as laws for the higher."[5]

Europe needs a new breed of rulers, a true aristocracy of masterful men, "a new *order of rank*." The superman is a new kind of man who breaks with accepted morality, which only negates life, and creates his own values. He does not repress his instincts but asserts them. A self-determining individual, he liberates himself from the fetters of old values and traditions and asserts his prerogative as master. Free of Christian guilt and throwing off the crushing burden of his own psychological past, he proudly affirms his own being; dispensing with the Christian "thou shalt not," he instinctively says, "I will." He dares to be himself. Because he is not like other people, traditional definitions of good and evil have no meaning for him. He does not allow his individuality to be stifled, but makes his own values, those that flow from his very being and enhance his life. He relishes and exudes power. He knows that life is purposeless but lives it laughingly, instinctively, adventurously, fully. The superman represents the highest form of life.

The superman exemplifies the ultimate fact of life, that "the most fearful and fundamental desire in man [is] his drive for power,"[6] that human beings crave and strive for power ceaselessly and uncompromisingly. It is perfectly natural for human beings to want to dominate nature and other human beings, even to inflict pain on them. This will to power is not a product of rational reflection but flows from the very essence of human existence. As the motivating force in human behavior, it governs everyday life and is the determining factor in political life. The enhancement of power brings supreme enjoyment: "the love of power is the demon of men. Let them have everything—health, food, a place to live, entertainment—they are and remain unhappy and lowspirited; for the demon waits and waits and will be satisfied. Take everything from them and satisfy this and they are almost happy—as happy as men and demons can be."[7] The masses, cowardly and envious, will condemn the superman as evil; this has always been their way. Thus, Nietzsche castigates democracy, because it "represents the disbelief in great human beings and an elite society,"[8] and Christianity, for imposing an unnatural morality, one that affirms meekness, humility, and compassion.

The German philosopher Arthur Schopenhauer (1788–1860) had declared that beneath the conscious intellect is the will, a striving, demanding, and imperious force that is the real determinant of human behavior. In contrast to Hegel, who identified ultimate reality with reason, Schopenhauer viewed will, an all-encompassing force that pervades even plants and animals, as the the essence of reality: "the will is the thing-in-itself, the inner content, the essence of the world. . . . every man is what he is through his will . . . for willing is the basis of his inner being."[9] In contrast to the philosophes, who saw human beings as fundamentally rational, Schopenhauer held that the intellect is merely a tool of an alogical and irrational will: "The intellect . . . . is unable to determine the will itself, for the will is wholly inaccessible to it, and, as we have seen, is for it inscrutable and impenetrable."[10] Life is an endless striving to fulfill ceaseless desires. Schopenhauer anticipated Freud when he declared that dark and blind animal impulses, not reason, are a human being's true essence. Schopenhauer sought to repress the will, which he considered to be the source of human un-happiness. He urged stifling this striving, aimless life-urge that keeps us in the throes of desire like an unquenchable thirst.

A profound pessimism underlay Schopenhauer's philosophy. If the will is not gratified, we suffer pain; if is is too easily satisfied, we experience terrible boredom. And fear of death gnaws us.

> Man, as the most complete objectification of that will, is . . . also the most necessitous of all beings: he is through and through concrete will-ing and needing; he is a concretion of a thousand [needs and wants]. With these he stands upon the earth, left to himself, uncertain about every-thing except his own need and misery. . . . With cautious steps and cast-ing anxious glances round him he pursues his path, for a thousand acci-dents and a thousand enemies lie in wait for him. Thus he went while yet a savage, thus he goes in civilised life; there is no security for him. The life of the great majority is only a constant struggle for this existence itself, with the certainty of losing it at last. But what enables them to endure this wearisome battle is not so much the love of life as the fear of death, which yet stands in the background as inevitable, and may come upon them at any moment.[11]

"I understand him as if he had written especially for me,"[12] Nietzsche said of Schopenhauer. Nietzsche learned from Schopen-hauer to appreciate the unconscious strivings and impulses that dom-inate human behavior, but he rejected Schopenhauer's negation of the will, his flight from life, and his pessimism. Regarding the will as a source of strength, the wellspring of human creativeness and accom-plishment, Nietzsche called for its heroic and joyful assertion. Affir-mation of the will permits us to redeem life from nothingness. Nietzsche saw a necessity for the expansion of energy and heroism, not a necessity for resignation and the pursuit of nirvana, as Schopen-hauer had advocated.

Supermen cast off all established values. Free of all restrictions, rules, and codes of behavior imposed by society, they create their own values. They burst upon the world propelled by that something that urges people to want, take, strike, create, struggle, seek, dominate. Supermen are people of restless energy who enjoy living dangerously, scorn meekness and humility, and dismiss humanitarian sentiments; they are noble warriors, hard and ruthless. Only a new elite, which distances itself from the masses and holds in contempt the Christian belief that all people are equal before God, can save European society from decadence. At times, Nietzsche declares that supermen, a new breed of nobles, will rule the planet; at other times, he states that they will demonstrate their superiority by avoiding public life, ignoring es-tablished rules, and refraining from contact with inferiors.

Nietzsche in Perspective   The influence of Nietzsche's philosophy is still a matter of controversy and conjecture. Nietzsche brilliantly expressed the spirit of an age in which all areas of thought and culture were pitting life force and soul against positivism and scientism, intuition and instinct against reason, and daring and adventure against bourgeois conformity, comfort, and smugness. Nietzsche discerned, says Franz Kuna, a British literary historian, "beneath the surface of modern life, dominated by knowledge and science, . . . vital energies which were wild, primitive and completely merciless."[13] The release of these vital energies in the twentieth century almost hurled Western civilization back to a state of barbarism.

Perhaps better than anyone else, Nietzsche grasped the crucial problem of modern society and culture—that with the death of God traditional moral values had lost their authority and binding power. In a world where nothing is true, all is permitted. Nietzsche foresaw that the future, an age of nihilism, would be violent and sordid. "For some time now our whole European culture has been moving as toward a catastrophe, with a tortured tension that is growing from decade to decade: restlessly, violently, headlong, like a river that wants to reach the end."[14]

Nietzsche is part of a general nineteenth-century trend that sought to affirm the human being and earthly aspirations rather than God or salvation. There is no God, Nietzsche declared, values and norms do not derive from a transcendental realm outside ourselves. We must respond to this crisis of existence, he said, by facing ourselves and our lives free of illusion, pretense and hypocrisy, by standing on our own two feet, and forging our own way. We do this, he said, by rejecting conventional beliefs and ways of living and choosing our own values— the values that we can feel and live by without deception or rationalization. Nietzsche's rejection of God, metaphysics, and all-embracing historical theories (Hegelianism and Marxism, for example) that attempt to impose rational patterns on the past and the present is crucial to the development of existentialism and postmodern thought (see Chapters 11 and 12).

But no social policy could be derived from Nietzsche's heroic individualism, which taught that "there are higher and lower men and that a single individual can . . . justify the existence of whole millennia."[15] Nietzsche thought only of great individuals, humanity's noblest specimens, who overcame nihilism by overcoming themselves, mediocrity, and the artificiality of all inherited values; the social community and social injustice did not concern him, and the average human being had no value for him. "The weak and ill-constituted shall perish: first principle of our philanthropy. And one shall help them to do so."[16] Surely these words offer no constructive guidelines for dealing with the problems of modern industrial civilization. Nor can we find anything helpful in Nietzsche's condemnation of equality. In *Thus Spake Zarathustra* (1883–85), the prophet declares: "With these preachers of equality will I not be mixed up and confounded. For thus speaketh justice *unto me:* 'Men are not equal.' And neither shall they become so! What would be my love to the Superman if I spoke otherwise."[17] Nietzsche's view that society is merely "a foundation and scaffolding by means of which a select class of beings may be able to elevate themselves to . . . a higher *existence*"[18] is a warrant for ruthless domination and exploitation.

Nietzsche had no constructive proposals for dealing with the disintegration of rational and Christian certainties. Instead, his vitriolic attack on European institutions and values, immensely appealing to central European intellectuals, who saw his philosophy as liberating an inner energy, helped erode the rational foundations of Western civilization. Thus, many young people, attracted to Nietzsche, welcomed World War I; they viewed it as an esthetic experience and thought that it would clear a path to a new heroic age. They took literally Nietzsche's words: "A society that definitely and *instinctively* gives up war and conquest is in decline"[19] and "Ye shall love peace as a means to new wars—and the short peace more than the long. . . . Ye say that it is the good cause which halloweth even war? I say unto you: it is the good war which halloweth every cause."[20]

Nazi theorists tried to make Nietzsche a forerunner of their movement. They sought from Nietzsche a philosophical sanction for their own will to power, contempt for the weak, ruthlessness, and glorification of action, as well as for their cult of the heroic and their Social Darwinist revulsion for human equality and endorsement of cruelty. Recasting Nietzsche in their own image, the Nazis viewed themselves as Nietzsche's supermen: the new aristocracy, members of a master race who, by force of will, would conquer all obstacles and reshape the world according to their self-created values. Were they not engaged in the liberation of the instincts and the "transvaluation of all values" that Nietzsche had urged, in which nothing is true and everything is permitted? Some German intellectuals were drawn to Nazism because it seemed a healthy affirmation of life, the life with a new purpose for which Nietzsche had called. Thus, Alfred Baeumler, a German academic and fervent National Socialist, lauded Nietzsche as the philosopher of heroic youth:

> The foundations of Christian morality—religious individualism, a guilty conscience, meekness, concern for the eternal salvation of the soul—all are absolutely foreign to Nietzsche. . . . The Mediterranean religion of salvation is alien to and far removed from his Nordic attitude.

He can understand man only as a warrior against Fate. . . . We call
Nietzsche the philosopher of heroism. . . . One must have the need to be
strong, otherwise one will never be. . . . We Germans . . . . understand the
"will to power." . . . If today we see German youth on the march under
the banner of the swastika, we are reminded of Nietzsche's . . . [appeal to
youth]. And if today we shout "Heil Hitler!" to this youth, at the same
time we are hailing Nietzsche.[21]

Nietzsche himself, detesting German nationalism and militarism,
scoffed at the notion of German racial superiority, disdained (despite
some unfortunate remarks) anti-Semitism, and denounced state-wor-
ship. He would have abhorred Hitler and been dismayed at the twisting
of his idea of the will to power into a prototype fascist principle. The
men that he admired were passionate but self-possessed individuals,
who, by mastering their own chaotic passions, would face life and
death courageously, affirmatively, and creatively. Such men make great
demands on themselves. Nevertheless, as Janko Lavrin points out,
"Practically all the Fascist and Nazi theories can find some support in
Nietzsche's texts, provided one gives them the required twist."[22] Un-
fortunately, Nietzsche's extreme and violent denunciation of Western
democratic principles, including equality, his praise of power, his call
for the liberation of the instincts, his elitism, which denigrates and
devalues all human life that is not strong and noble, and his spurning
of humane values provided a breeding ground for violent, antirational,
antiliberal, and inhumane movements. His philosophy is conducive to
a politics that knows no moral limits.

Fyodor Dostoevski

Like Nietzsche, Fyodor Dostoevski (1821–1881), Russian novelist and
essayist, attacked the fundamental outlook of liberals and socialists.
In contrast to their view that human beings are innately good, responsive to reason's promptings, and capable of constructing the good society through reason, Dostoevski saw human beings as inherently depraved, irrational, and rebellious.

Notes from Underground In *Notes from Underground* (1864), the
narrator, the Underground Man, rebels against the efforts of rational-
ists, humanists, positivists, liberals, utilitarians, and socialists to define human nature as essentially rational and good and to reform society so as to promote greater happiness. He rebels against science and
reason, against the entire liberal and socialist vision, and he does so
in the name of human subjectivity—the uncontainable, irrepres-
sible, whimsical, and foolish human will. Human nature, says the

Underground Man, is too volatile, too diversified, to be schematized
by the theoretical mind.

For the Underground Man, there are no absolute and timeless truths
that precede the individual and to which the individual should conform. There is only a terrifying world of naked wills vying with each
other. In such a world, people do not necessarily seek happiness, prosperity, and peace—all that is sensible and good for them, as "enlightened" thinkers would hold. To the rationalist who aims to eliminate
suffering and deprivation, Dostoevski replies that some people freely
choose suffering and depravity, because it gratifies them—for some,
"there is enjoyment even in a toothache"[23]—and are repelled by
wealth, peace, security, and happiness. So much for Bentham's pleasure
and pain principle. In order to assert his own individuality—to demonstrate that he can choose freely for himself—a man will even do
something stupid and self-injurious. Thus, out of spite, the Underground Man resists treatment for his liver ailment. He even protests
against the laws of nature. "Of course I cannot break through a wall by
battering my head against it . . . but I am not going to resign myself to
it simply because it is a stone wall and I am not strong."[24] Reason can
point out the absurdity of an action that is against our own interests,
but reason is an insignificant determinant of behavior.

The Underground Man insists that people do not want to be robots
in a rigorously regulated social order that creates a slot for everything.
They consider excessive intellectualizing—"over-acute consciousness"—a disease that keeps them from asserting their autonomy, their
"independent choice."

> . . . it seems that something that is dearer to almost every man than his
> greatest advantages must really exist . . . for which, if necessary, a man
> is ready to act in opposition to all laws, that is, in opposition to reason,
> honor, peace, prosperity. . . . One's own free unfettered choice, one's own
> fancy, however wild it may be, one's own fancy worked up at times to a
> frenzy—why that is that very "most advantageous advantage" which we
> have overlooked, which comes under no classification and through
> which all systems and theories are continually being sent to the
> devil. . . . What man needs is simply *independent* choice, whatever that
> independence may cost and wherever it may lead.[25]

It is this irrational will that defines the individual's uniqueness and
leads him to resist the blueprints drawn up by social theorists. If individuals do not act out of enlightened self-interest—if they constantly
act contrary to their own reasoned interests—then what hope is there
for social planners desirous of creating the "good" society?

> Oh tell me, who first declared, who first proclaimed, that man only does
> nasty things because he does not know his own real interests; and that

if he were enlightened, if his eyes were opened to his real normal interests, man would at once cease to do nasty things, would at once become
good and noble because, being enlightened and understanding his real
advantage, he would see his own advantage in the good and nothing else,
and we all know that not a single man can knowingly act to his own
disadvantage. Consequently, so to say, he would begin doing good
through necessity. Oh, the babe! Oh the pure, innocent child.[26]

The Underground Man maintains that by following irrational impulses and engaging in irrational acts, human beings assert their individuality; they prove that they are free. The Underground Man is totally free; he struggles to define his own existence according to his own
needs and not the standards and values created by others. He regards
freedom of choice as a human being's most priceless possession and
holds that choice derives not from the intellect but from impulses and
feelings that account for our essential individuality. For him, the "rational faculty . . . is . . . simply one-twentieth of all my faculties of
life";[27] life is more than reasoning, more than "simply extracting
square roots." In rejecting external security and liberal and socialist
concepts of progress—in aspiring to assert his own individuality even
if this means acting against his best interests—the Underground Man
shows that a powerful element of irrationality underlies human nature. In presenting freedom of the will as the supreme good, Dostoevski
raised the specter of a dangerous nihilism: the naked will aspiring to
self-realization respects no principle of truth and is bound by no morality. An unbridled freedom—which for the Underground Man is the
supreme good—can destroy all social relationships on which civilized
life depends. It can lead to both self-destruction and social chaos.

Dostoevski himself did not advocate a philosophy of will. He believed that irrational rebellion ended in self-destruction, that chaotic
human impulses were not the vehicle to genuine freedom and self-
affirmation. Ultimately, he sought a Christian solution to this fundamental human dilemma: faith in Christ and Christian love and altruism were the best guides to self-enrichment.

The Grand Inquisitor *The Brothers Karamazov* (1880), perhaps Dostoevski's greatest work, contains a powerful section, *The Grand Inquisitor*, that supplements the ideas treated in *Notes from Underground*. In *The Grand Inquisitor*, Dostoevski brilliantly explores
central questions of modern society: Do human beings, base and weak
by nature, really desire the gift of freedom of choice, given to them by
Christ? Does freedom of choice promote an anarchic individualism
that threatens to tear asunder the fabric of society?

The scene takes place in Seville in the sixteenth century, during the
infamous Spanish Inquisition, when heretics were burned "every day

to the glory of God." Christ returns to earth. The people recognize him and "He moves silently in their midst with a gentle smile of compassion. The sun of love burns in His heart, radiance, enlightenment and power shine from His eyes, and, shed on the people, stirs their hearts with responsive love."[28] But the Grand Inquisitor orders Christ's arrest, informing him, "I don't care to know whether it is You or only a semblance of Him, but tomorrow I will condemn You and burn You at the stake as the worst of heretics. And the very people who today kissed Your feet, tomorrow at the faintest sign from me will rush to heap up the embers of Your fire."[29]

The Grand Inquisitor visits Christ in the dungeon. The old man tells Christ that men and women cannot bear the gift of freedom—the ability to regulate one's life according to freely selected standards—that he had granted them. People "in their simplicity and natural unruliness cannot even understand" freedom; they fear and dread it. It is not freedom, says the Grand Inquisitor, but bread and security that people truly desire.

> . . . for the sake of that earthly bread the spirit of the earth will rise up against You and fight with You and will overcome You, and all will follow him. . . . In the end they will lay their freedom at your feet, and say to us, "Make us your slaves, but feed us." They will understand themselves, at last, that freedom and bread enough for all are inconceivable together.[30]

People also crave authority. They have a will to obey. They yearn to submit to a superior power that will dominate them. Unable to deal with freedom, says the Grand Inquisitor, people had surrendered it to the church, which instructs them how to live and act. The church has heretics executed because their plea for individuality threatens order.

Ultimately, it is human nature that works against freedom, says the Grand Inquisitor. People "can never be free, for they are weak, sinful, worthless, and rebellious. [They do] not have the strength to forego the earthly bread for the sake of the heavenly."[31] Freedom of choice, insists the Grand Inquisitor, has been a burden for human beings.

> So long as man remains free he strives for nothing so incessantly and so painfully as to find as quickly as possible someone to worship. But man seeks to worship what is established beyond dispute, so indisputably that all men would agree at once to worship it. . . . This craving for *community* of worship is the chief misery of every man individually and of all humanity from the beginning of time. For the sake of common worship they've slain each other with the sword. . . . I tell you that man is tormented by no greater anxiety than to find someone to whom he can hand over quickly that gift of freedom with which the unhappy creature is born. . . . Nothing is more seductive for man than his freedom of conscience, but at the same time nothing is a greater torture.[32]

You judged people too highly, the Grand Inquisitor tells Christ, in believing that they would freely embrace you. Human beings are really weak and base; they need to be led for their own good. "There are . . . only three powers that can conquer and capture the conscience of these impotent rebels forever, for their own happiness—those forces are miracle, mystery and authority. You rejected all three."[33] Therefore, the church has "corrected Your work," by teaching people

> that it is not the free judgment of their hearts, not love that matters, but a mystery which they must follow blindly, even against their conscience. . . . And men rejoiced that they were again led like a flock, and that the terrible gift that had brought them such suffering, was, at last, lifted from their hearts. . . . Why have You come now to hinder us?[34]

The paradox of freedom, compellingly stated in Dostoevski's fable, would haunt liberals in the twentieth century. Does freedom of choice plunge the soul into anguish? Is freedom a burden that human beings cannot tolerate? Will frightened and isolated souls yearn to replace freedom with miracle, mystery, and authority, particularly if these forces weld them into a community and promise them material security? Do people yearn to submit to and to be dominated by authority? Are the masses far "more satisfied by a doctrine tolerating no other beside itself, than by the granting of liberal freedom,"[35] as Hitler believed? Twentieth-century dictators who may never have read Dostoevski's fable instinctively grasped its meaning. In *The Grand Inquisitor*, Dostoevski anticipated the seductive power of the mass movements of our century.

Henri Bergson

Another thinker who reflected the growing preoccupation with the nonrational was Henri Bergson (1859–1941), a French philosopher of Jewish background. Just before World War I, Bergson was an immensely popular lecturer at the Collège de France, often attracting the elite of Parisian society. He considered converting to Catholicism, but in defiance of the rampant anti-Semitism in the 1930s, he retained his Jewish identity. He died in January 1941 from pneumonia contracted after waiting in line for several hours to be registered as a Jew in German-occupied Paris.

Originally attracted to positivism, Bergson turned away from the positivistic claim that science could explain everything and fulfill all human needs. Such an emphasis on the intellect, said Bergson, sacrifices spiritual impulses, imagination, and intuition and reduces the soul to a mere mechanism. The mind is not a collection of atoms

operating according to mechanical principles but an active consciousness with profound intuitive capacities.

Bergson insisted that scientific thinking is limited: it only gives us
a partial understanding of existence; it cannot penetrate to reality itself. The method of intuition, whereby the mind strives to become one
with the object, can tell us more about reality than the method of analysis employed by science. Entering into the object through intuition is
an avenue to truth that is closed to the calculations and measurements
of science. The knowledge conveyed by intuition surpasses that attained by science.

To his admirers, Bergson's philosophy liberated the person from the
constraints of positivism, mechanism, and materialism and showed
the creative potential of intuition, the mystical experience, and the
poetic imagination—those forces of life that resist categorization by
the scientific mind. It was a protest against modern technology and
bureaucracy, against all those features of mass society that seemed to
stifle individual uniqueness and spontaneity. It was an attempt to reaffirm the primacy of the individual in an increasingly mechanized and
bureaucratic world. Bergson's opponents, particularly Julien Benda (see
page 428), the noted French cultural critic, denounced Bergson for undermining and degrading analytical reason by proposing that intuition,
which is rooted in emotion, provided insight into absolute reality. Bergson's method, unlike the scientific method, said Benda, yielded no verifiable results.

Unlike Nietzsche's, Bergson's thought, which was too humane and
religious, did not provide spiritual sustenance to brutal twentieth-century totalitarian ideologies. However, the popularity of his irrational
intuitionism, with its depreciation of reason, was another indication
of the nonrational's unsuspected strength and appeal—another sign
that people were searching for new alternatives to the Enlightenment
world-view. In succeeding decades, this yearning would find its most
dangerous expression in totalitarian ideologies that politicized the irrational.

Georges Sorel

Nietzsche and Dostoevski proclaimed that irrational forces constitute
the essence of human nature; Bergson held that a nonrational intuition
provided insights unattainable by the scientific mentality. Georges
Sorel (1847–1922), who gave up engineering to follow intellectual pursuits, was a French social theorist who recognized the political potential of the nonrational. Sorel attended Bergson's lectures and was profoundly impressed with his devaluing of rationalism and his emphasis

on the power of inner force, what Sorel called "the psychology of the deeper life." Sorel recognized that this nonrational force could be harnessed for radical political ends.

Like Nietzsche, Sorel was disillusioned with contemporary bourgeois society, which he considered decadent, soft, unheroic, and life-denying. Whereas Nietzsche called for the superman to rescue society from decadence and mediocrity, Sorel placed his hopes in the proletariat. He saw workers as courageous and virile, bearers of higher values, noble and determined producers struggling against exploiters and parasites. Sorel hoped that the revolutionary radicalism of the working class would usher in a "society of heroes"—selfless workers-inventors, whose talent for artisanship and talent for innovation would promote progress.

Sorel wanted workers to destroy the existing bourgeois-liberal-capitalist order and to rejuvenate society, to infuse it with dynamic and creative energy and a sense of moral purpose. The overthrow of decadent bourgeois society would be accomplished through a general strike—a universal work stoppage that would bring down governments and give power to the workers. Sorel applauded violence, for it intensified the revolutionaries' dedication to the cause and spurred them to acts of heroism. It also accorded with his general conception that life is an unremitting battle and that history is a perpetual conflict between decay and vitality, between passivity and action. In his view, struggle purified, invigorated, and promoted creative change.

Sorel believed that the general strike had all the appeal of a great myth. What was important was not that the general strike actually take place, but that its image stir all the anticapitalist resentments of the workers and inspire them to carry out their revolutionary responsibilities. Sorel understood the extraordinary potency of myth: it structures and intensifies the feelings; it integrates and unifies people and channels their energy into heroic action. Was not the early Christians' resolve strengthened by the myths of eternal bliss in heaven and by the promise of Christ's second coming? asked Sorel. Because they appeal to the imagination and the feelings, myths are an effective way of organizing the masses, buoying up their spirits, and moving them to acts of heroism. By believing in the myth of the general strike, workers would soar above the moral decadence of bourgeois society and bear the immense sacrifices that their struggle calls for. The myth serves a religious function: it unites the faithful into a collectivity with one will and induces a heroic state of mind. That the myth does not meet the standards of logical thought is irrelevant, for it is not the intellect but faith and passion that spur people to heroic action. Thus, for Sorel, Marxism was not a scientifically accurate theory of history and of capitalist society, but "social poetry," a mythology that induced the proletarian masses to rebel. The chief responsibility of creative leaders is to provide the masses with the right myths at the right time: "There is probably in the mind of every man, hidden under the ashes, a quickening fire; the awakener is the man who stirs the ashes and thus makes the flames leap up."[36]

Like Marx, Sorel believed that the goals of the worker could not be achieved through peaceful parliamentary means; he too wanted no reconciliation between bourgeois exploiters and oppressed workers. The only recourse for workers was direct action and violence. However, Marx considered violence simply as a means to a revolutionary end and would dispense with it once the end was achieved. Regarding violence as ennobling, heroic, purifying, and sublime—a means of restoring grandeur to a flabby world—Sorel valued it as an end in itself.

Sorel's pseudoreligious exaltation of violence and mass action—action for its own sake—his condemnation of liberal democracy and rationalism, his recognition of the power and political utility of irrational and fabricated myths, and his vision of a heroic morality emerging on the ruins of a dying shabby bourgeois world found concrete expression in the fascist movements after World War I. Indeed, he lived long enough to express admiration for Mussolini's "astonishing comprehension of the Italian masses" and his "political genius." And the Duce claimed Sorel as a principal mentor. Just before the March on Rome in 1922, which gave him power, Mussolini stated in Sorelian terms: "We have created a Myth, a Myth that is a Faith, a passion. It does not need to be a reality, it is a stimulus and a hope, a belief and courage. Our Myth is the Nation, the grandeur of the nation, which we will make a concrete 'reality.'"[37] In 1926, Mussolini praised Sorel: "It is to Georges Sorel that I owe the most. . . . his theories on the technique of revolution contributed most to form the discipline, the energy and the power of the fascist cohorts."[38] The major difference between Sorel and Mussolini is that Sorel wanted the workers to take control of the means of production, something that Mussolini, the advocate of state power, never considered. Sorel, who regarded the state as a wicked institution, would have had difficulty with Mussolini's dictatorship.

Sorel also hailed Lenin's revolutionary radicalism, his sense of mission that was translated into action. Instilled with a new morale, the Russian workers, said Sorel at the time of the Bolshevik Revolution, could acquire immortal glory in their efforts to construct a new society of producers. For Sorel, the Bolsheviks had demonstrated the power of the myth of the proletariat; their achievement would inspire other revolutions in Europe.

Sorel heralded the age of mass political movements committed to revolutionary violence and of myths manufactured by propaganda experts determined to destroy the liberal-rational tradition of the Enlightenment. That Sorel's quest for a society of heroes to overcome bourgeois decadence appealed to intellectuals, says Jack J. Roth, was

> symptomatic of a profound intellectual and moral disturbance—the desertion by intellectuals (and those with intellectual pretensions) of the democratic idea. And their story was something of a tragedy. They had sought to evoke the "sublime." But their efforts, purposefully or not, had worked from 1914 to Auschwitz (along with others) to unleash the "beast."[39]

SIGMUND FREUD: THE WORLD OF THE UNCONSCIOUS

By demonstrating the human being's kinship with the animal world, Darwin had reduced humanity's self-esteem. Sigmund Freud (1856–1939), an Austrian-Jewish physician who spent most of his adult life in Vienna, diminished it still further by asserting in scientific language that reason is not the mainspring of human actions.

Although Freud never practiced Judaism and viewed all religious beliefs as illusions, he was very conscious of his ancestry, especially when confronted with anti-Semitism, and attributed his independence of thought to his Jewishness: "at an early age I was made familiar with the fate of being in the Opposition and of being put under the ban of the 'compact majority.' The foundations were thus laid for a certain degree of independence in judgment."[40]

In many ways, Freud was a child of the Enlightenment. Like the philosophes, he identified civilization with reason and regarded science as the avenue to knowledge. But in contrast to the philosophes, Freud focused on the massive power and influence of nonrational drives. Marx had argued that, although people believe that they think freely, in truth, their beliefs and thoughts reflect the outlook of the ruling class: economic considerations determine consciousness. Freud too held that our conscious thoughts, which we believe are freely arrived at, are, in truth, determined by hidden forces, namely unconscious impulses. Whereas Nietzsche glorified the irrational and approached it with a poet's temperament, Freud recognized its potential danger, sought to comprehend it scientifically, and wanted to regulate it in the interests of civilization. Unlike Nietzsche, Freud did not belittle the rational but always sought to salvage respect for reason. In a letter to the Austrian novelist Stefan Zweig, Freud said that the essential task of psychoanalysis was "to struggle with the demon" of

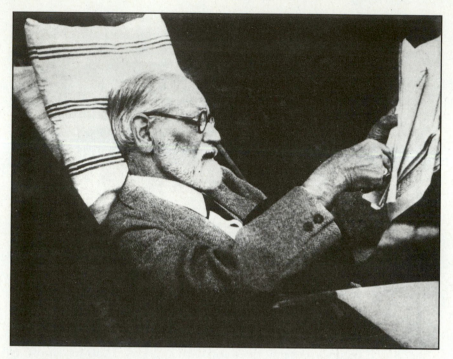

Sigmund Freud *(Culver Pictures)*

irrationality in a "sober way," to make it "a comprehensible object of science."[41] And by "a sober way," he meant the scientific method, not Bergson's intuition or Nietzsche's inspired insights: "there are no sources of knowledge of the universe other than the intellectual working-over of carefully scrutinized observations—in other words, what we call research—and alongside of it no knowledge derived from revelation, intuition, or divination."[42]

The Unconscious

Freud held that people are not fundamentally rational; human behavior is governed primarily by powerful inner forces that are hidden from consciousness. Much intense mental activity takes place within the human mind that is independent of and unknown to consciousness. These primitive drives, strivings, and thoughts harbored in the unconscious, rather than rational faculties, constitute the greater part of the mind; they influence our behavior often without our awareness so that we may not know the real reasons for our actions. We may think that a particular action of ours is motivated by friendship, duty, honor, or faith, but in reality and unknown to the conscious mind, a wish for power or self-punishment or a dependent need might be the true determinator of our behavior. For example, parents, with all sincerity, believe that they are punishing a child for his or her own good, but in reality they might derive sadistic pleasure from the beating. Freud considered not just the external acts of a person, but also the inner psychic reality that underlies human behavior.

Freud, of course, did not discover the unconscious. Romantic poets had sought the wellspring of creativity in a layer of mind below consciousness. The Greek tragedians, Shakespeare, Schopenhauer, Nietzsche, and Dostoevski, among others, had all penetrated the hidden and tangled world of the passions and marveled at its elemental power. Thus, Euripides described the forces that seethe within as "the bloody Fury raised by the fiends of Hell." Freud, who believed that artistic and literary creativity ultimately derives from primal instincts rooted in the unconscious, paid tribute to creative writers' intuition: "they are apt to know of a whole host of things between heaven and earth of which our philosophy has not yet let us dream. In their knowledge of the mind they are far in advance of us everyday people, for they draw upon sources which we have not yet opened up for science."[43] He described Nietzsche as a philosopher "whose guesses and intuitions often agree in the most astonishing way with the laborious findings of psychoanalysis."[44] He praised Schopenhauer's explanation of insanity: "What he says . . . about the struggle against accepting a distressing piece of reality coincides with my concept of repression . . . completely."[45] Freud's great achievement was to explore the unconscious methodically and systematically with the tools and temperament of a scientist.

After graduating from medical school, Freud specialized in the treatment of nervous disorders. By encouraging his patients to speak to him about their troubles, Freud was able to probe deeper into their minds. These investigations led him to conclude that childhood fears and experiences, often sexual in nature, accounted for neuroses—disorders in thinking, feeling, and behavior that interfere with everyday acts of personal and social life. Neuroses can take several forms, including hysteria, anxiety, depression, obsessions, and so on. So painful and threatening were these childhood emotions and experiences that his patients banished them from conscious memory to the realm of the unconscious. To understand and treat neurotic behavior, Freud said, it is necessary to look behind overt symptoms and bring to the surface emotionally charged experiences and fears—childhood traumas—that lie buried in the unconscious, along with primitive impulses.

Freud probed the unconscious by urging his patients to say whatever came to their minds. This procedure, called free association, rests on the premise that spontaneous and uninhibited talk reveals a person's underlying preoccupations, his or her inner world, those "demons" that are at the root of the person's emotional distress. A second avenue to the unconscious is the analysis of dreams. Dreams, said Freud, reveal an individual's secret wishes—often socially unacceptable desires and frightening memories. Too painful to bear, we lock them up in the deepest dungeons of the unconscious; these repressed thoughts and feelings constitute the greater part of the unconscious. But even in their cages, the demons remain active, continuing to haunt us, to generate conflicts. Our distress is real and even excruciating, but we do not know its source. Because these memories and feelings find an outlet in dreams, said Freud, the interpretation of dreams is the path *par excellence* to knowledge of the unconscious.

Freud held that the *id*, the subconscious seat of the instincts, is "a cauldron full of seething excitations" that constantly demand gratification. The id is "untamed passion"—primitive, infantile, asocial, and illogical. It knows no values, no morality; it has no awareness of good and evil. It is a restless and tormented force that perpetually strives for the gratification of its needs in accordance with the pleasure principle and without regard for others. Unable to endure tension, it demands sexual release, the termination of pain, the cessation of hunger. When the id is denied an outlet for its instinctual energy, people become frustrated, angry, and unhappy. Gratifying the id is our highest pleasure. But the full gratification of instinctual demands is detrimental to civilized life.

Conflict Between Civilization and Human Nature

Freud postulated a harrowing conflict between the restless strivings of our instinctual nature and the requirements of civilization. Civilization, for Freud, demands the renunciation of instinctual gratification and the mastery of animal instincts, a thesis he developed in *Civilization and Its Discontents* (1930). While Freud's thoughts in this work were no doubt influenced by the great tragedy of World War I (and perhaps by the terrible pain he suffered from cancer), the main theme could be traced back to his earlier writings. Human beings derive their highest pleasure from sexual fulfillment, said Freud, but unrestrained sexuality drains off psychic energy needed for creative artistic and intellectual life. Hence society, through the family, the priest, the teacher, and the police, imposes rules and restrictions on our animal nature. These rules, duties, and expectations are internalized; they become our conscience, or what Freud calls the *superego*. Freud posits an immensely painful and irremediable conflict between the id and the superego, for our instincts, unable to tolerate confinement in the unconscious, resist the regulations that the superego imposes on them. The very institutions and rules that preserve civilization are also the source of our discontent; society saddles us with expectations and rules that our human nature finds enormously difficult to fulfill.

The human being is caught in a tragic bind. Society's demand for the denial of full instinctual gratification causes terrible frustration; equally distressing, the violation of society's rules under the pressure of instinctual needs evokes terrible feelings of guilt. Either way people suffer; civilized life simply entails too much pain for people. It seems that the price we pay for civilization is neurosis.

Most people cannot endure the renunciation of instinctual satisfaction that civilization requires. There are times when our elemental human nature rebels against all the restrictions and *thou shalt not*s demanded by society, against all the misery and torment imposed by civilization. Some people seek escape from life's torments by isolating themselves from others or by systematically negating the instincts, as Eastern philosophies advocate. Others seek refuge in religion, which Freud viewed as a delusional transformation of reality; still others deal with the cruelties of life by a flight into neurotic illness. The path favored by Freud was intellectual and creative work; it provides a culturally valuable release for narcissistic and aggressive impulses. But always the pervasive power of the instincts remains a source of conflict between the individual and society.

What contributes further to our unhappiness, said Freud, is that "civilization imposes great sacrifices not only on man's sexuality but also on his aggressivity."[46] People are not good by nature as the philosophes had taught; on the contrary, they are "creatures among whose instinctual endowments is to be reckoned a powerful share of aggressiveness." Human beings have an aggressive desire to dominate others. Their first inclination is not to love their neighbor but to "satisfy their aggressiveness on him, to exploit his capacity for work without compensation, to use him sexually without his consent, to seize his possessions, to humiliate him, to cause him pain, to torture and to kill him."[47] During World War I, Freud wrote to a colleague: "What is happening in this war . . . the cruelties and injustices for which the most civilized nations are responsible . . . [proves], that the primitive savage and evil impulses of mankind have not vanished . . . [but] lie in wait for opportunities of becoming active once more."[48] In *Thoughts for the Times on War and Death* (1915), written at the height of World War I, Freud expressed similar sentiments:

murderers, who had the lust for killing in their blood, as perhaps, we ourselves have today. . . . The expression "Devil take him!", which so often comes to people's lips in joking anger and which really means "Death take him!", is in our unconscious a serious and powerful death-wish. Indeed our unconscious will murder even for trifles.[49]

Man is wolf to man, concluded Freud. "Who has the courage to dispute it in the face of all the evidence in his own life and in history?"[50] Civilization "has to use its utmost efforts in order to set limits to man's aggressive instincts," but "in spite of every effort these endeavors of civilization have not so far achieved very much."[51] People find it difficult to do without "the satisfaction of this inclination to aggression."[52] When circumstances are favorable, this primitive aggressiveness breaks loose and "reveals man as a savage beast to whom consideration towards his own kind is something alien."[53] We should not be surprised by the uncivilized behavior of people during war, wrote Freud in *Thoughts for the Times on War and Death*:

> In reality our fellow-citizens have not sunk so low as we feared, because they had never risen so high as we believed. The fact that . . . peoples and states mutually abrogated their moral restraints naturally prompted . . . individual citizens to withdraw for a while from the constant pressure of civilization and to grant a temporary satisfaction to the instincts which they had been holding in check.[54]

For Freud, "the inclination to aggression is an original self-subsisting disposition in man . . . that . . . constitutes the greatest impediment to civilization." Civilization attempts "to combine single human individuals and after that families, then races, peoples and nations into one great unity. . . . But man's natural aggressiveness instinct, the hostility of each against all and of all against each, opposes this program of civilization."[55] Destructive—that is, antisocial and anticultural impulses—drive people apart, threatening society with disintegration. For Freud, an unalterable core of human nature is ineluctably in opposition to civilized life. To this extent everyone is potentially an enemy of civilization.

Freud and the Philosophes

Freud's awareness of the irrational and his general pessimism regarding people's ability to regulate it in the interests of civilization did not lead him to break faith with the Enlightenment tradition. Unlike Nietzsche, Freud did not celebrate the irrational. He was too aware of its self-destructive nature for that. Civilization is indeed a burden, but people must bear it, for the alternative is far worse. Freud, says Peter Gay,

> had no use whatever for the celebration of irrational forces, or for the primitivism that would evade the dialectic of civilization by abandoning civilization altogether. He had not labored in the sickroom of the human mind to join the party of disease; he had not descended to the sewer of human nature to wallow in what he had found there. He was no devotee of the Id; he assigned no privileged position to that blind imperious agent of the will, and valued the organizing rationalism of the Ego—or the naysaying constraints of the superego as equally natural.[56]

In the tradition of the philosophes, Freud sought truth based on a scientific analysis of human nature and believed that reason was the best road to social improvement. Like the philosophes, he was critical of religion, regarding it as a pious illusion, a fairy tale that originated in the human being's inability to break away from a childlike dependency on a father.

> The common man cannot imagine this Providence otherwise than in the figure of an enormously exalted father. Only such a being can understand the needs of the children of men and be softened by their prayers and placated by the signs of their remorse. The whole thing is so patently infantile, so foreign to reality, that to anyone with a friendly attitude to humanity it is painful to think that the great majority of mortals will never be able to rise above this view of life.[57]

Freud drew a sharp distinction between science, whose conclusions are open to question, debate, and modification, and religion, which requires adherence to doctrines that contradict reason and experience. For both Freud and the philosophes, "there is no appeal to a court above that of reason."[58] It would be an illusion, declared Freud in *The Future of an Illusion* (1927), "to suppose that what science cannot give us we can get elsewhere."[59] Like the philosophes, Freud viewed religion as a barrier to progress and human betterment. Religious doctrines, he wrote, originated in "the ignorant times of the childhood of humanity . . . If we attempt to assign the place of religion in the evolution of mankind, it appears not as a permanent acquisition but as a counterpart to the neurosis which individual civilized men have to go through in their passage from childhood to maturity."[60] Also like the skeptical and anticlerical philosophes, Freud held that religion has not invariably made us more moral.

> Religion has clearly performed great services for human civilization. It has contributed much towards the taming of asocial instincts. But not enough. It has ruled human society for many thousands of years and has had the time to show what it can achieve. . . . It is doubtful whether men

were in general happier at a time when religious doctrines held unre-
stricted sway; more moral they certainly were not. . . . In every age immorality has found no less support in religion than morality has.[61]

Also like the philosophes, Freud was a humanitarian who sought to
relieve human misery by making people aware of their true nature,
particularly their sexuality. He wanted society to soften its overly re-
strictive sexual standards because they were injurious to mental
health. As a practicing psychiatrist, he tried to assist his patients in
dealing with emotional problems. One enduring consequence of the
Freudian revolution is the recognition of the enormous importance
played by childhood in the shaping of the adult's personality; the neurotic disorders that burden adults begin in early childhood. Freud urged
that we show greater concern for the emotional needs of children.

Although Freud undoubtedly was a child of the Enlightenment, in
crucial ways he differed from the philosophes. Regarding the Christian
doctrine of original sin as a myth, the philosophes had believed that
people's nature was essentially good. If people took reason as their
guide, evil could be eliminated. Freud, however, asserted in secular
terms, a gloomy view of human nature. In 1918, he concluded:

> . . . I have found little that is "good" about human beings on the whole.
> In my experience most of them are trash, no matter whether they pub-
> licly subscribe to this or that ethical doctrine or to none at all. That is
> something that you cannot say aloud or perhaps even think, though your
> experiences of life can hardly be different from mine. If we are to talk of
> ethics, I subscribe to a high ideal from which most of the human beings
> I have come across depart most lamentably.[62]

Freud saw evil as rooted in human nature rather than as a product of
a faulty environment. Education and better living conditions will not
eliminate evil, as the philosophes expected, nor will abolition of private property, as Marx had declared.

> The communists believe that they have found the path to deliverance
> from our evils. According to them, man is wholly good and is well-dis-
> posed to his neighbour; but the institution of private property has cor-
> rupted his nature. The ownership of private wealth gives the individual
> power, and with it the temptation to ill-treat his neighbour; while the
> man who is excluded from possession is bound to rebel in hostility
> against his oppressor. If private property were abolished, all wealth held
> in common . . . ill-will and hostility would disappear among men. . . .
> [T]he psychological premises on which the [communist] system is based
> are an untenable illusion. In abolishing private property we deprive the
> human love of aggression of one of its instruments, certainly a strong
> one, though certainly not the strongest; but we have in no way altered
> . . . anything in . . . [the] nature [of aggressiveness]. Aggressiveness was

not created by property. It reigned almost without limit in primitive times, when property was still very scanty, and it already shows itself in the nursery. . . . If we do away with personal rights over material wealth, there still remains prerogative in the field of sexual relationships, which is bound to become the source of the strongest dislike and the most violent hostility among men who in other respects are on an equal footing.[63]

For Freud, the socialists' earthly utopia, indeed, the whole Marxist system, was based on an illusion—a mistaken idealization of human nature. Like the Christian's heavenly kingdom, Marx's utopia was merely wishful thinking; it had no foundation in reality.

In the tradition of Socrates, the philosophes had defined the human being by the capacity to reason. They venerated reason; it had enabled Newton to unravel nature's mysteries and would permit people to achieve virtue and reform society. Freud's clinical studies led him to conclude that irrational emotions, not reason, dominate human behavior. The definition of the human being as fundamentally rational and good now seemed hopelessly naive. Nevertheless, Freud, wanted reason to prevail. "Our best hope for the future is that intellect—the scientific spirit, reason—may in process of time establish a dictatorship in the mental life of man. The nature of reason is a guarantee that afterwards it will not fail to give man's emotional impulses . . . the position they deserve."[64] Human beings cannot remain children forever, he said, but must rid themselves of illusions and be educated to reality. His famous words—"Where there is Id, there shall be Ego"—held out the hope that through reason human beings could acquire the strength to dispel those irrationalities that misgovern their lives. Freud wanted to raise to the level of consciousness hitherto unrecognized inner conflicts that caused emotional distress. Only such awareness enables individuals to resolve their neuroses. He also believed that the "dominance of reason will prove to be the strongest uniting bond among men and lead the way to further unions."[65]

But Freud who understood that reason's soft voice had to compete with the thunderous roars of the id was forever skeptical. His awareness of the immense pressures that civilization places on our fragile egos led him to break with the philosophes' optimism and to take a grim view of the present and the future.

> While mankind has made continual advances in its control over nature and may expect to make still greater ones, it is not possible to establish with certainty that a similar advance has been made in the management of human affairs; and probably at all periods, just as now once again, many people have asked themselves whether what little civilization has thus been acquired is indeed worth defending at all.[66]

Unlike Marx, Freud had no vision of utopia. The hostile, untamable character of human nature, with its murderous wishes, is an ever present obstacle to harmonious social relations. That Freud was hounded out of Vienna by the Nazis and his four sisters were murdered by them simply for being Jewish is a telling footnote to his view of human nature, the power of the irrational, and the fragility of civilization. Freud himself, who died shortly before the outbreak of World War II, probably would not have been surprised by the Holocaust. He would have regarded it as still another manifestation of human aggressiveness, "which is an indestructible feature of human nature."[67]

C. G. JUNG:
THE COLLECTIVE UNCONSCIOUS

Carl Gustav Jung (1875–1961), a Swiss psychiatrist with a broad interest in history, philosophy, mysticism, and mythology, also explored the world of the unconscious. For a few years, Jung collaborated with Freud but mounting disagreements between them—among other things, Jung criticized Freud for overemphasizing the role played by sexuality in human development and mental disorders—led to an irrevocable break in 1914, and Jung founded his own school of analytical psychology.

Jung contributed to psychological thought in two significant ways. First, he drew a distinction between two basic personality types: introverts, who are generally withdrawn, absorbed in their own inner lives; and extroverts who are apt to be outgoing and optimistic. The characteristics of introversion and extroversion are found to varying degrees within each person; a clear preponderance of one attitude over the other enables us to classify a person as an introverted or extroverted type. Jung developed these ideas in *The Psychological Types* (1921).

Second, he developed a theory of the collective unconscious that students of anthropology, religion, and mythology find particularly useful. Like Freud, Jung maintained that everyone has an unconscious that is the repository of painful feelings and ideas that are kept hidden from consciousness. Each individual's unconscious contains elements that are peculiar to that individual's own life story, his or her own unique history. This personal unconscious "rests upon a deeper layer, which does not derive from personal experience and is not a personal acquisition but is inborn."[68] This deeper layer, which Jung called the collective unconscious, "has contents and modes of behavior that are more or less the same everywhere and in all individuals. It is, in other words, identical in all men and thus constitutes a common psychic substrate of a suprapersonal nature which is present in everyone of us."[69] The collective unconscious contains universal images and symbols—Jung called them archetypes—that are archaic remnants of humanity's remotest past. Stored in the collective unconscious, said Jung, "is the whole spiritual heritage of mankind's evolution born anew in the brain structure of each individual."[70] The archetypes are a permanent part of human nature; as such, they continually influence our feelings, thoughts, and behavior.

The collective unconscious, said Jung, was formed in the primordial past through the human brain's continual interaction with the environment. It accounts for the fact that themes and images in the mythologies and art of far-separated peoples are strikingly similar and that the dreams and paintings of European mental patients contain material that closely resembles themes and images found in Eastern religious literature and art. Dreams, which are "involuntary, spontaneous products of the unconscious psyche . . . pure products of nature not falsified by any conscious purpose,"[71] are the main source of archetypes. Fantasies, myths, fairy tales, and the delusions and hallucinations of the insane also point to the existence of the collective unconscious.

Like Nietzsche, Jung warned that modern men and women have overvalued the intellect at the expense of deeply rooted feelings inherited from primitive ancestors. The gains of modern society have also entailed a great loss—the desacralization of the world has caused our spiritual life to fall into disrepair. We moderns have lost contact with myths and symbols, which, since primitive times, had been a source of emotional and spiritual sustenance. Jung held that religious feelings are central to the human psyche. Consequently, increased scientific comprehension of nature and the concomitant loss of religious myths and beliefs have left the modern individual disoriented and distressed, vulnerable to psychological disorders. An overvaluing of rational consciousness at the expense of inner psychic needs is detrimental to personality.

Jung maintained that modern men and women suffer from a sense of religious emptiness. Science has caused them to doubt inherited religious beliefs, but it provides no answer to questions of life's meaning. Modern man has the "feeling that he is a haphazard creature without meaning, and it is this feeling that prevents him from living his life with the intensity it demands if it is to be enjoyed to the full. Life becomes stale and is no longer the exponent of the complete man."[72] To surmount this spiritual void, to overcome the feeling of being adrift in a meaningless existence, Jung urged an inner experience, a journey into the interior realms of the unconscious. Such an encounter with one's psychic substrate was for Jung a religious experience.

SOCIOLOGICAL THOUGHT: CONFRONTING THE IRRATIONAL AND THE COMPLEXITIES OF MODERN SOCIETY

The end of the nineteenth century and the beginning of the twentieth mark the great age of sociological thought. The leading sociological thinkers of the period all regarded science as the only valid model for correct thinking, and all claimed that their thought rested on a scientific foundation. All were aware of the significance of the nonrational in the development of social life and institutions. They struggled with some of the crucial problems of modern society. How can society achieve coherence and stability when the customary associations and attachments that had characterized village life were ruthlessly dissolved by the rapidly developing industrial-urban-capitalist order and when religion no longer united people or provided them with unquestioned values? What are the implications of the nonrational for political life in an age of mass democracy? How can people preserve their individuality in a society that is becoming increasingly regimented? In many ways, twentieth-century dictatorships were responses to the dilemmas of modern society analyzed by these social theorists. And twentieth-century dictators would employ these social theorists' insights into groups and mass psychology for the purpose of gaining and maintaining power.

Emile Durkheim: Anomie

Émile Durkheim (1858–1917), a French scholar of Jewish background—he came from a long line of rabbis—and heir to Comte's vision of creating a science of society, was an important founder of modern sociology. Like Comte, he considered scientific thought the only valid model for modern society. A crucial element of Durkheim's thought was the effort to show that the essential ingredients of modern times—secularism, rationalism, and individualism—threaten society with disintegration. Traditional society was pervaded by the belief that the social order was derived from God, that a person's place and function were assigned by God and determined by birth, and that the inequalities of this world would be compensated for in the world to come. However, modern people, captivated by the principle of individualism, will not accept such restraints, said Durkheim. They seek to uplift themselves and demand that society allow them the opportunity. In the process, they reject or ignore the moral and social restraints that society requires, and this attitude leads to anarchy. Durkheim wanted to prevent modern society from disintegrating into a disconnected mass of self-seeking, antagonistic individuals. Like Rousseau, he held that the individual becomes fully human as a member of a community.

The weakening of those traditional ties, collective values, and common beliefs that had bound the individual to society constitutes for Durkheim, the crisis of modern society. To a Western world intrigued by scientific progress, Durkheim emphasized the spiritual malaise of modern society. Modern people, said Durkheim, suffer from *anomie*— a collapse of norms and values that produces disorientation. People do not feel integrated into a collective community and find no purpose in life, a condition that is detrimental to both the individual and the social order. In *Suicide* (1897), Durkheim maintained that "the exceptionally high number of voluntary deaths manifests the state of deep disturbances from which civilized societies are suffering and bears witness to its gravity."[73] The pathology of modern society is also demonstrated by a high level of boredom, anxiety, and pessimism.

Modern people are driven to suicide by intense competition and the disappointment and frustration resulting from unfulfilled expectations and lack of commitment to moral principles. People must limit their aspirations and exercise discipline over their desires and passions, said Durkheim. They must stop wanting more. Religion once spurred people toward discipline and restraint, but it no longer can.

Durkheim approved of modernity, but he noted that modern ways have not brought happiness or satisfaction to the individual. Modern scientific and industrial society requires a new moral system that will bind together the various classes into a cohesive social order giving meaning and purpose to human life and helping to overcome those feelings of restlessness and dissatisfaction that torment people. Like Saint-Simon, Durkheim called for a rational and secular system of morals to replace Christian dogma, which had lost its power to attract and to bind. If a rational and secular replacement for Christianity is not found, he said, society runs the risk of dispensing with moral beliefs altogether, and this vacuum it could not endure. Like the positivists, Durkheim insisted that the new moral beliefs must be discovered through the methods of science.

Durkheim hoped that occupational and professional organizations— updated medieval guilds—would integrate the individual into society and provide the moral force able to restrain the selfish interests of both employer and worker. By curbing egoism, fostering self-discipline, and promoting altruism, these organizations would provide substitutes for religion.

Durkheim focused on a crucial dilemma of modernity. On the one hand, modern industrial civilization has provided the individual with unparalleled opportunities for self-development and material improvement. On the other hand, the breakdown of traditional communal bonds caused by the spread of rationalism and individualism has produced a sense of isolation and alienation. In modern mass society, the individual feels like an outsider, a condition that has been exacerbated by the decline of Christianity. Twentieth-century totalitarian movements sought to integrate these uprooted and alienated souls into new collectivities—a proletarian state based on workers' solidarity or a racial state based on blood and soil.

Gaetano Mosca: Elites

Gaetano Mosca (1858–1941), an Italian social theorist, advanced the view that ruling elites are the basic feature of political societies. His principal work, *Elements of Political Science,* was first published in 1895; an enlarged third edition was issued in 1923 and later translated under the title *The Ruling Class.* In the positivist tradition, Mosca asserted that political and social theories must be removed from the realm of emotion, fancy, and imprecision; he sought to derive general laws of political behavior from an analysis of recorded facts.

Mosca argued that all societies are characterized by "two classes of people . . . a class that rules and a class that is ruled. The first class, always the less numerous . . . monopolizes power and enjoys the advantages that power brings." The organized minority imposes its will on the multitudes "in a manner that is now more or less legal, now more or less arbitrary and violent."[74] If the masses succeed in deposing the ruling class, "there would have to be another organized minority within the masses themselves to discharge the functions of a ruling class. Otherwise all organization, and the whole social structure, would be destroyed."[75] The ruling oligarchy is convinced that it has a right to its privileges and power, and the masses become resigned to their lowly station. In contrast to Marx, who held that the economically powerful always dominate political life, Mosca asserted that the nature of the ruling class depends on the way the society is organized. Thus, while in some societies the class possessing economic power predominates, in others warriors or a hereditary caste constitutes the ruling class. In modern society, said Mosca, salaried officials—state bureaucrats—are an important segment of the ruling elite.

Ruling minorities have in common a high level of organization, which enables their members to act in concert; by contrast, the disorganized masses, unable to unite against the minority, are perpetually reduced to powerlessness. Members of a ruling minority also possess wealth and superior intellectual and personality qualities—drive, ambition, and determination—that assist them in maintaining their dominance. In a view that closely resembled Marx's theory of ideology, Mosca held that the governing classes "do not justify their power exclusively by de facto possession of it, but try to find a moral and legal basis for it"[76]—the will of God or the will of the people. Such myths, or "universal illusions," purported to be based on universal principles,

> answer a real need in man's social nature; and this need, so universally felt, of governing and knowing that one is governed not on the basis of mere material or intellectual force, but on the basis of moral principle, has beyond any doubt a practical and real importance. . . . [A] universal illusion is a . . . social force that contributes powerfully to consolidating political organization and unifying peoples or even whole civilizations.[77]

Thus, for Mosca, the dominant class justifies and perpetuates its rule by cleverly asserting that it rests on principles widely held to be true.

It is a basic and unchangeable law of human nature that people struggle for pre-eminence, said Mosca. A corollary of this law is that the individual's struggle for pre-eminence is articulated on the social level into ruling elites and ruled majorities. A ruling class is a permanent feature of society; regardless of how the state is constituted, a narrow governing minority will always retain control. Oligarchic rule is the essential element of political life. Thus, Mosca rejected the democratic theory, best exemplified by Rousseau, that a government could be constituted in which political power is concentrated in an assembly of citizens who are fundamentally equal. He also rejected the socialist hope that in the future collectivist society the exploiter and the exploited will be no more and the state will cease to be an agent of a dominant class.

Mosca contended that those chosen to serve as representatives of the people in a democratic or socialist society will soon transform themselves into a ruling elite determined to preserve and protect their own special interests. To those who valued equality and placed hope and confidence in representative democracy as a just and rational way of resolving political tensions, Mosca's thought offered little consolation. It seemed that a small minority, through its control of political parties and the press, constituted the real rulers in a democratic society. Yet Mosca himself gradually turned from a critic to a skeptical defender of parliamentary institutions and did not support Mussolini's Fascist regime. In December 1925, when Mussolini was consolidating his power, Mosca rose from his seat in the Senate and declared: "I who have always criticized parliamentary government almost lament over its downfall."[78]

Vilfredo Pareto: Elites

Mosca's countryman, Vilfredo Pareto (1848–1923), an economist and sociologist, also focused on elites and the persistence of the nonrational in politics. Like Comte, Pareto aimed to construct a system of sociology on the model of the physical sciences. In *The Mind and Society* (1916), his most significant work, he concluded that social behavior does not rest primarily on reason but on nonrational instincts and sentiments. These deeply rooted and essentially changeless feelings are the fundamental elements in human behavior. While society may change, human nature remains essentially the same. Whoever aims to lead and to influence people must appeal not to logic but to elemental feelings. Most human behavior is nonrational, rooted in human instincts and sentiments.

Nonlogical considerations also determine the beliefs that people hold. Like Marx and Freud, Pareto believed that we cannot accept a person's word at face value. People do not act according to carefully thought-out theories. They act first from nonlogical motivations and then construct a rationalization to justify their behavior:

> . . . a very large number of human actions are not the outcome of reasoning. They are purely instinctive actions, although the man performing them experiences a feeling of pleasure in giving them, quite arbitrarily, logical causes. He is, generally speaking, not very exacting as to the soundness of this logic and is very easily satisfied by a semblance of rationality. Nevertheless, he would feel very uncomfortable if there were lacking a smattering of logic. . . .
>
> Human beings habitually make all their actions dependent on a small number of rules of conduct in which they have a religious faith. It is inevitable that this should be so, for the general mass of men possess neither the character nor the intelligence necessary for them to become capable of relating their actions to their real causes.[79]

Much of Pareto's work was devoted to studying the nonrational elements of human consciousness and the various beliefs invented to give the appearance of rationality to behavior that derives from feeling and instinct.

Pareto divided society into two strata: the elite and the masses. Elites have always existed, said Pareto, because human beings are unequal by nature and because the goods that all people seek cannot be shared equally. Because struggle is a general law of life, elites and masses will exist in all societies. Thus, Pareto rejected as naive Marx's vision of the end of the class struggle.

> Suppose collectivism to be established and that "capital" no longer exists; then only a particular form of class struggle will have disappeared

and new ones will emerge to replace it. New conflicts will appear between the different kinds of workers and the socialist state, between the intellectuals and the non-intellectuals, between the various politicians, between the politicians and those they administer, between innovators and conservatives, etc.[80]

In the tradition of Machiavelli, Pareto held that a successful ruling elite must, with cunning, and if necessary with violence, exploit the feelings and impulses of the masses to its own advantage. Democrats, he said, delude themselves in thinking that the masses are really influenced by rational argument. Pareto predicted that new political leaders would emerge who would master the people through propaganda and force, appealing always to sentiment rather than to reason. To this extent, Pareto was an intellectual forerunner of fascism, which preached an authoritarian elitism. Mussolini praised Pareto and proudly claimed him as a source of inspiration. To what degree Pareto, who died one year after Mussolini gained power, welcomed the fascist regime is a matter of conjecture. But the triumph of fascism did seem to confirm his convictions that democracy was ready to collapse, and that a small minority of determined men, willing to use violence, could gain control of the state if the holders of power were reluctant to counter with force.

Gustave Le Bon: Mass Psychology

Mosca and Pareto focused on ruling elites; Gustave Le Bon (1841–1931), a French social psychologist, concentrated on mass psychology as demonstrated in crowd behavior, a phenomenon of considerable importance in an age of accelerating industrialization and democriatization. "The substitution of the unconscious action of crowds for the conscious activity of individuals is one of the principal characteristics of the present age,"[81] Le Bon declared in the preface to *The Crowd* (1895). In the past, said Le Bon, rivalries between monarchs dominated Europe's political stage; "the opinion of the masses scarcely counted, and most frequently did not count at all."[82] But Europe has experienced a great transformation. "The age we are about to enter will in truth be the ERA OF CROWDS."[83] In this new age, "the voice of the masses has become predominant. . . . The destinies of nations are elaborated at present in the heart of the masses, and no longer in the councils of princes."[84] Organized in socialist parties, syndicates, and unions, the masses aspire to eliminate the upper classes and establish an egalitarian society. Their activities threaten civilization, which has "only been created and directed by a small intellectual aristocracy, never by crowds."[85]

Le Bon drew many examples of mass behavior from the French Revolution, but he also drew on the events of his own day, including the famous Boulanger episode in the late 1880s. General Georges Boulanger was idolized by various political factions, but particularly by royalists and nationalists eager to overthrow the Third French Republic. Viewing Boulanger as a man of destiny, a beloved leader, the Parisian crowds clamored for him to seize power. Had Boulanger launched an insurrection, noted Le Bon, he "might easily have found a hundred thousand men ready to sacrifice their lives for his cause."[86] It was just such a relationship between a leader and the masses that intrigued Le Bon.

Le Bon applied the term *crowd* to a group of people in which individuality is submerged in the mass and the individual loses control over his or her emotions. A psychological crowd could be a street mob, a political party, or a labor union. An agglomeration of individuals "presents new characteristics very different from those of the individuals composing it. The sentiments and ideas of all the persons in the gathering take one and the same direction, and their conscious personality vanishes."[87] The crowd acquires a collective mind, in which critical thinking is swamped and

> unconscious qualities obtain the upper hand. . . . [T]he individual forming part of a crowd acquires, solely from numerical considerations, a sentiment of invincible power which allows him to yield to instincts which, had he been alone he would perforce have kept under restraint. . . . [A] crowd being anonymous, and in consequence irresponsible, the sentiment of responsibility which always controls individuals disappears entirely.[88]

Gripped by the crowd's hypnotic power, an individual readily sacrifices personal interest to collective interest: "having entirely lost his conscious personality, he obeys all the suggestions of the operator who has deprived him of it, and commits acts in utter contradiction with his character and habits."[89] Becoming increasingly intolerant and fanatical, the crowd member "descends several rungs in the ladder of civilisation. Isolated, he may be a cultivated individual; in a crowd, he is a barbarian—that is, a creature acting by instinct."[90] These destructive instincts inherited from our primitive past are activated by the crowd. Assured of impunity, the individual gives free reign to them, something he is unable to do in the ordinary course of events. Crowd behavior demonstrates convincingly that "the part played by the unconscious in all our acts is immense and that played by reason very small"[91]—that in a contest with sentiment human reason is utterly powerless.

Le Bon also discussed the leaders of crowds and their means of persuasion. "A crowd is a servile flock that is incapable of ever doing without a master," said Le Bon. Leaders "are more frequently men of action than thinkers"; they are "morbidly nervous, excitable, . . . bordering on madness." Fanatically committed to their beliefs, they do not respond to logical argument. The masses, "always ready to listen to the strong-willed man,"[92] respond to the intensity of the leader's faith.

In 1898, three years after the publication of *The Crowd*, Le Bon wrote *The Psychology of Socialism*, in which he compared socialism to a religion promising worldly salvation. Socialism's triumph, he predicted, will be followed by "servitude, misery and Caesarism. . . . Intelligence and ability will be replaced by mediocrity. . . . It will be a hell, a terrible hell."[93] This argument had the support of French conservatives, who distrusted and feared the organized strength of the working class.

Both Mussolini and Hitler, who deliberately sought to seduce, manipulate, and dominate the masses, absorbed Le Bon's ideas, which had become commonplace in the early twentieth century. "I don't know how many times I have re-read *Psychologie des Foules* [*The Crowd*]," declared Mussolini. "It is an excellent work to which I frequently refer."[94] Hitler's analysis of the crowd—"sober reasoning determines their thoughts far less than emotion and feeling"—restates many of Le Bon's observations.

Graham Wallas: The Irrational in Politics

In *Human Nature and Politics* (1908), Graham Wallas (1858–1932), an English political scientist and Fabian socialist, concluded that political opinions and voting patterns were not the result of reasoning tested by experience but derived from a whole complex of impulses, habits, and prejudices. During election campaigns, said Wallas, a candidate eschews appeals to logical argument and plays on the voters' emotions instead. The candidate deliberately tries to gain the affection of voters by giving the appearance of friendliness, by displaying photographs of himself, by giving away prizes

> all under circumstances which offer little or no opportunity for the formation of a reasoned opinion of his merits, but many opportunities for the rise of a purely instinctive affection among those present. A simple-minded supporter whose affection has been so worked up will probably try to give an intellectual explanation of it. He will say that the man of whom he may really know nothing except that he was photographed in

a Panama hat with a fox-terrier is "the kind of man we want" and that therefore he has decided to support him.[95]

Wallas's views challenged the fundamental assumption of liberal democracy—that the average person has the ability to deal rationally with affairs of state—and seemed to buttress conservatives' apprehensions about the dangers of universal suffrage.

Max Weber: The Dilemma of Modernity

Probably the most prominent social thinker of the age and a leading shaper of modern sociology was Max Weber (1864–1920). To Weber, a German academic, modern Western civilization, unlike the other civilizations of the globe, had virtually eliminated myth, mystery, and magic from its conception of nature and society—the "disenchantment of the world," Weber called it. Modern westerners, said Weber, seek to master all things by calculation. This process of rationalization, or calculated knowledge and action, was most conspicuous in Western science, but it was also evident in politics, law, and economics.

Weber considered Western science an attempt to understand and master nature through reason. He viewed Western capitalism as an effort to organize work and production and to pursue profits in a deliberately methodical and calculating manner, unhampered by inherited traditions and sentiments. Workers are subject to rational discipline, to "scientific management." In the factory, "the psycho-physical apparatus of man is completely adjusted to the demands of the outer world, the tools, the machines—in short, it is functionalized, and the individual is shorn of his natural rhythm as determined by his organism; in line with the demands of work procedure, he is attuned to a new rhythm."[96] Western political life, too, has a marked rational character: the Western state has a rationally written constitution, rationally formulated law, and a bureaucracy of trained, technically efficient, government officials who administer the affairs of state according to rational rules and regulations. Justice is not dispensed by wise elders committed to sacred traditions; it involves neither oracles nor ordeals but, operating "like a technically rational machine," it proceeds from codified law and established procedures. Modern industrial capitalism requires a legal and administrative system, which, like a machine, functions in an efficient and predictable way. Even Western music, which is distinguished by a harmonic chord system and rigorously structured orchestrations, shows this process of rationalization.

The question of why the West, and not China or India, engaged in this process of rationalization intrigued Weber, and much of his scholarly effort went into answering it. Weber showed how various religious beliefs had influenced a people's understanding of nature, shaped its social and political institutions and economic behavior, and contributed to or blocked the development of rationalization. Weber's most famous thesis is that Protestantism, which saw work as a religious duty and hedonism as a sin and called for methodical self-control, the rational planning of one's life in accordance with God's will—produced an outlook that was conducive to the requirements of capitalism (see page 57). Capitalism, said Weber, is not a thirst for money, a merely acquisitive desire that has been exhibited since the early days of civilization. The distinguishing feature of capitalism is the rational organization of all business activities, including the labor force, so that profits are continuous and calculable. The Protestant ethic gave religious approval to methodical and patient work and to saving and reinvesting, for it saw worldly activity as a way of increasing God's glory, worldly success as a sign of God's blessing, and sloth and hedonism as offensive to God.

Weber understood the terrible paradox of reason. Reason accounts for brilliant achievements in science and economic life, but it also despiritualizes life by ruthlessly eliminating centuries-old traditions, denouncing deeply felt religious beliefs as superstition, and regarding human feelings and passions as impediments to clear thinking. The process of disenchantment has given people knowledge, but it has also made them soulless and their life meaningless. This is the dilemma of modern individuals, said Weber. Science cannot answer the ultimate questions of life—it cannot give men and women a purpose for living. And the burgeoning of bureaucracy in government, business, and education stifles individual autonomy.

The process of secularization and rationalization has fostered self-liberation, for it enabled human beings to overcome illusions and to take control over the environment and themselves. But it is also a means of self-enslavement, for it produces institutions, giant bureaucracies, that encouage uniformity and depersonalization. Modern officials, said Weber, are emotionally detached and concerned only with the efficient execution of tasks; such human feelings as compassion and affection are ruled out as hindrances to effectiveness. In the name of efficiency, people are placed in "iron cages," depriving them of their personal liberty and humanity.

> It is horrible to think that the world would one day be filled with nothing but those little cogs, little men clinging to little jobs and striving towards bigger ones. . . . This passion for bureaucracy . . . is enough to drive one to despair. It is as if in politics . . . we were deliberately to become men who need "order" and nothing but order, who become

nervous and cowardly if for one moment this order wavers, and helpless if they are torn away from their total incorporation in it. That the world should know no men but these: it is in such an evolution that we are already caught up, and the great question is, therefore, not how we can promote and hasten it, but what can we oppose to this machinery in order to keep a portion of mankind free from this parceling-out of the soul, from this supreme mastery of the bureaucratic way of life.[97]

The prospect exists that people would refuse to endure this violation of their spiritual needs and would reverse the process of disenchantment by seeking redemption in the irrational. Weber himself, however, was committed to the ideals of reason and personal freedom, which he felt were threatened by bureaucratic regimentation on the one hand and the irrational potentialities of human nature on the other. Like the philosophes, Weber believed that individuals fulfill themselves as human beings when they behave rationally and responsibly. Like Freud, he contended that social life is pervaded by tension and antagonism and that utopias are illusions: no golden age existed in the past, and there is none in store for us in the future. Also like Freud, he wanted people to commit themselves to scientific rationality and to base their actions on free choice. Such rational and morally autonomous individuals, he believed, are best able to face the challenges of modern life.

Like Freud, Weber was aware of the power of the nonrational in society. One expression of the irrational that he analyzed was the charismatic leader who attracts people by force of personality. Charismatic leaders may be religious prophets, war heroes, statesmen, or others who possess this extraordinary personality that attracts and dominates others. People yearn for charismatic leadership during times of crisis. The leader claims a mission—a sacred duty—to lead the people during the crisis; the leader's authority rests on the people's belief in the mission and their faith in the leader's remarkable abilities. A common allegiance to the charismatic leader unites the community. Weber's analysis of this phenomenon throws light on the popularity of twentieth-century dictators and demagogues. Weber proposed charismatic leadership for Germany, but not the kind identified with fascism. Successful leadership, said Weber, required passion directed by reason.

> For the problem is precisely: How can burning passion and a cool sense of proportion be forced to coexist in the same soul? Politics is made with the head, not with . . . the soul. And yet devotion to it can only be born and nourished from passion, if it is not to be a frivolous intellectual game, but humanely genuine action.[98]

THE MODERNIST MOVEMENT

At the same time that Freud and social theorists were breaking with the Enlightenment view of human nature and society, artists and writers were rebelling against traditional forms of artistic and literary expression that had governed European cultural life since the Renaissance. Their experimentations produced a great cultural revolution called *modernism*, which still profoundly influences the arts.

Breaking with Conventional Modes of Esthetics

In many ways, modernism was a restatement and expansion of the Romantic Movement, which had dominated European culture in the early nineteenth century. Both movements subjected to searching criticism cultural styles that had been formulated during the Renaissance and had roots in ancient Greece. But even more than romanticism, modernism cultivated an intense introspection—a heightened awareness of self. To a greater degree than the romantics, modernist writers sought to convey their own unique feelings and saw the intellect as a barrier to the free expression of elemental human emotions. To this extent, they were reacting against naturalism, which called for a detached study of people and social conditions and stressed a causal relationship between the individual and the environment. Their critique of naturalism paralleled the romantics' denunciation of eighteenth-century rationalism. More than their romantic predecessors, modernist artists and writers abandoned conventional literary and artistic models and experimented with new modes of expression. The consequence of their bold venture, says literary critic Irving Howe, was nothing less than the "breakup of the traditional unity and continuity of Western culture."[99]

Like Freud, modernist artists and writers went beyond surface appearances in search of a more profound reality hidden in the human psyche. French poet Arthur Rimbaud who anticipated this trend, wrote:

> The first study of the man who wants to be a poet is the knowledge of himself, complete. He looks for his soul, inspects it, tests it, learns it. . . .
> I say that one must be a *seer*, make oneself a *seer*.
> The Poet makes himself a *seer* by a long, gigantic and rational *derangement of all the senses*. All forms of love, of suffering, and madness. He searches himself. He exhausts all poisons in himself and keeps only

their quintessences. Unspeakable torture where he needs all his faith, all his superhuman strength, where he becomes among all men the great patient, the great criminal, the one accursed—and the supreme Scholar!—Because he reaches the *unknown.* Since he cultivated his soul, rich already, more than any man! He reaches the unknown, and when, bewildred, he ends by losing the intelligence of his visions, [at least] he has seen them.[100]

Writers such as Thomas Mann, Marcel Proust, James Joyce, August Strindberg, D. H. Lawrence, and Franz Kafka explored the inner life of the individual and the psychopathology of human relations. They dealt with the predicament of men and women who rejected the values and customs of their day, and they depicted the anguish of people burdened by guilt, torn by internal conflicts, and driven by an inner self-destructiveness. They also showed the overwhelming might of the irrational and the appeal of the primitive and, breaking with convention, dealt with sexual themes.

From the Renaissance through the Enlightenment and into the nineteenth century, Western esthetic standards had been shaped by the conviction that the universe embodied an inherent mathematical order. A corollary of this conception of the outer world as orderly and intelligible was the view that art should imitate reality. From the Renaissance on, says sociologist Daniel Bell, art was seen as "a mirror of nature, a representation of life. Knowledge was a reflection of what was 'out there' . . . a copy of what was seen."[101] Since the Renaissance, artists had deliberately made use of laws of perspective and proportion; musicians had used harmonic chords that brought rhythm and melody into a unified whole; writers had produced works according to a definite pattern that included a beginning, middle, and end.

Modernist culture, however, acknowledged no objective reality of space, motion, and time that means the same to all observers. Rather, reality can be grasped in many ways; a multiplicity of frames of reference apply to nature and human experience. Reality is the way the viewer perceives it to be through the prism of the imagination. "There is no outer reality," said the modernist German poet Gottfried Benn, "there is only human consciousness, constantly building, modifying, rebuilding new worlds out of its own creativity."[102] Modern art, for example, does not aspire to imitate nature. It is concerned less with the object itself than with how the artist transforms it—with the sensations that an object evokes in the artist's inner being and the meaning the artist's imagination imposes on reality. "Conscientious and exact imitation of nature does not create a work of art," wrote Emile Nolde, a German expressionist painter. "A work becomes a work of art when one re-evaluates the values of nature and adds one's own spirituality."[103] Swiss painter Paul Klee declared:

> Formerly we used to represent things visible on earth. . . . Today we re-
> veal the reality that is behind visible things, thus expressing the belief
> that the visible world is merely an isolated case in relation to the uni-
> verse and that there are many more other, latent realities. Things appear
> to assume a broader and more diversified meaning, often seemingly con-
> tradicting the rational experience of yesterday.[104]

Modern artists deliberately plunged into the world of the unconscious in search of the instinctual, the fantastic, the primitive, and the
mysterious, which they perceived as a higher and more profound reality than is grasped by analytical thought. What matters most to the
artist, said Klee, is not "the present state of outward appearances . . .
as accidentally fixed in time and space," but the artist's own "penetrating vision and intense depth of feeling."[105] The new norm "permits
the painter to proportion objects in accordance with the degree of plasticity he desires them to have,"[106] declared poet Guillaume Apollinaire.
And Maurice Denis, the prominent muralist, wrote:

> Art is no longer only a visual sensation which we record, only a pho-
> tograph . . . of nature. No, it is a creation of our spirit of which nature is
> only the occasion. Instead of "working with the eye, we search in the
> mysterious center of thought," as Gauguin said. . . . Thus we set free our
> sensibility, and art, instead of being a *copy*, became the *subjective defor-
> mation* of nature.[107]

Bell discusses the subjective nature of modern art:

> Modernism . . . denies the primacy of an outside reality, as given. It
> seeks either to rearrange reality, or to retreat to the self's interior, to pri-
> vate experience as the source of its concerns and aesthetic preoccupa-
> tions. . . . There is an emphasis on the self as the touchstone of under-
> standing and on the activity of the knower rather than the character of
> the object as the source of knowledge. . . . Thus one discerns the inten-
> tions of modern painting . . . to break up ordered space. . . . to bridge the
> distance between object and spectator, to 'thrust' itself on the viewer and
> establish itself immediately by impact.[108]

Dispensing with conventional forms of esthetics that stressed structure and coherence, modernism propelled the arts onto uncharted seas.
Recoiling from a middle-class, industrial civilization that prized rationalism, organization, clarity, stability, and definite norms and values, modernist writers and artists were fascinated by the bizarre, the
mysterious, the unpredictable, the primitive, the irrational, and the
formless. Writers, for example, experimented with new techniques to
convey the intense struggle between the conscious and the unconscious and to connote the aberrations and complexities of human personality and the irrationality of human behavior. In particular, they
devised a new way, the stream of consciousness, to exhibit the mind's

every level—both conscious reflection and unconscious strivings—and to capture how thought is punctuated by spontaneous outbursts, disconnected assertions, random memories, hidden desires, and persistent fantasies. In music, Igor Stravinsky experimented with atonality, and Arnold Schoenberg with primitive rhythms. When Stravinsky's ballet *The Rite of Spring* was performed in Paris in 1913, the theater audience rioted to protest the composition's use of primitive, jazzlike rhythms and its theme of ritual sacrifice.

Cultural Pessimism

Many people living in *la belle époque*—the end of the nineteenth century—viewed Western achievements in the arts and sciences as a triumph. But there were culture critics, like Nietzsche, who dismissed the era's outward brilliance as a facade; for them decadence, decline, and rot constituted the true reality. The theme of cultural degeneration and weariness with existence pervaded the works of several writers and artists. Thus French writer Ernest Caro wrote in 1878: "Never has the question of evil and that of life's value been argued with such passion as in our own time. . . . Is it true that the world is ill-begotten, that there is a radical, absolute, insuperable evil inherent in nature and mankind, that existence is a misfortune and that nothingness is better than being?"[109] The world being shaped by positivism and science, these culture critics said, reduced existence to a remorseless and sterile mechanism. Life was deprived of spirituality, poetry, imagination, and ultimate meaning. These thinkers saw their times as fraught with anguish, a struggle between the soul, yearning to discover a deeper and personal meaning to life, and a positivistic-mechanistic world-view, which debased the imagination and relegated the individual to the world of things.

The pessimism of this period had roots in Schopenhauer's philosophy. His chief work, *The World as Will and Idea* (1819), came to enjoy popularity in France, particularly after its translation in 1886. Other shapers of this spirit of pessimism and decadence were French poets Charles Baudelaire (1821–1867) and Arthur Rimbaud (1854–1891). Baudelaire's *Flowers of Evil* (1855) gave primacy to putrescence and decay, to melancholy and despair, and to the bizarre and perverted. When a revised edition of *Flowers of Evil*, was ready for publication, Baudelaire wrote to his mother that the work shows "my disgust and my hatred for everything."[110] Rimbaud, like Nietzsche and Baudelaire, had an intense disgust for bourgeois society, its materialism, hypocrisy, and sham respectability. He condemned conventional love, family, morality, and intellectualism. In the poem "What Does it Matter" (1872), he expressed his general revulsion at the world:

> Industrialists, princes, senates
> Perish! Power, justice, history: down with you! . . .
> Europe, Asia, America—disappear![111]

Modern Art

The modernist movement, which began near the end of the nineteenth century, was in full bloom before World War I and would continue to flower in the postwar world. Probably the clearest expression of the modernist viewpoint is found in art. In the late nineteenth century, artists began to turn away from standards that had characterized art since the Renaissance. No longer committed to depicting how an object appears to the eye, they searched for new forms of expression. The history of modern painting begins with impressionism, which covered the period from 1860 to 1886 and broke with traditional formulas of composition (the arrangement of figures and objects) and treatments of color and light. Impressionism centered in Paris, and its leading figures were Edouard Manet, Claude Monet, Camille Pissarro, Edgar Degas, and Pierre Auguste Renoir. Taking Pissarro's advice—"Don't proceed according to rules and principles but paint what you observe and feel"—impressionists tried to give their own immediate and personal impression of an object or an event. They tried to capture how movement, color, and light appeared to the eye at a fleeting instant.

Intrigued by the impact that light has on objects, impressionists left their studios for the countryside, where they painted nature under an open sky. They used bold colors and drew marked contrasts between light and dark to reflect how objects in intense sunlight seem to shimmer against their background.

In addition to landscapes, impressionists painted railways, bridges and boulevards, and people—in dance halls, cafés, theaters, and public gardens. Impressionist painters wanted to portray life as it was commonly experienced in a rapidly industrializing world. And always they tried to convey the momentary impression of an event or figure.

In the late 1880s and the 1890s, several artists went beyond impressionism. Called postimpressionists, they further revolutionized the artist's sense of space and color. Even more than the impressionists, they tried to make art a vivid emotional experience and to produce a personal impression of reality rather than a photographic copy of objects.

Paul Cézanne (1839–1906) sought to portray his visual perception of an object, not the object itself. In other words, to what is seen, the artist brings a personal appreciation, which his or her intelligence organizes into a work of art. When painting objects in a group, Cézanne deliberately distorted perspective, subordinating the appearance of an individual object to the requirements of the total design. Cézanne tried to demonstrate that an object, when placed together with other objects, is seen differently than when it stands alone.

No longer bound by classical art forms, artists examined non-Western art, searching for new forms of beauty and new ways of expression. The large number of artifacts and art objects coming into European capitals from Asia, Africa, and the Pacific area as souvenirs of nineteenth-century imperialist ventures and from anthropologists and ethnographers—stimulated interest in non-Western art. Paul Gauguin (1848–1903) saw beauty in carvings and fabrics made by such technologically backward people as the Marquesas Islanders. He discovered that very simple, even primitive, means of construction could produce works of great beauty.

A successful Parisian stockbroker, Gauguin abandoned the marketplace for art. He came to view bourgeois civilization as artificial and rotten. By severing human beings from the power of their own feelings, industrial civilization blunted the creative expression of the imagination and prevented people from attaining a true understanding of themselves. For these reasons, Gauguin fled to Tahiti. On this picturesque island, which was largely untouched by European ways, he hoped to discover humanity's original nature without the distortions and corruption of modern civilization.

The postimpressionists produced a revolution not only of space but also of color, as exemplified by Vincent van Gogh (1853–1890). The son of a Dutch minister, van Gogh was a lonely, tortured, and impetuous soul. For a short period, he served as a lay preacher among desperately poor coal miners. Moving to Paris in 1886, van Gogh came under the influence of the French impressionists. Desiring to use color in a novel way—his own way—van Gogh left Paris for the Mediterranean countryside, where he hoped to experience a new vision of sunlight, sky, and earth. Van Gogh used purer, brighter colors than artists had used before. He also recognized that color, like other formal qualities, could act as a language in and of itself. He believed that the local, or "real," color of an object does not necessarily express the artist's experience. Artists, according to van Gogh, should seek to paint things not as they are, but as the artists feel them. *The Starry Night* conveys his vision of a night sky, not with tiny points of lights, but with exploding and whirling stars in a vast universe, overwhelming the huddled dwellings built by human beings.

Practically unknown in his lifetime, van Gogh's art became extremely influential soon after his death. One of the first artists to be affected by his style was the Norwegian artist Edvard Munch (1863–1944), who discovered van Gogh's use of color while in Paris. In *The Dance of Life*, for example, Munch used strong, simple lines and intense color to explore unexpressed sexual stresses and conflicts. In *The Scream*, he deliberately distorted the human face and the sky, ground, and water to portray terror.

After the postimpressionists, art moved still further away from reproducing an exact likeness of a physical object or human being. Increasingly artists sought to penetrate deeper into the unconscious, which they saw as the source of creativity and the abode of a higher truth. Paul Klee described modern art in this way: "Each [artist] should follow where the pulse of his own heart leads. . . . Our pounding heart drives us down, deep down to the source of all. What springs from this source, whether it may be called dream, idea or phantasy—must be taken seriously."[112]

In Germany, the tendency to use color for its power to express psychological states continued in the work of artists known as German expressionists. Expressionists inherited Nietzsche's cultural pessimism—his view that society was decadent—as well as his plea for renewal through subjective creation. For them artistic creativity was a prelude to cultural liberation and renewal. Through art, they hoped to demonstrate pure vitality, to express, in the words of Ernst Ludwig Kirchner (1880–1938), "the richness and joy of living, . . . love as well as hatred."[113] In his *Reclining Nude* of 1909, Kirchner used strong, acid yellows and greens to evoke feelings of tension, stress, and isolation. He also used bold, rapid lines to define flat shapes, a technique borrowed from folk art and from non-Western native traditions.

In France, another group of avant-garde artists called the *fauves* (the wild beasts) used color with great freedom to express intense feelings and heightened energy. After examining the works of the fauves, a French critic wrote: "What is presented here . . . has nothing to do with painting; some formless confusion of colors, blue, red, yellow, green, the barbaric and naive spirit of the child who plays with the box of colors he has just got as a Christmas present."[114] Rebelling against new currents in painting, critics failed to recognize the originality and genius of the fauves.

Henri Matisse (1869–1954), the leading fauvist painter, freed color from every restriction. He painted broad areas with stunning pigment unrelated to the real colors of the subject. His brilliant use of color and design aroused a violent reaction; one New York critic described a Matisse exhibition as "ugliness that is most appalling . . . artistic degeneration . . . hideousness."[115]

Between 1909 and 1914, a new style called cubism was developed by Pablo Picasso (1881–1973) and Georges Braque (1882–1963). They explored the interplay between the flat world of the canvas and the three-dimensional world of visual perception. Like the postimpressionists, they sought to paint a reality deeper than what the eye sees at first glance. Cubist art presents objects from multiple viewpoints. The numerous fragmentary images of cubist art make one aware of the complex experience of seeing. One art historian describes cubism as follows: "The cubist is not interested in usual representational standards. It is as if he were walking around the object he is analyzing, as one is free to walk around a piece of sculpture for successive views. But he must represent these views at once."[116]

In *Les Demoiselles d'Avignon,* Picasso painted five nudes. In each instance the body is distorted in defiance of classical and Renaissance standards of beauty. The masklike faces show Picasso's debt to African art and, together with the angular shapes, deprive the subjects of individuality and personality. The head of the squatting figure combines a profile with a full face—Picasso's attempt to present multiple aspects of an object at the same time. In order to depict something from a multiple perspective, cubists deliberately deformed objects, distorting visual reality in deference to the artists' own sensibilities, their own artistic autonomy.

Throughout the period from 1890 to 1914, avant-garde artists were de-emphasizing subject matter and the representation of objects and stressing the expressive power of such formal qualities as line, color, and space. It is not surprising that some artists finally began to create work that did not refer to anything seen in the real world. Piet Mondrian (1872–1944), a Dutch artist, came to Paris shortly before World War I. There he saw the cubist art of Picasso and Braque. The cubists had compressed the imaginary depth in their paintings so that all objects seemed to be contained within a space only a few inches deep. They had also reduced subject matter to insignificance. It seemed to Mondrian that the next step was to get rid of illusionistic space and subject matter entirely. By eliminating from his painting any reference to the visible world, Mondrian helped to inaugurate abstract art.

Another founder of abstract art was Wassily Kandinsky (1866–1944), a Russian residing in Germany. Kandinsky gradually came to remove all traces of the physical world from his paintings to create a non-objective art that bears no resemblance to the natural world. In stating that he "painted . . . subconsciously in a state of strong inner tension,"[117] Kandinsky explicitly expressed a principal quality of modern art.

The revolution in art that took place near the turn of the twentieth century is reverberating still. After nearly a hundred years, these masters of modern art continue to inspire their audiences with their passion and vision. In breaking with the Renaissance view of the world as inherently orderly and rational, modern artists opened up new possibilities for artistic expression and exemplified the growing power and appeal of the nonrational in European life.

MODERN PHYSICS

Until the closing years of the nineteenth century, the view of the physical universe held by the Western mind rested largely on the classical physics of Newton and included the following principles: (1) time, space, and matter were objective realities that existed independently of the observer; (2) the universe was a giant machine whose parts obeyed strict laws of cause and effect; (3) the atom, indivisible and solid, was the basic unit of matter; (4) heated bodies emitted radiation in continuous waves; and (5) through further investigation, it would be possible to gain complete knowledge of the physical universe.

Between the 1890s and the 1920s, this view of the universe was shattered by a second Scientific Revolution. The discovery of x-rays by Wilhelm Konrad Roentgen in 1895, of radioactivity by Henri Bequerel in 1896, and of the electron by J. J. Thomson in 1897 led science to abandon the conception of the atom as a solid and indivisible particle. Rather than resembling a billiard ball, the atom consisted of a nucleus of tightly packed protons separated from orbiting electrons by empty space.

In 1900, Max Planck (1858–1947), a German physicist, proposed the quantum theory, which holds that a heated body does not radiate energy in a continuous unbroken stream, as had been believed, but in intermittent spurts or jumps called quanta. Planck's theory of discontinuity in energy radiation challenged a cardinal principle of classical physics that action in nature was strictly continuous.

In 1905, Albert Einstein (1879–1955), a German-Swiss physicist of Jewish lineage, substantiated and elaborated on Planck's theory by suggesting that all forms of radiant energy—light, heat, x-rays—moved through space in discontinuous packets of energy. Then, in 1913, Niels Bohr, a Danish scientist, applied Planck's theory of energy quanta to the interior of the atom and discovered that the Newtonian laws of motion could not fully explain what happened to electrons orbiting an atomic nucleus.

As physicists explored the behavior of the atom further, it became apparent that its nature was fundamentally elusive and unpredictable. They soon observed that radioactive atoms threw off particles and

Albert Einstein *(Lotte Jacobi Archives, University of New Hampshire)*

transformed themselves from atoms of one element into atoms of an entirely different element. But the transformation of a single atom in a mass of radioactive material could not be predicted according to inexorable laws of cause and effect. For example, it is known that over a period of 1,620 years half the atoms of the element radium decay and transform themselves into atoms of another element. It is impossible, however, to know when a particular atom in a lump of radium will undergo this transformation. Scientists can only make accurate predictions about the behavior of an aggregate of radium atoms; the transformation of any given atom is the result of random chance rather than of any known physical law. That we cannot predict when a particular radioactive atom will decay calls into question the notion of classical physics that physical nature proceeds in an orderly fashion, according to strict laws of cause and effect.

Newtonian physics says that, given certain conditions, we can predict what will follow. For example, if an airplane is flying north at four hundred miles per hour, we can predict its exact position two hours from now, assuming that the plane does not alter its course or speed.

Quantum mechanics teaches that in the subatomic realm we cannot predict with certainty what will take place; we can only say that, given certain conditions, it is *probable* that a certain event will follow. This principle of uncertainty was developed in 1927 by the German scientist Werner Heisenberg (1901–1976), who showed that it is impossible to determine at one and the same time both an electron's precise speed and its position. Science writer Alan E. Nourse explains:

> [Heisenberg showed] that the very act of attempting to examine [an] electron any more closely in order to be *more certain* of where it was and what it was doing at a given instant *would itself alter where the electron was and what it was doing at the instant in question.* Heisenberg, in effect, was saying that in dealing with the behavior of electrons and other elementary particles the laws of cause and effect do not and cannot apply, that all we can do is make predictions about them on the basis of probability and not a very high degree of probability at that. . . . the more certain we try to become about a given electron's *position* at a given instant, the wider the limits of probability we must accept with regard to what its *momentum* [speed] is at the same time, and vice versa. The more closely either one property of the electron or the other is examined, the more closely we approach certainty with regard to one property or the other, the more wildly uncertain the other property becomes. And since an electron can really only be fully described in terms of *both* its position and its momentum at any given instant, *it becomes utterly impossible to describe an electron at all* in terms of absolute certainties. We can describe it only in terms of uncertainties or probabilities.[118]

In the small-scale world of the electron, we enter a universe of uncertainty, probability, and statistical relationships. No improvement in measurement technique will dispel this element of chance and provide us with complete knowledge of the universe.

Although Einstein could not accept that a complete comprehension of reality was unattainable, his theory of relativity was instrumental in shaping modern physics; it altered classical conceptions of space and time. Newtonian physics had viewed space as a distinct reality, a stationary and motionless medium through which light traveled and matter moved. Time was viewed as a fixed and rigid framework that was the same for all observers and existed independently of human experience. For Einstein, however, neither space nor time had an independent existence; neither could be divorced from human experience. Once asked to explain briefly the essentials of relativity, Einstein replied: "It was formerly believed that if all material things disappeared out of the universe, time and space would be left. According to the relativity theory, however, time and space disappear together with the things."[119]

Contrary to all previous thinking, relativity theory holds that time differs for two observers traveling at different speeds. Imagine twin brothers involved in space exploration, one as an astronaut, the other as a rocket designer who never leaves earth. The astronaut takes off in the most advanced spaceship yet constructed, one that achieves a speed close to the maximum attainable in our universe—the speed of light. After traveling several trillion miles, the spaceship turns around and returns to earth. According to the experience of the ship's occupants, the whole trip took about two years. But when the astronaut lands on earth, he finds totally changed conditions. For one thing, his brother has long since died, for according to earth's calendars some two hundred years have elapsed since the rocket ship set out on its journey. Such illustration seemed to defy common sense and all experience, yet experiments supported Einstein's claims.

Motion, too, is relative. The only way we can describe the motion of one body is to compare it with another moving body. This means that there is no motionless, absolute, fixed frame of reference anywhere in the universe. The following passage by science writer Isaac Asimov illustrates Einstein's theory of the relativity of motion:

> Suppose we on the earth were to observe a strange planet ("Planet X"), exactly like our own in size and mass, go whizzing past us at 163,000 miles per second relative to ourselves. If we could measure its dimensions as it shot past, we would find that it was foreshortened by 50 per cent in the direction of its motion. It would be an ellipsoid rather than a sphere and would, on further measurement, seem to have twice the mass of the earth.
>
> Yet to an inhabitant of Planet X, it would seem that he himself and his own planet were motionless. The earth would seem to be moving past him at 163,000 miles per second, and it would appear to have an ellipsoidal shape and twice the mass of *his* planet.
>
> One is tempted to ask which planet would really be foreshortened and doubled in mass. but the only possible answer is: that depends on the frame of reference.[120]

In his famous equation, $E = mc^2$, Einstein showed that matter and energy are not separate categories but two different expressions of the same physical entity. The source of energy is matter; and the source of matter is energy. Tiny quantities of matter could be transformed into staggering amounts of energy. The atomic age was dawning.

The discoveries of modern physics transformed the world of classical physics. Whereas nature had been regarded as something outside the individual—an objective reality that existed independently of ourselves—modern physics teaches that our position in space and time determines what we mean by reality and that our very presence affects reality itself. When we observe a particle with our measuring instruments, we are interfering with it, knocking it off its course; we are participating in reality. Nor is nature fully knowable, as the classical physics of Newton had presumed. Uncertainty, probability, and even mystery are inherent in the universe.

We have not yet felt the full impact of modern physics, but there is no doubt that it has been part of a revolution in human perceptions. Jacob Bronowski, a student of science and culture, concludes:

> One aim of the physical sciences has been to give an exact picture of the material world. One achievement of physics in the twentieth century has been to prove that that aim is unattainable. . . . There is no absolute knowledge. . . . All information is imperfect. We have to treat it with humility. That is the human condition; and that is what quantum physics says. . . . The Principle of Uncertainty . . . fixed once and for all the realization that all knowledge is limited.[121]

That we cannot fully comprehend nature, that science provides us with only a tentative mental construct and not with the "truth" of nature itself, must inevitably make us less certain about our theories of human nature, government, history, and morality. That scientists must qualify and avoid absolutes has no doubt made us more cautious and tentative in framing conclusions about the individual and society. Like Darwin's theory of human origins, Freud's theory of human nature, and the transformation of classical space by modern artists, the modifications of the Newtonian picture by modern physicists contributed to the sense of uncertainty and disorientation that characterizes the twentieth century.

THE ENLIGHTENMENT TRADITION IN DISARRAY

Most nineteenth-century thinkers carried forward the spirit of the Enlightenment, particularly in its emphasis on reason and science and its concern for individual liberty and social reform. In the tradition of the philosophes, nineteenth-century thinkers regarded science as humanity's greatest achievement, believed that reason was common to humanity, and asserted that through reason society could be reformed. The spread of parliamentary government, the extension of education, the abolition of slavery and the end of serfdom, improvements in the standard of living, and the many advances in science and technology seemed to confirm the belief of the philosophes in humanity's future progress. These factors and the relative absence of conflicts between the Great Powers, say Edmund Stillman and William Pfaff,

> seemed to justify the optimism and confidence in progress that so deeply marked the beliefs of the century. For the nineteenth, more than the seventeenth or eighteenth, was the Enlightenment century, enjoying the fulfillment, at any rate, of that material faith and that conviction of man's ability to shape and perfect his condition which had originated in the great intellectual revolution of two hundred years earlier. In the nineteenth century the optimism that stemmed from the Enlightenment was gratified in a series of astonishing political, scientific, and social accomplishments.[122]

Thus, an entry in the *Larousse Dictionary* for 1875 read:

> Humanity is perfectible and it moves incessantly from the less good to better, from ignorance to science, from barbarism to civilization. . . . The idea that humanity becomes day by day better and happier is particularly dear to our own century. Faith in the law of progress is the true faith of our century.[123]

But at the same time, the Enlightenment tradition was being undermined. In the early nineteenth century, the romantics revolted against the Enlightenment's rational-scientific spirit in favor of human will and feelings; romantic nationalists valued the collective soul of the nation, ancient traditions rooted in a hoary and dateless past, over reason and individual freedom; and conservatives emphasized the limitations of reason and attacked the political agenda of the Enlightenment and the French Revolution.

In the closing decades of the century, the Enlightenment tradition was challenged by Social Darwinists, who glorified violence and saw conflict between individuals and between nations as a law of nature. They considered the right of the powerful to predominate to be a right of nature that is beyond good and evil. Echoing Sorel, several thinkers trumpeted the use of force in social and political controversies. A number of thinkers, rejecting the Enlightenment's view of people as fundamentally rational, held that subconscious drives govern human behavior more than reason does. Expressing contempt for reason, several of these thinkers celebrated impulses and instincts, which they regarded as the true essence of human beings and life; they glorified an irrational vitality that transcended considerations of good and evil. "I have always considered myself a voice of what I believe to be a greater renaissance—the revolt of the soul against the intellect—now beginning in the world,"[124] wrote Irish poet William Butler Yeats. German advocates of "life philosophy" explicitly called the mind "the enemy of the soul."

Even theorists who studied the individual and society in a scientific way pointed out that below a surface rationality lies a substratum of irrationality that constitutes a deeper reality. The conviction was growing that reason was a puny instrument in comparison with the volcanic strength of nonrational impulses, that these impulses pushed people toward destructive behavior and made political life precarious, and that the nonrational did not bend very much to education. The Enlightenment's image of the autonomous individual who makes rational decisions after weighing the choices (a fundamental premise of liberalism and democracy) no longer seemed tenable. Often the individual is not the master of his or her own person; human freedom is limited by human nature. Others argued that ideas of right, truth, and justice have no validity; rather, they are merely tools used by elites in their struggle to gain and maintain power. Opponents of liberalism and democracy utilized the theory of elites advanced by Mosca and Pareto, Le Bon's social psychology, and the new stress on human irrationality as proof that the masses were incapable of self-government and that they had to be led by their betters. Many intellectuals of the right employed the new social theories to devalue the individualist and rationalist bases of liberal democracy bequeathed by the Enlightenment.

At the beginning of the twentieth century, the dominant mood remained that of confidence in Europe's future progress and in the values of European civilization. However, certain disquieting trends were already evident; they would grow to crisis proportions in succeeding decades. Although few people may have realized it, the Enlightenment tradition was in disarray. The thinkers of the Enlightenment believed in an orderly, machinelike universe, in natural law and natural rights operating in the social world, in objective rules that gave form and structure to artistic productions, in the essential rationality and goodness of the individual, and in science and technology as instruments of progress. This coherent world-view, which had produced an attitude of certainty, security, and optimism, was in the process of dissolution by the early twentieth century. The common-sense Newtonian picture of the physical universe, with its inexorable laws of cause and effect, was altered. The belief in natural rights and objective standards governing morality was undermined, rules and modes of expression that were at the very heart of Western esthetics were abandoned, and confidence in human rationality and goodness was weakened. Science and technology were accused of forging a mechanical, bureaucratic, and materialistic world that stifled intuition and the feelings and so diminished the self. And to redeem the self, some urged heroic struggle, which could easily be channeled into a primitive nationalism and martial crusades.

Also challenged and rejected was the Enlightenment's view of progress. The philosophes had defined progress as the advancement of reason and freedom, the spread of education, improvement in the standard of living, and the elimination of war. By the turn of the century, many people rejected this image of progress. Stirred by nationalism's powerful emotional appeal, attracted to Social Darwinist ideas, and scornful of scientific rationalism, they equated progress with national power and viewed conflicts between nations and races as a fruitful law of nature and a creative force that rescued nations from materialism and mediocrity. Destructive thoughts and feelings, sometimes masked in the language of science, were ascending from the cellars and sewers of the human psyche.

The attack on the moral and intellectual values associated with the Enlightenment—the denunciation of reason, exaltation of force, quest for the heroic, and yearning for a new authority—constitutes the intellectual background of the fascist movements that emerged after World War I. Holding the Enlightenment tradition in contempt, and fascinated by power and violence, many people, including intellectuals, would exalt fascist ideas and lionize fascist leaders.

By the early twentieth century, the universe no longer seemed an orderly system, an intelligible whole, but something fundamentally inexplicable. Human nature, too, seemed intrinsically unfathomable and problematic. To the question "Who is man?" Greek philosophers, medieval scholastics, Renaissance humanists, and eighteenth-century philosophes had provided a coherent and intelligible answer. By the early twentieth century, Western intellectuals no longer possessed a clear and unified idea of who the human being was; individuals seemed strangers unto themselves, and life seemed devoid of an overriding purpose, a discoverable meaning. Science could perform many wonders, but it could not fulfill the deeply rooted human desire to endow the world and existence with meaning that is coherent, intelligible, and significant. The ground was crumbling beneath the great edifices of Western civilization, as Nietzsche sensed:

> Disintegration characterizes this time, and thus uncertainty: nothing stands firmly on its feet or on a hard faith in itself; one lives for tomorrow as the day after tomorrow is dubious. Everything on our way is slippery and dangerous, and the ice that still supports us has become thin: all of us feel the warm, uncanny breath of the thawing wind; where we will walk, soon no one will be able to walk.[125]

This radical, new disorientation created a sense of doubt, dissatisfaction, and uncertainty among some intellectuals. At the beginning of the twentieth century, says Dutch historian Jan Romein, "European man, who only half a century earlier had believed he was about to embrace an almost totally safe existence, and paradoxically did so in many ways, found himself before the dark gate of uncertainty."[126]

When the new century began, most Europeans remained optimistic about the future, some even holding that European civilization was on the threshold of a golden age. Few suspected that European civilization would soon be gripped by a crisis that threatened its very survival. The powerful forces of irrationalism that had been celebrated by Nietzsche, analyzed by Freud, and creatively expressed in modernist culture would erupt with devastating fury in twentieth-century political life, particularly in the form of extreme nationalism and racism, which extolled violence and elevated the soul and the heart over the intellect and reason.

Disoriented and disillusioned people searching for new certainties and values would turn to political ideologies that openly rejected reason, lauded war, and scorned the inviolability of the human person. Dictators, utilizing the insights into the unconscious and the nonrational advanced by Freud and social theorists, would succeed in manipulating the minds of the masses to an unprecedented degree.

These currents began to form at the end of the nineteenth century, but World War I brought them together into a tidal wave. World War I accentuated the questioning of established norms and the dissolution of Enlightenment certainties and caused many people to regard Western civilization as dying and beyond recovery. The war not only exacerbated the spiritual crisis of the preceding generation, it also shattered Europe's political and social order and gave birth to totalitarian ideologies that nearly obliterated the legacy of the Enlightenment.

NOTES

1. Friedrich Nietzsche, *The Birth of Tragedy*, trans. Francis Golffing (Garden City, N.Y.: 1956), pp. 111–112.
2. Friedrich Nietzsche, *Twilight of the Idols*, and *The Anti-Christ*, trans. R. J. Hollingdale (Baltimore: Penguin Books, 1968), secs. 5, 7, 43, pp. 117–118, 157.
3. Ibid., sec. 18, p. 128.
4. Friedrich Nietzsche, *The Genealogy of Morals*, trans. Horace B. Samuel, in *The Philosophy of Nietzsche* (New York: Modern Library, 1954), First Essay, sec. 12, p. 655.
5. Friedrich Nietzsche, *The Will to Power*, trans. Walter Kaufmann and R. J. Hollingdale, ed. Walter Kaufmann (New York: Vintage Books, 1968), sec. 861, pp. 458–459.
6. Ibid., sec. 720, pp. 383–384.
7. Quoted in R. J. Hollingdale, *Nietzsche* (London: Routledge and Kegan Paul, 1973), p. 82.

8. Nietzsche, *The Will to Power*, sec. 752, p. 397.

9. Arthur Schopenhauer, *The World as Will and Representation*, trans. E. F. J. Payne (Indian Hills, Colo: Falcon's Wing Press, 1956), I, 275, 292.

10. Ibid., p. 291.

11. Arthur Schopenhauer, *The World as Will and Idea*, in *Schopenhauer: Selections*, ed. DeWitt H. Parker (New York: Scribner's 1928), p. 331.

12. Quoted in Michael Fox, ed., *Schopenhauer: His Philosophical Achievement* (Totowa, N.J.: Barnes and Noble 1980), p. xvi.

13. Franz Kuna, "The Janus-Faced Novel: Conrad, Musil, Kafka, Mann," in *Modernism*, ed. Malcolm Bradbury and James McFarlane (Atlantic Highlands, N.J.: Humanities Press, 1978), p. 446.

14. Nietzsche, *The Will to Power*, preface, p. 3.

15. Nietzsche, *The Will to Power*, sec. 997, p. 518.

16. Nietzsche, *The Anti-Christ*, sec. 2, p. 116.

17. Friedrich Nietzsche, *Thus Spake Zarathustra*, sec. 29, in *The Philosophy of Nietzsche*, p. 108.

18. Friedrich Nietzsche, *Beyond Good and Evil*, sec. 258, in *The Philosophy of Nietzsche*, pp. 576–577.

19. Nietzsche, *The Will to Power*, sec. 728, p. 386.

20. Nietzsche, *Thus Spake Zarathustra*, sec. 10, pp. 47–48.

21. Excerpted in George L. Mosse, ed., *Nazi Culture* (New York: Grosset and Dunlap, 1966), p. 98, 100.

22. Janko Lavrin, *Nietzsche* (New York: Scribner's, 1971), p. 113.

23. Fyodor Dostoevski, *Notes from Underground* and *The Grand Inquisitor*, trans. Ralph E. Matlaw (New York: Dutton, 1960), p. 13. Translation copyright © 1960, 1988 by E. P. Dutton. Used by permission of the publisher, Dutton, an imprint of New American Library, a division of Penguin Books USA Inc.

24. Ibid., p. 12.

25. Ibid., pp. 20, 23.

26. Ibid., p. 18.

27. Ibid., p. 25.

28. Fyodor Dostoevski, *The Grand Inquisitor*, p. 122.

29. Ibid., p. 123.

30. Ibid., pp. 126–127.

31. Ibid., p. 127.

32. Ibid., pp. 128–129.

33. Ibid., pp. 129–130.

34. Ibid., p. 132.

35. Adolf Hitler, *Mein Kampf*, trans. Ralph Mannheim (Boston: Houghton Mifflin, 1962), p. 42.

36. Georges Sorel, *Reflections on Violence*, trans., T. E. Hulme and J. Roth (New York: Free Press, 1950), p. 35.

37. Quoted in Jack J. Roth, *The Cult of Violence: Sorel and the Sorelians* (Berkeley: University of California Press, 1980), p. 211.

38. Ibid., p. 224.

39. Ibid., p. 276.

40. Sigmund Freud, "An Autobiographical Study," in *The Standard Edition of the Complete Psychological Works of Sigmund Freud*, ed. James Strachey, 2nd ed. (London: Hogarth, 1959), XX, 9.

41. Quoted in Peter Gay, *Freud: A Life for Our Time* (New York: Norton, 1988), p. xvii.

42. Sigmund Freud, *New Introductory Lectures on Psychoanaly-*

sis, trans. James Strachey (New York: Norton, 1965), p. 159.

43. Sigmund Freud, "Delusions and Dreams in Jensen's 'Gradiva,'" trans. James Strachey in *The Standard Edition*, IX, 8.

44. Sigmund Freud, "An Autobiographical Study," in *The Standard Edition*, XX, 60.

45. Sigmund Freud, "On The History of the Psychoanalytic Movement," in *The Standard Edition*, XIV, 15.

46. Sigmund Freud, *Civilization and Its Discontents*, trans. and ed. James Strachey (New York: Norton, 1961), p. 62. By permission of W. W. Norton & Company, Inc. Copyright © 1961 by James Strachey. Copyright renewed 1989. Reprinted with permission from *The Standard Edition of Psychological Works of Sigmund Freud*, translated and edited by James Strachey, by Sigmund Freud Copyrights, The Institute of Psycho-Analysis and the Hogarth Press.

47. Ibid., p. 58.

48. Quoted in J. N. Isbister, *Freud: An Introduction to His Life and Work* (Cambridge, England: Polity Press, 1985), p. 203.

49. Sigmund Freud, "Thoughts for the Times on War and Death," in *The Standard Edition*, IV, 296–297.

50. Freud, *Civilization and Its Discontents*, p. 58.

51. Ibid., p. 59.

52. Ibid., p. 61.

53. Ibid., p. 59.

54. Freud, "Thoughts for the Times on War and Death," p. 285.

55. Freud, *Civilization and Its Discontents*, p. 69.

56. Peter Gay, *Freud, Jews, and Other Germans* (New York: Oxford University Press, 1978), p. 70.

57. Freud, *Civilization and Its Discontents*, p. 21.

58. Sigmund Freud, *The Future of an Illusion*, trans. W. D. Robson-Scott, rev. James Strachey (Garden City, N.Y.: Doubleday Anchor Books, 1964), p. 43.

59. Ibid., p. 92.

60. Freud, *New Introductory Lectures on Psychoanalysis*, p. 168.

61. Freud, *The Future of an Illusion*, pp. 60–62.

62. Quoted in Isbister, *Freud*, pp. 204–205.

63. Freud, *Civilization and Its Discontents*, pp. 59–61.

64. Freud, *New Introductory Lectures on Psychoanalysis*, p. 171.

65. Ibid.

66. Freud, *The Future of an Illusion*, p. 4.

67. Freud, *Civilization and Its Discontents*, p. 61.

68. Carl Gustav Jung, "The Archetypes and the Collective Unconscious," trans. R.F.C. Hull, in *The Collected Works of C. G. Jung*, 2nd ed., ed. Herbert Read et al. (Princeton, N.J.: Princeton University Press, 1968), IX, pt. 1, p. 3.

69. Ibid., p. 4.

70. Jung, *The Structure and Dynamics of the Psyche*, in *The Collected Works*, V, 158.

71. Jung, *The Archetypes and the Collective Unconscious*, p. 48.

72. Jung, *The Structure and Dynamics of the Psyche*, p. 380.

73. Émile Durkheim, *Suicide: A Study in Sociology*, trans. John Spaulding and George Simpson (New York: Free Press, 1951), p. 391.

74. Gaetano Mosca, *The Ruling Class*, trans. Hannah D. Kahn,

ed. Arthur Livingston (New York: McGraw-Hill, 1939), p. 50.

75. Ibid., p. 51.

76. Ibid., p. 70.

77. Ibid., p. 71.

78. Quoted in A. William Salomonne, *Italian Democracy in the Making* (Philadelphia: University of Pennsylvania Press, 1945), pp. xv–xvi.

79. Excerpted in S. Finer, ed., *Vilfredo Pareto: Sociological Writings*, trans. Derick Mirfin (New York: Praeger, 1966), pp. 124–127.

80. Quoted in Irving M. Zeitlin, *Ideology and the Development of Sociological Theory* (Englewood Cliffs, N.J.: Prentice-Hall, 1968), p. 165.

81. Gustave Le Bon, *The Crowd: A Study of the Popular Mind* (New York: Viking, 1960), p. 3.

82. Ibid., pp. 14–15.

83. Ibid., p. 14.

84. Ibid., p. 15.

85. Ibid., p. 18.

86. Ibid., p. xx.

87. Ibid., p. 23.

88. Ibid., p. 30.

89. Ibid., p. 31.

90. Ibid., p. 32.

91. Ibid., p. 7.

92. Ibid., p. 118.

93. Excerpted in Alice Widener, ed., *Gustave Le Bon: The Man and His Words* (Indianapolis: Liberty Press, 1979), p. 143.

94. Quoted in Robert A. Nye, *The Origin of Crowd Psychology* (Beverly Hills, Calif.: Sage, 1975), p. 178.

95. Graham Wallas, *Human Nature and Politics* (London: Constable, 1948), p. 31.

96. Max Weber, *Economy and Society*, ed. Guenther Roth and Claus Wittich (New York: Bedminister, 1968), p. 1156.

97. Quoted in Robert Nisbet, *The Social Philosophers* (New York: Crowell, 1973), p. 441.

98. Quoted in Arthur Mitzman, *The Iron Cage: An Historical Interpretation of Max Weber* (New York: Knopf, 1970), p. 250.

99. Irving Howe, ed., *The Idea of the Modern in Literature and the Arts* (New York: Horizon, 1967), p. 16.

100. *Complete Works of Rimbaud with Selected Letters*, trans. Wallace Fowlie (Chicago: University of Chicago Press, 1966), p. 307.

101. Daniel Bell, *The Cultural Contradictions of Capitalism* (New York: Basic Books, 1976), p. 110.

102. Quoted in Howe, *The Idea of the Modern*, p. 15.

103. Excerpted in Herschel B. Chipp, ed., *Theories of Modern Art* (Berkeley: University of California Press, 1968), p. 146.

104. Paul Klee, *The Inward Vision*, trans. Norbert Guterman (New York: Abrams, 1958), sec. 5, p. 8.

105. Paul Klee, *On Modern Art*, trans. Paul Findlay (London: Faber and Faber, 1948), p. 88.

106. Guillaume Apollinaire, *The Cubist Painters*, excerpted in *Aspects of the Modern European Mind*, ed. John Cruickshank (New York: Barnes and Noble, 1969), p. 171.

107. Excerpted in Chipp, *Theories of Modern Art*, p. 106.

108. Bell, *The Cultural Contradictions*, pp. 110,112.

109. Quoted in Jean Pierrot, *The Decadent Imagination, 1880–1900*, trans. Derek Coltman (Chicago: University of Chicago Press, 1980), p. 46.

110. Quoted in Roger L. Williams, *The Horror of Life* (Berkeley: University of California Press, 1980), p. 18.

111. *Complete Works of Rimbaud,* p. 125.

112. Klee, *On Modern Art,* p. 51.

113. Quoted in Donald E. Gordon, *Expressionism: Art and Idea* (New Haven, Conn.: Yale University Press, 1987), p. 2.

114. Quoted in Alfred H. Barr, Jr., ed., *Masters of Modern Art* (New York: Museum of Modern Art, 1954), p. 46.

115. Ibid., p. 47.

116. John Canady, *Mainstreams of Modern Art* (New York: Holt, 1961), p. 458.

117. Quoted in G. H. Hamilton, *Painting and Sculpture in Europe, 1880–1940* (Baltimore: Penguin Books, 1967), p. 133.

118. Alan Nourse, *Universe, Earth, and Atom* (New York: Harper and Row, 1969), pp. 554–555, 560.

119. Quoted in A.E.E. McKenzie, *The Major Achievements of Science* (London: Cambridge University Press, 1960), I, 310.

120. Isaac Asimov, *Asimov's Guide to Science* (New York: Basic Books, 1972), pp. 354–355.

121. Jacob Bronowski, *The Ascent of Man* (Boston: Little, Brown, 1973), p. 353.

122. Edmund Stillman and William Pfaff, *The Politics of Hysteria* (New York: Colophon Books, 1964), p. 26.

123. Quoted in Daniel Pick, *Faces of Degeneration* (Cambridge: Cambridge University Press, 1989), p. 12.

124. Quoted in Roland N. Stromberg, *Redemption by War* (Lawrence, Kans.: Regents Press of Kansas, 1982), p. 65.

125. Nietzsche, *The Will to Power,* p. 40.

126. Jan Romein, *The Watershed of Two Eras,* trans. Arnold J. Pomerans (Middletown, Conn.: Wesleyan University Press, 1978), p. 658.

SUGGESTED READING

Barr, Alfred, H., Jr., ed., *Masters of Modern Art* (1954).

Baumer, Franklin, *Modern European Thought* (1977).

Bradbury, Malcolm, and James McFarlane, eds., *Modernism, 1890–1930* (1974).

Chipp, Herschel B., ed., *Theories of Modern Art* (1968).

Davies, Alistair, *An Annotated Critical Bibliography of Modernism* (1982).

Fox, Michael, ed., *Schopenhauer: His Philosophical Achievement* (1980).

Gay, Peter, *Freud: A Life for Our Times* (1988).

Hamilton, G. H., *Painting and Sculpture in Europe, 1880–1940* (1967).

Hollingdale, R. J., *Nietzsche* (1973).

Howe, Irving, ed., *The Idea of the Modern in Literature and the Arts* (1967).

Hughes, H. Stuart, *Consciousness and Society* (1958).

Isbister, J. N., *Freud* (1985).

Kaufmann, Walter, *Nietzsche* (1956).

Lavrin, Janko, *Nietzsche* (1971).

Masur, Gerhard, *Prophets of Yester-day* (1961).

Mitzman, Arthur, *The Iron Cage: An Historical Interpretation of Max Weber* (1970).

Monaco, Paul, *Modern European Culture and Consciousness, 1870–1980* (1983).

Nelson, Benjamin, ed., *Freud and the Twentieth Century* (1957).

Pierrot, Jean, *The Decadent Imagination, 1880–1900* (1980).

Roazen, Paul, *Freud's Political and Social Thought* (1968).

Rosenthal, Bernice, ed., *Nietzsche in Russia* (1986).

Zeitlin, I. M., *Ideology and the Development of Sociological Theory* (1968).

Zukav, Gary, *The Dancing Wu Li Masters: An Overview of the New Physics* (1979).

10

Irrationalism in Political Thinking

Nietzsche's, Sorel's, and other culture critics' attacks on modern liberal civilization expressed a growing mood of discontent among intellectuals, artists, and youth at the turn of the century. These critics were rejecting what they considered a shallow intellectualism—a cold and calculating reason that suffocated the passions—in favor of a vital life-force that awakened the spirit. Disgusted with an ignoble, materialistic bourgeois society that crushed the soul and corrupted culture, and contemptuous of parliamentary government and political parties which elevated the mediocre into positions of power, they yearned for a life of heroism, nobility, danger, and idealism. The radical attack on the values of modern liberal civilization found its most dangerous expression in a surge of nationalistic and racist thinking. Extreme nationalists wanted to rescue existence from what they deemed to be a spiritually empty modern society by absorbing the individual into a revitalized and unified national community. In the process, nationalism grew more ethnocentric, belligerent, intolerant, irrational, and racist. The extreme nationalism of the late nineteenth and early twentieth centuries contributed to World War I and to the rise of fascism after the war; it was the seedbed of totalitarian nationalism.

The years 1914 to 1945, marked by world wars, totalitarianism, and mass extermination, were a sorry period for Western civilization. And it is a distressing truth that these developments had deep roots in European thought of the late nineteenth century. The glorification of the national community and the quest for the heroic fanned the flames of an aggressive nationalism and militarism that helped ignite World War I. The branding of the liberal-rational tradition as an enemy of the soul led to fascism; the single-minded conviction that society should be remolded in line with Marxist dogma formed the ideological foundation for Stalin's terror; and the propagation of racist theories paved the road to Auschwitz. While many intellectuals during this period struggled to preserve the tradition of reason and freedom, others either quickly abandoned these ideals to serve other masters or welcomed the opportunity to destroy what they had always hated.

FROM LIBERAL TO EXTREME NATIONALISM

In the first half of the nineteenth century, nationalism and liberalism went hand in hand. Liberals sought both the rights of the individual and national independence and unification. Liberal nationalists believed that a unified state free of foreign subjugation was in harmony with the principle of natural rights, and they insisted that love of country led to love of humanity. "With all my ardent love of my nation," said Francis Palacky, a Czech patriot, "I always esteem more highly the good of mankind and of learning than the good of the nation."[1] Addressing the Slavs, Giuseppe Mazzini declared: "We who have ourselves arisen in the name of our national right, believe in your right, and offer to help you to win it. But the purpose of our mission is the permanent and peaceful organization of Europe."[2]

As nationalism grew more extreme, however, its profound difference from liberalism became more apparent. Concerned exclusively with the greatness of the nation, extreme nationalists rejected the liberal emphasis on political liberty; they regarded liberty as an obstacle to national power. In the pursuit of national grandeur, nationalists denounced national minorities, particularly Jews, for corrupting the nation's soul and glorified war as a symbol of the nation's resolve and will. At the founding of the Nationalist Association in Italy in 1910, one leader declared:

> Just as socialism teaches the proletariat the value of class struggle, so we must teach Italy the value of international struggle. But international struggle is war? Well, then, let there be war! And nationalism will arouse the will for a victorious war . . . the only way to national redemption.[3]

Interpreting politics with the logic of emotions, extreme nationalists insisted that they had a sacred mission to regain lands once held in the Middle Ages, to unite with their kinfolk in other lands, or to rule over peoples considered inferior. They organized patriotic societies and created a cult of ancestors and a mystique of blood, soil, and a sacred national past. In these ancestral traditions and attachments, the nationalist found a higher reality akin to religious truth. Loyalty to the nation-state was elevated above all other allegiances. The nation-state became an object of religious reverence; the spiritual energies that formerly had been dedicated to Christianity were now channeled into the worship of the nation-state. In 1902, Friedrich Paulsen, a German philosopher, warned of nationalism's threat to reason and morality:

A supersensitive nationalism has become a very serious danger for all the peoples of Europe; because of it, they are in danger of losing the feeling for human values. Nationalism, pushed to an extreme, just like sectarianism, destroys moral and even logical consciousness. Just and unjust, good and bad, true and false, lose their meaning; what men condemn as disgraceful and inhuman when done by others, they recommend in the same breath to their own people as something to be done to a foreign country.[4]

By the beginning of the twentieth century, conservatives had become the staunchest advocates of nationalism, and the nationalism preached by conservative extremists was stripped of Mazzinian ideals of liberty, equality, and the fellowship of nations. Landholding aristocrats, generals, and clergy, often joined by big industrialists, saw nationalism as a convenient instrument for gaining a mass following in their struggle against democracy and socialism. Championing popular nationalist myths and dreams and citing Social Darwinist and racist doctrines, a newly radicalized right hoped to harness the instinctual energies of the masses, particularly the peasants and the lower middle class—shopkeepers, civil servants, white-collar workers—to conservative causes. Peasants, who viewed liberalism and Marxism as threats to traditional values, and the lower bourgeoisie, who feared the proletariat, were receptive to the rhetoric of ultranationalists, who denounced democracy and Marxism as barriers to national unity and Jews as aliens endangering the nation. Nationalism was presented as a victory of idealism over materialism, the subordination of class and personal interests to the general good of the nation.

Social Darwinists, who applied Darwin's biological theories to relations among nations, injected particularly dangerous elements into nationalism: the conviction that humanity was divided into superior and inferior races and the idea that national and racial conflicts produced progress. They maintained that nations and races were engaged in a struggle for survival in which only the fittest survive and deserve to survive. In their view, war was nature's stern way of eliminating the unfit. Karl Pearson, a British academic, stated in *National Life from the Standpoint of Science* (1900):

> History shows me only one way, and one way only in which a higher state of civilization has been produced, namely the struggle of race with race, and the survival of the physically and mentally fitter race. . . .
>
> . . . Let us suppose we could prevent the white man, if we liked, from going to lands of which the agricultural and mineral resources are not worked to the full; then I should say a thousand times better for him that he should not go than that he should settle down and live alongside the inferior race. The only healthy alternative is that he should go and completely drive out the inferior race. . . . I venture to assert, then, that the struggle for existence between white and red man . . . painful and even terrible as it was in its details, has given us a good far outbalancing its immediate evil. . . .
>
> The . . . great function of science in national life . . . is to show us . . . how the nation is a vast organism subject . . . to the great forces of evolution. There is a struggle of race against race and of nation against nation.
>
> The path of progress is strewn with the wrecks of nations; traces are everywhere to be seen of the [slaughtered remains] of inferior races. . . . Yet these dead people are, in very truth, the stepping stones on which mankind has arisen to the higher intellectual and deeper emotional life of today.[5]

"We are a conquering race," said U.S. Senator Albert J. Beveridge. "We must obey our blood and occupy new markets, and if necessary, new lands."[6] "War is a biological necessity of the first importance," exclaimed the Prussian General Friedrich von Bernhardi in *Germany and the Next War* (1911). Without war "an unhappy development will follow, which excludes every advancement of . . . all real civilization."[7]

Darwinian biology was used to promote the belief in Anglo-Saxon (British and American) and Teutonic (German) racial superiority. Social Darwinists attributed to racial qualities the growth of the British Empire, the expansion of the United States to the Pacific, and the extension of German power. The domination of other peoples—American Indians, Africans, Asians, Poles—was deemed the natural right of the superior race. British naturalist Alfred Russel Wallace, who arrived at the theory of evolution independently of Darwin, had written in 1864:

> The intellectual and moral, as well as the physical qualities of the European are superior; the same power and capacities which have made him rise in a few centuries from the condition of the wandering savage . . . to his present state of culture and advancement . . . enable him

when in contact with savage man, to conquer in the struggle for existence and to increase at his expense.[8]

And just before World War I the Pan-German Association, whose membership included professors, schoolteachers, journalists, lawyers, and
aristocrats, maintained:

> The racial-biological ideology tells us that there are races that lead and
> races that follow. Political history is nothing but the history of struggle
> among the leading races. Conquests, above all, are always the work of
> the leading races. Such men can conquer, may conquer, and shall con-
> quer.[9]

The theory of evolution was a great achievement of the rational
mind, but in the hands of the Social Darwinists it served to undermine
the Enlightenment tradition. Whereas the philosophes emphasized human equality, Social Darwinists divided humanity into racial superiors
and inferiors. Whereas the philosophes believed that states would increasingly submit to the rule of law to reduce violent conflicts, Social
Darwinists regarded racial and national conflict as a biological necessity, a law of history, and a means to progress. In propagating a tooth-
and-claw version of human and international relations, Social Darwinists dispensed with the humanitarian and cosmopolitan sentiments
of the philosophes and distorted the image of progress. Claiming to
rest on the authority of science, these views promoted territorial ag-
grandizement and military build-up and led many to welcome World
War I. The Social Darwinist notion of the struggle of races for survival
became a core doctrine of the Nazi party after World War I and provided
the "scientific" and "ethical" justifications for genocide.

EXTREME NATIONALISM IN GERMANY:
VOLKISH THOUGHT

Although nationalism was a common European phenomenon, it
proved particularly dangerous in Germany. The unification of Germany in 1870–71 turned the new state into an international power of
the first rank, upsetting the balance of power in Europe. How a strong,
united Germany would fit into European life was the crucial problem in the decades following the Franco-Prussian War. To German nationalists, the unification of Germany was both the fulfillment of
a national dream and the starting point of an even more ambitious
goal—the extension of German power in Europe and the world. As the
nineteenth century drew to a close, German nationalism became more

extreme. Believing that Germany must either grow or die, nationalists pressed the government to build a powerful navy, acquire colonies, gain a much greater share of the world's markets, and expand German interests and influence in Europe. Sometimes these goals were expressed in the language of Social Darwinism—that nations are engaged in an eternal struggle for survival and domination.

An ominous expression of German nationalism was Volkish thought. (*Volk* means "folk" or "people".) German Volkish thinkers sought to bind together the German people through a deep love of their language, traditions, and fatherland. These thinkers felt that the Germans were animated by a higher spirit than that found in other peoples. To Volkish thinkers, the Enlightenment and parliamentary democracy were foreign ideas that corrupted the pure German spirit. With fanatical devotion, Volkish thinkers embraced all things German—the medieval past, the German landscape, the simple peasant, the village—and denounced the liberal-humanist tradition of the West as alien to the German soul.

Volkish thought attracted Germans frightened by all the complexities of the modern age—industrialization, urbanization, materialism, party politics, and class conflicts. They feared an impersonal and overly rationalized capitalist system that destroyed ancient social forms and traditional virtues, seemed indifferent to their individual needs and communal traditions, and alienated people from themselves and each other. Seeing their beloved Germany transformed by these forces of modernity, Volkish thinkers yearned to restore the sense of community that they attributed to the preindustrial age. Only by identifying with their sacred soil and sacred traditions would Germans escape from the rootlessness and alienation of modern industrial society. A return to roots would restore authenticity to life and stimulate genuine cultural creativity. Only then could the different classes band together in an organic unity.

The Volkish movement had little support from the working class, which was concerned chiefly with improving its standard of living. It appealed mainly to farmers and villagers, who regarded the industrial city as a threat to native values and a catalyst for foreign ideas; to artisans and small shopkeepers, threatened by big business; and to scholars, writers, teachers, and students, who saw in Volkish nationalism a cause worthy of their idealism. The schools were leading agents for the dissemination of Volkish ideas.

Volkish thinkers looked back longingly to the Middle Ages, which they viewed as a period of social and spiritual harmony and reverence for national traditions. They also glorified the ancient Germanic tribes that overran the Roman Empire, contrasting their courageous and vigorous German ancestors with the effete and degenerate Romans. A few tried to harmonize ancient and heroic Germanic traditions with Christianity. This often meant expunging Jewish elements from Christianity.

Such attitudes led Germans to see themselves as a heroic people, fundamentally different from and better than the English and French. It also led them to regard German culture as unique—innately superior to and in opposition to the liberal-humanist outlook of the Enlightenment. Like their romantic predecessors, Volkish thinkers held that the German people and culture had a special destiny and a unique mission. They pitted the German soul against the Western intellect and juxtaposed feeling, intuition, and spirit to a drab, dissecting rationalism. They accused liberalism of fostering a vulgar materialism, an anarchic individualism, and a soul-stifling rational-scientific outlook, all of which separated people from the true genius, the peculiar character, of the German nation. To be sure, the Western humanist tradition had many supporters in Germany—German universities, after all, were leading centers of scholarship—but the counterideology of Volkish thought was becoming widespread. The radical nationalist, racist, irrational, and antiliberal outlook shaped by these Volkish thinkers in the late nineteenth century would undermine support for the democratic Weimar Republic established in Germany after World War I and provide Hitler with receptive listeners.

One shaper of the Volkish outlook was Wilhelm von Riehl (1823–1897), a professor at the University of Munich. He contrasted the artificiality of modern city life with the unspoiled existence in the German countryside. Another was Berthold Auerbach (1812–1882), who exalted the peasant as the ideal German. Paul de Lagarde (1827–1891), a professor of oriental languages, called for a German faith, different from Christianity, that would unite the nation; he saw the Jews as enemies of Germany. Julius Langbehn (1851–1907) lauded a mystical and irrational life force as superior to a soulless science and held that the Jews, rootless and devoid of spirituality, corrupted the German soul.

Richard Wagner (1813–1883), the great composer, expressed Volkish ideals in his music and writings. He glorified a pre-Christian Germanic past and called for the spiritual redemption of German society through art that stemmed from the rich soil of German tradition, particularly heroic legends and myths. For Wagner, modern society lacked soul. A cultural rebirth inspired by the common heritage of the Volk would unite a fragmented German nation and overcome the mediocrity, materialism, philistinism, and atomization of modern life. Wagner called for a revitalized Christianity. By this he meant a Germanized Christianity, a purified national faith centered on sacred ancient Germanic myths. In his later years, influenced by Gobineau's racial theories (see the next section), Wagner warned that race mixing produced cultural decline.

Wagner attracted fervent disciples, who revered the master as an artistic genius and prophet of Germanism. Wagnerians helped to popularize Volkish ideas and were active members of several Volkish and racist societies, including the Pan-German Association, that taught the inherent superiority of the German Volk. The Nazis later praised Wagner's music and treatment of Germanic myths for brilliantly expressing the inner feelings and hopes of the German Volk. Hitler, who had memorized long passages from Wagner's works, hailed Wagner as Germany's great culture hero, and Wagner's still active disciples, seeking to promote a link between the master's world-view and National Socialism, praised Hitler for possessing a "genuine folk soul." On the radio and at mass meetings, the Nazis played Wagner's music in order to create an electrically charged atmosphere for their propaganda.

RACIAL THEORISTS

Volkish thinkers were especially attracted to racist doctrines. Racist thinkers held that race was the key to history, and that not only physical features, but also moral, esthetic and intellectual qualities distinguished one race from another. In their view, a race retained its vigor and achieved greatness when it preserved its purity; intermarriage between races was contamination that would result in genetic, cultural, and military decline. Unlike liberals, who held that anyone who accepted German law was a member of the German nation, Volkish thinkers, argued that a person's nationality was a function of his or her "racial soul" or "blood." On the basis of this new conception of nationality, racists argued that Jews, no matter how many centuries their ancestors had dwelt in Germany, could never think and feel like Germans and should be deprived of citizenship.

Like their Nazi successors, Volkish thinkers claimed that the German race was purer than, and therefore superior to, all other races; its superiority was revealed in such physical characteristics as blond hair, blue eyes, and fair skin—all signs of inner qualities lacking in other races. German racists claimed that the Germans were descendants of ancient Aryans. (The Aryans emerged some four thousand years ago, probably between the Caspian Sea and the Hindu Kush Mountains. Intermingling with others, the Aryans lost whatever identity as a people they might have had.) After discovering similarities between core European languages—Latin, Greek, and German—and ancient Persian and Sanskrit (the language of the fair-skinned conquerors of India), nineteenth-century scholars believed that these languages all stemmed from a common tongue spoken by the Aryans. From there, some leaped to the unwarranted conclusion that the Aryans constituted a distinct race endowed with superior racial qualities.

Arthur de Gobineau

A key figure in the shaping of racist thinking was Arthur de Gobineau (1816–1882), a French writer and political thinker. In *Essay on the Inequality of Human Races* (1853–55), Gobineau, often referred to as the "Father of Racism," held that three basic races, each with its own distinguishing features, existed in the world: the yellow, the black, and the white. He organized the races in a hierarchy of ability and value, with the white race at the apex. The yellow race, he said, was concerned with material prosperity and excelled in commerce, but it had little physical energy, was inclined to apathy, and lacked the imagination for theorizing. The black race had well-developed senses, especially taste and smell, but a weak intellect. The white race was gifted with energetic intelligence. White people possessed noble virtues— honor, spiritedness, a love of liberty—generally lacking in other races. They also had a monopoly of beauty and strength.

Marx saw class as the key to history; for Gobineau it was race. In the Dedication to his *Essay*, he wrote: "I was gradually penetrated by the conviction that the racial question overshadows all other problems of history, that it holds the key to them all."[10] Racial factors accounted for the rise and fall of civilization. The white race, particularly the Aryans, had created high civilization, but miscegenation had caused this civilization to decline.

Gobineau was not well received in France, but gradually he gained a following in Germany. Wagner, who befriended Gobineau, and Wagner's devoted followers, the Bayreuth Circle, employed Gobineau's theories to support their belief in a superior German race. Ludwig Scheemann, a Wagnerian, established the Gobineau Society, which promoted Gobineau's racial outlook, as did the Pan-German Association and other Volkish and nationalist groups. Gobineau himself was no anti-Semite; however, German anti-Semites of the late nineteenth and early twentieth centuries made use of his theory of racial decay to justify their hatred of Jews. In their view, Jews were the racial inferiors who were corrupting the blood of the superior Aryan race and undermining German culture. Excerpts from Gobineau's works were later printed by the Nazis for schoolchildren.

Houston Stewart Chamberlain

Volkish thinkers embraced the ideas of Houston Stewart Chamberlain
(1855–1927), an Englishman whose devotion to Germanism led him to
adopt German citizenship. An ardent admirer of Wagner's music,
Chamberlain became an active member of the Bayreuth Circle. (After
divorcing his first wife, he married Wagner's daughter in 1908.) He regarded Wagner as the highest expression of German creativity. Contact
with the Wagnerians' anti-Semitism intensified Chamberlain's own
dislike of Jews. He came to see Jew and German as dialectical opposites
locked in a struggle of world-historical significance—a theme that he
developed in his major work, *Foundations of the Nineteenth Century*
(1899).

In *Foundations*, Chamberlain attempted to assert in scientific fashion that races differed not only physically but also morally, spiritually,
and intellectually and that the struggle between races was the driving
force of history. He held that the Germans, descendants of the ancient
Aryans, were physically superior and bearers of a higher culture. He
attributed Rome's decline to the dilution of its racial qualities through
miscegenation. The blond, blue-eyed, long-skulled Germans, possessing the strongest strain of Aryan blood and distinguished by an inner
spiritual depth, were the true ennoblers of humanity.

Denying that Christ was a Jew, Chamberlain hinted that Christ was
of Aryan stock. According to Chamberlain, the goal of the Jew was "to
put his foot upon the neck of all the nations of the world and be Lord
and possessor of the whole earth."[11] Chamberlain saw Aryan and Jew
as pitted against each other in a titanic struggle. As agents of a spiritually empty capitalism and divisive liberalism, the Jews, said Chamberlain, were undermining German society. Materialistic, cowardly,
and devious, they were the very opposite of the idealistic, heroic, and
faithful Germans.

Chamberlain's book was enormously popular in Germany. Pan-German and other Volkish-nationalist organizations frequently cited it.
Kaiser Wilhelm II called *Foundations* a "hymn to Germanism" and
read it to his children. "Next to the national liberal historians like
Heinrich von Treitschke and Heinrich von Sybel," concludes German
historian Fritz Fischer, "Houston Stewart Chamberlain had the greatest influence upon the spiritual life of Wilhelmine Germany."[12]

Chamberlain's racist and anti-Semitic views make him a spiritual
forerunner of Nazism, and he was praised as such by Alfred Rosenberg,
the leading Nazi racial theorist in the early days of Hitler's movement.
Josef Goebbels, the Nazi propagandist, hailed Chamberlain as a "path-
breaker" and "pioneer" after meeting him in 1926. In 1923, Chamber-

lain, then sixty-eight years old, met Hitler, whose movement was still in its formative stage. Chamberlain subsequently praised Hitler as the savior of the Reich, and Hitler visited Chamberlain on his deathbed and attended his funeral.

ANTI-SEMITISM: THE POWER, APPEAL, AND DANGER OF MYTHICAL THINKING

German racial nationalists singled out Jews as the most wicked of races and a deadly enemy of the German people. Anti-Semitism, which was widespread in late nineteenth century Europe, provides a striking example of the perennial appeal, power, and danger of mythical thinking—of elevating to the level of objective truth ideas that have no basis in fact but provide coherent and emotionally satisfying explanations of life and history. Anti-Semitic organizations and political parties sought to deprive Jews of their civil rights, and anti-Semitic publications proliferated. The radical right saw Jew-hatred as a popular formula for mobilizing and uniting all social classes—a precondition for strengthening the nation and overcoming democratic and socialist movements. By propagating the myth of the wicked Jew, the radical right demonstrated the truth of Sorel's insight that people are moved and united by myths that simplify and clarify the complexities of the modern world.

German conservatives deliberately fanned the flames of anti-Semitism to win the masses over to conservative and nationalist causes. The Christian Social Workers' party, founded in 1878 by Adolf Stöcker, a prominent Protestant preacher, engaged in anti-Semitic agitation in order to recruit the lower bourgeoisie to the cause of the Protestant church and the Prussian monarchy. The party denounced Jews as capitalists and deicides and blamed them for all of Germany's problems. "Jewry is a drop of alien blood in our people's body,"[13] he declared, and hoped that a future "liberator" would take up the fight against Jewry. In German-speaking Austria, Karl Lueger, a leader of the Christian Social party, founded by conservative German nationalists, and mayor of Vienna from 1897 to 1910, exploited anti-Semitism to win elections in the overwhelmingly Catholic city. Georg von Schönerer, founder of the German National party in Austria, wanted to eliminate Jews from all areas of public life. His followers wore watch chains with pictures of hanged Jews attached.

Christian Anti–Semitism

Anti-Semitism had a long and bloodstained history in Europe, stemming both from an irrational fear and hatred of outsiders with noticeably different ways and from the commonly accepted myth that the Jews as a people were collectively and eternally cursed for rejecting Christ. Since the early days of their religion, Christians saw Jews as the murderers of Christ—an image that promoted terrible anger and hatred. Several of the early Church Fathers venomously attacked the Jews and Judaism. Origen (c. 195–c. 251) maintained that "the blood of Jesus falls not only on the Jews of the time but on all generations of Jews up to the end of time." In the late fourth century, Saint John Chrysostom held that the Jews were "the most miserable of men, inveterate murderers, destroyers, men possessed by the Devil, their rituals are criminal and impure, their religion is a disease."

Since the Devil was very real to early and medieval Christians, the Jews became identified with all that was evil. Christians developed a mindset, concludes the Rev. Robert A. Everett, that was "unable to see anything positive in Judaism. . . . Judaism and the Jewish people came to have no real value for Christians except as a negative contrast to Christianity."[14] Because of this "teaching of contempt," the Christian ethic of love did not extend to the Jews.

> . . . once it is established that God has cursed the Jews, how can one argue that Christians should love them? If Jews have been fated by God to have . . . a long history of suffering, who are Christians to alter their history by doing anything to relieve Jewish suffering? The theology of victimization thus precludes Christian love as a basis of relating to Jews.[15]

The "diabolization of the Jew," which bore no relationship to the actual behavior of Jews or to their highly ethical religion, and the "theology of victimization," which held that Jews were collectively and eternally punished for denying Christ, became powerful myths. Over the centuries, these myths poisoned Christians' hearts and minds against Jews, prompting innumerable humiliations and persecutions.

During the Middle Ages, people believed and spread incredible tales about Jews. They accused Jews of torturing and crucifying Christian children in order to use their blood for ritual purposes, of stabbing the communion bread until it ran with Christ's blood, of poisoning wells to kill Christians, of worshiping and serving the Devil, and of organizing a secret government that conspired to destroy Christianity. Periodically, mobs humiliated, tortured, and massacred Jews, and rulers expelled them from their kingdoms. Often barred from owning land and excluded from the craft guilds, medieval Jews concentrated in trade and moneylending—occupations that frequently earned them greater hostility.

The policy of the medieval church toward the Jews was that they should not be harmed, but that they should live in degradation. The humiliated and persecuted Jew was a potent sign of the consequence of rejecting Christ, another reminder of the Church Triumphant. Hence, the Fourth Lateran Council barred Jews from public office, required them to wear a distinguishing badge on their clothing, and ordered them to remain off the streets during festivals. Christian art, literature, and religious instruction depicted the Jews in a derogatory manner. The Jew, "the seed of Satan," appeared in the company of the Devil or wore the Devil's horns and tail. Deeply etched into the minds and hearts of Christians, the distorted image of the Jew as a contemptible creature persisted in the popular mentality into the twentieth century. Medieval Christian anti-Semitism, which saw the Jew as vile and Judaism as repulsive—which had stamped the Jew with the mark of Cain—fertilized the soil for modern anti-Semitism.

Modern Anti-Semitism: Old Hatreds Intensified

By the sixteenth century, Jews in a number of lands were forced by law to live in separate quarters of the town called *ghettos*. In the nineteenth century, under the aegis of the liberal ideals of the Enlightenment and the French Revolution, Jews gained legal equality in most European lands. They could leave the ghetto and participate in many activities that had been closed to them. Traditionally an urban people, the Jews, who were concentrated in the leading cities of Europe, took advantage of this new freedom and opportunity. Motivated by the fierce desire of outsiders to prove their worth, aided by deeply embedded traditions that valued education and family life, and conditioned by many centuries of poverty and surviving by their wits in a hostile environment, Jews were admirably prepared to compete in a society where effort and talent counted more than birth or religion. Jews achieved striking success as entrepreneurs, bankers, lawyers, journalists, doctors, scientists, scholars, and performers. For example, in 1880, Jews, who constituted about 10 percent of the Viennese population, accounted for 38.6 percent of the medical students and 23.3 percent of the law students in Vienna. Viennese cultural life before World War I was to a large extent shaped by Jewish writers, musicians, critics, and patrons. All but one of the major banking houses were Jewish. German Jews gained prominence in law, medicine, and journalism and were active in the retail trades, particularly department stores. By the 1930s,

30 percent of the Nobel Prize winners in Germany were Jews, although Jews accounted for less than 1 percent of the population. The meteoric rise of the Jews stirred up resentment among Gentiles. But most European Jews—peasants, peddlers, and laborers—were quite poor. Perhaps five to six thousand Jews of Galicia in Austria-Hungary died of starvation annually, and many Russian Jews fled to the United States to escape from desperate poverty. But the anti-Semites saw only "Jewish influence," "Jewish manipulation," and "Jewish domination." Aggravating anti-Semitism among Germans was the flight of thousands of Russian-Polish Jews into Austria and Germany. Poor, speaking a different language (Yiddish), and having noticeably different customs, these Jews triggered primitive fears and hatreds.

Like other bourgeois, the Jews who were members of the commercial and professional classes gravitated toward liberalism. Moreover, as victims of persecution, Jews naturally favored societies that were committed to the liberal ideals of legal equality, toleration, the rule of law, and equality of opportunity. As strong supporters of parliamentary government and the entire system of values associated with the rational-humanist tradition of the Enlightenment, the Jews became targets of conservatives and Volkish thinkers, who repudiated the humanistic and cosmopolitan outlook of liberalism and professed a militant nationalism. German historian Karl Dietrich Bracher concludes: "Anti-Semitism was a manifestation of a rejection of the 'West' with which Jews were identified . . . . because the Enlightenment and democracy were essential preconditions for their acceptance and progress."[16]

Conservatives, including staunch Christians, interpreted Jewish emancipation as a victory for the Enlightenment and liberalism, which they despised. Nationalists denounced Jews as interlopers, a foreign Asiatic tribe in their midst—even though the Jewish presence in Germany went back to Roman times. In 1847, the playwright Heinrich Laube wrote: "In recent time a foreign element has penetrated everywhere in our midst, and into literature as well. This is the Jewish element. I call it foreign with emphasis; for the Jews are an Oriental nation as totally different from us today as they were two thousand years ago."[17]

The thought processes of Volkish anti-Semites demonstrate the mind's monumental capacity for irrational thinking. Anti-Semites invented a mythical evil that could be blamed for all the social and economic ills caused by the rapid growth of industry and cities and for all the new ideas that were undermining the Old Order. Their anxieties and fears concentrated on the Jews, to whom they attributed everything they considered evil in the modern age, all that threatened their traditional way of life and corrupted the German Volk. To these people, the great changes occurring in Germany did not stem from impersonal historical forces but were the work of Jews, who had uncanny powers. They regarded Jews as international conspirators who were plotting to dominate Germany and the world. This accusation was a secularized and updated version of the medieval demonological myth that Jews, in the service of Satan, were plotting to destroy Christendom. In an extraordinary display of irrationality, Volkish thinkers held that Jews throughout the world were gaining control over political parties, the press, and the economy in order to dominate the planet.

The myth of a Jewish world conspiracy found its culminating expression in the notorious forgery *The Protocols of the Elders of Zion*. The *Protocols* was written in France in the 1890s by an unknown author in the service of the Russian secret police, which sought to justify the tsarist regime's anti-Semitic policies. Drawing upon earlier anti-Semitic conspiracy works—and one work that had nothing to do with Jews but attributed ambitions of world domination to Napoleon III—the forger concocted a tale of a meeting of Jewish elders in the Jewish cemetery of Prague. In these eerie surroundings, the elders plot to take over the world.

First published in Russia in 1903, the *Protocols* was widely distributed after World War I and widely believed. Defeat in World War I and a revolution that replaced the Kaiser's government with an unpopular democratic republic made many Germans receptive to the *Protocols'* message. To them the *Protocols* provided convincing evidence that the Jews were responsible for starting the war, for Germany's defeat, and for the revolution that toppled the monarchy. In 1924, a Jewish observer described the book's impact in postwar Germany:

> In Berlin I attended several meetings which were entirely devoted to the *Protocols*. The speaker was usually a professor, a teacher, an editor, a lawyer or someone of that kind. The audience consisted of members of the educated class, civil servants, tradesmen, former officers, ladies, above all students. . . . Passions were whipped up to a boiling point. . . . [The Jew] was the cause of all ills—those who had made the war and brought about the defeat and engineered the revolution, those who had conjured up all our suffering. This enemy . . . slunk about in the darkness, one shuddered to think what secret designs he was harboring. . . . I observed the students. . . . Now young blood was boiling, eyes flashed, fists clenched, hoarse voices roared applause or vengeance. . . . German scholarship allowed belief in the genuineness of the *Protocols* and in the existence of a Jewish world-conspiracy to penetrate ever more deeply into all the educated sections of the German population, so that now it is simply ineradicable.[18]

Even after the *Protocols* was exposed as a forgery, it continued to be translated and distributed. For anti-Semites, the myth of a Jewish world-conspiracy had become an integrating principle that provided satisfying answers to the crucial questions of existence.

Jew-hatred was extremely popular among conservatives and nationalists in Wilhelmine Germany. Anti-Semitic publications proliferated and some, like Wilhelm Marr's *The Victory of Judaism over Germanism* (1879) and Theodor Fritsch's *The Anti-Semitic Catechism* (1887) went through numerous printings and editions. Anti-Semitism gained considerable respectability in Germany, for it was preached by prominent university scholars, including Paul de Lagarde and Heinrich von Treitschke, by the prominent Protestant pastor, Adolf Stöcker, by politicians, and by the immensely popular Wagner.

In *Judaism in Music,* first published in 1850 under a pseudonym and republished in 1869 under his own name, Wagner, who resented the prominence of the Jewish composers Felix Mendelssohn and Giacomo Meyerbeer, asserted that Jews debased German music. They could not possess or express the feelings that animated the German soul; they had their own folk soul, which had been shaped by a degenerate culture. Devoid of a creative imagination and concerned only with self-centered materialist pursuits, said Wagner, Jews could only have a destructive influence on German culture. In later essays, published in the Wagnerian journal, the *Bayreuther Blätter,* Wagner's anti-Semitism grew even more vitriolic and racist.

In the Middle Ages, Jews had been persecuted and humiliated primarily for religious reasons. In the nineteenth century, national-racial considerations supplemented a traditional, biased Christian perception of Jews and Judaism. However, whereas Christian anti-Semites believed that, through conversion, Jews could escape the curse of their religion, racial anti-Semites, who used the language of science to justify their hatred, said that Jews were indelibly stained and eternally condemned by their genes. Their evil and worthlessness derived from inherited racial characteristics, which could not be altered by conversion. Thus, Hermann Ahlwardt, an anti-Semitic deputy (and author of *The Desperate Struggle Between Aryan and Jew,* 1890) stated in a speech before the German Reichstag in 1895:

> If one designates the whole of Jewry, one does so in the knowledge that the racial qualities of this people are such that in the long run they cannot harmonize with the racial qualities of the Germanic peoples and that every Jew who at this moment has not done anything bad may nevertheless under the proper conditions do precisely that, because his racial qualities drive him to do it . . . the Jews . . . operate like parasites.[19]

German anti-Semitic organizations and political parties failed to get the state to pass anti-Semitic laws, and by the early 1900s, these groups had declined in political power and importance. But the mischief had been done. In the minds of many Germans, even in respectable circles, the image of the Jew as an evil and dangerous creature had been firmly planted. It was perpetuated by the schools, youth groups, the Pan-German Association, and an array of racist pamphlets and books. Anti-Semites of the late nineteenth century had constructed an ideological foundation on which Hitler would later build his movement. In words that foreshadowed Hitler, Paul de Lagarde said of the Jews: "One does not have dealings with pests and parasites: one does not rear them and cherish them; one destroys them as speedily as possible."[20]

"The Sleep of Reason"

The Jewish population of Germany was quite small: in 1900 it was only about 497,000, or 0.95 percent, of the total population of 50,626,000. Jews were proud of their many contributions to German economic and intellectual life. They considered themselves patriotic Germans and regarded Germany as an altogether desirable place to live—a place of refuge in comparison with Russia, where Jews lived in terrible poverty and suffered violent attacks. It is, of course, absurd to believe that a nation of 50 million was threatened by a half a million citizens of Jewish birth, or that the 11 million Jews of the world (by 1900) had organized to rule the planet. Despite the paranoia of the anti-Semite, the German Jews and the Jews in the rest of Europe were quite powerless. There were scarcely any Jews in the ruling circles of governments, armies, civil services, or heavy industries. As events were to prove, the Jews, with no army or state, were the weakest of peoples. But the race mystics, convinced that they were waging a war of self-defense against a satanic foe, were impervious to rational argument. Anti-Semites, said Theodor Mommsen, the great nineteenth-century German historian, would not listen to

> logical and ethical arguments. . . . They listen only to their own envy and hatred, to the meanest instincts. Nothing else counts for them. They are deaf to reason, right, morals. One cannot influence them. . . . [Anti-Semitism] is a horrible epidemic, like cholera—one can neither explain nor cure it.[21]

Racial myths and stereotypes provided people with a comprehensive world-view, an interpretation of life and history that fulfilled the yearning for coherence and meaning, around which they could integrate their thinking. True believers derived a feeling of significance and worth from these racial myths, for they could measure themselves against their polar opposite. True believers also felt that they were engaged in a noble struggle of universal significance: protecting the

Aryan race and its civilization from a deadly enemy. By cloaking their hatred in the mantle of science—nature demands that the favored race triumph over the wicked race—racists could view persecution and even liquidation coldly, matter-of-factly, undeterred by human values or conscience.

Racial nationalism, a major element in nineteenth-century intellectual life, attacked and undermined the Enlightenment tradition. Rejecting the principle of equality, racial anti-Semites judged people not by their accomplishments or character but by their "blood," over which the individual had no control. Blood determines the way a person thinks, talks, behaves, and creates, they said. Scorning toleration, racists advocated legal discrimination and took pleasure in vilification and persecution. Although racist thinkers claimed that their theories were rooted in science, ultimately they derived from primordial feelings. Racists distorted reason and science to demonize and condemn an entire people and to justify humiliation and persecution. They succeeded in presenting a racial ideology fraught with unreason and hate as something virtuous and idealistic. That many people, including the educated and the enlightened, accepted these doctrines was an ominous sign for Western civilization. The sleep of reason does indeed beget monsters, as Spanish painter Francisco de Goya had warned in the early nineteenth century. The popularity of racist ideas showed how tenuous the rational tradition of the Enlightenment is, how receptive the mind is to dangerous myths and demagogic appeals, how easily idealism is debased and science abused, and how readily human behavior can degenerate into inhumanity.

WORLD WAR I

Before 1914, the dominant mood in Europe was one of pride in the accomplishments of Western civilization and confidence in its future progress. Advances in science and technology, the rising standard of living, the spread of democratic institutions, the expansion of social reform, the increase in literacy for the masses, and Europe's position of power in the world—all contributed to a sense of optimism. Other reasons for optimism were that, since the defeat of Napoleon, Europe had avoided a general war, and since the Franco-Prussian War (1870–71), the Great Powers had not fought each other. Reflecting on the world he knew before World War I, Arnold J. Toynbee (see Chapters 11 and 12) recalled that his generation

> expected that life throughout the World would become more rational, more humane, and more democratic and that, slowly but surely, political

democracy would produce greater social justice. We had also expected that the progress of science and technology would make mankind richer, and that this increasing wealth would gradually spread from a minority to a majority. We had expected that all this would happen peacefully. In fact we thought that mankind's course was set for an earthly paradise, and that our approach towards this goal was predestined for us by historical necessity.[22]

Few people recognized that the West's outward achievements masked an inner turbulence, which was propelling Western civilization toward a cataclysm. The European state system was failing. In the early nineteenth century, liberals had believed that redrawing the political map of Europe on the basis of nationality would promote peaceful relations among states. But quite the reverse occurred. By 1914, national states, answering to no higher power, were fueled by an explosive nationalism and were grouped into alliances that faced each other with ever-mounting hostility. Nationalist thinkers propagated pseudoscientific racial and Social Darwinist doctrines that glorified conflict and justified the subjugation of other peoples. Nationalist passions, overheated by the popular press and expansionist societies, poisoned international relations. Committed to enhancing national power, statesmen lost sight of Europe as a community of nations sharing a common civilization. Caution and restraint gave way to belligerency in foreign affairs.

War as Celebration

The surge of a belligerent nationalism and the failure of the European state system was paralleled by a cultural crisis. Some European intellectuals attacked the rational tradition of the Enlightenment and celebrated the primitive, the instinctual, and the irrational. Increasingly, young people grew attracted to philosophies of life and action that ridiculed liberal bourgeois values and viewed war as a purifying and ennobling experience. "If only there were a war, even an unjust one," wrote George Heym, a young German writer in 1912. "This peace is so rotten."[23] In 1912, a survey of Parisian students between the ages of eighteen and twenty-five indicated that

the most cultivated elite among young people . . . find in warfare an aesthetic ideal of energy and strength. They believe that "France needs heroism in order to live." 'Such is the faith,' comments Monsieur Tourolle, 'which consumes modern youth. How many times in the last two years have we heard this repeated: 'Better war than this eternal waiting!' There is no bitterness in this avowal, but rather a secret hope. War! The word has taken on a sudden glamour. . . . These young men impute to it all the beauty with which they are in love and of which they have been deprived by ordinary life. Above all, war, in their eyes, is the occasion for the most noble of virtues, those which they exalt above all others: energy, mastery, and sacrifice for a cause which transcends ourselves.[24]

Colonial wars, colorfully portrayed in the popular press, ignited the imagination of bored factory workers and daydreaming students and reinforced a sense of duty and an urge for gallantry among soldiers and aristocrats. These "splendid" little colonial wars helped fashion an attitude that made war acceptable, if not laudable. Yearning to break loose from their ordinary lives and to embrace heroic values, many Europeans regarded violent conflict as the highest expression of individual and national life. The prominent German historian Heinrich von Treitschke (1834–1896) expressed the fuzzy militarist idealism that pervaded German universities:

> Most undoubtedly war is the one remedy for an ailing nation. Social selfishness and party hatreds must be [silenced] before the call of the State when its existence is at stake. Forgetting himself, the individual must only remember that he is a part of the whole, and realize the unimportance of his own life compared with the common weal.
> The grandeur of war lies in the utter annihilation of puny man in the great conception of the State, and it brings out the full magnificence of the sacrifice of fellow-countrymen for one another. . . .
> It is war which fosters the political idealism which the materialist rejects. What a disaster for civilization it would be if mankind blotted its heroes from memory. . . . To appeal from this Judgment to Christianity would be sheer perversity, for does not the Bible distinctly say that the ruler shall rule by the sword, and again that greater love hath no man than to lay down his life for his friend? To Aryan races, who are before all things courageous, the foolish preaching of everlasting peace has always been vain. They have always been men enough to maintain with the sword what they have attained through the spirit. . . . only the exhausted, spiritless, degenerate periods of history have toyed with the idea [of perpetual peace].[25]

Although technology was making warfare more brutal and dangerous, Europe retained a romantic illusion about combat. "Even if we end in ruin, it was beautiful,"[26] commented General Erich von Falkenhayn, the future chief of the German General Staff, on those stirring days just prior to the outbreak of World War I.

Although Europe was seemingly progressing in the art of civilization, the mythic power of nationalism and the primitive appeal of conflict were driving European civilization to the abyss. Few people recognized the potential crisis—certainly not the statesmen, whose reckless blundering allowed the Continent to stumble into war.

In early August, when war was certain, an extraordinary phenomenon occurred. Crowds gathered in capital cities and expressed their loyalty to the fatherland and their readiness to fight. It seemed as if people wanted violence for its own sake. It was as if war provided an escape from the dull routine of classroom, job, and home; from the emptiness, drabness, mediocrity, and pointlessness of bourgeois society; from the materialism and philistinism of a society that valued money, possession, and organization over the forces of life that pulsate within; from "a world grown old and cold and weary,"[27] said Rupert Brooke, a young British poet. To some, war was a "beautiful . . . sacred moment" that satisfied an "ethical yearning."[28]

To many people, war seemed a healthy and heroic antidote to what was regarded as an unbearably decadent and soul-destroying bourgeois world—an attitude that was very prevalent among youth and intellectuals in the years just prior to 1914. Ernst Jünger, a German novelist and essayist who had left school and volunteered for duty at the age of nineteen, exemplified this mood in his war memoir, *The Storm of Steel:*

> We had grown up in a material age and in each one of us there was the yearning for great experience, such as we had never known. The war had entered into us like wine. We had set out in a rain of flowers to seek the death of heroes. The war was our dream of greatness, power, and glory. There is no lovelier death in the world . . . anything rather than stay at home. . . . I had set out to the war gaily, . . . thinking we were to hold a festival on which all the pride of youth was lavished.[29]

But more significantly, the outpouring of patriotic sentiments demonstrated the immense power that nationalism exercised over the European mind. With extraordinary success, nationalism welded millions of people into a collectivity ready to devote body and soul to the nation, especially during its hour of need. Devotion to the nation had become the noblest of all earthly ideals.

Even socialists, whose loyalty was supposed to be given to an international workers' movement—"the proletariat has no fatherland," Marx and Engels had written in the *Communist Manifesto*—devoted themselves to their respective nations. Class bonds proved far weaker than did ties to country, which stirred deeper and more primitive tribal instincts. Benedetto Croce, the prominent Italian historian-philosopher, observed: "The war has demonstrated that the international struggle always takes precedence over the social, that the actors of world history are peoples and states, not classes."[30]

In Paris, men marched down the boulevards singing the stirring words of the French national anthem, the "Marseillaise," while women showered young soldiers with flowers. A participant in these days recalls: "Young and old, civilian and military men burned with the same excitement. . . . Beginning the next day, thousands of men eager to fight would jostle one another outside recruiting offices, waiting to join up. . . . The word 'duty' had a meaning for them, and the word 'country' had regained its splendor."[31] Similar scenes occurred in Berlin. "It is a joy to be alive," editorialized one newspaper. "We wished so much for this hour. . . . The sword which has been forced into our hand will not be sheathed until our aims are won and our territory extended as far as necessity demands."[32]

Soldiers bound for battle acted as if they were going off on a great adventure. "My dear ones, be proud that you live in such a time and in such a nation and that you . . . have the privilege of sending those you love into so glorious a battle,"[33] wrote a young German law student to his family. The young warriors yearned to do something noble and altruistic, to win glory, to experience life at its most intense; they viewed the war as a means of self-discovery.

Many of Europe's most distinguished intellectuals—and not just those of the radical right, but also liberals and socialists—were captivated by the martial mood, sharing Rupert Brooke's sentiments: "Now God be thanked Who had matched us with His hour,/And caught our youth, and wakened us from sleeping."[34] In October 1914, Max Weber, the greatest sociologist of the prewar generation, wrote: "This war is with all its ugliness great and wonderful, it is worthwhile experiencing it."[35] And he expressed regret that he was too old to go to the front. In November 1914, Thomas Mann, the distinguished German writer, saw the war as "purification, liberation . . . an enormous hope"; [it] set the hearts of poets aflame. . . . How could the artist, the soldier in the artist, not praise God for the collapse of a peaceful world with which he was fed up, so exceedingly fed up."[36] To the prominent German historian Friedrich Meinecke, August 1914 was "one of the great moments of my life which suddenly filled my soul with the deepest confidence in our people and the profoundest joy."[37]

Besides being gripped by a thirst for excitement and a quest for the heroic, many intellectuals welcomed the war because it unified the nation in a noble spirit of fraternity and self-sacrifice. It was a return, some felt, to the organic roots of human existence, a way of overcoming a sense of individual isolation. "How shall we react to the war?" asked Adolf von Harnack, the distinguished student of religion. "Calmly, resolutely, and with exultation. Petty egoisms will disappear and there will only be room for the broad view of life. We are entering a period that will fill us with the joy of sacrifice."[38] Stefan Zweig (1881–1942), an Austrian writer, recalled the intense feelings of fraternity and solidarity that gripped Vienna in August 1914:

As never before, thousands and hundreds of thousands felt what they should have felt in peace time, that they belonged together. A city of two million, a country of nearly fifty million, in that hour felt that they were participating in world history, in a moment which would never recur, and that each one was called upon to cast his infinitesimal self into the glowing mass, there to be purified of all selfishness. All differences of class, rank, and language were flooded over at that moment by the rushing feeling of fraternity. Strangers spoke to one another in the streets, people who had avoided each other for years shook hands, everywhere one saw excited faces. Each individual experienced an exaltation of his ego, he was no longer the isolated person of former times, he had been incorporated into the mass, he was part of the people, and his person, his hitherto unnoticed person, had been given meaning. The petty mail clerk . . . the cobbler, had suddenly achieved a romantic possibility in life; he could become a hero, and everyone who wore a uniform was already being cheered by the women. . . . But it is quite possible that a deeper, more secret power was at work in this frenzy. So deeply, so quickly did the tide break over humanity that, foaming over the surface, it churned up the depths, the subconscious primitive instincts of the human animal—that which Freud so meaningfully calls "the revulsion from culture," the desire to break out of the conventional bourgeois world of codes and statutes, and to permit the primitive instincts of the blood to rage at will.[39]

Some intellectuals viewed the war as a quest for authenticity—an opportunity to experience the life of the spirit and to fulfill the inner self—which adherents of "life philosophy" had been advocating. These intellectuals believed that the war would spiritually regenerate a decadent and artificial European society. It would liberate the spirit from pettiness and ignominy imposed upon it by bourgeois materialism and resurrect glory, nobility, and heroism; it would awaken a spirit of self-sacrifice and give life an overriding purpose; it would rid the nation of wickedness, selfishness, and hypocrisy and cleanse Europe of its spiritual and racial impurities; and would elevate the artistic impulse to a higher level of creativity. From the war would emerge a higher civilization, morally, esthetically, and spiritually reborn.

Thus, a generation of European youth marched off to war joyously, urged on by their teachers and cheered by a delirious nation. But it must be emphasized that the soldiers who went to the front singing and the statesmen and generals who welcomed war or did not try hard enough to prevent it expected a short, decisive, gallant conflict. Virtually no one envisioned what World War I turned out to be—four years of barbaric, senseless bloodletting. But although their gloomy words were drowned out by the cheers of deluded idealists, chauvinists, and fools, there were prophets who realized that Europe was stumbling into darkness. "The lamps are going out all over Europe," said British Foreign Secretary Edward Grey. "We shall never see them lit again in our lifetime."

The War and European Consciousness

"There will be wars as never before on earth," predicted Nietzsche. World War I bore him out. Modern technology enabled the combatants to kill with unprecedented efficiency; modern nationalism infused both civilians and soldiers with the determination to fight until the enemy was totally beaten. The modern state, exercising wide control over its citizens, mobilized its human, material, and spiritual resources to wage total war. As the war hardened into a savage and grueling fight, the statesmen did not press for a compromise peace but rather demanded ever more mobilization, ever more escalation, and ever more sacrifices. The Great War profoundly altered the course of Western civilization, deepening the spiritual crisis that had produced it. How could one speak of the inviolability of the individual when Europe had become a slaughterhouse, or of the primacy of reason when nations permitted the slaughter to go unabated for four years? How could the mind cope with this spectacle of a civilization turning against itself, destroying itself in an orgy of organized violence? A young French soldier, shortly before he was killed at Verdun, expressed the mood of disillusionment that gripped the soldiers in the trenches: "Humanity is mad! It must be mad to do what it is doing. What a massacre! What scenes of horror and carnage, I cannot find words to translate my impressions. Hell cannot be so terrible. Men are mad!"[40] The war, said British poet Robert Graves provoked an "inward scream" that still reverberates. Now only the naive could believe in continuous progress. Western civilization had entered an age of violence, anxiety, and doubt that still persists.

World War I was a great turning point in the history of the West. The war left many with the gnawing feeling that Western civilization had lost its vitality and was caught in a rhythm of breakdown and disintegration. It seemed that Western civilization was fragile and perishable, that Western people, despite their extraordinary accomplishments, were never more than a step or two away from barbarism. Surely, any civilization that could allow such a senseless slaughter to last four years had entered its decline and could look forward only to the darkest of futures.

European intellectuals were demoralized and disillusioned. The orderly, peaceful, rational world of their youth had come crumbling down. The Enlightenment world-view, weakened in the nineteenth century by the assault of romantics, Social Darwinists, extreme nationalists, race mystics, and glorifiers of the irrational, was now disintegrating. The enormity of the war had shattered faith in the capacity of reason to deal with crucial social and political questions. It appeared that civilization was fighting an unending and seemingly hopeless battle against the irrational elements in human nature and that war would be a recurring phenomenon in the twentieth century.

Confidence in the future gave way to doubt. The old beliefs in the perfectibility of humanity, the blessings of science, and ongoing progress seemed an expression of naive optimism. A.J.P. Taylor concludes:

> The First World War was difficult to fit into the picture of a rational civilization advancing by ordered stages. The civilized men of the twentieth century had outdone in savagery the barbarians of all preceding ages, and their civilized virtues—organization, mechanical skill, self-sacrifice—had made war's savagery all the more terrible. Modern man had developed powers which he was not fit to use. European civilization had been weighed in the balance and found wanting.[41]

Western civilization had lost its spiritual center. French writer Paul Valéry summed up the mood of a troubled generation, for whom the sun seemed to be setting on the Enlightenment:

> The storm has died away, and still we are restless, uneasy as if the storm were about to break. Almost all the affairs of men remain in a terrible uncertainty. We think of what has disappeared and we are almost destroyed by what has been destroyed; we do not know what will be born, and we fear the future, not without reason. We hope vaguely, we dread precisely; our fears are infinitely more precise than our hopes; we confess that the charm of life is behind us. There is no thinking man . . . who can hope to dominate this anxiety, to escape from this impression of darkness . . . . But among all these injured things is the Mind. The Mind has indeed been cruelly wounded; its complaint is heard in the hearts of intellectual men; it passes a mournful judgment on itself. It doubts itself profoundly.[42]

This disillusionment heralded a loss of faith in liberal-democratic values that contributed to the widespread popularity of fascist ideologies in the postwar world. Having lost confidence in the power of reason to solve the problems of the human community, in liberal doctrines of individual freedom, and in the institutions of parliamentary democracy, many people turned to fascism as a simple saving faith. Far from making the world safe for democracy, as President Woodrow Wilson and other liberals had hoped, World War I gave rise to totalitarian movements, which nearly destroyed democracy.

The war produced a generation of young people who had reached their maturity in combat. Violence had become a way of life for millions of soldiers hardened by battle and for millions of civilians aroused by four years of propaganda. The astronomical casualty figures—some 10 million dead and 21 million wounded—had a brutalizing effect. Violence, cruelty, suffering, and even wholesale death seemed to be natural and acceptable components of human existence. The sanctity of the individual seemed to be liberal and Christian claptrap.

The fascination with violence and contempt for life lived on in the postwar world. Many returned veterans yearned for the excitement of battle and the fellowship of the trenches—what one French soldier called "the most tender human experience." After the war, a young English officer recalled: "There was an exaltation, in those days of comradeship and dedication, that would have come in few other ways. And so, to those of us who had ridden with Don Quixote and Rupert Brooke on either hand, the Line is sacred ground, for there we saw the vision splendid."[43] A fraternal bond united the men of the trenches. But many veterans also shared a primitive attraction to war's fury. The brutalizing effect of the war is seen in this statement by a German soldier for whom the war had never ended:

> People told us that the War was over. That made us laugh. We ourselves are the War. Its flame burns strongly in us. It envelops our whole being and fascinates us with the enticing urge to destroy. We . . . marched onto the battlefields of the postwar world just as we had gone into battle on the Western Front: singing, reckless, and filled with the joy of adventure as we marched to the attack; silent, deadly, remorseless in battle.[44]

The Great War's veterans made ideal recruits for extremist political movements that replicated wartime fellowship, glorified action, and promised to rescue society from a decadent liberalism. Both Hitler and Mussolini, themselves ex-soldiers imbued with the ferocity of the front, knew how to appeal to veterans. The lovers of violence and the harbingers of hate who became the leaders of fascist parties would come within a hairsbreadth of destroying Western civilization.

However, while the experience of the trenches led some veterans to embrace an aggressive militarism, others were determined that the horror should never be repeated. Tortured by the memory of the Great War, European intellectuals wrote pacifist plays and novels and signed pacifist declarations. In the 1930s, an attitude of "peace at any price" discouraged resistance to Nazi Germany in its bid to dominate Europe.

World War I was total war—it encompassed the entire nation and had no limits. States demanded total victory and total commitment from their citizens. They regulated industrial production, developed sophisticated propaganda techniques to strengthen morale, and exercised ever greater control over the lives of their people, organizing and disciplining them like soldiers. This total mobilization of nations' human and material resources provided a model for future dictators. With ever greater effectiveness and ruthlessness, dictators would centralize power and manipulate thinking.

THE RISE OF FASCISM

Liberals viewed the Great War as a conflict between freedom and autocracy and expected an Allied victory to accelerate the spread of democracy throughout Europe. In the immediate aftermath of the war, it seemed that liberalism would continue to advance as it had in the nineteenth century. The collapse of the autocratic German and Austrian empires had led to the formation of parliamentary governments throughout eastern and central Europe. Yet within two decades, in an extraordinary turn of events, democracy seemed in its death throes. In Spain, Portugal, Italy, and Germany, and in all the newly created states of central and eastern Europe except Czechoslovakia, democracy collapsed and various forms of authoritarian government emerged. The defeat of democracy and the surge of authoritarianism was best exemplified by the triumph of totalitarian fascist movements in Italy and Germany.

The emergence of fascist movements in more than twenty European lands after World War I was a sign that liberal society was in a state of disorientation and dissolution. The cultural pessimism, anti-intellectualism, and contempt for liberal values voiced by many intellectuals and nationalists before the war found expression after the war in the anti-democratic and irrational fascist ideologies that altered European political life. Fascism marked the culmination of the dangerous trends inherent in the extreme nationalism and radical conservatism of the late nineteenth century.

As a Europe-wide phenomenon, fascism was a response to a postwar society afflicted by spiritual disintegration, economic dislocation, political instability, and thwarted nationalist hopes. It was an expression of fear that the Bolshevik Revolution would spread westward. It was also an expression of hostility to democratic values and a reaction to the failure of liberal institutions to solve crushing problems of modern industrial society. Regarding liberalism as bankrupt and parliamentary government as futile, many people yearned for a military dictatorship. To fascists and their sympathizers, democracy seemed an ineffective, spiritless, and decaying old order ready to be overthrown.

In their struggle to bring down the liberal state, fascist leaders aroused primitive impulses and tribal loyalties and made use of myths and rituals to mobilize and manipulate the masses. With many liberal-rational certainties destroyed by the Great War, people were receptive to irrational ideas. Organizing their propaganda with the rigor of a military campaign, fascists stirred and dominated the masses and confused and undermined their democratic opposition, eroding its will to resist. Fascists were most successful in countries with weak democratic traditions. Having no patience for parliamentary procedures or sympathy for democratic principles, the people in these countries were drawn to demagogues who exuded charisma and promised direct action.

Fascist movements were marked by a determination to eradicate liberalism and Marxism—to undo the legacy of the French Revolution of 1789 and the Bolshevik Revolution of 1917. Fascists believed that theirs was a spiritual revolution—that they were initiating a new era in history and building a new civilization on the ruins of liberal democracy. "We stand for a new principle in the world," said Mussolini. "We stand for the sheer categorical, definitive, antithesis to the world of democracy . . . to the world which still abides by the fundamental principles laid down in 1789."[45] Repudiating the liberal concepts of the worth and dignity of each person and political freedom secured through parliamentary politics, fascists championed a collectivist ideology that focused on the nation's special needs. The chief principle of Nazism, said Hitler, "is to abolish the liberal concept of the individual and the Marxist concept of humanity, and to substitute for them the *Volk* community, rooted in the soil and united by the bond of its common blood."[46]

Fascists accused liberal society of despiritualizing human beings—of transforming them into materialistic creatures, whose highest ideal was money making and whose souls were deadened to noble causes, heroic deeds, and self-sacrifice. Idealistic youth and intellectuals rejoiced in fascism's activism and its glorification of the heroic; they saw it as a revolt against the mediocrity of mass society and a reaffirmation of the highest human spiritual qualities—heroism and dedication to one's people.

Fascists regarded Marxism as another enemy, for class conflict divided the nation. To fascists, the Marxist call for workers of the world to unite meant the death of the national community. Fascism, by contrast, would reintegrate the proletariat into the nation and end class hostilities, which divide and weaken the state and its people. By making people of all classes feel that they were a needed part of the nation, fascism offered a solution to the problems of insecurity and isolation in modern industrial society.

In contrast to liberalism and Marxism, fascism attacked the rational tradition of the Enlightenment and exalted will, race, feeling, and instinct. Intellectual discussion and critical analysis, said fascists, cause national divisiveness; reason promotes doubt, enfeebles the will, and hinders instinctive, aggressive action. Glorifying action for its own sake, fascists aroused and manipulated brutal and primitive impulses and carried into politics the combative spirit of the trenches. They formed private armies, which attracted veterans—many of them rootless, brutal, and maladjusted men, who sought to preserve the loyalty, camaraderie, altruism, excitement, and violence of the front. For these men war remained the father of all things. In both Italy and Germany battle-hardened veterans welcomed an opportunity to wear the uniforms of the fascist militia (Black Shirts in Italy and Brown Shirts in Germany), parade in the streets, and do battle with socialist and labor-union opponents. Fascism made a continual appeal to the emotions as a means of integrating the national community. This flow of emotion fueled irrational and dangerous desires and beliefs, which blocked critical judgment and responsible action.

Fascism exalted the leader who intuitively grasped what was best for the nation, and it called for rule by an elite of dedicated party members. The leader and the party would relieve the individual of the need to make decisions. "[N]ever before have the peoples thirsted for authority, direction, order, as they do now,"[47] wrote Mussolini. Holding that the liberal stress on individual freedom promoted competition and conflict that shattered national unity, fascists pressed for monolithic unity— one leader, one party, one ideology, and one national will.

The proliferation of fascist movements demonstrated that the habits of democracy are not quickly learned or easily retained. Particularly during times of crisis, people lose patience with parliamentary discussion and constitutional procedures, sink into nonrational modes of thought and behavior, and are easily manipulated by unscrupulous politicians. For the sake of economic or emotional security and national grandeur, they will often willingly sacrifice political freedom. Fascism starkly manifested the immense power of the irrational; it humbled liberals, making them permanently aware of the tenuousness of reason and the fragility of freedom.

HITLER'S WORLD-VIEW

Mussolini's fascism exhibited much bluster and braggadocio, but fascist Italy did not have the industrial and military strength or the total commitment of the people necessary to threaten the peace of Europe. Nazism, on the other hand, demonstrated a demonic quality that nearly destroyed Western civilization. The impact of Hitler's sinister,

Adolf Hitler *(The Bettmann Archive)*

fanatical, and obsessive personality was far greater on the German movement than was Mussolini's character on Italian fascism. Also contributing to the demonic radicalism of Nazism were certain deeply rooted German traditions that were absent in Italy: Prussian militarism, adoration of the power-state, and belief in the special destiny of the German Volk. These traditions made the German people's attachment to Hitler and Nazi ideology much stronger than was the Italian people's devotion to Mussolini and his party.

Some historians view Hitler as an unprincipled opportunist and a brilliant tactician who believed in nothing but cleverly manufactured and manipulated ideas that were politically useful in his drive for power. To be sure, Hitler was not concerned with the objective truth of an idea but with its potential political usefulness; nor was he a systematic thinker like Marx. Whereas communism claimed the certainty of science and held that it would reform the world in accordance with rational principles, Hitler proclaimed the higher validity of blood, instinct, and will and regarded the intellect as an enemy of the soul. Nevertheless, these crude and shallow ideas, made a remarkably consistent ideology. As Hajo Holborn notes, Hitler's fanaticism revealed an inner coherence:

> Hitler was a great opportunist and tactician, but it would be quite wrong to think that ideology was to him a mere instrumentality for gaining power. On the contrary, Hitler was a doctrinaire of the first order. Throughout his political career he was guided by an ideology . . . which from 1926 onward [did] not show any change whatsoever.[48]

Hitler's thought comprised a patchwork of nineteenth-century anti-Semitic, Volkish, Social Darwinist, antidemocratic, anti-Marxist, and antimodernist ideas. From these ideas, many of which enjoyed wide popularity, Hitler constructed a world-view rooted in myth. Given to excessive daydreaming and never managing to "overcome his youth with its dreams, injuries, and resentments,"[49] Hitler sought to make the world accord with his fantasies—struggles to the death between races, a vast empire ruled by a master race, a thousand-year Reich.

In its intent, Nazism was a deliberate rejection of the core values of modern liberal civilization. Hitler understood his world historical role better than did his adversaries.

> To the Christian doctrine of the infinite significance of the individual human soul and of personal responsibility, I oppose with icy clarity the saving doctrine of the nothingness of the individual human being, and of the continued existence in the visible immortality of the nation. . . . Providence has ordained that I should be the greatest liberator of humanity. . . . I am freeing man from the restraints of an intelligence that has taken charge; from the dirty and degrading self-mortification of a chimera called conscience and morality and from the demands of a freedom and personal independence which only a very few could bear.[50]

Racial Nationalism

Nazism rejected both the Judeo-Christian and the Enlightenment traditions and sought to found a new world order based on racial nationalism. For Hitler, race was the key to understanding world history. "All great cultures of the past perished only because the originally creative race died out from blood poisoning," he wrote. "A state which in this age of racial poisoning dedicates itself to the care of its best racial elements must some day become lord of the earth."[51] He believed that Western civilization was at a critical juncture. Liberalism was dying, and Marxism, that "Jewish invention," as he called it, would inherit the future unless it was opposed by an even more powerful world-view.

"With the conception of race National Socialism will carry its revolution and recast the world,"[52] said Hitler. As the German barbarians had overwhelmed a disintegrating Roman Empire, a reawakened, racially united Germany, led by men of iron will, would carve out a vast European empire and would deal a decadent liberal civilization its death-blow. It would conquer Russia, eradicate communism, and reduce to serfdom the subhuman Slavs, "a mass of born slaves who feel the need of a master."[53]

In the tradition of German Volkish thinkers, Hitler sharply distinguished between *Kultur* and civilization. Germanic *Kultur*, which binds the individual in a mystical way to his people and land, is superior to the rational tradition, which is the essence of Western civilization. He declared: "Civilization means the application of reason to life. Goethe, Schiller, Kant are reflections of the western mind. The patriots prefer to seek 'life forces,' the irrational impulses, which seem to them more characteristic of the German mind."[54] This glorification of irrational life forces, exemplified by a racial mythology that saw Germans as racially and culturally superior, is the centerpiece of National Socialist ideology. German cultural life had been characterized by a tendency to spiritualize existence—to disdain materialism and egoism and to discover one's soul in the ideal. Nazism, which described itself as the triumph of will, spirit, and idealism, both perverted and showed the limitations of this tradition.

Also in the tradition of Volkish nationalists and crude Social Darwinists, Hitler divided the world into superior and inferior races and pitted them against each other in a struggle for survival. This fight for life was a law of nature and of history. In Hitler's view, the Germans, descendants of ancient Aryans, possessed superior racial characteristics; a nation degenerates and perishes if it allows its blood to be contaminated by intermingling with lower races. Conflict between races was desirable, for it strengthened and hardened racial superiors; it made them ruthless—a necessary quality in this Darwinian world. As a higher race, the Germans were entitled to conquer and subjugate other races. Germany must have *Lebensraum* ("living space") by expanding eastward at the expense of the racially inferior Slavs.

The Jew as the Embodiment of Evil

An obsessive and virulent anti-Semitism dominated Hitler's mental outlook. In waging war against the Jews, Hitler believed that he was defending Germany from its worst enemy. Everything Hitler despised—liberalism, intellectualism, pacifism, parliamentarianism, internationalism, communism, modern art, and individualism—he attributed to Jews. "Two worlds face one another," said Hitler in a statement that clearly reflects the mythical character of his thought, "the men of God and the men of Satan! The Jew is the anti-man, the creature of another god. He must have come from another root of the human race. I set the Aryan and the Jew over and against each other."[55]

For Hitler the Jew was the mortal enemy of racial nationalism. The moral outlook of the ancient Hebrew prophets, which affirmed individual worth and made individuals morally responsible for their actions, was totally in opposition to Hitler's morality, which subordinated the individual to the national community. He once called conscience a Jewish invention. The prophetic vision of the unity of humanity under God and of equality, justice, and peace were also in opposition to Hitler's belief that all history is a pitiless struggle between races. The strongest and most ruthless deserve to survive; the weak must perish.

Hitler's anti-Semitism also served a functional purpose. By concentrating all evil in one enemy, "the conspirator and demonic" Jew, Hitler provided true believers with a simple, all-embracing, and emotionally satisfying explanation for all their misery. Racial and anti-Semitic myths gave their believers an interpretation of life and history that fulfilled the mind's yearning for meaning; people could integrate their thinking around such beliefs. By defining themselves as the racial and spiritual opposites of the "vile Jew," true believers of all classes derived a feeling of significance and worth and felt joined together in a mystical Volkish union. By seeing themselves engaged in a heroic battle against a single enemy who embodied evil, they would strengthen their will. Even failures and misfits could gain self-respect. Anti-Semitism provided insecure and hostile people with defenseless but recognizable targets on whom to focus their antisocial feelings, bearing out the wisdom of Freud's insight: "It is always possible to bind together a considerable number of people in love, so long as there are people left over to receive the manifestation of their aggressiveness."[56]

The surrender to crude and irrational myths served to disorient the intellect and to unify the nation. When the mind accepts an image such as Hitler's image of Jews as vermin, germs, and satanic conspirators, it has lost all capacity for critical judgment and objectivity. Such a disoriented mind is ready to believe and to obey, to be manipulated and led, to brutalize and to tolerate brutality; it is ready to be absorbed into the collective will of the community. That many people, including intellectuals and members of the elite, accepted these racial ideas shows the enduring power of mythical thinking and the vulnerability of reason. In 1933, the year Hitler took power, Felix Goldmann, a German-Jewish writer, commented astutely on the irrational character of Nazi anti-Semitism: "The present-day politicized racial anti-Semitism is the embodiment of myth, . . . nothing is discussed . . . only felt, . . . nothing is pondered critically, logically or reasonably, . . . only inwardly perceived, surmised. . . . We are apparently the last [heirs] . . . of the Enlightenment."[57]

Propaganda

Hitler understood that in an age of political parties, universal suffrage, and a popular press—the legacies of the French and Industrial revolutions—the successful leader must win the support of the masses. To gain this support, Hitler consciously applied and perfected elements of circus showmanship, church pageantry, American advertising, and the techniques of propaganda that the Allies had effectively used to stir their populations during the war. To be effective, said Hitler, propaganda must be aimed principally at the emotions. Intuitively, Hitler grasped the power and importance of the unconscious and the irrational in human behavior—the key idea of modern psychology, sociology and modernist culture. The masses are not moved by scientific ideas or by objective and abstract knowledge, he said, but by primitive feelings, terror, force, and discipline. Propaganda must reduce everything to simple slogans incessantly repeated and must concentrate on one enemy. The masses are aroused by the spoken, not the written, word—by a storm of hot passion erupting from the speaker "which like hammer blows can open the gates to the heart of the people."[58]

The most effective means of stirring the masses and strengthening them for the struggle ahead, said Hitler, is the mass meeting. Surrounded by tens of thousands of people and excited by the will power, strength, and unflagging determination radiating from the speaker, he wrote in *Mein Kampf*, individuals lose their sense of individuality and no longer see themselves as isolated. They become members of a community bound together by an esprit de corps reminiscent of the trenches during the Great War. Bombarded by the cheers of thousands of voices and by marching units, banners, and explosive oratory, individuals become convinced of the truth of the party's message and the movement's irresistibility. Their intellects overwhelmed and their resistance lowered, they lose their previous beliefs and are carried along on a wave of enthusiasm. "The man who enters such a meeting doubting and wavering leaves it inwardly reinforced; he has become a link to the community."[59]

At mass meetings, Hitler was a spellbinder who gave stunning performances. His pounding fists, throbbing body, wild gesticulations, hypnotic eyes, rage-swollen face, and repeated frenzied denunciations of the Treaty of Versailles, Marxism, the Jews, and the Weimar Republic inflamed and mesmerized the audience. Hitler immediately grasped the innermost feelings of his audience—its resentments and its longings. As one early admirer recalled, "The intense will of the man, the passion of his sincerity seemed to flow from him into me. I experienced an exaltation that could be likened only to religious conversion."[60] Hitler's career attests to the brilliance of Nietzsche's insight into demagogic behavior:

> In all great deceivers one thing is noteworthy to which they owe their power. In the actual act of deception, with all their preparations, the dreadful voice, expression, and mien . . . they are overcome by their *belief in themselves*; it is this, then, which speaks so miraculously, so wonderfully and persuasively to the spectators. . . . For men believe in the truth of everything that is visibly, strongly believed in.[61]

TOTALITARIANISM

In the 1930s the term totalitarianism was used to describe the Fascist regime in Italy, the National Socialist regime in Germany, and the communist regime in the Soviet Union. To a degree that far exceeds the ancient tyrannies and early modern autocratic states, these dictatorships aspired to and, with varying degrees of success, attained control over the individual's consciousness and behavior and all phases of political, social, and cultural life. To many people it seemed that a crises-riddled democracy was dying and that the future belonged to these dynamic totalitarian movements.

Totalitarianism is a twentieth-century phenomenon, for such all-embracing control over the individual and society could only be achieved in an age of modern ideology, technology, and bureaucracy. The totalitarian state was more completely established in Germany and the Soviet Union than in Italy, where cultural and historic conditions impeded the realization of the totalitarian goal of monolithic unity and total control.

In *Totalitarian Dictatorship and Autocracy* (1956), Carl J. Friedrich and Zbigniew K. Brzezinski viewed fascist and communist dictatorships as "historically unique and *sui generis*,"[62]—different in nature from ancient oriental despotisms, the Roman Empire, the tyrannies of the Renaissance city-states, or the absolute monarchies of modern Europe. "Broadly speaking, totalitarian dictatorship is a new development; there has never been anything quite like it before." They contended further that "fascist and communist totalitarian dictatorships are basically alike."[63] The ideological aims and social and economic policies of Hitler and Stalin differed fundamentally. However, both

Soviet Russia and Nazi Germany shared the totalitarian goal of total domination of the individual and institutions and both employed similar methods to achieve it.

Mussolini's Italy is more accurately called authoritarian, for the party-state either did not intend to control all phases of life or lacked the means to do so. Moreover, Mussolini hesitated to use the ruthless methods that Hitler and Stalin employed so readily. The industrialists, the large landowners, the church, and, to some extent, even the army never fell under the complete domination of the party. Life in Italy was less regimented and the individual less fearful than in Nazi Germany or communist Russia. Nor did the regime possess the minds of its subjects with the same thoroughness as the Nazis did in Germany. The Italian people might cheer Mussolini, but few were willing to die for him.

On close analysis, too, the Nazi state appears less totalitarian than the Soviet Union under Stalin. In practice, the Nazi state was not a coherent and monolithic political system held together by commands issuing from a single center of power. Rather, the nation was composed of organizations and individuals competing with one another for influence, power, and plunder. Moreover, unlike the Soviet regime, the Nazi state did not entirely destroy the old elites, who continued to play important roles in the state bureaucracy, the military, and industry.

Totalitarianism and Liberal Democracy

Striving for total unity, control, and obedience, the totalitarian dictatorship is the antithesis of liberal democracy. It abolishes all competing political parties, suppresses individual liberty, eliminates or regulates private institutions, and utilizes the modern state's bureaucracy and technology to impose its ideology and enforce its commands. The party-state determines what people should believe—what values they should hold. There is no room for individual thinking, private moral judgment, or individual conscience. The individual possesses no natural rights that the state must respect. The Fascist conception of the state is all-embracing, said Mussolini, and outside of the state "no human or spiritual values can exist, much less have value."[64] The state regards individuals merely as building blocks, the human material to be hammered and hewed into a new social order. It seeks to create an efficiently organized and stable society—one whose subjects do not raise troublesome questions or hold unorthodox opinions.

Nevertheless, the totalitarian dictatorship is also an unintended consequence of liberal democracy; it emerged in an age in which—as a consequence of the French and Industrial revolutions—the masses had become a force in political life. The totalitarian leader seeks to gain and preserve power by harnessing mass support. Hitler, in particular, built a party within the existing constitutional system and exploited the electoral process in order to overthrow the democratic government. As Goebbels cynically stated, "We have openly declared that we use democratic methods only to gain power and that once we had it we would ruthlessly deny our opponents all those chances we had been granted when we were in the opposition."[65] Unlike previous dictatorial regimes, the dictatorships of both the left and the right sought to legitimatize their rule by gaining the masses' approval. They both claimed that their governments were higher and truer expressions of the people's will. "This government is, in the truest sense of the word, a people's government,"[66] stated Goebbels. Nazism, which assimilated many popular nineteenth-century Volkish, romantic, nationalist, and racist ideas, commanded greater mass support than did Soviet communism, which had to be forced on the unreceptive Russian people by a resolute minority. Both dictatorships established their rule in the name of the people—the German Volk or the Soviet proletariat. And each presented itself as the sole interpreter of the general will—that which is best for the nation. Thus, in 1939, a Nazi theorist declared that the German leader-state constituted a higher and truer form of a people's government, for it

> is founded on the recognition that the true will of the people cannot be disclosed through parliamentary votes . . . but that the will of the people in its pure and uncorrupted form can only be expressed through the Führer. . . . The Führer is the bearer of the people's will. . . . In his will the will of the people is realized.[67]

Cult of the Leader

A distinctive feature of totalitarianism is the overriding importance given the leader, who is seen as infallible and invincible. "Mussolini is always right," was a favorite Fascist slogan. "Mussolini goes forward with confidence in a halo of myth, almost chosen by God, indefatigable and infallible, the instrument employed by Providence for the creation of a new civilization,"[68] wrote philosopher Giovanni Gentile. Hitler was seen as the incarnation of the German Volk. He was sent by destiny to lead the people: his intuition grasped the needs of the German nation and his will would assure the nation's triumph. "He stands like a statue grown beyond the measure of earthly man,"[69] is the way Nazi propaganda described Hitler. At camps and rallies, young people chanted: "We were slaves; we were outsiders in our own country. So were we before Hitler united us. Now we would fight against Hell itself for our leader."[70]

The Third Reich was organized as a leader-state, in which Hitler, the Fuehrer, embodied and expressed the will of the people. Proclaiming that Hitler and his ruling elite always identified with and served the German nation, the Nazi state demanded the people's complete obedience and supreme loyalty. Because the Fuehrer knew what was best for the nation—his intuition and will were virtually infallible—he deserved to have total power. Viewing individual liberty as a barrier to national unity and effective action by the state, the Nazi leader-state insisted that there could be no rights of the individual that the government must respect. As a Nazi political theorist stated, "The authority of the Fuehrer is total and all-embracing. . . . it embraces all members of the German community. . . . The Fuehrer's authority is subject to no checks or controls; it is circumscribed by no . . . individual rights; it is . . . overriding and unfettered."[71]

Idolization of the leader flowed naturally from Italian fascism and German National Socialism, ideologies rooted in nonrational hero-worship and a glorification of nation, war, and will. A personality cult is not native to Marxism, whose authority rests on a doctrine claiming scientific validity. Marxist theory placed supreme authority in the party, the vanguard of the proletariat, and rejected any notion of a supreme leader. Both Marx and Engels had explicitly rejected personal adulation. "Out of hatred for any cult of personality," wrote Marx, "I never allowed publication of the laudatory messages with which I was pestered. . . . I never even sent answers, except for a few rebukes."[72] However, the fact that Stalin was able to inject it into Marxism shows how crucial the personality cult is to totalitarianism.

Soviet propaganda made a cult of Stalin—"Father, Leader, Friend, and Teacher," "Greatest Genius of All Times and Peoples"—that bordered on deification. Stalin, says Roy A. Medvedev, a Soviet scholar, sought to create "a 'socialist religion' *with* a god. And the all-powerful, all-knowing, all-holy god of the new religion was himself, Stalin."[73] In 1935, a Soviet writer expressed religious-like adulation for Stalin:

> Centuries will pass and the generations still to come will regard us as the happiest of mortals, as the most fortunate of men, because we . . . were privileged to see Stalin, our inspired leader. Yes, and we regard ourselves as the happiest of mortals because we are the contemporaries of a man who never had an equal in world history. The men of all ages will call on thy name, which is strong, beautiful, wise and marvellous. Thy name is engraven on every factory, every machine, every place on the earth, and in the hearts of all men.[74]

The masses' slavish adulation of the leader and their uncritical acceptance of the dogma that the leader or the party is always right promote loyalty, dedication, and obedience and distorts rational thinking. Thus, when Stalin died in 1953, millions of Russians wept. To these deluded Russians, Stalin, who had murdered and deported millions, was still the "Beloved Father."

Ideology

Totalitarian leaders want more than power for its own sake; in the last analysis, they seek to transform the world according to an all-embracing ideology, a set of convictions and beliefs, which, says Hannah Arendt, "pretend[s] to know the mysteries of the whole historical process—the secrets of the past, the intricacies of the present, the uncertainties of the future."[75] The ideology constitutes a higher and exclusive truth, based on a law of history or social development, that, says Karl Dietrich Bracher, "reduce[s] the past and the future to a single historical principle of struggle, no matter whether by state, nation, people, race, or class."[76] The ideology contains a dazzling vision of the future—a secular New Jerusalem—that strengthens the will of the faithful and attracts converts. "This utopian and chiliastic outlook of totalitarian ideologies," declare Friedrich and Brzezinski, "gives them a pseudoreligious quality. In fact, they often elicit in the less critical followers a depth of conviction and a fervor of devotion usually found only among persons inspired by a transcendent faith."[77] Like a religion, the totalitarian ideology provides its adherents with beliefs that make society and history intelligible, that explain all of existence in an emotionally gratifying way. The ideology satisfies a human yearning for absolutes. It creates true believers who feel that they are participating in a great cause—a heroic fight against evil—that gives meaning to their lives. Thus, Lev Kopelev tells us about his days as a true believer: "The party became our church militant, bequeathing to all mankind eternal salvation, eternal peace and the bliss of earthly paradise. . . . The works of Marx, Engels and Lenin were accepted as holy writ, and Stalin was the infallible high priest."[78]

Social theorist Ernest Becker reflects on the relationship between ideological commitment and a yearning for meaning:

> Man transcends death . . . by finding a meaning for his life, some kind of larger scheme into which he fits; he may believe he has fulfilled God's purpose, or done his duty to his ancestors, or family, or achieved something which has enriched mankind. This is how man assures the expansive meaning of his life. . . .[W]hat man fears is not so much extinction, but extinction *with insignificance.* Man wants to know that his life has somehow counted . . . in a larger scheme of things . . . . I think it is time for social scientists to catch up with Hitler as a psychologist, and to

realize that men will do anything for a heroic belonging to a victorious cause if they are persuaded about the legitimacy of that cause.[79]

Like a religion, the totalitarian party gives isolated and alienated individuals a feeling of camaraderie, a complete sense of belonging; it enables individuals to lose themselves in the comforting and exhilarating embrace of a mass movement. Bakunin, the radical anarchist, had sensed the seductive power of the community when he stated: "I do not want to be *I*, I want to be *We*."[80]

Nazi racial ideology called for the integration and revitalization of the German racial community and the formation of a new society in which a person's status would depend not on wealth or birth but on service to the Volk. Devotion to the Volk would overcome class antagonisms, and a corrosive Jewish influence would be permanently eliminated. The new, racially united Germany would liberate itself from the humiliation of a lost war and a vindictive treaty, extend its power over the European continent, and dominate racial inferiors.

Soviet ideology combined the traditional Marxist goal of a classless society free of exploitation with the need to build a strong Russia. In opposition to Leon Trotsky, his principal rival for succeeding Lenin, Stalin considered the industrialization of Russia, not world revolution, as the party's most pressing goal. Without building up Soviet power, reasoned Stalin, Russia would be destroyed by its capitalist enemies.

Not only did the totalitarian religion-ideology supply followers with a cause that claimed absolute goodness; it also provided a Devil. For the Soviets, the source of evil and the cause of all the people's hardships were the degenerate capitalists, the traitorous Trotskyites, or the saboteurs and foreign agents, who impeded the realization of the socialist society. For the Nazis, the Devil was the conspirator Jew. These "evil" ones must be eliminated in order to realize the totalitarian movement's vision of the future. Thus, totalitarian regimes liquidate large segments of the population designated as "enemies of the people." Historical necessity or a higher purpose demands and justifies their liquidation. The appeal to historical necessity has all the power of a great myth. Presented as a world-historical struggle between the forces of good and the forces of evil, the myth incites fanaticism and numbs the conscience. Seemingly decent people engage in terrible acts of brutality with no remorse, convinced that they are waging a war against evil. Lev Kopelev, who participated in the forced collectivization of agriculture, recalls that the suffering of the kulaks "was excruciating to see and hear. . . . And even worse to take part in it. . . . And I persuaded myself, explained to myself, I mustn't give in to debilitating pity. We were realizing historical necessity."[81]

And again:

Our great goal was the universal triumph of Communism, and for the sake of that goal everything was permissible—to lie, to steal, to destroy hundreds of thousands and even millions of people, all those who were hindering our work or could hinder it, everyone who stood in the way.[82]

The Nazis mythically described the world as a battleground between divine and demonic powers, between the forces of light and the forces of darkness, symbolized by the Jew. In 1947, SS Captain Dieter Wisliceny, soon to be executed for war crimes, astutely analyzed the meaning of Nazi anti-Semitism. He described it

as a mystical and religious view which sees the world as ruled by good and bad powers. According to this view the Jews represented the evil principle. . . . It is absolutely impossible to make any impression on this outlook by means of logical or rational argument. It is a sort of religiosity. . . . Against this world of evil the race-mystics set the world of good, of light, incarnated in blond, blue-eyed people who were supposed to be the source of all capacity for creating civilization. . . . Now these two worlds were alleged to be locked in a perpetual struggle. . . . The usual view of Himmler [head of the SS] is that he was an ice-cold, cynical politician. . . . [In reality] Himmler was a mystic who embraced this worldview with religious fanaticism.[83]

Totalitarians are utopians inspired by idealism; they seek the salvation of their nation, of their race, or of humanity. They believe that the victory of their cause will usher in the millennium, a state of harmony and bliss. Such a vision is attractive to people burdened by economic insecurity or spiritual disorientation. The history of our century demonstrates how easily utopian beliefs can be twisted into paranoid fantasies, and idealistic sentiments transformed into murderous fanaticism.

Shaping a "New Man"

Unlike earlier autocratic regimes, the totalitarian dictatorship is not satisfied with its subjects' outward obedience; it demands the masses' unconditional loyalty and enthusiastic support. It strives to control the inner person: to shape thoughts, feelings, and attitudes in accordance with the party ideology, which becomes an official creed. It seeks to create a "new man," one who dedicates himself body and soul to the party and its ideology, a true believer stirred by a mission. Goebbels expressed this totalitarian goal: "It is not enough to reconcile people more or less to our regime, to move them towards a position of neutrality towards us, we want rather to work on people until they are addicted to us."[84] So too did an anonymous Nazi poet:

> We have captured all the positions
> And on the heights we have planted
> The banners of our revolution.
> You had imagined that was all that we wanted.
> We want more
> We want all
> Your hearts are our goal.
> It is your souls we want.[85]

The totalitarian state seeks to fashion subjects who believe that the party's ideology is the supreme authority; its doctrines provide the final answers to the ultimate questions of history and life. Such unquestioning, faithful subjects can be manipulated by the party. The disinterested search for truth, justice, and goodness—the exploration of those fundamental moral, political, and religious questions that have characterized the Western intellectual tradition for centuries—is abandoned. Truth, justice, and goodness are what the party deems them to be, and ideological deviation is forbidden. "Propaganda does not have anything to do with truth!" Goebbels told his staff during World War II. "We serve truth by serving a German victory."[86]

Intellectuals and creative artists are simply conveyors of official truths, "engineers of human souls," Stalin called them. "From now on it will not be your job to determine whether something is true but whether it is in the spirit of the National Socialist revolution,"[87] the Nazi minister of culture told university professors. Intellectual life is reduced to facilitating the smooth implementation of the ruling party's all-embracing blueprint. Intellectuals in totalitarian society, said Isaiah Berlin, are "technically trained believers who look on the human beings at their disposal as material which is infinitely malleable."[88]

The totalitarian dictatorship deliberately politicizes all areas of human activity. Ideology pervades works of literature, history, philosophy, art, and even science. It dominates the school curriculum and influences everyday speech and social relations. The state is concerned with everything its citizens do: there is no distinction between public and private life, and every institution comes under the party-state's authority. "The only people who still have a private life in Germany are those who are asleep,"[89] declared a high-ranking Nazi. The state relies on propaganda and a vast bureaucracy to deprive people of their capacity for independent thought and judgment, to manipulate people to think, to feel, and to act in conformity with the official ideology. It utilizes the media, parades, mass meetings, sports, theatrical performances, the cinema to keep the population in a state of ideological arousal.

Terror

If voluntary support for the regime cannot be generated by indoctrination, then the state unhesitatingly resorts to terror and violence to compel obedience. People live under a constant strain. Fear of the secret police is ever present; it produces a permanent state of insecurity, which induces people to do everything that the regime asks of them and to watch what they say and do.

Totalitarian regimes find no difficulty in recruiting people to staff the police and bureaucracies engaged in terror. Some recruits, like the activist Kopelev quoted earlier, are true believers committed to the party's ideology; others see an unparalleled opportunity to advance their careers. Still others, concludes George Kennan, are failures and misfits, resentful and brutal people driven by dark instincts:

> They are the ghouls of human society . . . [who, in difficult times, come] slinking out of the shadows, ready to take over, ready to flog, to intimidate, to torture, to do all those things in the company of armed men, and preferably against unarmed ones, that help to give them the illusion of success and security, that dispel for the moment the nightmare of inadequacy by which they are haunted.[90]

THE HOLOCAUST: THE NADIR OF REASON

The West has forged the instruments of reason that make possible a rational comprehension of physical nature and human culture. Nevertheless, despite the value that westerners have given to reason, they have shown a frightening capacity for irrational behavior and a persistent attachment to mythical modes of thought—to ideas that fly in the face of reason, logic, and even sanity. The twentieth century, an era of sophisticated science and high culture, contains numerous examples of the preponderance of mythical thought over rational thought and of deliberate revolts against reason. The history of our century demonstrates anew that reason operates only partially in the world of social and political life.

Idealists and Bureaucrats

The Holocaust—the extermination of European Jewry during World War II—starkly illustrates the limitations of reason and the immense power of the irrational. The SS, who carried out mass murder with fanatical zeal and bureaucratic efficiency, saw themselves as idealists charged with a noble mission to rid the world of worthless life—human devils, poisonous bacteria that were infecting the Volk. These race mystics believed that they were engaged in a life-and-death struggle with evil itself, as the following tract issued by SS headquarters during World War II indicates:

> Just as night rises up against the day, just as light and darkness are eternal enemies, so the greatest enemy of world-dominating man is man himself. The sub-man—that creature which looks as though biologically it were of absolutely the same kind, endowed by Nature with hands, feet and a sort of brain, with eyes and mouth—is nevertheless a totally different, a fearful creature, is only an attempt at a human being with a quasi-human face, yet in mind and spirit lower than any animal. Inside this being a cruel chaos of wild, unchecked passions: a nameless will to destruction, the most primitive lusts, the most undisguised vileness. A sub-man—nothing else! . . . Never has the sub-man granted peace, never has he permitted rest. . . . To preserve himself he needed mud, he needed hell, but not the sun. And this underworld of sub-men found its leader: the eternal Jew![91]

In exterminating the Jewish people, the Nazis believed that they were righteous souls defending the sacred Volk and civilization itself from fiendish foes. They were also symbolically destroying the essential values of the Enlightenment tradition—reason, freedom, equality, toleration, compassion, and individualism—which they despised and with which the Jews, because of their unique historical experience, were identified. They were also trying to cut out the very root of Western civilization's ethical tradition, which Hitler and the SS regarded as a mortal danger to Nazi racial ideology. As Father Jean Dujardin, a French priest, explains,

> . . . ethical Judaism invented and introduced, through Christianity in particular, an ethic of absolute respect for life, of the equal worth of men, of the brotherhood of man. It invented, as Hitler himself said, "Conscience." This ethic is totally incompatible with the idea of a hierarchy of races. Hitler also knew that Judaism introduced monotheism into the history of humanity. This monotheism is unacceptable. Because of its "moral demands," it . . . . is a radical condemnation of all idolatries and therefore of the idolatry of race. . . . So the Jews had to be eliminated . . . for what their existence symbolized.[92]

Many of the SS were ideologues committed to racist doctrines, which they believed were supported by the laws of biology. They were driven by a utopian vision of a new world order founded on a Social Darwinist fantasy of racial hierarchy. To realize this vision of ultimate good, they had to destroy the Jews, whom Nazi ideology designated as the source of all evil.

Other SS and their army of collaborators were simply ordinary people doing their duty as they had been trained to do, following orders
the best way they knew how, morally indifferent bureaucrats concerned with techniques and effectiveness, and careerists and function-
aries seeking to impress superiors with their ability to get the job done.
These people quickly adjusted to the routine of mass murder. Thus,
the thousands of German railway workers "treated the Jewish cattle-
car transports as a special business problem that they took pride in
solving so well."[93] German physicians who selected Jews for the gas
chambers were concerned only with the technical problems, and those
doctors who performed unspeakable medical experiments on Jews
viewed their subjects as laboratory animals. German industrialists
who worked Jewish slave laborers to death considered only cost effectiveness in their operations. So too did the firms that built the gas
chambers and the furnaces, whose durability and effectiveness they
guaranteed. An eyewitness reports that engineers from Topf and Sons
who experimented with different combinations of corpses decided that
"the most economical and fuel-saving procedure would be to burn the
bodies of a well-nourished man and an emaciated woman or vice versa,
together with that of a child, because, as the experiments had established, in this combination, once they had caught fire, the dead would
continue to burn without any further coke being required."[94] Rudolf
Hoess, the commandant of Auschwitz, who exemplified the bureaucratic mentality, tells us how his gas chambers were more efficient
than those used at Treblinka because they could accommodate far
more people. The Germans were so concerned with efficiency and cost
that—to conserve ammunition or gas and not to slow down the pace
from the time victims were ordered to undress until they were hurried
into the chambers—toddlers were taken from their mothers and
thrown live into burning pits or mass graves.

When the war ended, the SS murderers and those that assisted them
returned to families and jobs, resuming a normal life free of remorse
and untroubled by guilt. Several high-ranking Nazis, like Hoess and
Adolf Eichmann, who had organized the deportations to the death
camps, expressed no feelings of wrongdoing at their trials or before
their executions. They insisted that they should not be faulted for
doing what the state had legally authorized. "The human ability to
normalize the abnormal is frightening indeed,"[95] observes sociologist
Rainer C. Baum. Mass murderers need not be psychopaths. It is a "dis-
turbing psychological truth," notes Robert Jay Lifton, that "ordinary
people can commit demonic acts."[96]

Believing that they were cleansing Europe of a lower form of life,
a contemptible and dangerous people that was a mortal threat to
the German race, Nazi executioners performed their evil work with

dedication and resourcefulness, with assembly-line precision, and with moral indifference—a terrible testament to human irrationality and wickedness. Using the technology and bureaucracy of a modern state, the Germans, with scrupulous attention to technical problems, systematically slaughtered approximately 6 million Jews—two-thirds of the Jewish population of Europe. Some 1.5 million of the murdered were children; nearly 90 percent of the Jewish children in German-controlled Europe perished.

The Holocaust was heightened irrationality and organized evil on an unprecedented scale. Auschwitz, Treblinka, Sobibor, and the other death factories represent the triumph of human irrationality over reason—the surrender of the mind to a bizarre racial mythology that provided a metaphysical and pseudoscientific justification for mass murder. But they also represent the ultimate perversion of reason. A calculating reason manufactured and organized lies and demented beliefs into a structured system with its own inner logic and employed sophisticated technology and administrative techniques to destroy human beings spiritually and physically. Science and technology, which had been venerated as the great achievement of the Western mind, made mass extermination possible. The destructive power inherent in reason was unforeseen by the philosophes.

The Failure of European Culture

The Holocaust reveals a depth of wickedness and irrationality in human beings that compels thinking people to question the basic assumptions of Enlightenment humanism: the efficacy of reason, science, and education, and the essential goodness of human nature. The venerable humanist tradition of learning, high culture, and cultivated taste proved to be a very fragile barrier against human bestiality. How do we explain the fact that commanders of the *Einsatzgruppen*—the murder squads that slaughtered some 2 million Russian Jews—43 percent of whom had doctorate degrees, "were among the most highly educated of all the leaders of the Third Reich"? That several prominent figures in the bureaucracy of death listened to or played Mozart and Beethoven, read Goethe, visited art museums? That their love of high culture remained unaffected by their vile deeds? Elie Wiesel, a survivor and sensitive interpreter of the Holocaust, reflects on this point:

> Most of the killers of the *Einsatzgruppen* had college degrees. They knew what they were doing before they did it, while they did it, and after they did it. These people went to school ten, fifteen, twenty years to get a doctorate. How could they kill children—poor innocent, beautiful Jewish children—in the presence of their mothers? They were men of cul-

ture. They were educated. All the books they had read in college, all the ideas they had absorbed, all the music they had loved: is it possible that their education presented no problem to them? Is it possible that their knowledge was no obstacle?[97]

Scientists committed to rigorous objectivity also surrendered to myth's enticements. Thus, Nobel Prize laureate Johannes Stark advocated an "Aryan physics" and sought to cleanse German science of its "Jewish spirit." He stated that

> natural science is overwhelmingly a creation of the Nordic-Germanic blood component of the Aryan peoples. Anyone who . . . compares the faces of outstanding natural scientists will find the common Nordic-Germanic features in almost all of them. The ability to observe and respect facts, in complete disregard of the "I," is the most characteristic feature of the scientific activity of German types. . . . The Jewish spirit is wholly different in its orientation. . . . it is not able to rise to authentic creative work, to great discoveries in the natural sciences. . . . True, Heinrich Hertz made the great discovery of electromagnetic waves, but he was not a full-blooded Jew. He had a German mother, from whose side his spiritual endowment may well have been conditioned.[98]

Anthropologists and psychologists wrote "learned" treatises attesting to Jewish inferiority and endorsed Nazi racial laws and policies. Eugen Fisher, professor of anthropology at the University of Berlin, told an audience of French intellectuals in Paris in 1941, shortly after the Nazi invasion of Russia, that the "morals and actions of the Bolshevist Jews bear witness to such a monstrous mentality that we can only speak of inferiority and of beings of another species."[99]

Some thinkers with a religious bent interpret the Holocaust as proof of the failure of secularism and humanism, the very foundations of modern Western civilization. These interpreters regard Nazism as a neopagan religion that filled a spiritual vacuum caused by the decline of Christianity. For them, Nazism and the Holocaust were the consequence of westerners dethroning God and installing the human being as the ultimate authority—and eventually erecting and worshiping human idols. Hence the cult of the nation, the cult of the race, and the cult of the leader. These sinful acts culminated in a predictable disaster. Humanism, which made the individual, not God, the center of existence, and gave supreme value to human reason rather than to God's commands, could not contain Nazism's demonic evil.

To this critique of modern secularism and humanism, it could be replied that believing Christians also embraced Hitler and Nazism, participated in the slaughter of innocents, and saw no conflict between their faith and their deeds. At least one member of the *Einsatzgruppen* was a pastor, several chaplains witnessed the mass murder and remained silent, and some murderers solemnly celebrated Christmas. The Jews of Slovakia were deported while Father Jozef Tiso, a Catholic priest, headed the government, and Croatian priests actively participated in the persecution and slaughter of Jews and Serbs. Nor did the German churches find the moral courage to protest first the humiliation and persecution of Jews and then their deportation and extermination. Both the Enlightenment and the Christian traditions had failed the West.

The Holocaust has compelled Christian thinkers to confront hard and disquieting questions: To what extent did centuries old Christian anti-Semitism—"the teaching of contempt"—prepare the way for Nazi racial anti-Semitism? Did this religiously fomented anti-Judaism help shape an attitude of mind that led the Nazis to single out the Jews as a contemptible people? Did it lead many Germans in the 1930s, including members of the clergy and prominent theologians, to endorse Nazi legislation that stripped Jews of their civil rights, deprived them of their employment, and inflicted on them numberless humiliations? Did it spur people during the war, particularly in eastern Europe, where a vulgar anti-Semitism was rampant, to give tacit approval to the mass murder of Jews, to assist the Nazis, and even to celebrate the executions—"with cheers and laughter" noted one German officer as Lithuanians systematically beat their Jewish fellow citizens to death in front of a festive crowd? Did it desensitize people, including large numbers of the clergy, to Jewish suffering and even made them interpret the the deportation and slaughter of Jews as divine punishment for the crucifixion and for the Jews' rejection of Christ as messiah?* Did it cause some of the murderers to believe that they were doing God's work? "It is senseless to conceal that the roots of the Holocaust are reaching very deep in the history of the Christian Church and its theology,"[100] declares German theologian Paul Gerhard Aring. In recent decades, Christian thinkers have striven to examine these religious roots and to interpret the meaning of the Holocaust for Christianity. They have also struggled to rid Christian teachings and attitudes of a historic anti-Jewish bias, which, argues Eliezer Berkovits, "poisoned the very soul of. . . Western man with Jew-hatred."[101]

In Germany and throughout Nazi-occupied Europe, there could be found practicing Christians, including clergy steeped in Christian teachings, and intellectuals educated in the tradition of high culture who willingly endorsed and propagated Nazi ideology, even when the cattle cars were transporting innocents to death camps. It is a "dark secret," says literary critic David H. Hirsch, that

---

*There were, of course, Christians who opposed the persecution of Jews and some who risked their lives to hide Jews. These "righteous Gentiles" included members of the clergy.

European high culture in its most advanced phase not only was power-less to prevent the construction and implementation of death camps, but actually provided the ideological base on which the death camps were built. . . . The sad fact . . . is that neither European humanism, nor phi-losophy, nor religion, nor learning, nor music, nor art helped to prevent the degradation that European culture wrought upon itself. . . . [T]he cri-sis in Western culture was (and is) . . . the ease with which Europe was Nazified and . . . the rules of civilized human behavior . . . tampered with.[102]

NOTES

1. Quoted in Hans Kohn, *Pan-Slavism* (Notre Dame, Ind.: University of Notre Dame Press, 1953), pp. 66–67.
2. Ibid., p. 44.
3. Quoted in Edward R. Tannen-baum, *1900: The Generation Before the Great War* (Garden City: N.Y.: Doubleday, 1976), p. 337.
4. Quoted in Friedrich Meinecke, *The German Catastrophe* (Boston: Beacon Press, 1963), pp. 23–24.
5. Karl Pearson, *National Life from the Standpoint of Science*, excerpted in *Sources of the Western Tradition*, ed. Marvin Perry et al., 2nd ed. II, 215–216.
6. Quoted in H. W. Koch, "Social Darwinism in the 'New Imperialism,'" in *The Origins of the First World War*, ed. H. W. Koch (New York: Taplinger, 1972), p. 345.
7. Friedrich von Bernhardi, *Germany and the Next War*, trans. Allen H. Powles (New York: Longman's, Green, 1914) p. 18.
8. Quoted in John C. Greene, *The Death of Adam* (New York: Mentor Books, 1961), p. 313.
9. Quoted in Horst von Maltitz, *The Evolution of Hitler's Germany* (New York: MacGraw Hill, 1973), p. 33.
10. Excerpted in Michael D. Biddiss, ed., *Gobineau: Selected Political Writings* (New York: Harper Torchbooks, 1970), p. 41.
11. Quoted in Geoffrey G. Field, *Evangelist of Race: The Germanic Vision of Houston Stewart Chamberlain* (New York: Columbia University Press, 1981), p. 90.
12. Ibid., p. 225.
13. Quoted in Gilmer W. Blackburn, *Education in the Third Reich* (Albany: State University of New York Press, 1985), p. 144.
14. Excerpted in Randolph Braham, ed., *The Origins of the Holocaust: Christian Anti-Semitism* (New York: Institute for Holocaust Studies of the City University of New York, 1986), p. 36.
15. Ibid., p. 37.
16. Karl Dietrich Bracher, *The German Dictatorship*, trans. Jean Steinberg (New York: Praeger, 1970), p. 36.
17. Quoted in Jacob Katz, *The Darker Side of Genius: Richard Wagner's Anti-Semitism* (Hano-

ver, N.H.: University Press of New England, 1986), p. 19.

18. Quoted in Norman Cohn, *Warrant for Genocide* (New York: Harper Torchbooks, 1967), pp. 186–187.

19. Quoted in Raul Hilberg, *The Destruction of European Jews* (Chicago: Quadrangle, 1967), pp. 10–11.

20. Quoted in Helmut Krausnick et al., eds., *Anatomy of the SS State*, trans. Richard Barry et al. (London: Collins, 1968), p. 9.

21. Quoted in Peter G. J. Pulzer, *The Rise of Political Anti-Semitism in Germany and Austria* (New York: Wiley, 1964), p. 299.

22. Arnold J. Toynbee, *Surviving the Future* (New York: Oxford University Press, 1971), pp. 106–107.

23. Quoted in Roland N. Stromberg, *Redemption by War* (Lawrence, Kans.: Regents Press of Kansas, 1982), p. 24.

24. Excerpted in John W. Boyer and Jan Goldstein, eds., *Twentieth-Century Europe*, Vol. 9, in *University of Chicago Readings in Western Civilization* (Chicago: University of Chicago Press, 1987), p. 26.

25. Heinrich von Treitschke, *Politics*, trans. Blanche Dugdale and Torbend Bille, ed. Hans Kohn (New York: Harcourt, Brace, and World, 1963), pp. 39–40.

26. Quoted in James Joll, "The Unspoken Assumptions," in H. W. Koch, ed., *The Origins of the First World War* (New York: Taplinger, 1972), p. 325.

27. From "Peace," in *Collected Poems of Rupert Brooke* (New York: Dodd, Mead, 1941), p. 111.

28. Quoted in Joachim C. Fest, *Hitler* (New York: Harcourt Brace Jovanovich, 1973), p. 66.

29. Ernst Jünger, *The Storm of Steel*, trans. Basil Creighton (London: Chatto and Windus, 1929; New York: Howard Fertig, 1974), pp. 1, 315.

30. Quoted in Stromberg, *Redemption by War*, p. 136.

31. Roland Dorgeles, "After Fifty Years," excerpted in *Promise of Greatness*, ed. George A. Panichas (New York: John Day, 1968), pp. 14–15.

32. Quoted in Barbara Tuchman, *The Guns of August* (New York: Dell, 1962), p. 145.

33. Quoted in Robert G. L. Waite, *Vanguard of Nazism* (New York: Norton, 1969), p. 22.

34. From "Peace," in *Collected Poems of Rupert Brooke*, p. 111.

35. Quoted in J. P. Mayer, *Max Weber and German Politics* (London: Faber and Faber, 1944), p. 74.

36. Quoted in Peter Gay, *Freud: A Life for Our Time* (New York: Norton, 1988), p. 345.

37. Quoted in James Joll, "1914: The Unspoken Assumptions," in Koch, *The Origins of the First World War*, p. 318.

38. Quoted in Ronald Taylor, *Literature and Society in Germany, 1918–1945* (Totowa, N.J.: Barnes and Noble, 1980), p. 4.

39. Stefan Zweig, *The World of Yesterday* (New York: Viking, 1970), pp. 223–224.

40. Quoted in Alistair Horne, *The Price of Glory* (New York: Harper, 1967), p. 240.

41. A. J. P. Taylor, *From Sarajevo to Potsdam* (New York: Harcourt, Brace and World, 1966), pp. 55–56.

42. Paul Valéry, *Variety* (New York:

Harcourt, Brace, 1927), pp. 27–28.

43. Quoted in Modris Eksteins, *Rites of Spring: The Great War and the Birth of the Modern Age* (New York: Doubleday Anchor Books, 1989), p. 232.

44. Quoted in Robert G. L. Waite, *Vanguard of Nazism* (New York: Norton, 1969), p. 42.

45. Quoted in Zeev Sternhill, "Fascist Ideology," in Walter Laqueur, ed., *Fascism: A Reader's Guide* (Berkeley: University of California Press, 1976), p. 338.

46. Quoted in John Weiss, *The Fascist Tradition* (New York: Harper and Row, 1967), p. 9.

47. Quoted in Laqueur, *Fascism: A Reader's Guide*, p. 318.

48. Hajo Holborn, *Germany and Europe* (Garden City, N.Y.: Doubleday Anchor Books, 1971), p. 215.

49. Joachim C. Fest, *Hitler*, trans. Richard and Clara Winston (New York: Harcourt, Brace, Jovanovich, 1974), p. 548.

50. Hermann Rauschning, *Voice of Destruction* (New York: Putnam's, 1940), pp. 225–232.

51. Adolf Hitler, *Mein Kampf*, trans. Ralph Mannheim (Boston: Houghton Mifflin, 1962), p. 289.

52. Quoted in Alan Bullock, *Hitler: A Study in Tyranny* (New York: Harper Torchbooks, 1964), p. 400.

53. *Hitler's Secret Conversations, 1941–1944*, with an introductory essay by H. R. Trevor Roper (New York: Farrar, Strauss and Young, 1953), p. 28.

54. Quoted in J. Lucien Radel, *Roots of Totalitarianism* (New York: Crane Russak, 1975), p. 10.

55. Quoted in Lucy S. Dawidowicz, *The War Against the Jews, 1933–1945* (New York: Holt, Rinehart and Winston, 1975), p. 21.

56. Sigmund Freud, *Civilization and Its Discontents*, trans. and ed. James Strachey (New York: Norton, 1962), p. 61. By permission of W. W. Norton & Company, Inc. Copyright © 1961 by James Strachey. Copright renewed 1989.

57. Quoted in Uri Tal, "Consecration of Politics in the Nazi Era," in *Judaism and Christianity Under the Impact of National Socialism*, eds. Otto Dov Kulka and Paul R. Mendes Flohr, (Jerusalem: Historical Society of Israel, 1987), p. 70.

58. Hitler, *Mein Kampf*, p. 107.

59. Ibid., p. 479.

60. Quoted in Fest, *Hitler*, p. 162.

61. Friedrich Nietzsche, *Human All-Too-Human*, vol. 6, *The Complete Works of Friedrich Nietzsche*, ed. Oscar Levy, trans. Helen Zimmern (London: Foulis, 1910), pt. 1, sec. 52, p. 71.

62. Carl J. Friedrich and Zbigniew K. Brzezinski, *Totalitarian Dictatorship and Autocracy* (New York: A. Praeger, 1961), p. 5.

63. Ibid., p. 7.

64. Quoted in Laqueur, *Fascism: A Reader's Guide*, p. 318.

65. Quoted in Karl J. Newman, *European Democracy Between the Wars* (Notre Dame, Ind.: University of Notre Dame Press, 1971), p. 276.

66. Quoted in Richard Taylor, "Goebels and the Function of Propaganda," in *Nazi Propaganda*, ed. David Welch (Totowa, N.J.: Barnes and Noble, 1983), p. 36.

67. Ernst Rudolf Huber, *Constitutional Law of the Greater Germany*, excerpted in *Readings on Fascism and National Socialism*, selected by members of the Department of Philosophy, University of Colorado (Denver: Swallow, n. d.), p. 17.

68. Quoted in Max Gallo, *Mussolini's Italy* (New York: Macmillan, 1973), p. 218.

69. Quoted in Fest, *Hitler*, p. 532.

70. Quoted in T. L. Jarman, *The Rise and Fall of Nazi Germany* (New York: New York University Press, 1956), p. 182.

71. Quoted in Krausnick et al., *Anatomy of the SS State*, p. 128.

72. Quoted in Roy A. Medvedev, *Let History Judge*, trans. Colleen Taylor (New York: Knopf, 1972), p. 149.

73. Ibid., p. 151.

74. Excerpted in T. H. Rigby, ed., *Stalin* (Englewood Cliffs, N.J.: Prentice-Hall, 1960), p. 311.

75. Hannah Arendt, *The Origins of Totalitarianism* (New York: World, Meridian Books, 1958), p. 469.

76. Karl Dietrich Bracher, *The Age of Ideologies*, trans. Erwald Osers (New York: St. Martin's, 1984), p. 83.

77. Friedrich and Brzezinski, *Dictatorship and Aristocracy*, p. 13.

78. Lev Kopelev, *The Education of a True Believer*, trans. Gary Kern (New York: Harper, 1980), p. 251.

79. Ernest Becker, *Escape from Evil* (New York: Free Press, 1975), pp. 3–4, 142.

80. Quoted in Arendt, *Origins of Totalitarianism*, p. 330.

81. Lev Kopelev, *The Education of a True Believer*, p. 235.

82. Lev Kopelev, *No Jail for Thought*, trans. and ed. Anthony Austin (London: Martin Secker and Warburg, 1977), p. 11.

83. Cohn, *Warrant for Genocide*, p. 180.

84. Quoted in Welch, ed., *Nazi Propaganda*, p. 5.

85. Quoted in J. S. Conway, *The Nazi Persecution of the Churches* (New York: Basic Books, 1968), p. 202.

86. Welch, *Nazi Propaganda*, p. 5.

87. Quoted in Karl Dietrich Bracher, *The German Dictatorship*, trans. Jean Steinberg (New York: Praeger, 1970), p. 268.

88. Isaiah Berlin, *Four Essays on Liberty* (New York: Oxford University Press, 1969), p. 29.

89. Quoted in Detlev J. K. Peukert, *Inside Nazi Germany*, trans. Richard Deveson (New Haven, Conn.: Yale University Press, 1982), p. 237.

90. George F. Kennan, "Totalitarianism in the Modern World," in *Totalitarianism*, ed. Carl J. Friedrich (New York: Grosset and Dunlap, Universal Library, 1964), p. 23.

91. Quoted in Cohn, *Warrant for Genocide*, p. 188.

92. Father Jean Dujardin, "The Shoa—What Should It Teach?" in *Remembering for the Future: The Impact of the Holocaust and Genocide on Jews and Christians*, papers presented at an international scholars' conference held in Oxford, England, 1988 (Oxford: Pergamon Press, 1988), supplementary vol., p. 82.

93. Konnilyn G. Feig, *Hitler's Death Camps* (New York: Holmes and Meir, 1979), p. 37.

94. Quoted in Steven T. Katz, "Technology and Genocide: Technology as a 'Form of Life,'" in *Echoes from the Holocaust*,

eds. Alan Rosenberg and Gerald E. Meyers (Philadelphia: Temple University Press, 1988), p. 281.

95. Rainer C. Baum, "Holocaust: Moral Indifference as the Form of Modern Evil," in *Echoes from the Holocaust* p. 83

96. Robert J. Lifton, *The Nazi Doctors* (New York: Basic Books, 1968). p. 5.

97. Excerpted in Irving Abrahamson, ed., *Against Silence: The Voice and Vision of Elie Wiesel* (New York: Holocaust Library, 1985), I, 119.

98. Excerpted in George L. Mosse, ed., *Nazi Culture* (New York: Grosset and Dunlap, 1966), pp. 266–267.

99. Quoted in Benno Müller-Hill, *Murderous Science*, trans. George Fraser (Oxford: Oxford University Press, 1988), p. 46.

100. Paul Gerhard Aring, "The Challenge to the Christian Community in Germany: Faith, Theology and Practice after the 'Holocaust,'" in *Remembering for the Future*, I, 556.

101. Eliezer Berkovits, "Understanding the Present—to Save the Future," in *Remembering for the Future*, supplementary volume, p. 33.

102. David H. Hirsch, *The Deconstruction of Literature* (Hanover: N.H.: University Press of New England, 1991), pp. 71, 77.

SELECTED READING

Berenbaum, Michael and John K. Roth, eds. *Holocaust: Religious and Philosophical Implications* (1989).

Bracher, Karl Dietrich, *The German Dictatorship* (1970).

———, *The Age of Ideologies* (1984).

Bucheim, Heim, *Totalitarian Rule* (1968).

Cohn, Norman, *Warrant for Genocide* (1967).

Conquest, Robert, *The Harvest of Sorrow: Soviet Collectivization and the Terror-Famine* (1986).

Friedrich, Carl J. ed., *Totalitarianism* (1954).

Friedrich, Carl J. and Zbigniew K. Brzezinski, eds., *Totalitarian Dictatorship and Autocracy* (1956).

Jackel, Eberhard, *Hitler's Weltanschauung* (1972).

Koch, H. W., ed., *The Origins of the First World War* (1972).

Maltitz, Horst von, *The Evolution of Hitler's Germany* (1973).

Mosse, George L., *Nazi Culture* (1966).

———, *Toward the Final Solution* (1978).

———, *The Crisis of German Ideology* (1964).

———, *Germans & Jews* (1970).

Pulzer, Peter G. J., *The Rise of Political Anti-Semitism in Germany and Austria* (1964).

Rosenberg, Alan and Gerald E. Myers, eds., *Echoes from the Holocaust: Philosophical Reflections on a Dark Time* (1988).

Stromberg, Roland N., *Redemption by War: The Intellectuals and 1914* (1982).

Tucker, Robert C., ed., *Stalinism: Essays in Historical Interpretation* (1977).

11

Thought and Culture in an Era of World Wars and Totalitarianism

The presuppositions of the Enlightenment, already eroding in the decades prior to the Great War, seemed near collapse after 1918—another casualty of trench warfare. Economic distress, particularly during the Great Depression, also profoundly disoriented the European mind. Westerners no longer possessed a frame of reference, a common outlook for understanding themselves, their times, or the past. The core principles of Western civilization—the self-sufficiency of reason, the inviolability of the individual, and the existence of objective norms and values— no longer seemed binding or inspiring.

This crisis of consciousness evoked a variety of responses. Having lost faith in the essential meaning of Western civilization, some intellectuals turned their backs on it or found escape in their art. Others sought a new hope in the Soviet experiment. While some tried to reaffirm the liberal-rational-humanist tradition of the Enlightenment, others castigated this tradition as a failure and embraced antidemocratic ideas, including fascism. Christian thinkers, repelled by the secularism, materialism, and rootlessness of the modern age, urged westerners to find renewed meaning and purpose in their ancestral religion. A philosophical movement called existentialism sought to make life authentic in a world stripped of universal values. The atrocities committed during World War II contributed further to the Western mind's radical disorientation.

INTELLECTUALS AND ARTISTS IN TROUBLED TIMES

Postwar Pessimism

After the Great War, Europeans looked at themselves and their civilization differently. It seemed that in science and technology they had unleashed powers that they could not control, and belief in the stability and security of European civilization appeared to be an illusion. Also illusory was the expectation that reason would banish surviving signs of darkness, ignorance, and injustice and usher in an age of continual progress. European intellectuals felt that they were living in a "broken world." In an age of heightened brutality and mobilized irrationality, the values of old Europe seemed beyond recovery. "All the great words," wrote D. H. Lawrence "were canceled out for that generation."[1] The fissures discernible in European civilization before World War I had grown wider and deeper. To be sure, Europe also had its optimists—those who found reason for hope in the League of Nations and in the easing of international tensions in the mid–1920s. However, the Great Depression, the triumph of totalitarianism, and the gathering war clouds in the mid-1930s intensified feelings of doubt and disillusionment.

The somber mood that gripped European intellectuals in the immediate postwar period had been anticipated by Freud in a series of papers published in 1915 under the title "Thoughts for the Times on War and Death." The war, said Freud, stripped westerners of those cultural superimpositions that had served to contain a murderous primeval aggressiveness and threatened to inflict irreparable damage on European civilization.

> We cannot but feel that no event has ever destroyed so much that is precious in the common possessions of humanity, confused so many of the clearest intelligences or so thoroughly debased what is highest . . . . the war in which we had refused to believe broke out, and it brought— disillusionment. . . . It tramples in blind fury on all that comes in its way, as though there were to be no future and no peace among men after it is over. It cuts all the common bonds between the contending peoples, and threatens to leave a legacy of embitterment that will make any renewal of these bonds impossible for a long time to come.[2]

A pessimistic outlook also pervaded Freud's *Civilization and Its Discontents* (1930), in which he held that civilized life was forever threatened by the antisocial and irrational elements of human nature (see Chapter 9). Other expressions of pessimism abounded. "We are living today under the sign of the collapse of civilization,"[3] declared humanitarian Albert Schweitzer in 1923. Paul Valéry stated: "We modern civilizations have learned to recognize that we are mortal like the others. . . . We feel that a civilization is as fragile as life."[4] In 1932, German philosopher Karl Jaspers noted that "There is a growing awareness of imminent ruin tantamount to a dread of the approaching end of all that makes life worthwhile."[5] The novels of Aldous Huxley rejected a belief in progress and expressed a disenchantment with the modern world. Ernest Hemingway's *The Sun Also Rises* (1926) described a lost postwar generation. Erich Maria Remarque's *All Quiet on the Western Front* (1929) expressed the disorientation of young men whose humanity had been diminished by four years of death and brutality. In the following passage, a German soldier ponders the war's impact on youth.

> I am twenty years old; yet I know nothing of life but despair, death, fear, and fatuous superficiality cast over an abyss of sorrow. I see how peoples are set against one another, and in silence, unknowingly, foolishly, obediently, innocently slay one another. I see that the keenest brains of the world invent weapons and words to make it yet more refined and enduring. . . . all my generation is experiencing these things with me. . . . What do they expect of us if a time ever comes when the war is over? Through the years our business has been killing. . . Our knowledge of life is limited to death. What will happen afterwards?[6]

In the "Second Coming" (1919), William Butler Yeats conveyed this sense of dark times:

> Mere anarchy is loosed upon the world,
> The blood-dimmed tide is loosed, and everywhere
> The Ceremony of innocence is drowned;
> The best lack all conviction, while the worst
> Are full of passionate intensity.
> Surely some revelation is at hand
> Surely the Second Coming is at hand.[7]

T. S. Eliot's "The Wasteland" (1922) expressed the feeling of desolation, futility, and uncertainty felt by many of the war generation. In his image of a collapsing European civilization, Eliot creates a macabre scenario. Hooded hordes, modern-day barbarians, swarm over plains and lay waste cities. Jerusalem, Athens, Alexandria, Vienna, and London—each once a great spiritual or cultural center—are now "falling towers." Amid this destruction, one hears "high in the air/Murmur of maternal lamentation."[8]

Jung stated in *Modern Man in Search of a Soul* (1933):

> I believe I am not exaggerating when I say that modern man has suffered an almost fatal shock, psychologically speaking, and as a result has

fallen into profound uncertainty. . . .The revolution in our conscious outlook brought about by the catastrophic results of the World War, shows
itself in our inner life by the shattering of our faith in ourselves and our
own worth. . . . I realize only too well that I am losing my faith in the
possibility of a rational organization of the world, the old dream of the
millennium, in which peace and harmony should rule has grown pale.[9]

In 1936, Dutch historian Johan Huizinga wrote in a chapter entitled
"Apprehension of Doom":

> We are living in a demented world. And we know it . . . . Everywhere
> there are doubts as to the solidity of our social structure, vague fears of
> the imminent future, a feeling that our civilization is on the way to
> ruin. . . . almost all things which once seemed sacred and immutable
> have now become unsettled, truth and humanity, justice and reason. . . .
> The sense of living in the midst of a violent crisis of civilization, threat-
> ening complete collapse, has spread far and wide. . . . How naive the glad
> and confident hope of a century ago, that the advance of science and the
> general extension of education assured the progressive perfection of so-
> ciety, seems to us today![10]

Shortly after the start of World War II, Franz Alexander, a psychiatrist
educated in Hungary and living in the United States since 1931, reflected on Europe after World War I in *Our Age of Unreason:*

> I saw the world of my youth rapidly disintegrate and standards and ideals
> which had become second nature to me vanish. Like most European ob-
> servers of these eventful years I saw that a cultural epoch was in the
> process of dissolution. What would follow was not clear, but much
> clearer was what was specifically disappearing, the highest values I had
> known; science and artistic creation for their own sakes, the gradual
> improvement of human relations by the use of knowledge and reason
> were giving way to a chaotic sense of insecurity, fear, and distrust. . . .
> Everyone expected the worst, was worried, strained, and was concerned
> with . . . his uncertain future.[11]

The most influential expression of pessimism was Oswald Spengler's *The Decline of the West.* Published in July 1918, as the Great
War was drawing to a close, the first volume appeared and achieved
instant notoriety, going through fourteen printings by 1920. The second volume appeared in 1922. The work was particularly well received
in Spengler's native Germany, shattered by defeat. Spengler viewed history as an assemblage of many different cultures, which, like living
organisms, experience birth, youth, maturity, and death. What contemporaries pondered most was Spengler's insistence that Western civilization had entered its final stage and that its death could not be
averted.

Spengler defined a culture as a spiritual orientation that pervades a people's literature, art, religion, philosophy, politics, and economics; each culture has a distinctive style that distinguishes it from another culture. The ancient Greeks, said Spengler, viewed themselves as living in a clearly defined and finite world. Hence, classical sculpture was characterized by the life-sized nude statue, architecture by the temple with small columns, and political life by the small city-state rather than by a kingdom or an empire. Modern westerners, said Spengler, have a different cultural orientation—a Faustian urge to expand, to reach out. Thus, Europeans developed perspectival art, which permits distance to be depicted on a canvas; they sailed the oceans, conquered vast regions of the globe, and communicated over great distances by telephone and telegraph.

Spengler maintained that cultures, like biological organisms, pass through necessary stages: a heroic youth, a creative maturity, and a decadent old age. In its youth, during the Renaissance, said Spengler, Western culture experienced the triumphs of Michelangelo, Shakespeare, and Galileo; in its maturity, during the eighteenth century, it reached its creative height in the music of Mozart, the poetry of Goethe, and the philosophy of Kant. But now, Faustian culture, entering old age, shows signs of decay—a growing materialism and skepticism, a disenchanted proletariat, rampant warfare and competition for empire, and decadent art forms. "Of great painting or great music there can no longer be for Western people, any question,"[12] concluded Spengler.

To an already troubled Western world, Spengler offered no solace. The West, like other cultures and like any living organism, is destined to die; its decline is irreversible, its death inevitable, and the symptoms of degeneration are already evident. Spengler's gloomy prognostication buttressed the fascists, who claimed that they were building a a new and finer civilization on the ruins of a decadent liberal democracy and that the choice was between them and the Bolsheviks.

Literature and Art: Innovation, Disillusionment, and Social Commentary

Postwar pessimism did not prevent writers and artists from perpetuating the cultural innovations initiated before the war. In the works of D. H. Lawrence, Marcel Proust, André Gide, James Joyce, Franz Kafka, T. S. Eliot, and Thomas Mann, the modernist movement achieved a brilliant flowering. Often these writers gave expression to the troubles and uncertainties of the postwar period.

Franz Kafka *(German Information Center)*

Franz Kafka (1883–1924), whose major novels, *The Trial* and *The Castle*, were published after his death, did not receive recognition until after World War II. Yet perhaps better than any other novelist of his generation, Kafka grasped the dilemma of the modern age. There is no apparent order or stability in Kafka's world. Human beings strive to make sense out of life, but everywhere ordinary occurrences thwart them. They are caught in a bureaucratic web that they cannot control; they live in a nightmare society dominated by oppressive, cruel, and corrupt officials and amoral torturers. In Kafka's world, cruelty and injustice are accepted facts of existence, power is exercised without limits, and victims cooperate in their own destruction. Traditional values and ordinary logic do not operate. A world, thought to be secure, stable, and purposeful falls apart.

In *The Trial*, Josef K., an ordinary man who has no consciousness of wrongdoing, is arrested. "K. lived in a country with a legal constitution, there was universal peace, all the laws were in force; who dared seize him in his own dwelling?"[13] Josef K. is never told the reason for his arrest, and he is eventually executed, a victim of institutional evil that breaks and destroys him "like a dog." In these observations, Kafka foretold the character of the emerging totalitarian state. (Kafka's three sisters perished in the Holocaust.)

Kafka, a German-speaking Jew in the alien Slav environment of Czechoslovakia, was intimidated by a tyrannical father. He died at an early age from tuberculosis. Immediately after his death, Milena Jesenská described her lover: "He was a hermit, a man of insight who was frightened by life. . . . He saw the world as being full of invisible demons which assail and destroy defenseless man. . . . All his works describe the terror of mysterious misconceptions and guiltless guilt in human beings."[14]

In voicing his own deep anxieties, Kafka expressed the feelings of alienation and isolation that characterize the modern individual. He explored life's dreads and absurdities, offering no solutions or consolation. In Kafka's works, people are defeated and unable to comprehend the irrational forces that contribute to their destruction. Although the mind yearns for coherence, Kafka tells us that uncertainty, if not chaos, governs human relationships. We can be certain neither of our own identities nor of the world we encounter, for human beings are the playthings of unfathomable forces, too irrational to master. A brooding pessimism about the human condition pervades Kafka's work. One reason for the intensified interest in Kafka after World War II, observes Angel Flores, "is that the European world of the late 30's and 40's with its betrayals and concentration camps, its resulting cruelties and indignities, bore a remarkable resemblance to the world depicted by Kafka in the opening decades of the century. History seems to have imitated the nightmarish background evoked by the dreamer of Prague."[15]

Before World War I, German writer Thomas Mann (1875–1955) had earned a reputation for his short stories and novels, particularly *Buddenbrooks* (1901), which portrayed the decline of a prosperous bourgeois family. During the war, Mann remained a staunch conservative, who considered democracy "foreign and poisonous to the German character. . . . I am deeply convinced that the . . . 'authoritarian state' is and remains the one that is proper and becoming to the German people, and the one they basically want."[16] After the war, he drew closer to liberalism, supporting the Weimar Republic and attacking the Nazi cult of irrationalism.

In *Mario and the Magician* (1930), Mann explicitly attacked Italian fascism and implied that it would have to be resisted by arms. In 1931, two years before Hitler took power, Mann wrote an article, entitled "An Appeal to Reason," in which he described National Socialism and the extreme nationalism it espoused as a rejection of the Western rational tradition and a regression to primitive and barbaric modes of behavior. The nationalism of the day, he said, is

> something quite different from the nationalism of the nineteenth century, with its bourgeois, strongly cosmopolitan and humanitarian cast. It is distinguished in its character by ... its absolute unrestraint, its orgiastic, radically anti-humane, frenziedly dynamic character. ...
>
> Everything is possible, everything is permitted as a weapon against human decency. ... Fanaticism turns into a means of salvation, ... politics becomes an opiate for the masses, ... and reason veils her face.[17]

After Hitler's seizure of power, Mann went to Switzerland and eventually to the United States, where he remained a staunch foe of totalitarianism. In 1938, he denounced Nazism for its

> extreme contempt for humanity ... [and for] turning a nation into an unthinking war-machine in order to control free and thinking citizens. ... Their delight in the abuse of people is dirty and pathological. ... [There is] contempt of pure reason, the denial and violation of truth in favor of power and the interests of the state, the appeal to the lower instincts, to so-called 'feeling', the release of stupidity and evil from the discipline of reason and intelligence, the emancipation of blackguardism—in short a barbarous mob movement.[18]

In describing the crisis of reason that afflicted his generation, he pointed out the surrender "to admiration of the unconscious, to a glorification of instinct. ... And the bad instincts have accordingly been enjoying a heyday. We have seen instead of pessimistic conviction deliberate malice. Intellectual recognition of bitter truth turns into hatred and contempt for mind itself."[19]

In *The Magic Mountain*, begun in 1912 and completed in 1924, Mann reflected on the decomposition of bourgeois European civilization. The novel is set in a Swiss sanitarium, just prior to World War I. The patients, drawn from several European lands, suffer from tuberculosis and are diseased in spirit as well as body. The sanitarium symbolizes Europe. It is the European psyche that is sick and rushing headlong into a catastrophe.

One patient, the Italian Ludovico Settembrini, stands for the humanist ideals of the Enlightenment: reason, individual liberty, and progress. Although Mann is sympathetic to these ideals, he also indicts

Settembrini for his naive faith in progress, his shallow view of human nature, which gives little significance to the will, and his lofty rhetoric. Overestimating the power of the rational, Settembrini foolishly believes that people will mend their ways once they are enlightened by reason. Thus, he even claims that he cured a sick person merely by looking at him "rationally." Settembrini represents a decaying liberalism.

Pitted against Settembrini is Leo Naphta, a Spanish-trained Jesuit of Jewish-Polish descent who represents the revolt against reason in Mann's generation. Naphta rejects completely the Italian's liberal-humanist values. He is an authoritarian who insists that people do not need freedom, but rather authority and discipline imposed by state or church; he is a fanatic who subscribes to torture and terror as a means of imposing authority. Convinced that the dictatorship of the proletariat is the means of salvation demanded by the age, Naphta embraces Marxism. Borrowing from medieval mysticism, Nietzschean irrationalism, and Marxist militancy, he attacks every facet of the existing liberal order.

Mynheer Peeperkorn, a wealthy Dutch planter from Java, is nonintellectual, illogical, and inarticulate, but he radiates pure vitality and emotional intensity. This charismatic personality dwarfs the humanist Settembrini and the authoritarian Naphta and dominates the patients, who find him irresistible.

The Magic Mountain, which ends with the advent of World War I, raised, but did not resolve, crucial questions. Was the epoch of rational-humanist culture drawing to a close? Did bourgeois Europe welcome its spiritual degeneration in the same way that some of the patients in the sanitarium had a will-to-illness? How could Europe rescue itself from decadence?

D. H. Lawrence (1885–1930), the son of an illiterate British coal miner, was saddened and angered by the consequences of industrial society—the deterioration of nature, tedious work divorced from personal satisfaction, and a life-denying quest for wealth and possessions. He looked back longingly on preindustrial England and wanted people to reorient their thinking away from moneymaking and suppression of the instincts. In *Lady Chatterley's Lover* (1928) and other works, he dealt with the clash between industrial civilization and the needs of human nature, between regimentation and passion.

Like nineteenth-century romantics, Lawrence found a higher truth in deep-seated passion than in reason. This led him to rail against Christianity for stifling human sexuality. Like Nietzsche, he believed that excessive intellectualizing destroyed the life-affirming, instinctual part of human nature. In 1913, he wrote:

> My great religion is a belief in the blood, the flesh, as being wiser than
> the intellect. We can go wrong in our minds, but what our blood feels
> and believes and says is always true. The intellect is only a bit and a
> bridle. What do I care about knowledge. All I want is to answer to my
> blood without fribbling intervention of mind, or moral, or what not. . . .
> We have got so ridiculously mindful that we never know that we our-
> selves are anything.[20]

Many writers, shattered by World War I, disgusted by fascism's growing strength, and moved by the terrible suffering of the depression, became committed to social and political causes. Erich Maria Remarque's *All Quiet on the Western Front* (1929) was one of many
antiwar novels. In *The Grapes of Wrath* (1939), John Steinbeck captured the suffering of American farmers driven from their land by the
Dust Bowl and foreclosure during the depression. George Orwell's
Road to Wigan Pier (1937) recorded the bleak lives of English coal miners. Orwell (see pages 431–433) showed how poverty stifles the human
spirit and how idle it is to talk about the higher things in life and about
political freedom to the hungry and the destitute. Ignazio Silone, who
was expelled from fascist Italy, combined Christian ethics with socialist idealism in his novels, particularly *Bread and Wine* (1937). Few issues stirred the conscience of intellectuals as did the Spanish Civil
War, and many of them volunteered to fight with the Spanish Repub-
licans against the fascists. Ernest Hemingway's *For Whom the Bell
Tolls* (1940) expressed their sentiments.

The new directions taken in art before World War I—abstractionism
and expressionism—continued in the postwar decades. Picasso,
Mondrian, Kandinsky, Matisse, Rouault, Braque, Modigliani, and
other masters continued to refine their styles. In addition, new art
trends emerged, mirroring the trauma of a generation that had experienced the war and lost faith in Europe's moral and intellectual
values.

In 1915, in Zurich, artists and writers founded a movement called
Dada to express their revulsion against the war and the civilization
that spawned it. From neutral Switzerland the movement spread to
Germany and Paris. Dadaists expressed contempt for established artistic and literary standards and rejected both God and reason. "Through
reason man becomes a tragic and ugly figure," said one Dadaist;
"beauty is dead," said another. Dada shared in the postwar mood of
disorientation and despair. Disdaining a civilization that had given rise
to the world war, Dadaists viewed life as essentially futile and absurd
(Dada is a nonsense term). They celebrated the irrational and the instinctual and cultivated indifference. "The acts of life have no beginning or end. Everything happens in a completely idiotic way," declared

the poet Tristan Tzara, one of Dada's founders and its chief spokesman. Tzara elevated spontaneity above reason:

> What good did the theories of the philosophers do us? Did they help us to take a single step forward or backward? . . . . We have had enough of the intelligent movements that have stretched beyond measure our credulity in the benefits of science. What we want now is spontaneity because everything that issues freely from ourselves, without the intervention of speculative ideas, . . . represents us.[21]

For Dadaists the world was nonsensical and reality disordered; hence, they offered no solutions to anything. "Like everything in life, Dada is useless,"[22] said Tzara.

Dadaists showed their contempt for art (one art historian calls Dada "the first anti-art movement on record"[23]) by deliberately producing works seemingly devoid of artistic value. Marcel Duchamp's shovel is an example, as is his *Mona Lisa with a Mustache.* Despite the Dadaists' nihilistic aims and "calculated irrationality," says art historian H. W. Janson, "there was also liberation, a voyage into unknown provinces of the creative mind." Thus, Duchamp's painting with the nonsense title *Tu m'* was "dazzlingly inventive [and] far ahead of its time."[24]

Dada ended as a formal movement in 1924 and was succeeded by surrealism. Surrealists inherited from Dada a disdain for reason; they stressed fantasy and made use of Freudian insights and symbols in their art to reproduce the raw state of the unconscious and to arrive at truths beyond reason's grasp. André Breton, a surrealist French poet, expressed the surrealists' fascination with the irrational:

> We still live under the reign of logic, but the methods of logic are applied nowadays only to the resolution of problems of secondary interest. . . . Under color of civilization, under the pretext of progress all that rightly or wrongly may be regarded as fantasy or superstition has been banished from the mind, all uncustomary searching after truth has been proscribed. It is only by what must seem sheer luck that there has recently been brought to light an aspect of mental life—to my belief by far the most important—with which it was supposed that we no longer had any concern. All credit for these discoveries must go to Freud. . . . The imagination is perhaps on the point of reclaiming its rights.[25]

To penetrate the interior of the mind, said Breton, writers should "write quickly without any previously chosen subject, quickly enough not to dwell on and not to be tempted to read over what . . . [they] have written."[26] Writing should not be dictated by the intellect but should flow automatically from the unconscious. Surrealists tried to portray the world of fantasy and hallucination, the marvelous and the spontaneous. Breton urged artists to live their dreams, even if it meant seeing "a horse galloping on a tomato." In their attempt to break through the constraints of rationality in order to reach a higher reality—that is, a "surreality"—leading surrealists like Max Ernst (1891–1976), Salvador Dali (1904–1989), and Joan Miró (1893–1983) produced works of undeniable artistic merit.

Artists, like writers, expressed a social conscience. George Grosz combined a Dadaist sense of life's meaninglessness with a new realism to depict the moral degeneration of middle-class German society. In *After the Questioning* (1935), Grosz, then living in the United States, dramatized Nazi brutality; in *The End of the World* (1936), he expressed his fear of an impending second world war. Max Beckmann's service in the German army during World War I made him acutely aware of violence and brutality, which he expressed in *The Night* (1918–19) and other paintings. Designated a "degenerate artist" by the Nazis, Beckmann went into exile in Holland. In his etchings of maimed, dying, and dead soldiers, German artist Otto Dix produced a powerful visual indictment of the Great War's cruelty and suffering. Still another German artist, Käthe Kollwitz, showed a deep compassion for the sufferer—the unemployed, the hungry, the ill, the politically oppressed. In *Guernica* (1937), Picasso memorialized the Spanish village decimated by the fascists' saturation bombing during the Spanish Civil War. In the *White Crucifixion* (1938), Marc Chagall, a Russian-born Jew who had settled in Paris, depicted the terror and flight of Jews in Nazi Germany.

In a series of paintings, *The Passion of Sacco and Vanzetti* (1931–1932), American artist Ben Shahn showed his outrage at the execution of two radicals. William Gropper's *Migration* (1932) dramatized the suffering of the same dispossessed farmers described in Steinbeck's novel, *The Grapes of Wrath*. Philip Evergood, in *Don't Cry Mother* (1938–1944), portrayed the apathy of starving children and their mother's terrible helplessness.

ANTIDEMOCRATIC THOUGHT

A growing pessimism and disillusionment with traditional liberal-democratic values led many intellectuals to turn to fascism or communism as salvationist ideologies. "[I]t remains a paradoxical phenomenon," observes Karl Dietrich Bracher, "that writers and artists, philosophers and intellectuals, who more than anyone else are dependent on freedom and uncontrolled thought, seem to develop a strange weakness for revolutionary but intellectually closed systems of ideas."[27] And George Lichtheim points out, "it is a myth that the Nazi movement represented only 'the mob.' It had conquered the universities before it triumphed over society. The SS leaders were for the most part academically trained."[28] The appeal of fascism to intel- lectuals shattered the liberal assumption that educated people would reject irrational beliefs and support humanitarian causes.

Many intellectuals saw in fascism a way of awakening the soul and regenerating artistic creativity that had been deadened by a bourgeois civilization whose highest ideals were money and possessions. They hoped that these goals would be realized through the spiritual unity of the nation, the principal aim of fascism. Some intellectuals were at- tracted by fascism's activism (that not the word, but the deed gives life meaning), its elitism and cult of the hero (Nietzschean superman with the will to lead and to create), and its praise of war (the most genuine of life's experiences).

In Germany, right-wing intellectuals—Spengler, Ernst and Friedrich Georg Jünger, Ludwig Klage, Moeller van den Bruck and others—at- tacked the democratic Weimar Republic. They viewed it as the triumph of mediocrity and a barrier to the true unity of the German nation. Regarding democracy as the root cause of the disintegration of German society, they advocated authoritarian rule. In the tradition of nineteenth-century Volkish thinkers, they had contempt for reason and political freedom and glorified instincts, blood, the racial soul, soil, and the folk community—the nonrational wellspring of the true Ger- man spirit. In the brittle disunity and disorientation of German soci- ety, advocates of "life philosophy" searched for community and cer- tainty in the special qualities of the German soul. And in their view, the intellect was the soul's enemy, a barrier to grasping instinctual truths that emanated from the German Volk.

The Weimar Republic, said the conservative right, was out of har- mony with German tradition. Germany, they argued, should reject Western liberal democracy—a product of Anglo-Saxon materialism— and create an authoritarian government that would overcome a divi- sive individualism, provide order and authority, and revive the German virtues of heroism, community, and idealism. Friedrich Georg Jünger's *The Rise of the New Nationalism* (1926) expressed the radical conserv- atives' conception of Germany's high cultural mission:

> The new nationalism is born of the new awareness of blood-bonded community; it wants to make the promptings of the blood prevail. The new nationalism wants to strengthen the blood bonds and form them into a new state. Those who are part of an alien blood community . . . are excluded. They have to be driven out because they weaken the rich and fertile body of the nation that nourishes everything of signifi- cance. . . . Nationalism must apply its force to the masses and try to set them afire. . . . These means are neither parliaments nor parties, but rather military units mobilized by a fierce loyalty to a leader. . . . The

intensity of their discipline is the decisive factor. Next comes the urgent task to create a mighty organization covering all of Germany and to seize the reins of government. The community of blood is given the highest priority. . . . It recognizes no European community, no common human- ity. . . . We want the sharpest separation of races. The new state, ob- viously, will be authoritarian, . . . all-surpassing . . . the new steel-like instrument of power. . . . That state shall be the mold for the nation's blood-bound will to power. For that reason the nationalist movement urges the annihilation of all political forms of liberalism. No more par- ties, parliaments, elections![29]

Radical conservative intellectuals were heirs of the romantic, irra- tional, and antimodernist strain of German nationalism. Like their nineteenth-century Volkish predecessors, they revolted against many features of the modern world—liberalism and rationalism—and looked back longingly to a distant mythical past. They aspired to protect the Volk from the corrupting influences of liberalism, which they viewed as hostile to life. They posited a militaristic, active, and heroic life and the spiritual unity of the nation as antidotes to the soullessness, arti- ficiality, and fragmentation of modern liberal society. Some intellec- tuals of the right were often contemptuous of Hitler, viewing him as a man from the mob. Nevertheless, by turning many Germans against the republic and democracy, radical conservatives helped prepare peo- ple's minds to accept National Socialism. German historian Kurt Son- theimer concludes:

> The submission of a large part of German intellectual society to the National Socialist *Weltanschauung* . . . would have been inconceivable without the anti-democratic intellectual movement that preceded it and that, in its contempt for everything liberal, had blunted people's sensi- bilities to the inviolable rights of the individual and the preservation of human dignity. . . . Nothing is more dangerous in political life than the abandonment of reason. The intellect must remain the controlling, reg- ulating force in human affairs. The anti-democratic intellectuals of the Weimar period betrayed the intellect to 'Life.' They despised reason and found more truth in myth or in the blood surging in their veins. . . . Had they a little more reason and enlightenment, these intellectuals might have seen better where their zeal was leading them and their country.[30]

Attracted to this irrational philosophy of life and struggle, many German intellectuals welcomed the destruction of the Weimar Repub- lic, which they derisively called "the republic of reason," and the triumph of National Socialism, which they viewed as a national awak- ening, a true expression of the German soul. Hoping for a resurgence of a German folk tradition, some intellectuals hailed Hitler as Ger- many's savior. Thus, Martin Heidegger (see pages 446–447), a leading philosopher, who was elected Rector of Freiburg University by an almost unanimous vote of the faculty (purged of Jews) in April 1933, praised the new regime for attempting a radical transformation of German society and urged students to dedicate themselves to this process. "Do not let principles and 'ideas' be the rule of your existence," he told them. "The Fuehrer himself, and he alone, is the German reality of today, and of the future, and of its law."[31]

For Heidegger, Nazism contained an inner truth: it bound together the German people in a love for the land. Such love and unity, he felt, countered the soul-destroying rationality of the machine age. Idealization of the Volk heritage would help overcome the alienation of modern society.

Many German university professors lauded Hitler's racial and antidemocratic theories, preached them to their students, and justified the new regime. It is also true that some of these same people later became disillusioned and turned their backs on the Nazi state. A number went into exile, some were sent to concentration camps or executed, and several were involved in the July 20, 1944, plot to assassinate Hitler.

Several English-speaking writers, including Wyndham Lewis, Ezra Pound, T. S. Eliot, W. B. Yeats, and D. H. Lawrence, attacked democracy and expressed sympathy for fascist ideas, at least until England was threatened by Nazi power. English thinkers built on the powerful tradition of British antidemocratic thought that included Edmund Burke's hostility to the French Revolution, Thomas Carlyle's adulation of the heroic leader, and a long-standing elitist scorn of democracy for undermining high cultural standards. "Democracy is dead and force claims its ancient right," wrote Yeats in 1921. "With democracy has died too the old political generalisations."[32] Two years later, he warned that "generations to come will have for their task, not the widening of liberty, but recovery from its errors—the building up of authority, the restoration of discipline, the discovery of a life sufficiently heroic to live without the opium dream."[33] Such thinkers saw fascist leaders—at least in fascism's early stages—as heroic figures who were rescuing society from rule by the unfit masses and imposing a stable order that would foster cultural creativity. Some hoped that a fascist-type regime would give creative artists proper recognition, including a leadership role in political life.

France had several fascist or neofascist organizations by the late 1930s, including the *Parti populaire français*, the *Croix de feu*, the *Jeunesses patriotes*, the *Solidarité française*, and Charles Maurras' *Action français*, that attracted many young people and intellectuals. French fascism had its spiritual roots in the long-standing conservative hostility to the Enlightenment and the French Revolution, the integral nationalism preached by Maurice Barres (1862–1923) and Charles Maurras (1868–1952), the clerical, nationalist, and aristocratic rejection of the Third French Republic and of democracy, and a deeply embedded anti-Semitism, which grew more virulent at the time of the Dreyfus affair.

During World War II, a number of prominent French intellectuals, including Pierre Drieu la Rochelle (1893–1945), and Louis-Ferdinand Céline (1894–1961) collaborated with the Nazi occupiers. Drieu la Rochelle, a cultivated poet, novelist, and essayist, was attracted to fascism's dynamism, its cult of action, heroism, virility, and youth. Believing that a hedonistic liberalism and egalitarian Marxism had drained France of its will and vitality, Drieu saw fascism as a means to spiritual regeneration, a way of overcoming decadence. Fascism would replace a spiritually bankrupt leadership with a new and virile elite. His empathy for fascism also derived from a romantic temperament. He regarded fascism as passionate; it awakened the soul and stimulated the instincts. It was a revolution of the spirit—the triumph of idealism over materialism, of will over rationalism. Such an outlook led him to blame France's defeat in 1940 on a debilitating rationalism: "France has been destroyed by a rationalism that has reduced its genius. Today rationalism is beaten. One can only rejoice at rationalism's discomfort."[34]

COMMUNISM: "THE GOD THAT FAILED"

The economic misery of the depression and the rise of fascist barbarism led many intellectuals to find a new hope, even a secular faith, in communism. They praised the Soviet Union for supplanting capitalist greed with socialist cooperation, for recognizing the dignity of work and replacing a haphazard economic system marred by repeated depressions with one based on planned production, and for providing employment for everyone when joblessness was endemic in capitalist lands. Seduced by Soviet propaganda and desperate for an alternative to crisis-ridden democracy, these intellectuals saw the Soviet Union as a champion of peace and social justice.

American literary critic Edmund Wilson said that in the Soviet Union one felt at the "moral top of the world where the light never really goes out."[35] British political theorists Sidney and Beatrice Webb declared that there was no other country "in which there is actually so much widespread public criticism and such incessant reevaluation of its shortcomings as in the USSR."[36] To these intellectuals, it seemed that in the Soviet Union a vigorous and healthy civilization was emerging and that only communism could stem the tide of fascism. For many, however, the attraction was short-lived. Sickened by Stalin's purges and terror, the denial of individual freedom, and the suppression of truth, they came to view the Soviet Union as another totalitarian state and communism as another "god that failed."

One such intellectual was Arthur Koestler (1905–1983). Born in Budapest of Jewish ancestry and educated in Vienna, Koestler worked as a correspondent for a leading Berlin newspaper chain. He joined the Communist party at the very end of 1931 because he "lived in a disintegrating society thirsting for faith," was sensitized by the depression, and saw communism as the "only force capable of resisting the inrush of the primitive [Nazi] horde."[37] Koestler visited the Soviet Union in 1933, experiencing firsthand both the starvation brought on by forced collectivization and the propaganda that grotesquely misrepresented life in Western lands. Although his faith was shaken, he did not break with the party until 1938, in response to Stalin's liquidations.

In *Darkness at Noon* (1941), Koestler explored the attitudes of the Old Bolsheviks, who were imprisoned, tortured, and executed by Stalin. These dedicated Communists had served the party faithfully— many were heroes of the Revolution—but Stalin, fearing opposition, hating intellectuals, and driven by megalomania, denounced them as enemies of the people. In *Darkness at Noon,* the leading character, the imprisoned Rubashov, is a composite of the Old Bolsheviks. Although innocent, and without being physically tortured, Rubashov publicly confesses to political crimes that he never committed.

Rubashov is aware of the suffering that the party has brought to the Russian people:

> ... in the interests of a just distribution of land we deliberately let die of starvation about five million farmers and their families in one year. ... [to liberate] human beings from the shackles of industrial exploitation ... we sent about ten million people to do forced labour in the Arctic regions and the jungles of the East, under conditions similar to those of antique galley slaves. ... to settle a difference of opinion, we know only one argument: death. ... Our poets settle discussions on questions of style by denunciations to the secret police. ... The people's standard of life is lower than it was before the Revolution, the labour conditions are harder, the discipline is more inhuman. ... Our Press and our schools cultivate Chauvinism, militarism, dogmatism, conformism and ignorance. The arbitrary power of the Government is unlimited, and unexampled in history. Freedom of the Press, of opinion and of movement are as thoroughly exterminated as though the proclamation of the Rights of Man had never been. We have built up the most gigantic police apparatus, with informers made a national institution, and with the most refined scientific system of physical and mental torture. We whip the groaning masses of the country towards a theoretical future happiness which only we can see.[38]

Pained by his own complicity in the party's crimes, including the betrayal of friends, Rubashov questions the party's philosophy that the individual should be subordinated, and if necessary, sacrificed to the regime. Nevertheless, Rubashov remains the party's faithful servant; true believers do not easily break with their faith. By confessing to treason, Rubashov performs his last service for the revolution: for the true believer, everything—truth, justice, and the sanctity of the individual—is properly sacrificed to the party.

REAFFIRMING THE CHRISTIAN WORLD-VIEW

By calling into question core liberal beliefs—the essential goodness of human nature, the primacy of reason, the efficacy of science, and the inevitability of progress—the Great War led some thinkers to find in Christianity an alternative view of the human experience and the crisis of the twentieth century. Christian thinkers, including Karl Barth, Christopher Dawson, Paul Tillich, Reinhold Niebuhr, Jacques Maritain, and T. S. Eliot, asserted the reality of evil in human nature. They assailed liberals and Marxists for holding too optimistic a view of human nature and human reason, for postulating a purely rational and secular philosophy of history, and for anticipating an ideal society within the realm of historical time. For these thinkers, the Christian conception of history as a clash between human will and God's commands provided an intelligible explanation for the tragedies of the twentieth century. Karl Barth (1886–1968), the Swiss-German Protestant theologian, called for a reaffirmation of the Christ of faith, the uniqueness of Christianity, and the spiritual power of divine revelation. The true meaning of history, he said, is not to be found in the liberal view of the progress of reason and freedom or the Marxist conception of economic determinism. Rather, it derives from the fact that history is the arena in which the individual's faith is tested.

Jacques Maritain (1882–1973), a leading Catholic thinker, denounced core elements of the modern outlook—the self-sufficiency of the individual, the autonomy of the mind, and a nonreligious humanism—and urged revivifying the Christian philosophy of Thomas Aquinas, which, he said, successfully harmonized faith and reason. A strong advocate of political freedom, Maritain stressed the link between modern democracy and the Christian Gospels, which proclaimed "the natural equality of all men, children of the same God and redeemed by the same Christ . . . [and] the inalienable dignity of every soul fashioned in the image of God."[39] He insisted that "the democratic state of mind and . . . the democratic philosophy of life requires the energies of the Gospel to penetrate secular existence, taming the irrational to reason."[40] These energies would control the human propensity for self-centeredness, wickedness, and hatred of others. To survive, secular democracy needs to be infused with Christian love and compassion.

Christopher Dawson (1889–1970), an English Catholic thinker, stressed the historic ties between Christianity and Western civilization. In 1933, he wrote that "If our civilization is to recover its vitality or even to survive, it must cease to neglect its spiritual roots and must realize that religion is not a matter of personal sentiment . . . but . . . the very heart of social life and the root of every living culture."[41]

In 1934, British historian Arnold Toynbee (1889–1970) published the first three volumes of his monumental work, *A Study of History*, in which he tried to account for the rise, growth, breakdown, and disintegration of civilization. The next three volumes were published in 1939, and volumes seven to ten in 1954. The first six volumes were written at a time when Western civilization seemed to be breaking down. The world wars, the Great Depression, and totalitarianism had shattered Toynbee's Victorian optimism and his confidence in traditional liberal beliefs in reason, human nature, science, and technology. From his comparative study of all the world's civilizations, living and dead, Toynbee arrived at universal principles that apply to civilization in general. He concluded that civilizations rise and grow when a creative minority successfully responds to challenges. Conversely, a civilization declines when its leadership deteriorates and it no longer responds imaginatively to challenges, thereby disrupting the process of growth. Three broad patterns characterize a civilization in disintegration:

1. States sharing the same civilization wear each other out in warfare until a single half-dead state is left.
2. To preserve its power, the once-creative minority relies increasingly on force and oppression, causing it to lose the allegiance of the masses. Thus society is divided into three groups: a dominant but uncreative minority, an oppressed and alienated internal proletariat, and an external proletariat consisting of barbarian war bands on the borders.
3. In a last gasp of creativity, the dominant minority creates a universal state, i.e., the Roman Empire—which temporarily slows down the process of disintegration. In an act of momentous significance for the future, the disinherited and exploited internal proletariat gives rise to a universal church, i.e., Christianity. In Toynbee's view,

a civilization's breakdown provides an opportunity for spiritual growth.

Underlying Toynbee's philosophy of history was a religious orientation, for he saw religious prophets as humanity's greatest figures and higher religions as humanity's greatest achievement. Thus, he regarded the Middle Ages as a spiritual advance over a decadent Greco-Roman civilization and the emergence of modern secular civilization from the womb of the Middle Ages as spiritual regression. In the tradition of the Hebrew prophets and Christian thinkers, Toynbee held that history was "ultimately a quest for the vision of God in History."[42] He interpreted the crises of the modern West in religious terms, attributing the problems of Western civilization to its breaking away from Christianity and its embracing of "false idols," particularly the national state which, he said, had become the object of westerners' highest reverence.

Toynbee regarded nationalism as a primitive religion that induces people to revere the national community rather than God. This deification of the "parochial"—tribal or local—community, he said, intensifies the brutal side of human nature and sets people against people. To Toynbee, Nazism was the culmination of the worst elements in modern European nationalism, "the consummation . . . of a politico-religious movement, the pagan deification and worship of parochial human communities which had been gradually gaining ground for more than four centuries in the Western world at large."[43] The moral catastrophe of Nazism, he said, demonstrates the inadequacy of liberal humanism, for the Enlightenment tradition proved a feeble barrier to Nazism's rise and spread. The secular values of the Enlightenment divorced from Christianity are insufficient to restrain human nature's basest impulses. It is now impossible to retain a "belief in the inevitable progress of a secularized Western civilizaton and in the self-perfectibility of a graceless human nature."[44]

Toynbee held that the spiritual vacuum created by the West's turning away from Christianity was filled by ideologies, the most dangerous of which was nationalism. Still another idol, technology, attracted westerners who had broken with their ancestral religion. But because human nature remains as sinful as ever, human beings have misused technology.

For the West to save itself, said Toynbee, it must abide by the spiritual values of the world's religious prophets. While Toynbee attributed the highest value to religion, in a strict sense he was not a Christian. He did not accept the Virgin Birth or the Resurrection, and viewed Jesus not as divine but as a great human soul. The essence of Christianity for him was not dogma but the noble ideal that "self-sacrificing love is the most powerful of all the spiritual impulses known to us."[45] Moreover, Toynbee was a religious pluralist, who gave value to the prophets of all the world's higher religions—Judaism, Christianity, Islam, Hinduism, and Buddhism.

REAFFIRMING THE IDEALS OF FREEDOM AND REASON

The rise of fascism and Stalin's terror frightened intellectuals committed to the Enlightenment tradition. These thinkers tried to reaffirm the ideals of rationality and freedom that had been trampled on by the totalitarian movements.

Julien Benda

In *The Treason of the Intellectuals* (1927), Julien Benda (1867–1956), a French cultural critic of Jewish background, castigated intellectuals for intensifying hatred between nations, classes, and political factions. "Our age is indeed the age of the *intellectual organization of political hatreds*,"[46] he wrote. By fomenting political extremism rather than affirming the Western rational-humanist tradition, said Benda, these intellectuals have betrayed their responsibility. They do not pursue justice or truth but proclaim that "even if our country is wrong, we must think of it in the right."[47] They scorn outsiders, extol harshness and action, and proclaim the superiority of instinct and will to intelligence; or they "assert that the intelligence to be venerated is that which limits its activities within the bounds of national interest."[48] The logical end of this xenophobia, said Benda, "is the organized slaughter of nations and classes."[49]

Ortega y Gasset

José Ortega y Gasset (1883–1955), descendant of a noble Spanish family and a professor of philosophy, gained international recognition with the publication of *Revolt of the Masses* (1930). Ortega held that European civilization, the product of a creative elite, was degenerating into barbarism because of the growing power of the masses, who lack the mental discipline and commitment to reason to preserve Europe's intellectual and cultural traditions. Ortega did not equate the masses with the working class and the elite with the nobility; it was an attitude of mind, not a class affiliation, that distinguished the "mass-man" from the elite. The mass-man, said Ortega, has a commonplace mind and does not set high standards for himself. He is inert until driven by an external compulsion. Faced with a problem, he "is satisfied with thinking the first thing he finds in his head" and "crushes . . . everything that is different, everything that is excellent, individual, qualified, and select. Anybody who is not like everybody, who does not think like everybody, runs the risk of being eliminated."[50] Such intellectually vulgar people, declared Ortega, cannot understand or preserve the processes of civilization. The fascists exemplify this revolt of the masses:

> Under fascism there appears for the first time in Europe a type of man who does not want to give reasons or to be right, but simply shows himself resolved to impose his opinions. This is the new thing: the right not to be reasonable, the "reason of unreason." Hence I see the most palpable manifestation of the new mentality of the masses, due to their having decided to rule society without the capacity for doing so.[51]

The mass-man, said Ortega, does not respect the tradition of reason; he does not enter into rational dialogue with others or defend his opinions logically.

> [Because his thoughts are] nothing more than appetites in words. . . . the mass-man would feel himself lost if he accepted discussion. . . . Hence the "new thing" in Europe is to have done with discussions and detestation is expressed for all forms of intercommunion which implies acceptance of objective standards, ranging from conversation to Parliament, and taking in science. This means that there is renunciation of the common life based on culture which is subject to standards and a return to the common life of barbarism.[52]

The mass-man rejects reason and glorifies violence—the ultimate expression of barbarism. If European civilization is to be rescued from fascism and communism, said Ortega, the elite must sustain civilized values and provide leadership to the masses.

Ernst Cassirer

Ernst Cassirer (1874–1945), a German philosopher of Jewish lineage, emigrated after Hitler came to power, eventually settling in the United States. A staunch defender of the Enlightenment tradition, Cassirer wrote in 1932, just prior to Hitler's triumph:

> More than ever before, it seems to me, the time is again ripe for applying . . . self-criticism to the present age, for holding up to it that bright clear mirror fashioned by the Enlightenment. . . . The age which

venerated reason and science as man's highest faculty cannot and must not be lost even for us. We must find a way not only to see that age in its own shape but to release again those original forces which brought forth and molded this shape.[53]

In his last work, *The Myth of the State* (1946), Cassirer described Nazism as the triumph of mythical thinking over reason. The Nazis, said Cassirer, cleverly manufactured myths—of the race, the leader, the party, the state—that disoriented the intellect. Germans who embraced these myths surrendered their capacity for independent judgment, leaving themselves vulnerable to manipulation by the Nazi leadership. Cassirer warned:

> In politics we are always living on volcanic soil. We must be prepared for convulsions and eruptions. In all critical moments of man's social life, the rational forces that resist the rise of old mythical conceptions are no longer sure of themselves. In these moments the time of myth has come again. For myth has not been really vanquished and subjugated. It is always there, lurking in the dark and waiting for its hour and opportunity. This hour comes as soon as the other binding forces of man's social life . . . lose their strength and are no longer able to combat the demonic mythical powers.[54]

To contain the destructive powers of political myths, Cassirer urged strengthening the rational-humanist tradition and called for the critical study of political myths, for "in order to fight an enemy you must know him. . . . We should carefully study the origin, the structure, the methods, and the technique of the political myths. We should see the adversary face to face in order to know how to combat him."[55]

Erich Fromm

Like Cassirer and many other German-Jewish intellectuals, Erich Fromm (1900–1980), a social theorist and psychoanalyst, settled in the United States after the Nazi seizure of power. In *Escape from Freedom* (1941), Fromm sought to explain the triumph of Nazism within the larger context of European history. With the end of the Middle Ages, he said, the individual grew increasingly independent of external authority and experienced new possibilities for personal development. The individual's role in the social order was no longer rigorously determined by birth; increasingly the world was explained in natural terms, freeing people from magic, mystery, and authority; and the possibility for the full development of human potential here on earth was proclaimed. In the political sphere, this new orientation culminated in the democratic state. However, while westerners were becoming more "independent, self-reliant, and critical," they also became "more isolated, alone, and afraid."[56]

During the Middle Ages, said Fromm, the individual derived a sense of security from a structured social system that clearly defined the role of clergy, lords, serfs, and guildsmen and from the Christian world-view that made life and death purposeful. Modern westerners have lost this sense of security, said Fromm. Dwelling in vast cities, threatened by economic crises, and no longer comforted by the medieval conception of life's purpose, they often are tormented by doubts and overwhelmed by feelings of aloneness and insignificance. People try to overcome this "burden of freedom" by surrendering themselves to a person or power that they view "as being overwhelmingly strong"; they trade freedom for security by entering into "a symbiotic relationship that overcomes . . . aloneness."[57]

Because modern industrial society has made the individual feel powerless and insignificant, concluded Fromm, fascism is a constant threat. Fromm would meet the challenge of fascism by creating social conditions that lead the individual to be free and yet not alone, to be critical and yet not filled with doubts, to be independent and yet feel an integral part of humankind. After World War II, in *Man for Himself* (1947), he stated:

> The idea of the dignity and power of man, which gave man the strength and courage for the tremendous accomplishments of the last few centuries, is challenged by the suggestion that we have to revert to the acceptance of man's ultimate powerlessness and insignificance. This idea threatens to destroy the very roots from which our civilization grew. . . .
> I have written this book with the intention of reaffirming the validity of humanistic ethics.[58]

George Orwell

A British novelist and political journalist, George Orwell (1903–1950) wrote two powerful indictments of totalitarianism: *Animal Farm* (1945) and *1984* (1949). In *Animal Farm*, based in part on his experiences with communists during the Spanish Civil War, Orwell satirized the totalitarian regime built by Lenin and Stalin in Russia. In *1984*, written while he was dying of tuberculosis, Orwell, who was deeply committed to reason, human dignity, and freedom, warned that these great principles are now permanently menaced by the concentration and abuse of political power.

The society of 1984 is ruled by the Inner Party, which constitutes some 2 per cent of the population. Heading the Party is Big Brother—most likely a mythical figure created by the ruling elite to satisfy people's yearning for a leader. The Party indoctrinates people to love Big Brother, whose picture is everywhere. Party members are conditioned to accept unquestioningly the Party's orthodoxy, with all its contradictions, twists, and reversals. Doublethink, the prescribed way of thinking, brainwashes people into holding two contradictory beliefs simultaneously and believing that they are both true. The Party's philosophy of government is revealed in three slogans: WAR IS PEACE, FREEDOM IS SLAVERY, IGNORANCE IS STRENGTH. The Ministry of Truth resorts to thought control to dominate and manipulate the masses and to keep Party members loyal and subservient. Independent thinking is destroyed. Objective truth no longer exists. Truth is whatever the Party decrees at the moment. If the Party were to proclaim that two plus two equals five, it would have to be believed.

In the past, tyrants, despots, and dictators claimed that their rule benefited the people. Representing the ruling elite, Dostoevski's Grand Inquisitor (see pages 305–306) insists that the childlike masses are unfit to govern themselves; for their own good, they must be ruled by those who know better. In the tradition of the Grand Inquisitor, the rulers of Hitler's Germany and Stalin's Russia held that the Party ruled in the name of a higher good. Orwell's ruling elite, however, does not pretend to govern in the interests of humanity. It wants power because dominating others, which includes torture and humiliation, is the highest form of pleasure, something that Nietzsche had suggested.

> The Party seeks power entirely for its own sake. We are not interested in the good of others; we are interested solely in power. . . . The real power, the power we have to fight for day and night, is not power over things but over men. . . . Power is in tearing human minds to pieces and putting them together again in new shapes of your own choosing.[59]

Anyone thinking prohibited thoughts is designated a Thoughtcriminal, a crime punishable by death. The Thought Police's agents are ubiquitous, using hidden microphones and telescreens to check on Party members for any signs of deviance from the Party's rules and ideology. On posters displaying Big Brother's picture, the words BIG BROTHER IS WATCHING YOU are written. Believing that "who controls the past controls the future,"[60] the Ministry of Truth alters old newspapers to make the past accord with the Party's current doctrine. In this totalitarian society of the future, all human rights are abolished, people are arrested merely for their thoughts, and children spy on their parents. The society is brutalized by processions of chained prisoners of war, by public mass executions, and by the Two Minutes Hate ritual, which arouses the participants to a frenzy against the Party's enemies. A steady supply of cheap gin and pornographic literature keeps the masses (proles) dull-witted and out of political mischief. A member of the Inner Party describes the Party's totalitarian ambition—Orwell's frightening vision of the future that could befall us.

> Do you begin to see, then, what kind of world we are creating? . . . . Already we are breaking down the habits of thought which have survived from before the Revolution. We have cut the links between child and parent, and between man and man, and between man and woman. No one dares trust a wife or a child or a friend any longer. But in the future there will be no wives and no friends. Children will be taken from their mothers at birth, as one takes eggs from a hen. The sex instinct will be eradicated. Procreation will be an annual formality like the renewal of a ration card. . . . There will be no loyalty, except loyalty toward the Party. There will be no love except the love of Big Brother. There will be no art, no literature, no science. When we are omnipotent we shall have no more need of science. There will be no curiosity. . . . All competing pleasures will be destroyed. But always . . . there will be the intoxication of power, constantly increasing and constantly growing subtler. Always, at every moment, there will be the thrill of victory, the sensation of trampling on an enemy who is helpless. If you want a picture of the future, imagine a boot stamping on a human face—forever.[61]

Orwell's antiutopian novel focuses on Winston Smith, who works for the Ministry of Truth and is arrested by the Thought Police for harboring anti-party sentiments. Smith rebels against the Party in order to reclaim his individuality and think and feel in his own way rather than according to the party's dictates. Tortured brutally, humiliated, and brainwashed, Smith confesses to crimes that both he and the Party know he did not commit.

> He became simply a mouth that uttered, a hand that signed whatever was demanded of him. His sole concern was to find out what they wanted him to confess, and then to confess it quickly, before the bullying started anew. . . . He confessed that he had murdered his wife, although he knew, and his questioners must have known, that his wife was still alive.[62]

The Party, seeks to capture the mind, to transform people into robots. O'Brien of the Thought Police tells Smith: "You will be hollow. We shall squeeze you empty, and then we shall fill you with ourselves."[63] Thus, the Party does not kill Smith but "reshapes" him, "cures" him by breaking his will and transforming him into a true believer in Big Brother. Smith comes to believe that "the struggle was finished. He had won the victory over himself. He loved Big Brother."[64]

TRENDS IN PHILOSOPHY

All the leading schools of philosophy in the first half of the twentieth century—pragmatism, logical positivism, phenomenology, and existentialism—were concerned with fundamental philosophical questions: What is truth? Is truth relative or absolute? Can the mind arrive at truth?

Pragmatism

A major movement of thought in the early twentieth century, particularly in the United States, pragmatism sought to resolve social problems through empirical analysis and rejected an approach that attempted to explain reality by means of a metaphysical formula such as that put forth by Hegel. American philosopher William James (1842–1910), a principal founder of pragmatism, denied the existence of absolutes—that "ideas possessed truth just in proportion as they approach to being copies of the Absolute's eternal way of thinking."[65] For James, truth was not something inert, a "stagnant property" that, once we possess it, we stop thinking about. The truth of an idea, he said, is found in its usefulness and effectiveness in solving a problem and in enabling human beings to cope successfully with their environment. The pragmatist, said James, asks: What difference does this idea, which we think of as true, make in our lives? Does it agree with the observable world? Is it a useful instrument for explaining experience and guiding our actions? When applied to particular experiences, does it enable us to make valuable connections?

The leading exponent of pragmatism was American philosopher John Dewey (1859–1952). Breaking with his early attachment to Hegelian idealism, Dewey based his philosophical outlook on the naturalist suppositions and the empirical-experimental approach of modern science. Idealism errs, said Dewey, because its reflections are too divorced from the human being's actual experiences with the world and because it postulates a single unified cosmic principle as the essence of reality, when in fact human life involves a plurality of experiences, each with its own distinctive character. There is no absolute truth, no immutable and eternal verities, no essence of reality. Therefore, thought should not be a quest for eternal truths or ultimate meaning. Its objective is not certainty but greater clarity and understanding of our presuppositions, facts, and conclusions. It is the instrument—Dewey referred to his philosophy as "instrumentalism"—that we bring to bear on current issues. Knowledge is a useful tool that helps us solve critical social and economic problems. In the tradition of modern science, Dewey contended that the pursuit of knowledge is a self-correcting process; we must submit our findings before the bar of reason and experience and alter them on the basis of new evidence and insights.

Dewey viewed science as the West's greatest achievement. It offered a way of thinking and doing, he said, that should be applied to the problems of the human community. Scientific thinking is the best form of inquiry developed by humanity. It provides us with reliable knowledge and an effective method for evaluating beliefs, traditions, and institutions, for analyzing a situation, and for acting intelligently—for reconstructing old ideas and for initiating social and cultural change. It is the task of philosophy to transfer to human and moral subjects the method of inquiry—hypothesis, observation, and experimental testing—that has enabled us to understand physical nature with such expertise.

From the ancient Greeks, said Dewey, Western civilization inherited the belief in the superiority of contemplative thought over doing; the objective of knowledge was to enter a realm of fixed, changeless, and ultimate truths, whose existence precedes the knower. Thinkers devoted their intellectual energies to sublime abstractions: Truth, Being, Reality. Dewey considered this a barren activity. For him, thought was operational; it could not be separated from activity, from doing. Ideas are not unquestionable truths, but provisional hypotheses whose value has to be tested. We judge the merit of ideas and beliefs by applying them and diagnosing their consequences. We want to know an idea's effectiveness in restructuring a given environment and resolving a specific problem. In *Reconstruction in Philosophy* (1920), Dewey wrote:

> It is no longer enough for a principle to be elevated, noble, universal and hallowed by time. It . . . must justify itself by its works, present and potential. Such is the inner meaning of the modern appeal to experience as an ultimate criterion of value and validity. . . .
> . . . notions, theories, systems, no matter how elaborate and self-consistent they are, must be regarded as hypotheses. They are to be accepted as bases of actions which test them, not as finalities. To perceive this fact is to abolish rigid dogmas from the world. It is to recognize that conceptions, theories and systems of thought are always open to development through use. . . . They are tools. As in the case of all tools, their value resides not in themselves but in their capacity to work shown in the consequences of their use.[66]

Dewey saw the purpose of philosophy as the advancement of social progress. In holding that the human condition could be improved through the application of creative intelligence to political, social, and economic problems, Dewey exemplified the spirit of modern democracy. He valued democracy because it recognizes the intrinsic worth of the individual and seeks the individual's development. "Democracy has many meanings, but if it has a moral meaning, it is found in resolving that the supreme test of all political institutions and industrial arrangements shall be the contribution they make to the all-around growth of every member of the community."[67] Like all democrats, Dewey believed that the masses were capable of thinking and acting responsibly, that they did not require the authoritarian leadership of "a superior few":

> The foundation of democracy is faith in the capacities of human nature; faith in human intelligence and in the power of pooled and cooperative experience. It is not belief that these things are complete but that if given a show they will grow and be able to guide collective action. Every autocratic and authoritarian scheme of social action rests on a belief that the needed intelligence is confined to a superior few, who because of inherent natural gifts are endowed with the ability and the right to control the conduct of others.[68]

Convinced that democracy's success depends on the existence of an enlightened and civic-minded citizenry, Dewey stressed the importance of education and proposed fundamental educational reforms. He criticized contemporary educational practice for treating the child as a passive vessel into which the teacher poured knowledge; such an approach stifled intellectual development. A properly conceived education, he said, recognizes that the child is naturally inquisitive, imaginative, and active; the student "learns by doing," by actively experiencing and participating in the learning process. Young people should engage in activities that require making connections between actions and consequences. Thinking is triggered by a conscious effort to resolve a real problem, not by rote learning. A fundamental premise of his philosophy of education is that people who are properly trained in problem solving will be able to improve the conditions of existence. Dewey also wanted education to prepare a person to live as a productive member of a group. Dewey's educational theory had a profound influence on schooling in the United States.

Logical Positivism and Analytic Philosophy

Instrumentalism provided a frame of reference for dealing with current social problems, and Dewey saw himself as a social reformer. Analytic philosophy, like instrumentalism, valued the sciences but had virtually no application to social issues. It aspired solely to prove or disprove all assertions by using the empirical method of science and the strict logic of mathematical thinking as standards of verification. Analytic philosophers contended that the critical analysis of language is the central concern of philosophy. Both instrumentalist and analytical philosophy shared a common disdain for metaphysics, which they regarded as unverifiable speculation.

A principal development in the evolution of analytic philosophy was the emergence of logical positivism at the University of Vienna in the 1920s. Logical positivists were a group of scientifically and mathematically oriented thinkers who considered themselves heirs of David Hume's empiricism and of nineteenth-century philosophers, scientists, and logicians who rejected metaphysics and regarded the scientific method as the avenue to knowledge. The leading figures identified with the Vienna Circle were Moritz Schlick, a scientist-philosopher; Rudolf Carnap, a logician; Otto Neurath, a sociologist; and the mathematicians Hans Hahn and Kurt Gödel. The group maintained contacts with philosophers in other European countries. As Nazism spread in central Europe, several members sought refuge in Britain and the United States.

Ludwig Wittgenstein (1889–1951), a brilliant and eccentric Austro-English thinker, did not himself belong to the circle but, through his consultations with key members, profoundly influenced logical positivism. Wittgenstein, who had studied with Bertrand Russell (see below) in England, wrote down his philosophical thoughts while serving in the Austrian army during World War I. Captured by the Italians, he sent the manuscript to Russell from a prisoner-of-war camp. Entitled *Tractatus Logico-Philosophicus*, it was published in 1922. In this work—he somewhat altered his views in a later work, *Philosophical Investigations*, published in 1953—Wittgenstein argued that philosophy should not go beyond what can meaningfully be said. Philosophy does not produce a body of truths; it provides no picture of reality. It can only speak about the propositions of natural science, clarifying the terminology and conclusions attained by science. The clarification of language—the logical analysis of a statement—is philosophy's essential function. He called the propositions of theology, ethics, esthetics, and metaphysics "nonsensical" because the matters of which they speak transcend reality, the world of actual facts; they exceed what can be said by the logic of language. In the concluding section of *Tractatus*, Wittgenstein states: "What we cannot speak about we must pass over in silence."

A second center of logical positivism was in England. The leading British philosophers identified with the movement were Gilbert Ryle

(1900–1976) and A. J. Ayer (1910–1989). British logical positivists drew on the ideas of Bertrand Russell (1872–1970) and G. E. Moore (1873–1958), two Cambridge University philosophers of the early twentieth century, who had attacked the grand metaphysical systems built by British Hegelians. Both Russell and Moore objected to the imprecise and obscure language employed by these idealists. A renowned mathematician, Russell wanted language to have the precision of mathematics; Moore argued that many of the statements made by metaphysicians could not pass the test of common sense.

Logical positivists dismissed the propositions of metaphysics as meaningless because their truth or falsehood could not be verified by experience. They put forth a doctrine called the *verifiability principle,* which was applied to statements purporting to say something factual. To be of value, such statements—for example, "the distance between New York City and Los Angeles is 3,000 miles"—must make a point that could be demonstrated to be true or false on the basis of empirical observation. However, argued the logical positivists, many of the great questions that have intrigued philosophers—Does God exist? Is there an eternal and transcendent realm of Being? Do human beings have an immortal soul? What is justice?—do not meet this standard. The answers proposed cannot be proven or disproven. Such questions, then, are cognitively meaningless; they contain no truth and do not advance knowledge about reality. Thus, Ayer held that "all utterances about the nature of God are nonsensical," and he viewed ethical concepts—for instance, "Stealing money is wrong"—as "pure expressions of feeling" that "as such do not come under the category of truth and falsehood." We cannot argue about the validity of moral principles. "We merely praise or condemn them in the light of our own feelings."[69]

Logical positivists insisted that philosophy must dismiss the assertions put forth by traditional metaphysical systems because they cannot be confirmed or rejected on the basis of sense experience. Metaphysicians claim to teach knowledge that is of a higher value than that of empirical science, wrote Carnap, but in reality metaphysical propositions

> assert nothing, they contain neither knowledge nor error, they lie completely outside the field of knowledge, of theory, outside the discussion of truth or falsehood. . . . The danger lies in the *deceptive* character of metaphysics; it gives the illusion of knowledge without actually giving any knowledge. This is the reason why we reject it.[70]

Hegelian idealism, theology, mysticism, and other expressions of metaphysical thinking distort and obfuscate, said logical positivists, because they postulate a reality that transcends the world of science and common sense. They are merely expressions of feeling and do not belong to any branch of science or philosophy. Thus, Ayer held that "no statement which refers to a 'reality' transcending the limits of all possible sense-experience can possibly have any literal significance; from which it must follow that the labours of those who have striven to describe such a reality have all been devoted to the production of nonsense."[71] The first chapter of his important book, *Language, Truth and Logic* (1936), is entitled "The Elimination of Metaphysics."

Like Dewey and other pragmatists, logical positivists attacked metaphysical ideas put forth as true by traditional philosophy. Unlike Dewey, however, they did not reject the idea of truth itself. Certainty does exist, they said, but it can only be apprehended through rigorous scientific and mathematical analysis. Also unlike Dewey, logical positivists were unconcerned with political, social, economic, religious, or ethical issues. They assigned to philosophy a very narrow task: serving as a tool for science by sedulously promoting a scientific outlook. (In the Middle Ages, we recall, philosophy was viewed as the handmaiden of theology.)

Logical positivists maintained that philosophy could not compete with the various scientific disciplines as a means of acquiring knowledge, but that it can assist science in its pursuit of truth by clarifying the meaning and usage of the language employed by science. It can determine what can and cannot be said. Philosophy has the duty to point out that certain things are inexpressible; propositions that transcend reality also transcend the limits of language. According to logical positivists, such a rigorous analysis of the meaning of words and propositions on the basis of the verifiability principle would enable us to dismiss meaningless propositions, clear up ambiguities, and reject falsehoods. For them philosophy was a department of logic. Moritz Schlick (1882–1936), a leading member of the Vienna Circle, said that philosophy

> must be defined as *the activity of meaning*. Philosophy is an activity, not a science, but this activity, of course is at work in every single science continually, because before the sciences can discover the truth or falsity of a proposition they have to get at the meaning first. And sometimes in the course of their work they are surprised to find . . . that they have been using words without a perfectly clear meaning, and then they will have to turn to the philosophical activity of clarification, and they cannot go on with the pursuit of truth before the pursuit of meaning has been successful. In this way philosophy is an extremely important factor within science.[72]

Logical positivism was soon absorbed into the the broader movement of analytic philosophy, which became the dominant philosophy in British and American universities in the decades after World War II. Academic philosophers, engaging in linguistic analysis, produced a large number of technical works analyzing words and statements in minutest detail. Linguistic analysis has come under attack in recent years, and its influence is receding, as T. Z. Lavine notes:

> There is a growing sense in the philosophical world that this analytic philosophy . . . has been a failure. . . . Philosophy is no longer about the world, but only about the language with which we speak about the world. Analytic philosophy . . . . has been . . . [in] isolation from the vitality of the intellectual culture and from the issues of public and personal life. Cut off from these affairs of human life, the analytic philosopher has no contribution to make to them, beyond occasionally noting a linguistic misusage. There is thus a growing impatient criticism of analytic philosophy that it is out of touch with the vital matters of human life, with the things which concern us most. . . . Specifically within the area of ethics and political philosophy, in which philosophy has traditionally had the function of providing norms, standards, and ideals, analytic philosophy has reduced these areas to language games and the way words like right or good or justice are used, not how they should be used.[73]

Phenomenology

Phenomenology, another philosophical movement, is identified with the Austro-German philosopher Edmund Husserl (1859–1938). Shortly after receiving a Ph.D. in mathematics, Husserl, largely due to the influence of Franz Brentano, whose lectures on theoretical psychology he had attended in Vienna, decided to devote himself to philosophy. He taught at three German universities, including the University of Freiburg, from which he retired in 1929. With the growing influence of Nazism, Husserl, because of his Jewish ancestry, was shunned by his former students, and, after 1933, he was barred from engaging in academic activities at the university. Husserl had a profound influence on existentialist thinkers, particularly Jean-Paul Sartre, Maurice Merleau-Ponty, and Martin Heidegger, his student at Freiburg.

Husserl believed that the Western mind was in a state of crisis—he entitled his last major work, *Philosophy and the Crisis of European Man* (1935). The reason for this intellectual crisis, he said, is that westerners no longer believe in absolute truth; they reject the view that philosophical inquiry can disclose rational certainty. Husserl was protesting against pragmatists and naturalists who argued that the pursuit of ultimate truth is a misguided activity, that truth is what is operationally effective, what works. He also denounced historicists for making ideals, norms, and values relative, that is, for viewing them not as timeless truths, but as transient and temporally conditioned products of a particular culture in a particular stage of its historical development.

Husserl sought to discover for philosophy the same indubitable certainty that Husserl found in mathematics. This quest for verifiable truth was the overriding passion in his life. An entry in his diary in l906 reads: "I have been through enough torments from lack of clarity and from doubt that wavers back and forth. . . . Only one need absorbs me: I must win clarity else I cannot live; I cannot bear life unless I can believe that I shall achieve it."[74] Husserl believed fervently that there are norms and values deriving from reason that give an ultimate purpose and meaning to life. He was also convinced that we can acquire knowledge of essential being, of essences.

Husserl hoped to realize this quest for certainty by examining the basic structures of mental activity, to discover the essence of consciousness that pervades all knowing. We have a conscious awareness of something, insists Husserl. The objects of our consciousness do exist for us; the ego acts as if it is directed to an object. Phenomenology is concerned with the systematic investigation of consciousness and its objects; it analyzes how conscious subjects know objects and how human consciousness experiences and perceives all types of phenomena. Phenomenology seeks to discover the structures common to the activity of consciousness itself. Knowledge of the ultimate forms of mental activity that constitutes our conscious acts is a prerequisite for comprehending ourselves and the world.

In pursuing this aim, phenomenology strives to be rigorously scientific, rejecting any conclusion that cannot be verified. ("Philosophy as Rigorous Science" was the title of an essay Husserl wrote in 1911.) Husserl struggled to produce a method that would assure scientific rigor for philosophic inquiry. However, his "scientific philosophy" was based on the premise that the methodology employed by the natural sciences to explain the physical world of facts and hard data does not apply to our psychic life, for the activity of consciousness is not corporeal, it is not a physical datum that is measurable and quantifiable, but something entirely unique. When we examine the realm of consciousness—the human being as a thinking and spiritual subject, the author of culture—a different methodology is required.

Husserl intended to pioneer a science of phenomenology that would produce objectively and universally valid knowledge. Through a rigorous investigation of consciousness itself and the objects it perceives, phenomenology would uncover the essential nature of our spiritual being and penetrate beneath the superficial qualities of phenomena to their very essence, to the thing itself. Such an absolute foundation for scientific and philosophical knowledge—something that Descartes had sought—would permit us to create a universal science that unifies all existence. Philosophy, "the loftiest of all sciences," would be able to fulfill its historic mission: the achievement of pure and absolute knowledge.

Husserl insisted that phenomenology must be distinguished from all the empirical sciences, for it has its own peculiar method of philosophical investigation. The procedures developed by Husserl for exploring consciousness and its interaction with phenomena are extremely complex. They are also subject to criticism from a scientific point of view, although Husserl did insist that we must philosophize without presuppositions that prejudice the investigation and cautioned against reaching beyond the available evidence.

The value Husserl gave to the subjectivity of experience, particularly his notion of the *life-world*—how meaning is acquired from the conscious subject's perception of, reaction to, and organization of daily experiences—had a profound impact on existentialism.

Existentialism

The philosophical movement that best exemplified the anxiety and uncertainty of Europe in an era of world wars and totalitarianism was existentialism. Like writers and artists, existentialist philosophers were responding to a European civilization that seemed to be in the throes of dissolution. What route should people take in a world where old values and certainties had dissolved, where universal truth was rejected and God's existence was denied? How could people cope in a society where they were menaced by technology, manipulated by impersonal bureaucracies, and overwhelmed by anxiety? If the universe is devoid of any overarching meaning, what meaning could one give to one's own life? These questions were at the crux of existentialist philosophy. Although existentialism was most popular after World War II, expressing the anxiety and despair of many intellectuals who had lost confidence in reason and progress, several of its key works were written prior to the war or during it.

Basic Principles Existentialism does not lend itself to a single definition, for its principal theorists did not adhere to a common body of doctrines. For example, some existentialists were atheists, like Jean-Paul Sartre, or omitted God from their thought, like Martin Heidegger; others, like Karl Jaspers, believed in God but not in Christian doctrines; still others, like Gabriel Marcel and Nikolai Berdyaev, were Christians, and Martin Buber was a believing Jew. Perhaps the essence

Jean-Paul Sarte *(Lipnitzki-Viollet)*

of existentialism appears in the following principles, although not all existentialists would subscribe to each point or agree with the way it is expressed.

1. Reality defies ultimate comprehension; there are no timeless truths, essences that exist independently of and prior to the individual human being. Our existence precedes and takes precedence over any presumed essences. The moral and spiritual values that society tries to impose cannot define the individual person's existence.
2. Reason alone is an inadequate guide to living, for people are more than thinking subjects who approach the world through critical analysis. They are also feeling and willing beings, who must participate fully in life and experience existence directly, actively, passionately. Only in this way does one live wholly and authentically.
3. Thought must not merely be abstract speculation—just knowing things is not enough. Rather, thought must have a bearing on life; it must be translated into deeds.

4. Human nature is problematic and paradoxical, not fixed or constant; each person is like no other. Self-realization comes when one affirms one's own uniqueness. The human being, as Nietzsche said, is an "indeterminate animal." The individual's nature, declared Karl Jaspers, "presents a domain of limitless possibilities. Mankind's nature consists in aspiration and daring to choose and to enter paths none of which is the only prescribed or valid one."[75] One becomes less than human when one permits one's life to be determined by a mental outlook—a set of rules and values—imposed by others.

5. We are alone. The universe is indifferent to our expectations and needs, and death is ever stalking us. Awareness of this elementary fact of existence evokes a sense of overwhelming anxiety and depression.

6. Existence is essentially absurd. There is no purpose to our presence in the universe. We simply find ourselves here; we do not know and will never find out why. Compared with the eternity of time that preceded our birth and will follow our death, the short duration of our existence seems trivial and inexplicable. And death, which irrevocably terminates our existence, testifies to the ultimate absurdity of life.

7. We are free. We must face squarely the fact that existence is purposeless and absurd. In doing so, we can give our life meaning. It is in the act of choosing freely from among different possibilities that the individual shapes an authentic existence. There is a dynamic quality to human existence; the individual has the potential to become more than he or she is.

Nineteenth-Century Forerunners   Three nineteenth-century thinkers—Søren Kierkegaard (1813–1855), Fyodor Dostoevski (see Chapter 9), and Friedrich Nietzsche (see Chapter 9)—were the principal nineteenth-century forerunners of existentialism. Their views of reason, will, truth, and existence greatly influenced twentieth-century existentialists.

Kierkegaard   Søren Kierkegaard, a Danish religious philosopher and Lutheran pastor, held that self-realization as a human being comes when the individual takes full responsibility for his or her life; the individual does this by choosing one way of life over another. In making choices, said Kierkegaard, the individual overcomes the agonizing feeling that life in its deepest sense is nothingness.

For Kierkegaard, the highest truth is that human beings are God's creatures. However, God's existence cannot be demonstrated by reason; the crucial questions of human existence can never be resolved in a logical and systematic way. The individual does not know God through disinterested reflection but by making a passionate commitment to him. In contrast to Christian apologists who sought to demonstrate that Christian teachings did not conflict with reason, Kierkegaard denied that Christian doctrines were objectively valid; for him, Christian beliefs were absurd and irrational and could not be harmonized with reason. The true Christian, said Kierkegaard, commits himself to beliefs that are unintelligible; with confidence, he plunges into the absurd. But through this leap of faith, he conquers despair and gives meaning to his own existence.

Twentieth-century existentialists took from Kierkegaard the idea that an all-consuming dread is the price of existence. "I stick my finger into existence—it smells of nothing. Where am I? What is this thing called the world? Who is it who has lured me into the thing, and now leaves me here? Who am I? How did I come into world? Why was I not consulted?"[76] The sense that we live in a meaningless world drives us to the edge of the abyss. This overwhelming dread can cause us to flee from life and to find comfort in delusions, but it can also spark courage, for it is an opportunity to make a commitment. For both Kierkegaard and twentieth-century existentialists, the true philosophical quest is a subjective experience: the isolated individual, alone and without help, choosing a way of life, struggling with his or her own being to make a commitment. Only in this way does the individual become a whole person. Kierkegaard's dictum "it is impossible to exist without passion"—that our actions matter to us—is at the heart of existentialism.

Dostoevski Although existentialist themes pervade several of Dostoevski's works, it is in *Notes from Underground* that he treats explicitly the individual's quest for personal freedom, identity, and meaning and the individual's revolt against established norms—themes that are crucial to the outlook of twentieth-century existentialists.

Nietzsche For several reasons, Friedrich Nietzsche was an important forerunner of existentialism. Nietzsche held that modern westerners had lost all their traditional supports. Philosophical systems are merely expressions of an individual's own being and do not constitute an objective representation of reality: there is no realm of being that is the source of values, and there are no Platonic Ideals or universal truths that are apprehended through reason. Nor does religion provide truth, for the foundations for belief have been destroyed beyond repair. God is dead, even though we are not fully aware of his demise. It is an essential truth of human existence that we live in a godless and absurd world. No transcendental values, rules, or authority exists outside of human beings.

To overcome nothingness, said Nietzsche, individuals must define life for themselves and celebrate it fully, instinctively, and heroically. Nietzsche's insistence that individuals confront existence squarely, without hypocrisy, and give meaning to it—their own meaning—was vital to the shaping of existentialism.

Phenomenology and Existentialism   Husserl's emphasis on what he called "psychical subjectivity," or the I as the subject of experience, links phenomenology with existentialism. Like Husserl, existential-ists contended that the methods employed by chemists and biologists to comprehend the material world cannot explain human conscious-ness. Like Husserl, they gave priority to the life-world (see page 442) over the physical world described by science. Also like Husserl, they regarded the individual as a conscious and active subject who imposes meaning and value on existence. Sartre, the leading French existen-tialist, rejected Husserl's search for absolutes, focusing instead on how the individual, tossed into a world that is devoid of certainty, struggles to give meaning to his or her life.

Martin Heidegger   German philosopher Martin Heidegger (1889–1976), generally regarded as the central figure in the development of twentieth-century existentialist thought, presents a problem to stu-dents of philosophy. First, Heidegger rejected being classified as an ex-istentialist. Second, he wrote in a nearly incomprehensible style that obscured his intent. Third, in 1933 Heidegger, recently appointed rector of the University of Freiburg by Hitler's government, joined the Na-tional Socialist party and publicly praised Hitler and the Nazi regime (see pages 421–422). He did so despite the fact that Husserl, his es-teemed teacher to whom he had dedicated *Being and Time* (1927), his *magnum opus,* had been humiliated by the Nazis for his Jewish ances-try. The following year, Heidegger resigned as rector and gave no fur-ther support to the Third Reich, but he retained his membership in the party until the end of the war, still found things to praise in Nazism, and, after the war, never renounced his service to the Third Reich. Hei-degger's dalliance with Nazism caused some thinkers either to dismiss him or to minimize his importance as a philosopher.

Heidegger's *Being and Time* (1927), is a pathbreaking work in twen-tieth-century philosophy. In it Heidegger asked: What does it mean to be human, to say I am? Most people shun this question, said Heideg-ger; consequently they live unauthentically, merely accepting a way of life set by others. Such people, he said, have "fallen from being"; they do not reflect on their existence or recognize the various possibilities and choices that life offers. Rather, they flee from their own selves and accept without reflection society's values. Neither their actions nor their goals are their own. They have forfeited a human being's most distinctive qualities: freedom and creativity.

To live authentically, declared Heidegger, the individual has to face explicitly the problem of Being; that is, one has to determine one's own existence, create one's own possibilities, and make choices and commitments. We must do this in the face of the agonizing fact that the world has neither an ontological meaning nor a moral structure. Choosing, said Heidegger, is not just a matter of disengaged thought, for the human creature is more than a conscious knower. The authentic life encompasses the feelings, as well as the intellect; it is a genuine expression of a person's whole being.

Coming to grips with death, said Heidegger, provides us with the opportunity for an authentic life. The trauma of our mortality and finiteness, the image of the endless void in which Being passes into non-Being, overwhelms us with dread; we come face to face with the insignificance of human existence, with the directionless lives that we pursue. To escape this dread, said Heidegger, some people simply immerse themselves in life's petty details or adopt the values prescribed by others. But dread of death is also an opportunity. It can put us in touch with our own uniqueness, our own Being, permitting us to take hold of our own existence and to make life truly our own.

The authentic life requires, said Heidegger, that we see ourselves within the context of historical time, for we cannot escape from the fact that our lives are bound by conditions and outlooks inherited from the past. Human beings are thrown into a world that is not of their own making, said Heidegger; they dwell in a particular society that carries with it the weight of the past and the tensions and conflicts of the present. Without knowledge of these conditions, he declared, events and things will always impose themselves on us, and we will not have the courage to reject conventions that are not of our own making.

Karl Jaspers   Karl Jaspers (1883–1969), a German psychiatrist turned philosopher, was a leading figure in the existentialist movement. Jaspers came into disfavor with the Nazi regime (he advocated liberal-humanist values and his wife was Jewish), and in 1937 he lost his position as professor of philosophy at Heidelberg University. Like Kierkegaard, Jaspers held that philosophy and science cannot provide certainty. Also like Kierkegaard, he sought to discover the genuine self through an encounter with life. Like Heidegger, he held that while death makes us aware of our finitude, thereby promoting anxiety, it also goads us to focus on what is truly important and to do so immediately. Jaspers insisted that the individual has the power to choose; to be aware of this freedom and to use it is the essence of being human. He declared in 1930:

> Man is always something more than what he knows of himself. He is not what he is simply once for all, but is a process; he is . . . endowed with possibilities through the freedom he possesses to make of himself what he will by the activities on which he decides.[77]

Feelings of guilt and anxiety inevitably accompany free will, said Jaspers. Nevertheless, we must have the courage to make a choice, for it is in the act of choosing that the individual shapes his or her true self.

Jaspers rejected revealed religion, dogmas, and the authority of churches, but he did postulate what he called "philosophical faith." He thought of human existence as an encounter with Transcendence— "the eternal, indestructible, the immutable, the source [that] . . . can be neither visualized nor grasped in thought."[78] Jaspers did not equate Transcendence with God in the conventional sense, but the concept is laden with theistic qualities. Although not a traditional Christian, Jaspers was no atheist.

Jean-Paul Sartre   The outlook of several French existentialists—Jean-Paul Sartre (1905–1980), Maurice Merleau-Ponty (1908–1961), Albert Camus (1913–1960), and Simone de Beauvoir (1908–1986)—was shaped by their involvement in the resistance to Nazi occupation during World War II. Sartre, the leading French existentialist, said that their confrontation with terror and torture taught them "to take evil seriously." Evil is not the effect of ignorance that might be remedied by knowledge or of passions that might be controlled, said Sartre; rather, it is a central fact of human existence and is unredeemable. Facing capture and death, the members of the French Resistance understood what it is to be a solitary individual in a hostile universe. Living on the cutting edge of life, they rediscovered the essence of human freedom: they could make authentic choices. By saying no to the Nazis and resisting them, they confronted existence squarely. They faced the central problem that concerned Sartre: what does it mean to be a human being?

Sartre served in the French army at the outbreak of World War II and was captured by the Germans. Released after the French surrender, he taught philosophy while serving in the Resistance. His principal philosophical work, *Being and Nothingness* (1943), shows the strong influence of phenomenology. In addition to his philosophical writings, Sartre, gained international acclaim for his novels and plays, many of them, particularly *Nausea* (1938) and *No Exit* (1944), written from an existentialist point of view.

In contrast to Kierkegaard and Jaspers, Sartre defined himself as an

atheist and saw existentialism as a means of facing the consequences
of a godless universe. Atheistic existentialism, he said, begins with the
person and not with God, a pre-established ethic, or a uniform conception of human nature. For Sartre, existence precedes essence, that is,
there are no values that precede the individual metaphysically or
chronologically to which he or she must conform. There exists no
higher realm of Being and no immutable truths that serve as ultimate
standards of virtue. It is unauthentic to submit passively to established
values that one did not participate in making. The individual has nothing to cling to; he or she is thrown into the world "with no support
and no aid."[79] It is the first principle of existence, said Sartre, that we
must each choose our own ethics, define ourselves, and give our own
meaning to our own existence. Through our actions, we decide how
we shall create ourselves. We are what we do, said Sartre; each individual is "nothing else than the ensemble of his acts, nothing else than
his life. . . . man's destiny is within himself."[80] As conscious beings,
we are totally responsible for defining our lives and for giving them
meaning and value.

> Not only is man what he conceives himself to be but he is also only
> what he wills himself to be. . . . Man is nothing else but what he makes
> of himself. . . . existentialism's first move is to make every man aware of
> what he is and to make the full responsibility of his existence rest on
> him.[81]

In Sartre's view, a true philosophy does not engage in barren discourses on abstract themes. Rather, it makes commitments and incurs
risks. We are not objectified instruments, determined and shaped by
material forces, as Marxism teaches. (Later, Sartre sought to integrate
existentialism with Marxism.) Nor do unconscious drives determine
our actions, as Freud contended. Rather, we live in a world of our own
making. We alone, as free conscious beings, are responsible for who we
are and for the feelings that torment, trap, and immobilize us. True,
the conditions in which we find ourselves impinge on our existence,
but it is up to us to decide what we shall do about these conditions.
Thus, said Sartre, a French man or woman had to choose between
being a patriot or a traitor during the German occupation.

We have the capacity to plunge decisively, audaciously into life and
constantly to recreate ourselves. We have no control over the fact that
we exist; existence is simply given to us. But each individual does decide his or her own peculiar essence. We do so by the particular way
we choose to live. The realization that we have the freedom to decide
for ourselves what meaning we give to our lives can be liberating and
exhilarating. But it can also fill us with a dread that immobilizes or
that leads us to seek refuge in a role selected for us by others. When

we abdicate this responsibility of choosing a meaning for our lives, said Sartre, we live in "bad faith."

Albert Camus   Reared and educated in French-ruled Algeria, Albert Camus (1908–1957) gained an instant reputation in 1942 with the publication of *The Stranger*, a short novel, and *The Myth of Sisyphus*, a philosophical essay. During World War II, he served in the French Resistance. His most important works in the decade after the war were two works of fiction—*The Plague* (1947) and *The Fall* (1956)—and *The Rebel* (1951), a set of interpretive essays on historical, philosophical, and esthetic topics.

Camus dealt with the existential theme of the individual struck by the awareness of God's nonexistence. "But it so happens that there is no more father, no more rule!"[82] says a character in *The Fall*. Camus is concerned with how we react to our own impending rendezvous with an eternity of nothingness. Does this mean that my life is without meaning? That my actions do not matter? Camus rejected both suicide and nihilism as responses to this absurdity of existence. Even though existence has no higher meaning and the universe is indifferent to us, we must still accept "the desperate encounter between human inquiry and the silence of the universe."[83] Ultimately, Camus saw a moralistic humanism that promoted fraternity and dignity as a worthwhile response to the absurdity of the human condition. Human beings should aspire to serve "those few values without which a world . . . isn't worth living in, without which a man . . . is not worthy of respect."[84]

In *The Stranger*, Meursault, an insignificant French shipping clerk, kills an Algerian Arab for no particular reason. It was as if shooting him or not shooting him came to the same thing. Convicted and sentenced to death, Meursault examines his own life, which he has lived without awareness, imagination, passion, or commitment, as revealed in the novel's opening lines: "Maman died today. Or yesterday, maybe, I don't know."[85] Meursault displays a shocking indifference to his mother's death not because of any hate for her but simply because this is the way he lives. Neither her death nor his own life is very important to him. Committed to nothing, moved by nothing, unable to find value in anything, and not given to introspection or reflection, he merely lives passively from day to day, a stranger to himself and to life. His behavior seems to illustrate the essential absurdity of life, its lack of transcendent value, and the universe's benign indifference to us.

For Camus, neither religion nor philosophy provides a basis for human values or can tell us with certainty what is right or wrong. No final authority can be found in a transcendental heaven or in reason's dictates. Thus, when a priest tries to make Meursault aware of his guilt and his spiritual needs, the condemned man responds: "He seemed so certain, about everything, didn't he. And yet none of his certainties was worth one hair of a woman's head."[86] Values may not be absolute or eternal, maintained Camus, but he did urge living by values that advanced human dignity and warm human relations.

Religious Existentialism   Several thinkers are classified as religious existentialists, among them Nikolai Berdayev (1874–1948), an exile from communist Russia, Martin Buber (1878–1965), a Jew who fled Nazi Germany; and Gabriel Marcel (1889–1973), a French Catholic. During World War I, Marcel served with the French Red Cross, accounting for soldiers missing in battle. This shattering experience brought the sensitive thinker face to face with the tragedy of human existence. A growing concern with the spiritual life led him to convert to Catholicism in 1929.

The modern individual, said Marcel in 1933, "tends to appear to himself and to others as an agglomeration of functions."[87] A person is viewed as an entrepreneur, a laborer, a consumer, a citizen. The hospital serves as a repair shop, and death "becomes objectively and functionally the scrapping of what has ceased to be of use and must be written off as a total loss." In such a functional world, maintained Marcel, people are valued for what they produce and possess. If they do not succeed as merchants, bookkeepers, or ticket takers, people judge them and they judge themselves as personal failures. Such an outlook suffocates spirituality and deprives the individual of the joy of existence. It produces an "intolerable unease" in the individual "who is reduced to living as though he were in fact submerged by his function. . . . Life in a world centered on function is liable to despair because in reality this world is *empty*, it rings hollow."[88]

Marcel wanted people to surpass a functional and mechanical view of life and to explore the mystery of existence—to penetrate to a higher level of reality. He held that one penetrates ultimate reality when one overcomes egocentricity and exists for others, when one loves and is loved by others. When we exist through and for others, when we treat another person not as an object performing a function but as a "thou" who matters to us, we soar to a higher level of existence. When we are actively engaged with others in concrete human situations, we fulfill ourselves as human beings; when we actively express love and fidelity toward others, life attains a higher meaning. Such involvement with others, said Marcel, provides us with a glimpse of a transcendent reality and is a testimony to God's existence. Marcel maintained that faith in God overcomes anxiety and despair, which characterize the modern predicament. It also improves the quality of human relationships, for if we believe that all people matter to God they are more likely to matter to us.

THE MODERN PREDICAMENT

The process of fragmentation that had showed itself in European thought and the arts at the end of the nineteenth century accelerated after World War I. Increasingly, philosophers, writers, and artists expressed disillusionment with the rational-humanist tradition of the Enlightenment. They no longer shared the Enlightenment's confidence either in reason's capabilities or in human goodness, and they viewed perpetual progress as an illusion.

For some thinkers, the crucial problem was the great change in the European understanding of truth. Since the rise of philosophy in ancient Greece, Western thinkers had believed in the existence of objective, universal truths—truths that were inherent in nature and applied to all peoples at all times. (Christianity, of course, also taught the reality of truth as revealed by God.)

It was held that such truths—the natural rights of the individual, for example—could be apprehended by the intellect and could serve as a standard for individual aspirations and social life. The recognition of these universal principles, it was believed, compels people to measure the world of the here and now in the light of rational and universal norms and to institute appropriate reforms. It was the task of philosophy to reconcile human existence with the objective order.

During the nineteenth century, the existence of universal truth came into doubt. A growing historical consciousness led some thinkers to maintain that what people considered truth was merely a reflection of their culture at a given stage in history—their perception of things at a specific point in the evolution of society and human consciousness. These thinkers held that universal truths were not woven into the fabric of nature. There are no natural rights of life, liberty, and property that constitute the individual's birthright; there are no standards of justice or equality that are inherent in nature and ascertainable by reason. It was people, said these thinkers, who elevated the beliefs and values of an age to the status of objective truth. The normative principles, which for the philosophes of the Enlightenment constituted a standard for political and social reform and a guarantee of human rights, were no longer linked to the natural order, to an objective reality that could be confirmed by reason. As Hannah Arendt noted, "We certainly no longer believe, as the men of the French Revolution did, in a universal cosmos of which man was a part and whose natural laws he had to imitate and conform to."[89]

This radical break with the traditional attitude toward truth contributed substantially to the crisis of European consciousness that marked the first half of the twentieth century. Values and beliefs, either those inherited from the Enlightenment or those taught by Christianity, no longer gave Europeans a sense of certainty and security. People were left without a normative order to serve as a guide for living—an outlook that fosters nihilism.

Between Condorcet's paean to progress and our century's testimony of pain, the consciousness of Europe had been altered. The self-assured confidence in the future gave way to doubt and despair. The unswerving faith in reason was shattered. Whereas the philosophes possessed beliefs whose certainty seemed self-evident, the twentieth century, devoid of a unity of outlook, knows largely incoherence, doubt, and confusion. "Twentieth-century man," wrote Arthur Koestler in 1953, "has no answer to the question of the meaning of life, because socially and metaphysically he does not know where he belongs."[90]

By the early twentieth century, the attitude of westerners toward reason had undergone a radical transformation. Some thinkers who placed their hopes in the rational tradition of the Enlightenment were distressed by reason's inability to resolve the tensions and conflicts of modern industrial society. Moreover, the growing recognition of the nonrational—of human actions determined by hidden impulses—led people to doubt that reason plays the dominant role in human behavior. The intellect does not seem autonomous, self-regulating, a sovereign master; more often than not, it is subject to the rebellious demands of unconscious drives and impulses. Now we cannot escape from the feeling that men's and women's propensity for goodness, their capacity to improve society, their potential for happiness are severely limited by an inherent irrationality—indeed, that civilization itself is threatened by our instinctual needs, as Freud proclaimed.

We now recognize that the irrational, to which thinkers of the Enlightenment had paid little attention, is a permanent and ineradicable feature of human nature and social life. Nonrational factors pervade our personal life, religious beliefs, esthetic tastes, and political commitments. To dismiss the instinctual, to thwart the nonrational side of our nature, may lead to psychic distress, as Freud maintained; or to a stifling of our creative capacities, as Nietzsche claimed; or even to a deadening of our moral sentiments, as Rousseau warned. We cannot have civilization without reason, and yet we cannot live by reason alone. This irrational side of human nature throws into confusion the blueprints of philosophers and social planners. Can we provide for instincts and feelings without undermining the rationality upon which modern civilization rests? Emphasizing the autonomy and sovereignty of reason and the uniformity of human nature, the philosophes were largely untroubled by this problem.

Other thinkers viewed the problem of reason differently. They assailed an attitude of mind that found no room for Christianity because its teachings did not pass the test of reason and science. The horrors of the twentieth century have led some thinkers to question the core feature of the modern age—secular rationality—and to urge reorienting thinking around the transcendental—God and moral absolutes.

Some have attacked reason for fashioning a technological and bureaucratic society that devalued and crushed human passions and stifled individuality. These thinkers insisted that human beings cannot fulfill their potential—cannot live wholly—if their feelings are denied. They agreed with D. H. Lawrence's critique of rationalism: "The attribution of rationality to human nature, instead of enriching it, now seems to me to have impoverished it. It ignored certain powerful and valuable springs of feeling. Some of the spontaneous, irrational outbursts of human nature can have a sort of value from which our schematism was cut off."[91]

Thinkers pointed out that reason was a double-edged sword; it could demean, as well as ennoble, the individual. They attacked all theories that subordinated the individual to a rigid system. They denounced positivism for reducing human personality to psychological laws, and Marxism for making social class a higher reality than the individual. They rebelled against political collectivization, which regulated individual existence according to the needs of the corporate state, and they assailed modern technology and bureaucracy, creations of the rational mind, for fashioning a social order that devalued and depersonalized the individual, denying people an opportunity for independent growth and a richer existence. These thinkers held that modern industrial society, in its drive for efficiency and uniformity, deprived people of their uniqueness and reduced flesh and blood human beings to cogs in a mechanical system.

Responding to the critics of reason, other philosophers maintained that it was necessary to reaffirm respect for the rational tradition first proclaimed by the ancient Greeks and given its modern expression by the Enlightenment philosophes. Reason, said these thinkers, was indispensable to civilization. What they advocated was perpetually broadening the scope of reason to accommodate the insights into human nature advanced by the romantics, Nietzsche, Freud, modernist writers and artists, and others who explored the world of feelings, will, and the subconscious; and perpetually humanizing reason so that it never reduces a human being to a thing.

The consciousness of Europe, already profoundly damaged by World

War I, was again grievously wounded by the Hitler years. The Nazi era showed how fragile is the Western tradition of freedom, reason, and human dignity. The popularity of fascism in many European lands demonstrated that liberty is not appealing to many people—that, at any rate, there are many things that they consider more important. It seems that without much reluctance people will trade freedom for security or national grandeur. In 1939, John Dewey reflected on this dilemma:

> Does freedom in itself and in the things it brings with it seem as important as security of livelihood; as food, shelter, clothing, or even as having a good time? . . . How do the fruits of liberty compare with the enjoyments that spring from a feeling of union, of solidarity, with others? Will men surrender their liberties if they believe that in doing so they will obtain the satisfaction that comes from a sense of fusion with others and that respect by others which is the product of strength furnished by solidarity?[92]

A painful lesson of the Nazi era is that the irrational cannot be underestimated or neglected. Rather, it must be understood and confronted. Thus, H. A. Hodges concludes:

> There are many nonrational factors at work in human experience and activity. . . . It has been given to our age to explore this aspect of human life more deeply and fully than was ever done before, and the result is indeed unsettling. But it is also laid upon us to face the music honestly, and to find a way to go on being human without yielding to a Leader or a Party, or a doctrine which is set above criticism.[93]

To confront the irrational—to find a constructive outlet for its creative energies and to cope with its destructive capacities—remains one of the great challenges of our time.

The Nazi assault on reason and freedom demonstrated anew the precariousness of Western civilization. It would forever cast doubt on the Enlightenment conception of human goodness, secular rationality, and the progress of civilization through advances in science and technology. It bears out Walter Lippmann's insight that "men have been barbarians much longer than they have been civilized. They are only precariously civilized, and within us there is the propensity, persistent as the force of gravity, to revert under stress and strain, under neglect or temptation, to our first natures."[94] The future envisioned by the philosophes seemed further away than ever.

In the decades shaped by world wars and totalitarianism, intellectuals raised questions that went to the heart of the dilemma of modern life. How can civilized life be safeguarded against human irrationality, particularly when it is channeled into political ideologies that idolize the state, the leader, the party, or the race? Do human beings dread freedom of choice, as the Grand Inquisitor in Dostoevski's *Brothers Karamazov* insists, preferring instead the certainty of ideological belief, as the popularity of fascist movements seemed to demonstrate? How can individual human personality be rescued from a relentless rationalism that reduces human nature and society to mechanical systems and seeks to regulate the individual as it would any material object? Do we as human beings have the moral and spiritual resolve to use properly the technological and scientific creations of modern civilization, or will they devour us? Do the values associated with the Enlightenment provide a sound basis on which to integrate society? Can the individual find meaning in what many now consider a meaningless universe?

NOTES

1. Quoted in Barbara Tuchman, *The Guns of August* (New York: Dell, 1962), p. 440.
2. Sigmund Freud, "Thoughts for the Times on War and Death," in the *Standard Edition of the Complete Psychological Works of Freud*, ed., James Strachey (London: Hogarth Press, 1957), XIV, 275, 278.
3. Quoted in Franklin L. Baumer, "Twentieth-Century Visions of the Apocalypse," *Cahiers d'Histoire Mondiale* (Journal of World History), 1, No. 3 (January 1954), 624.
4. Excerpted in Marvin Perry et al., ed., *Sources of the Western Tradition*, 2nd ed. (Boston: Houghton Mifflin, 1991), II, 284.
5. Quoted in Baumer, "Twentieth-Century Visions of the Apocalypse," p. 624.
6. Erich Maria Remarque, *All Quiet on the Western Front*, trans. A. W. Wheen (Boston: Little, Brown, 1929), p. 224.
7. W. B. Yeats, "The Second Coming," in *Collected Poems of W. B. Yeats* (New York: Macmillan, 1956), pp. 184–185. Reprinted with permission of Macmillan Publishing Company from *The Poems of W. B. Yeats: A New Edition*, edited by Richard J. Finneran. Copyright © 1924 by Macmillan Publishing Company, renewed 1952 by Bertha Georgie Yeats.
8. T. S. Eliot, "The Waste Land," in *Collected Poems, 1909–1962* (New York: Harcourt, Brace, 1970), p. 67.
9. Carl Gustav Jung, *Modern Man in Search of a Soul*, trans. W. S. Dell and Cary F. Baynes (New York: Harcourt, Brace, 1933), pp. 231, 234–235.
10. Johan Huizinga, *In the Shadow of Tomorrow* (London: Heinemann, 1936), pp. 1–3.
11. Franz Alexander, *Our Age of Unreason* (Philadelphia: Lippincott, 1942), p. 7.

12. Oswald Spengler, *The Decline of the West*, trans. Charles F. Atkinson (London: Allen and Unwin, 1926), p. 40.

13. Franz Kafka, *The Trial*, trans. Willa and Edward Muir (New York: Knopf, 1957), p. 7.

14. Quoted in Harold Bloom, ed., *Franz Kafka: The Trial* (New York: Chelsea House, 1987), p. 1.

15. Angel Flores, ed., *The Kafka Problem* (New York: Gordian Press, 1975), p. xxi.

16. Thomas Mann, *Reflections of a Non-Political Man*, trans. Walter D. Morris (New York: Ungar, 1983), p. 16.

17. Thomas Mann, "An Appeal to Reason," excerpted in Perry, *Sources of the Western Tradition*, 2nd, II, 351–352.

18. Thomas Mann, *Coming Victory of Democracy* (New York: Knopf, 1938), pp. 30–31.

19. Thomas Mann, "Schopenhauer," in *Essays of Three Decades*, trans. H. T. Lowe-Porter (New York: Knopf, 1968), p. 409.

20. Henry T. Moore, ed., *The Collected Letters of D. H. Lawrence* (New York: Viking, 1962), I, 180.

21. Tristan Tzara, "Lecture on Dada (1922)," trans. Ralph Mannheim, *The Dada Painters and Poets*, ed. Robert Motherwell (New York: Witterborn, Schultz, 1951), pp. 250, 248.

22. Ibid., p. 251.

23. Edward Lucie-Smith, in Donald Carrol and Edward Lucie-Smith, *Movements in Modern Art* (New York: Horizon Press, 1973), p. 49.

24. H. W. Janson, *History of Art*, 2nd ed. (Englewood Cliffs, N.J.: Prentice-Hall, 1977), p. 661.

25. André Breton, *Surrealism and Painting*, excerpted in *Theories of Modern Art*, ed. Herschel B. Chipp (Berkeley: University of California Press, 1968), pp. 413–414.

26. André Breton, *What Is Surrealism?* trans. David Gascoyne (London: Faber and Faber, 1936), p. 62.

27. Karl Dietrich Bracher, *The Age of Ideologies*, trans. Ewald Osers (New York: St. Martin's, 1982), p. 153.

28. George Lichtheim, *The Concept of Ideology and Other Essays* (New York: Vintage Books, 1967), p. 228.

29. Friedrich Georg Jünger, *The Rise of the New Nationalism*, freely trans. by T. H. Von Laue, excerpted in Perry, *Sources of the Western Tradition*, II, 239.

30. Kurt Sontheimer, "Anti-Democratic Thought in the Weimar Republic," in *The Path to Dictatorship, 1918–1933*, trans. John Conway with an introduction by Fritz Stern (Garden City, New York: Doubleday Anchor Books, 1966), pp. 47–49.

31. Quoted in Victor Farias, *Heidegger and Nazism* (Philadelphia: Temple University Press, 1989), p. 118.

32. Quoted in Grattan Freyer, *W. B. Yeats and the Anti-Democratic Tradition* (Totowa, N.J.: Barnes and Noble, 1981), p. 94.

33. Ibid., p. 95.

34. Quoted in Robert Soucy, *Fascist Intellectual: Drieu La Rochelle* (Berkeley: University of California Press, 1979), p. 241.

35. Quoted in David Caute, *The Fellow Travellers* (New York: Macmillan, 1973), p. 64.

36. Ibid., p. 92.

37. Richard Crossman, ed., *The God*

That Failed (New York: Bantam Books, 1951), pp. 15, 21.

38. Arthur Koestler, *Darkness at Noon* (New York: Macmillan, 1941), pp. 158–159.

39. Jacques Maritain, *Christianity and Democracy* (New York: Scribner's, 1944), p. 44.

40. Ibid., p. 62.

41. Quoted in C. T. McIntire, ed., *God, History, and Historians* (New York: Oxford University Press, 1977), p. 9.

42. Arnold J. Toynbee, *A Study of History* (New York: Oxford University Press, 1963–64), X, 42.

43. Arnold J. Toynbee, *Survey of International Affairs, 1933* (London: Oxford University Press, 1934), p. 111.

44. Arnold J. Toynbee, *A Study of History*, VIII, 269.

45. Arnold J. Toynbee, *Experiences* (New York: Oxford University Press, 1969), p. 135.

46. Julien Benda, *The Betrayal of the Intellectuals*, trans. Richard Aldington (Boston: Beacon, 1955), p. 21.

47. Ibid., p. 38.

48. Ibid., p. 122.

49. Ibid., p. 162.

50. José Ortega y Gasset, *The Revolt of the Masses* (New York: Norton, 1957), pp. 63, 18.

51. Ibid., p. 73.

52. Ibid., pp. 73–74.

53. Ernst Cassirer, *The Philosophy of the Enlightenment*, trans. Fritz C. A. Koelln and James P. Pettegrove (Boston: Beacon, 1955), pp. xi–xii.

54. Ernst Cassirer, *The Myth of the State* (New Haven, Conn.: Yale University Press, 1946), p. 280.

55. Ibid., p. 296.

56. Erich Fromm, *Escape from Freedom* (New York: Avon Books, 1965), p. 124.

57. Ibid., pp. 173, 246.

58. Erich Fromm, *Man for Himself* (New York: Rinehart, 1947), pp. 5, 7.

59. George Orwell, *1984* (New York: Harcourt Brace, 1949; paperback, New American Library, 1961), pp. 266, 269–270.

60. Ibid., p. 251.

61. Ibid., p. 217, 219–220.

62. Ibid., p. 200.

63. Ibid., p. 211.

64. Ibid., p. 245.

65. William James, *Pragmatism* (New York: Longman's, Green, 1931), p. 200.

66. John Dewey, *Reconstruction in Philosophy* (New York: Henry Holt, 1920), pp. 48, 145.

67. Ibid., p. 186.

68. Excerpted in Joseph Ratner, ed., *Intelligence in the Modern World: John Dewey's Philosophy* (New York: Modern Library. 1939), p. 402.

69. A. J. Ayer, *Language, Truth and Logic* (New York: Dover, 1952), pp. 108, 112.

70. Rudolf Carnap, *Philosophy and Logical Syntax* (London: Kegan Paul, Trench, Trubner, 1935), pp. 29, 31.

71. Ayer, *Language, Truth, and Logic*, p. 34.

72. Excerpted in Richard M. Rorty, ed., *The Linguistic Turn* (Chicago: University of Chicago Press, 1967), pp. 50–51.

73. T. Z. Lavine, *From Socrates to Sartre: The Philosophical Quest* (New York: Bantam Books, 1984), pp. 409–410.

74. Quoted in W. T. Jones, *A History of Western Philosophy*, vol. 4, *Kant to Wittgenstein and Sartre*,

2nd ed. (New York: Harcourt, Brace and World, 1969), pp. 390–391.

75. Excerpted in W. Warren Wagar, ed., *Science, Faith and Man: European Thought Since 1914* (New York: Harper Torchbooks, 1968), p. 129.

76. Quoted in Lavine, *From Socrates to Sartre*, p. 322.

77. Karl Jaspers, *Man in the Modern Age*, trans. Eden and Cedar Paul (Garden City, N.Y.: Doubleday Anchor Books, 1951), p. 159.

78. Quoted in John Macquarie, *Existentialism* (Baltimore: Penguin Books, 1973), p. 246.

79. Jean-Paul Sartre, *Existentialism*, trans. Bernard Frechtman (New York: Philosophical Library, 1947), p. 28.

80. Ibid., pp. 38, 42.

81. Ibid., pp. 18–19.

82. Albert Camus, *The Fall*, trans. Justin O'Brien (New York: Knopf, 1956), p. 134.

83. Albert Camus, *The Rebel*, trans. Anthony Bower (New York: Knopf, 1956), p. 6.

84. Quoted in Germaine Brée, *Camus* (New Brunswick, N.J.: Rutgers University Press, 1961), p. 9.

85. Albert Camus, *The Stranger*, trans. Matthew Ward (New York: Vintage Books, 1988), p. 3.

86. Ibid., p. 120.

87. Gabriel Marcel, "On the Ontological Mystery," in *The Philosophy of Existentialism*, trans. Manya Harari (Secaucus, N.J.: Citadel Press, 1980), p. 10.

88. Ibid., p. 12.

89. Quoted in Harry S. Kariel, *In Search of Authority* (Glencoe, Ill.: Free Press, 1964), p. 246.

90. Arthur Koestler, "A Guide to Political Neuroses," in *The Trail of the Dinosaur and Other Essays* (London: Hutchison, 1970), p. 140.

91. Quoted in Anthony Arblaster, *The Rise and Decline of Western Liberalism* (Oxford: Blackwell, 1984), p. 81.

92. John Dewey, *Freedom and Culture* (New York: Putnam's, 1939), pp. 3–4.

93. Quoted in Alan Sica, *Weber, Irrationality and Social Order* (Berkeley: University of California Press, 1988), pp. 18–19.

94. Walter Lippmann, *The Public Philosophy* (Boston: Little, Brown, 1955), p. 86.

SUGGESTED READING

Ayer, A. J., *Philosophy in the Twentieth Century* (1982).

Barrett, William, *Irrational Man* (1958).

Blackham, H. J., *Six Existentialist Thinkers* (1952).

———, ed., *Reality, Man and Existence* (1965).

Cain, Seymour, *Gabriel Marcel* (1963).

Cassirer, Ernst, *The Myth of the State* (1946).

Cooper, David E. *Existentialism* (1990).

Cruickshank, John, ed., *Aspects of the Modern European Mind* (1969).

Flores, Angel, ed., *The Kafka Problem* (1975).

Grene, Marjorie, *Sartre* (1973).

Kaufmann, Walter, ed., *Existentialism from Dostoevsky to Sartre* (1956).

Lavine, T. Z., *From Socrates to Sartre* (1984).

McIntire, C. T., ed., *God, History, and Historians* (1977).

McIntire, C. T. and Perry, Marvin, eds., *Toynbee Reappraisals* (1989).

Macquarrie, John, *Existentialism* (1972).

Pawel, Ernst, *The Nightmare of Reason* (1984).

Roth, Jack, ed., *World War I: A Turning Point in Modern History* (1967).

Wagar, W. Warren, ed., *European Thought Since 1914* (1968).

Waterhouse, Roger, ed., *A Heidegger Critique* (1981).

IV

THE CONTEMPORARY AGE

12

From Modern to Postmodern

It is still too early to attempt a synthesis of recent and contemporary trends of Western thought. More time is needed to assess which current developments will have more than a passing influence. This concluding chapter focuses on *postmodernism*, a loosely defined term encompassing recent developments in the arts and thought that seem, in some ways at least, to mark a break with the past. The chapter also considers some themes of great interest in previous periods—technological society, Marxism, and human rights—that have continued to concern intellectuals.

SOME THEMES FROM THE PAST

Critique of Technological Society

Nineteenth- and early-twentieth-century thinkers had expressed concern about the threat modern industrial society posed to individual autonomy. Max Weber warned about the "iron cage" of bureaucracy, which threatened to objectify and manipulate the individual in the interests of technical efficiency. In recent decades, several thinkers, including French social theorist Jacques Ellul, German philosopher Martin Heidegger, English historian Arnold J. Toynbee, German-American psychoanalyst Erich Fromm, American social theorist Lewis

Mumford, and thinkers associated with the Frankfurt School (see below) expanded upon the earlier critique. They warned that in modern technology we have conjured up a monster that can ruin our planet, destroy our bodies, and deaden our human spirit. In striving for maximum efficiency and output, they said, industrial society effaces individual autonomy and discards humanistic values.

In *The Technological Society* (1964), Ellul concluded:

> The machine has made itself master of the heart and brain. . . . What is important is to go higher and faster; the object of the performance means little. The act is sufficient unto itself. Modern man can think only in terms of figures, and the higher the figures, the greater his satisfaction. He looks for nothing beyond the marvelous escape mechanism that technique has allowed him, to offset the very repressions caused by the life technique forces him to lead. He is reduced, in the process, to a near nullity. Even if he is not a worker on the assembly line, his share of autonomy and individual initiative becomes smaller and smaller.[1]

Our technological, bureaucratic, and consumer society, said Fromm in *The Revolution of Hope* (1968),

> reduces man to an appendage of the machine, ruled by its very rhythm and demands. It transforms him into *Homo consumens*, the total consumer, whose only aim is to *have* more and to *use* more. This society produces many useless things, and to the same degree many useless people. Man, as a cog in the production machine, becomes a thing, and ceases to be human. He spends his time doing things in which he is not interested, with people in whom he is not interested, producing things in which he is not interested; and when he is not producing, he is consuming. He is the eternal suckling with the open mouth "taking in," without . . . inner activeness whatever . . . industry forces on him.[2]

Toynbee argued that the monotony of work in factory and bureaucracy, as well as urban blight—noise, traffic jams, dirt, and ugliness—causes great psychological stress. The human being, who "is not a cipher, not a reference-number, not a computer-card [but] a living soul,"[3] cannot tolerate depersonalization and separation from nature. We are engaged in a new type of warfare, he said, which may in reality be the Third World War—"a war not between states or peoples, but between personality and technology."[4] Toynbee, who thought spaciously about the past and had a religious bent, held that technology has become for the modern age an object of worship, and as God warned, human beings pay a heavy price for idolization. We can learn to use technology for human ends, he said, only if we are guided by spiritual values.

Attacks on modern industrial society also came from within the Marxist tradition, particularly from thinkers associated with the Institute for Social Research founded in 1923 at the University of Frankfurt. Since most of its chief members were Jewish, the Institute transferred its headquarters to New York after Hitler came to power, but after the war it returned to Germany. Among the leading figures of the Frankfurt School were Max Horkheimer, Walter Benjamin, Theodor Adorno, and Herbert Marcuse. Focusing on the humanist elements found in Marx's earlier works and influenced by the emphasis in psychoanalysis on human subjectivity and self-development, these thinkers, known as critical theorists, denounced both Soviet and capitalist technocracy for fashioning a totally administered society that obliterates individuality and reduces people to social atoms. Thus, in *Dialectic of Enlightenment* (1947), Adorno and Horkheimer argued that reason, which the philosophes had employed to attack myth and religion in order to promote human liberation, has turned against itself, becoming a means of subjugating individuals to the planning, organizing, and disciplining mechanisms of modern technocracy. And for this the Enlightenment is to blame, they said, for it advocated an instrumental reason that sought technical mastery over nature and society and considered suspect whatever did not conform to a standard of computation and utility. Such an attitude alienated human beings from nature, permitted the domination of some human beings by others, and turned the individual into an abstraction, an impersonal component of a conceptual system. The ideological foundations of totalitarianism are found within the philosophy of the Enlightenment.

These attacks on materialistic and repressive bourgeois culture and on coercive and oppressive authority, particularly as formulated by Herbert Marcuse, who saw revolutionary violence as the means to human liberation, influenced the New Left radicalism that swept across college campuses in the United States, Germany, and France in the 1960s. Many students and intellectuals sought to create an alternative society, a counterculture that would preserve individual autonomy and the possibility of self-realization against the relentless growth and demands of technocracy. In *The Greening of America* (1970), a sympathetic analysis of the youth culture, which was still prominent then, Charles A. Reich empathized with this revulsion against the demands of modern technocracy:

> Technology and production can be great benefactors of man, but they are mindless instruments; if undirected they roll along with a momentum of their own. In our country they pulverize everything in their path: the landscape, the natural environment, history, and tradition, the amenities and civilities, the privacy and spaciousness of life, beauty, and the fragile, slow-growing social structures which bind us together. Organization and bureaucracy, which are applications of technology to social

institutions, increasingly dictate how we shall live our lives, with the logic of organization taking precedence over any other values. . . .

Work and living have become more and more pointless and empty. . . . For most Americans, work is mindless, exhausting, boring, servile, and hateful, something to be endured while 'life' is confined to 'time off.' At the same time our culture has been reduced to the grossly commercial; all cultural values are for sale, and those that fail to make a profit are not preserved. Our life activities have become plastic, vicarious, and false to our genuine needs, activities fabricated by others and forced upon us. . . .

Beginning with school, if not before, an individual is systematically stripped of his imagination, his creativity, his heritage, his dreams, and his personal uniqueness, in order to style him into a productive unit for a mass, technological society. Instinct, feeling, and spontaneity are repressed by overwhelming forces.[5]

The New Left radicals condemned bourgeois values as ruthless competition and exploitation, vulgar materialism, and repressed sexuality, and they expressed hate for coercive authority and impersonal bureaucracies—the so-called "system" or "establishment." Denouncing all forms of oppression (some regarded work, academic discipline, and prohibitions on drug use as oppressive), they urged exploration of new, freer, more authentic, and individualistic lifestyles. They also called for a global response to worldwide problems: overpopulation, a deteriorating environment, poverty, and nuclear weapons. Some identified with black militants in the United States and with Third World leaders, including Mao and Castro, and wanted to reshape the United States according to a Cuban or Chinese model. Also fueling their rage was the highly unpopular Vietnam War. In 1968, this rage against the system and a desire to create a new and liberating culture exploded into open rebellion in Paris and other leading cities. This movement, which consisted largely of middle-class youths, many of them no doubt simply spoiled and rebellious adolescents, nevertheless pointed to "a profound crisis of faith in the values that had inspired democratic societies for many decades,"[6] concludes Leszek Kolakowski, a leading student of Marxism.

Marxism: The End of an Ideal?

Marxists were very prominent in Western intellectual life, particularly in France, after World War II. For example, in his essay "Marxism and Existentialism" (1957), Sartre asserted an immanent relationship between his existentialist outlook and Marxism. At the same time, however, certain developments—Khrushchev's revelations of Stalin's crimes (1956), the brutal suppression of the Hungarian revolution (1956), and the publication of Milovan Djilas's *The New Class* (1957)—caused a growing dismay among Marxists. Djilas, a long-time Yugoslav communist who turned critic of Marxist theory and practice in 1953, debunked the myth of the classless society and indicted the communist system in the Soviet Union:

> Earlier revolutions, particularly the so-called bourgeois ones, attached considerable significance to the establishment of individual freedoms immediately following cessation of the revolutionary terror. The final results of earlier revolutions were often greater legal security and greater civil rights. This cannot be said of the Communist revolution. . . . no other revolutions promised so much and accomplished so little. . . .
>
> In contrast to earlier revolutions, the Communist revolution, conducted in the name of doing away with classes, has resulted in the most complete authority of any single new class. Everything else is a sham and an illusion. . . . This new class, . . . the political bureaucracy, . . . may be said to be made up of those who have special privileges and economic preference of the administrative monopoly they hold. . . . Only in a Communist state are a number of both specified and unspecified positions reserved for members of the party.[7]

For much of the 1960s and 1970s many, social theorists and philosophers identified with Marxism and expanded Marxist scholarship. But the Soviet invasion of Czechoslovakia in 1968, which smothered in the cradle a reform movement that sought Marxism "with a human face," further exposés of Stalinism by Russian intellectuals, including poet Yevgeny Yevtushenko and novelist Alexander I. Solzhenitsyn, and the fanaticism, repression, and sheer stupidity displayed during China's Cultural Revolution added to the dismay of Marxists. Increasingly, socialist theorists, including adherents of the Frankfurt School, held that Marx's enduring value lay in his vision of a truly free and self-affirming human being and in his attempt to overcome exploitation, as well as the individual's alienation from work, from his or her own self, and from others. Existing communist regimes, with their monolithic state machines, the theorists insisted, represented the negation of Marx's humanist vision.

The sudden and unexpected collapse of communism in Eastern Europe in 1989 seemed to discredit Marxism irrevocably. Reformers in Eastern European lands liberated from communist oppression expressed revulsion with the socialist past and a desire to regenerate their countries with an infusion of Western liberal ideals and institutions. Vaclav Havel, a frequently imprisoned dissident playwright who was elected president of a free Czechoslovakia in 1989, expressed this disillusionment with the past and hope for a new democratic future:

The worst of it is that we live in a spoiled moral environment. We have become morally ill because we are used to saying one thing and thinking another. We have learned not to believe in anything, not to care about each other, to worry only about ourselves. . . . The previous regime, armed with a proud and intolerant ideology, reduced people into the means of production. . . . . Many of our citizens died in prison in the 1950's. Many were executed. Thousands of human lives were destroyed.

Perhaps you are asking what kind of republic I am dreaming about. I will answer you: a republic that is independent, free, democratic, a republic with economic prosperity and also social justice.[8]

Is Marxism a failed ideology propped up only by brutal repression in the few surviving communist regimes? Is "scientific socialism," which claimed to have deciphered the essential meaning and direction of history, neither scientific nor relevant to current needs? Is it merely another idea that had been given too much credence and is now ready to be swept into the dustbin of history? Daniel Chirot, a student of international relations, reflects on the decline of the socialist ideal:

The central idea of socialism, that economies controlled by the "people" acting through governments can bring about more rapid progress than market driven ones, is in disgrace. The goal of radical egalitarianism is recognized as a vain dream that can only turn into a totalitarian nightmare if attempts are made to enforce it. Destroying old ruling classes and replacing them by a socialist bureaucracy only creates a new ruling class. The fantastic projection of so many intellectuals' dreams onto the industrial working class, which endowed that class with a purity, internationalism, selflessness, and rationality no class could ever possess, has been exposed as a sham. In any case, the old industrial working class is in decline in the advanced industrial countries and it cannot be the dominant class of the future. All of this has meant that "scientific socialism" . . . has been shown to be neither scientific nor the wave of the future.[9]

Francis Fukuyama suggests that the decline of communism and the end of the Cold War reveal a larger process at work—"the ultimate triumph of Western liberal democracy."

The twentieth century saw the developed world descend into a paroxysm of ideological violence, as liberalism contended first with the remnants of absolutism, then bolshevism and fascism, and finally an updated Marxism that threatened to lead to the ultimate apocalypse of nuclear war. But the century that began full of self-confidence in the ultimate triumph of Western liberal democracy seems at its close to be returning full circle to where it started: . . . to an unabashed victory of economic and political liberalism. The triumph of the West, of the Western *idea*, is evident first of all in the total exhaustion of viable systematic alternatives to Western liberalism. . . . What we may be witnessing . . . is the end point of mankind's ideological evolution and the universalization of Western liberal democracy as the final form of government.[10]

In another address, Havel sees the end of communism as the end of a way of thinking that is characteristic of the modern West—that society can be explained and organized according to a theoretical model claiming the certainty of science. Echoing the view of postmodernists (discussed later in this chapter), Havel regards this aspect of the modern outlook as inherently dangerous:

> The modern era has been dominated by the culminating belief . . . that the world—and Being as such—is a wholly knowable system governed by a finite number of universal laws that man can grasp and rationally direct for his own benefit. This era, beginning with the Renaissance and developing from the Enlightenment . . . was characterized by rapid advances in rational, cognitive thinking.
>
> This, in turn, gave rise to the proud belief that man, as the pinnacle of everything that exists, was capable of objectively describing, explaining and controlling everything that exists, and of possessing the one and only truth about the world. . . . It was an era of ideologies, doctrines, interpretations of reality, an era in which the goal was to find a universal theory of the world and thus a universal key to unlock its prosperity.
>
> Communism was the perverse extreme of this trend. It was an attempt, on the basis of a few propositions masquerading as the only scientific truth, to organize all of life according to a single model, and to subject it to central planning and control regardless of whether or not that was what life wanted.
>
> The fall of Communism can be regarded as a sign that modern thought—based on the premise that the world is objectively knowable, and that knowledge so obtained can be absolutely generalized—has come to its final crisis. . . . The end of Communism is a serious warning to all mankind. It is a signal that the era of arrogant, absolutist reason is drawing to a close.[11]

Human Rights

The modern struggle for human rights, which was initiated during the Enlightenment, advanced by the French Revolution, and embodied in liberalism, continues in the contemporary age. Two crucial developments in this struggle are the civil rights movement in the United States and the feminist movement. Spokespersons for these movements have used ideas formulated by Western thinkers in earlier struggles for liberty and equality. Thus, one reason for the success of Martin Luther King's policy of direct action was that he both inspired and shamed white America to live up to its Judeo-Christian and democratic principles. In his famous "Letter from Birmingham City Jail," King expressed the immanent link between his movement and the Western tradition:

> One day the South will know that when these disinherited children of God sat down at lunch counters they were in reality standing up for the best in the American dream and the most sacred rules in our Judeo-Christian heritage, and thusly, carrying our whole nation back to those great wells of democracy which were dug deep by the Founding Fathers in the formulation of the Constitution and the Declaration of Independence.[12]

Feminist organizations, which first arose in advanced Western lands in the nineteenth century, continue their agitation for complete equality, and in recent years they have proliferated worldwide. A seminal work in the history of feminism after World War II was *The Second Sex* (1949), written by Simone de Beauvoir (1908–1986), French philosopher and long-time companion of Jean-Paul Sartre. It described the role of women in a traditional society, in which the majority of women were married, depended on men for their role in society, and were tied to their homes and their children; only a minority of women (including the author) led independent lives. Because the forces of social tradition were controlled by men, de Beauvoir said, women were relegated to a secondary place in the world. She argued that despite considerable changes in their social status women were still prevented from becoming autonomous individuals and taking their places as men's equals. Marriage was still expected to be women's common destiny, with their identity defined in relation to their husbands. In discussing the status of newly independent women, de Beauvoir held that, because of their failure to escape the psychological trap of secondary status, they lacked confidence and creativity in their work. The ideas expressed in this work, illustrated in the following passage, became central to the contemporary feminist movement.

> Woman has always been man's dependent, if not his slave; the two sexes have never shared the world in equality. And even today woman is heavily handicapped, though her situation is beginning to change. Almost nowhere is her legal status the same as man's, and frequently it is much to her disadvantage. Even when her rights are legally recognized in the abstract, long-standing custom prevents their full expression in the mores. In the economic sphere men and women can almost be said to make up two castes; other things being equal, the former hold the better jobs, get higher wages, and have more opportunity for success than their new competitors. In industry and politics they have a great many more positions and they monopolize the most important posts. . . . At the present time, when women are beginning to take part in the affairs of the world, it is still a world that belongs to men.[13]

Simone de Beauvoir *(Michel Phillippot/Sygma)*

The Women's Liberation Movement that emerged in the 1960s and 1970s demanded more than political and legal equality, the goal of earlier feminists. Viewing history and culture from a woman's perspective, feminists challenged and rejected many biased traditions that had governed male-female relations for centuries. They fought for divorce rights, made rape and sexual harassment major concerns, questioned the double standard in sexual behavior, and campaigned for access to abortion. Scholars specializing in the new field of women's studies are providing new and valuable insights in art, literature, sociology, and other disciplines.

POSTMODERNISM

The term *postmodern*, which first came into vogue in the 1970s, has various meanings. Some scholars and critics use it to describe the avant-garde developments in the arts and architecture—the new and eclectic styles that perpetuated early twentieth-century cultural trends but also transformed and transcended them. Thus, postmodern architecture moves away from the modern style exemplified by the Bauhaus movement of the 1920s. Mies Van Der Rohe and Le Corbusier, the principal exponents of the movement, sought technologically efficient structures, buildings that were harmonious, uniform, functional, impersonal, and unencumbered with frills or ornamentation. This pragmatic and austere design dominated public housing and office buildings after World War II. By contrast, postmodern architecture is eclectic and pluralistic: it deliberately combines incongruous styles and revives bits and pieces from the past (a medieval square, a classical column) to create a collage of differences. It rejects the mass-produced uniformity and homogeneity—described as dull and monotonous by critics—that marked urban design after World War II. Instead, it seeks to give visual expression to the wide diversity of individuals, the heterogeneity and plasticity of lifestyles, and the spontaneity, incongruity, dissonance, and anxiety that characterize contemporary city life. Postmodern urban architecture aspires to be a collage, for, after all, that is what the city truly is. Postmodern art, too, is more pluralistic than its predecessor. This diversity is expressed by mixing incompatible styles, by superimposing one theme on another that is completely unrelated, and by grouping apparently widely differing themes. For example, Robert Rauschenberg's *Tracer* contains contemporary street scenes, army helicopters, two floating cubes, and a reproduction of Rubens's *Toilet of Venus.* Postmodern art also incorporates past traditions, recognizes the esthetic potential of the banal (Andy Warhol's soup can), and takes its subjects from popular culture (Roy Lichtenstein's comic book art and Warhol's movie stars). Rock music has been called "the most representative of postmodern cultural forms"[14] because it articulates a plurality of ethnic and cultural identities, is intertwined with heterogeneous fashion styles, appeals to youth, and employs new sound and visual technologies.

The term *postmodern* is also used to describe recent developments in thought: structuralism and particularly poststructuralism. Historians of ideas view these movements as marking a fundamental break with the humanist tradition that emerged in the Renaissance and achieved full expression in the Enlightenment. This tradition, which gave central place to the autonomous self and to independent reason, has been called into question. As Silvio Gaggi points out, postmodernism can also mean *posthumanism.*

> When *postmodern* is used this way, the suggestion is that certain fundamental premises of the humanist tradition—the confidence in reason

as a faculty enabling humans to come to an understanding of the universe, the belief in the existence of the self and the acceptance of the individual as the primary existential entity—have been . . . rejected as no longer tenable.[15]

Postmodernism's radical critique of the autonomous self, reason's primacy, objective science, universal norms, and progress through reason constitutes still another attack on the Enlightenment tradition.

Structuralism

Starting in the 1960s, existentialism, which had gained wide popularity immediately after World War II, was superseded by a new movement of thought called structuralism. As with existentialism, France was the center of structuralism. Among the French thinkers who employed structuralist approaches—even though some may have denied being structuralists—were anthropologist-philosopher Claude Lévi-Strauss, historian Michel Foucault, literary critic Roland Barthes, Marxist theorist Louis Althusser, and psychoanalyst Jacques Lacan.

Structuralism held that the structure of the human mind—ways of thinking that are common to all human beings—underlay all cultural expressions. Structuralism owed a great debt to Ferdinand de Saussure (1857–1913), who pioneered the science of linguistics. He viewed a language as a self-contained system. Each component of the language—grammar, syntax—performs a specific function within the system, like each piece in a game of chess, and is specifically related to the other components. It is because language contains such an inner coherence, an underlying structure, that people speaking the same language can instantly understand each other even if words are arranged in a novel way. Although the surface structures of the world's languages seem to differ widely from each other, nevertheless, suggested American linguist Noam Chomsky (b. 1928), all languages do in fact resemble each other; when we go beyond surface appearances and explore their "deep structures," he said, we observe that languages, to a large extent, have general properties. There is a system of rules, a "general form of language," that underlines each particular language, said Chomsky. Chomsky speculated that this phenomenon— a general grammar that applies to all languages—points to fundamental structures of the brain designed by evolution. We are born with an innate ability to absorb the rules of language just as baby birds are programmed to learn the song of their species.

Building on the insight provided by linguistics, structuralists asked: What are the hidden structures, "conceptual schemes," embodied in human institutions, customs, and thought? So far, they said, the social sciences have dealt only with surface phenomena. In contrast, structuralists sought to uncover the deep, hidden infrastructures, or fundamental properties, that are contained in literary and philosophical works, ancient myths, and social relations and that tie together the component parts into a coherent system. Structuralists shared with Marx and Freud the conviction that we must seek a deeper, hidden reality—which for Marx meant economic forces and for Freud, psychological forces—that determines and explains surface phenomena.

Often called "the father of structuralism," Claude Lévi-Strauss (b. 1908) was born in Belgium, the grandson of a rabbi, and studied in Paris. From 1934 to 1939, he taught anthropology in Brazil, where he had an opportunity to study primitive tribes. After teaching in New York from 1942 to 1945, he returned to France and enjoyed a brilliant academic career there. In several works, particularly *The Elementary Structures of Kinship* (1969), *Tristes Tropiques* (1955), and the *Savage Mind* (1962), Lévi-Strauss argued that in a given society all cultural modes—table manners, kinship systems, myths, literature, art, and so forth—are interrelated. They are all manifestations of underlying structures that give coherence and unity to these cultural expressions and enable us to see that society as an organic whole. Found in all societies, these deep structures are ultimately expressions of basic thought processes that are universal. Existing independently of and determining consciousness in a way that the individual is unaware of, they are clues to the very essence or structure of the mind itself. "[T]he apparent arbitrariness of the mind, its supposedly spontaneous flow of inspiration, and its seemingly uncontrolled inventiveness," declared Lévi-Strauss, "imply the existence of laws operating at a deeper level. . . . [I] am guided by the search for the constraining structures of the mind."[16] It is because human beings share common thought structures, maintained Lévi-Strauss, that the various myths of the world resemble each other and that modern poems and ancient myths possess similar internal structures. Human beings are linked more by common mental characteristics than they are divided by cultural, racial, or class considerations.

Structuralists sought to uncover the general rules, or invariant structures, governing the various disciplines—language, art, literature, psychology, anthropology. For structuralists, hidden mechanisms rooted in the human mind generate cultural patterns, literary and artistic creations, and political systems. In their view, culture is ultimately determined by unconscious mental structures—by the brain's ordering mechanisms—shared by all human beings, and it was this peculiar ability of the mind that was the object of their investigation.

For structuralists, human beings are not ultimately self-determining subjects—the central assumption of European thought since Descartes—but agents of these universal mental structures. We are shaped by unconscious predispositions that are manifested in language and cultural life. No subject consciously devises these structures, and they are not present in the conscious thoughts of their users. There is "a kind of necessity . . . underlying the illusions of liberty,"[17] declared Lévi-Strauss, who emphasized not the individual as conscious self but as a social creature bound by genetics and culture, by systems with their own identifiable patterns. These structures, which underlie the conscious activity of the individual, he said, are the true objects of study. Human beings function in a world of large-scale social structures that no one planned and that cannot be undone by human intervention. Because structuralism diminished the role of the autonomous individual in human culture and history, it has been called antihumanistic.

Stressing timeless mental structures rather than change and development, structuralists also minimized the importance of history. They denied that history reveals any overarching pattern—Marxism's march to socialism, for example—and they rejected all theories of historical progress. Thus, Lévi-Strauss did not view as progress humanity's movement from a primitive state to civilization and was often critical of modern Western civilization. He castigated the modern West for a ruthless economic drive that placed self-interest before a respect for the environment and for other cultures. It cannot be said that structuralist thinkers ever discovered the hidden structures governing the human mind, and the movement itself faded, passing into poststructuralism.

Poststructuralism

Like structuralists, poststructuralists diminished the significance of the individual, but unlike structuralists, they did not believe that scientific objectivity or the attainment of truth was possible. Poststructuralists, particularly French intellectuals Michel Foucault (some of his writings also show a strong structuralist influence), Jean-François Lyotard, and Jacques Derrida, were greatly influenced by Nietzsche's antipathy to theoretical systems that claimed to have grasped an essential truth. Above all, Nietzsche affirmed "becoming"—that all is process and development—and rejected the very idea of "being"—that there are permanent, static truths knowable to the mind. Poststructuralists inherited Nietzsche's repudiation of metahistory—the view that history is a rational process, a continuous movement toward some goal—in its liberal (the progress of reason and freedom), Hegelian (the unfolding of Spirit), or Marxian (the triumph of socialism) format. Postmodernists in general deny that history reveals an identifiable pattern, and they reject all attempts to impose an overarching synthesis on the past. Thus, Lyotard defines postmodernism as "incredulousness towards metanarratives"—a repudiation of all-encompassing theoretical systems and master plans that purport to give meaning to life and history.

Poststructuralists also draw from Nietzsche's critique of conformity and authority based on accepted values. Like Nietzsche, poststructuralists seek to discredit or delegitimate values and beliefs associated with modernity and to strike out in new directions. In the tradition of Nietzsche, they repudiate all grand theories of metaphysics, all grand historical syntheses, all transcendental morality, and all ideologies that seek to provide legitimacy to existing viewpoints, judgments, or authority. For poststructuralists, all is flux and process: there is no being, only becoming. There are no universal norms, no unity of vision, no totalizing systems, no intellectual center points, no permanence, but only heterogeneity, dissolution, discontinuity, fragmentation, irresolution, and change. There is no social or historical progress, but only movement and accumulation. We cannot speak of "objective" knowledge or truth. Truth-claims, said Foucault, are merely a means of exercising and legitimating power over others. Like propaganda, from which they are indistinguishable, truth-claims are designed to serve the interests of the powerful.

In addition, poststructuralist thinkers were influenced by the Frankfurt School, Heidegger, and others who warned that theories claiming metaphysical certainty encase the individual in a straitjacket, reducing the person to an object that can be manipulated. They share with these predecessors a fear of mechanized rationality and of a totally administered society.

Also flowing into poststructuralism was the the youth culture that fueled the uprisings in 1968. Poststructuralists share the disdain that the radical left of the 1960s had for bourgeois society and for coercive authority; its yearning to emancipate people from repressive systems, both institutional and ideological; and its positive view of cultural diversity.

Poststructuralism is closely identified with deconstruction, a technique for reading literary and philosophic works developed by Derrida. Derrida rejected two basic assumptions of structuralism: that there are general laws, invariant structures, underlying human activity; and that a work of philosophy or literature contains a set meaning that the mind can apprehend and relate to others. Derrida developed his views in three works published in 1967 (*Of Grammatology; Speech and Phenomena;* and *Writing and Difference*) and in several later works.

Derrida held that a rigorous reading of a text—one that analyzes all aspects of language, including metaphors, the etymology of words, symbols, inadvertent puns, Freudian slips—shows that a text's underlying arguments and premises are fundamentally ambiguous, inconsistent, and contradictory. Derrida argued that deconstructive readings, such as the kind he attempted of Plato, Rousseau, Freud, and others, refute the naive assumption that a text contains a set of self-evident meanings intended by the author. Rather, the text tells a story that differs from and may even be opposed to the one the author may have intended. One reason for this is that language itself is elusive—the same word used at different times produces divergent meanings. Because words and rhetorical systems are inherently slippery, language cannot be trusted to convey an intended meaning; all supposed logical arguments are suspect. There is an inherent discrepancy between what the author may have intended and what the content of the text reveals. Simply stated, deconstructionists hold that it is impossible for language to say what the author means. Moreover, authors cannot help acting as mouthpieces of the dominant ideology of the day; unwittingly, their words are used to sustain the privileged and to suppress the powerless. In effect, the authors do not control their words but are controlled by them.

Deconstruction shatters the conventional belief that the author is a unified stable self and that his or her work possesses a coherent, stable, and inner logic and an intended meaning—that the words on paper have a one-to-one correspondence with ideas or images in the author's mind. No correct meaning can be ascribed to a text; meanings are indeterminate, uncertain, ambiguous. Deconstruction denies the possibility of determining truth or certainty. Facts are unverifiable; no rational principle exists either in a text or in the universe. Thus, in deciphering and reinterpreting texts, deconstructionists seek to unmask and debunk accepted meanings, but not to provide new authoritative ones; to raise problems but not to provide solutions.

Deconstruction signifies both the "death of the author" and the "death of the subject." It negates the view that the individual is a sovereign rational subject capable of participating in sustained rational discourse, that objectivity is a realizable goal, and that words can reliably communicate thoughts and relate experience. Deconstructionists deny that language is an instrument over which we have control, that moral judgments are possible, that the mind, making use of accumulated wisdom, is progressing to a truer understanding of reality, and that society can be rationally understood and rationally reformed.

As David Lehman, author of a study of Paul de Man,* America's
leading disciple of Derrida, points out, deconstruction serves to depre-
ciate the entire corpus of learning that for centuries had been the main-
stay of the Western humanist tradition. He notes that deconstructionists are not "interested in the moral dimension of a novel or poem, or
in evaluating the degree of its artistic success, or in treating the ideas
and the values it promotes. . . . It is retrograde in the highest degree to
imagine that Shakespeare's heroes and Jane Austin's heroines resemble
actual human beings and may therefore have something to teach us
about the conduct of our lives."[18] For deconstructionists, the canonical
books of Western thought are not creative works of art possessing an
inherent worth, works of insight, inspiration, and stylistic excellence
that the reader should approach with respect. Rather, deconstructionists seek to discredit, expose as fraudulent, or relegate as obsolete ideas
and ideals that are at the heart of the Western tradition, particularly in
its modern form, and to dismiss standards of esthetics as irrelevant.
The thrust of the deconstructionists, says critic Sven Birkerts, "is to
demolish the deeply rooted conceptions of the Enlightenment, pre-
sumably so that the culture can evolve in new directions. Deconstruction itself offers no signposts for this evolution, only a method of taking things apart. In this, Deconstructionists are like members of a
terrorist sect."[19]

Postmodernism: New Possibilities or Dangerous Nihilism?

Postmodernists reject universal principles and seek the dismantling of
all systems and beliefs. Recognition that we live in a centerless universe, they say, fosters a creative cultural diversity and an exciting
plasticity in lifestyles. It compels us to acknowledge the legitimacy of
a plurality of perspectives and to scrutinize ideas constantly, for at bottom all interpretations are subjective, and all knowledge is relative and
fallible.

In the postmodern view, Enlightenment rationality, with its underlying assumption that reason can uncover rational norms by which to
measure and alter institutions, traditions, and beliefs, has proven to be
an instrument of human oppression. All attempts to subject the indi-

*Born in Belgium, Paul de Man came to the United States after World War II and had
a brilliant career at Yale University as a professor of literature. As the foremost exponent of deconstruction in America, he had many devoted admirers. After his death
in 1983, it was learned that he had written propaganda, including anti-Semitic pieces,
for the Nazis during World War II.

vidual to a religious, political, economic, or moral system claiming to rest on the certainty of reason or faith provide theoretical justification for entrenched elites to dominate, coerce, and repress others. Truth-claims are both a mask for power and a means of coercion. A disavowal of truth and a disdain for the ideological strife that scarred our century leads postmodernists to call for an end to "redemptive politics of any kind and . . . all utopianism or messianic movements."[20]

Knowing that no outlook rests on a firm foundation, that the quest for meaning or truth is fruitless, and that no criteria permit us to say that one interpretation is superior to another, they argue, offers the human being radically new possibilities. Knowing that we live in an open-ended world which rejects monist, final, and fixed world-views, can lead us to concentrate creatively on contemporary experience. It can also make us both appreciate more and tolerate nonconventional and improvisational approaches to life. When that happens, the danger of totalitarianism and political fanaticism can lessen, since they rely on a particular view of truth.

Aside from denying the existence of universal norms, postmodernists argue that the idea of the sovereign and rational human being—a basic principle of liberal humanism—is a modern myth. Eliminating the concept of the self-determining individual reduces the importance that humanism gives to reason's search for truth and to social planning. It also exposes as naive humanist confidence in people's capacity to improve the human condition through collective action—that is, to direct history. During the Renaissance, a new view of the human being emerged that differed markedly from the medieval view. Postmodernists are redefining the individual for a new age. Political scientist Pauline Marie Rosenau provides a composite of the "postmodern individual," who seeks liberation from transcendental norms, humanist values, traditional affiliations and loyalties, and community rules.

> The post-modern individual is relaxed and flexible, oriented toward feeling and emotions, interiorization, and holding a "be yourself" attitude. S/he is an active human being constituting his/her own social reality, pursuing a personal quest for meaning but making no truth claims for what results. S/he looks to fantasy, humor, the culture of desire, and immediate gratification. Preferring the temporary over the permanent, s/he is contented with a "live and let live" (in the present) attitude. More comfortable with the spontaneous than the planned, the post-modern individual is also fascinated with tradition, the antiquated, . . . the exotic, the sacred, the unusual, and the place of the local rather than the general or the universal. Post-modern individuals are concerned with their own lives, their particular personal satisfaction, and self-promotion. Less concerned with old loyalties and modern affiliations such as marriage, family, church, and nation, they are more oriented toward their own needs.

> . . . The post-modern individual is characterized by an absence of strong singular identity. . . . S/he is a floating individual with no distinct reference points or parameters. . . . The post-modern individual is wary of general rules, comprehensive norms, hegemonic systems of thought.
>
> The post-modern individual calls for the end of certitude, reasoned argument, modern rationality, objective modern science, . . . and art subject to evaluation on the basis of standard criteria.[21]

Thinkers committed to traditional Western ideals decry the post-structuralist dismantling of values, denial of objectivity, and repudiation of the Enlightenment's goal of the rational improvement of society. They denounce deconstruction as an insidious attack on the great works of Western literature. Are there no standards by which we can judge the esthetic merit or lack of merit of a poem or a novel? Do authors have so little control over their words that all stated meanings are suspect? Is language so elusive that we must treat all texts as fundamentally unintelligible—as unsolvable puzzles—and must equate reading a text with getting stuck in a revolving door?

Poststructuralism's radical critique of self-sufficient reason, say these critics, erodes the foundations of democratic government, which rests on rational discourse. It also promotes a dangerous nihilism, in which all is permissible. Is there no free will that allows us to rise above impulse, no autonomous subject responsible for its behavior? Are there no moral norms by which we can condemn genocide, cannibalism, infanticide, torture, slavery, religious or racial persecution, rape, incest, child abuse, drug abuse, or drunken driving? Are there no criteria by which we can characterize something as an improvement—as progress?

THE ENLIGHTENMENT PROJECT IN A POSTMODERN AND GLOBAL AGE

In his discussion of Jürgen Habermas, a leading German social theorist of the late twentieth century and a defender of what Habermas calls the "Enlightenment project," Richard J. Bernstein describes the crisis of our age to which Habermas responded:

> . . . we live in an era when there is a suspicion of reason, and the very idea of universal validity claims that can be justified through argument. There is a rage against humanism and the Enlightenment legacy. . . . From all sides, we hear of "the end of philosophy," "the end of the individual," and even the "end of Western civilization."[22]

In recent years, modern Western civilization has come under severe attack by religious thinkers, by postmodernists, and by advocates of Third World peoples.

Some religious thinkers criticize the modern age for its espousal of secular rationality, the central legacy of the Enlightenment. These thinkers argue that reason without God degenerates into an overriding concern for technical efficiency: an attitude of mind that produces Auschwitz, the Gulag, weapons of mass destruction, and the plundering and polluting of the environment. Without God, the self degenerates into selfish competition, domination, exploitation, and unrestrained hedonism. Human dignity conceived purely in secular terms does not permit us to recognize the *thou* of another human being—to see our neighbor as someone who has been dignified by God. By taking the sacred out of life, we end up with spiritual emptiness and gnawing emotional distress. These critics of the Enlightenment tradition urge a reorientation of thinking around God and transcendent moral absolutes; otherwise, they argue, liberal democracy cannot resist the totalitarian temptation or overcome human wickedness. David Walsh summarizes the position of those who regard modernity as a dead end and seek a resurgence of the spiritual and the transcendent.

> No longer can we naively subscribe to the fundamental conceit from which modernity began: that human beings are capable of providing their own moral and political order. The conception of a secular society, existing without reference to any transcendental source and drawing its legitimacy entirely from humanity's autonomous self-determination, has begun to lose its appeal. That experiment has run its course. Having been brought to its limits in the twentieth century, its bankruptcy has become fully exposed. Virtually everywhere we look, the old confidence in secular rationality has been broken. . . . Faced with the evident inability of reason to provide the ultimate justification and motivation for order, modern human beings have again begun to look toward the source of order that lies beyond the self. A remarkable opening of the soul is taking place, as we increasingly come to realize that we are not the self-sufficient ground of our own existence. . . . [Modernity] furnished the justification for the unprecedented cruelty and the unlimited menace of our own time. . . . [We now recognize that] evil is not simply the responsibility of this or that dictator, political system, or specific set of circumstances. The problems lie deeper in the nature of modern civilization itself. The spiritual vacuum at its core has finally been confronted.[23]

Postmodernists argue that modernity founded on the Enlightenment legacy, which had once been viewed as a progressive force emancipating the individual from unreasonable dogmas, traditions, and authority, has become a source of repression through its own creations:

technology, bureaucracy, consumerism, materialism, the nation-state, ideologies, and a host of other institutions, procedures, and norms. An aversion to a technoscientific culture and its rational-logical methodology leads postmodernists to reject the principle of objectivity in the social sciences and to give great weight to the subjective: to feelings, intuition, fantasy, to the poetry of life. Postmodernists contend that the logical evaluation of data, no matter how carefully attempted, and reasoned arguments, no matter how logical they seem, reveal only personal preferences and biases. In their view, science has no greater claim to truth than does religion, myth, or witchcraft. In a world marked by cultural diversity and individual idiosyncrasies, there are no correct answers, no rules that apply everywhere and for everyone. Moreover, like those who point out the dangers of reason not directed by spiritual values, postmodernists argue that reason fosters oppressive governments, military complexes, and stifling bureaucracies. Nor has it solved our problems.

Postmodernists also express their disdain for Western humanism, which ascribes an inherent dignity to human beings, urges the full development of the individual's potential, and regards the rational, self-determining human being as the center of existence. Postmodernists argue that humanism has failed: socialism's humanist vision ended in Stalinism, and liberal humanism, like Christianity, did not prove to be a barrier to Nazism. They note that in our own day the rational-humanist tradition has failed to solve the problems of overpopulation, worldwide pollution, world hunger, and poverty that ravage our planet. Nor has reason coped successfully with the blight, homelessness, violence, racial tensions, or drug addiction that are destroying our cities. Moreover, postmodernists contend that the Western tradition, which has been valued as a great and creative human achievement, is fraught with gender, class, and racial bias. They see it as merely a male, white, Eurocentric interpretation of things. The West's vaunted ideals, they claim, are really a cloak of hypocrisy intended to conceal, rationalize, and legitimate the power, privileges, and preferences of white European male elites.

Postmodernists and other critics of Western civilization, particularly those who identify with people of color throughout the globe, call into question the intrinsic worth of the entire tradition of humanist learning and culture. They point to the modern West's historic abuses—slavery, imperialism, racism, ethnocentrism, sexism, class exploitation, and the ravaging of the environment. They accuse westerners of marginalizing the poor, women, and people of color—whom they have viewed as the "other"—of arrogantly exalting Western values and achievements, and of belittling and even destroying indigenous peoples and cultures of the world. Finding Western civilization intrinsically flawed, some critics seek a higher wisdom in non-Western—African, Asian, or Native American—traditions.

However, defenders of the Enlightenment heritage argue that this heritage, with all its flaws, still has a powerful message for us. They caution against devaluing and undermining the modern West's unique achievements:

> The tradition of *reason*, which makes possible a scientific understanding of the physical universe, the utilization of nature for human betterment, and the identification and reformation of irrational and abusive institutions and beliefs
>
> The tradition of *political freedom*, which is the foundation of democratic institutions
>
> The tradition of *subjective freedom*, which asserts the individual's capacity for ethical autonomy
>
> The tradition of *humanism*, which regards individuals as active subjects, with both the right and the capacity to realize their full human potential
>
> The tradition of *equality*, which demands equal treatment under the law for every individual
>
> The tradition of *human dignity*, which affirms the inviolable integrity and worth of the human personality—the driving force behind what is now a global struggle for human rights
>
> The tradition of *social justice*, which insists that the community has a moral obligation to assist the needy and the unfortunate

Jacques Ellul offers this answer to the intellectuals who express their disdain for the West and exalt the other civilizations of the world:

> I am not criticizing or rejecting other civilizations and societies. . . . The thing . . . that I am protesting against is the silly attitude of western intellectuals in hating their own world and then illogically exalting all other civilizations. Ask yourself this question: If the Chinese have done away with binding the feet of women, and if the Moroccans, Turks, and Algerians have begun to liberate their women, whence did the impulse to these moves come from? From the West, and nowhere else! Who invented the "rights of man"?
>
> . . . the essential, central, undeniable fact is that the West was the first civilization in history to focus attention on the individual and on freedom. . . . The West, and the West alone, is responsible for the movement that has led to the desire for freedom. . . .
>
> Today men point the finger of outrage at slavery and torture. Where did that kind of indignation originate? What civilization or culture cried out that slavery was unacceptable and torture scandalous? Not Islam, or Buddhism, or Confucius, or Zen, or the religions and moral codes of Africa and India! The West alone has defended the inalienable rights of the

human person, the dignity of the individual. . . . The West attempted to apply in a conscious, methodical way the implications of freedom.

. . . the West discovered what no one else had discovered: freedom and the individual. . . . I see no other satisfactory model that can replace what the West has produced.[24]

In *Freedom in the Making of Western Culture* (1991), sociologist Orlando Patterson declares that freedom, Western civilization's "preeminent ideal," was historically almost totally unknown in the non-Western world.

> For most of human history, and for nearly all of the non-Western world prior to Western contact, freedom was, and for many still remains, anything but an obvious or desirable goal. Other values and ideals were, or are, of greater importance to them—values such as the pursuit of glory, honor, and power for oneself or one's family and clan, nationalism and imperial grandeur, militarism and valor in warfare, filial piety, the harmony of heaven and earth, the spreading of the "true faith," nirvana, hedonism, altruism, justice, equality, material progress—the list is endless. But almost never, outside the contact of Western culture and its influence, has it included freedom.[25]

Joseph Campbell, in his essay "The Separation of East and West" (1961), was even more emphatic regarding the uniqueness of the West's achievement.

> It is not easy for Westerners to realize that the ideas recently developed in the West of the individual, his selfhood, his rights, and his freedom, have no meaning whatsoever in the Orient. . . . They would have meant nothing to the peoples of early Mesopotamian, Egyptian, Chinese or Indian civilizations. They are, in fact repugnant to the ideals, the aims and orders of life, of most of the peoples of the earth. And yet . . . they are the truly great 'new thing' that we do indeed represent to the world that constitutes our Occidental revelation of a properly human spiritual ideal, true to the highest potentiality of our species.[26]

Creating these values is the great achievement of the Western mind. Their roots are ultimately found in the West's Greek or Judeo-Christian heritages, but it was the philosophes of the Enlightenment who clearly articulated them for the modern age. To be sure, these ideals are a goal, not a finished achievement, and nothing should make us more appreciative of their preciousness or more alert to their precariousness than examining their violation and distortion over the course of centuries. George Steiner reminds us that "Auschwitz, . . . the Gulag, [and] the systematic incineration from the air of great cities evolved from the inside the politics, the technologies and the vocabularies of European culture."[27] It is equally true that every age has to rethink the Western tradition in order to find ways of utilizing constructively the insights gleaned from experience and advances in knowledge.

Therefore, it is crucial in this age of globalism, with its heightened sense of ethnic and cultural diversity, that westerners become sensitized to the histories and traditions of all cultures and root out permanently all racist and sexist ideas that have gravely poisoned Western perceptions and history. Furthermore, as advocates of postmodernism urge, we need to be wary of ideologies that claim to have discovered the meaning of history and of life and to be more open to alternative lifestyles, more willing to recognize the authenticity of different voices. And, as numerous thinkers have stressed, we must be ever alert to the dangers inherent in modern technology and bureaucracy.

But it is just as crucial in an era of global interdependence and tension that we continuously affirm and vitalize the core values of our own heritage. We must not permit this priceless legacy to be deconstructed away into meaninglessness or contemptuously negated as the ideological tool of oppressive elites. The history of our century demonstrates that when we lose confidence in this heritage we risk losing our humanity, and civilized life is threatened by organized barbarism. What British historian J. H. Plumb says of reason applies as well to the other ideals that constitute the Western *idea:*

> Man's success has derived from his application of reason, whether this has been to technical or to social questions. And it is the duty of the historian to teach this, to proclaim it, to demonstrate it in order to give humanity some confidence in a task that will still be cruel and long—the resolution of the tensions and antipathies that exist within the human species.[28]

NOTES

1. Jacques Ellul, *The Technological Society*, trans. John Wilkinson (New York: Vintage Books, 1964), pp. 302–303.
2. Erich Fromm, *The Revolution of Hope* (New York: Bantam, 1968), pp. 39–40.
3. Arnold J. Toynbee, *Cities on the Move* (New York: Oxford University Press, 1970), p. 245.
4. Quoted in Marvin Perry, *Arnold Toynbee and the Crisis of the West* (Washington, D.C.: University Press of America, 1982), p. 74.
5. Charles A. Reich, *The Greening of America* (New York: Random House, 1970), pp. 7–9.
6. Leszek Kolakowski, *Main Currents of Marxism*, vol. 3, *The*

Breakdown (New York: Oxford University Press, 1987), p. 490.

7. Milovan Djilas, *The New Class* (New York: Praeger, 1957), pp. 27, 31, 36, 38, 72.

8. *New York Times*, January 2, 1990, p. A 13.

9. Daniel Chirot, "After Socialism, What?" *Contention*, 1 (Fall 1991), 30

10. Francis Fukuyama, "The End of History," *The National Interest*, (Summer 1989), 3–4.

11. *New York Times*, March 1, 1992, Week in Review section, p. 15. Copyright © 1992 by the New York Times Company. Reprinted by permission.

12. Excerpted in *The Essential Writings and Speeches of Martin Luther King, Jr.*, ed. James M. Washington (New York: Harper Collins, 1991), p. 302.

13. Simone de Beauvoir, *The Second Sex*, trans. H. M. Parshley (New York: Knopf, 1953), p. xx.

14. Steven Connor, *Postmodernist Culture* (Oxford: Blackwell, 1989), p. 186.

15. Silvio Gaggi, *Modern/Postmodern* (Philadelphia: University of Pennsylvania Press, 1989), pp. 18–19.

16. Claude Lévi-Strauss, *The Raw and the Crooked* (New York: Harper, 1969), p. 10.

17. Ibid.

18. David Lehman, *Signs of the Times: Deconstruction and the Fall of Paul de Man* (New York: Poseidon Press, 1991), pp. 53, 57.

19. Quoted in Ibid., p. 78.

20. Quoted in Pauline Marie Rosenau, *Post-Modernism and the Social Sciences* (Princeton: Princeton University Press, 1992), p. 65. Copyright © 1992 by Princeton University Press. Reprinted by permission of Princeton University Press.

21. Ibid., pp. 53–56.

22. Richard J. Bernstein, ed., *Habermas and Modernity* (Cambridge, Mass.: MIT Press, 1985) p. 25.

23. David Walsh, *After Ideology: Recovering the Spiritual Foundations of Freedom* (New York: Harper Collins, 1990), pp. 1–3.

24. Jacques Ellul, *The Betrayal of the West*, trans. Matthew J. O'Connell (New York: Seabury, 1978), pp. 16–19, 29, 49.

25. Orlando Patterson, *Freedom in the Making of Western Culture* (New York: Basic Books, 1991), p. x.

26. Joseph Campbell, *Myths to Live By* (New York: Bantam Books, 1973), p. 61.

27. Quoted in David H. Hirsch, *The Deconstruction of Literature: Criticism After Auschwiz* (Hanover, N.H.: University Press of New England), p. 245.

28. J. H. Plumb, *The Death of the Past* (Boston: Houghton Mifflin, 1970), p. 142.

SUGGESTED READING

Connor, Steven, *Postmodernist Culture* (1989).

De George, Fernande M. and Richard T. De George, eds., *The Structuralists: From Marx to Lévi-Strauss* (1972).

Gaggi, Silvio, *Modern/Postmodern* (1989).

Harland, Richard, *Superstructuralism* (1987).

Harvey, David, *The Condition of Postmodernity* (1989).

Hirsch, David H., *The Deconstruction of Literature* (1991).

Lehman, David, *Signs of the Times: Deconstruction and the Fall of Paul de Man* (1991).

Megill, Allan, *Prophets of Extremity* (1985).

Rose, Margaret A., *The post-modern and the post-industrial* (1991).

Rosenau, Pauline M., *Post-Modernism and the Social Sciences* (1992).

Sarup, Madan, *An Introductory Guide to Post-Structuralism and Post-Modernism* (1989).

Shapiro, Gary, ed., *After the Future: Postmodern Times and Places* (1990).

Silverman, Hugh J., ed., *Derrida and Deconstruction* (1989).

Surrock, John, ed., *Structuralism and Since* (1979).

Index